GOLF U.S.A.

A Guide to the Best Golf Courses and Resorts

COREY SANDLER

CB

CONTEMPORARY BOOKS

Library of Congress Cataloging-in-Publication Data

Sandler, Corey, 1950–
    Golf U.S.A. : a guide to the best golf courses and resorts / Corey Sandler.
      p.   cm.
    Includes index.
    ISBN 0-8092-2644-8
    1. Golf courses—United States—Directories.   2. Golf resorts—United States—
Directories.   I. Title: Golf USA.   II. Title.

GV981 .S28   2000
796.352'06'873—dc21

00-20088

To Willie and Tessa, my favorite links.

This book is not authorized or endorsed by any attraction or business described in its pages. All attractions, product names, or other works mentioned in this book are trademarks or registered trademarks of their respective owners or developers and are used in this book strictly for editorial purposes and to the benefit of the trademark owner; no commercial claim to their use is made by the author or the publisher.

Cover photograph: Cypress Point Golf Course, Pebble Beach, California
Copyright © Panoramic Images/Gerald French

GV981
.S28
2000

Published by Contemporary Books
A division of NTC/Contemporary Publishing Group, Inc.
4255 West Touhy Avenue, Lincolnwood (Chicago), Illinois 60712-1975 U.S.A.
Copyright © 2000 by Word Association, Inc.
Printed in the United States of America
International Standard Book Number: 0-8092-2644-8
00 01 02 03 04 05 LB 18 17 16 15 14 13 12 11 10 9 8 7 6 5 4 3 2 1

Contents

Acknowledgments

Dozens of hardworking and creative people helped move my words from the keyboard to the pages of this book.

Among the many to thank are editor Adam Miller of Contemporary Books. Thanks to Linda Gray, our original champion, and publisher John Nolan.

Julia Anderson managed the editorial and printing processes with professionalism and good humor.

Thanks to the golf courses, resorts, hotels, equipment makers, mail-order companies, and attractions that offered discount coupons to our readers.

Special thanks to ace copy editor, Val Elmore. As always, Janice Keefe ran the office and the author with good humor. Thanks also to Dan Keefe, the office golf pro.

And finally, thanks to you for buying this book. We all hope you find it of value; we'd appreciate it if you would let us know how we can improve the book in future editions.

You can send us a letter at the address that follows; enclose a self-addressed stamped envelope if you'd like a reply. No phone calls, please.

Econoguide Travel Books
P.O. Box 2779
Nantucket, MA 02584

We're also available over the Internet at www.econoguide.com. To send us electronic mail, use this address: info@econoguide.com.

Chapter 1

A Guide to the Best Golf Courses and Resorts

Welcome to the 2000–2001 edition of *Golf U.S.A.: A Guide to the Best Golf Courses and Resorts*. Here you'll find more than 2,500 of the best public, resort, and semi-private courses in the nation.

This is not a guide to windswept and dusty $5 courses where you'll play with make-it-yourself clubs and second-hand balls. Instead, the goal is to help you get the most for your money and make the best use of your time.

We've collected information on the best public, resort, and semiprivate courses at any price, along with details of how to get the most for your money—no matter how much you spend—on equipment. You'll also find valuable advice on how to travel in economic style from coast to coast.

And we offer a selection of money-saving coupons. There is no connection between the information in this book and the coupons we publish, except that everything between the covers is intended to save you money.

Pardon us for saying so, but we think the cost-effectiveness of this book speaks for itself. You should easily be able to save several times the cover price, and have a good time doing so.

Golf Is a Simple Game, Right?

At its most basic, golf is a very simple and inexpensive game:

1. Hammer a peg into the ground.
2. Place a ball on top of the peg.
3. Swing a stick at the ball.
4. Aim the flight of the ball at a hole in the ground a few hundred yards away, trying not to hit the trees, the water, and other golfers.

That was about all that was required back when the game was new, and the basic concept still holds. There are about 26.4 million American golfers among us now, up about 50 percent from a decade ago, according to 1999 figures from the National Golf Foundation. Of that number, about 5.4 million are pretty serious about their sport, playing 25 or more rounds per year.

About half of American golfers are between the ages of 18 and 39. Another

20 percent are in their 40s, and 25 percent are seniors, age 50 and older. Women make up about 22 percent of U.S. golfers.

According to the foundation, there are more than 16,000 courses of all description in the United States, including regulation, par-3, and executive courses. Florida tops the list of states with 1,198 courses, followed by California (955), Michigan (930), Texas (860), and New York (857). And finally, if you're trying to determine the highest concentration of golf holes per 100,000 population in metropolitan areas, you'll want to stay in the southeast: Myrtle Beach, SC (721), Naples, FL (548), Wilmington, NC (331), Ft. Pierce/Port St. Lucie, FL (328), and Ft. Myers/Cape Coral, FL (318).

Spending the Green

From the tee to the ball to the club to the golfer to the spectacular golf resort, the price of entry and the complexity of the sport have soared like a well-struck drive from an elevated tee.

Golfers spend $15 billion per year on equipment and greens fees, according to foundation studies. Of that amount, $2.2 billion is spent on golf clubs. Average spending depends on frequency of play, with avid golfers (25 or more rounds per year) spending about $1,710 each year, moderate golfers (8 to 24 rounds) about $719, and the occasional golfer (less than 8 rounds per year) about $183.

You can pay $150 or more for a round of golf at a fancy resort, with $50 gloves holding a $500 custom-fitted titanium wood, and wear a monogrammed $300 golfing ensemble that makes you look just like Tiger or the Shark or the Golden Bear or some other pro star with a colorful nickname.

Or you can pay $15 for 18 holes at a well-maintained municipal course, wear a pair of slacks from the closet and a tee shirt from Kmart and tee off with an off-the-shelf club purchased from a discount store.

Either way, you're swinging a stick at a ball on a peg. And the ball costs a buck or two, no matter how pricey the rest of your golfing setup.

Think About the Game

Before you pick up the telephone to make reservations for the golfing vacation of your dreams, stop and think about the important details of your personal dream.

Ask yourself the following questions, and remember that there are no right or wrong answers. The only penalty comes from not asking them at all.

1. *What kind of a golf course and resort do I want to visit?* Do you want to go to an easy course where you can boost your ego by shooting the lowest score of your golfing career? Or would you rather visit one of America's most difficult courses, where your score will climb into the stratosphere but, oh, what stories you'll be able to tell at the 19th hole when you return home?

2. *Is price an object?* The courses in this book, all of them selected as above average, range from as low as $10 per round to $150 and even more. It's all golf, and there are some classic challenges and gorgeous locations at the less-

expensive courses; it's up to you to decide whether a brand name is worth the extra fare.

3. *When I spend the night, do I require a luxurious resort setting, or is a clean Motel Cheapo acceptable?* There are many advantages to staying at a world-class resort, especially if you are in mixed company (golfers and nongolfers) or if you plan to stay in one area for an extended period of time and want to make use of other amenities. And, as I will point out in Chapter 3 on hotels, a luxury resort is not always that much more expensive than a strip motel if you plan to play golf at the resort's course. You'll have to do the math yourself, based on your own preferences and plans.

4. *Must I travel in high season?* The warm spring of Florida and much of the South is a huge lure to frostbitten northerners. But sometimes it seems as if the entire state of New Hampshire is in line in front of you at the tee . . . and airline, auto rental, hotel, and greens fees are at their highest.

5. *Am I willing to spend a little bit of time to save a lot of money?* If so, read on; you'll find all of the information you need to make the most of your money and time on a golfing vacation.

About the Course Ratings

In Chapter 5, you'll find information on more than 2,500 public, resort, and semiprivate courses around the nation. To make the cut, the course had to be above average to exceptional, and open to visitors.

We based our ratings on published reviews and reports by players. Golf courses are awarded from one to four golf balls, as follows:

☺	Worth a Visit
☺☺	Above Average
☺☺☺	Exceptional
☺☺☺☺	Very Best

We show you the best courses open to the public, and the best deals—a combination of highest quality and most reasonable rates. Look for these labels in the listings:

BEST	*Golf U.S.A.'s* Best Courses
DEAL	*Golf U.S.A.'s* Best Golfing Deals
STATE	*Golf U.S.A.'s* Best Courses in the State

There are nearly 350 *Golf U.S.A.* Best and State courses. The *Golf U.S.A.* Deal icon is awarded to any course that is ranked as Exceptional or Very Best and is priced at bargain or budget levels of less than $40 for a round of golf. There are more than 700 *Golf U.S.A.* Deals spread across the country.

Golf U.S.A. includes only those golf courses or resorts that are open to the public. That doesn't mean, alas, that you will be able to walk up to the pro shop at 9 A.M. and claim an immediate starting time. In fact, at the height of the season, some of the most popular public courses are booked up for weeks in advance. Call ahead of time—at the same time you make your travel plans—to arrange a reservation, and try to avoid those days sure to be busy, including most holidays and Saturdays.

We also include listings for semiprivate (or semipublic, if you prefer) courses. These are membership clubs that offer a limited number of slots to visitors; availability may be limited to specific days or times, or you may be able to obtain a reservation for any slot not already spoken for by a member.

Finally, there are the resort courses that usually give priority to guests at the resort itself or a limited number of nearby hotels. Depending on the course, they will either offer a discounted rate for resort guests, or a premium rate for visitors not staying at the resort.

You should plan on calling any golf course or resort before you show up to play a round. In addition to the convenience of having an arranged tee-off time, remember that hours and days of operation, rates, and other details are subject to change. Every year a number of courses go private, too, closing off access to non-members or invited guests.

The codes in the listings are:

P	Public Course
R	Resort Course
SP	Semiprivate Course

You'll also find listings on regularly offered discounts, including seasonal rates, special prices for weekdays or twilight hours, and accommodations for senior and junior golfers.

Low season at golf courses varies, depending on the weather and regional practice. In the Northeast, Midwest, and mountainous regions, low season often means early spring when the snows have finally melted and again in the late fall as the air turns cold and storm clouds gather. In the hotter climes of the South and the desert West, the low season may be declared during the heart of the summer in July and August when only mad dogs, Englishmen, and the most dedicated of golfers brave the midday sun.

Discounts noted in the listings include:

W	Weekdays
L	Low Season
R	Resort Guests
T	Twilight
S	Seniors
J	Juniors

The range of greens fees for courses in *Golf U.S.A.* are indicated by symbols from bargain to very expensive and beyond to exclusive. Remember that rates are always subject to change, and the direction is almost always upward.

The rates indicate a typical discount rate and standard full rate. Be sure to ask about discount rates when you call for a reservation.

Here are the price ranges for the listings in this book:

$	Bargain	Less than $20
$$	Budget	About $20 to $39
$$$	Moderate	About $40 to $59
$$$$	Expensive	About $60 to $79
$$$$$	Very Expensive	About $80 to $100
$$$$$$	Exclusive	More than $100

You will see price icons for greens on every course, and another price icon if there is an additional charge for rental of a cart. If this information was unavailable to us, we've indicated that you should "Inquire" at the course for rental rates.

Then we have the essential statistics for the courses. We begin by organizing courses by region within each state. In larger states, regions can cover several hundred square miles; consult a map or make a phone call to be sure your golfing goal is a reasonable drive (by car) from where you live or where you're staying. Confirm directions to the course when you call to make a reservation.

Other information in the listings includes the number of holes (we list only courses with 18 or more holes). Next is the par. For 18-hole courses we tell you the pars from the back and front tees; for 27-hole courses the par is indicated from the back tees only. Yardage is listed from the front and back tees for 18-hole courses and the back tees only for 27-hole challenges.

The rating tells you the USGA course rating from the back and front tees for 18-hole courses and the back tees for 27-hole courses. The same pattern is used to report the USGA slope rating.

Finally, you'll learn the course's official season and its published high season. You'll want to call to check on the schedule of hours for a course before you go, however. Call the phone number listed for each course.

Buying Golf Equipment

Titleist golf balls are the same whether you buy them at full list price from the pro shop just before tee time or by mail at deep discount. So, too, are golf accessories, clothing, and even clubs.

In general, you'll find the highest prices on golf equipment at pro shops or at full-service retail shops. You'll also likely find the best service.

The best deals on equipment are often available through a mail-order operation or at a discount store, including golf-only shops as well as sporting goods superstores and general merchandisers.

You will have to decide, though, whether the service you receive from a competent golf retailer—including repair of grips and other minor repairs—might make it worthwhile to buy your clubs locally.

Be sure to compare guarantees and service promises from anyone who tries to sell you equipment. There are some instances where mail-order sources offer both the best price and the best support after the sale; other times you may find that mail-order operations want to take your order only and have little in the way of advice to offer.

I am a big fan of mail-order purchases in certain situations. During the years, I have purchased tens of thousands of dollars' worth of items over the phone, from sporting equipment to video cameras to personal computers to a car. Before I read out the digits on my credit card, though, I ask a ton of questions about the product and the store's current availability, billing and shipping policies, product return and warranty procedures, and anything else I can think of. My theory is this: if they won't respond to my questions before they have my money, what would make me think they would respond after they've deposited my money in their bank account?

Always use a credit card when you purchase by mail order; doing so gives you some legal rights to recover money in the event of nonperformance by the seller, and some contractual rights to get your credit card company's assistance if you have a problem.

You'll find a selection of coupons from some direct marketers of golfing equipment in this book; you'll find other listings for mail-order companies in golf magazines, in newspapers, and on the Internet.

Outlet stores offer another important way to shop for equipment and clothing. Some outlet stores are operated by manufacturers and others by discounters. As with any other purchase, compare their prices with full retail prices and spend your money wisely.

Used Equipment, Recycled Balls, and X-Outs

One good way to save money on practice equipment or to outfit a beginner is to buy used equipment. You may find clubs at a tag sale or listed in the classified ads. Check with local pro shops and retail stores to see if they have used demo or rental sets available for sale.

In recent years we have also seen the growth of used sporting goods stores that specialize in buying and reselling last year's clubs, outgrown boots and skis, and all of that other stuff that clutters our basements. A used driver with a few minor knicks on the head will look identical to a new driver after it has been around the course a few times.

And did you ever wonder just how many perfectly good balls sit at the bottom of the pond at your favorite course? Well, there may be thousands . . . or they may have been recently harvested by one of many companies that clean them up and resell them at a deep discount.

Another way to save money is to purchase X-out balls, which are new balls marked with an *X* or other symbol through the brand name to indicate a defect. In theory, an X-out ball is sold at a discount because of cosmetic flaws—misprints, off colors, or mottled covers. That means you should be able to use the ball in your game and pocket the price difference. Unfortunately, there may be other problems that are not so benign: imperfect covers, improper weight, or off-center construction.

You should have no problem using X-out balls on the driving range or even in an informal round. You may not want to use an X-out on your one and only game at a spectacular resort, or in a competition.

The Best Days to Go Golfing

Some of the best days to play golf are during the off-season (which varies from place to place) or when others have other things to do, including Easter Sunday, Christmas Day (if the course is open), New Year's Day, Mother's Day, and any day when there is an important sporting event going on. You might try hitting the links on the afternoon of Super Bowl Sunday, for example.

Although the Fourth of July may be a glorious day on Cape Cod, in the Colorado Rockies, or in Saratoga Springs, it may be an unbearably hot day in Palm Springs, West Palm Beach, or Houston. Likewise, a warm and sunny March or October day in Orlando may be a miserably wet and cold day in Minnesota.

Therein lies one money-saving strategy for the exceptionally hardy golfer: courses in sun spots including Florida, the deep South, and southern California often offer significant discounts in the heart of the summer, and courses in colder climes will have value pricing in the spring and fall (and sometimes snowless winter) while full rates are charged in the fair days of summer.

Special Golf Services

The world of golf seems to exist in a perpetual state of imbalance: there are either too many golfers seeking too few tee times, or too many golf courses and not enough golfers.

The first situation can ruin your golfing vacation or clean out your wallet; the second situation can work to your benefit. But sometimes the place where you want to play turns out to be the spot where it is the most difficult to obtain a reservation.

Tee-Time Services

One way to obtain a tee time at the most popular courses is to use a reservation service. These companies usually arrange for blocks of time at courses in their area and offer them to their clients. At some of the nation's most popular courses, using a service may be the only way to obtain a tee time.

Some services make their money by charging a commission to the golf courses; others will charge you a fee by adding a premium to the regular greens fee.

Be sure you go over the ground rules and are quoted a bottom line price before you agree to a deal from a tee-time service.

In some situations, you may even be able to obtain a discounted greens fee through one of these services, especially during off-season periods. The service may have some reservations it needs to unload at the last minute, or a golf course may cut its rates for clients of the service to fill up a slow day. Don't hesitate to ask for a discount—asking costs nothing, and you just may be rewarded for your effort.

Discount Cards

There are a number of national and regional discount programs that offer reduced greens fees, two-for-the-price-of-one deals, and other special programs for golfers. In general, you will find that the programs offer discounts during low-season periods and at courses that are less popular than those on everyone's leader board of the best of the best. But that doesn't mean there aren't great deals available, or that you won't find the perfect course at a discounted price.

There are three types of discount programs we have seen:

1. *Nonprofit organizations.* The American Lung Association and other groups have offered discount golf programs at the local, regional, or national level.
2. *Golf and travel clubs.* A number of commercial organizations, including travel packagers, golf magazines, and others, sell discount golf cards.
3. *Groups of golf courses.* Corporate families of courses, including those at Walt Disney World in Florida and the Robert Trent Jones Golf Trail in Alabama, regularly offer multiday or annual discount passes. Elsewhere, you will find discount golf cards offered by associations of golf courses within a particular area.

Pay attention to small print on any discount card offer; not all discounts or special offers are as great a deal as they appear. Look for the following:

1. *Exclusion periods.* Are the discounts valid only at twilight on rainy Thursdays in February, or can you use the card at any time?
2. *Limitations.* Can you only use the card once at each course that participates? Must each golfer in your party have an individual card?
3. *Hidden charges.* Some discount cards promise free or half-price greens fees, but include in the small print a requirement that you rent a golf cart at the full rate.

As with any other purchase, compare prices with and without the discount cards. Some of the programs are great deals, while others are a triple bogey on a par 3.

About the Special Offers in This Book

Be sure to check the discount coupons at the back of this book. The companies represented there promise money-saving offers for *Golf U.S.A.* readers. The presence of a coupon in this section is not in any way related to the author's opinions published in this book.

Chapter 2
How to Save Money on Air Travel and Golf Packages

We're heading south to Orlando for a not-that-untypical mixed-sports cross-generation family holiday. There's golf courses all around, water sports, baseball spring training, and, of course, the sprawling Walt Disney World complex.

To begin with, flights to Orlando are generally very reasonable because of the huge numbers of tourists that head to the theme parks and other attractions there. Our tickets cost $349 each for the round-trip from Boston, which is not too bad for the spring peak season to Florida. (We could have flown for $248 by driving just a bit out of the way to Providence, Rhode Island.) The businessman across the aisle will suffer through the same mystery meal, watch the same crummy movie, and arrive at Orlando at the same millisecond we do. The only difference will be the fact that he paid $976.50 for his ticket because he traveled on short notice and within a business week.

Somewhere else on this plane there is a couple who were bumped off a previous flight because of overbooking. I figure they are happily discussing where to use the two free round-trip tickets they received in compensation.

Up front in first class, where the food is ever so slightly better and you arrive a millisecond earlier, someone who apparently has more money than they know what do to with is sitting in a leather seat that costs $1,266.50 to rent for a few hours. Also in the first class cabin: a family of four is traveling on free tickets earned through Mom's frequent flier plan.

Back in the cheap(er) seats, we're flying on an excursion rate ticket that extends over a weekend and was purchased more than two weeks ahead of the flight; in most circumstances, that's the key to cheap tickets.

And on my trip back home, I may choose to try to improve on the less-convenient reservation I was forced to accept when I bought that cut-rate ticket. How will I do this? Read on.

Alice in Airlineland

In today's strange world of air travel, there is a lot of room for the dollarwise and clever traveler to wiggle. You can pay an inflated full price, you can take advantage of the lowest fares, or you can play the ultimate game and parlay tickets into free travel. In this chapter, I'll show you how to do each.

Recent years have been good for the airlines, but there are still some great bargains available to the careful shopper.

There are three golden rules: When it comes to saving hundreds of dollars on travel, be flexible, be flexible, and be flexible. Here's how to translate that flexibility into extra dollars in your pocket:

• Be flexible about when you choose to travel. Go during the off-season or low-season when airfares, hotel rooms, and other attractions are offered at substantial discounts. Try to avoid school vacations, including the prime summer travel months of July and August, unless you enjoy a lot of company. However, if you can stand the heat, the summer is a great time to go to the hot spots of Florida, Texas, and southern California to play in the semicool early mornings or late afternoons of the off-season.

• Be flexible about the day of the week you travel. In many cases you can save hundreds of dollars by bumping your departure date one or two days in either direction. Ask your travel agent or airline ticket agent for current fare rules and restrictions.

The days of lightest air travel are generally midweek, Saturday afternoon, and Sunday morning. The busiest days are Sunday evening, Monday morning, and Friday afternoon and evening.

In general, you will receive the lowest possible fare if your stay includes all day Saturday; this class of tickets are called excursion fares. Airlines use this as a way to exclude business travelers from the cheapest fares, assuming that businesspeople will want to be home by Friday night.

• Be flexible about the hour of your departure. There is generally lower demand—and therefore lower prices—for flights that leave in the middle of the day or very late at night. The highest rates are usually assigned to breakfast-time (7 A.M.–11 A.M.) and cocktail-hour (4 P.M.–7 P.M.) departures.

• Be flexible on the route you will take, and be willing to put up with a change of plane or stopover. Once again, you are putting the law of supply and demand in your favor. For example, a non-stop flight from Boston to Orlando for a family of four may cost hundreds more than a flight from Boston that includes a change of planes in Atlanta (a Delta hub) before proceeding on to Florida.

(You should also understand that in airline terminology, a "direct" flight does not necessarily mean a "non-stop" flight. Non-stop means the plane goes from Point A to Point B without stopping anywhere else. A direct flight may go from Point A to Point B, but may include a stopover at Point C or at more than one airport along the way. A connecting flight means that you must get off the plane at an airport enroute and change to another plane.)

• Consider flying on one of the deep-discount airlines, but don't let economy cloud your judgment. Some carriers are simply better run than others. Read the newspapers, check with a trusted travel agent, and use common sense. As far as we're concerned, the best thing about the cheapo airlines is the pressure they put on the established carriers to lower prices or even to match fares on certain flights. Look for the cheapest fare you can find and then call your favorite big airline and see if it will sell you a ticket at the same price—it just might work.

> **Checking in again.** Having a boarding pass issued by a travel agent is not the same as checking in at the airport. You'll still need to show your ticket at the counter so the agent knows you're there.

• Don't overlook the possibility of flying out from a different airport either. For example, metropolitan New Yorkers can find domestic flights from La Guardia, Newark, or White Plains as an alternative to Kennedy Airport. Suburbanites of Boston might want to consider flights from Worcester or Providence as possibly cheaper alternatives to Logan Airport. (In the true example I gave at the start of this chapter, a family of four could have saved $400 by driving to Providence instead of Boston, an easy alternative for much of New England.) Chicago has O'Hare and Midway. From Southern California there are major airports at Los Angeles, Orange County, Burbank, and San Diego.

• Plan way ahead of time and purchase the most deeply discounted advance tickets, which usually are noncancelable. Most carriers limit the number of discount tickets on any particular flight. Although there may be plenty of seats left on the day you want to travel, they may be offered at higher rates.

• In a significant change during the past few years, most airlines have modified nonrefundable fares to be noncancelable. What this means is that if your plans change or you are forced to cancel your trip, your tickets retain their value and can be applied against another trip. At the start of 2000, most airlines charged a fee of about $75 to reissue a ticket.

• If you're feeling adventurous, you can take a big chance and wait for the last possible moment, keeping in contact with charter tour operators and accepting a bargain price on a leftover seat and hotel reservation. You may also find that some airlines will reduce the prices on leftover seats within a few weeks of your departure date; don't be afraid to check with the airline regularly, or ask your travel agent to do it for you. In fact, some travel agencies have automated computer programs that keep a constant electronic eagle eye on available seats and fares.

• Take advantage of special discount programs such as senior citizens' clubs, military discounts, or offerings from other organizations to which you may belong.

If you are in the over-60 category, you may not even have to belong to a group such as AARP; simply ask the airline ticket agent if there is a discount available. You may have to prove your age or show a membership card when you pick up your ticket or boarding pass.

Air Wars

Airlines are forever gnashing their teeth and weeping about huge losses brought about by cutthroat competition. And then they regularly turn around and drop their prices radically with major sales.

I'm not going to waste time worrying about the bottom line of the airlines; it's my wallet and yours I want to keep full.

Therefore, the savvy traveler keeps an eye out for airline fare wars all the time. Read the ads in daily newspapers and keep an ear open to news broadcasts that often cover the outbreak of price wars. If you have a good relationship with a travel agent, you can ask to be notified of any good fare deals.

And in this electronic age, become a regular visitor to Internet web pages devoted to airline reservations, as well as to on-line newsletters that cover travel issues. You can also sign up for e-mail notification of changes in airfare. Some major airlines even offer to send you a message when they offer special fares or discounts.

The most common times for airfare wars are in the weeks leading up to the travel industry's off-season. Look for sales in late summer for flights in the period between Labor Day and Thanksgiving and again in the fall to cover the slow winter season with the exception of Christmas, New Year's, and Presidents' Day holiday periods.

There are three important strategies to employ here:

1. Hold off on vacation travel plans for as long as you can. If you're lucky, you'll be able to snare a discount fare. Don't wait too long, though—the deepest standard discounts are usually for tickets purchased at least 21 days before the date of travel. And remember that the chances for a fare sale for Memorial Day weekend or Thanksgiving are very slim, and in fact tickets may be hard to obtain at any price.

2. Consider grabbing a discount-fare ticket even if your travel dates are not firm. In most cases (be sure to check with the airline) you will be able

Torrey Pines Golf Course, San Diego, California
James Blank photo courtesy of the San Diego Convention & Visitors Bureau

to adjust dates for a small penalty of about $75; the final price of the ticket should still be less than a regular fare.

3. Ask for a refund on previously purchased tickets if fares go down for the period of your travel. The airline may refund the difference, or you may be able to reticket your itinerary at the new fare, paying a penalty of $75 or so for cashing in the old tickets. Be persistent—if the difference in fare is significant, it may be worthwhile to make a visit to the airport to meet with a supervisor at the ticket counter.

Another money-saving strategy involves the use of discount coupons distributed directly by the airlines, or through third parties such as supermarkets, catalog companies, and direct marketers. A typical coupon offers $50 or $100 off full fares or certain types of discount fares. It has been my experience that these coupons are often less valuable than they seem—while they are certainly better than paying full fare, they often result in a price that is higher than other readily available discounts. Read the fine print carefully and be sure to ask ticket agents if the price they quote you with the coupon is higher than another fare for which you qualify.

Convention Fares

If you are traveling to a convention that happens to take place near the golf course of your dreams, you may be able to get in on a discount with a particular airline that was negotiated by the group. In fact, you may not need any affiliation at all with a convention group to take advantage of the special rates offered. All the airline will ask is the name or number of the discount plan for the convention; the ticket agent is almost certainly not going to ask to see your union card or funny hat.

Check with conventions and visitors bureaus at your destination to see if any large groups are traveling when you plan to fly. Is this sneaky? Yes. But we think it is also sneaky and underhanded for an airline to charge hundreds of dollars more for the seats to the left and right of the one we're sitting in. Here are a few more tips:

• Consider doing business with discounters, known in the industry as consolidators or, less flatteringly, as bucket shops. These companies buy the airlines' slow-to-sell tickets in volume and resell them to consumers at rock-bottom prices. Look for their ads in the classified listings of many Sunday newspaper travel sections and through some online web pages.

Be sure to study and understand the restrictions; there may be stiff penalties for changes or cancellations, or changes may not be permitted at all. And consolidator tickets are sold for a particular flight on a particular airline; if you miss your plane, you may find yourself completely out of luck. In most instances, the airline would have no obligation to put you on another flight. That said, I have used consolidator tickets several times without problems.

• A bit more in the shadows are ticket brokers who specialize in the resale of frequent flier coupons and other free or almost-free tickets. Most airlines attempt to prohibit the resale or transfer of free tickets from the original ticket holder to a second or third party; the fact is that very rarely are they successful in preventing such reuse. However, I can't recommend that you take this sort of risk; you could end up in an airport waving a worthless piece of paper at a gate agent who has no obligation to do anything for you at all.

Bidding for a Ticket

Among many new wrinkles introduced in the age of the Internet is the travel auction. One leader in this field is www.priceline.com. Their pitch goes something like this: "Tell us where you want to travel, which days, and how much you'd like to pay. We'll let you know if any airline accepts your offer."

It's an interesting concept, and one that holds the potential of significant savings for some travelers if, and it's a big if, you can accept the limitations of the system. Here are some of those limits:

• In most cases, you cannot specify a time of day to travel. You can expect that airlines will try to fill their least-attractive slots, which may include very early, late night, or overnight flights.

• You can't choose a particular airline. Although the auction companies do have arrangements with major airlines, they also produce tickets for some of the lesser lines.

• If you make an offer, you have to back it up with a credit card and you must accept whatever flight arrangements are offered. And the tickets are generally non-refundable or non-cancellable.

• Finally, don't expect to get tickets for free. You'll likely find that airlines will not accept bids that are much below their lowest advertised price; the advantage of services such as Priceline is that you can obtain such fares even when they are "officially" sold out. And don't forget that you'll have to pay departure and airport taxes on top of the accepted bid price.

A Loophole Closes a Bit

The biggest change to hit the airline industry in recent years had nothing to do with fancy new jetliners, improved service, or (heaven forbid) a decent airborne meal. Instead it was the near-universal end to transferable tickets.

In days of old, all you needed to board the plane was your ticket, like an admission ticket to the theater. Travelers were often able to resell or give away unneeded nested ticket pairs, promotional free tickets, or frequent flier passes.

But in the fall of 1995, the federal government called a security alert at the nation's airports because of perceived threats from the Middle East and elsewhere. As part of a package that included elimination of some parking spaces directly in front of terminals, increased scrutiny of carry-on and checked baggage, and other measures, airline check-in agents began asking for a photo ID for each ticket holder and comparing that name against the ticket.

Although the security alert was reduced later in the year (subject to future reinstatement), most airlines have continued to ask for identification. Why? Industry observers noted that airlines took to this practice with particular relish, and news reports said that some of the major carriers found they were earning a significant increase in profits by blocking the use of tickets issued under another name.

Standing Up for Standing By

One of the little-known secrets of air travel on most airlines and most types of tickets is the fact that travelers who have valid tickets are allowed to stand by for flights other than the ones for which they have reservations; if there are empty seats on the flight, standby ticket holders are permitted to board.

Some airlines are very liberal in their acceptance of standbys within a few days of the reserved flight, while others will charge a fee for changes in itinerary. And some airport agents are stricter about the regulation than others.

Here's what I do know: if I cannot get the exact flight I want for a trip, I make the closest acceptable reservations available after that flight and then show up early at the airport and head for the check-in counter for the flight I really want to take. Unless you are seeking to travel during an impossibly overbooked holiday period or arrive on a bad weather day when flights have been canceled, your chances of successfully standing by for a flight are usually pretty good.

Call the airline a day before the flight and check on availability. Some clerks are very forthcoming with information; many times I have been told something like, "There are 70 open seats on that flight."

Be careful with standby maneuvers if your itinerary requires a change of plane en route; you'll need to check the availability of seats on all of the legs of your journey.

And a final note: be especially careful about standing by for the very last flight of the night. If you somehow are unable to get on that flight, you're stuck for the night.

My personal strategy usually involves making a reservation for that last flight and standing by for one or more earlier flights on the same day.

Your Consumer Rights

The era of airline deregulation has been a mixed blessing for the industry and the consumer. After a period of wild competition based mostly on price, we now are left with fewer but larger airlines and a dizzying array of confusing rules. The U.S. Department of Transportation and its Federal Aviation Administration (FAA) still regulate safety issues. Almost everything else is between you and the airline.

Policies on fares, cancellations, reconfirmation, check-in requirements, and compensation for lost or damaged baggage or for delays all vary by airline.

Your rights are limited and defined by the terms of the contract you make with an airline when you buy your ticket. You may find the contract included with the ticket you purchase, or the airlines may "incorporate terms by reference" to a separate document, which you will have to request to see.

Whether you are buying your ticket through a travel agent or dealing directly with the airline, here are some important questions to ask:

Double indemnity. Your home owner's or renter's insurance policy may include coverage for theft of your possessions while you travel, making it unnecessary to purchase a special policy. Check with your insurance agent.

Second chance. Tour cancellations are rare. Most tour operators, if forced to cancel, will offer another package or other incentives as a goodwill gesture. If a charter flight or charter tour is canceled, your money must be refunded within 14 days.

- Is the price guaranteed, or can it change from the time of the reservation until you actually purchase the ticket?
- Can the price change between the time you buy the ticket and the date of departure?
- Is there a penalty for cancellation of the ticket?
- Can the reservation be changed without penalty, or for a reasonable fee? Be sure you understand the sort of service you are buying.
- Is this a nonstop flight, a direct flight (an itinerary where your plane will make one or more stops en route to its destination), or a flight that requires you to change planes one or more times?
- What seat has been issued? Do you really want the center seat in a three-seat row, between two strangers?

You might also want to ask your travel agent:

- Is there anything I should know about the financial health and viability of this airline?
- Are you aware of any threats of work stoppages or legal actions that could ruin my trip?

Overbooking

Overbooking is a polite industry term for the legal business practice of selling more than an airline can deliver. It all stems, alas, from the rudeness of many travelers who neglect to cancel flight reservations that will not be used. Airlines study the patterns on various flights and city pairs and apply a formula that allows them to sell more tickets than there are seats on the plane in the expectation that a certain percentage of ticket holders will not show up for one reason or another.

But what happens if everyone holding a reservation shows up? Someone will be left behind.

The involuntary bump list will begin with passengers who check in late. Airlines must ask for volunteers before bumping any passengers who have followed the rules on check-in.

Now, assuming that no one is willing to give up a seat just for the fun of it, the airline will offer some sort of compensation—either a free ticket or cash, or both. It is up to the passenger and the airline to negotiate a deal.

Some air travelers, including this author, look forward to an overbooked flight when their schedules are flexible. My most profitable score: $4,000 in vouchers on a set of four $450 international tickets. The airline was desperate to clear a large block of seats, and it didn't matter to us if we arrived home a few hours late. We received the equivalent of three tickets for the price of one, and you can bet that we'll hope to earn some more free travel on future tickets purchased with those vouchers.

The U.S. Department of Transportation's consumer protection regulations set some minimum levels of compensation for passengers who are bumped from a flight as a result of overbooking.

If you are bumped involuntarily, the airline must provide a ticket on its next available flight. Unfortunately, there is no guarantee there will be a seat on that plane, or that it will arrive at your destination at a convenient time.

If the airline can get you on another flight that will get you to your destination within one hour of the original arrival time, no compensation need be paid. If you are scheduled to get to your destination more than one hour but less than two hours late, you're entitled to receive an amount equal to the one-way fare of the oversold flight, up to $200. If the delay is more than two hours, the bumpee will receive an amount equal to twice the one-way fare of the original flight, up to $400.

It is not considered bumping if a flight is canceled because of weather, equipment problems, or the lack of a flight crew. You are also not eligible for compensation if the airline substitutes a smaller aircraft for operational or safety reasons, or if the flight involves an aircraft that has 60 seats or less.

How to Get Bumped

Why in the world would you want to be bumped? Well, perhaps you'd like to look at missing your plane as an opportunity to earn a little money for your time instead of an annoyance. Is a two-hour delay worth $100 an hour to you? For the inconvenience of waiting a few hours on the way home a family of four might receive a voucher for $800—that could pay for a week's hotel plus a heck of a meal at the airport.

If you're not in a rush to get to your destination—or to get back home—you might want to volunteer to be bumped. We wouldn't recommend doing this on the busiest travel days of the year, or if you are booked on the last flight of the day, unless you are also looking forward to a free night in an airport motel.

Traveling with golf clubs. Many major airlines make special accommodations for golf bags. They may offer a free cardboard box to surround your case, or a heavy plastic bag to encase your clubs; some even sell special travel bags made of canvas or nylon that cover your equipment. Call your airline in advance to find out what it may have available; confirm that bags are offered at the airport where you will start your trip. Finally, add at least 30 minutes to your preflight check-in time to take care of packing business.

You can protect your own equipment. You might consider purchasing a hard travel case to cover your clubs. Consider wrapping your clubs in padding—bubble plastic or foam rubber will do, but so will your underwear, socks, and sweaters.

Finally, consult with your home insurance agent to see what coverage you already have on your belongings while you travel. If you make several vacation trips each year, it may be worthwhile to purchase a relatively inexpensive rider to your home owner's or renter's policy to cover your equipment beyond the basic liability of the airlines.

Flyer beware. Charter flights operate independently of scheduled carriers. If you are on a trip that combines scheduled and non-scheduled flights, or two unrelated charter flights, a delay or cancellation of one flight may cause you to lose out on your next flight.

For that reason, it may make sense to avoid such combinations, or to leave extra hours or even days between connections. Some tour operators offer travel-delay insurance that pays for accommodations or alternative travel arrangements necessitated by certain types of delays.

And, if you are using a scheduled airline to connect with a charter flight or vice versa, your baggage will not be transferred automatically. You must make the transfer yourself.

How to Book a Package or Charter Flight

If possible, use a travel agent—preferably one you know and trust from prior experience. In general, the tour operator pays the travel agent's commission. Some tour packages, however, are available only from the operator who organized the tour; in certain cases, you may be able to negotiate a better price by dealing directly with the operator, although you are giving up one layer of protection for your rights.

Pay for your ticket with a credit card; this is a cardinal rule for almost any situation in which you are prepaying for a service or product.

Realize that charter airlines don't have large fleets of planes available to substitute in the event of a mechanical problem or an extensive weather delay. They may or may not be able to arrange for a substitute plane from another carrier.

If you are still willing to try a charter after all of these warnings, check the bottom line once more before you sign the contract. First of all, is the air travel significantly less expensive than the lowest nonrefundable fare from a scheduled carrier? (Remember that you are, in effect, buying a nonrefundable fare with most charter flight contracts.)

Have you included taxes, service charges, baggage transfer fees, or other charges the tour operator may put into the contract?

Are the savings significantly more than the 10 percent by which the charter operator may boost the price—without your permission? Do any savings come at a cost of time? Put a monetary value on your time.

Finally, don't buy a complete package until you have compared it with the à la carte cost of such a trip. Call the hotels offered by the tour operator, or similar ones in the same area, and ask them a simple question: "What is your best price for a room?" Be sure to mention any discount programs that are applicable, including AAA or other organizations. Do the same for car rental agencies, and remember to place a call to any area attractions you plan to visit to get current prices.

And, of course, don't overlook the discount coupons for hotels, motels, restaurants, and attractions that are included in this book.

About Travel Agencies

Here's my advice about travel agents, in a nutshell: get a really good one, or go it alone. Good travel agents remember who they work for: you.

Of course there is a built-in conflict of interest here, because the agent is in most cases paid by someone else. Agents receive a commission on airline tickets, hotel reservations, car rentals, and many other services they sell you. The more they sell (or the higher the price), the more they earn.

I would recommend you start the planning for any trip by calling the airlines and a few hotels and finding the best package you can put together for yourself. Then make a call to your travel agency and ask them to do better.

If your agent contributes knowledge or experience, comes up with dollar-saving alternatives to your own package, or offers some other kind of convenience, then go ahead and book through the agency. If, as I often find, you know a lot more about your destination and are willing to spend a lot more time to save money than the agent will, do it yourself.

There is one special type of travel agency worth considering. A number of large agencies offer their customers rebates on part of their commissions. Some of these companies cater only to frequent fliers who will bring in a lot of business; other rebate agencies offer only limited services to clients.

You can find discount travel agencies through many major credit card companies (Citibank and American Express among them) or through associations and clubs. Some warehouse shopping clubs have rebate travel agencies.

And if you establish a regular relationship with your local travel agency and bring them enough business to make them glad to see you walk through their door, don't be afraid to ask them for a discount equal to a few percentage points.

Kids in midair. If you are flying with children, discuss with your airline or travel agent any special needs you might have. These might include a request for a bulkhead seat to give children a little extra room for fidgeting (although you will lose the storage space underneath the seat in front of you) or special meals (most airlines offer a child's meal of a hot dog or hamburger upon request, which may be more appealing to a youngster than standard airline cuisine).

Be sure to pack a special utility bag for young children and carry it on board the plane. Extra diapers in the baggage compartment won't help you at all in an emergency at 25,000 feet. Include formula, food, and snacks as well as a few toys and books to occupy young ones.

Changes in altitude at takeoff and landing may cause some children discomfort in their ears. Try to teach them to clear their ears with an exaggerated yawn. Bubble gum or candy, or a bottle for babies, can help too.

And finally, keep in touch with your travel agent or tour operator. In many cases, your agent can anticipate major changes before departure time and let you know how the changes will affect your plans. Many operators will try hard to keep you from demanding a refund if you find a major change unacceptable. They may offer a discount or an upgrade on a substitute trip or adjust the price of the changed tour.

Golf Packages

Some of the best deals for golfers can be found by booking a package golf tour from a resort, or from a specialized travel agency or tour packager.

The packages often bring together discounted airfare, cheap car rentals, off-rate hotel rooms, and free or deeply discounted greens fees. That's the good news.

The potential bad news is that you have to pay attention to the details of the package to make certain it is a better deal than an à la carte vacation you assemble for yourself or an equivalent level of convenience and luxury.

Here is an example of a package to Hilton Head Island offered by one major packager:

- Round-trip air transportation to Hilton Head or Savannah from major East Coast and Midwest locations
- Accommodations for three nights
- Rental car with unlimited mileage
- Four daily greens fees with guaranteed advance tee times

Low-season rates (summer in Hilton Head) are as low as $499 per person at a motel and up to $629 at a resort at one of the name golf courses. High-season rates (spring in Hilton Head) range from about $559 to $699 per person.

This particular package has a relatively small amount of fine print, although some of the elements are important: the participating golf resorts all require rental of a golf cart at an additional fee of $15 to $19 per person; some of the tonier golf resorts may add an unspecified surcharge, and rental car taxes, fees, and insurance.

Some other notes include penalties of up to $150 if reservations have to be changed after documents have been issued, and a cancellation policy that includes the following:

- Up to 45 days before departure, $25 per person cancellation fee
- Within 45 to 15 days before departure, $100 per person cancellation fee, plus any applicable air-, hotel-, car-, or golf-related penalties (with the penalties not specified in the brochure)
- Within 15 days and up to 72 hours before departure, $150 per person cancellation fee, plus any applicable air-, hotel-, car-, or golf-related penalties
- Within 72 hours of departure, forfeiture of the full advance payment

Does this mean that golf packages are not a good deal? Absolutely not. It just means that you have to study the fine print very carefully. The more onerous the cancellation fees, the more valuable a cancellation insurance policy becomes.

And finally, don't be afraid to attempt to negotiate with a tour packager for a better deal or better conditions. Some companies may have contractual obligations with airlines, hotels, and courses; they may be willing to cut their rates close to departure dates.

Drive, He Said?

Everyone's conception of the perfect vacation is different, but for me, I draw a distinction between getting there and being there. I want the getting there part to be as quick and simple as possible, and the being there part to be as long as I can manage and afford. Therefore, I fly to just about any destination that is more than a few hundred miles from my home. The cost of driving, hotels, meals en route, and general physical and mental wear and tear rarely equals a deeply discounted excursion fare.

If you do drive, though, you can save a few dollars by using the services of AAA or another major automobile club. Before you head out, spend a bit of time and money to make certain your vehicle is in traveling shape: a tune-up and fully inflated, fully inspected tires will certainly save gas, money, and headaches.

If you plan to travel by bus or train, be aware that the national carriers generally have the same sort of peak and off-peak pricing as the airlines. The cheapest time to buy tickets is when the fewest people want them.

Renting a Car

Renting a car can be a liberating experience, freeing you from the hassles of finding a taxi, allowing you to explore the area at will, permitting you to rent a less-expensive hotel room a bit of a drive away from the golf resort, and giving you the freedom to drive to that exciting restaurant—the one with better food and better prices than those offered by room service.

Renting a car can also be an anchor around your neck. You'll need to find a place to park, a set of maps of the area, and the location of gas stations. Finally, you'll need to leave time on getaway day to fill up the tank and drop off the car.

I recommend you sit down with a piece of paper and a pencil and calculate the value of a rental car. Expect to pay somewhere between $30 and $50 per day for a small car—plus tax, gas, and parking. Compare the bottom line with the cost of taxis, shuttle services (does your hotel offer a free service?), and even with the cost of hiring a car and driver for a few hours.

The best policy. Consider, carefully, trip-cancellation insurance. The policies reimburse you for lost deposits or prepayments if you must cancel a trip because you or certain specified members of your family become ill. Read the policy to understand the circumstances under which the company will pay.

Don't buy more coverage than you need; if your tour package costs $5,000 but you would lose only $1,000 in a cancellation, then the amount of the insurance payoff required is just $1,000.

Some policies will pay health and accident benefits while on vacation, excluding any preexisting conditions.

And be sure you understand your airline's policies on cancellations. You may be able to reschedule a flight or even receive a refund after payment of a service charge. Some airlines will give full refunds or free rescheduling if you can prove a medical reason.

If your trip is based on refundable tickets and cancelable hotel reservations you don't need trip-cancellation insurance at all—the policy won't pay you anything at all if you can get your money back without it.

I generally find that renting a car is more expensive than using a taxi or car service for most travel in and near major cities and resorts, but I prefer to pay the extra money for the freedom to explore at will. Renting a car is usually a cost-effective decision when you have a long distance to travel between airport and resort, or from hotel to golf course.

Saving Money at the Rental Counter

Car rental companies will try—with varying levels of pressure—to convince you to purchase special insurance coverage. They'll tell you it's "only" $7 or $9 per day. What a deal! That works out to about $2,500 or $3,330 per year for a set of rental wheels. Of course the coverage is intended primarily to protect the rental company, not you.

Before you travel, check with your insurance agent to determine how well your personal automobile policy will cover a rental car and its contents. We strongly recommend you use a credit card that offers rental car insurance; such insurance usually covers the deductible below your personal policy. The extra auto insurance by itself is usually worth an upgrade to a gold card or other extra-service credit card.

The only sticky area comes for those travelers who have a driver's license but no car, and therefore no insurance. Again, consult your credit card company and your insurance agent to see what kind of coverage you have, or what kind you need.

Your travel agent may be of assistance in finding the best rates; you can make a few phone calls by yourself too. Rental rates generally follow the same structure. I have obtained rates as low as $59 a week for a tiny subcompact (a convertible, no less) in low season in Florida.

Although it is theoretically possible to rent a car without a credit card, you will find it a rather inconvenient process. If the rental agency cannot hold your credit card account hostage, it will often require a large cash deposit— perhaps as much as several thousand dollars—before it will give you the keys.

Be aware that the least-expensive car rental agencies usually do not have their stations at the airport itself. You will have to wait for a shuttle bus to take you from the terminal to the rental lot, and you must return the car to that same outlying area at the end of your trip. This may add about 20 to 30 minutes to your arrival and departure schedule.

Pay attention, too, when the rental agent explains the gas policy. The most common plan says that you must return the car with a full tank; if the agency must refill the tank, you will be billed a service charge plus what is usually a very high per-gallon rate.

Other optional plans include one where the rental agency sells you a full tank when you first drive away and takes no note of how much gas remains when you return the car. Unless you somehow manage to return the car with the engine running on fumes, you are in effect making a gift to the agency with every gallon you bring back.

I prefer the first option, which requires making it a point to refill the tank on the way to the airport on getaway day.

Chapter 3
Hotels

A Place to Lay Your Head

Let us start out by saying that some travelers—let's call them type A people—consider a hotel to be a place to catch a minimal amount of shut-eye and store their stuff between expeditions. They want their hotel clean, convenient, . . . and cheap. They don't care whether the television has rabbit ears or 32 cable channels, whether there is a health club, or whether the view out the window is an asphalt parking lot. Amenities don't mean very much to the type A who arrives at 11 P.M. and departs each morning at 7 A.M. for the links.

For others—type B folk—the place they stay is one of the main aspects of the vacation. They demand large rooms with three telephones, two television sets with satellite channels, in-room saunas, on-call massage therapists, spectacular restaurants and room service, extravagant furnishings, and million-dollar views of the beach, the golf course, or the mountain peaks.

There is nothing wrong with either preference, unless you are a type A person forced to pay for a view you never see and a swimming pool you never visit, or a type B person unhappily stuck in an economy motel without HBO and room service.

So, the first decision you should make in planning a vacation is to decide what level of luxury you are willing to pay for. But before you make a reservation, you should also perform a cost/benefit analysis for the trip you have in mind.

Here's a hypothetical comparison of five hotel options for a golfing vacation, using typical prices from in and around a four-star golf resort in Arizona.

Example 1

Economy Motel: Public Golf, Economy Dining

Basic room (per person, double-occupancy)	$30
Breakfast and dinner at economy restaurants	$20

Greens fee at public golf course $30
Car rental (per person, for two golfers) $30
                                            Total: $110 per person per night

Example 2

Economy Motel: Resort Golf, Economy Dining
Basic room (per person, double-occupancy) $30
Breakfast and dinner at economy restaurants $20
Greens fee at resort golf course $100
Car rental (per person, for two golfers) $30
                                            Total: $180 per person per night

Example 3

Luxury Golf Resort: Resort Golf, Economy Dining
Luxury room (per person, double-occupancy) $75
Breakfast and dinner at economy restaurants $20
Discounted resort greens fee for guests $75
Car rental (per person, for two golfers) $30
                                            Total: $200 per person per night

Example 4

Luxury Golf Resort: Resort Golf, Fine Dining
Luxury room (per person, double-occupancy) $75
Breakfast and dinner at resort restaurants $50
Discounted resort greens fee for guests $75
Car rental (not needed)   0
                                            Total: $200 per person per night

Example 5

Luxury Golf Resort: Resort Golf Package
Luxury room (per person, double-occupancy) $250
Breakfast and dinner on modified American plan   0
Unlimited resort greens fee (included)   0
Car rental (not needed)   0
                                            Total: $250 per person per night

What can be learned from this one comparison?

The least-expensive option is to stay at an economy motel, eat at economy restaurants, and visit a reasonably priced public course. You knew that, right?

But things become more complicated when your goal is to play at one of America's premier resorts. The best deal might be found at a luxury resort that offers discounts on golf rounds or even a golf resort that offers a package, including golf and other amenities, such as lessons, practice time, and more.

A few more notes: car rental is included in Examples 1, 2, and 3 because travelers will need to get to the courses and to restaurants. I have removed the cost of a car rental from Examples 4 and 5 because golfers should be able to make use of the resort's facilities to get to the course and restaurants; most luxury resorts offer courtesy transportation to nearby airports for guests.

In my experience, I have found that modified American plan packages (breakfast and dinner included in room rates) are often priced above the value I would place on those meals, but that's a purely subjective judgment.

Other elements that you should consider are health clubs, pools, tennis courts, jogging tracks, and other amenities. You may also want to take note of attractions for nongolfers in your party (be sure to seek credit for any golf greens fees that will not be used). Families who travel together might want to consider the appeal of courses located within or near major attractions. Mom or dad can go golfing for the day while the kids and the nongolfing spouse can visit such places as Walt Disney World, Williamsburg, Disneyland, and Las Vegas.

Negotiating for a Room

Notice the title of this section; it's not called "Buying a Room." The fact of the matter is that hotel rooms, like almost everything else, are subject to negotiation and change.

Here is how to pay the highest possible price for a hotel room: walk up to the front desk without a reservation and say, "I'd like a room." Unless the "No Vacancy" sign is lit, you may be charged the rack rate, which is the published maximum nightly charge. You not only want to avoid paying the rack rate, you want to pay the lowest possible price.

Before you head for your vacation, spend an hour on the phone and call half a dozen hotels that seem to be in the price range you're comfortable with. (Consider membership in AAA; you can use their annual tour books as starting points for your research.)

Start by asking for the room rate. Then ask the reservation clerk for the hotel's best rate. Does that sound like an unnecessary second request? Trust us, it's not. I can't begin to count the number of times the rates have dropped substantially when I asked a second time.

True story: I once called the reservation desk of a major hotel chain and asked for the rates for a night at a Chicago location. "That will be $149 per night," I was told. "Ouch," I said. "Oh, would you like to spend less?" the reservation clerk asked. I admitted that I would, and she punched a few keys on her keyboard. "They have a special promotion going on. How about $109 per night?" she asked.

Not bad for a city hotel, I reasoned, but still I hadn't asked the big question. "What is your best rate?" I asked. "Oh, our best rate? That would be $79," said the agent.

> **Here's my card.** Membership in AAA brings some important benefits for the traveler, although you may not be able to apply the club's usual 10 percent discount on top of whatever hotel rate you negotiate. (It doesn't hurt to ask, though.) Be sure to request a tour book and maps from AAA, even if you plan to fly; AAA maps are much better than those given by car rental agencies.
>
> If you are age 50 or older, consider membership in AARP (American Association of Retired Persons) for discounts on hotel, car rental, and travel packages. A number of hotels have their own senior discount programs as well.

Weekly, not weakly.
Are you planning to stay for a full week? Ask for the weekly rate. If the reservation clerk says there is no such rate, ask to speak to someone in charge; the manager may be willing to shave a few dollars per day off the rate for a long-term stay.

Safety first. The small safes available in some hotels can be valuable to the traveler; be sure to inquire whether there is a service charge for their use. I've been in hotels that apply the charge whether I used the safe or not; look over your bill at checkout and object to any charges that are not proper. In any case, I'd suggest that any objects that are so valuable that you feel it necessary to lock them up should probably be left at home.

"OK, I'll take it," I told the clerk. "I'm a AAA member, by the way." Another pause. "That's fine, Mr. Sandler. The nightly room rate will be $71.10. Have a nice day."

When you feel you've negotiated the best deal you can over the phone, make a reservation at the hotel of your choice. Be sure to go over the dates and prices one more time, and obtain the name of the person you spoke with and a confirmation number if available.

But wait. When you show up at your hotel on the first night, stop and look at the marquee outside and see if the hotel is advertising a discount rate. Many hotels in major tourist areas adjust their prices based on day-to-day visitor levels. It is not uncommon to see prices change by $10 or more during the course of a day.

Here's where you need to be bold. Walk up to the desk as if you do not have a reservation, and ask the clerk: "What is your best room rate for tonight?" If the rate you are quoted is less than the rate in your reservation, you are now properly armed to ask for a reduction in your room rate.

Similarly, if the room rate advertised out front on the marquee drops during your stay, don't be shy about asking that your charges be reduced. Just be sure to ask for the reduction before you spend another night at the old rate, and obtain the name of the clerk who promises a change. If the hotel tries a lame excuse such as "That's only for new check-ins," you can offer to check out and then check back in again. That will usually work; you can always check out and go to the hotel across the road that will usually match the rates of its competitor.

And here is the way to make the most informed choice, but try it in the low season only. Arrive at your destination without a reservation, and then cruise the motel strip. Check the outdoor marquees for discount prices. I make notes. Make a few phone calls to the ones you found attractive. Once again, be sure to ask for the best price. The later in the day you search for a room, the more likely you are to find a hotel ready to make a deal.

Dialing for Dollars

By now I hope you realize that you must be aggressive in your negotiations with a reservation clerk. Sometimes you also need to be very persistent.

A few years back, a major travel magazine conducted a survey of hotel rates and found wide discrepancies between the prices quoted by central toll-free services, reservations clerks at a particular hotel, and travel agents. The survey was indecisive; no one source consistently yielded the lowest prices.

The magazine's recommendation was to use the services of a travel agent you trust, and request that the agent verify the lowest rate with a direct call. The agent can check the computer first and then compare against the hotel's offer.

How to Protect Against an Unfulfilled Hotel Reservation

A reservation guarantees you a place to stay, right? Well . . . *usually*.

At busy times of the year, hotels hope to operate at or near capacity. And like airlines and car rental companies, a hotel may even take more reservations than it has rooms, figuring that a certain percentage of people will cancel at the last minute or fail to show up. Nevertheless, it is still possible that you can show up at the front desk with your reservation in hand and find out there is no room at the inn.

First of all, let's understand one of the deep, dark little secrets of hotels: in most cases it is almost impossible for a hotel to oust guests who stay beyond their reserved length of stay. The manager can object, the chambermaids can refuse to deliver fresh towels, and room service can take forever to deliver dinner (well, they do that anyway, but you get the idea). Hotels may have to resort to a court order to remove someone who refuses to go peacefully. (I'm not going to suggest this as a strategy, but it is true that some brazen travelers will accept a one-night-only reservation on the day before a sold-out convention and then stay as long as they want.)

How can you protect yourself from losing a room? Guarantee your room for late arrival using a major credit card; by itself this gives you a bought-and-paid-for contract for a room that should be honored, and some credit card companies go even further to add guarantees of their own. If you have any doubts about availability of rooms, call the hotel directly to make a reservation instead of using an 800 number; this is generally a good practice anyhow, since you may sometimes find better prices by calling directly.

If you are a member of a hotel frequent-guest program, use the priority reservation services of the program. (The same applies for car rental services—if you are in a club, use the special number you receive to increase your clout.)

The policies at various hotels differ, but you should be able to make some demands if your reservation is not honored. Start by asking for a suite or a

Clearing the air. If you don't indulge, ask for a nonsmoking room at check-in. With luck, the air will be somewhat cleaner and furniture coverings and drapes somewhat fresher.

Wrong numbers. Be sure you understand a hotel's telephone billing policy. Some establishments allow free local calls, while others charge as much as a dollar for such calls. (I'm especially unhappy with service charges for 800 numbers.) Be sure to examine your bill carefully at checkout and make sure it is correct. I strongly suggest you obtain a telephone credit card and use it when you travel.

Northstar-at-Tahoe's high altitude, 18-hole resort golf course features a wide-open front nine and a technical, tree-lined back nine.

David Madison photo courtesy of Northstar-at-Tahoe

business-class room (at the same rate you were quoted for your original reservation). If that doesn't work, insist that the hotel find you another room of equal or better quality nearby. The hotel should provide transportation to the other hotel if you need it, and if it's a good operation it may offer to give you one or more nights free.

Keep notes of the names of the front-desk personnel and manager and don't be shy about writing to the customer service department of any national chain involved—it may earn you a free room in the future.

Discount Hotel Deals

It should be pretty clear by now that I shudder at the thought of paying full price for travel and hotel arrangements. Here are a few steps every travel shopper should follow:

• Join an association that offers discounts at participating hotel chains and individual locations. These include the AAA and CAA automobile clubs, AARP, and professional groups.

• Use credit cards that offer special discounts to their members; American Express and Discover cards are among the many companies that regularly offer special deals.

• Check into wholesale buying clubs such as Price Club, Costco, BJ's, and others that may offer special deals to members.

• If you are a frequent traveler, consider joining a membership club associated with major hotel chains. Some of these clubs offer discounts off nightly rates, or they may reward you with free nights after a certain number of paid visits.

Discount Hotel Companies

One other avenue to explore is hotel booking services and hotel consolidators. These companies may have made special arrangements with individual hotels to allow them to offer discounted rates at off-peak times of the year, or they may have actually committed to purchase and resell blocks of rooms around the country.

As with any other special offer, be sure to compare the rates offered you with other deals. I suggest you begin by finding the lowest possible rate by yourself. Then call a discount company to see if it has a better deal to offer.

The timing of your reservation entails a metaphorical roll of the dice. You may find that last-minute availability is limited to the most expensive properties. Or you may find a discount company that has some rooms it needs to unload or lose money on.

One of these companies is the Hotel Reservations Network, which claims savings of up to 65 percent at hotels in cities that include Anaheim, Boston, Chicago, Los Angeles, Miami, New Orleans, New York, Orlando, San Diego, and San Francisco.

Here are some discount hotel companies:

Hotel Reservations Network
(800) 964-6835
www.hoteldiscount.com

TravelNow
(800) 568-1972
www.TravelNow.com

Capitol Reservations
(800) 847-4832
http://hotelsdc.com/reserv.html.

A Selection of Some of America's Best Golf Courses

There is no way to make everyone happy with a list of the top golf courses in the country. Some golfer will swear that a barely known, barely maintained muni course up the street is one of America's secret dreams. Others will try to justify their multi-thousand-dollar vacation trip to a dream course in Hawaii or California by rhapsodizing about the perfect placement of the trees and the hillocks and the plushness of the towels in the locker room.

The real answer is this: the best golf course in America is the one that thrilled with its challenge, its beauty, its variety, and the overall quality of the experience for *you.*

Our list of the *Golf U.S.A.* Top 10 is drawn from truly subjective experiences of friends, acquaintances, golf pros, golf writers, and anyone else we could corner to discuss the subject. The list may not be exactly the same as the one you would draw up, but you've got to admit it would be a lot of fun to work your way down the list over the coming year. Fore!

ⓞⓞⓞⓞ *Golf U.S.A.* **Top 10** ⓞⓞⓞⓞ

1. **Pebble Beach Golf Links.** Pebble Beach, California
2. **Pinehurst Resort No. 2.** Pinehurst, North Carolina
3. **Spyglass Hill Golf Course.** Pebble Beach, California
4. **Cascades at The Homestead.** Hot Springs, Virginia
5. **Harbour Town Golf Links.** Hilton Head Island, South Carolina
6. **Mauna Kea Beach Golf Course.** Kamuela (Hawaii), Hawaii
7. **Cog Hill Golf Club #4.** Lemont, Illinois
8. **Kiawah Island Resort Ocean Course.** Kiawah Island, South Carolina
9. **Tournament Players Club Stadium Course at Sawgrass.** Ponte Vedra Beach, Florida
10. **The Prince, Princeville Resort.** Princeville (Kauai), Hawaii

Chapter 4
Golf Travelers' Most Frequently Asked Questions

One of the most welcome additions to our publishing lexicon comes from the world of the Internet, where common-interest groups on almost any conceivable topic introduce themselves with lists of frequently asked questions, known in the computer world as FAQs.

I'm committed to the world of paper and ink; books travel so much better than PCs (no batteries or extension cords), and dropping a book into the bathtub is much less of a catastrophe than drowning a laptop computer. However, I'm not above borrowing a good idea when I see one. So, here are the golfing FAQs, just the FAQs.

Golf Equipment

Even a great golfer needs the right equipment. What constitutes the right equipment? Read on.

Clubs

1. *What is a* wood, *and why are some of them made of materials that never grew in a forest?* The classic definition of a wood is a club for use when distance down the fairway or a carry across a body of water is more important than accuracy. Originally such clubs were made of solid wood, but there are now woods made of laminated timber, metal, and advanced man-made substances such as graphite.

Wooden woods usually are made of persimmon for solid heads that are turned using a master model or on an automated lathe; laminated heads are made of thin veneers of wood that are pressure-formed and turned on a lathe. There is little difference in performance or feel between the two types of wooden woods, although a laminated club may be sturdier than a solid one.

Metal woods generally are made of cast metal including stainless steel, aluminum, and more exotic materials such as titanium. The club heads are usually hollow when first cast; they are then precisely balanced—or sometimes purposely made off-balance to achieve a certain effect—when they are filled with polyurethane or other compounds.

31

Because the metal in the metal woods is usually cast pretty thin, it is sometimes subject to being crushed or dented. One way to get around this is to make the metal wood slightly smaller but with thicker walls, a so-called midsize head; another solution involves the use of plastic, graphite, or harder metal face inserts in the sweet spot of metal woods.

Graphite, which has increasingly become the material of choice for club shafts, is also used for molding woods. Graphite woods usually are about the same weight as wood or metal woods, but because the material is about 40 percent lighter than steel the resulting club is much larger. As such, it gives the golfer a larger sweet spot, which may be a comfort for some players, and is a bit more forgiving for slightly off-center hits.

By the way, some especially strong and accurate swingers on the pro tour will use a 1- or 2-iron off the tee on some holes.

2. *What is meant by the "loft" of a club?* Loft is a measurement of the angle of the club face compared with a flat surface beneath it. A club with 0 degrees of loft is perpendicular to the ground; a 1-wood usually has between 8 and 12 degrees of loft.

3. *What is an* iron, *and are any of them made from that basic element?* Irons, used when accuracy is more important than distance, originally were made of iron. Today few are. More common are stainless steel irons. Some are made of aluminum, and the newest thing is the forged titanium iron, promising greater accuracy and distance than iron irons. Irons are either cast or forged.

A cast club is created by pouring molten metal into a mold that includes markings and design elements. A form of cast club is the cavity back iron, which distributes the weight of the head around its perimeter and yields a large sweet spot that is more forgiving of off-center shots.

A forged club is made by hammering and otherwise shaping a superheated chunk of metal; the completed piece must then go through a finishing process that includes milling and grinding. A form of forged iron is a muscleback, or blade, design that is formed in such a way as to distribute the weight of the iron across all of the head, producing a small sweet spot in its center. This makes a properly hit shot fly straight and long, but penalizes any off-center hit. Some golfers believe that a muscleback iron delivers a truer feel.

4. *What do the numbers on clubs mean?* The numbers evolved over time as more weapons were added to the golfer's arsenal, but they generally refer to the relative loft of a club—the lower the number, the lower the loft and the "longer" the club. A low-loft long club is supposed to deliver the greatest distance at the cost of accuracy; a higher number means higher loft—meaning shorter distance and better accuracy.

5. *Is there a standard "set" of clubs?* A golfer is supposed to have no more than 14 clubs in a set—you can have less but not more. The makeup of your optimal set should vary according to your strength and abilities as well as the particular challenges you expect to see on the course you are playing.

A typical set might include:

Woods: 1, 3, and 5
Irons: 3, 4, 5, 6, 7, 8, 9, and a pitching wedge
Putter

Some players will sacrifice a 5-iron or a 6-iron for a sand wedge, especially when playing on beachlike courses.

6. *What kind of shaft should stand between the grip and the club?* If you think about its function, you'll realize that the shaft is actually the most complex part of a golf club. It has to be strong yet light, able to transfer the power of your swing to the club and ball yet able to flex properly, and it must be the proper length for varying skill levels and sizes of golfers. Designers talk about weight, stiffness, torque, and flex points.

Shafts were originally made of wood, but these are mostly relegated to the antique shelves these days. More common now are steel, graphite, or titanium. Stainless steel or carbon steel shafts are drawn to the proper length, thickness, and wall design, and then hardened and chrome plated. The flex of the shaft typically is adjusted by making it thinner at the grip (more likely to flex) and thicker at the club. Steel shafts have the advantage of carrying an identical or similar feel from one club in a set to another, and they are generally the least expensive and most durable.

Graphite shafts generally are made by wrapping graphite tape around a form, which is later cut and polished. Graphite shafts are noticeably lighter than steel, and able to dampen the vibration transmitted up the shaft by contact with the ball or ground. Graphite shafts, though, can vary in feel from one club in a set to another; they are also more expensive than steel. Even more expensive are graphite shafts with filament winding, which is supposed to combine the light weight and feel of graphite with the consistency of steel.

Most expensive are titanium shafts, which are light and strong; some players find them too stiff.

7. *How do I judge the stiffness of a shaft?* As with any other piece of equipment, whatever works best for you is the right thing. Experts say that the faster your swing speed the stiffer the shaft you should use (this is to prevent the club head from lagging behind the shaft as it meets the ball). Conversely, slower swingers can benefit from the extra kick a flexible shaft will deliver.

Shafts are often rated by manufacturers as R (regular), S (stiff), and X (extra stiff). There are also A (men's flexible) and L (ladies' flexible) classes.

In general, a beginner and someone with a less-than-awesome swing will benefit from a lightweight, high-flex shaft that will drive the ball further.

A more technical way to rate a shaft is to list its frequency, a measure of the number of vibration cycles per minute for the shaft. The stiffer the shaft, the faster its vibration rate; an extra-stiff shaft vibrates at about 270 cycles.

Let's talk about *torque.* Let's do the twist, which is what a shaft's torque is all about. In general, the stiffer the shaft the less torque the club will have. Steel shafts typically have a torque rating of about 2.5 degrees, a relatively slight potential twisting action. Graphite shafts are twistier, usually ranging from about 3.5 to 5.5 degrees of torque. Some exotic graphite shafts extend beyond this range in either direction.

8. *What's the purpose of flex points?* The flex point, also called the kick point or the bend point, is the place where a shaft will bend. A high flex point will result in a low trajectory. A low flex point will tend to make the ball fly higher; the shaft will feel as if it whips the club into the ball.

9. *How do I get a grip for myself?* Even the seemingly minor issue of how to hold onto your club can become as complicated as any other part of golfing equipment. Golf grips are typically made of rubber, leather, or cord. They are available in standard, oversized, and undersized versions.

The original design for grips used cowhide or calfskin leather. These are soft and comfortable with a bit of tackiness that helps you hold onto the club. Leather grips are a bit more expensive than man-made materials and may require professional installation and repair.

Rubber grips are usually a composition material made up of rubber and granulated cork. The advantage of rubber includes its lower price, ease of installation, and the ability to mold into the grip markers for hand placement and other special comfort and playability features.

Cord grips add fabric or man-made filament to a rubber grip to create a nonslip surface, especially valuable in wet, hot, or humid weather. A variation is a half-cord grip that puts smooth rubber at thumb level and corded rubber where the fingers wrap around.

Grip sizes can be adjusted with padding or tape on the shaft beneath the grip. Alternatively, you can order your grips in special sizes.

Oversized grips can be more comfortable for certain players, especially those with arthritis or other problems or those who have extra-large paws. The overlarge grip may reduce hand movement, increasing a tendency to slice.

An undersized grip is geared toward women and others with smaller hands. The hand is more likely to move, increasing a tendency to hook.

10. *What kind of putter should I use?* That's easy: use the one that lets you sink the ball into the cup under all imaginable conditions. If you think about it, the humble putter is probably the most important club in your bag. On a typical course, about 60 percent of the shots are pitches, chips, or putts; any golfer who neglects the short game is due for a lifetime of high scores. You'll use a putter on just about every hole, and if you can learn to shave a stroke off every traverse of the green, you'll lower your score by 18.

Putters come in a bewildering set of shapes, but are basically of one of three designs: blades, mallets, and perimeter-weighted heads. The simple blade uses a small, flat surface and in the hands of an expert putter offers a great deal of precision in aiming. For the rest of us, seeking to improve on our limited skills, there are also mallets which use a larger, rounder clubhead, and perimeter-weighted clubs that balance the weight of the club around a large central sweet spot; both of these designs are intended to make putts move straighter.

11. *How do I select the best clubs for me?* The best suggestion is to combine some informed advice with some real-world testing. In other words, ask a golf pro, golf equipment salesperson, or good golfer you know and trust about the latest and greatest equipment, as well as the oldest and most-proven.

The next step is to try out the clubs. Beg or borrow—don't steal—a set from the golf shop, the pro shop at a golf club, or a friend. You might be able to rent a set from a golf club too. Play a round or two with the clubs.

It would be wonderful if you suddenly found that the new clubs shaved a dozen strokes off your typical game. In fact, you may find that the new clubs feel so very different from your current set that your score goes up. What you are looking for are cures for known problems, an improved feel, and an overall better match between the equipment and your abilities.

12. *Should I purchase a custom-fitted or custom-built set of clubs?* In the best of all possible worlds, a custom-fitted or custom-built set of clubs would be standard. That's because no two golfers are the same height, and no two golfers have identical strength, ability, or preferences.

Off-the-shelf sets are assembled based on a club manufacturer's definition of an average golfer; you will find sets of clubs best suited for rank amateurs, competent longtime players, and pro-level players. Although prices will fit within a wide range, off-the-shelf sets are relatively less expensive than custom sets.

A custom-built set is one that is manufactured specifically for a single golfer. It may include nonstandard shaft lengths, customized weighting, special grips, and other accommodations. Parts for the clubs can be made by a club maker or can be ordered from a name-brand manufacturer and assembled to meet your needs. No matter how you cut it, buying custom-built clubs is the most expensive way to go.

In between is a custom-fit set. This is a set that is made up of ready-made components selected to match your particular needs. For example, you can order nonstandard lengths from most major name-brand club makers. Or you can mix and match club lengths and weights within a set.

Whether you end up buying your clubs from the pro shop or from a retail or mail-order operation, a visit to your local pro—especially one who is familiar with your game—can help you save money and time.

13. *Should I have my clubs adjusted and maintained?* In a word, yes. Any competent technician can adjust the shaft length of your clubs to help you strike the ball squarely. Shafts can be shortened by cutting or in many cases lengthened with an insert.

Another valuable service is an adjustment to the grip to make sure it fits your hands. Grips can be built up with tape on the shaft. You can also purchase replacement grips for most shafts.

Older irons with worn grooves can be rejuvenated to restore your ability to apply backspin.

14. *Can I build my own clubs?* Yes. A number of club makers sell components—club heads, shafts, and grips—that you can assemble by yourself. You'll find listings in some of the golf magazines. You may be able to save some money this way, but you'll need to do your own research for advice on customization.

Balls

1. *My local pro shop has golf balls for sale with prices from about a buck to $5 each. Will an expensive ball make me a star on the PGA Tour?* No, but it might help the owner of your pro shop make a boat payment.

Let's start with the numbers: some golfers are willing to spend thousands of dollars on a set of clubs, hundreds on clothing, hundreds on greens fees . . . but everyone ends up swinging at a ball that sells for just a few dollars.

Approximately 2.3 million balls are sold worldwide every day—about 832 million a year. Two-thirds of the ball sales are made in the American market. The average retail price of a ball is about $2.50, but some are sold for about half that and others for twice the price. Insiders say that balls—no matter what the selling price—cost less than 50 cents to manufacture.

Ball makers have tried mightily during the past decade to make the simple golf ball more complicated and expensive. In 1985, only 147 ball designs were officially accepted for play in tournaments. Today, that number has passed more than 1,500. (In 1996, leading golfer Greg Norman took himself out of a tournament when he apparently used a ball that was mislabeled.)

Consider this: In 1968, the average length of a drive on the pro tour was 258 yards; in 1995, it was 263 yards. That's about a 2 percent increase, which most observers credit to the improved physical condition of today's players, not to improved equipment.

2. *What kind of balls are legal for play?* There are two basic designs: three-piece, used by nearly every professional golfer, and two-piece, used by nearly everyone else.

The three-piece ball has a solid or liquefied center that is wound with rubber threads and then covered with a synthetic balata outer surface. Balata is a latexlike dried juice of trees in the sapodilla family. Today, real balata is hard to find; instead, there are synthetic substitutes that have the same properties.

A balata ball is more expensive, has a short life span, cuts easily, and goes out of round after just a few solid hits. But it supposedly has a superior feel and offers more control to those golfers able to apply hooks, slices, and spins at will to fade or draw a shot or apply backspin.

Two-piece balls have a solid plastic center and a plastic cover, usually based on Surlyn (courtesy of a DuPont factory instead of a noble tree). Less expensive and less likely to cut or nick, a Surlyn ball goes farther than a three-piece ball, but it is harder to control.

Use whichever type of ball works best for you. Some experts say that golfers who shoot in the 70s generally prefer the three-piece ball because they can better control the flight of the ball. For the rest of us, two-piece balls will (in theory) fly longer and straighter.

3. *Can a manufacturer stuff the ball with feathers or flubber?* Yes, more or less. The official specifications say that a golf ball cannot weigh more than 1.62 ounces and cannot be smaller than 1.68 inches in diameter. The balls also must pass a test with a golf swing machine: they can't have an initial velocity off the club face of more than 250 feet per second, and can't travel more than 280 yards when hit by the machine.

So, a basketball-sized ball filled with feathers just might qualify.

4. *What about those cute dimples?* First of all, they're not just cute; they are essential to the flight of the ball. The purpose of the dimples is to make the ball aerodynamically appropriate, pulling air over the top and creating pressure underneath, which makes the ball fly somewhat like an airplane wing. The number of dimples has varied from a few hundred to nearly a thousand. The common range for officially accepted balls is from 318 to 552.

5. *What about the compression rating for golf balls?* You think you're under pressure when you step up to the tee? Inside your golf ball, the core is under extreme pressure; typical golf balls are given compression ratings between 80 and 100, with 90 a common choice. There is no proven correlation between compression and the distance or accuracy of a shot, although some golfers claim to be able to feel a difference between high- and low-rated balls.

6. *Which type of ball should I use?* The one you can drive the farthest, approach the green with the most accuracy with, and putt with deadeye aim. Some players can discern no difference between the most expensive balls on the market and the scuffs they find on the driving range; others are more particular about the golf ball they choose than anything else in their lives.

Hitting the Ball with the Club

1. *Why do my drives not fly straight to where I aim them?* If we were able to solve that problem with just a few words here, we could become instant millionaires—so rich we could afford to hire someone else to play golf for us.

Aside from missing the ball—which none of us has ever done, right?—the most common problems are hooks and slices, pushes and pulls, and fades or draws. These are not always problems, though, since capable golfers can purposely change their swing to direct the ball for a tricky shot.

2. *What is a hook and how is it different from a slice?* A slice happens when the ball is given a sidespin that makes it curve in flight from left to right, generally costing you a bit of distance as well as putting you in danger of landing in the rough.

A hook is the opposite of a slice.

A slice happens when the club face strikes the ball open several degrees relative to the club path. A hook is caused by striking the ball with the club face a bit closed on contact.

Other causes of slices are an outside-to-in swing plane, an incomplete hand release, or a collapsed left wrist. You might also slice if you place the ball too far back in your stance.

A hook can come about from an inside-to-out swing plane, an early hand release, or a bowed left wrist. Placing the ball too far forward in your stance also contributes to your chances of shooting a hook.

The best way to fix a hook or a slice is to seek professional help. A competent instructor or pro should be able to diagnose the source of your problem.

Better players can purposely add a slice to bend a drive around a dogleg to the right, or a hook to go the other direction.

3. *What is a push and how is it different from a pull?* A push is a ball that has very little sidespin and a straight flight path but ends up to the right of the target.

A pull is the opposite of a push, with a straight shot ending up to the left of the target.

4. *What is a fade and how is it different from a draw?* A fade is a straight shot with just a bit of sidespin that gives it left-to-right travel at the end of its flight. Because the forward energy of the ball is greater than the slight

sidespin, the fade of the ball doesn't take effect until it slows down near the end of its flight. A fade is accomplished by a straight swing aimed at the target with the club face open just a few degrees at impact.

A draw is the opposite of a fade, with a small amount of right-to-left travel at the end of its flight. A draw is accomplished by a straight swing aimed at the target with the club face closed just a few degrees at impact.

Handicap, Course, and Slope Ratings

1. *What is a USGA handicap index?* A handicap is one way to equalize the level of skill among a party of golfers, across a large tournament of contestants, or between you and Tiger Woods, Greg Norman, and whoever is the PGA star of the day.

In formal terms, a handicap is an estimation of a player's expected performance on a standardized course (more about that later). A handicap of 0 means a player can be expected to shoot par on an ordinary course. A handicap of 18 means the player can be expected to average a stroke over par on an ordinary course.

In practical terms, players subtract their handicap from actual strokes at the end of a round for a net score.

The next step is to find a way to compare performance on one course with another; we'll get to slope and course ratings in a moment.

Sea Trail Golf Links, Sunset Beach, North Carolina
Courtesy of the North Carolina Division of Travel and Tourism

2. *How do I obtain an official USGA handicap index?* The only way to receive a rating is to be assigned one by a golf club that subscribes to the USGA system. The handicap is based on the average of your 10 best scores among the last 20 rounds you have played.

You don't necessarily have to become a member of an exclusive and expensive golf club for the purpose, though; there are golf clubs at many public courses that charge only modest fees and often afford you special privileges, including reduced greens fees and preferred tee times. Clubs don't even necessarily have to be associated with a golf course, but can run traveling competitions and events at a number of locations.

There is also another way to obtain a close equivalent to a USGA handicap. The quick reference allowance (QRA) can be used by a tournament committee for ranking players. The QRA takes the three best scores made in the last year on a regulation course with a par of 68 or higher. Also included are any scores made in a tournament during the past two years. The QRA is calculated as the second-best score, minus 70 for men or minus 73 for women.

3. *What do the USGA course and slope ratings mean?* The United States Golf Association (USGA) attempts to create a way to compare one golfer with another, and one golf course with another.

Courses are rated based on criteria set up by the USGA; the ratings are supposed to be performed by authorized golf associations rather than the particular club itself.

A yardage rating classifies the difficulty of play based only on yardage; as such it does not take into account obstacles and terrain and other natural and unnatural elements of the design that can make a 4,500-foot killer and a 7,500-foot cream puff. The rating is expressed as the score a scratch player would be expected to make when playing a course of average difficulty.

A scratch player is defined by the USGA as an amateur player who plays to the standard of the stroke-play qualifiers competing in the U.S. Amateur Championship. A male scratch golfer can hit tee shots an average of 250 yards and can reach a 470-yard hole in two shots. This generally equates to a player with a 0 handicap up to about a 2 handicap. A female scratch golfer is an amateur player who plays to the standard of the match-play qualifiers in the U.S. Women's Amateur Championship and can hit tee shots an average of 210 yards and can reach a 400-yard hole in two shots.

Another important rating, though not often published, is the bogey rating. First of all, a bogey golfer is a player who is about a stroke above par, specifically one who has a USGA handicap index between 17.5 and 22.4 for men and between 21.5 and 26.4 for women; a male bogey golfer can be expected to hit tee shots an average of 200 yards and reach a 370-yard hole in two shots, while a female bogey golfer can hit tee shots of 150 yards and reach a 280-yard hole in two shots.

A bogey rating is an evaluation of the difficulty of a course for a bogey golfer under normal course and weather conditions and includes yardage and obstacles to the extent they affect scoring. It is calculated as the average of the better half of a bogey golfer's scores under normal playing conditions. We'll come to the importance of the bogey rating in a moment.

A USGA course rating is a classification of the playing difficulty of a course under normal course and weather conditions, specifically taking into account yardage and other obstacles that affect the scoring ability of a scratch player. The course rating is expressed in strokes.

Note that a yardage rating and USGA course rating are not the same as par, and not directly related to that measure.

The slope rating classifies the relative difficulty of a course for players with handicaps above scratch. The lowest slope rating is 55 and the highest is 155, and the average slope rating for men and women is 113.

In case you were wondering, here's how a slope rating is calculated: the difference between the bogey rating and the course rating is multiplied by 5.381 for men and 4.24 for women.

Courses make available a conversion chart that relates the slope rating to the USGA handicap of individual players. Ratings are also listed for each of the various sets of tees at a course. Golfers check the chart at the course to see where their handicap index falls on the chart; at a difficult course, your handicap will be adjusted upward, and at an easier-than-average course it will be adjusted downward.

The course ratings also take into account play from the back and front tees, again with the aim of equalizing play among golfers of different skill levels.

The Toughest Courses in America

Based on the slope rating, which are the most difficult courses in America? The top end of the rating chart is set at 155, and a handful of courses come very close to the ceiling with ratings from championship tees.

Here's a somewhat selective listing of 35 of the most difficult 18-hole courses in America.

⊚⊚⊚⊚ *Golf U.S.A.* 35 Toughest Public Courses ⊚⊚⊚⊚

1. **Westin La Paloma Country Club.** Tucson, Arizona	155/155
2. **Kiawah Island Resort.** Ocean Course, Kiawah Island, South Carolina	152/133
3. **Blackwolf Run Golf Club.** Whistling Straights Course, Kohler, Wisconsin	152/132
4. **Marriott's Bay Point Resort.** Lagoon Legend Course, Panama City Beach, Florida	152/127
5. **PGA West.** TPC Stadium Course, La Quinta, California	151/124
6. **Blackwolf Run Golf Club.** River Course, Kohler, Wisconsin	151/128
7. **Thunder Hill Golf Club.** South Madison, Ohio	151/127
8. **Redhawk Golf Club.** Temecula, California	149/124
9. **Spyglass Hill Golf Course.** Pebble Beach, California	147/133
10. **Thoroughbred Golf Club.** Rothbury, Michigan	147/126
11. **Troon North Golf Club.** Monument, Pinnacle. Scottsdale, Arizona	147/128
12. **Grand Traverse Resort.** Bear Course, Acme, Michigan	146/137
13. **Breckenridge Golf Club.** Breckenridge, Colorado	146/118

14. **Ventana Canyon Golf and Racquet Club.** Mountain Course,
    Tucson, Arizona   146/117
15. **The Prince Golf Club.** Princeville, Kauai, Hawaii   145/127
16. **Desert Falls Country Club.** Palm Desert, California   145/124
17. **Wilderness Valley Golf Club.** Black Forest Course, Gaylord,
    Michigan   145/131
18. **Quicksilver Golf Club.** Midway, Pennsylvania   145/115
19. **North Port National Golf Club.** Lake Ozark, Missouri   145/122
20. **Shattuck Golf Course.** Jaffrey, New Hampshire   145/139
21. **Fox Creek Golf Club.** Edwardsville, Illinois   144/134
22. **Hulman Links Golf Course.** Terre Haute, Indiana   144/127
23. **Treetops Sylvan Resort.** Jones Masterpiece Course, Gaylord,
    Michigan   144/123
24. **Stoney Creek Golf Club.** East Stoney Creek, North Carolina   144/123
25. **Poppy Hills Golf Course.** Pebble Beach, California   144/131
26. **Elk Ridge Golf Club.** Atlanta, Michigan   143/130
27. **Blackwolf Run Golf Club.** Meadow Valleys Course, Kohler,
    Wisconsin   143/125
28. **Marriott's Tan-Tar.** Oaks Course, Osage Beach, Missouri   143/103
29. **The Golf Courses at Kenton County.** Independence, Kentucky   143/123
30. **Bluffs on Thompson Creek Golf Club.** St. Francisville, Louisiana 143/123
31. **La Purisma Golf Course.** Lompoc, California   143/131
32. **Makalei Hawaii Country Club.** Kailua-Kona, Hawaii   143/125
33. **Sentryworld Golf Course.** Stevens Point, Wisconsin   142/126
34. **Tapawingo National Golf Club.** St. Louis, Missouri   141/139
35. **Bald Head Island Club.** Bald Head Island, North Carolina   139/117

Pebble Beach Golf Links
Photo © Joann Dost, courtesy Pebble Beach Golf Links

Chapter 5
Golf U.S.A. State-by-State

The East

Connecticut

Delaware

Maine

Maryland

Massachusetts

New Hampshire

New Jersey

New York

Pennsylvania

Rhode Island

Vermont

Virginia

Washington, D.C.

Connecticut

Golf in Connecticut can be very green and very busy in the spring and summer.

The **Richter Park Golf Club** in Danbury, a bit more than an hour from New York City, is a not-so-hidden jewel where it can be quite difficult to obtain a tee time if you are not a local resident; still, it's worth a try.

Sterling Farms Golf Club in Stamford is another surprisingly lush municipal course, again with restrictions on out-of-towners. Also worth a visit is the **Crestbrook Park Golf Course** in Watertown, just north of Waterbury. In the Hartford area is the **Tallwood Country Club** in Hebron, a green and watery course.

Elmridge Golf Course recently added a second 18 holes, River Ridge in Griswold, just north of the Foxwoods Casino. **Tashua Knolls** in Trumbull has plans to add another 9 to its facilities.

Some Connecticut courses manage to stay open year-round, with deep discounts in the winter. In the snowbelts of the state, courses may close in the heart of the winter.

Look for highest prices in the heart of the summer, with the best deals in the coolest months.

Golf U.S.A. Leader Board: Best Public Course in Connecticut

☺☺☺☺   Richter Park Golf Club

Golf U.S.A. Leader Board: Best Deals in Connecticut

$$/☺☺☺	Blackledge Country Club (Anderson, Gilead, Links)
$$/☺☺☺	Cedar Knob Golf Club
$$/☺☺☺	Crestbrook Park Golf Course
$$/☺☺☺	Lyman Orchards Golf Club (Robert Trent Jones Course)
$$/☺☺☺	Pequabuck Golf Club
$$/☺☺☺	Pine Valley Country Club
$$/☺☺☺	Portland Golf Course
$$/☺☺☺	Ridgefield Golf Course
$$/☺☺☺	Rockledge Country Club
$$/☺☺☺	Shennecossett Municipal Golf Course
$$/☺☺☺	Simsbury Farms Golf Club
$$/☺☺☺	H. Smith Richardson Golf Course
$$/☺☺☺	Stanley Golf Club (Blue, Red, White)
$$/☺☺☺	Sterling Farms Golf Club
$$/☺☺☺	Tallwood Country Club
$$/☺☺☺	Timberlin Golf Club
$$/☺☺☺	Tunxis Plantation Country Club (Red, Green)

Connecticut Golf Guide

Stamford

P	**Sterling Farms Golf Club**	Greens:	$$–$$$	W L T S J
☺☺☺	Newfield Ave., Stamford. (203) 329-7888	Carts:	$–$$	
DEAL	18 holes. Par 72/73. Yards: 6,410/5,600	Rating:	71.7/72.6	
	Year-round. High: July–Aug.	Slope:	127/121	

Bridgeport Area

P	**Candlewood Valley Country Club**	Greens:	$–$$	W T S
☺☺	Danbury Rd., New Milford. (860) 354-9359	Carts:	$–$$	
	18 holes. Par 72/72. Yards: 6,295/5,403	Rating:	70.3/70.9	
	Apr.–Dec. High: May–Sept.	Slope:	120/126	

Key to Symbols

Rating: 1 to 4 Golf Balls

☺	Worth a Visit		
☺☺	Above Average		
☺☺☺	Exceptional		
☺☺☺☺	Very Best		

Course Type

P	Public
R	Resort
SP	Semiprivate

BEST	*Golf U.S.A.* Best American Courses
DEAL	*Golf U.S.A.* Best Golfing Deals
STATE	*Golf U.S.A.* Best in State

Price Ranges

$	<$20	Bargain
$$	$20–$39	Budget
$$$	$40–$59	Moderate
$$$$	$60–$79	Expensive
$$$$$	$80–$100	Very Expensive
$$$$$$	$100+	Exclusive

Discounts

W	Weekdays
L	Low Season
R	Resort Guests
T	Twilight
S	Seniors
J	Juniors

Connecticut Golf Guide

P ☺☺☺ DEAL	**H. Smith Richardson Golf Course** Morehouse Hwy., Fairfield. (203) 255-7300 18 holes. Par 72/72. Yards: 6,676/5,764 Mar.-Nov. High: May-Oct.	Greens: $ W Carts: $$ Rating: 71.0/72.8 Slope: 124/127
P ☺☺	**Tashua Knolls Golf Course** Tashua Knolls Lane, Trumbull. (203) 261-5989 18 holes. Par 72/72. Yards: 6,540/5,454 Mar.-Dec. High: May-Sept.	Greens: $$ W S J Carts: $$ Rating: 71.9/71.7 Slope: 125/124
P ☺☺	**Whitney Farms Golf Course** Shelton Rd., Monroe. (203) 268-0707 18 holes. Par 72/73. Yards: 6,714/5,480 Mar.-Dec. High: June-Aug.	Greens: $$$ W Carts: Incl. Rating: 72.4/72.9 Slope: 135/134

New Haven Area

P ☺☺	**Grassy Hill Country Club** Clark Lane, Orange. (203) 795-1422 18 holes. Par 70/71. Yards: 6,208/5,209 Mar.-Dec. High: Apr.-Oct.	Greens: $$ W S Carts: $ Rating: 70.5/71.1 Slope: 122/118
P ☺☺	**Orange Hills Country Club** Racebrook Rd., Orange. (203) 795-4161 18 holes. Par 71/74. Yards: 6,451/6,080 Mar.-Nov. High: May-Oct.	Greens: $$ W Carts: $$ Rating: 71.2/71.5 Slope: 116/121

New London/Norwich Area

P ☺☺	**Elmridge Golf Course** 229 Elmridge Rd., Pawcatuck. (860) 599-2248 *Red/Blue/White* 27 holes. Par 71/72/71. Yards: 6,347/6,650/6,311 Mar.-Dec. High: May-Sept.	Greens: $$ W L T Carts: $$ Rating: 121/117/115 Slope: 72.3/70.8/70.5
P ☺☺	**River Ridge Golf Course** Rte. 164, Griswold (860) 376-3268 18 holes. Par 72/72. Yards: 6,436/5,340 Mar.-Dec. High: May-Sept.	Greens: $$ W L T Carts: $$ Rating: 70.6/71.0 Slope: 126/118
P ☺☺	**Norwich Golf Course** New London Turnpike, Norwich. (860) 889-6973 18 holes. Par 71/71. Yards: 6,191/5,104 Apr.-Dec. High: May-Aug.	Greens: $$ W Carts: $ Rating: 69.6/70.2 Slope: 123/118
P ☺☺☺ DEAL	**Shennecossett Municipal Golf Course** Plant St., Groton. (860) 445-0262 18 holes. Par 71/71. Yards: 6,562/5,671 Year-round. High: July-Aug.	Greens: $$ W Carts: $ Rating: 69.1/72.4 Slope: 121/122

Waterbury/Watertown/Bristol Area

P ☺☺☺ DEAL	**Crestbrook Park Golf Course** Northfield Rd., Watertown. (860) 945-5249 18 holes. Par 71/75. Yards: 5,696/6492/6098 Apr.-Dec. High: June-Aug.	Greens: $$ W S J Carts: $$ Rating: 73.6/69.9/73.8 Slope: 128/121/128
SP ☺☺☺ DEAL	**Pequabuck Golf Club** School St., Pequabuck. (860) 583-7307 18 holes. Par 69/72. Yards: 6,015/5,374 Apr.-Dec. High: May-Sept.	Greens: $$$ Carts: $$ Rating: 68.7/70.3 Slope: 115/118

Danbury Area

P ☺☺☺☺ BEST	**Richter Park Golf Club** Aunt Hack Rd., Danbury. (203) 748-5743 18 holes. Par 72/72. Yards: 6,744/5,114 Apr.-Nov. High: June-Aug.	Greens: $$-$$$ T S J Carts: $$ Rating: 73.3/69.8 Slope: 134/126

Connecticut Golf Guide

P ☺☺☺ DEAL	**Ridgefield Golf Course** Ridgebury Rd., Ridgefield. (203) 748-7008 18 holes. Par 71/74. Yards: 6,444/5,124 Apr.–Nov. High: June–Aug.	Greens: $$$ T S J Carts: $$ Rating: 70.9/70.76 Slope: 123/119

Hartford Area

P ☺☺	**Bel Compo Golf Club** Nod Rd., Avon. (860) 678-1679 18 holes. Par 71/71. Yards: 6,779/5,171 Apr.–Nov. High: May–Sept.	Greens: $$ W S J Carts: $ Rating: 71.9/69.5 Slope: 125/116
P ☺☺☺ DEAL	**Blackledge Country Club** West St., Hebron. (860) 228-0250 *Anderson/Gilead/Links* 27 holes. Par 72/72/72. Yards: 6,787/6,718/6,701 Mar.–Dec. High: June–Aug.	Greens: $$ W L T S J Carts: $ Rating: 72.3/NA/NA Slope: 123/NA/NA
P ☺☺☺ DEAL	**Cedar Knob Golf Club** Billings Rd., Somers. (860) 749-3550 18 holes. Par 72/74. Yards: 6,734/5,784 Year-round. High: Apr.–Sept.	Greens: $ W L S J Carts: $ Rating: 72.3/73.8 Slope: 119/126
P ☺☺	**Hunter Memorial Golf Club** Westfield Rd., Meriden. (203) 634-3366 18 holes. Par 71/72. Yards: 6,700/5,764 Mar.–Dec. High: June–Aug.	Greens: $–$$ W S J Carts: $$ Rating: 71.9/72.7 Slope: 124/131
SP ☺☺	**Lyman Orchards Golf Club** Rt. 157, Middlefield. (860) 349-8055 *Gary Player Course* 18 holes. Par 70/71. Yards: 5,763/6,325 Mar.–Nov. High: May–Oct.	Greens: $$/$$$ W T S Carts: Incl. and required Rating: 71.2/69.6 Slope: 131/128
☺☺☺ DEAL	*Robert Trent Jones Course* 18 holes. Par 72/72. Yards: 6,200/6,614	Greens: $$/$$$ Carts: $ Rating: 71.2/69.3 Slope: 127/123
P ☺☺	**Millbrook Country Club** Pigeon Hill Rd., Windsor. (860) 688-2575 18 holes. Par 71/73. Yards: 6,258/5,715 Apr.–Nov. High: May–Oct.	Greens: $$ Carts: $ Rating: 71.0/71.0 Slope: 125/124
P ☺☺☺ DEAL	**Pine Valley Country Club** Welch Rd., Southington. (860) 628-0879 18 holes. Par 71/73. Yards: 6,325/5,482 Mar.–Dec. High: June–Aug.	Greens: $$ Carts: $ Rating: 70.6/72.0 Slope: 123/122
SP ☺☺☺ DEAL	**Portland Golf Course** Bartlett St., Portland. (860) 342-6107 18 holes. Par 71/71. Yards: 6,213/5,039 Mar.–Dec. High: May–Oct.	Greens: $$ W S J Carts: $ Rating: 70.8/68.6 Slope: 124/118
P ☺☺☺ DEAL	**Rockledge Country Club** S. Main St., W. Hartford. (860) 521-3156 18 holes. Par 72/74. Yards: 6,436/5,434 Apr.–Dec. High: June–July	Greens: $–$$ S Carts: $ Rating: 71.1/72.7 Slope: 129/129
P ☺☺☺ DEAL	**Simsbury Farms Golf Club** Old Farms Rd., West Simsbury. (860) 658-6246 18 holes. Par 72/72. Yards: 6,421/5,439 Apr.–Nov. High: May–Sept.	Greens: $$ Carts: $$ Rating: 71.1/70.1 Slope: 124/117
P ☺☺☺ DEAL	**Stanley Golf Club** Hartford Rd., New Britain. (860) 827-8144 *Blue/Red/White* 27 holes. Par 72/71. Yards: 6,453/6,138 Apr.–Dec. High: June–Sept.	Greens: $$ W Carts: $$ Rating: 71.1/71.6 Slope: 115/118

Connecticut Golf Guide

P ☺☺☺ DEAL	**Tallwood Country Club** North St., Rte. 85. Hebron. (860) 646-3437 18 holes. Par 72/72. Yards: 6,366/5,430 Mar.–Dec. High: May–Sept.	Greens: $$ Carts: $ Rating: 70.2/70.6 Slope: 123/121	L
P ☺☺☺ DEAL	**Timberlin Golf Club** Ken Bates Dr., Kensington. (860) 828-3228 18 holes. Par 72/72. Yards: 6,733/5,477 Apr.–Nov. High: June–Sept.	Greens: $–$$ Carts: $ Rating: 72.2/72.0 Slope: 129/125	S J
P ☺☺☺ DEAL	**Tunxis Plantation Country Club** Town Farm Rd., Farmington. (860) 677-1367 *Green Course* 18 holes. Par 70. Yards: 5,958 Apr.–Nov. High: May–Aug.	Greens: $$ Carts: $$ Rating: 68.1 Slope: 117	S J
☺☺	*White Course* 18 holes. Par 72/72. Yards: 6,241	Rating: 69.2 Slope: 117	

Delaware

The brief list of courses in this small state is led by the **Three Little Bakers Country Club** in Wilmington, formerly a private course in the hills with some very difficult challenges, especially on the back nine. Even with a monopoly at the high end of the market in the state, it is offered at bargain rates.

Also highly recommended is **Ron Jaworski's Garrisons Lake Golf Club**, an older course that has grown with age; visitors can play there during the week.

Delaware's generally moderate climate allows most courses to remain open year-round. Look for deepest discounts in fall through winter, with peak rates in effect from about May to September.

Golf U.S.A. Leader Board: Best Public Courses in Delaware

☺☺☺ Three Little Bakers Country Club

☺☺☺ Ron Jaworski's Garrisons Lake Golf Club

Golf U.S.A. Leader Board: Best Deal in Delaware

$$/☺☺☺ Three Little Bakers Country Club

Delaware Golf Guide

P ☺	**Del Castle Golf Course** McKennans Church Rd., Wilmington. (302) 995-1990 18 holes. Par 72/72. Yards: 6,625/5,369 Year-round. High: Apr.–Nov.	Greens: $–$$ Carts: $–$$ Rating: 70.4/70.9 Slope: 116/116	W L T S J
P ☺	**Ed "Porky" Oliver Golf Course** N. DuPont Rd., Wilmington. (302) 571-9041 18 holes. Par 69/71. Yards: 6,115/5,674 Year-round. High: May–Sept.	Greens: $$ Carts: $$ Rating: 69.8/71.8 Slope: 118/121	W L T S J
P ☺☺☺ STATE	**Ron Jaworski's Garrisons Lake Golf Club** Smyrna. (302) 653-6349 18 holes. Par 72/72. Yards: 7,028/5,460 Year-round. High: June–Aug.	Greens: $$ Carts: Incl. Rating: 73.1/71.6 Slope: 127/126	W L T S
SP ☺☺☺ DEAL STATE	**Three Little Bakers Country Club** Foxcroft Dr., Wilmington. (302) 737-1877 18 holes. Par 71/72. Yards: 6,609/5,209 Year-round. High: Apr.–Oct.	Greens: $$$ Carts: Incl. Rating: 71.9/70.5 Slope: 130/121	W L T S J

Maine

The king of the hill among public and resort courses in Maine is **Sugarloaf**, near the ski area of the same name in Carrabassett Valley. It's a spectacular and challenging mountain course carved out of the woods; each hole is isolated as a form of golfer's green tunnel vision, limiting your attention to one hole at a time. Sugarloaf has been polishing plans for an additional course for several years.

In Rockport you'll find the **Samoset Resort**, a gorgeous ocean course along the rocky coast of Penobscot Bay. The course has its very own lighthouse and Atlantic views from 13 holes. The resort has plans for a 200-room addition, and possibly a redesign of the stunning course in coming years.

Penobscot Valley is a classic, older course.

Near the middle of the state is **Waterville**, a superb semiprivate challenge that also captures a spot on the *Golf U.S.A.* Deals list.

Snow can pile up pretty high in winter, followed by the spring mud season. Most courses are open from about April to November, with peak rates and best conditions in the short but sweet summer, from June through early September.

Golf U.S.A. Leader Board: Best Public Courses in Maine

☺☺☺ Samoset Resort Golf Club
☺☺☺☺ Sugarloaf Golf Club
☺☺☺☺ Waterville Country Club

Golf U.S.A. Leader Board: Best Deals in Maine

$$/☺☺☺   Aroostock Valley Country Club
$$/☺☺☺   Biddeford Saco Golf Club
$$/☺☺☺   Kebo Valley Golf Course
$$/☺☺☺   Sable Oaks Golf Club
$$/☺☺☺   Val Halla Golf Course
$$/☺☺☺☺ Waterville Country Club

Maine Golf Guide

Northern Maine

SP ☺☺☺ DEAL	**Aroostock Valley Country Club** Russell Rd., Fort Fairfield. (207) 476-8083 18 holes. Par 72/72. Yards: 6,304/5,393 May–Oct. High: July–Aug.	Greens: $$ L Carts: $ Rating: 69.9/70 Slope: 117/117	
P ☺	**Mingo Springs Golf Course** Proctor Rd. and Rte. 4, Rangeley. (207) 864-5021 18 holes. Par 70/70. Yards: 6,014/5,158 May–Oct. High: July–Sept.	Greens: $$ Carts: $-$$ Rating: 66.3/67.4 Slope: 109/110	
R ☺☺☺☺ BEST	**Sugarloaf Golf Club** RR 1, Carrabassett Valley. (207) 237-2000 18 holes. Par 72/72. Yards: 6,910/5,309 May–Oct. High: July-Oct.	Greens: $$$$$ L R T J Carts: $ Rating: 74.4/73.7 Slope: 151/136	
R ☺☺	**Va Jo Wa Golf Course** Walker Rd., Island Falls. (207) 463-2128 18 holes. Par 72/72. Yards: 6,223/5,065 May–Oct. High: July–Sept.	Greens: $$ R T Carts: Inquire Rating: 70.4/69.6 Slope: 121/115	

Maine Golf Guide

Bangor Area

P
☺☺
Bangor Municipal Golf Course
Webster Ave., Bangor. (207) 941-0232
18 holes. Par 71/71. Yards: 6,345/5,173
Apr.–Nov. High: June–Aug.

Greens: $ W T
Carts: Inquire
Rating: 67.9/69.1
Slope: 112/111

P
☺☺☺
DEAL
Kebo Valley Golf Course
Eagle Lake Rd., Bar Harbor. (207) 288-3000
18 holes. Par 70/72. Yards: 6,131/5,440
Apr.–Nov. High: July–Aug.

Greens: $$ L
Carts: $
Rating: 69.0/72.0
Slope: 130/121

SP
☺☺☺☺
Penobscot Valley Country Club
Main St., Orono. (207) 866-2423
18 holes. Par 72/74. Yards: 6,445/5,796
Apr.–Oct. High: June–Aug.

Greens: $$–$$$
Carts: $
Rating: 70.5/73.9
Slope: 126/128

Augusta Area

SP
☺☺
Rockland Golf Club
Old County Rd., Rockland. (207) 594-9322
18 holes. Par 70/73. Yards: 6,121/5,572
Apr.–Oct. High: June–Sept.

Greens: $$ T
Carts: $$
Rating: 67.8/71.8
Slope: 115/119

SP
☺☺☺☺
DEAL
STATE
Waterville Country Club
Oakland. (207) 465-9861
18 holes. Par 70/73. Yards: 6,427/5,381
Apr.–Nov. High: May–Sept.

Greens: $$$
Carts: $$
Rating: 69.6/71.3
Slope: 124/119

Portland Area

R
☺☺
Bethel Inn and Country Club
Broad St., Bethel. (207) 824-6276, (800) 654-0125
18 holes. Par 72/72. Yards: 6,663/5,280
May–Oct. High: July–Aug.

Greens: $$$ W L R T
Carts: $$
Rating: 72.3/71.4
Slope: 133/129

SP
☺☺☺
DEAL
Biddeford Saco Golf Club
Old Orchard Rd., Saco. (207) 282-5883
18 holes. Par 71/72. Yards: 5,845/5,053
Apr.–Nov. High: June–Aug.

Greens: $$–$$$ W T
Carts: $$
Rating: 68.5/69.2
Slope: 114/110

SP
☺☺
Cape Arundel Golf Club
Old River Rd., Kennebunkport. (207) 967-3494
18 holes. Par 69/70. Yards: 5,869/5,134
Apr.–Oct. High: July–Sept.

Greens: $$
Carts: $$
Rating: 67.0/68.6
Slope: 117/106

P
☺☺
Dutch Elm Golf Club
Brimstone Rd., Arundel. (207) 282-9850
18 holes. Par 72/73. Yards: 6,244/5,384
Apr.–Nov. High: July–Aug.

Greens: $$ W L R T S
Carts: Inquire
Rating: 71.1/70.1
Slope: 125/115

R
☺☺
Poland Spring Country Club
Rte. 26, Poland Spring. (207) 998-6002
18 holes. Par 71/74. Yards: 6,450/5,856
Apr.–Oct. High: June–Aug.

Greens: $ R
Carts: $
Rating: 68.2/71.6
Slope: 119/117

P
☺☺
Riverside Municipal Golf Course
Riverside St., Portland. (207) 797-3524
18 holes. Par 72/72. Yards: 6,450/5,640
Apr.–Nov. High: July–Aug.

Greens: $ S J
Carts: $
Rating: 69.5/70.7
Slope: 115/112

P
☺☺☺
DEAL
Sable Oaks Golf Club
S. Portland. (207) 775-6257
18 holes. Par 70/72. Yards: 6,359/4,786
Apr.–Dec. High: Apr.–Sept.

Greens: $$ T W
Carts: $$
Rating: 71.8/67.4
Slope: 138/116

P
☺☺☺
DEAL
Val Halla Golf Course
Val Halla Rd., Cumberland. (207) 829-2225
18 holes. Par 72/72. Yards: 6,567/5,437
Apr.–Oct. High: June–Sept.

Greens: $–$$ W S J
Carts: Inquire
Rating: 71.1/70.4
Slope: 126/116

P	**Willowdale Golf Club**	Greens: $ T
☺☺	Willowdale Rd., Scarborough. (207) 883-9351	Carts: $
	18 holes. Par 70/70. Yards: 5,980/5,344	Rating: 68.7/73.7
	Apr.–Oct. High: July–Aug.	Slope: 110/112

Central Coast

R	**Samoset Resort Golf Club**	Greens: $$$$$–$$$$$$ L R
☺☺☺	Warrenton St., Rockport. (207) 594-1431	Carts: Incl.
BEST	18 holes. Par 70/72. Yards: 6,018/5,087	Rating: 69.7/70.1
	Apr.–Nov. High: June–Sept.	Slope: 125/120

Maryland

Hog Neck on the DelMarVa Peninsula is a spectacular, demanding challenge with sand and water on the front nine, and long, narrow fairways on the way home. And you'll save a bit of green, since it is listed on the *Golf U.S.A.* Best Deals list.

Queenstown Harbor, southeast of Baltimore, offers beautiful river settings.

Most courses in Maryland manage to stay open year-round. Expect the best conditions and peak prices from about April through October.

Golf U.S.A. Leader Board: Best Public Courses in Maryland

☺☺☺☺   Hog Neck Golf Course
☺☺☺☺   Queenstown Harbor Golf Links (River)

Golf U.S.A. Leader Board: Best Deals in Maryland

$$/☺☺☺	Black Rock Golf Course
$/☺☺☺	Breton Bay Golf and Country Club
$$/☺☺☺	Eagle's Landing Golf Club
$$/☺☺☺	Enterprise Golf Course
$$/☺☺☺	Harbourtowne Golf Resort & Country Club
$$/☺☺☺☺	Hog Neck Golf Course
$/☺☺☺	Mount Pleasant Golf Club
$/☺☺☺	Pine Ridge Golf Course
$$/☺☺☺	Redgate Municipal Golf Course
$$/☺☺☺	River Run Golf Club
$$/☺☺☺	Wakefield Valley Golf & Conference Center

Western Maryland

R	**The Golf Club at Wisp**	Greens: $$$ T S J
☺☺☺	Marsh Hill Rd., McHenry. (301) 387-4911	Carts: Incl.
	18 holes. Par 72/72. Yards: 7,122/5,542	Rating: 73.0/72.0
	Apr.–Oct. High: July–Sept.	Slope: 137/128

Hagerstown Area

P	**Black Rock Golf Course**	Greens: $–$$ T S J
☺☺☺	Mt. Aetna Rd., Hagerstown. (301) 791-3040	Carts: $
DEAL	18 holes. Par 72/74. Yards: 6,646/5,179	Rating: 70.7/64.7
	Year-round. High: May–Sept.	Slope: 124/112

Baltimore Area

SP	**Bay Hills Golf Club**	Greens: $$ T
☺☺	Bay Hills Dr., Arnold. (410) 974-0669	Carts: Incl.

Maryland Golf Guide

	18 holes. Par 70/70. Yards: 6,423/5,029 Year-round. High: Apr.–Oct.	Rating: Slope:	70.8/69.2 118/121
SP ☺☺	**Beaver Creek Country Club** Mapleville Rd., Hagerstown. (301) 733-5152 18 holes. Par 72/73. Yards: 6,878/5,636 Year-round. High: May–Oct.	Greens: $–$$ W L R T Carts: $ Rating: 71.6/71.4 Slope: 120/124	
P ☺☺	**Clustered Spires Golf Course** Gas House Pike, Frederick. (301) 694-6249 18 holes. Par 72/72. Yards: 6,769/5,230 Year-round. High: Apr.–Oct.	Greens: $–$$ W T S J Carts: $ Rating: 70.5/70.0 Slope: 115/124	
P ☺☺	**Diamond Ridge Golf Course** Ridge Rd., Woodlawn. (410) 944-6607 18 holes. Par 70/72. Yards: 6,550/5,833 Year-round. High: Apr.–Oct.	Greens: $ T S J Carts: $ Rating: 71.0/73.2 Slope: 120/123	
P ☺☺☺☺ BEST DEAL	**Hog Neck Golf Course** Old Cordova Rd., Easton. (410) 822-6079 18 holes. Par 72/72. Yards: 7,000/5,500 Feb.–Dec. High: Apr.–Oct.	Greens: $$–$$$ W L T J Carts: $ Rating: 73.7/71.3 Slope: 131/125	
P ☺☺☺ DEAL	**Mount Pleasant Golf Club** Hillen Rd., Baltimore. (410) 254-5100 18 holes. Par 71/73. Yards: 6,757/5,294 Year-round. High: June–Aug.	Greens: $ W T S J Carts: $ Rating: 71.8/69.4 Slope: 119/118	
P ☺☺☺ DEAL	**Pine Ridge Golf Course** Dulaney Valley Rd., Lutherville. (410) 252-1408 18 holes. Par 72/72. Yards: 6,820/5,732 Year-round. High: Mar.–Oct.	Greens: $ W T S J Carts: Inquire Rating: 72.0/72.0 Slope: 122/120	
P ☺☺☺	**Queenstown Harbor Golf Links** 310 Links Lane Queenstown. (410) 827-6611 *Lakes Course* 18 holes. Par 71/71. Yards: 6,537/4,606 Year-round. High: Apr.–Oct.	Greens: $$$$–$$$$$ W T J Carts: Incl. Rating: 71.0/66.6 Slope: 124/111	
☺☺☺☺ STATE	*River Course* 18 holes. Par 72/72. Yards: 7,110/5,026	Rating: 74.2/69.0 Slope: 138/123	
P ☺☺	**Rocky Point Golf Club** Back River Neck Rd., Essex. (410) 391-2906 18 holes. Par 72/74. Yards: 6,785/5,510 Year-round. High: Apr.–Sept.	Greens: $ W T S J Carts: $ Rating: 72.3/73.1 Slope: 122/121	
R ☺☺	**Turf Valley Hotel and Country Club** Turf Valley Rd., Ellicott City. (410) 465-1504 *North Course* 18 holes. Par 71/71. Yards: 6,633/5,600 Year-round. High: Apr.–Oct.	Greens: $$–$$$ W L R T Carts: Incl. Rating: 69.5/71.8 Slope: 117/124	
☺☺	*East Course* 18 holes. Par 71/71. Yards: 6,592/5,564	Rating: 72.0/71.6 Slope: 128/131	
☺☺	*South Course* 18 holes. Par 70/72. Yards: 6,323/5,572	Rating: 69.2/72.8 Slope: 113/126	
SP ☺☺☺ DEAL	**Wakefield Valley Golf & Conference Center** Fenby Farm Rd., Westminster. (410) 876-6662 27 holes. Par 72/72/72. Yards: 6,933/7,038/6,823 Mar.–Dec. High: June–Sept.	Greens: $$ L T S J Carts: Incl. Rating: 74.4/74.1/73.6 Slope: 139/138/139	

Washington, D.C., Area

| SP
☺☺☺ | **Breton Bay Golf and Country Club**
Rte. 3, Leonardtown. (301) 475-2300 | Greens: $$ J
Carts: $ | |

Maryland Golf Guide

DEAL	18 holes. Par 72/73. Yards: 6,933/5,457 Mar.–Dec. High: May–Aug.	Rating: Slope:	73.0/70.1 126/117

P
☺☺☺
DEAL

Enterprise Golf Course
Enterprise Rd., Mitchellville. (301) 249-2040
18 holes. Par 72/72. Yards: 6,586/5,157
Year-round. High: Mar.–Oct.

Greens: $–$$　　W L T S J
Carts: $$
Rating: 71.7/69.6
Slope: 128/114

P
☺☺

Glenn Dale Country Club
Old Prospect Hill Rd., Glenn Dale. (301) 464-0904
18 holes. Par 70/70. Yards: 6,282/4,809
Year-round. High: Apr.–Oct.

Greens: $$　　L T S J
Carts: $$
Rating: 70.0/67.2
Slope: 115/107

R
☺☺☺
DEAL

Harbourtowne Golf Resort & Country Club
Rte. 33, St. Michaels. (410) 745-5183, (800) 446-9066
18 holes. Par 70/71. Yards: 6,320/5,036
Year-round. High: Apr.–Oct.

Greens: $$　　L R
Carts: $
Rating: 69.5/68.5
Slope: 120/113

P
☺☺

Needwood Golf Course
Needwood Rd., Derwood. (301) 948-1075
18 holes. Par 70/72. Yards: 6,254/5,112
Year-round. High: May–Sept.

Greens: $–$$　　S J
Carts: $$
Rating: 69.1/69.2
Slope: 113/105

P
☺☺

Northwest Park Golf Course
Layhill Rd., Wheaton. (301) 598-6100
18 holes. Par 72/74. Yards: 7,185/6,325
Year-round. High: June–Aug.

Greens: $　　T S J
Carts: $
Rating: 74.0/74.5
Slope: 122/126

P
☺☺

Poolesville Golf Course
W. Willard Rd., Poolesville. (301) 428-8143
18 holes. Par 71/73. Yards: 6,757/5,599
Year-round. High: June

Greens: $–$$　　S J
Carts: Inquire
Rating: 72.3/71.4
Slope: 123/118

P
☺☺☺
DEAL

Redgate Municipal Golf Course
Avery Rd., Rockville. (301) 309-3055
18 holes. Par 71/71. Yards: 6,432/5,271
Year-round. High: Apr.–Nov.

Greens: $–$$　　S J
Carts: $
Rating: 71.7/70.2
Slope: 131/121

P
☺☺☺
DEAL

River Run Golf Club
Beauchamp Rd., Berlin. (410) 641-7200
18 holes. Par 71/71. Yards: 6,705/5,002
Year-round. High: Apr.–Oct.

Greens: $–$$　　W L R T
Carts: $
Rating: 70.4/73.1
Slope: 128/117

SP
☺☺☺☺

Swan Point Golf Club
Swan Point Blvd., Issue. (301) 259-0047
18 holes. Par 72/72. Yards: 6,290/5,009
Mar.–Dec. High: June–Sept.

Greens: $$–$$$$　　W L T S J
Carts: Incl.
Rating: 70.5/69.3
Slope: 128/116

P
☺☺

Trotters Glen Golf Course
Batchellors Forest Rd., Olney. (301) 570-4951
18 holes. Par 72/72. Yards: 6,220/4,983
Year-round. High: June–Aug.

Greens: $–$$　　W L
Carts: $$
Rating: 69.3/68.2
Slope: 113/111

P
☺☺

Twin Shields Golf Club
Roarty Rd., Dunkirk. (410) 257-7800
18 holes. Par 70/70. Yards: 6,321/5,305
Year-round. High: Apr.–Oct.

Greens: $$　　W L
Carts: $$
Rating: 68.2/67.0
Slope: 118/113

SP
☺☺

University of Maryland Golf Course
University Blvd., College Park. (301) 403-4299
18 holes. Par 71/72. Yards: 6,654/5,563
Year-round. High: Apr.–Oct.

Greens: $$　　W L T S J
Carts: $
Rating: 71.7/71.1
Slope: 120/117

P
☺☺

Wicomico Shores Municipal Golf Course
Rte. 234, Chaptico. (301) 934-8191
18 holes. Par 72/72. Yards: 6,482/5,460
Year-round. High: May–Sept.

Greens: $　　W T S J
Carts: $
Rating: 70.7/68.3
Slope: 120/120

DelMarVa Peninsula

R ☺☺	**The Bay Club** Libertytown Rd., Berlin. (800) 229-2582 18 holes. Par 72/72. Yards: 6,958/5,609 Year-round. High: Apr.–Oct.	Greens: $$–$$$ W L R T Carts: Incl. Rating: 73.1/71.3 Slope: 126/118
SP ☺☺☺	**The Beach Club Golf Links** Deer Park Rd., Berlin. (410) 641-4653 18 holes. Par 72/72. Yards: 7,020/5,167 Year-round. High: Apr.–Oct.	Greens: $$–$$$ L T Carts: Incl. Rating: 73.0/69.0 Slope: 128/117
SP ☺☺	**Cambridge Country Club** Horns Point Rd., Cambridge. (410) 228-4808 18 holes. Par 72/73. Yards: 6,387/5,416 Year-round. High: May–Oct.	Greens: $$ R Carts: Inquire Rating: 69.3/71.0 Slope: 113/118
P ☺☺☺ DEAL	**Eagle's Landing Golf Club** Eagle's Nest Rd., Berlin. (410) 213-7277 18 holes. Par 72/72. Yards: 7,003/4,896 Year-round. High: Apr.–Oct.	Greens: $–$$ W L T Carts: $ Rating: 74.3/69.3 Slope: 126/115
SP ☺☺	**Nassawango Country Club** Nassawango Rd., Snow Hill. (410) 632-3144 18 holes. Par 72/73. Yards: 6,644/5,760 Year-round. High: May–Oct.	Greens: $$ L Carts: $ Rating: 70.2/72.1 Slope: 125/125
SP ☺☺	**Nutters Crossing Golf Club** S. Hampton Bridge Rd., Salisbury. (410) 860-4653 18 holes. Par 70/70. Yards: 6,033/4,800 Year-round. High: Apr.–Oct.	Greens: $$ T Carts: Incl. Rating: 67.1/66.5 Slope: 115/110
R ☺☺	**Ocean City Golf and Yacht Club** Berlin. (410) 641-1779 *Bayside Course* 18 holes. Par 72/72. Yards: 6,526/5,396 Year-round. High: Apr.–Oct.	Greens: $–$$ W L Carts: $ Rating: 71.7/71.3 Slope: 121/119
☺☺	*Seaside Course* 18 holes. Par 73/75. Yards: 6,520/5,456	Rating: 70.9/73.1 Slope: 115/119

Massachusetts

The Bay State's golfing shrine is located among the shrub pines, sand dunes, fog, and wind of Cape Cod; three of the state's best public and resort courses are located there. The championship Blue Course along the ocean at **New Seabury** includes No. 3, which is surrounded by water on three sides. The **Captains**, in Brewster, winds its way through a thick scrub pine forest. It's also on our *Golf U.S.A.* Deals list. The gorgeous **Farm Neck** hugs the shore of Martha's Vineyard.

In the hills around the Connecticut River above Springfield is the well-regarded **Crumpin-Fox Club**, named after a long-defunct soda company that occupied the site. It offers breathtaking views from some of its elevated tees. And all the way west in the Green Mountains along the New York border is the **Taconic Golf Club.**

Some courses, including many on Cape Cod and along the southern coast, try to stay open year-round, although snow closures do occur. Massachusetts's snowbelt includes Worcester and the Berkshire Mountains to the west. For the rest of the state, a realistic season is from April through early December. The high season at most courses runs from about May through September.

Golf U.S.A. Leader Board: Best Public Courses in Massachusetts

◔◔◔   Captains Golf Course
◔◔◔◔   Crumpin-Fox Club
◔◔◔◔   Farm Neck Golf Club
◔◔◔◔   New Seabury Country Club (Blue)
◔◔◔◔   Taconic Golf Club

Golf U.S.A. Leader Board: Best Deals in Massachusetts

$$/◔◔◔   Atlantic Country Club
$$/◔◔◔   Bayberry Hills Golf Course
$$/◔◔◔   Cape Cod Country Club
$$/◔◔◔   Captains Golf Course
$$/◔◔◔   Cranberry Valley Golf Course
$$/◔◔◔   Dennis Highlands Golf Course
$$/◔◔◔   Dennis Pines Golf Course
$$/◔◔◔   Gardner Municipal Golf Course
$$/◔◔◔   George Wright Golf Course
$$/◔◔◔   Maplegate Country Club
$$/◔◔◔   Oak Ridge Golf Club
$$/◔◔◔   Olde Barnstable Fairgrounds Golf Course
$$/◔◔◔   Stow Acres Country Club (North, South)
$$/◔◔◔   Trull Brook Golf Course
$$/◔◔◔   Wachusett Country Club
$$/◔◔◔   Waubeeka Golf Links

Massachusetts Golf Guide

Western Massachusetts

SP
◔◔◔◔
STATE
Taconic Golf Club
Meacham St., Williamstown. (413) 458-3997
18 holes. Par 71/71. Yards: 6,614/5,202
Apr.–Nov.
Greens: $$$$$$
Carts: Incl.
Rating: 69.9/71.7
Slope: 127/127

SP
◔◔◔
Wahconah Country Club
Orchard Rd., Dalton. (413) 684-1333
18 holes. Par 71/73. Yards: 6,567/6,223
Apr.–Nov.
Greens: $$$
Carts: $$
Rating: 70.2/71.9
Slope: 126/123

P
◔◔◔
DEAL
Waubeeka Golf Links
New Ashford Rd., S. Williamstown. (413) 458-8355
18 holes. Par 72/72. Yards: 6,296/5,086
Apr.–Nov. High: July–Aug.
Greens: $–$$ L J
Carts: Inquire
Rating: 70.9/71.2
Slope: 127/111

Springfield Area

P
◔◔◔◔
STATE
Crumpin-Fox Club
Parmenter Rd., Bernardston. (413) 648-9101
18 holes. Par 72/72. Yards: 7,007/5,432
Apr.–Nov. High: June–Oct.
Greens: $$$$ R J
Carts: $
Rating: 73.8/71.5
Slope: 141/131

SP
◔◔◔
Hickory Ridge Country Club
W. Pomeroy Lane, Amherst. (413) 253-9320
18 holes. Par 72/72. Yards: 6,794/5,340
Apr.–Nov. High: May–Sept.
Greens: $$–$$$ W J
Carts: $$
Rating: 72.5/70.3
Slope: 129/117

P
◔◔◔
Oak Ridge Golf Club
S. Westfield St., Feeding Hills. (413) 789-7307
Greens: $–$$ W L T J
Carts: $

Massachusetts Golf Guide

DEAL	18 holes. Par 70/70. Yards: 6,819/5,307 Mar.–Dec. High: June–Sept.	Rating: Slope:	71.2/70.0 124/NA

P ☺☺	**Westover Golf Course** South St., Granby. (413) 547-8610 18 holes. Par 72/72. Yards: 6,610/5,600 Apr.–Dec. High: June–Sept.	Greens: $ Carts: $ Rating: 71.9/71.9 Slope: 129/117	L J

Worcester Area

SP ☺☺	**Blissful Meadows Golf Club** Chockalog Rd., Uxbridge. (508) 278-6133 18 holes. Par 72/72. Yards: 6,656/5,072 Apr.–Nov. High: May–Oct.	Greens: $–$$ Carts: $ Rating: NA Slope: 120	L T S

P ☺☺☺ DEAL	**Gardner Municipal Golf Course** Eaton Dr., Gardner. (978) 632-9703 18 holes. Par 71/75. Yards: 6,106/5,653 Apr.–first snow. High: June–Sept.	Greens: $–$$ Carts: $ Rating: 68.9/71.7 Slope: 124/122	W T J

SP ☺☺☺ DEAL	**Wachusett Country Club** Prospect St., West Boylston. (508) 835-4453 18 holes. Par 72/NA. Yards: 6,608/6,216 Apr.–Nov. High: May–Oct.	Greens: $$ Carts: $$ Rating: 71.7/70.0 Slope: 124/120	W L T

SP ☺☺	**Westminster Country Club** Ellis Rd., Westminster. (978) 874-5938 18 holes. Par 71/71. Yards: 6,491/5,453 Apr.–Nov. High: May–Sept.	Greens: $$ Carts: $$ Rating: 70.9/70.0 Slope: 133/115	T

Boston Area

P ☺☺	**Bradford Country Club** Chadwick Rd., Bradford. (978) 372-8587 18 holes. Par 70/70. Yards: 6,469/4,939 Apr.–Dec. High: May–Sept.	Greens: $–$$ Carts: $ Rating: 72.8/67.8 Slope: 141/129	L

P ☺☺	**Colonial Country Club** Audubon Rd., Wakefield. (781) 245-9300 18 holes. Par 70/72. Yards: 6,565/5,280 Apr.–Dec. High: May–Sept.	Greens: $$$$ Carts: Incl. Rating: 72.8/70.5 Slope: 130/119	L T S J

P ☺☺☺ DEAL	**George Wright Golf Course** West St., Hyde Park. (617) 364-9679 18 holes. Par 70/70. Yards: 6,440/5,131 Year-round. High: June–Aug.	Greens: $$ Carts: $$ Rating: 69.8/68.8 Slope: 127/111	W S J

P ☺☺	**Lakeville Country Club** Clear Pond Rd., Lakeville. (508) 947-6630 18 holes. Par 72/72. Yards: 6,274/5,297 Year-round. High: May–Sept.	Greens: $$ Carts: $$ Rating: 70.1/68.5 Slope: 123/118	

P ☺☺☺ DEAL	**Maplegate Country Club** Maple St., Bellingham. (508) 966-4040 18 holes. Par 72/72. Yards: 6,815/4,852 Apr.–Dec. High: May–Sept.	Greens: $–$$ Carts: $$$ Rating: 74.2/70.2 Slope: 133/124	W L T J

P ☺☺☺	**New England Country Club** Paine St., Bellingham. (508) 883-2300 18 holes. Par 71/71. Yards: 6,430/4,908 Apr.–Nov. High: June–Sept.	Greens: $$–$$$ Carts: Incl. Rating: 70.8/68.7 Slope: 130/121	W L T

P ☺☺	**Sagamore Springs Golf Club** Main St., Lynnfield. (781) 334-6969 18 holes. Par 70/70. Yards: 5,936/4,784 Mar.–Dec. High: June–Sept.	Greens: $$ Carts: $ Rating: 68.6/66.5 Slope: 119/112	L S

P ☺☺☺	**Shaker Hills Golf Club** Shaker Rd., Harvard. (978) 772-2227	Greens: $$$ Carts: Incl.	T

	18 holes. Par 71/71. Yards: 6,850/5,001	Rating:	72.3/67.9
	Apr.–Nov. High: June–Sept.	Slope:	135/121

P	**Stow Acres Country Club**	Greens:	$$	W L T S J
☺☺☺	Randall Rd., Stow. (978) 568-1100	Carts:	$$	
DEAL	*North Course*	Rating:	72.8/70.6	
	18 holes. Par 72/72. Yards: 6,939/6,011	Slope:	130/130	
	Mar.–Dec. High: Apr.–Nov.			

☺☺☺	*South Course*	Rating:	71.8/70.5
DEAL	18 holes. Par 72/72. Yards: 6,520/5,642	Slope:	120/118

R	**Tara Ferncroft Country Club**	Greens:	$$$$
☺☺☺	Ferncroft Rd., Danvers (978) 777-5614	Carts:	Incl.
	18 holes. Par 72/73. Yards: 6,601/6,213	Rating:	72.4/72.7
	Apr.–Dec. High: May–Oct.	Slope:	133/133

P	**Trull Brook Golf Course**	Greens:	$$	L T
☺☺☺	River Rd., Tewksbury. (978) 851-6731	Carts:	$$	
DEAL	18 holes. Par 72/72. Yards: 6,335/5,165	Rating:	68.5/70.2	
	Mar.–Nov. High: June–Aug.	Slope:	115/118	

Cape Cod/Martha's Vineyard

P	**Atlantic Country Club**	Greens:	$$	T
☺☺☺	Little Sandy Pond Rd., Plymouth. (508) 888-6644	Carts:	$	
DEAL	18 holes. Par 72/72. Yards: 6,728/4,918	Rating:	73.0/68.9	
	Mar.–Dec. High: June–Aug.	Slope:	131/116	

SP	**Ballymeade Country Club**	Greens:	$$$–$$$$	W L T S
☺☺☺	Falmouth Woods Rd., N. Falmouth. (508) 540-4005	Carts:	Incl.	
	18 holes. Par 72/72. Yards: 6,928/5,001	Rating:	74.3/69.9	
	Year-round. High: June–Aug.	Slope:	139/119	

P	**Bass River Golf Course**	Greens:	$–$$	L T
☺☺	Highbank Rd., South Yarmouth. (508) 398-9079	Carts:	$$	
	18 holes. Par 72/72. Yards: 6,129/5,343	Rating:	79.3/69.9	
	Year-round. High: May–Sept.	Slope:	122/115	

SP	**Bayberry Hills Golf Course**	Greens:	$$	L T
☺☺☺	W. Yarmouth Rd., W. Yarmouth. (508) 394-5597	Carts:	$$	
DEAL	18 holes. Par 72/72. Yards: 6,573/5,323	Rating:	71.7/69.7	
	Apr.–Dec. High: May–Oct.	Slope:	125/119	

P	**Cape Cod Country Club**	Greens:	$$	W L T
☺☺☺	Theater Rd., Hatchville. (508) 563-9842	Carts:	$$	
DEAL	18 holes. Par 71/72. Yards: 6,404/5,348	Rating:	70.6/68.8	
	Year-round. High: Mar.–Oct.	Slope:	120/116	

P	**Captains Golf Course**	Greens:	$$–$$$	L T
☺☺☺	Freeman's Way, Brewster. (508) 896-5100	Carts:	Inquire	
BEST	18 holes. Par 72/72. Yards: 6,794/5,388	Rating:	72.7/70.5	
DEAL	Mar.–Dec. High: May–Oct.	Slope:	130/117	

P	**Cranberry Valley Golf Course**	Greens:	$$	L T
☺☺☺	Oak St., Harwich. (508) 430-7560	Carts:	$$	
DEAL	18 holes. Par 72/72. Yards: 6,745/5,518	Rating:	71.9/71.3	
	Year-round. High: Mar.–Nov.	Slope:	129/115	

P	**Dennis Highlands Golf Course**	Greens:	$$	L T
☺☺☺	Old Bass River Rd., Dennis. (508) 385-8347	Carts:	$$	
DEAL	18 holes. Par 71/71. Yards: 6,464/4,927	Rating:	70.4/67.4	
	Year-round. High: Apr.–Nov.	Slope:	118/112	

P	**Dennis Pines Golf Course**	Greens:	$$	L T
☺☺☺	E. Dennis. (508) 385-8547	Carts:	$$	
DEAL	18 holes. Par 72/73. Yards: 7,029/5,798	Rating:	71.9/73.7	
	Year-round. High: Apr.–Nov.	Slope:	127/122	

Massachusetts Golf Guide

SP ☺☺☺☺ STATE	**Farm Neck Golf Club** Farm Neck Way, Oak Bluffs. (508) 693-3057 18 holes. Par 72/72. Yards: 6,807/5,004 May–Dec. High: July–Aug.	Greens: Carts: Rating: Slope:	$$$$$ L $$ 72.1/68.3 129/120
P ☺☺	**Highland Golf Links** Highland Light Rd., N. Truro. (508) 487-9201 18 holes. Par 70/72. Yards: 5,299/4,587 Apr.–Nov. High: June–Sept.	Greens: Carts: Rating: Slope:	$$ $$ 65.0/66.6 103/109
P ☺☺	**Hyannis Golf Club at Iyanough Hills** Rte. 132, Hyannis. (508) 362-2606 18 holes. Par 71/72. Yards: 6,514/5,149 Year-round. High: June–Sept.	Greens: Carts: Rating: Slope:	$$$ S $ 70.2/69.0 121/125
R ☺☺☺☺ BEST	**New Seabury Country Club** Shore Dr. W., Mashpee. (508) 477-9110 *Blue Course* 18 holes. Par 72/72. Yards: 7,200/5,764 Year-round. High: July–Aug.	Greens: Carts: Rating: Slope:	$$$$–$$$$$$ L T $ 75.3/73.8 130/128
☺☺☺	*Green Course* 18 holes. Par 70/70. Yards: 6,035/4,827	Rating: Slope:	69.0/67.6 120/112
R ☺☺☺	**Ocean Edge Golf Club** Villages Dr., Brewster. (508) 896-5911 18 holes. Par 72/72. Yards: 6,665/6,127 Mar.–Dec. High: June–Sept.	Greens: Carts: Rating: Slope:	$$–$$$ W L R J $ 71.9/68.7 129/125
P ☺☺☺ DEAL	**Olde Barnstable Fairgrounds Golf Course** Rte. 149, Marstons Mills. (508) 420-1141 18 holes. Par 71/71. Yards: 6,479/5,122 Year-round. High: Apr.–Nov.	Greens: Carts: Rating: Slope:	$$ W T $$ 70.7/69.2 123/118
SP ☺☺	**Quashnet Valley Country Club** Old Barnstable Rd., Mashpee. (508) 477-4412 18 holes. Par 72/72. Yards: 6,602/5,094 Year-round. High: Apr.–Oct.	Greens: Carts: Rating: Slope:	$$–$$$ L T $ 71.7/70.3 132/119
SP ☺☺	**Round Hill Country Club** Round Hill Rd., E. Sandwich. (508) 888-3384 18 holes. Par 71/70. Yards: 6,300/4,800 Year-round. High: May–Oct.	Greens: Carts: Rating: Slope:	$$$ L T Incl. 71.4/68.1 124/115

Fall River Area

P ☺☺	**Swansea Country Club** Market St., Swansea. (508) 379-9886 18 holes. Par 72/72. Yards: 6,840/5,239 Year-round. High: May–Sept.	Greens: Carts: Rating: Slope:	$$ L T Inquire 72.7/69.3 124/109

New Hampshire

The Granite State has a nice selection of fine public and resort golf courses. At the front of the pack is the very difficult **Shattuck Golf Course** in Jaffrey, east of Keene.

In the picturesque White Mountains, you'll find the **North Conway Country Club**, shoehorned in among the hills.

By the sea, near Portsmouth, you'll find the windswept **Portsmouth Country Club**, complete with a new clubhouse added in 1999.

The Manchester and Concord area, big cities by New Hampshire standards, offers two first-class courses: the **Country Club of New Hampshire**, in a thickly wooded wilderness setting in North Sutton at the base of Mount Kearsarge, and the **Eastman Golf Links**, a hilly challenge in Grantham.

Sky Meadow is a low mountain course in Nashua, just 30 miles north of Boston, with spectacular views in all directions. Another handsome setting is the rolling **Bretwood Golf Course** in Keene.

Five of New Hampshire's best coexist on the *Golf U.S.A.* Deals list: Bretwood, Country Club of New Hampshire, Eastman Golf Links, North Conway Country Club, and Shattuck Golf Course.

The New England winters limit golf course schedules in New Hampshire to April through November. Peak season rates are in effect from about May through late September.

Golf U.S.A. Leader Board: Best Public Courses in New Hampshire

☺☺☺☺	Bretwood Golf Course
☺☺☺	Country Club of New Hampshire
☺☺☺	Eastman Golf Links
☺☺☺	North Conway Country Club
☺☺☺☺	Portsmouth Country Club
☺☺☺☺	Shattuck Golf Course

Golf U.S.A. Leader Board: Best Deals in New Hampshire

$$/☺☺☺☺	Bretwood Golf Course
$$/☺☺☺	Campbell's Scottish Highlands Golf Course
$$/☺☺☺	Country Club of New Hampshire
$$/☺☺☺	Eastman Golf Links
$$/☺☺☺	Hanover Country Club
$$/☺☺☺	John H. Cain Golf Club
$$/☺☺☺	North Conway Country Club
$$/☺☺☺	Overlook Country Club
$$/☺☺☺	Passaconaway Country Club
$$/☺☺☺☺	Shattuck Golf Course

New Hampshire Golf Guide

Northern New Hampshire

R	**The Balsams Grand Resort**	Greens:	$$$	R
	Rte. 26, Dixville Notch. (603) 255-4961	Carts:	$	
☺☺☺	*Panorama Golf Club*	Rating:	73.9/67.8	
	18 holes. Par 72/72. Yards: 6,804/5,069	Slope:	136/115	
	May–Oct. High: July–Aug.			

R	**Mount Washington Golf Course**	Greens:	$$	R
☺☺☺	Rte. 302, Bretton Woods. (603) 278-1000	Carts:	$$	
	18 holes. Par 71/71. Yards: 6,638/5,336	Rating:	68.0/70.6	
	May–Oct. High: July–Sept.	Slope:	113/118	

SP	**North Conway Country Club**	Greens:	$$	L T S J
☺☺☺	Norcross Circle, N. Conway. (603) 356-9391	Carts:	$$	
DEAL	18 holes. Par 71/71. Yards: 6,659/5,530	Rating:	71.9/71.4	
STATE	May–Oct. High: June–Oct.	Slope:	126/120	

New Hampshire Golf Guide

P ☺☺	**White Mountain Country Club** Ashland Rd., Ashland. (603) 536-2227 18 holes. Par 71/73. Yards: 6,464/5,410 Apr.–Nov. High: May–Sept.	Greens: $–$$ Carts: $ Rating: 70.4/69.6 Slope: 122/118	T

Lebanon Area

P ☺☺☺ DEAL	**Hanover Country Club** Rope Ferry Rd., Hanover. (603) 646-2000 18 holes. Par 69/73. Yards: 5,876/5,468 Apr.–Nov. High: June–Sept.	Greens: $$ Carts: $ Rating: 68.7/72.7 Slope: 118/127	T

Portsmouth Area

P ☺☺	**Pease Golf Course** Portsmouth. (603) 433-1331 18 holes. Par 71/71. Yards: 6,346/5,243 Apr.–Nov. High: June–Aug.	Greens: $$ Carts: $$ Rating: 70.8/69.9 Slope: 128/120	
SP ☺☺☺☺ STATE	**Portsmouth Country Club** Greenland. (603) 436-9719 18 holes. Par 72/76. Yards: 7,050/6,202 Apr.–Nov. High: June–Sept.	Greens: $$$$ Carts: $$ Rating: 74.5/77.1 Slope: 127/135	T
SP ☺☺	**Rochester Country Club** Church St., Gonic. (603) 332-9892 18 holes. Par 72/73. Yards: 6,596/5,414 Apr.–Nov. High: June–Aug.	Greens: $$–$$$ Carts: Incl. Rating: 72.2/70.4 Slope: 125/123	

Keene Area

P ☺☺☺☺ DEAL STATE	**Bretwood Golf Course** East Surry Rd., Keene. (603) 352-7626 *North Course* 18 holes. Par 72/72. Yards: 6,974/5,140 Apr.–Nov. High: June–Oct.	Greens: $$ Carts: $$ Rating: 73.7/71.5 Slope: 136/120	W T
☺☺☺☺	*South Course* 18 holes. Par 72/71. Yards: 6,952/4,990 Apr.–Nov. High: June.–Oct.	Rating: 73.1/70.1 Slope: 139/121	
SP ☺☺☺	**Keene Country Club** West Hill Rd., Keene. (603) 352-9722 18 holes. Par 72/75. Yards: 6,200/5,900 Apr.–Nov. High: May–Sept.	Greens: $$$ Carts: Incl. Rating: 69.4/72.2 Slope: 124/130	
P ☺☺☺☺ DEAL STATE	**Shattuck Golf Course** Dublin Rd., Jaffrey. (603) 532-4300 18 holes. Par 71/71. Yards: 6,764/4,632 Apr.–Oct. High: June–Sept.	Greens: $$$–$$$$ Carts: $ Rating: 74.1/73.1 Slope: 145/139	W L T

Manchester/Concord Area

P ☺☺	**Beaver Meadow Golf Club** Beaver Meadow Dr., Concord. (603) 228-8954 18 holes. Par 72/72. Yards: 6,356/5,519 Apr.–Nov. High: May–Sept.	Greens: $–$$ Carts: Inquire Rating: 70.0/71.8 Slope: 121/123	W T J
P ☺☺	**Candia Woods Golf Links** South Rd., Candia. (603) 483-2307 18 holes. Par 71/73. Yards: 6,530/5,582 Mar.–Dec. High: June	Greens: $$ Carts: $ Rating: 70.9/71.7 Slope: 121/127	W L T J
P ☺☺☺ DEAL STATE	**Country Club of New Hampshire** Kearsarge Valley Rd., N. Sutton. (603) 927-4246 18 holes. Par 72/72. Yards: 6,743/5,416 Apr.–Nov. High: July–Sept.	Greens: $$ Carts: $ Rating: 71.6/71.7 Slope: 125/127	W T
SP ☺☺☺	**Eastman Golf Links** Grantham. (603) 863-4500	Greens: $$ Carts: $	

DEAL	18 holes. Par 71/73. Yards: 6,731/5,369	Rating:	73.5/71.9
STATE	May–Nov. High: July–Sept.	Slope:	137/128

P	**Green Meadow Golf Club**	Greens:	$$	W L T S J
	Steele Rd., Hudson. (603) 889-1555	Carts:	Inquire	
☺	*North Course*	Rating:	67.6/68.3	
	18 holes. Par 72/72. Yards: 6,495/5,102	Slope:	109/113	
	Mar.–Dec. High: Apr.–Aug.			

P	**Jack O'Lantern Resort**	Greens:	$$	W R T
☺☺	Rte. 3, Woodstock. (603) 745-3636	Carts:	$	
	18 holes. Par 70/70. Yards: 5,829/4,725	Rating:	67.5/67.5	
	May–Oct.	Slope:	113/113	

SP	**John H. Cain Golf Club**	Greens:	$-$$	W L T
☺☺☺	Unity Rd., Newport. (603) 863-7787	Carts:	$	
DEAL	18 holes. Par 71/71. Yards: 6,415/4,738	Rating:	72.4/63.8	
	Apr.–Nov. High: July–Sept.	Slope:	134/112	

SP	**Laconia Country Club**	Greens:	$$$$$
☺☺☺	Elm St., Laconia. (603) 524-1273	Carts:	Incl.
	18 holes. Par 72/72. Yards: 6,483/5,552	Rating:	71.7/72.1
	Apr.–Nov. High: June–Sept.	Slope:	128/125

P	**Overlook Country Club**	Greens:	$$	T
☺☺☺	Overlook Dr., Hollis. (603) 465-2909	Carts:	$$	
DEAL	18 holes. Par 71/72. Yards: 6,290/5,230	Rating:	69.7/70.4	
	Apr.–Dec. High: June–Aug.	Slope:	130/126	

P	**Passaconaway Country Club**	Greens:	$$	W L T S J
☺☺☺	Midway Ave., Litchfield. (603) 424-4653	Carts:	Inquire	
DEAL	18 holes. Par 71/72. Yards: 6,855/5,369	Rating:	72.2/70.3	
	Apr.–Dec. High: May–Sept.	Slope:	126/118	

P	**Waukewan Golf Club**	Greens:	$$	L
☺☺	Meredith. (603) 279-6661	Carts:	$$	
	18 holes. Par 71/73. Yards: 5,735/5,010	Rating:	67.1/67.7	
	May–Oct. High: June–Sept.	Slope:	120/112	

P	**Windham Golf and Country Club**	Greens:	$$
☺☺	Londonderry Rd., Windham. (603) 434-2093	Carts:	$
	18 holes. Par 72/72. Yards: 6,442/5,127	Rating:	71.3/69.1
	Year-round. High: May–Oct.	Slope:	136/123

Nashua Area

P	**Amherst Country Club**	Greens:	$$	T S
☺☺	Ponemah Rd., Amherst. (603) 673-9908	Carts:	$	
	18 holes. Par 72/74. Yards: 6,520/5,532	Rating:	71.0/74.2	
	Mar.–Dec. High: May–Oct.	Slope:	123/129	

P	**Campbell's Scottish Highlands Golf Course**	Greens:	$$	W T S
☺aa	Brady Ave., Salem. (603) 894-4653	Carts:	$	
DEAL	18 holes. Par 71/71. Yards: 6,249/5,056	Rating:	69.5/68.4	
	Apr.–Nov. High: July–Aug.	Slope:	120/114	

P	**Sagamore-Hampton Golf Club**	Greens:	$$	L
☺☺	North Rd., North Hampton. (603) 964-5341	Carts:	Inquire	
	18 holes. Par 71/71. Yards: 6,084/5,008	Rating:	67.4/71.5	
	Apr.–Dec. High: May–Sept.	Slope:	111/110	

New Jersey

The very best of the Garden State includes two very green and challenging courses north of Philadelphia: **Hominy Hill**, a *Golf U.S.A.* Deal, in Colts Neck, home of more than 100 bunkers, and **Howell Park**, in Farmingdale.

Just outside of Atlantic City is the sandy **Blue Heron Pines Golf Club**.

In northwest New Jersey, 50 miles west of New York City, there are the outstanding White and Blue courses of **Flanders Valley** in Flanders. Another 18 holes is scheduled to open in Jefferson in the spring of 2001.

In southern New Jersey, many courses hope to stay open year round, while others are limited to a season from about March through early December. At most courses, peak season rates are in effect from about April through September.

Golf U.S.A. Leader Board: Best Public Courses in New Jersey

ꙮꙮꙮꙮ Blue Heron Pines Golf Club
ꙮꙮꙮꙮ Flanders Valley Golf Course (White, Blue)
ꙮꙮꙮꙮ Hominy Hill Golf Course
ꙮꙮꙮꙮ Howell Park Golf Course

Golf U.S.A. Leader Board: Best Deals in New Jersey

$$/ꙮꙮꙮ   Buena Vista Country Club
$$/ꙮꙮꙮ   Farmstead Golf and Country Club (Clubview, Lakeview, Valleyview)
$$/ꙮꙮꙮꙮ Hominy Hill Golf Course
$$/ꙮꙮꙮ   Ocean County Golf Course at Atlantis
$$/ꙮꙮꙮ   Rancocas Golf Club
$$/ꙮꙮꙮ   Sunset Valley Golf Course

New Jersey Golf Guide

Northern New Jersey/Newark Area

P ꙮꙮ	**Ash Brook Golf Course** Raritan Rd., Scotch Plains. (908) 668-8503 18 holes. Par 72/72. Yards: 6,962/5,661 Year-round. High: Mar.–Oct.	Greens: Carts: Rating: Slope:	$$ $ 72.2/71.8 117/119	W
P ꙮꙮꙮ	**Beaver Brook Country Club** Rte. 31 South, Clinton. (908) 735-4022 18 holes. Par 72/72. Yards: 6,601/5,438 Mar.–Dec. High: June–Aug.	Greens: Carts: Rating: Slope:	$$–$$$ $$ 71.7/71.7 125/122	T
SP ꙮꙮꙮ	**Bowling Green Golf Club** Schoolhouse Rd., Oak Ridge. (973) 697-8688 18 holes. Par 72/72. Yards: 6,689/4,966 Mar.–Dec. High: Apr.–Sept.	Greens: Carts: Rating: Slope:	$$–$$$ $ 73.0/68.4 136/116	W T
SP ꙮꙮꙮ	**Crystal Springs Golf Club** Crystal Springs Rd., Hamburg. (973) 827-1444 18 holes. Par 72/72. Yards: 6,808/5,888 Apr.–Nov. High: May–Sept.	Greens: Carts: Rating: Slope:	$$–$$$$ Incl. 74.1/69.7 137/126	W T
P ꙮꙮꙮ DEAL	**Farmstead Golf and Country Club** Lawrence Rd., Lafayette. (973) 383-1666 *Clubview/Lakeview/Valleyview* 27 holes. Par 71/69/68. Yards: 6,680/6,221/6,161 Apr.–Nov. High: May–Oct.	Greens: Carts: Rating: Slope:	$$ Inquire 71.3/68.4/67.0 118/112/112	T S
P ꙮꙮꙮ	**Flanders Valley Golf Course** Pleasant Hill Rd., Flanders. (973) 584-5382 *Red/Gold*	Greens: Carts: Rating:	$$–$$$$ $$ 71.6/71.8	W T S

18 holes. Par 72/72. Yards: 6,770/5,540
Apr.–Nov. High: May–Aug.

| | | Slope: | 126/123 |

ⓖⓖⓖⓖ   *White/Blue*   Rating: 72.3/71.6
STATE   18 holes. Par 72/72. Yards: 6,765/5,534   Slope: 126/121

P
Great Gorge Country Club
Rte. 517, McAfee. (973) 827-5757
ⓖⓖⓖ   *Lake/Quarry/Rail*
27 holes. Par 71/71/72. Yards: 6,819/6,826/6,921
Mar.–Nov. High: May–Oct.

Greens: $$$–$$$$ W L T S
Carts: Incl.
Rating: 73.4/72.8/73.5
Slope: 132/128/129

P
ⓖⓖ
Green Knoll Golf Course
Garretson Rd., Bridgewater. (908) 722-1301
18 holes. Par 71/72. Yards: 6,443/5,324
Mar.–Nov. High: May–Sept.

Greens: $$ S J
Carts: $$
Rating: 70.5/71.1
Slope: 120/124

SP
ⓖⓖ
High Mountain Golf Club
Ewing Ave., Franklin Lakes. (201) 891-4653
18 holes. Par 71/71. Yards: 6,347/5,426
Apr.–Nov. High: May–Oct.

Greens: $$ W T
Carts: Incl.
Rating: 69.5/70.0
Slope: 118/117

SP
ⓖⓖ
Jumping Brook Golf and Country Club
Jumping Brook Rd., Neptune. (908) 922-6140
18 holes. Par 72/72. Yards: 6,591/5,316
Year-round. High: May–Sept.

Greens: $$ W T S J
Carts: $
Rating: 71.4/71.2
Slope: 122/118

SP
ⓖⓖ
Old Orchard Country Club
Monmouth Rd., Eatontown. (908) 542-7666
18 holes. Par 72/72. Yards: 6,588/5,575
Year-round. High: May–Sept.

Greens: $–$$ W L T S
Carts: $$
Rating: 70.5/70.8
Slope: 116/115

P
ⓖⓖ
Paramus Golf Club
Paramus Rd., Paramus. (201) 440-6079
18 holes. Par 71/70. Yards: 6,212/5,241
Year-round. High: Apr.–Nov.

Greens: $$ W S
Carts: $$
Rating: 69.1/72.0
Slope: 118/117

P
ⓖⓖ
Quail Brook Golf Course
New Brunswick Rd., Somerset. (908) 560-9528
18 holes. Par 71/72. Yards: 6,591/5,385
Year-round. High: May–Sept.

Greens: $$ S J
Carts: $$
Rating: 70.8/69.9
Slope: 119/115

P
ⓖⓖⓖ
River Vale Country Club
Rivervale Rd., River Vale. (201) 391-2300
18 holes. Par 72/74. Yards: 6,470/5,293
Mar.–Nov. High: June–Sept.

Greens: $$$–$$$$$ L T
Carts: Incl.
Rating: 70.1/68.6
Slope: 116/107

P
ⓖⓖ
Spooky Brook Golf Course
Elizabeth Ave., Somerset. (908) 873-2242
18 holes. Par 71/72. Yards: 6,612/5,376
Year-round. High: May–Sept.

Greens: $$ S J
Carts: $$
Rating: 70.5/73.5
Slope: 113/120

P
ⓖⓖⓖ
DEAL
Sunset Valley Golf Course
W. Sunset Rd., Pompton Plains. (201) 835-1515
18 holes. Par 70/70. Yards: 6,483/5,274
Apr.–Dec. High: May–Sept.

Greens: $–$$ T S
Carts: $$
Rating: 71.7/70.8
Slope: 129/123

SP
ⓖⓖⓖ
Woodlake Golf and Country Club
New Hampshire Ave., Lakewood. (908) 367-4500
18 holes. Par 72/74. Yards: 6,766/5,557
Year-round. High: May–Aug.

Greens: $$–$$$ W L T
Carts: Incl.
Rating: 72.5/72.2
Slope: 126/120

Trenton Area

SP
ⓖⓖ
Cranbury Golf Club
Southfield Rd., Cranbury. (609) 799-0341
18 holes. Par 71/72. Yards: 6,312/5,545
Year-round. High: May–Sept.

Greens: $$ W L T J
Carts: $
Rating: 70.0/72.0
Slope: 117/118

SP ☺☺	**Cream Ridge Golf Club** Rte. 539, Cream Ridge. (609) 259-2849 18 holes. Par 71/71. Yards: 6,630/5,101 Year-round. High: May–Sept.	Greens: Carts: Rating: Slope:	$–$$ $$ 72.3/72.3 119/119	W L T S J
P ☺☺	**Spring Meadow Golf Course** Atlantic Ave., Farmingdale. (908) 449-0806 18 holes. Par 72/76. Yards: 5,953/5,310 Year-round. High: Apr.–Oct.	Greens: Carts: Rating: Slope:	$ $$ 68.1/69.7 113/114	W T S

Cherry Hill/Philadelphia Suburbs

P ☺☺☺ DEAL	**Buena Vista Country Club** Rte. 40, Buena. (609) 697-3733 18 holes. Par 72/72. Yards: 6,869/5,651 Year-round. High: May–Oct.	Greens: Carts: Rating: Slope:	$$ $ 73.5/72.2 131/128	W L T
SP ☺☺	**Golden Pheasant Golf Club** Eayrestown Rd., Medford. (609) 267-4276 18 holes. Par 72/72. Yards: 6,273/5,105 Year-round. High: Apr.–Oct.	Greens: Carts: Rating: Slope:	$–$$ $ 68.1/68.4 119/114	W T S
P ☺☺☺☺ DEAL STATE	**Hominy Hill Golf Course** Mercer Rd., Colts Neck. (732) 462-9222 18 holes. Par 72/72. Yards: 7,049/5,794 Mar.–Dec. High: May–Oct.	Greens: Carts: Rating: Slope:	$$$ $$ 74.2/73.6 131/129	W T S J
P ☺☺☺☺ STATE	**Howell Park Golf Course** Yellow Brook Rd., Farmingdale. (732) 938-4771 18 holes. Par 72/72. Yards: 6,916/5,722 Mar.–Dec. High: Apr.–Oct.	Greens: Carts: Rating: Slope:	$$–$$$ $$ 73.4/73.0 128/127	W T
P ☺☺	**Ramblewood Country Club** Mt. Laurel. (609) 235-2118 *Red/White/Blue* 27 holes. Par 72/72/72. Yards: 6,883/6,624/6,723 Year-round. High: Apr.–Oct.	Greens: Carts: Rating: Slope:	$$$ Inquire 72.9/71.1/72.1 130/129/130	W L T S
P ☺☺☺ DEAL	**Rancocas Golf Club** Willingboro. (609) 877-5344 18 holes. Par 71/72. Yards: 6,634/5,284 Year-round. High: Apr.–Nov.	Greens: Carts: Rating: Slope:	$$–$$$ Incl. 73.0/73.0 130/127	W L T S J
SP ☺☺	**Ron Jaworski's Eagles' Nest Country Club** Woodbury-Glassboro Rd., Sewell. (609) 468-3542 18 holes. Par 71/71. Yards: 6,376/5,210 Year-round. High: Apr.–Oct.	Greens: Carts: Rating: Slope:	$–$$ $ 71.3/71.2 130/125	W L T S
SP ☺☺	**Willow Brook Country Club** Bridgeboro Rd., Moorestown. (609) 461-0131 18 holes. Par 72/72. Yards: 6,457/5,028 Year-round. High: May–Sept.	Greens: Carts: Rating: Slope:	$$ $ 71.2/68.3 125/110	W L T S

Jersey Shore

SP ☺☺	**Ocean Acres Country Club** Buccaneer Lane, Manahawkin. (609) 597-9393 18 holes. Par 72/72. Yards: 6,548/5,412 Year-round. High: June–Aug.	Greens: Carts: Rating: Slope:	$–$$ $$ 70.5/70.7 120/118	L T

Atlantic City Area

SP ☺☺	**Avalon Country Club** Rte. 9N, Cape May Court House. (609) 465-4653 18 holes. Par 71/72. Yards: 6,325/4,924 Year-round. High: May–Sept.	Greens: Carts: Rating: Slope:	$$–$$$ Incl. 70.3/70.7 122/122	W L T J
P ☺☺☺☺ STATE	**Blue Heron Pines Golf Club** Galloway. (609) 965-4653 18 holes. Par 72/72. Yards: 6,777/5,053 Year-round. High: May–Oct.	Greens: Carts: Rating: Slope:	$$$$$–$$$$$$ Incl. 73.0/68.4 136/116	W L T

P	**Brigantine Golf Links**	Greens:	$$$	L R T
◯◯	Roosevelt Blvd., Brigantine. (609) 266-1388	Carts:	Incl.	
	18 holes. Par 72/72. Yards: 6,520/6,233	Rating:	NA	
	Year-round. High: May–Sept.	Slope:	123/120	
SP	**Cape May National Golf Club**	Greens:	$$–$$$$	W L T J
◯◯◯	Rte. 9, Cape May. (609) 884-1563	Carts:	Incl.	
	18 holes. Par 71/71. Yards: 6,857/4,696	Rating:	72.9/68.8	
	Year-round. High: May–Oct.	Slope:	136/115	
P	**Cedar Creek Golf Course**	Greens:	$–$$	W T S J
◯◯	Tilton Blvd., Bayville. (908) 269-4460	Carts:	$$	
	18 holes. Par 72/72. Yards: 6,325/5,173	Rating:	71.2/72.5	
	Year-round. High: May–Sept.	Slope:	115/116	
R	**Greate Bay Resort and Country Club**	Greens:	$$$$	L R T
◯◯◯	Mays Landing Rd., Somers Point. (609) 927-0066	Carts:	Incl.	
	18 holes. Par 71/71. Yards: 6,750/5,495	Rating:	72.3/70.6	
	Year-round. High: May–Sept.	Slope:	130/126	
R	**Marriott's Seaview Resort**	Greens:	$$–$$$$$	L T
	S. New York Rd., Absecon. (609) 748-7680	Carts:	Incl.	
◯◯◯	*Bay Course*	Rating:	69.0/70.7	
	18 holes. Par 71/72. Yards: 6,263/5,586	Slope:	113/115	
	Year-round.			
◯◯◯	*Pines Course*	Rating:	73.0/73.2	
	18 holes. Par 71/75. Yards: 6,885/5,837	Slope:	132/128	
P	**Ocean County Golf Course at Atlantis**	Greens:	$–$$	T S J
◯◯◯	Tuckerton. (609) 296-2444	Carts:	$$	
DEAL	18 holes. Par 72/72. Yards: 6,845/5,579	Rating:	73.6/71.8	
	Year-round. High: Aug.	Slope:	134/124	
P	**Pinelands Golf Club**	Greens:	$–$$	W L T
◯	S. Mays Landing Rd., Winslow. (609) 561-8900	Carts:	$	
	18 holes. Par 71/71. Yards: 6,224/5,375	Rating:	69.7/70.4	
	Year-round. High: May–Nov.	Slope:	114/119	

Southern New Jersey

P	**Centerton Golf Club**	Greens:	$	W L T
◯◯	Almond Rd., Elmer. (609) 358-2220	Carts:	$$	
	18 holes. Par 71/71. Yards: 6,725/5,525	Rating:	69.2/71.5	
	Year-round. High: May–Aug.	Slope:	120/120	
P	**Holly Hills Golf Club**	Greens:	$$	W L T J
◯◯	Freisburg Rd., Alloway. (609) 455-5115	Carts:	$	
	18 holes. Par 72/72. Yards: 6,376/5,056	Rating:	70.8/68.0	
	Year-round. High: Apr.–Oct.	Slope:	120/114	

New York

The Empire State, despite the image of the concrete canyons of New York City, is actually a very green place with a lot of open space and mountain ranges.

The best of the public and resort courses include the famed Adirondack Mountain courses at the **Sagamore Golf Club** in Bolton Landing, which have been restored to their original difficult 1928 Donald Ross design. There is also the memorable pine-lined **Saratoga Spa Golf Course** in Saratoga Springs.

Around Syracuse in central New York are the rolling forests and impossibly green lakes of **Green Lakes State Park Golf Club** in Fayetteville, and the **Radisson Greens Golf Club** in Baldwinsville.

Wayne Hills Country Club winds through the trees in Lyons, east of Rochester; in 1999, the club began adding tons of white sand.

The Southern Tier around Binghamton features the **En-Joie Golf Club** in Endicott, home of the B.C. Open and a handsome challenge.

The rolling Catskill Mountains, about 100 miles from New York City, have a few memorable courses at the Borscht Belt resorts, including the monstrous Monster Course at the **Concord Resort Hotel** in Kiamesha Lake, and the spectacular mountain Lake/Valley/Vista triumvirate at the **Grossinger Resort** in Liberty.

Courses near New York City can be very crowded, and very slow to play; come early, or drive out of the city a bit to save waiting at the course.

Finally, there are two notable courses on Long Island: the very difficult, hilly Black Course at **Bethpage State Park** in Farmingdale (the site of the U.S. Open in 2002), and the rolling links-like beach challenge of **Montauk Downs State Park**, at the end of the island in Montauk, 100 miles east of New York City.

No fewer than seven courses coexist on the *Golf U.S.A.* Best and *Golf U.S.A.* Deals lists: Bethpage State Park, En-Joie, Green Lakes State Park, Montauk Downs State Park, Radisson Greens, Saratoga Spa, and Wayne Hills.

Adirondack and Catskill Mountain courses (and many in western New York in and around Buffalo and Niagara Falls) operate from about April through October, with peak rates in effect from about June through August.

Many courses elsewhere in the state attempt to operate year-round, while others are open from March through December. Peak rates are in effect likewise from June through August.

Golf U.S.A. Leader Board: Best Public Courses in New York

◎◎◎◎ Bethpage State Park Golf Courses (Black)
◎◎◎◎ Concord Resort Hotel (Monster)
◎◎◎   En-Joie Golf Club
◎◎◎   Green Lakes State Park Golf Club
◎◎◎◎ Grossinger Resort (Lake, Valley, Vista)
◎◎◎◎ Montauk Downs State Park Golf Course
◎◎◎◎ Radisson Greens Golf Club
◎◎◎◎ The Sagamore Golf Club
◎◎◎   Saratoga Spa Golf Course
◎◎◎◎ Wayne Hills Country Club

Golf U.S.A. Leader Board: Best Deals in New York

$/◎◎◎   Amsterdam Municipal Golf Course
$/◎◎◎   Arrowhead Golf Course
$/◎◎◎◎   Bethpage State Park Golf Courses (Black, Blue, Green, Red)
$$/◎◎◎   Blue Hill Golf Club
$$/◎◎◎   Bluff Point Golf & Country Club
$$/◎◎◎   Centerpointe Country Club
$$/◎◎   Chautauqua Golf Course (Hill, Lake)

$$/☺☺☺	Conklin Players Club
$$/☺☺☺	Crab Meadow Golf Club
$/☺☺☺	Craig Wood Golf Course
$$/☺☺☺	Deerfield Country Club
$$/☺☺☺	Deerwood Golf Course
$/☺☺☺	Durand Eastman Golf Course
$/☺☺☺	Dutch Hollow Country Club
$/☺☺☺	Endwell Greens Golf Club
$$/☺☺☺	En-Joie Golf Club
$$/☺☺☺	Foxfire Golf Club
$/☺☺☺	Green Lakes State Park Golf Club
$$/☺☺☺	Hiland Golf Club
$$/☺☺☺	Malone Golf Club (East, West)
$/☺☺☺	Mark Twain Golf Club
$$/☺☺☺☺	Montauk Downs State Park Golf Course
$$/☺☺☺	Nevele Country Club
$$/☺☺☺	Peek'n Peak Resort
$$/☺☺☺☺	Radisson Greens Golf Club
$$/☺☺☺	Rock Hill Country Club
$/☺☺☺	Saratoga Spa Golf Course
$$/☺☺☺	Segalla Country Club
$$/☺☺☺	Shadow Pines Golf Club
$/☺☺☺	Sheridan Park Golf Club
$$/☺☺☺	Smithtown Landing Golf Club
$/☺☺☺	Soaring Eagles Golf Club
$$/☺☺☺	Spring Lake Golf Club
$$/☺☺☺	Swan Lake Golf Club
$$/☺☺☺	Tarry Brae Golf Club
$$/☺☺☺	Tennanah Lake Golf & Tennis Club
$/☺☺☺	Terry Hills Golf Course
$$/☺☺☺	Thendara Golf Club
$$/☺☺☺	Thomas Carvel Country Club
$$/☺☺☺	Town of Walkill Golf Club
$$/☺☺☺	Tri County Country Club
$$/☺☺☺	Watertown Golf Club
$$/☺☺☺☺	Wayne Hills Country Club
$$/☺☺☺	Whiteface Golf Club
$/☺☺☺	Willowbrook Country Club

New York Golf Guide

Buffalo Area

P ☺☺	**Beaver Island State Park Golf Club** Beaver Island SP, Grand Island. (716) 773-4668 18 holes. Par 72/72. Yards: 6,700/6,200 Apr.–Nov. High: July–Aug.	Greens: $ Carts: $ Rating: 69.8 Slope: 108	W S J
R ☺☺	**Byrncliff Golf Club** Rte. 20A, Varysburg. (716) 535-7300	Greens: $ Carts: Incl.	L R T S

	18 holes. Par 72/73. Yards: 6,688/5,243	Rating:	70.3/73.1
	Apr.–Nov. High: June–Aug.	Slope:	115/119

R	**Chautauqua Golf Course**	Greens:	$–$$	W L T
	Rte. 394, Chautauqua. (716) 357-6211	Carts:	$	
☺☺☺	*Hill Course*	Rating:	70.9/69.1	
DEAL	18 holes. Par 72/72. Yards: 6,542/5,076	Slope:	113/108	
	Apr.–Nov. High: June–Aug.			

☺☺☺	*Lake Course*	Rating:	70.2/70.2
DEAL	18 holes. Par 72/74. Yards: 6,449/5,426	Slope:	112/112

P	**Deerwood Golf Course**	Greens:	$–$$	W T
☺☺☺	Sweeney St., N. Tonawanda. (716) 695-8520	Carts:	$	
DEAL	18 holes. Par 72/73. Yards: 6,948/6,150	Rating:	73.0/75.0	
	Apr.–Dec. High: June–Aug.	Slope:	117/123	

R	**Holiday Valley Resort**	Greens:	$–$$	L
☺☺	Rte. 219, Ellicottville. (716) 699-2346	Carts:	$	
	18 holes. Par 72/73. Yards: 6,555/5,381	Rating:	71.3/74.0	
	Apr.–Oct. High: June–Sept.	Slope:	125/115	

P	**Hyde Park Golf Course**	Greens:	$	S J
☺	Porter Rd., Niagara Falls. (716) 297-2067	Carts:	Inquire	
	18 holes. Par 70/70. Yards: 6,400/5,700	Rating:	70.0/72.0	
	Apr.–Nov. High: June–Sept.	Slope:	110/110	

P	**Rothland Golf Course**	Greens:	$	W L T S
	Clarence Center Rd., Akron. (716) 542-4325	Carts:	$	
☺☺	*Red/Gold/White*	Rating:	70.2/68.7/68.1	
	27 holes. Par 72/72/72. Yards: 6,486/6,216/6,044	Slope:	112/110/112	
	Apr.–Nov. High: June–Sept.			

P	**Sheridan Park Golf Club**	Greens:	$	W T
☺☺☺	Center Park Dr., Tonawanda. (716) 875-1811	Carts:	$	
DEAL	18 holes. Par 71/74. Yards: 6,534/5,656	Rating:	71.5/74.0	
	Apr.–Nov. High: June–Aug.	Slope:	116/116	

P	**Terry Hills Golf Course**	Greens:	$	L T S
☺☺☺	Clinton St., Batavia. (716) 343-0860	Carts:	$	
DEAL	18 holes. Par 72/72. Yards: 6,072/5,107	Rating:	69.2/68.4	
	Mar.–Nov. High: June–Aug.	Slope:	110/108	

SP	**Tri County Country Club**	Greens:	$$$	T
☺☺☺	Rte. 39, Forestville. (716) 965-9723	Carts:	$	
DEAL	18 holes. Par 71/72. Yards: 6,639/5,577	Rating:	70.9/70.5	
	Apr.–Oct. High: July–Aug.	Slope:	118/113	

P	**Willowbrook Country Club**	Greens:	$	W L T S
☺☺☺	Lake Ave., Lockport. (716) 434-0111	Carts:	$	
DEAL	18 holes. Par 71/71. Yards: 6,018/5,713	Rating:	68.9/67.7	
	Apr.–Nov. High: June–Aug.	Slope:	112/112	

Rochester Area

R	**Bristol Harbour Golf Club**	Greens:	$$$	W L R T S J
☺☺☺	Senaca Point Rd., Canandaigua. (716) 396-2460	Carts:	Incl.	
	18 holes. Par 72/72. Yards: 6,700/5,500	Rating:	72.6/73.0	
	Apr.–Nov. High: June–Sept.	Slope:	126/126	

SP	**Centerpointe Country Club**	Greens:	$–$$	W L T S
☺☺☺	Brickyard Rd., Canandaigua. (716) 924-5346	Carts:	Incl.	
DEAL	18 holes. Par 71/71. Yards: 6,787/5,225	Rating:	72.2/69.9	
	Apr.–Nov. High: June–Aug.	Slope:	119/112	

SP	**Deerfield Country Club**	Greens:	$–$$	L S
☺☺☺	Craig Hull Dr., Brockport. (716) 392-8080	Carts:	$	

DEAL	27 holes. Par 72/72. Yards: 7,083/6,300	Rating:	73.9/72.4
	Apr.–Oct. High: June–Aug.	Slope:	138/127

P	**Durand Eastman Golf Course**	Greens:	$	W L S J
☺☺☺	Kings Hwy. N., Rochester. (716) 266-0110	Carts:	$	
DEAL	18 holes. Par 70/72. Yards: 6,003/5,785	Rating:	68.8/71.7	
	Apr.–Nov. High: June–Aug.	Slope:	111/109	

P	**Eagle Vale Golf Course**	Greens:	$$	W L S J
☺☺	Nine Mile Point Rd., Fairport. (716) 377-5200	Carts:	Incl.	
	18 holes. Par 70/72. Yards: 5,584/5,801	Rating:	71/73	
	Apr.–Dec. High: June–Aug.	Slope:	121/121	

P	**Genesee Valley Golf Course**	Greens:	$	L T S J
	E. River Rd., Rochester. (716) 424-2920	Carts:	$	
☺	*New Course*	Rating:	NA/67.7	
	18 holes. Par 72/72. Yards: 5,270/5,270	Slope:	93.0/100	
	Apr.–Nov. High: June–July			

☺	*Old Course*	Rating:	69.3/73.2
	18 holes. Par 71/77. Yards: 6,374/5,561	Slope:	104/102

R	**Glen Oak Golf Course**	Greens:	$$–$$$	W L T S
☺☺☺	Smith Rd., E. Amherst. (716) 688-5454	Carts:	Incl.	
	18 holes. Par 72/72. Yards: 6,730/5,561	Rating:	72.4/71.9	
	Apr.–Nov. High: June–Aug.	Slope:	129/118	

P	**Lima Golf & Country Club**	Greens:	$	W L S
☺☺	Plank Rd., Lima. (716) 624-1490	Carts:	$	
	18 holes. Par 72/74. Yards: 6,338/5,624	Rating:	69.2/74.0	
	Apr.–Oct. High: June–Sept.	Slope:	115/117	

R	**Peek'n Peak Resort**	Greens:	$$	W S
☺☺☺	Olde Rd., Clymer. (716) 355-4141	Carts:	$	
DEAL	18 holes. Par 72/72. Yards: 6,427/4,835	Rating: 70.1/67.5		
	Apr.–Nov. High: June–Sept.	Slope: 128/116		

☺☺	*New Course*	Rating:	70.1/67.5
	18 holes. Par 72/72. Yards: 6,427/4,835	Slope:	128/119

P	**Shadow Lake Golf & Raquet Club**	Greens:	$–$$	W L T S
☺☺	Five Mile Line Rd., Penfield. (716) 385-2010	Carts:	$	
	18 holes. Par 71/72. Yards: 6,164/5,498	Rating:	68.5/70.5	
	Mar.–Dec. High: June–Aug.	Slope:	111/112	

P	**Shadow Pines Golf Club**	Greens:	$$	W L S
☺☺☺	Whalen Rd., Penfield. (716) 385-8550	Carts:	Incl.	
DEAL	18 holes. Par 72/72. Yards: 6,763/5,292	Rating:	72.4/70.4	
	Apr.–Oct. High: June–Aug.	Slope:	125/123	

SP	**Wayne Hills Country Club**	Greens:	$$–$$$	W
☺☺☺☺	Gannett Rd., Lyons. (315) 946-6944	Carts:	Incl.	
DEAL	18 holes. Par 72/73. Yards: 6,854/5,556	Rating:	73.2/71.1	
STATE	Apr.–Nov. High: May–Sept.	Slope:	131/119	

SP	**Wild Wood Country Club**	Greens:	$–$$	L S
☺☺	W. Rush Rd., Rush. (716) 334-5860	Carts:	$$	
	18 holes. Par 71/72. Yards: 6,431/5,368	Rating:	69.7/71.4	
	Apr.–Oct. High: July–Aug.	Slope:	124/122	

SP	**Winged Pheasant Golf Links**	Greens:	$–$$	W R S J
☺☺	Sand Hill Rd., Shortsville. (716) 289-8846	Carts:	$$	
	18 holes. Par 70/72. Yards: 6,400/5,835	Rating:	69.0/72.0	
	Mar.–Nov. High: June–Aug.	Slope:	118/119	

Syracuse/Central New York

P	**Arrowhead Golf Course**	Greens:	$	S J
☺☺☺	E. Taft Rd., E. Syracuse. (315) 656-7563	Carts:	$	

New York Golf Guide

DEAL		18 holes. Par 72/73. Yards: 6,700/5,156 Apr.–Nov. High: May–Sept.	Rating: Slope:	70.9/68.5 113/109

P ☺☺	**Battle Island Golf Course** Rte. 48, Battle Island State Park, Fulton. (315) 592-3361 18 holes. Par 72/72. Yards: 5,973/5,561 Apr.–Nov.	Greens: Carts: Rating: Slope:	$ $ 67.9/68.7 109/NA	W S J
SP ☺☺	**Camillus Country Club** Bennetts Corners Rd., Camillus. (315) 672-3770 18 holes. Par 73/73. Yards: 6,368/5,573 Apr.–Nov. High: June–Aug.	Greens: Carts: Rating: Slope:	$ $ 70.1/71.4 115/110	W L S J
P ☺☺☺ DEAL	**Conklin Players Club** Conklin Rd., Conklin. (607) 775-3042 18 holes. Par 72/72. Yards: 6,772/4,699 Apr.–Nov. High: May–Oct.	Greens: Carts: Rating: Slope:	$–$$ $ 72.5/67.8 127/116	W L S
P ☺	**Drumlins West Golf Club** Nottingham Rd., Syracuse. (315) 446-5580 18 holes. Par 70/70. Yards: 6,030/4,790 Apr.–Nov. High: May–Aug.	Greens: Carts: Rating: Slope:	$ $$ 68.2/71.0 111	S J
SP ☺☺☺ DEAL	**Dutch Hollow Country Club** Benson Rd., Owasco. (315) 784-5052 18 holes. Par 71/72. Yards: 6,400/5,045 Apr.–Nov. High: May–Sept.	Greens: Carts: Rating: Slope:	$ $ 70.3/68.5 120/116	W L T S J
P ☺☺	**Elm Tree Golf Course** State Rte. 13, Cortland. (607) 753-1341 18 holes. Par 70/73. Yards: 6,103/5,520 Apr.–Nov. High: June–Aug.	Greens: Carts: Rating: Slope:	$ $ 68.5/66.3 98.5/99	W L R T S J
P ☺☺☺ DEAL	**Foxfire Golf Club** Village Blvd., Baldwinsville. (315) 638-2930 18 holes. Par 72/72. Yards: 6,887/5,405 Mar.–Nov. High: June–Aug.	Greens: Carts: Rating: Slope:	$–$$ $ 72.8/71.5 127/115	S J
P ☺☺☺ DEAL STATE	**Green Lakes State Park Golf Club** Green Lakes Rd., Fayetteville. (315) 637-0258 18 holes. Par 71/74. Yards: 6,212/5,481 Apr.–Nov. High: May–Sept.	Greens: Carts: Rating: Slope:	$ $$ 68.4/70.6 113/120	S
P ☺☺	**Liverpool Golf and Country Club** Morgan Rd., Liverpool. (315) 457-7170 18 holes. Par 71/69. Yards: 6,412/5,487 Year-round. High: Apr.–Nov.	Greens: Carts: Rating: Slope:	$–$$ $ 70.7/69.3 114/113	W L T S J
P ☺☺	**Massena Country Club** Rte. 131, Massena. (315) 769-2293 18 holes. Par 71/75. Yards: 6,602/5,361 May–Oct. High: June–Aug.	Greens: Carts: Rating: Slope:	$$ $$ 70.1/71.4 110/111	L T
SP ☺☺☺☺ DEAL STATE	**Radisson Greens Golf Club** Potter Rd., Baldwinsville. (315) 638-0092 18 holes. Par 72/73. Yards: 7,010/5,543 Apr.–Nov. High: May–Sept.	Greens: Carts: Rating: Slope:	$$ $ 73.3/70.0 135/124	W S
SP ☺☺☺☺	**Seven Oaks Golf Club** East Lake Rd., Hamilton. (315) 824-1432 18 holes. Par 72/72. Yards: 6,915/5,315 Apr.–Oct. High: June–Aug.	Greens: Carts: Rating: Slope:	$$–$$$ $ 73.0/72.0 127/128	W R

Utica-Rome Area

P ☺☺	**Domenico's Golf Course** Church Rd., Whitesboro. (315) 736-9812 18 holes. Par 72/75. Yards: 6,715/5,458 Mar.–Nov. High: May–Aug.	Greens: Carts: Rating: Slope:	$ $ 70.5/71.5 118/NA	W T

New York Golf Guide

SP ☺☺	**Rome Country Club** Rte. 69, Rome. (315) 336-6464 18 holes. Par 72/75. Yards: 6,775/5,505 Year-round. High: May–Aug.	Greens: **$–$$** W Carts: **$$** Rating: 71.8/70.4 Slope: 125/NA
SP ☺☺☺ DEAL	**Thendara Golf Club** Rte. 28, Thendara. (315) 369-3136 18 holes. Par 72/73. Yards: 6,426/5,755 May–Oct. High: July–Sept.	Greens: **$$** T Carts: Inquire Rating: 70.8/72.8 Slope: 124/121

Adirondack Region

P ☺☺	**Adirondack Golf & Country Club** Peru. (518) 643-8403, (800) 346-1761 18 holes. Par 72/72. Yards: 6,851/5,069 Mar.–Dec. High: July–Aug.	Greens: **$–$$** W L T S J Carts: Inquire Rating: 71.9/67.9 Slope: 123/115
SP ☺☺☺ DEAL	**Bluff Point Golf & Country Club** Bluff Point Dr., Plattsburgh. (518) 563-3420 18 holes. Par 72/72. Yards: 6,309/5,295 Apr.–Nov. High: June–Sept.	Greens: **$$** L T Carts: Incl. Rating: 70.6/71.0 Slope: 122/121
P ☺☺☺ DEAL	**Craig Wood Golf Course** Rte. 73, Lake Placid. (518) 523-9811 18 holes. Par 72/72. Yards: 6,534/5,500 May–Oct. High: July–Aug.	Greens: **$** R T Carts: **$** Rating: 70.6/70.2 Slope: 114/118
R ☺☺	**Lake Placid Resort** Mirror Lake Dr., Lake Placid. (518) 523-4460 *Lower Course* 18 holes. Par 70/74. Yards: 6,235/5,658 May–Oct. High: July–Aug.	Greens: **$$$$** L R T J Carts: **$$** Rating: 69.0/73.0 Slope: 115/113
☺☺	*Upper Course* 18 holes. Par 70/75. Yards: 5,852/5,463	Rating: 69.0/72.0 Slope: 115/NA
SP ☺☺☺ DEAL	**Malone Golf Club** Country Club Rd., Malone. (518) 483-2926 *East Course* 18 holes. Par 72/73. Yards: 6,545/5,224 Apr.–Oct. High: June–Aug.	Greens: **$$** T Carts: **$$** Rating: 71.5/69.9 Slope: 123/117
☺☺☺ DEAL	*West Course* 18 holes. Par 71/71. Yards: 6,592/5,272	Rating: 71.4/70.1 Slope: 124/119
R ☺☺	**Thousand Islands Golf Club** Cty. Rd. 100, Wellesley Island. (315) 482-9454 18 holes. Par 72/74. Yards: 6,302/5,240 Apr.–Nov. High: June–Sept.	Greens: **$$** W L R T J Carts: **$$** Rating: 69.2/68.5 Slope: 118/114
SP ☺☺☺ DEAL	**Watertown Golf Club** Watertown. (315) 782-4040 18 holes. Par 72/73. Yards: 6,309/5,492 Apr.–Oct. High: June–Aug.	Greens: **$$** T Carts: **$** Rating: 69.4/67.9 Slope: 113/114
R ☺☺☺ DEAL	**Whiteface Golf Club** Lake Placid. (518) 523-2551 18 holes. Par 71/72. Yards: 6,285/5,482 May–Oct. High: July–Aug.	Greens: **$$** L R T J Carts: **$** Rating: 71.5/73.9 Slope: 123/113

Albany/Capital District

P ☺☺	**Alban Hills Country Club** Alban Hills Dr., Johnstown. (518) 762-3717 18 holes. Par 70/70. Yards: 6,005/5,094 Apr.–Nov. High: June–Sept.	Greens: **$** W T S J Carts: **$** Rating: 66.3/67.6 Slope: 103/105

New York Golf Guide

P	**Amsterdam Municipal Golf Course**	Greens:	$	S
😊😊😊	Upper Van Dyke Ave., Amsterdam. (518) 842-4265	Carts:	$	
DEAL	18 holes. Par 71/74. Yards: 6,370/5,352	Rating:	70.2/70.2	
	Apr.–Nov. High: July–Aug.	Slope:	120/110	

SP	**Ballston Spa Country Club**	Greens:	$$$	
😊😊😊	Rte. 67, Ballston Spa. (518) 885-7935	Carts:	Incl.	
	18 holes. Par 71/74. Yards: 6,290/5,504	Rating:	69.6/68.3	
	Apr.–Nov. High: June–Sept.	Slope:	124/122	

SP	**Hiland Golf Club**	Greens:	$$$	W L T
😊😊😊	Haviland Rd., Queensbury. (518) 761-4653	Carts:	$	
DEAL	18 holes. Par 72/72. Yards: 6,632/5,677	Rating:	72.5/72.5	
	Apr.–Nov. High: June–Sept.	Slope:	133/123	

P	**The New Course at Albany**	Greens:	$	T
😊😊	O'Neil Rd., Albany. (518) 489-3526	Carts:	$	
	18 holes. Par 71/71. Yards: 6,179/4,990	Rating:	69.4/72.0	
	Apr.–Nov. High: June–Aug.	Slope:	117/113	

R	**The Sagamore Golf Club**	Greens:	$$$$$$	R
😊😊😊😊	Sagamore Rd., Bolton Landing. (518) 644-9400	Carts:	Incl.	
STATE	18 holes. Par 70/70. Yards: 6,771/5,211	Rating:	73.8/73.0	
	Apr.–Nov. High: May–Sept..	Slope:	137/122	

P	**Saratoga Spa Golf Course**	Greens:	$	S J
😊😊😊	Saratoga Spa SP, Saratoga Springs. (518) 584-2006	Carts:	Inquire	
DEAL	18 holes. Par 72/72. Yards: 7,078/5,611	Rating:	73.7/72.5	
STATE	Apr.–Nov. High: June–Aug.	Slope:	130/122	

P	**Schenectady Golf Course**	Greens:	$	S J
😊😊	Oregon Ave., Schenectady. (518) 382-5155	Carts:	$	
	18 holes. Par 72/72. Yards: 6,570/5,275	Rating:	71.1/68.1	
	Apr.–Nov. High: May–Aug.	Slope:	123/115	

Catskill Region

R	**Concord Resort Hotel**	Greens:	$$$	W R T
	Kiamesha Lake. (914) 794-4000	Carts:	Incl.	
😊😊😊	*International Golf Course*	Rating:	72.2/73.6	
	18 holes. Par 71/71. Yards: 6,619/5,554	Slope:	127/125	
	Apr.–Nov. High: June–Sept.			

😊😊😊😊	*Monster Golf Course*	Greens:	$$$$–$$$$$$	W R T
BEST	18 holes. Par 72/72. Yards: 7,471/6,548	Carts:	Incl.	
		Rating:	76.4/78.5	
		Slope:	142/144	

R	**Grossinger Resort**	Greens:	$$$$	W T
	Rte. 52 E., Liberty. (914) 292-9000	Carts:	Incl.	
😊😊😊😊	*Lake/Valley/Vista*	Rating:	73.5/72.5/72.1	
STATE	27 holes. Par 72/70/72. Yards: 6,714/6,964/6,536	Slope:	134/133/132	
	Apr.–Nov. High: June–Sept.			

R	**Kutsher's Country Club**	Greens:	$$$	R T
😊😊😊	Kutsher Rd., Monticello. (914) 794-6000	Carts:	Incl.	
	18 holes. Par 71/71. Yards: 6,510/5,676	Rating:	74.3/72.0	
	Apr.–Nov. High: July–Aug.	Slope:	126/122	

R	**Nevele Country Club**	Greens:	$$	W R T
😊😊😊	Rte. 209, Ellenville. (800) 647-6000	Carts:	Inquire	
DEAL	18 holes. Par 70/70. Yards: 6,600/4,600	Rating:	71.9/71.1	
	Apr.–Dec. High: May–Sept.	Slope:	128/126	

P	**Tarry Brae Golf Club**	Greens:	$–$$	W L T
DEAL	Pleasant Valley Rd., S. Fallsburg. (914) 434-2620	Carts:	Inquire	

☺☺☺	18 holes. Par 72/76. Yards: 6,888/5,610 Apr.–Nov. High: June–Sept.	Rating: Slope:	73.4/72.2 129/120

R ☺☺☺ DEAL	**Tennanah Lake Golf & Tennis Club** Hankins Rd., Roscoe. (607) 498-5502 18 holes. Par 72/74. Yards: 6,769/5,797 May–Oct. High: June–Aug.	Greens: Carts: Rating: Slope:	$$ $$ 73.7/74.7 132/131	W R T S J

Binghamton/Southern Tier

SP ☺☺	**Canasawacta Country Club** Norwich. (607) 336-2685 18 holes. Par 70/71. Yards: 6,271/5,166 Apr.–Oct. High: June–Aug.	Greens: Carts: Rating: Slope:	$–$$ $ 69.9/68.8 120/114	L T J

P ☺☺☺ DEAL STATE	**En-Joie Golf Club** W. Main St., Endicott. (607) 785-1661 18 holes. Par 72/74. Yards: 7,016/5,205 Mar.–Dec. High: May–Sept.	Greens: Carts: Rating: Slope:	$–$$ $ 73.0/69.8 125/118	W L S J

P ☺☺☺ DEAL	**Endwell Greens Golf Club** Sally Piper Rd., Endwell. (607) 785-4653 18 holes. Par 72/76. Yards: 7102/5,382 Apr.–Nov. High: May–Aug.	Greens: Carts: Rating: Slope:	$ Inquire 73.6/70.6 121/117	W L S

P ☺☺	**The Links at Hiawatha Landing** Marshland Rd., Apalachin. (607) 687-6952 18 holes. Par 72/72. Yards: 7,067/5,101 Apr.–Nov. High: June–Sept.	Greens: Carts: Rating: Slope:	$$–$$$ Incl. 73.5/68.4 131/113	W L T

☺☺☺ DEAL	**Mark Twain Golf Club** Corning Rd., Elmira. (607) 737-5770 18 holes. Par 72/76. Yards: 6,829/5,571 Apr.–Oct. High: June–Aug.	Greens: Carts: Rating: Slope:	$ $ 73.6/72.3 123/121	W T S J

P ☺☺☺ DEAL	**Soaring Eagles Golf Club** Middle Rd., Horseheads. (607) 739-0551 18 holes. Par 72/72. Yards: 6,625/4,930 Apr.–Nov. High: June–Sept.	Greens: Carts: Rating: Slope:	$ $$ 71.6/67.5 117/108	T S J

New York City/Northern Suburbs

SP ☺☺☺ DEAL	**Blue Hill Golf Club** Blue Hill Rd., Pearl River. (914) 735-2094 18 holes. Par 72/72. Yards: 6,471/5,651 Mar.–Dec. High: June–Sept.	Greens: Carts: Rating: Slope:	$$ $$ 70.6/70.6 116/117	W T

P ☺☺	**Dunwoodie Golf Club** Wasylenko Lane, Yonkers. (914) 968-2771 18 holes. Par 70/72. Yards: 5,815/4,511 Apr.–Dec. High:June–July.	Greens: Carts: Rating: Slope:	$$–$$$ $$ 68.3/67.8 117/117	T S J

SP ☺☺☺	**Garrison Golf Club** Rte. 9, Garrison. (914) 424-3605 18 holes. Par 72/70. Yards: 6,470/5,041 Apr.–Nov. High: June–Aug.	Greens: Carts: Rating: Slope:	$$–$$$ $ 71.3/69.3 130/122	W T S

R ☺☺☺	**Hanah Country Club** Rte. 30, Margaretville. (914) 586-4849 18 holes. Par 72/72. Yards: 7,033/5125 Apr.–Oct. High: June–July	Greens: Carts: Rating: Slope:	$$–$$$ Included 73.5/69.7 133/123	W L R T S

SP ☺☺	**IBM Mid-Hudson Valley Golf Course** South Rd., Poughkeepsie. (914) 433-2222 18 holes. Par 72/72. Yards: 6,691/4,868 Mar.–Dec. High: Mar.–Dec.	Greens: Carts: Rating: Slope:	$$ $$ 72.4/67.9 130/117	W T J

P ☺☺☺	**Island Green Country Club** Amenia. (914) 373-9200	Greens: Carts:	$$ $$	L T S J

New York Golf Guide

DEAL	18 holes. Par 72/72. Yards: 6,617/5,601		Rating:	70.3/72.3
	Apr.–Nov. High: May–Sept.		Slope:	129/129

P	**James Baird State Park Golf Club**		Greens:	$	L T S J
☺☺	Freedom Plains Rd., Pleasant Valley. (914) 473-6200		Carts:	$$	
	18 holes. Par 71/74. Yards: 6,616/5,541		Rating:	71.3/75.2	
	Apr.–Nov. High: May–Aug.		Slope:	124/131	

P	**La Tourette Golf Club**		Greens:	$$	T S J
☺☺	Richmond Hill Rd., Staten Island. (718) 351-1889		Carts:	$$	
	18 holes. Par 72/72. Yards: 6,692/5,493		Rating:	70.7/70.9	
	Year-round. High: May–Sept.		Slope:	119/115	

P	**McCann Memorial Golf Club**		Greens:	$$	S J
☺☺	Wilbur Rd., Poughkeepsie. (914) 471-3917		Carts:	$$	
	18 holes. Par 72/72. Yards: 6,524/5,354		Rating:	72.0/71.4	
	Mar.–Dec. High: Apr.–Oct.		Slope:	128/123	

P	**Mohansic Golf Club**		Greens:	$$–$$$	W T S J
☺☺	Baldwin Rd., Yorktown Heights. (914) 962-4049		Carts:	$$	
	18 holes. Par 70/75. Yards: 6,500/5,594		Rating:	69.9/75.2	
	Apr.–Dec. High: June–Aug.		Slope:	120/127	

P	**Pelham–Split Rock Golf Course**		Greens:	$	W T S J
	Shore Rd., Bronx. (718) 885-1258		Carts:	$	
☺	*Pelham Course*		Rating:	69.6/NA	
	18 holes. Par 71/71. Yards: 6,991/5,634		Slope:	114/115	
	Year-round. High: May–Sept.				

☺	*Split Rock Course*		Rating:	71.9/71.7
	18 holes. Par 71/71. Yards: 6,714/5,509		Slope:	125/122

SP	**Putnam Country Club**		Greens:	$–$$	W T S J
☺☺	Hill St., Mahopac. (914) 628-4200		Carts:	$	
	18 holes. Par 71/73. Yards: 6,774/5,799		Rating:	72.1/73.7	
	Apr.–Nov. High: June–Sept.		Slope:	131/132	

P	**Saxon Woods Golf Course**		Greens:	$–$$$	W T S J
☺☺	Mamaroneck Ave., Scarsdale. (914) 725-3814		Carts:	$$	
	18 holes. Par 71/73. Yards: 6,397/5,617		Rating:	70.2/71.2	
	Apr.–Dec. High: June–Aug.		Slope:	119/120	

P	**Spook Rock Golf Course**		Greens:	$$–$$$	T
☺☺	Suffern. (914) 357-3085		Carts:	$$	
	18 holes. Par 72/72. Yards: 6,894/4,953		Rating:	73.1/68.1	
	Apr.–Nov. High: May–Sept.		Slope:	127/118	

P	**Stony Ford Golf Club**		Greens:	$$	W L T S
☺☺	Rte. 416, Montgomery. (914) 457-4949		Carts:	$$	
	18 holes. Par 72/72. Yards: 6,651/5,856		Rating:	72.4/74.0	
	Apr.–Nov. High: May–Sept.		Slope:	129/129	

P	**Thomas Carvel Country Club**		Greens:	$$	W L T S
☺☺☺	Ferris Rd., Pine Plains. (518) 398-7101		Carts:	Incl.	
DEAL	18 holes. Par 73/75. Yards: 7,025/5,066		Rating:	73.5/69.0	
	Apr.–Nov. High: June–Sept.		Slope:	127/115	

P	**Town of Walkill Golf Club**		Greens:	$$	W T S
☺☺☺	Sands Rd., Middletown. (914) 361-1022		Carts:	$	
DEAL	18 holes. Par 72/72. Yards: 6,437/5,171		Rating:	71.2/69.7	
	Apr.–Nov. High: June–Aug.		Slope:	122/119	

P	**Van Cortlandt Golf Club**		Greens:	$–$$	T S J
☺	Van Cortlandt Park, Bronx. (718) 543-4595		Carts:	$$	
	18 holes. Par 70/70. Yards: 6,122/5,421		Rating:	68.9/73.0	
	Year-round. High: Apr.–Oct.		Slope:	112/120	

New York Golf Guide

SP ☺☺☺	**Villa Roma Country Club** Villa Roma Rd., Callicoon. (914) 887-5097 18 holes. Par 71/72. Yards: 6,231/4,791 Apr.–Nov. High: May–Sept.	Greens: Carts: Rating: Slope:	$$–$$$ Incl. 70.3/68.8 119/113	W R T S

Long Island

P ☺☺	**Bergen Point Country Club** Bergen Ave., W. Babylon. (516) 661-8282 18 holes. Par 71/71. Yards: 6,637/5,707 Mar.–Dec. High: June–Oct.	Greens: Carts: Rating: Slope:	$–$$ $ 71.4/71.8 120/122	W L T S J
P ☺☺☺☺ BEST DEAL	**Bethpage State Park Golf Courses** Farmingdale. (516) 249-4040 *Black Course* 18 holes. Par 71/71. Yards: 7,295/6,281 Year-round. High: May–Sept.	Greens: Carts: Rating: Slope:	$$ $$ 76.6/71.4 148/134	W L T S J
☺☺☺ DEAL	*Blue Course* 18 holes. Par 72/72. Yards: 6,684/6,213	Rating: Slope:	71.7/75.0 124/129	
☺☺☺ DEAL	*Green Course* 18 holes. Par 71/71. Yards: 6,267/5,903	Rating: Slope:	69.5/73.0 121/126	
☺☺☺ DEAL	*Red Course* 18 holes. Par 70/70. Yards: 6,756/6,198	Rating: Slope:	72.2/75.1 127/130	
☺☺	*Yellow Course* 18 holes. Par 71/71. Yards: 6,339/5,966	Rating: Slope:	70.1/72.2 121/123	
P ☺☺☺ DEAL	**Crab Meadow Golf Club** Waterside Ave., Northport. (516) 757-8800 18 holes. Par 72/72. Yards: 6,613/5,845 Mar.–Dec. High: Apr.–Sept.	Greens: Carts: Rating: Slope:	$$ $$ 70.9/72.6 118/120	T S J
P ☺	**Eisenhower Park Golf** Eisenhower Park, E. Meadow. (516) 572-0200 *Blue Course* 18 holes. Par 72/72. Yards: 6,026/5,800 Year-round. High: May–Oct.	Greens: Carts: Rating: Slope:	$–$$ $$ 68.7/74.1 112/122	W L S
☺☺	*Red Course* 18 holes. Par 72/72. Yards: 6,756/5,449	Rating: Slope:	71.5/69.8 119/115	
☺	*White Course* 18 holes. Par 72/72. Yards: 6,269/5,920	Rating: Slope:	69.5/71.4 115/117	
SP ☺☺	**Hauppauge Country Club** Veterans Memorial Hwy., Hauppauge. (516) 724-7500 18 holes. Par 72/74. Yards: 6,525/5,925 Year-round. High: May–Sept.	Greens: Carts: Rating: Slope:	$$ Inquire 71.0/75.5 122/131	W L T S
P ☺☺	**Indian Island Country Club** Riverside Dr., Riverhead. (516) 727-7776 18 holes. Par 72/72. Yards: 6,374/5,545 Mar.–Jan. High: May–Sept.	Greens: Carts: Rating: Slope:	$-$$ $$ 70.3/71.3 122/122	L T S J
R ☺☺	**Marriott's Golf Club at Wind Watch** Vanderbilt Motor Pkwy., Hauppauge. (516) 232-9850 18 holes. Par 71/71. Yards: 6,563/5,175 Year-round. High: Apr.–Oct.	Greens: Carts: Rating: Slope:	$$–$$$$ Incl. 71.0/68.6 138/118	L R T J
P ☺☺	**Middle Island Country Club** Yapank Rd., Middle Island. (516) 924-5100 *Dogwood/Oaktree/Spruce* 27 holes. Par 72/72/72. Yards: 6,934/7,027/7,015 Year-round. High: Apr.–Oct.	Greens: Carts: Rating: Slope:	$$ $ 73.4/73.4/73.4 128/128/128	

New York Golf Guide

P	Montauk Downs State Park Golf Course	Greens:	$$	T S
☺☺☺☺	S. Fairview Ave., Montauk. (516) 668-1100	Carts:	$–$$	
BEST	18 holes. Par 72/72. Yards: 6,762/5,797	Rating:	73.3/74.2	
DEAL	Year-round. High: June–Oct.	Slope:	135/132	

P	Oyster Bay Town Golf Course	Greens:	$$$	W L T S J
☺☺☺	Southwood Rd., Woodbury. (516) 677-5960	Carts:	Inquire	
	18 holes. Par 70/70. Yards: 6,351/5,109	Rating:	71.5/70.4	
	Year-round. High: Apr.–Oct.	Slope:	131/126	

P	Rock Hill Country Club	Greens:	$$$	W L T S J
☺☺☺	Clancy Rd., Manorville. (516) 878-2250	Carts:	Incl.	
DEAL	18 holes. Par 71/72. Yards: 7,050/5,390	Rating:	73.7/71.4	
	Year-round. High: May–Sept.	Slope:	128/121	

P	Smithtown Landing Golf Club	Greens:	$–$$	W L
☺☺☺	Landing Ave., Smithtown. (516) 360-7618	Carts:	$	
DEAL	18 holes. Par 72/72. Yards: 6,114/5,263	Rating:	69.4/70.1	
	Year-round. High: May–Sept.	Slope:	129/126	

P	Spring Lake Golf Club	Greens:	$$	W T
☺☺☺	E. Bartlett Rd., Middle Island. (516) 924-5115	Carts:	$	
DEAL	18 holes. Par 72/72. Yards: 7,048/5,732	Rating:	73.2/70.0	
	Year-round. High: Apr.–Oct.	Slope:	128/120	

P	Sunken Meadow State Park Golf Club	Greens:	$	S
	Sunken Meadow SP, Kings Park. (516) 269-5351	Carts:	Inquire	
☺☺	*Blue/Red/Green*	Rating:	73.2/73.6/73.2	
	27 holes. Par 71/72/71. Yards: 6,100/6,165/6,185	Slope:	120/120/119	
	Apr.–Nov. High: Apr.–Sept.			

P	Swan Lake Golf Club	Greens:	$$–$$$	T
☺☺☺	River Rd., Manorville. (516) 369-1818	Carts:	$$	
DEAL	18 holes. Par 72/72. Yards: 7,011/5,245	Rating:	72.5/69.0	
	Year-round. High: Apr.–Oct.	Slope:	121/112	

P	Timber Point Golf Course	Greens:	$–$$	W L T S J
	Great River Rd., Great River. (516) 581-2401	Carts:	$$	
☺	*Red/White/Blue*	Rating:	72.9/71.9/70.6	
	27 holes. Par 72/72/72. Yards: 6,642/6,525/6,441	Slope:	121/116/116	
	Year-round. High: June–Aug.			

P	West Sayville Golf Club	Greens:	$$	W L T S J
☺☺	Montauk Hwy., W. Sayville. (516) 567-1704	Carts:	$$	
	18 holes. Par 72/72. Yards: 6,715/5,387	Rating:	72.5/71.2	
	Year-round. High: May–Sept.	Slope:	124/119	

Pennsylvania

In Oxford, 55 miles southwest of Philly, you'll find **Wyncote**, a very difficult links-style course.

Center Valley near Allentown offers an interesting course with contrasting front and back nines, the first set open and the last tight.

Some courses smell of pines, others of money; at the **Hershey Country Club** the prevailing odor is chocolate. It's an old-style club in Hershey near Harrisburg, with modern amenities and maintenance. The West Course is the better of two courses, with the East just slightly behind. In Lebanon, about 15 miles east of Hershey, is **Royal Oaks**, a challenging links course in superb shape.

In State College is the **Toftrees Resort**, where every very wooded hole presents a different challenge and view.

Near Pittsburgh are the very tight **Champion Lakes** in Bolivar, and **Tom's Run** in Blairsville, home of nearly 100 sand traps.

Residents of both the *Golf U.S.A.* Best and the *Golf U.S.A.* Deals list are Center Valley, Champion Lakes, and Royal Oaks.

Many courses in Pennsylvania are open year-round, with peak rates in effect from about March to September.

Mountain-region courses and those around Lake Erie have a season from March to November, with peak rates usually charged from April to September.

Golf U.S.A. Leader Board: Best Public Courses in Pennsylvania

◎◎◎◎ Center Valley Club
◎◎◎◎ Champion Lakes Golf Course
◎◎◎◎ Eagle Lodge Country Club
◎◎◎◎ Hershey Country Club (West)
◎◎◎◎ Royal Oaks Golf Course
◎◎◎◎ Toftrees Resort
◎◎◎◎ Tom's Run Golf Course
◎◎◎◎ Wyncote Golf Club

Golf U.S.A. Leader Board: Best Deals in Pennsylvania

$/◎◎◎   Bavarian Hills Golf Course
$$/◎◎◎   Bucknell Golf Club
$$/◎◎◎   Butler's Golf Course
$$/◎◎◎   Carroll Valley Golf Resort (Mountain View, Carroll Valley)
$$/◎◎◎   Cedarbrook Golf Course (Gold)
$$/◎◎◎◎   Center Valley Club
$$/◎◎◎◎   Champion Lakes Golf Course
$$/◎◎◎   Chestnut Ridge Golf Club
$/◎◎◎   Downing Golf Course
$/◎◎◎   Downriver Golf Club
$/◎◎◎   Edgewood in the Pines Golf Course
$/◎◎◎   Emporium Country Club
$$/◎◎◎   Fairview Golf Course
$/◎◎◎   Flying Hills Golf Course
$$/◎◎◎   Foxchase Golf Club
$$/◎◎◎   Greencastle Greens Golf Club
$$/◎◎◎   Hawk Valley Golf Club
$$/◎◎◎   Heritage Hills Golf Resort
$$/◎◎◎   Honey Run Golf and Country Club
$$/◎◎◎   Iron Masters Country Club
$$/◎◎◎   Locust Valley Golf Club
$$/◎◎◎   Mayfield Golf Club
$/◎◎◎   Mill Race Golf Course
$/◎◎◎   Mohawk Trails Golf Course
$/◎◎◎   North Hills Municipal Golf Course

$$/☺☺☺	Penn National Golf Club
$$/☺☺☺	Pennsylvania State University Golf Course (Blue)
$$/☺☺☺	Pine Acres Country Club
$$/☺☺☺	Riverside Golf Course
$$/☺☺☺☺	Royal Oaks Golf Course
$$/☺☺☺	South Hills Golf Club
$$/☺☺☺	State College Elks Country Club
$$/☺☺☺	Stone Hedge Country Club
$/☺☺☺	Sugarloaf Golf Club
$/☺☺☺	Tam O'Shanter Golf Club
$$/☺☺☺	Tamiment Resort and Conference Center
$$/☺☺☺	Upper Perk Golf Course
$/☺☺☺	White Deer Park and Golf Course (Challenge)
$$/☺☺☺	White Tail Golf Club
$$/☺☺☺	Wilkes-Barre Golf Club

Pennsylvania Golf Guide

Erie Area

P	**Cross Creek Resort**	Greens:	$$	W L
	Titusville. (814) 827-9611	Carts:	$	
☺☺	*North Course*	Rating:	68.6	
	18 holes. Par 70/70. Yards: 6,495/5,285	Slope:	112/108	
	Apr.–Oct. High: June–Aug.			

P	**Downing Golf Course**	Greens:	$	L T
☺☺☺	Troupe Rd., Harborcreek. (814) 899-5827	Carts:	$	
DEAL	18 holes. Par 72/74. Yards: 7,175/6,259	Rating:	73.0/74.4	
	Year-round. High: Mar.–Nov.	Slope:	114/115	

P	**Erie Golf Club**	Greens:	$	T
☺☺	Old Zuck Rd., Erie. (814) 866-0641	Carts:	$	
	18 holes. Par 69/72. Yards: 5,682/4,977	Rating:	67.2/68.2	
	Mar.–Nov. High: Apr.–Oct.	Slope:	111/109	

P	**North Hills Municipal Golf Course**	Greens:	$$	W L T
☺☺☺	N. Center St., Corry. (814) 664-4477	Carts:	Incl.	
DEAL	18 holes. Par 71/72. Yards: 6,108/5,057	Rating:	71.0/71.4	
	Apr.–Oct. High: July–Aug.	Slope:	115/119	

P	**Riverside Golf Course**	Greens:	$$	W L T
☺☺☺	Cambridge Springs. (814) 398-4537	Carts:	Incl.	
DEAL	18 holes. Par 71/72. Yards: 6,334/5,286	Rating:	69.7/69.5	
	Mar.–Oct. High: June–Sept.	Slope:	119/116	

Scranton/Wilkes-Barre Area

P	**Edgewood in the Pines Golf Course**	Greens:	$$	W L T
☺☺☺	Edgewood Rd., Drums. (717) 788-1101	Carts:	Incl.	
DEAL	18 holes. Par 72/72. Yards: 6,721/5,184	Rating:	71.9/69.9	
	Apr.–Nov. High: May–Aug.	Slope:	130/118	

P	**Glen Brook Country Club**	Greens:	$$	W L R T S
☺☺	Glenbrook Rd., Stroudsburg. (717) 421-3680	Carts:	Incl.	
	18 holes. Par 72/72. Yards: 6,536/5,234	Rating:	71.4/69.4	
	Apr.–Nov. High: May–Oct.	Slope:	123/117	

R	**Mill Race Golf Course**	Greens:	$	W S J
☺☺☺	Benton. (717) 925-2040	Carts:	$	
DEAL	18 holes. Par 70/71. Yards: 6,096/4,791	Rating:	68.6/68.3	
	Mar.–Nov. High: May–Aug.	Slope:	126/122	

Pennsylvania Golf Guide

R ☺☺☺	**Mount Airy Lodge Golf Course** Woodland Rd., Mount Pocono. (717) 839-8811 18 holes. Par 72/73. Yards: 6,426/5,771 Apr.–Nov. High: May–Sept.	Greens: $$$$ Carts: $ Rating: 71.4/73.3 Slope: 130/120	W R T
P ☺☺	**Pocono Manor Inn and Golf Club** Pocono Manor. (717) 839-7111 *East Course* 18 holes. Par 72/75 Yards: 6,540/6,002 Apr.–Nov. High: May–Oct.	Greens: $$–$$$ Carts: Incl. Rating: 69/NA Slope: 118/NA	W R T
☺☺	*West Course* 18 holes. Par 72/72. Yards: 6,857/5,706	Rating: 72.3/NA Slope: 117/NA	
R ☺☺	**Shawnee Inn and Golf Resort** River Rd., Shawnee-on-Delaware. (717) 421-1500 *Blue/Red/White* 27 holes. Par 72/72/72. Yards: 6,589/6,665/6,800 Apr.–Nov. High: May–Aug.	Greens: $$–$$$$ Carts: Incl. Rating: 72.4/72.8/72.2 Slope: 131/129/132	W L R T
SP ☺☺	**Skytop Lodge Golf Club** Skytop. (717) 595-8910 18 holes. Par 71/75. Yards: 6,256/5,683 Apr.–Oct. High: June–Sept.	Greens: $$–$$$ Carts: $ Rating: 70.2/72.8 Slope: 121/122	R
P ☺☺☺ DEAL	**Stone Hedge Country Club** Tunkhannock. (717) 836-5108 18 holes. Par 71/71. Yards: 6,644/5,046 Apr.–Dec. High: May–Sept.	Greens: $–$$ Carts: $ Rating: 71.9/69.9 Slope: 124/122	W L T S
P ☺☺☺ DEAL	**Sugarloaf Golf Club** Sugarloaf. (717) 384-4097 18 holes. Par 72/72. Yards: 6,845/5,620 Mar.–Nov. High: July–Aug.	Greens: $ Carts: $$ Rating: 73.0/72.8 Slope: 122/120	T
R ☺☺☺ DEAL	**Tamiment Resort and Conference Center** Bushkill Falls Rd., Tamiment. (717) 588-6652 18 holes. Par 72/72. Yards: 6,858/5,598 Apr.–Nov. High: May–Sept.	Greens: $$ Carts: $ Rating: 72.7/71.9 Slope: 130/124	W L R T J
SP ☺☺	**Water Gap Golf Club** Mtn. Rd., Delaware Water Gap. (717) 476-0200 18 holes. Par 72/74. Yards: 6,237/5,199 Mar.–Nov. High: July–Sept.	Greens: $$–$$$ Carts: Incl. Rating: 69.0/69.0 Slope: 124/120	W
P ☺☺☺ DEAL	**Wilkes-Barre Golf Club** Wilkes-Barre. (717) 472-3590 18 holes. Par 72/74. Yards: 6,912/5,690 Apr.–Nov. High: June–Aug.	Greens: $$ Carts: $ Rating: 72.8/73.2 Slope: 125/115	W L T S J

North Central Pennsylvania

P ☺☺☺ DEAL	**Bavarian Hills Golf Course** Mulligan Rd., St. Mary's. (814) 834-3602 18 holes. Par 71/73. Yards: 6,290/4,845 Year-round. High: June–Aug.	Greens: $ Carts: $ Rating: 68.8/67.2 Slope: 126/115	T J
SP ☺☺	**Corey Creek Golf Club** U.S. Rte. 6 E., Mansfield. (717) 662-3520 18 holes. Par 72/72. Yards: 6,571/4,920 Apr.–Nov. High: May–Oct.	Greens: $–$$ Carts: $ Rating: 71.1/66.0 Slope: 120/110	W L T
SP ☺☺☺ DEAL	**Emporium Country Club** Cameron Rd., Emporium. (814) 486-7715 18 holes. Par 72/72. Yards: 6,032/5,233 Mar.–Nov. High: Apr.–Sept.	Greens: $–$$ Carts: $ Rating: 68.5/69.0 Slope: 118/115	W

Pennsylvania Golf Guide

SP ☺☺☺ DEAL	**Pine Acres Country Club** W. Warren Rd., Bradford. (814) 362-2005 18 holes. Par 72/72. Yards: 6,700/5,600 Apr.–Oct. High: June–Aug.	Greens: $–$$ W L Carts: $ Rating: 70.3/72.3 Slope: 120/120
P ☺☺☺ DEAL	**White Deer Park and Golf Course** Montgomery. (717) 547-2186 *Challenge Course* 18 holes. Par 72/72. Yards: 6,605/4,742 Year-round. High: May–Sept.	Greens: $ W L S J Carts: $ Rating: 71.6/68.4 Slope: 133/125
☺☺	*Vintage Course* 18 holes. Par 72/72. Yards: 6,405/4,843	Rating: 69.7/68.5 Slope: 122/120

Pittsburgh Area

P ☺☺☺ DEAL	**Butler's Golf Course** Rock Run Rd., Elizabeth. (412) 751-9121 18 holes. Par 72/74. Yards: 6,606/5,560 Year-round. High: Apr.–Oct.	Greens: $–$$ W L T S J Carts: $ Rating: 70.3/70.8 Slope: 115/119
P ☺☺	**Castle Hills Golf Course** W. Oakwood Way, New Castle. (724) 652-8122 18 holes. Par 72/73. Yards: 6,415/5,784 Mar.–Dec. High: May–Sept.	Greens: $ L S J Carts: $ Rating: 69.7/73.3 Slope: 118/113
P ☺☺☺ DEAL	**Cedarbrook Golf Course** Belle Vernon. (724) 929-8300 *Gold Course* 18 holes. Par 72/72. Yards: 6,701/5,211 Year-round. High: Apr.–Sept.	Greens: $–$$ L S J Carts: $ Rating: 71.6/68.6 Slope: 135/123
☺☺	*Red Course* 18 holes. Par 71/71. Yards: 6,100/4,600	Rating: 67.2/64.6 Slope: 118/107
P ☺☺☺☺ DEAL STATE	**Champion Lakes Golf Course** Bolivar. (724) 238-5440 18 holes. Par 71/74. Yards: 6,608/5,556 May–Nov. High: May–Sept.	Greens: $$ W L Carts: $ Rating: 72.3/72.1 Slope: 133/127
P ☺☺☺ DEAL	**Chestnut Ridge Golf Club** Blairsville. (724) 459-7188 18 holes. Par 72/72. Yards: 6,321/5,132 Apr.–Nov. High: May–Sept.	Greens: $$ W Carts: $ Rating: 70.7/70.2 Slope: 129/119
R ☺☺	**Conley's Resort Inn** Pittsburgh Rd., Butler. (724) 586-7711 18 holes. Par 72/72. Yards: 6,200/5,625 Year-round. High: Apr.–Oct.	Greens: $–$$ W L R T S Carts: $ Rating: 69.0/69.0 Slope: 110/110
P ☺☺	**Donegal Highlands Golf Club** Donegal. (724) 423-7888 18 holes. Par 72/72. Yards: 6,153/5,884 Mar.–Nov. High: June–Aug.	Greens: $ W L S J Carts: $ Rating: 69.6/65.7 Slope: 126/118
P ☺☺	**Fox Run Golf Course** River Rd., Beaver Falls. (724) 847-3568 18 holes. Par 72/72. Yards: 6,488/5,337 Year-round. High: May–Sept.	Greens: $ L S Carts: Inquire Rating: 69.6/67.3 Slope: 113/108
R ☺☺☺	**Golf Club at Hidden Valley** Craighead Dr., Hidden Valley. (814) 443-6454 18 holes. Par 72/72. Yards: 6,589/5,027 Apr.–Nov. High: June–Aug.	Greens: $$–$$$ W L R T Carts: Incl. Rating: 73.5/69.2 Slope: 142/129
P ☺☺	**Hickory Heights Golf Club** Hickory Heights Dr., Bridgeville. (412) 257-0300	Greens: $$ W L T S J Carts: Inquire

18 holes. Par 72/72. Yards: 6,531/5,002 Year-round. High: Apr.–Oct.	Rating: 71.6/65.0 Slope: 131/115

P
☺☺
Lenape Heights Golf Course	Greens: $ W
Ford City. (724) 763-2201 18 holes. Par 71/71. Yards: 6,145/4,869 Mar.–Nov. High: Apr.–Sept.	Carts: $ Rating: 69.0/67.4 Slope: 120/114

R
☺☺
Linden Hall Golf Club	Greens: $–$$ W L R S J
Dawson. (724) 529-2366 18 holes. Par 72/77. Yards: 6,675/5,900 Mar.-Dec. High: June-Aug.	Carts: $$ Rating: 71.8/73.6 Slope: 122/123

P
☺☺☺
DEAL
Mayfield Golf Club	Greens: $–$$ W
Rte. 68, Clarion. (814) 226-8888 18 holes. Par 72/72. Yards: 6,990/5,439 Apr.–Oct. High: June–Aug.	Carts: $ Rating: 73.0/71.0 Slope: 117/118

P
☺☺
Meadowlink Golf Club	Greens: $ W L S
Bulltown Rd., Murrysville. (724) 327-8243 18 holes. Par 72/72. Yards: 6,139/5,103 Year-round. High: Apr.–Sept.	Carts: $ Rating: 68.2/66.9 Slope: 125/118

P
☺☺☺
DEAL
Mohawk Trails Golf Course	Greens: $ W L S
New Castle. (724) 667-8570 18 holes. Par 72/72. Yards: 3,126/3,198 Mar.–Dec. High: May–Sept.	Carts: $ Rating: 70.6/69.0 Slope: 108/106

P
☺☺
Mount Odin Park Golf Club	Greens: $
Mt. Odin Park Dr., Greensburg. (724) 834-2640 18 holes. Par 70/72. Yards: 5,395/4,733 Year-round. High: Apr.–Sept.	Carts: $ Rating: 65.0/68.0 Slope: 108/104

R

☺☺☺
Nemacolin Woodlands Resort	Greens: $$$–$$$$ W L T
Rte. 40E, Farmington. (724) 329-6111 *The Links Golf Club* 18 holes. Par 71/71. Yards: 6,814/4,835 Apr.–Nov. High: May–Oct.	Carts: Incl. Rating: 73.0/67.3 Slope: 131/115

☺☺
Mystic Rock Golf Club	Greens: $$$$$ L
18 holes. Par 72/72. Yards: 6,832/4,800	Carts: Incl. Rating: 75.0/68.8 Slope: 146/125

SP
☺☺
North Fork Golf and Tennis Club	Greens: $ S J
Johnstown. (814) 288-2822 18 holes. Par 72/72. Yards: 6,470/5,762 Apr.–Oct. High: June–Aug.	Carts: $ Rating: 71.1/72.0 Slope: 124/114

P
☺☺
Oakbrook Golf Course	Greens: $
Stoystown. (814) 629-5892 18 holes. Par 71/73. Yards: 5,935/5,530 Apr.–Nov. High: June–Aug.	Carts: Inquire Rating: 67.4/70.4 Slope: 109/113

P
☺☺
Pittsburgh North Golf Club	Greens: $–$$ L S J
Bakerstown Rd., Bakerstown. (724) 443-3800 18 holes. Par 72/72. Yards: 7,021/5,075 Year-round. High: June–Aug.	Carts: $ Rating: 68.8/68.3 Slope: 128/114

P
☺☺☺
Quicksilver Golf Club	Greens: $$$$ L T S J
Quicksilver Rd., Midway. (724) 796-1811 18 holes. Par 72/74. Yards: 7,085/5,067 Mar.–Dec. High: May–Oct.	Carts: Incl. Rating: 75.7/68.6 Slope: 145/115

R
☺☺☺
Seven Springs Mountain Resort Golf Course	Greens: $$$–$$$$ W L R T
Champion. (814) 352-7777 18 holes. Par 71/72. Yards: 6,360/4,934 Apr.–Oct. High: July–Aug.	Carts: Incl. Rating: 70.6/68.3 Slope: 116/111

Pennsylvania Golf Guide

P ☺☺	**Springdale Golf Club** Uniontown. (724) 439-4400 18 holes. Par 70/71. Yards: 6,100/5,350 Year-round. High: July–Aug.	Greens: Carts: Rating: Slope:	$ $ 67.5/68.5 115/115	W L S
P ☺☺☺ DEAL	**Tam O'Shanter Golf Club** Rte. 18 M, Hermitage. (724) 981-3552 18 holes. Par 72/76. Yards: 6,537/5,385 Mar.–Nov. High: June–Sept.	Greens: Carts: Rating: Slope:	$ $ 69.4/70.2 121/113	W L R S J
P ☺☺☺☺ STATE	**Tom's Run Golf Course** Blairsville. (724) 459-7188 18 holes. Par 72/72. Yards: 6,812/5,363 Apr.–Nov. High: June–Sept.	Greens: Carts: Rating: Slope:	$$$–$$$$ Incl. 73/71.2 134/126	W

Allentown/Reading/Bethlehem Area

P ☺☺	**Allentown Municipal Golf Course** Tilghman St., Allentown. (610) 395-9926 18 holes. Par 73/73. Yards: 7,085/5,635 Year-round. High: May–Sept.	Greens: Carts: Rating: Slope:	$ $$ 72.0/71.3 127/123	L T S J
P ☺☺	**Arrowhead Golf Course** Weavertown Rd., Douglassville. (610) 582-4258 *Red/White* 18 holes. Par 71/71. Yards: 6,002/6,002 Year-round.	Greens: Carts: Rating: Slope:	$ $ 68.9/73.4 116/124	W L T
P ☺☺	**Bethlehem Municipal Golf Club** Illicks Mills Rd., Bethlehem. (610) 691-9393 18 holes. Par 72/72. Yards: 6,830/5,119 Year-round. High: Mar.–Oct.	Greens: Carts: Rating: Slope:	$–$$ $ 70.6/69.1 112/NA	W T S J
P ☺☺	**Blackwood Golf Course** Red Corner Rd., Douglassville. (610) 385-6922 18 holes. Par 70/70. Yards: 6,403/4,826 Year-round. High: May–Sept.	Greens: Carts: Rating: Slope:	$ Inquire 68.6/62.0 115/95	W L T S
SP ☺☺☺	**Buck Hill Golf Club** Buck Hill Falls. (717) 595-7730 *White/Blue/Red* 27 holes. Par 72/70/70. Yards: 6,450/6,150/6,300 Apr.–Nov. High: June–Sept.	Greens: Carts: Rating: Slope:	$$–$$$ $ 71.0/69.8/70.4 126/120/122	T
P ☺☺☺☺ DEAL STATE	**Center Valley Club** Center Valley Pkwy., Center Valley. (610) 791-5580 18 holes. Par 72/72. Yards: 6,916/4,925 Apr.–Dec.	Greens: Carts: Rating: Slope:	$$$$ Incl. 74.1/63.8 135/107	T
P ☺☺☺ DEAL	**Fairview Golf Course** Rte. 72, Quentin. (717) 273-3411 18 holes. Par 71/73. Yards: 6,227/5,221 Year-round. High: May–Sept.	Greens: Carts: Rating: Slope:	$–$$ $ 69.2/72.9 106/115	W L T S J
P ☺☺☺ DEAL	**Flying Hills Golf Course** Village Center Dr., Reading. (610) 775-4063 18 holes. Par 70/70. Yards: 6,023/5,176 Year-round. High: Mar.–Sept.	Greens: Carts: Rating: Slope:	$ $ 68.2/68.8 118/118	W L
P ☺☺	**Macoby Run Golf Course** McLeans Station Rd., Green Lane. (215) 541-0161 18 holes. Par 72/NA. Yards: 6,319/NA Year-round. High: May–Sept.	Greens: Carts: Rating: Slope:	$ $ 69.5/NA 118/NA	L T S J
P ☺☺	**Rich Maiden Golf Course** Fleetwood. (610) 926-1606 18 holes. Par 69/70. Yards: 5,635/5,145 Year-round. High: Apr.–Sept.	Greens: Carts: Rating: Slope:	$ $ 63.7/65.1 97/99	L T S

Pennsylvania Golf Guide

P	Wedgewood Golf Club	Greens:	$$	W L T S
☺☺	Limeport Pike, Coopersburg. (610) 797-4551	Carts:	Incl.	
	18 holes. Par 71/72. Yards: 6,162/5,622	Rating:	68.8/65.8	
	Year-round. High: Apr.–Sept.	Slope:	122/108	

P	White Tail Golf Club	Greens:	$–$$	W T S J
☺☺☺	Klein Rd., Bath. (610) 837-9626	Carts:	$	
DEAL	18 holes. Par 72/72. Yards: 6,432/5,152	Rating:	70.6/65.3	
	Apr.–Dec. High: May–Sept.	Slope:	128/113	

P	Willow Hollow Golf Course	Greens:	$	W T S J
☺☺	Prison Rd., Leesport. (610) 373-1505	Carts:	$	
	18 holes. Par 70/70. Yards: 5,810/4,435	Rating:	67.1/NA	
	Year-round. High: May–Sept.	Slope:	105/90	

Altoona Area

P	Downriver Golf Club	Greens:	$	W T J
☺☺☺	Everett. (814) 652-5193	Carts:	$	
DEAL	18 holes. Par 72/73. Yards: 6,855/5,513	Rating:	70.5/71.6	
	Apr.–Nov. High: June–Sept.	Slope:	115/118	

SP	Iron Masters Country Club	Greens:	$$	W
☺☺☺	Roaring Spring. (814) 224-2915	Carts:	$	
DEAL	18 holes. Par 72/75. Yards: 6,644/5,683	Rating:	72.2/73.6	
	Apr.–Dec. High: June–Aug.	Slope:	130/119	

Harrisburg/York Area

P	Blue Mountain View Golf Course	Greens:	$	W L S J
☺☺	Blue Mtn. Dr., Fredericksburg. (717) 865-4401	Carts:	$$	
	18 holes. Par 71/73. Yards: 6,010/4,520	Rating:	68.2/64.9	
	Year-round. High: Apr.–Sept.	Slope:	110/101	

P	Briarwood Golf Club	Greens:	$–$$	W L R T S
	W. Market St., York. (717) 792-9776	Carts:	$	
☺☺	*East Course*	Rating:	69.7/67.8	
	18 holes. Par 72/72. Yards: 6,550/5,120	Slope:	116/112	
	Year-round. High: Mar.–Oct.			

☺☺	*West Course*	Rating:	69.7/67.4	
	18 holes. Par 70/70. Yards: 6,300/4,820	Slope:	119/112	

SP	Bucknell Golf Club	Greens:	$$	
☺☺☺	Rte. 1, Lewisburg. (717) 523-8193	Carts:	$	
DEAL	18 holes. Par 70/71. Yards: 6,268/5,330	Rating:	70.0/70.5	
	Mar.–Nov. High: June–Aug.	Slope:	132/128	

P	Carroll Valley Golf Resort	Greens:	$–$$	W L R
☺☺☺	*Mountain View Course.* Fairfield. (717) 642-5848	Carts:	$	
DEAL	18 holes. Par 71/70. Yards: 6,343/5,024	Rating:	70.2/68.2	
	Mar.–Nov. High: Apr.–Oct.	Slope:	122/113	

☺☺☺	*Carroll Valley Course.* Fairfield. (717) 642-8252	Greens:	$$	L R
DEAL	18 holes. Par 71/72. Yards: 6,633/5,005	Carts:	$	
	Year-round. High: Apr.–Oct.	Rating:	71.2/67.6	
		Slope:	120/114	

P	Cedar Ridge Golf Course	Greens:	$	L T
☺☺	Barlow Two Taverns Rd., Gettysburg. (717) 359-4480	Carts:	$	
	18 holes. Par 72/NA. Yards: 6,132/5,546	Rating:	69.5/69.3	
	Year-round. High: Apr.–Nov.	Slope:	114/114	

P	Greencastle Greens Golf Club	Greens:	$–$$	W L T S J
☺☺☺	Castlegreen Dr., Greencastle. (717) 597-1188	Carts:	$	
DEAL	18 holes. Par 72/74. Yards: 6,892/5,305	Rating:	72.6/70.3	
	Year-round. High: Apr.–Oct.	Slope:	129/124	

Pennsylvania Golf Guide

P ☺☺	**Grandview Golf Club** Carlisle Rd., York. (717) 764-2674 18 holes. Par 72/73. Yards: 6,639/5,578 Year-round. High: Apr.–Oct.	Greens: Carts: Rating: Slope:	$–$$ W L R T $ 70.5/71.1 119/120
R ☺☺☺ DEAL	**Heritage Hills Golf Resort** Mt. Rose Ave., York. (717) 755-4653 18 holes. Par 71/71. Yards: 6,330/5,075 Year-round. High: Apr.–Sept.	Greens: Carts: Rating: Slope:	$$ L T S $ 70.8/68.9 122/110
R ☺☺☺	**Hershey Country Club** E. Derry Rd., Hershey. (717) 533-2464 *East Course* 18 holes. Par 71/71. Yards: 7,061/6,363 Year-round. High: May–Oct.	Greens: Carts: Rating: Slope:	$$$$$ T Incl. 73.6/71.6 128/127
☺☺☺☺ STATE	*West Course* 18 holes. Par 73/76. Yards: 6,860/5,908	Greens: Carts: Rating: Slope:	$$$$$$ Incl. 73.1/74.7 131/127
P ☺☺☺	**Country Club of Hershey South** West Derry Rd., Hershey. (717) 534-3450 18 holes. Par 71/72. Yards: 6,204/4,856 Year-round. High: May–Oct.	Greens: Carts: Rating: Slope:	$–$$$ W T Incl. 69.9/69.6 121/107
SP ☺☺☺ DEAL	**Honey Run Golf and Country Club** S. Salem Church Rd., York. (717) 792-9771 18 holes. Par 72/72. Yards: 6,797/5,583 Year-round. High: May–Aug.	Greens: Carts: Rating: Slope:	$$ W L R T S J $ 72.4/74.0 123/125
P ☺	**Manada Golf Club** Grantville. (717) 469-2400 18 holes. Par 72/72. Yards: 6,705/5,276 Year-round. High: Apr.–Sept.	Greens: Carts: Rating: Slope:	$ W L T S J $ 70.7/68.8 117/111
SP ☺☺☺ DEAL	**Penn National Golf Club** Fayetteville. (717) 352-3000 18 holes. Par 72/72. Yards: 6,959/5,367 Year-round. High: May–Oct.	Greens: Carts: Rating: Slope:	$–$$ L T S J $ 73.2/70.1 129/116
P ☺☺☺ DEAL	**Pennsylvania State University Golf Course** W. College Ave., State College. (814) 865-4653 *Blue Course* 18 holes. Par 72/72. Yards: 6,525/5,128 Mar.–Nov. High: June–Sept.	Greens: Carts: Rating: Slope:	$–$$ T $ 72.0/69.8 128/118
☺☺	*White Course* 18 holes. Par 70/70. Yards: 6,008/5,212	Rating: Slope:	68.2/69.4 115/116
P ☺☺☺☺ DEAL STATE	**Royal Oaks Golf Course** W. Oak St., Lebanon. (717) 274-2212 18 holes. Par 71/71. Yards: 6,486/4,795 Year-round. High: Apr.–Nov.	Greens: Carts: Rating: Slope:	$$–$$$ W L Incl. 71.4/66.9 121/109
P ☺☺☺ DEAL	**South Hills Golf Club** Westminster Ave., Hanover. (717) 637-7500 *South/North/West* 27 holes. Par 71/71. Yards: 6,315/6,709/6,478 Year-round. High: May–Oct.	Greens: Carts: Rating: Slope:	$–$$ W L T $ 70.5/71.8/70.4 121/122/124
SP ☺☺☺ DEAL	**State College Elks Country Club** Rte. 322, Boalsburg. (814) 466-6451 18 holes. Par 71/72. Yards: 6,358/5,125 Apr.–Nov. High: May–Sept.	Greens: Carts: Rating: Slope:	$$ $$ 70.9/70.2 123/119

Pennsylvania Golf Guide

R ☺☺☺☺ STATE	**Toftrees Resort** State College. (814) 238-7600 18 holes. Par 72/72. Yards: 7,018/5,555 Year-round. High: June–Sept.	Greens: $$$–$$$$ W L T J Carts: Incl. Rating: 74.3/71.8 Slope: 134/126
SP ☺☺	**Towanda Country Club** Towanda. (717) 265-6939 18 holes. Par 71/76. Yards: 6,100/5,600 Apr.–Nov. High: May–Sept.	Greens: $ S J Carts: $$ Rating: 68.0/67.0 Slope: 119/102
P ☺	**Valley Green Golf Course** Valley Green Rd., Etters. (717) 938-4200 18 holes. Par 71/71. Yards: 6,000/5,500 Mar.–Nov. High: Apr.–Oct.	Greens: $ W L T S J Carts: $ Rating: 67.0/67.0 Slope: 110/109

Philadelphia Area

SP ☺☺	**Center Square Golf Club** Rte. 73, Center Square. (610) 584-5700 18 holes. Par 71/73. Yards: 6,342/5,648 Year-round. High: Apr.–Nov.	Greens: $–$$ L T S Carts: $$ Rating: 69.6/71.4 Slope: 116/117
P ☺☺	**Cool Creek Country Club** Cool Creek Rd., Wrightsville. (717) 252-3691 18 holes. Par 71/71. Yards: 6,521/5,703 Year-round. High: Apr.–Oct.	Greens: $–$$ W L R T S J Carts: $ Rating: 71.1/72.6 Slope: 118/118
P ☺☺	**Five Ponds Golf Club** W. St. Rd., Warminster. (215) 956-9727 18 holes. Par 71/71. Yards: 6,760/5,430 Year-round. High: Apr.–Sept.	Greens: $–$$ W L T S Carts: $ Rating: 71.0/70.1 Slope: 121/117
P ☺☺	**Fox Hollow Golf Club** Trumbauersville Rd., Quakertown. (215) 538-1920 18 holes. Par 71/71. Yards: 6,595/5,411 Year-round. High: May–Sept.	Greens: $–$$ W L T S J Carts: $ Rating: 70.2/67.0 Slope: 117/106
P ☺☺☺ DEAL	**Foxchase Golf Club** Stevens Rd., Stevens. (717) 336-3673 18 holes. Par 72/72. Yards: 6,689/4,690 Year-round. High: Apr.–Oct.	Greens: $–$$ W L T S J Carts: Incl. Rating: 72.7/66.9 Slope: 124/116
P ☺☺	**General Washington Golf Course** Egypt Rd., Audubon. (610) 666-7602 18 holes. Par 70/72. Yards: 6,300/5,300 Year-round. High: Apr.–Oct.	Greens: $–$$ L T S J Carts: $ Rating: 67.5/67.4 Slope: NA
P ☺☺☺ DEAL	**Hawk Valley Golf Club** Crestview Dr., Denver. (717) 445-5445 18 holes. Par 72/72. Yards: 6,743/5,422 Year-round. High: Apr.–Nov.	Greens: $–$$ J Carts: $ Rating: 70.3/70.2 Slope: 132/119
P ☺☺	**Limekiln Golf Club** Limekiln Pike, Ambler. (215) 643-0643 *Red/White/Blue* 27 holes. Par 70/70/70. Yards: 6,213/6,415/6,176 Year-round. High: May–July	Greens: $$ T S Carts: $ Rating: 67.8/68.7/NA Slope: 114/114/NA
P ☺☺☺ DEAL	**Locust Valley Golf Club** Locust Valley Rd., Coopersburg. (610) 282-4711 18 holes. Par 72/74. Yards: 6,451/5,444 Mar.–Dec. High: May–Sept.	Greens: $–$$ L T S Carts: $ Rating: 71.0/71.3 Slope: 132/121
P ☺☺	**Moccasin Run Golf Course** Schoff Rd., Atglen. (610) 593-7341 18 holes. Par 72/72. Yards: 6,336/5,275 Year-round. High: Apr.–Oct.	Greens: $–$$ W L T S J Carts: $ Rating: 69.0/67.7 Slope: 113/113

R ☺☺☺	**Mountain Laurel Golf Club** Rte. 534 and 180, White Haven. (717) 443-7424 18 holes. Par 72/72. Yards: 6,798/5,631 Apr.–Nov. High: June–Aug.	Greens: Carts: Rating: Slope:	$$$ W L R T S Incl. 72.3/71.9 113/113
SP ☺☺	**Mountain Manor Inn and Golf Club** Creek Rd., Marshall's Creek. (717) 223-1290 *Blue/Yellow* 18 holes. Par 71/71. Yards: 6,233/5,079 Apr.–Oct.	Greens: Carts: Rating: Slope:	$–$$ W L R T $$ 68.5/68.5 115/115
☺☺	*Orange/Silver* 18 holes. Par 72/72. Yards: 6,426/5,146	Rating: Slope:	71.0/71.5 132/124
SP ☺☺	**Northampton Valley Country Club** Rte. 232, Richboro. (215) 355-2234 18 holes. Par 70/71. Yards: 6,377/5,586 Year-round. High: Apr.–Oct.	Greens: Carts: Rating: Slope:	$–$$ W T S $ 69.2/70.0 123/118
P ☺☺	**Overlook Golf Course** Lititz Pike, Lancaster. (717) 569-9551 18 holes. Par 70/71. Yards: 6,100/4,962 Year-round. High: May–Aug.	Greens: Carts: Rating: Slope:	$–$$ L S $ 69.2/68.4 110/113
P ☺☺	**Pickering Valley Golf Club** S. White Horse Rd., Phoenixville. (610) 933-2223 18 holes. Par 72/72. Yards: 6,530/5,235 Year-round. High: Apr.–Oct.	Greens: Carts: Rating: Slope:	$–$$ W T S Incl. 70.3/64.5 122/111
P ☺☺☺ DEAL	**Upper Perk Golf Course** Rte. 663 and Ott Rd., Pennsburg. (215) 679-5594 18 holes. Par 71/71. Yards: 6,381/5,249 Mar.–Dec. High: May–Sept.	Greens: Carts: Rating: Slope:	$–$$ W L T S J $$ 70.0/69.6 117/113
P ☺	**Valley Forge Golf Club** N. Gulf Rd., King of Prussia. (610) 337-1776 18 holes. Par 71/73. Yards: 6,200/5,668 Mar.–Nov. High: June–July	Greens: Carts: Rating: Slope:	$–$$ $ 68.9/71.1 107
SP ☺☺☺☺ STATE	**Wyncote Golf Club** Wyncote Dr., Oxford. (610) 932-8900 18 holes. Par 72/72. Yards: 7,012/5,454 Year-round. High: May–Oct.	Greens: Carts: Rating: Slope:	$$$–$$$$$ W T S J $ 74.0/71.6 130/126

Rhode Island

The small state of Rhode Island is limited in public golf course offerings, but visitors can count on at least three memorable places to play. The **North Kingstown Municipal Golf Course** lies alongside a Navy air base and the ocean, making for plenty of man-made and natural challenges. The **Richmond Country Club** feels like a very different place, stretching deep into the pines.

The **Triggs Memorial** course dates back to a Donald Ross design of 1927. It is a difficult challenge with a wee bit of a Scottish feel.

All three—North Kingstown, Richmond, and Triggs—also win spots on the *Golf U.S.A.* Deals list.

Courses in Rhode Island are generally open from March through November, with peak rates in effect in the summer months from June to September.

Golf U.S.A. Leader Board: Best Public Courses in Rhode Island

☺☺☺   North Kingstown Municipal Golf Course

◎◎◎   Richmond Country Club
◎◎◎   Triggs Memorial Golf Course

Golf U.S.A. Leader Board: Best Deals in Rhode Island

$$/◎◎◎   Exeter Country Club
$$/◎◎◎   North Kingstown Municipal Golf Course
$$/◎◎◎   Richmond Country Club
$$/◎◎◎   Triggs Memorial Golf Course

Rhode Island Golf Guide

Providence/Newport Area

P ◎◎	**Country View Golf Club** Colwell Rd., Harrisville. (401) 568-7157 18 holes. Par 70/70. Yards: 6,067/4,755 Mar.–Nov. High: June–Sept.	Greens: Carts: Rating: Slope:	$–$$ $$ 69.2/67.0 119/105	W L T S
P ◎◎	**Cranston Country Club** Burlingame Rd., Cranston. (401) 826-1683 18 holes. Par 71/72. Yards: 6,750/5,499 Mar.–Dec. High: May–Sept.	Greens: Carts: Rating: Slope:	$$ $ 72.4/NA 124/NA	T S
P ◎◎◎ DEAL	**Exeter Country Club** Ten Rod Rd., Exeter. (401) 295-1178 18 holes. Par 72/72. Yards: 6,919/5,733 Mar.–Nov. High: June–Sept.	Greens: Carts: Rating: Slope:	$$ $ 72.3/72.1 123/115	L T
P ◎◎	**Foster Country Club** Johnson Rd., Foster. (401) 397-7750 18 holes. Par 72/74. Yards: 6,187/5,500 Apr.–Nov. High: May–Aug.	Greens: Carts: Rating: Slope:	$–$$ $ 69.5/70.0 114/112	
SP ◎◎	**Green Valley Country Club** Union St., Portsmouth. (401) 849-2162 18 holes. Par 71/71. Yards: 6,830/5,459 Mar.–Dec. High: May–Sept.	Greens: Carts: Rating: Slope:	$$ $$ 72.0/69.5 126/120	W T
SP ◎◎	**Laurel Lane Golf Course** Laurel Lane, W. Kingston. (401) 783-3844 18 holes. Par 71/70. Yards: 5,806/5,381 Year-round High: June–Sept.	Greens: Carts: Rating: Slope:	$$ $$ 67.6/66.2 120/113	T
P ◎◎◎ DEAL STATE	**North Kingstown Municipal Golf Course** Callahan Rd., N. Kingstown. (401) 294-0684 18 holes. Par 70/70. Yards: 6,161/5,227 Apr.–Nov. High: May–Oct.	Greens: Carts: Rating: Slope:	$$ $$ 69.3/69.5 123/115	W L T
P ◎◎◎ DEAL STATE	**Richmond Country Club** Sandy Pond Rd., Richmond. (401) 364-9200 18 holes. Par 71/71. Yards: 6,826/4,974 Apr.–Nov. High: June–Sept.	Greens: Carts: Rating: Slope:	$$ $$ 72.1/70.4 121/113	W T
P ◎◎◎ DEAL STATE	**Triggs Memorial Golf Course** Chalkstone Ave., Providence. (401) 521-8460 18 holes. Par 72/72. Yards: 6,596/5,598 Year-round. High: June–Aug.	Greens: Carts: Rating: Slope:	$$ $$ 72.9/73.1 128/123	L S
P ◎◎	**Winnapaug Country Club** Shore Rd., Westerly. (401) 596-1237 18 holes. Par 72/72. Yards: 6,345/5,113 Year-round. High: June–Sept.	Greens: Carts: Rating: Slope:	$$ $$ 70.6/69/1 118/110	T

Vermont

You'll find a very green mountain challenge at **Gleneagles Golf Course** in Manchester Village in southern Vermont's ski region. A bit farther east is the **Mount Snow Golf Club** in West Dover, a hilly challenge in the ski area and home to a well-respected golf school.

The **Stratton Mountain Resort** is a bit farther north, home of the handsome and well-maintained Lake/Mountain/Forest nines, which feature views of the green off-season ski runs above.

In the central part of the state is the **Rutland Country Club**, an attractive course at the base of the mountains.

In the north-central region is the **Sugarbush Golf Course** in Warren, set at the base of Sugarbush Mountain and surrounded by spectacular forest and hills. East of Rutland, in lovely covered-bridge country, is the **Woodstock Country Club**, a sandy course situated just behind the picturesque Woodstock Inn in the Kedron Valley.

Most courses in Vermont operate on a snow-country schedule. Expect peak rates from about June to August.

For a classic taste of New England, golf packages are available at the traditional Equinox Hotel or the elegant Charles Orvis Inn at The Equinox in Manchester Center. The golfing high season in snow country runs from about May to November; the rest of the year is high season for skiing. Rates including golf start at about $205 midweek, $248 weekends per person for double rooms.

One advantage to golfing in snow country, though, is the abundance of off-season hotels and guest houses near the ski areas. Look for nightly rates, not including golf, of $50–$100.

Another option is to stay in a ski chalet at one of Vermont's winter resorts. For example, the Killington Resort offers golf packages from mid-May to mid-October. Rates, including motel room, breakfast, and golf, are as low as $79 per person for double-occupancy rooms, with deluxe suites about $100 per person. Luxury condos with kitchens rent for as little as $95 for a one-bedroom unit, to about $200 for a three- or four-bedroom unit.

Golf U.S.A. Leader Board: Best Public Courses in Vermont

☺☺☺	Gleneagles Golf Course
☺☺☺	Mount Snow Golf Club
☺☺☺☺	Rutland Country Club
☺☺☺	Stratton Mountain Resort (Lake, Mountain, Forest)
☺☺☺	Sugarbush Golf Course
☺☺☺	Woodstock Country Club

Golf U.S.A. Leader Board: Best Deals in Vermont

$$/☺☺☺	Country Club of Barre
$$/☺☺☺	Crown Point Country Club
$$/☺☺☺	Killington Golf Course
$$/☺☺☺	Proctor-Pittsford Country Club

Photo © Bob Perry, courtesy of Killington Ski & Summer Resort, Killington, Vermont

Vermont Golf Guide

St. Albans

P
☺☺
Champlain Country Club
St. Albans. (802) 527-1187
18 holes. Par 70/70. Yards: 6,237/5,225
Apr.–Oct. High: July–Aug.

Greens: $$ W T
Carts: $$
Rating: 69.9/70.4
Slope: 123/117

Burlington Area

R
☺☺
Basin Harbor Golf Club
Basin Harbor Rd., Vergennes. (802) 475-2309
18 holes. Par 72/72. Yards: 6,513/5,745
May–Oct. High: July–Aug.

Greens: $$ W L R T J
Carts: $$
Rating: 71.5/74.8
Slope: 122/125

SP
☺☺
Kwiniaska Golf Club
Spear St., Shelburne. (802) 985-3672
18 holes. Par 72/72. Yards: 7,037/5,632
Apr.–Nov. High: June–Aug.

Greens: $$ T
Carts: $$
Rating: 72.5/72.6
Slope: 128/119

SP
☺☺
Newport Country Club
Pine Hill Rd., Newport. (802) 334-2391
18 holes. Par 72/72. Yards: 6,117/5,312
Apr.–Oct. High: July–Aug.

Greens: $$ T
Carts: $
Rating: 69.4/70.5
Slope: 109/111

SP
☺☺
Rocky Ridge Golf Club
Ledge Rd., Burlington. (802) 482-2191
18 holes. Par 72/72. Yards: 6,000/5,230
Apr.–Nov. High: July–Aug.

Greens: $ T
Carts: $$
Rating: 69.1/68.7
Slope: 124/110

R
☺☺
Stowe Golf Course
Cape Cod Rd., Stowe. (802) 253-4893
18 holes. Par 72/72. Yards: 6,206/5,346
May–Oct. High: July–Sept.

Greens: $$$ T
Carts: $
Rating: 69.3/70.1
Slope: 117/118

R
☺☺☺
STATE
Sugarbush Golf Course
Warren. (802) 583-6725
18 holes. Par 72/72. Yards: 6,464/5,231
May–Oct. High: July–Oct.

Greens: $$$ W L R T J
Carts: $
Rating: 71.7/70.4
Slope: 128/119

Vermont Golf Guide

Montpelier/Barre Area

| P
☺☺☺
DEAL | **Country Club of Barre**
Plainfield Rd., Barre. (802) 476-7658
18 holes. Par 71/71. Yards: 6,240/5,431
Apr.–Oct. High: June–Aug. | Greens: $$
Carts: $
Rating: 70.2/71.7
Slope: 123/119 | |

Rutland Area

| R
☺☺☺
DEAL | **Killington Golf Course**
Killington Rd., Killington. (802) 422-6700
18 holes. Par 72/72. Yards: 6,326/5,108
May–Oct. | Greens: $$$
Carts: $
Rating: 70.6/71.2
Slope: 126/123 | T J |

| P
☺☺☺
DEAL | **Proctor-Pittsford Country Club**
Corn Hill Rd., Pittsford. (802) 483-9379
18 holes. Par 70/72. Yards: 6,052/5,446
Apr.–Nov. High: July–Aug. | Greens: $$
Carts: $
Rating: 69.4/66.1
Slope: 121/115 | T |

| SP
☺☺☺☺
STATE | **Rutland Country Club**
North Grove St., Rutland. (802) 773-3254
18 holes. Par 70/71. Yards: 6,134/5,368
Apr.–Oct. High: June–Aug. | Greens: $$$$
Carts: Incl.
Rating: 69.7/71.6
Slope: 125/125 | |

| R

☺☺☺
STATE | **Stratton Mountain Resort**
Stratton Mountain. (802) 297-4114
Lake/Mountain/Forest
27 holes. Par 72/72/72. Yards: 6,526/6,478/6,602
May–Oct. High: July–Aug. | Greens: $$$–$$$$
Carts: $
Rating: 71.2/71.2/72.0
Slope: 125/126/125 | W L R J |

| R
☺☺☺
STATE | **Woodstock Country Club**
The Green, Woodstock. (802) 457-6674
18 holes. Par 69/71. Yards: 6,001/4,924
May–Nov. High: July–Aug. | Greens: $$$–$$$$
Carts: $
Rating: 69.0/67.0
Slope: 121/113 | W L R T |

Southern Vermont

| SP
☺☺☺
DEAL | **Crown Point Country Club**
Weathersfield Center Rd., Springfield. (802) 885-1010
18 holes. Par 72/72. Yards: 6,572/5,542
Apr.–Oct. High: May–Sept. | Greens: $$–$$$
Carts: $$
Rating: 72.0/71.3
Slope: 123/117 | W T J |

| R
☺☺☺
STATE | **Gleneagles Golf Course**
Rte. 7A, Manchester Village. (802) 362-3223
18 holes. Par 71/71. Yards: 6,423/5,396
May–Oct. | Greens: $$$$–$$$$$
Carts: $
Rating: 71.1/71.4
Slope: 128/122 | T |

| SP
☺☺☺☺ | **Haystack Golf Club**
Spyglass Dr., Wilmington. (802) 464-8301
18 holes. Par 72/74. Yards: 6,549/5,471
May–Oct. High: July–Aug. | Greens: $$$–$$$$
Carts: Incl.
Rating: 71.1/71.4
Slope: 128/122 | W L R J |

| R
☺☺☺
STATE | **Mount Snow Golf Club**
West Dover. (802) 464-5642
18 holes. Par 72/72. Yards: 6,894/5,436
May–Oct. High: July–Aug. | Greens: $$$
Carts: $
Rating: 73.3/72.8
Slope: 130/121 | L R T J |

Virginia

The Cascades Course at the **Homestead Resort** in far western Virginia at the base of the Allegheny Mountains is a famous but still-hidden mountain gem, probably the best course in the state. In Wintergreen, west of Charlottesville, is the Stoney Creek at Wintergreen Course at the **Wintergreen Resort**, a superior challenge at the foot of the Blue Ridge Mountains. Its front nine are located in a former cornfield and the back nine in a deep forest; also at Wintergreen is the Devil's Knob Golf Club, a well-regarded mountain course.

In Williamsburg, the Gold Course at the **Golden Horseshoe Golf Club** is an exceptional challenge in the historic colonial town, with a more modern island green at No. 16. The Blue/Gold Course at **Ford's Colony** in Williamsburg is a handsome test of golfing skills. Ford's Colony plans to expand the Blue Course with another nine holes in mid-2000. Another excellent, tricky challenge is the River Course at the **Kingsmill Resort** in Williamsburg near the Busch Gardens theme park; it includes several watery challenges, including the sometimes foggy James River on the way home.

The Golden Eagle Course at the **Tides Inn** near Chesapeake Bay in Irvington has a lot of water, including a pair of long carries and some 120 bunkers.

Most courses in temperate Virginia are open year-round, with peak rates usually in effect from April to October. Mountain-region resorts, including the Homestead Resort in Hot Springs, are open from April to October, with peak rates in effect for much of the operating year.

The Kingsmill Resort in Williamsburg, a rolling green golfing heaven, has off-season pricing on its rooms and suites from December through April.

The famed Golden Horseshoe at the Williamsburg Inn has value-season pricing in January and February; leisure prices in March, June, September, and early November; summer rates in July and August; and highest peak rates in April, May, and October, and at Thanksgiving. Rates per person for rooms and unlimited golf vary from $176 during value season to $351 at peak times. To save more money, you can stay at the not-quite-as-posh Williamsburg Woodlands or the Governor's Inn, where golf and room deals run from a high season (mid-March to mid-November) of about $150 per person to about $120 in other months.

Golf U.S.A. Leader Board: Best Public Courses in Virginia

๏๏๏๏	Ford's Colony Country Club (Blue, Gold)
๏๏๏๏	Golden Horseshoe Golf Club (Gold)
๏๏๏๏	The Homestead Resort (Cascades)
๏๏๏๏	Kingsmill Resort (River)
๏๏๏๏	The Tides Inn (Golden Eagle)
๏๏๏๏	Wintergreen Resort (Devil's Knob, Stoney Creek)

Golf U.S.A. Leader Board: Best Deals in Virginia

$$/๏๏๏	Bristow Manor Golf Club
$$/๏๏๏	Bryce Resort Golf Course
$$/๏๏๏	Caverns Country Club
$$/๏๏๏	Draper Valley Golf Club
$/๏๏๏	The Hamptons Golf Course
$$/๏๏๏	Hanging Rock Golf Club
$/๏๏๏	Lakeview Golf Course
$$/๏๏๏	Lee's Hill Golfer's Club
$$/๏๏๏	Meadows Farms Golf Course
$/๏๏๏	Newport News Golf Club at Deer Run (Cardinal, Deer Run)
$$/๏๏๏	Olde Mill Golf Course

$$/☺☺☺	Pohick Bay Regional Golf Course
$$/☺☺☺	Reston National Golf Course
$$/☺☺☺	River's Bend Golf Course
$$/☺☺☺	Royal Virginia Golf Club
$$/☺☺☺	Shenandoah Crossing Resort and Country Club
$/☺☺☺	Sleepy Hole Golf Course
$/☺☺☺	Suffolk Golf Course
$$/☺☺☺	Sycamore Creek Golf Course
$/☺☺☺	Wolf Creek Golf and Country Club

Virginia Golf Guide

Washington, D.C., Area

P
☺☺
Algonkian Regional Park Golf Course
Sterling. (703) 450-4655
18 holes. Par 72/72. Yards: 7,015/5,795
Year-round. High: May–Dec.

Greens: $–$$ W R S J T
Carts: $$
Rating: 73.5/74.0
Slope: 125/113

P
☺☺☺
DEAL
Bristow Manor Golf Club
Valley View Dr., Bristow. (703) 368-3558
18 holes. Par 72/73. Yards: 7,102/5,527
Year-round. High: Mar.–Nov.

Greens: $$$–$$$$ W L T S J
Carts: Incl.
Rating: 72.9/71.7
Slope: 129/126

R
☺☺☺
DEAL
Bryce Resort Golf Course
Basye. (540) 856-2124
18 holes. Par 71/71. Yards: 6,261/5,240
Mar.–Dec. High: May–Aug.

Greens: $–$$ W L R T
Carts: $
Rating: 68.8/70.1
Slope: 122/120

R
☺☺☺
DEAL
Caverns Country Club
Airport Rd., Luray. (540) 743-7111
18 holes. Par 72/72. Yards: 6,499/5,499
Year-round. High: Apr.–June, Sept.–Oct.

Greens: $–$$
Carts: $
Rating: 71.2/72.4
Slope: 117/120

P
☺☺
Herndon Centennial Golf Club
Ferndale Ave., Herndon. (703) 471-5769
18 holes. Par 71/71. Yards: 6,445/5,025
Year-round. High: May–Sept.

Greens: $$ W S J
Carts: $$
Rating: 68.7/69.0
Slope: 116/121

R
☺☺☺
Lansdowne Golf Club
Woodridge Pkwy., Lansdowne. (703) 729-4071
18 holes. Par 72/72. Yards: 7,057/5,213
Year-round. High: Apr.–Nov.

Greens: $$$$ L R
Carts: Incl.
Rating: 74.0/75.0
Slope: 130/134

P
☺☺☺
DEAL
Lee's Hill Golfer's Club
Old Dominion Pkwy., Fredericksburg. (540) 891-0111
18 holes. Par 72/72. Yards: 6,805/5,064
Year-round. High: Apr.–Oct.

Greens: $$–$$$ W L T S J
Carts: Incl.
Rating: 72.4/68.2
Slope: 128/115

P

☺☺☺
DEAL
Meadows Farms Golf Course
Flat Run Rd., Locust Grove. (540) 854-9890
Island Green/Longesthole/Waterfall
27 holes. Par 72/72. Yards: 7,005/6,058/6,871
Year-round. High: Apr.–Sept.

Greens: $$ L T S
Carts: Incl.
Rating: 73.2/68.9/72.7
Slope: 129/123/123

P
☺☺☺
DEAL
Pohick Bay Regional Golf Course
Gunston Rd., Lorton. (703) 339-8585
18 holes. Par 72/72. Yards: 6,405/4,948
Year-round. High: Mar.–Nov.

Greens: $$ W L J S
Carts: $
Rating: 71.7/68.9
Slope: 131/121

P
☺☺☺
DEAL
Reston National Golf Course
Sunrise Valley Dr., Reston. (703) 620-9333
18 holes. Par 71/72. Yards: 6,871/5,886
Year-round. High: Apr.–Oct.

Greens: $$$–$$$$ W L T S J
Carts: $
Rating: 72.9/74.3
Slope: 126/132

Virginia Golf Guide

P ◎◎	**South Wales Golf Course** Jeffersonton. (540) 451-1344 18 holes. Par 71/73. Yards: 7,077/5,020 Year-round. High: Apr.–Oct.	Greens: Carts: Rating: Slope:	$–$$ $$ 73.2/68.5 123/104	W L T S
SP ◎◎	**Stoneleigh Golf Club** Prestwick Court, Round Hill. (540) 338-4653 18 holes. Par 72/71. Yards: 6,709/4,837 Year-round. High: Apr.–Oct.	Greens: Carts: Rating: Slope:	$$$ Incl. 73.1/69.9 141/118	W T
P ◎◎	**Twin Lakes Golf Course** Clifton Rd., Clifton. (703) 631-9099 18 holes. Par 73/73. Yards: 7,010/5,935 Year-round. High: May–Sept.	Greens: Carts: Rating: Slope:	$$ $$ 73.0/72.6 121/118	W S J

Northern Virginia

SP ◎◎◎	**Shenandoah Valley Golf Club** 134 Gold Club Cir., Front Royal. (540) 635-3588 *Red-White/White-Blue/Red-Blue* 27 holes. Par 71/71/72. Yards: 6,121/6,330/6,399 Year-round. High: Mar.–Oct.	Greens: Carts: Rating: Slope:	$$–$$$ Incl. 69.6/70.7/71.1 122/122/126	W L T
R ◎◎	**The Shenvale** New Market. (540) 740-3181 27 holes. Par 71/71/71. Yards: 6,595/6,297/6,358 Year-round. High: Apr.–Oct.	Greens: Carts: Rating: Slope:	$–$$ $ 71.1/70.1/70.1 120/119/117	L R T

Charlottesville Area

P ◎◎◎	**Birdwood Golf Course** Rte. 250 W., Charlottesville. (804) 293-4653 18 holes. Par 72/72. Yards: 6,865/5,041 Year-round. High: Apr.–Oct.	Greens: Carts: Rating: Slope:	$$$ $ 73.1/72.4 132/122	
SP ◎◎◎ DEAL	**Lakeview Golf Course** Rte. 11, Harrisonburg. (540) 434-8937 *Lake/Peak/Spring* 27 holes. Par 72/72/72. Yards: 6,517/6,640/6,303 Year-round. High: Apr.–Oct.	Greens: Carts: Rating: Slope:	$ $ 71.0/71.3/70.9 119/121/120	T
P ◎◎◎ DEAL	**Royal Virginia Golf Club** Dukes Rd., Hadensville. (540) 457-2041 18 holes. Par 72/NA. Yards: 7,106/NA Year-round. High: Dec.–Feb.	Greens: Carts: Rating: Slope:	$–$$ $ 73.4/NA 131/NA	W L T S
R ◎◎◎ DEAL	**Shenandoah Crossing Resort and Country Club** Rte. 2, Gordonsville. (540) 832-9543 18 holes. Par 72/72. Yards: 6,192/4,713 Year-round. High: May–Sept.	Greens: Carts: Rating: Slope:	$$ Incl. 69.8/66.5 119/111	W L T S J
R ◎◎◎◎ STATE	**Wintergreen Resort** Wintergreen. (800) 266-2444 *Devil's Knob Golf Club* 18 holes. Par 70/70. Yards: 6,576/5,060 Apr.–Oct. High: May–Oct.	Greens: Carts: Rating: Slope:	$$$–$$$$ $ 71.7/68.6 130/118	W L R
◎◎◎◎ BEST	*Stoney Creek at Wintergreen* *Monocan-Shamokin/Shamokin-Tucahoe/Tucahoe-Monocan* 27 holes. Par 72/72/72. Yards: 7,005/6,998/6,951	Rating: Slope:	74.0/73.8/74.0 132/130/130	

Richmond Area

P ◎◎	**Belmont Golf Course** Hilliard Rd., Richmond. (804) 266-4929 18 holes. Par 71/73 Yards: 6,350/5,418 Year-round. High: Apr.–Oct.	Greens: Carts: Rating: Slope:	$–$$ $ 70.6/72.6 126/130	S J
SP ◎◎	**Birkdale Golf and Country Club** Royal Birkdale Dr., Chesterfield. (804) 739-8800	Greens: Carts:	$$ Incl.	W L R T S J

	18 holes. Par 71/71. Yards: 6,544/4,459	Rating:	71.1/NA	
	Year-round. High: May–Oct.	Slope:	122/NA	

P	**The Crossings Golf Club**	Greens:	$$–$$$	W L S J
☺☺☺	Virginia Center Pkwy., Glen Allen. (804) 261-0000	Carts:	Incl.	
	18 holes. Par 72/72. Yards: 6,619/5,625	Rating:	70.7/73.2	
	Year-round.	Slope:	126/128	

P	**Glenwood Golf Club**	Greens:	$–$$	W T S J
☺☺	Creighton Rd., Richmond. (804) 226-1793	Carts:	$	
	18 holes. Par 71/75. Yards: 6,464/5,197	Rating:	70.0/72.1	
	Year-round. High: May–Oct.	Slope:	114/120	

SP	**Mill Quarter Plantation Golf Course**	Greens:	$–$$	W L R T S J
☺☺	Mill Quarter Dr., Powhatan. (804) 598-4221	Carts:	Inquire	
	18 holes. Par 72/72. Yards: 6,970/5,280	Rating:	73.2/NA	
	Year-round. High: Apr.–Sept.	Slope:	127/109	

SP	**River's Bend Golf Course**	Greens:	$–$$	W T S J
☺☺☺	Hogans Alley, Chester. (804) 530-1000	Carts:	$	
DEAL	18 holes. Par 71/71. Yards: 6,671/4,932	Rating:	71.9/67.8	
	Year-round. High: Apr.–Oct.	Slope:	132/117	

P	**Sycamore Creek Golf Course**	Greens:	$$	W L T S J
☺☺☺	Manakin Rd., Manakin Sabot. (804) 784-3544	Carts:	Incl.	
DEAL	18 holes. Par 70/70. Yards: 6,256/5,149	Rating:	69.7/64.6	
	Year-round. High: Apr.–Oct.	Slope:	124/114	

Southwest Virginia

SP	**Wolf Creek Golf and Country Club**	Greens:	$	W L R T S J
☺☺☺	Rte. 1, Bastian. (703) 688-4610	Carts:	$	
DEAL	18 holes. Par 71/71. Yards: 6,215/4,788	Rating:	68.7/71.0	
	Year-round. High: Apr.–Oct.	Slope:	107/128	

Roanoke Area

P	**Draper Valley Golf Club**	Greens:	$–$$	W L
☺☺☺	Rte. 1, Draper. (703) 980-4653	Carts:	$	
DEAL	18 holes. Par 72/72. Yards: 7,046/4,793	Rating:	73.3/65.6	
	Year-round. High: Mar.–Nov.	Slope:	125/113	

P	**Hanging Rock Golf Club**	Greens:	$–$$	W L R T S J
☺☺☺	Red Lane, Salem. (703) 389-7275	Carts:	$	
DEAL	18 holes. Par 72/72. Yards: 6,828/4,463	Rating:	72.3/62.6	
	Year-round. High: Apr.–Oct.	Slope:	125/106	

R	**The Homestead Resort**	Greens:	$$$$$–$$$$$$	L R T J
	Hot Springs.	Carts:	$	
☺☺☺☺	*Cascades Course.* (540) 839-1776	Rating:	72.9/70.3	
BEST	18 holes. Par 70/70. Yards: 6,659/5,041	Slope:	136/124	
	Apr.–Oct. High: May–Oct.			

☺☺☺	*The Old Course.* (540) 839-1776	Greens:	$$$–$$$$	L R T J
	18 holes. Par 72/72. Yards: 6,211/4,852	Carts:	$	
		Rating:	69.7/67.7	
		Slope:	120/116	

☺☺☺	*Lower Cascades Course.* (540) 839-1776	Greens:	$$$$	L R T J
	18 holes. Par 72/70. Yards: 6,579/4,686	Carts:	$	
		Rating:	72.2/66.2	
		Slope:	127/110	

R	**Olde Mill Golf Course**	Greens:	$$	W L R T
☺☺☺	Rte. 1, Laurel Fork. (703) 398-2211	Carts:	$	
DEAL	18 holes. Par 72/72. Yards: 6,833/4,876	Rating:	72.7/70.4	
	Year-round. High: Apr.–Oct.	Slope:	127/134	

Williamsburg Area

R	**Ford's Colony Country Club**	Greens:	$$$$$–$$$$$$	W L R T
	Ford's Colony Dr., Williamsburg. (757) 258-4130	Carts:	Incl.	
☺☺☺☺	*Black Heath Course*	Rating:	71.8/62.9	
STATE	18 holes. Par 71/71. Yards: 6,621/4,605	Slope:	133/112	
	Year-round. High: Apr.–Oct.			
☺☺☺	*Red/White Course*	Rating:	72.3/73.2	
	18 holes. Par 72/72. Yards: 6,755/5,614	Slope:	126/132	
R	**Golden Horseshoe Golf Club**	Greens:	$$$$–$$$$$	L R T
	S. England St., Williamsburg. (757) 220-7696	Carts:	Incl.	
☺☺☺☺	*Gold Course*	Rating:	73.6/70.6	
BEST	18 holes. Par 71/71. Yards: 6,817/5,168	Slope:	138/127	
	Year-round. High: Apr.–Oct.			
☺☺☺☺	*Green Course*	Rating:	73.4/69.3	
	18 holes. Par 72/72. Yards: 7,120/5,348	Slope:	134/109	
R	**Kingsmill Resort**	Greens:	$$$$$–$$$$$$	L R T
	Kingsmill Rd., Williamsburg. (757) 253-3906	Carts:	Incl.	
☺☺☺	*Plantation Course*	Rating:	71.3/67.9	
	18 holes. Par 72/72. Yards: 6,543/4,880	Slope:	119/116	
	Year-round. High: Apr.–Oct.			
☺☺☺☺	*River Course*	Rating:	73.3/67.5	
STATE	18 holes. Par 71/71. Yards: 6,853/4,646	Slope:	137/116	
☺☺	*Woods Course*	Rating:	72.7/68.7	
	18 holes. Par 72/72. Yards: 6,784/5,140	Slope:	131/120	

Newport/Norfolk/Virginia Beach Area

P	**The Hamptons Golf Course**	Greens:	$	W L S J
☺☺☺	Butler Farm Rd., Hampton. (757) 766-9148	Carts:	$	
DEAL	27 holes. Par 71/71/70. Yards: 6,401/6,283/5,940	Rating:	69.9/69.4/67.8	
	Year-round. High: Mar.–Sept.	Slope:	110/110/106	
P	**Hell's Point Golf Course**	Greens:	$$–$$$	W L R T
☺☺☺	Atwoodtown Rd., Virginia Beach. (757) 721-3400	Carts:	Incl.	
	18 holes. Par 72/72. Yards: 6,966/5,003	Rating:	73.3/71.2	
	Year-round. High: May–Aug.	Slope:	130/116	
SP	**Honey Bee Golf Club**	Greens:	$$–$$$	W L T S J
☺☺☺	S. Indian Blvd., Virginia Beach. (757) 471-2768	Carts:	Incl.	

Key to Symbols

Rating: 1 to 4 Golf Balls

☺	Worth a Visit
☺☺	Above Average
☺☺☺	Exceptional
☺☺☺☺	Very Best

BEST *Golf U.S.A.* Best American Courses
DEAL *Golf U.S.A.* Best Golfing Deals
STATE *Golf U.S.A.* Best in State

Course Type

P	Public
R	Resort
SP	Semiprivate

Price Ranges

$	<$20	Bargain
$$	$20–$39	Budget
$$$	$40–$59	Moderate
$$$$	$60–$79	Expensive
$$$$$	$80–$100	Very Expensive
$$$$$$	$100+	Exclusive

Discounts

W	Weekdays
L	Low Season
R	Resort Guests
T	Twilight
S	Seniors
J	Juniors

| | 18 holes. Par 72/72. Yards: 6,705/4,929 | Rating: | 69.6/67.0 | |
| | Year-round. High: Mar.–Oct. | Slope: | 123/104 | |

SP ☺☺☺	**Kiln Creek Golf and Country Club**	Greens:	$$–$$$	W L
	Brick Kiln Blvd., Newport News. (757) 988-3220	Carts:	Incl.	
	18 holes. Par 72/72. Yards: 6,888/5,313	Rating:	73.4/69.5	
	Year-round. High: Apr.–Oct.	Slope:	130/119	

P	**Newport News Golf Club at Deer Run**	Greens:	$	W L S J
	Jefferson Ave., Newport News. (757) 886-7925	Carts:	$	
☺☺☺	*Cardinal Course*	Rating:	70.9/62.8	
DEAL	18 holes. Par 72/72. Yards: 6,645/4,789	Slope:	118/102	
	Year-round. High: Apr.–Nov.			

| ☺☺☺ | *Deer Run Course* | Rating: | 73.7/70.0 | |
| DEAL | 18 holes. Par 72/72. Yards: 7,206/5,295 | Slope: | 133/113 | |

P ☺☺	**Red Wing Lake Golf Course**	Greens:	$$	S J
	Prosperity Rd., Virginia Beach. (757) 437-4845	Carts:	$	
	18 holes. Par 72/72. Yards: 7,080/5,285	Rating:	73.7/68.1	
	Year-round. High: Apr.–Oct.	Slope:	125/102	

P ☺☺☺	**Sleepy Hole Golf Course**	Greens:	$	W S J
	Sleepy Hole Rd., Suffolk. (757) 538-4100	Carts:	$	
DEAL	18 holes. Par 71/72. Yards: 6,695/5,121	Rating:	71.7/64.8	
	Year-round. High: Apr.–Oct.	Slope:	122/108	

P ☺☺	**Stumpy Lake Golf Club**	Greens:	$	W L T S J
	E. Indian River Rd., Virginia Beach. (757) 467-6119	Carts:	$	
	18 holes. Par 72/72. Yards: 6,800/5,200	Rating:	72.2/67.1	
	Year-round. High: Apr.–Oct.	Slope:	119/97	

P ☺☺☺	**Suffolk Golf Course**	Greens:	$	S J
	Holland Rd., Suffolk. (757) 539-6298	Carts:	$	
DEAL	18 holes. Par 72/72. Yards: 6,340/5,561	Rating:	70.3/71.1	
	Year-round. High: May–Sept.	Slope:	121/112	

R	**The Tides Inn**	Greens:	$$$–$$$$	W L R
	Golden Eagle Dr., Irvington. (804) 438-5501	Carts:	$	
☺☺☺☺	*Golden Eagle Golf Course*	Rating:	74.3/70.9	
STATE	18 holes. Par 72/72. Yards: 6,963/5,261	Slope:	134/126	
	Mar.–Dec. High: Apr.–Oct.			

R	**The Tides Lodge Resort and Country Club**	Greens:	$$–$$$	W L R T
	St. Andrews Lane, Irvington. (804) 438-6200	Carts:	$	
☺☺☺	*The Tartan Course*	Rating:	71.5/69.2	
	18 holes. Par 72/72. Yards: 6,586/5,121	Slope:	124/116	
	Mar.–Dec. High: May–Oct.			

P ☺☺	**Woodlands Golf Course**	Greens:	$	S J
	Woodland Rd., Hampton. (757) 727-1195	Carts:	$	
	18 holes. Par 69/69. Yards: 5,482/4,399	Rating:	64.6/64.8	
	Year-round. High: Apr.–Sept.	Slope:	99/100	

Washington, D.C.

It's hard to believe that there are a handful of golf courses within the tight con-
fines of the District of Columbia—none are so lavish as to warrant a congressional investigation, but at least you can air out your bag of clubs while on a
business or tourist visit.

The best of the courses is probably the **Langston Golf Course**, which also
wins a spot on the *Golf U.S.A.* Deals list. The Blue Course at the **East Potomac
Park Golf Course** has great views of the city skyline, although the course has
become a bit bedraggled. The new 9-hole Par 3 Red Course was due to open in

the spring of 2000. Finally, there is the **Rock Creek Park Golf Course**, a short, tight challenge in the city's best-known greensward.

You can expect courses to stay open year-round, although weather and conditions can be pretty grim in the winter and wiltingly hot in the summer. High season runs from late spring through the end of summer.

Golf U.S.A. Leader Board: Best Public Course in Washington, D.C.

☺☺ Langston Golf Course

Golf U.S.A. Leader Board: Best Deals in Washington, D.C.

$/☺☺	East Potomac Park Golf Course
$/☺	Langston Golf Course
$/☺	Rock Creek Park Golf Course

Washington, D.C., Golf Guide

P	**East Potomac Park Golf Course**	Greens:	$–$$	W S	
	Ohio Dr., Washington. (202) 554-7660	Carts:	$		
☺☺	*Blue Course*	Rating:	68.5		
	18 holes. Par 72/72. Yards: 6,599/5,274	Slope:	109		
	Year-round. High: May–Sept.				
P	**Langston Golf Course**	Greens:	$	W S	
☺☺	Benning Rd. N.E., Washington. (202) 397-8638	Carts:	$		
STATE	18 holes. Par 72/72. Yards: 6,340/6,100	Rating:	69.6/70		
	Year-round. High: Mar.–Oct.	Slope:	115/115		
P	**Rock Creek Park Golf Course**	Greens:	$	W S	
☺	16th & Rittenhouse St. N.W., Washington. (202) 882-7332	Carts:	$		
	18 holes. Par 65/65. Yards: 4,715/NA	Rating:	62.5/65.5		
	Year-round. High: June–Aug.	Slope:	112/102		

The Central States

Illinois	Missouri
Indiana	Nebraska
Iowa	North Dakota
Kansas	Ohio
Kentucky	South Dakota
Michigan	West Virginia
Minnesota	Wisconsin

Illinois

The best of the public courses in the Land of Lincoln is probably No. 4 at **Cog Hill Golf Club** in Lemont, southwest of Chicago. Players say they need every club in their bag to survive its numerous sand and water hazards.

Two attractive courses are the tree-lined Woodside and Lakeside nines at **Cantigny Golf** in Wheaton, west of Chicago. Other Illinois courses of note include **Kemper Lakes** in Long Grove, north of Chicago, a woods-meadow-lake combination with some very technically demanding holes; **Pine Meadow** in Mundelein, also to the north; and the **George W. Dunne**, another woodsy wonderland.

All the way over in the northwest corner near Dubuque in the Mississippi River Valley are the winning North and South courses of **Eagle Ridge**. The ridge overlooks Lake Galena.

The best of our *Golf U.S.A.* Deals include the **Aldeen Golf Club**, **Balmoral Woods**, and **Heritage Bluffs**.

Some of the courses in Illinois operate year-round, especially those in the southern part of the state, particularly those near St. Louis. Elsewhere expect courses to be open from about April through November. Statewide peak rates are in effect during late spring and summer months.

Golf U.S.A. Leader Board: Best Public Courses in Illinois

◎◎◎◎ Cantigny Golf (Woodside, Lakeside, Hillside)
◎◎◎◎ Cog Hill Golf Club (No. 4)
◎◎◎◎ Eagle Ridge Inn and Resort (North, South)
◎◎◎ George W. Dunne National Golf Course
◎◎◎◎ Kemper Lakes Golf Course
◎◎◎◎ Pine Meadow Golf Club

Golf U.S.A. Leader Board: Best Deals in Illinois

$$/◎◎◎◎	Aldeen Golf Club
$$/◎◎◎	Balmoral Woods Country Club
$$/◎◎◎	Belk Park Golf Club
$$/◎◎◎	Big Run Golf Club
$$/◎◎◎	Blackberry Oaks Golf Course
$$/◎◎◎	Bonnie Brook Golf Club
$$/◎◎◎	Bon Vivant Country Club
$$/◎◎◎	Cog Hill Golf Club (No. 2)
$$/◎◎◎	Edgebrook Country Club
$$/◎◎◎	Fox Bend Golf Course
$$/◎◎◎	Fox Creek Golf Club
$$/◎◎◎	Glenwoodie Country Club
$$/◎◎◎◎	Heritage Bluffs Golf Course
$/◎◎◎	Hickory Point Golf Club
$$/◎◎◎	The Ledges Golf Club
$/◎◎◎	Lick Creek Golf Course
$$/◎◎◎	Marengo Ridge Golf Club
$$/◎◎◎	Naperbrook Golf Course
$/◎◎◎	Newman Golf Course
$$/◎◎◎	The Oak Club of Genoa
$$/◎◎◎	The Orchards Golf Club
$/◎◎◎	Park Hills Golf Club (West)
$$/◎◎◎	Pinecrest Golf & Country Club
$/◎◎◎◎	Prairie Vista Golf Course
$$/◎◎◎	Prairieview Golf Course
$$/◎◎◎	The Rail Golf Club

$$/☺☺☺	Rend Lake Golf Course
$$/☺☺☺	Sandy Hollow Golf Course
$$/☺☺☺	Schaumburg Golf Course
$$/☺☺☺	Silver Lake Country Club (South)
$$/☺☺☺	Springbrook Golf Course
$$/☺☺☺	Steeple Chase Golf Club
$$/☺☺☺	Timber Trails Country Club
$$/☺☺☺	Village Greens of Glen Ellyn
$$/☺☺☺	Wedgewood Golf Course
$/☺☺☺	Westview Golf Course

Illinois Golf Guide

Dubuque Area

R	**Eagle Ridge Inn and Resort**	Greens:	$$$$$–$$$$$$ L R T
	Galena. (815) 777-5200	Carts:	$
☺☺☺☺	*North Course*	Rating:	73.4/72.9
BEST	18 holes. Par 72/72. Yards: 6,836/5,578	Slope:	134/127
	Apr.–Nov. High: May–Oct.		
☺☺☺☺	*South Course*	Rating:	72.7/72.4
BEST	18 holes. Par 72/72. Yards: 6,762/5,609	Slope:	134/128
☺☺☺☺	*The General*	Rating:	73.8/66.7
	18 holes. Par 72/72 Yards: 6,820/5,335	Slope:	137/119
P	**Lacoma Golf Course**	Greens:	$
	Timmerman Rd., E. Dubuque. (815) 747-3874	Carts:	$
☺☺	*Blue Course*	Rating:	718/70.0
	18 holes. Par 71/71. Yards: 6,705/5,784	Slope:	123/117
	Mar.–first snow. High: May–Sept.		
☺☺	*Red/Gold Course*	Rating:	63.5/63.8
	18 holes. Par 69/69. Yards: 5,552/4,895	Slope:	105/102
P	**The Ledges Golf Club**	Greens:	$–$$ W L T S J
☺☺☺	McCurry Rd., Roscoe. (815) 389-0979	Carts:	$
DEAL	18 holes. Par 72/72. Yards: 6,740/5,881	Rating:	72.5/74.1
	Apr.–Oct. High: May–Aug.	Slope:	129/129
P	**Prairieview Golf Course**	Greens:	$$ W T S J
☺☺☺	N. River Rd., Byron. (815) 234-4653	Carts:	$$
DEAL	18 holes. Par 72/72. Yards: 6,893/5,658	Rating:	72.3/71.6
	Apr.–Oct. High: June–Aug.	Slope:	123/117

Rock Island

P	**Highland Springs Golf Course**	Greens:	$ W T S J
☺☺	35th St. W., Rock Island. (309) 787-5814	Carts:	Inquire
	18 holes. Par 72/72. Yards: 6,884/5,875	Rating:	73.0/69.0
	Apr.–Oct. High: June–Aug.	Slope:	118/NA

Chicago Area

P	**Aldeen Golf Club**	Greens:	$$–$$$ W T
☺☺☺☺	Reid Farm Rd., Rockford. (815) 282-4653	Carts:	$$
DEAL	18 holes. Par 72/72. Yards: 7,058/5,038	Rating:	73.9/69.2
	Apr.–Oct. High: June–Aug.	Slope:	130/116
P	**Arboretum Golf Club**	Greens:	$$ W L
☺☺	Half Day Rd., Buffalo Grove. (847) 913-1112	Carts:	Inquire
	18 holes. Par 72/72. Yards: 6,477/5,039	Rating:	71.1/68.7
	Mar.–Dec. High: June–Aug.	Slope:	132/118

Illinois Golf Guide

P ☺☺☺ DEAL	**Balmoral Woods Country Club** Crete. (708) 672-7448 18 holes. Par 72/72. Yards: 6,683/5,282 Mar.–Nov. High: June–Aug.	Greens: Carts: Rating: Slope:	$$$ Incl. 72.6/71.8 131/117	W L T S
P ☺☺	**Bartlett Hills Golf Course** W. Oneida, Bartlett. (630) 837-2741 18 holes. Par 71/71. Yards: 6,482/5,488 Year-round. High: Apr.–Sept.	Greens: Carts: Rating: Slope:	$–$$ $ 71.2/71.8 124/121	W L T S J
P ☺☺☺ DEAL	**Big Run Golf Club** W. 135th St., Lockport. (815) 838-1057 18 holes. Par 72/74. Yards: 6,690/5,975 Apr.–Nov. High: June–Aug.	Greens: Carts: Rating: Slope:	$$$ $$ 72.2/74.8 139/133	L T J
P ☺☺☺ DEAL	**Blackberry Oaks Golf Course** Kennedy Rd., Bristol. (630) 553-7170 18 holes. Par 72/72. Yards: 6,258/5,230 Apr.–Nov. High: June–Aug.	Greens: Carts: Rating: Slope:	$$ $$ 69.8/70.1 121/119	T S J
P ☺☺☺ DEAL	**Bonnie Brook Golf Club** N. Lewis Ave., Waukegan. (847) 360-4730 18 holes. Par 72/73. Yards: 6,701/5,559 Apr.–Nov. High: May–Sept.	Greens: Carts: Rating: Slope:	$–$$ $$ 72.4/72.2 126/124	T S
P ☺☺	**The Burr Hill Club** Burr Rd., St. Charles. (630) 584-8236 18 holes. Par 72/72. Yards: 6,640/5,111 Year-round. High: May–Aug.	Greens: Carts: Rating: Slope:	$–$$ $ 72.5/70.9 128/120	W L T
P ☺☺☺☺ BEST	**Cantigny Golf** Mack Rd., Wheaton. (630) 668-3323 *Woodside/Lakeside/Hillside* 27 holes. Par 72/72/72. Yards: 6,709/6,625/6,760 Apr.–Oct. High: June–Aug.	Greens: Carts: Rating: Slope:	$$$$ 73.1/71.8/72.8 136/131/130	S J
P ☺☺☺	**Carillon Golf Club** S. Carillon, Plainfield. (815) 886-2132 18 holes. Par 71/71. Yards: 6,607/5,194 Mar.–Nov. High: June–Sept.	Greens: Carts: Rating: Slope:	$$–$$$ Incl. 71.1/68.4 121/108	W L T S J
P ☺☺	**Cog Hill Golf Club** Archer Ave., Lemont. (630) 257-5872 *No. 1* 18 holes. Par 71/72. Yards: 6,314/5,530 Year-round. High: Apr.–Oct.	Greens: Carts: Rating: Slope:	$$–$$$ $$ 69.8/71.4 118/119	W L T J
☺☺☺ DEAL	*No. 2* 18 holes. Par 72/72. Yards: 6,262/5,484	Rating: Slope:	69.8/70.5 120/115	
☺☺	*No. 3* 18 holes. Par 72/71. Yards: 6,423/5,306	Rating: Slope:	69.9/69.5 116/112	
☺☺☺☺ BEST	*No. 4* 18 holes. Par 72/72. Yards: 6,940/5,889	Greens: Carts: Rating: Slope:	$$$$$$ Incl. 75.4/74.7 142/133	
P ☺☺	**Deer Creek Golf Club** University Park. (708) 672-6667 18 holes. Par 72/72. Yards: 6,755/5,835 Year-round. High: May–Sept.	Greens: Carts: Rating: Slope:	$–$$ $ 72.4/73.2 124/120	W T S J
SP ☺☺☺	**Edgebrook Country Club** Sudyam Rd., Sandwich. (815) 786-3058	Greens: Carts:	$$ $	L

DEAL	18 holes. Par 72/72. Yards: 6,100/5,134 Year-round. High: June–Aug.	Rating: Slope:	70.4/64.5 123/106
P ☺☺☺ DEAL	**Fox Bend Golf Course** Rte. 34, Oswego. (630) 554-3939 18 holes. Par 72/72. Yards: 6,800/5,400 Mar.–Dec. High: May–Sept.	Greens: $$ W L T S J Carts: $ Rating: 72.1/70.1 Slope: 124/116	
P ☺☺	**Fox Run Golf Links** Plum Grove Rd., Elk Grove Village. (847) 980-4653 18 holes. Par 70/70. Yards: 6,287/5,288 Apr.–Nov. High: June–Aug.	Greens: $$ W T Carts: $$ Rating: 70.5/70.2 Slope: 119/116	
P ☺☺☺ BEST	**George W. Dunne National Golf Course** S. Central, Oak Forest. (708) 614-2600 18 holes. Par 72/72. Yards: 7,170/5,535 Mar.–Dec. High: May–Aug.	Greens: $$–$$$ W T S J Carts: $$ Rating: 75.1/71.4 Slope: 135/121	
P ☺☺	**Gleneagles Golf Club** McNulty Rd., Lemont. (630) 257-5466 *Red Course* 18 holes. Par 70/74. Yards: 6,090/6,090 Mar.–Dec. High: June–Aug.	Greens: $$ L T S Carts: Inquire Rating: 67.6/71.3 Slope: 112/111	
☺☺	*White Course* 18 holes. Par 70/75. Yards: 6,250/6,080	Rating: 70.1/72.3 Slope: 120/114	
P ☺☺☺ DEAL	**Glenwoodie Country Club** 193rd and State, Glenwood. (708) 758-1212 18 holes. Par 72/72. Yards: 6,715/5,176 Year-round. High: Apr.–Sept.	Greens: $–$$ W L T S J Carts: $ Rating: 71.8/68.4 Slope: 120/108	
R ☺☺	**The Golf Club at Oak Brook Hills** Midwest Rd., Oak Brook. (630) 850-5530 18 holes. Par 70/69. Yards: 6,372/5,152 Mar.–Nov. High: Apr.–Sept.	Greens: $$$–$$$$ W L T S Carts: Inquire Rating: 70.4/69.2 Slope: 122/114	
P ☺☺☺	**Golf Club of Illinois** Edgewood Rd., Algonquin. (847) 658-4400 18 holes. Par 71/71. Yards: 7,011/4,896 Mar.–Nov. High: May–Sept.	Greens: $$$–$$$$ W L T S J Carts: Incl. Rating: 74.6/68.6 Slope: 133/115	
P ☺☺☺☺ DEAL	**Heritage Bluffs Golf Course** W. Bluff Rd., Channahon. (815) 467-7888 18 holes. Par 72/72. Yards: 7,106/4,967 Apr.–Oct. High: May–Sept.	Greens: $$$ W T S J Carts: Incl. Rating: 73.9/68.4 Slope: 138/114	
P ☺☺	**Highland Park Country Club** Park Ave. W., Highland Park. (847) 433-9015 18 holes. Par 70/70. Yards: 6,522/5,353 Apr.–Nov. High: May–Sept.	Greens: $$$ W L T Carts: $ Rating: 72.1/71.8 Slope: 130/122	
P ☺☺	**Highland Woods Golf Course** N. Ela Rd., Hoffman Estates. (847) 202-0340 18 holes. Par 72/72. Yards: 6,995/5,895 Mar.–Dec. High: May–Sept.	Greens: $$ W T Carts: $$ Rating: 72.5/72.0 Slope: 129/125	
P ☺☺	**Hilldale Golf Club** Ardwick Dr., Hoffman Estates. (847) 310-1100 18 holes. Par 71/72. Yards: 6,432/5,409 Apr.–Nov. High: June–Aug.	Greens: $$ W L T S Carts: $ Rating: 71.3/72.1 Slope: 125/121	
P ☺	**Hughes Creek Golf Club** Spring Valley Dr., Elburn. (630) 365-9200 18 holes. Par 72/72. Yards: 6,506/5,561 Apr.–Nov. High: June–Aug.	Greens: $–$$ W L T S J Carts: $ Rating: 70.9/71.7 Slope: 117/115	

Illinois Golf Guide

R ☺	**Indian Lakes Resort** W. Schick Rd., Bloomingdale. (630) 529-0200 *East Course* 18 holes. Par 72/72. Yards: 6,890/5,031 Apr.–Nov. High: June–Sept.	Greens: $$-$$$ W L T R Carts: Incl. Rating: 72.4/70.5 Slope: 120/117
☺	*West Course* 36 holes. Par 72/72. Yards: 6,901/5,088	Rating: 72.1/71.1 Slope: 123/120
P ☺☺	**Ingersoll Memorial Golf Club** Daisyfield Rd., Rockford. (815) 987-8834 18 holes. Par 71/74. Yards: 5,991/5,140 Apr.–Oct.	Greens: $-$$ T Carts: $$ Rating: 68.2/73.3 Slope: 108/108
P ☺☺☺☺ BEST	**Kemper Lakes Golf Course** Old McHenry Rd., Long Grove. (847) 320-3450 18 holes. Par 72/72. Yards: 7,217/5,638 Apr.–Nov. High: June–Aug.	Greens: $$$$$$ Carts: Incl. Rating: 75.7/67.9 Slope: 140/125
P ☺☺☺	**Klein Creek Golf Club** Pleasant Hill Rd., Winfield. (630) 690-0101 18 holes. Par 72/72. Yards: 6,673/4,509 Apr.–Nov. High: June–Sept.	Greens: $$$-$$$$ W Carts: Incl. Rating: 71.9/66.2 Slope: 127/110
P ☺☺☺ DEAL	**Marengo Ridge Golf Club** Harmony Hill Rd., Marengo. (815) 923-2332 18 holes. Par 72/73. Yards: 6,636/5,659 Mar.–Dec. High: May–Sept.	Greens: $-$$ W L T S J Carts: $ Rating: 71.4/72.2 Slope: 122/120
R ☺☺	**Marriott's Lincolnshire Resort** Lincolnshire. (847) 634-5935 18 holes. Par 72/72. Yards: 6,313/4,892 Apr.–Oct. High: May–Sept.	Greens: $$-$$$ W L T Carts: Incl. Rating: 71.1/68.9 Slope: 129/117
P ☺☺☺	**Midlane Country Club** W. Yorkhouse Rd., Wadsworth. (847) 244-1990 18 holes. Par 72/72. Yards: 7,073/5,635 Mar.–Nov. High: June–Sept.	Greens: $$-$$$ W L T S Carts: Inquire Rating: 74.4/72.7 Slope: 132/124
P ☺☺☺ DEAL	**Naperbrook Golf Course** 111th St., Plainfield. (630) 378-4215 18 holes. Par 72/72. Yards: 6,755/5,381 Mar.–Dec. High: June–Aug.	Greens: $$ W L T S J Carts: $$ Rating: 71.2/69.5 Slope: 120/112
P ☺☺	**Oak Brook Golf Club** York Rd., Oak Brook. (630) 990-3032 18 holes. Par 72/72. Yards: 6,541/5,341 Mar.–Dec. High: Apr.–Sept.	Greens: $$ T Carts: $ Rating: 71.2/70.9 Slope: 121/120
P ☺☺☺ DEAL	**The Oak Club of Genoa** Ellwood Greens Rd., Genoa. (815) 784-5678 18 holes. Par 72/72. Yards: 7,032/5,556 Mar.–Dec. High: May–Sept.	Greens: $$ W L T S Carts: Incl. Rating: 74.1/72.5 Slope: 135/127
P ☺☺☺	**Odyssey Golf Course** S. Ridgeland, Tinley Park. (708) 429-7400 18 holes. Par 72/72. Yards: 7,095/5,554 Apr.–Nov. High: June–Aug.	Greens: $-$$$ W L T Carts: Incl. Rating: 73.1/69.3 Slope: 131/116
P ☺☺	**Old Oak Country Club** S. Parker Rd., Lockport. (708) 301-3344 18 holes. Par 71/72. Yards: 6,535/5,274 Apr.–Dec. High: June–Sept.	Greens: $$ W L T S J Carts: $ Rating: 70.1/NA Slope: 124/NA
P ☺☺☺☺	**Orchard Valley Golf Club** W. Illinois Ave., Aurora. (630) 907-0500	Greens: $$$ T S J Carts: $$

	18 holes. Par 72/72. Yards: 6,745/5,162 Apr.–Oct. High: June–Sept.	Rating: Slope:	72.2/70.1 132/118

P
◎◎

Palatine Hills Golf Course
W. Northwest Hwy., Palatine. (847) 359-4020
18 holes. Par 72/72. Yards: 6,800/5,975
Apr.–Nov. High: June–Aug.

Greens: $$–$$$ W L T
Carts: $
Rating: 71.6/73.1
Slope: 120/119

P

◎◎◎
DEAL

Park Hills Golf Club
W. Stephenson, Freeport. (815) 235-3611
West Course
18 holes. Par 72/73. Yards: 6,622/5,940
Apr.–Nov. High: June–Aug.

Greens: $–$$ W J
Carts: $
Rating: 71.3/76.2
Slope: 121/127

◎◎

East Course
18 holes. Par 72/72. Yards: 6,477/5,401

Rating: 69.9/69.8
Slope: 116/115

P
◎◎◎◎
BEST

Pine Meadow Golf Club
Mundelein. (847) 566-4653
18 holes. Par 72/72. Yards: 7,141/5,203
Mar.–Dec. High: Apr.–Oct.

Greens: $$$$ T J
Carts: $$
Rating: 74.6/70.9
Slope: 138/125

P
◎◎◎
DEAL

Pinecrest Golf & Country Club
Algonquin Rd., Huntley. (847) 669-3111
18 holes. Par 72/72. Yards: 6,636/5,061
Mar.–Dec. High: June–Aug.

Greens: $$ T S J
Carts: $
Rating: 71.4/68.9
Slope: 119/112

P
◎◎◎

Plum Tree National Golf Club
Lembcke Rd., Harvard. (815) 943-7474
18 holes. Par 72/72. Yards: 6,648/5,954
Apr.–Dec. High: Apr.–Dec.

Greens: $$–$$$ L T S
Carts: $
Rating: 72.9/74.9
Slope: 128/132

P
◎◎

Poplar Creek Country Club
Hoffman Estates. (847) 884-0219
18 holes. Par 72/72. Yards: 6,108/5,386
Mar.–Nov. High: June–Aug.

Greens: $$ T S J
Carts: $
Rating: 69.6/69.9
Slope: 124/118

P
◎◎◎◎

Prairie Landing Golf Course
W. Chicago. (630) 208-7600
18 holes. Par 72/72. Yards: 6,862/4,859
Apr.–Nov. High: May–Sept.

Greens: $$$$$ L T J
Carts: Incl.
Rating: 73.8/69.3
Slope: 131/119

P
◎◎

Randall Oaks Golf Club
Binnie Rd., Dundee. (847) 428-5661
18 holes. Par 71/71. Yards: 6,160/5,379
Apr.–Nov. High: June–Aug.

Greens: $–$$ W T S J
Carts: $
Rating: 67.7/70.3
Slope: 113/110

SP
◎◎◎

Ruffled Feathers Golf Club
Lemont. (630) 257-1000
18 holes. Par 72/72. Yards: 6,878/5,273
Mar.–Nov. High: Apr.–Oct.

Greens: $$$–$$$$$ W L T
Carts: Incl.
Rating: 73.1/66.1
Slope: 134/105

P

◎◎

St. Andrews Golf and Country Club
W. Chicago. (630) 231-3100
Lakewood Course
18 holes. Par 72/72. Yards: 6,666/5,353
Year-round. High: May–Sept.

Greens: $$ W L T J
Carts: $$
Rating: 71.1/69.4
Slope: 121/114

◎◎

St. Andrews Course
18 holes. Par 71/71. Yards: 6,759/5,138

Rating: 71.2/68.2
Slope: 118/110

P
◎◎◎
DEAL

Sandy Hollow Golf Course
Rockford. (815) 987-8836
18 holes. Par 71/76. Yards: 6,228/5,883
Apr.–Oct. High: June–Aug.

Greens: $–$$ T
Carts: $$
Rating: 69.4/72.8
Slope: 113/113

Illinois Golf Guide

P ☺☺☺ DEAL	**Schaumburg Golf Course** N. Roselle Rd., Schaumburg. (847) 885-9000 27 holes. Par 71/71. Yards: 6,522/4,885 Apr.–Dec. High: June–Aug.	Greens: Carts: Rating: Slope:	$$ $ 70.6/67.2 117/114	W T S J

P ☺☺☺	**Seven Bridges Golf Club** Woodridge. (630) 964-7777 18 holes. Par 72/72. Yards: 7,118/5,277 Apr.–Nov. High: May–Oct.	Greens: Carts: Rating: Slope:	$$$–$$$$$ Incl. 74.4/69.8 132/118	

P ☺☺	**Silver Lake Country Club** 82nd Ave., Orland Park. (708) 349-6940 *North Course* 18 holes. Par 72/77. Yards: 6,826/5,719 Mar.–Jan. High: Apr.–Oct.	Greens: Carts: Rating: Slope:	$$ $ 71.9/72.5 116/116	W L T S J

☺☺☺ DEAL	*South Course* 18 holes. Par 70/72. Yards: 5,948/5,138	Rating: Slope:	67.9/69.3 108/109	

P ☺☺	**Spartan Meadows Golf Club** Elgin. (847) 931-5950 18 holes. Par 72/72. Yards: 6,853/5,353 Apr.–Nov. High: May–Sept.	Greens: Carts: Rating: Slope:	$–$$ $$ 72.7/70.3 123/116	W L T S J

P ☺☺☺ DEAL	**Springbrook Golf Course** 83rd St., Naperville. (630) 420-4215 18 holes. Par 72/73. Yards: 6,896/5,850 Mar.–Dec.	Greens: Carts: Rating: Slope:	$$ $$ 72.6/72.7 124/125	W L T S J

P ☺☺☺ DEAL	**Steeple Chase Golf Club** N. La Vista Dr., Mundelein. (847) 949-8900 18 holes. Par 72/72. Yards: 6,827/4,831 Apr.–Nov. High: May–Sept.	Greens: Carts: Rating: Slope:	$–$$$ $ 73.1/68.1 129/113	W T S J

P ☺☺	**Sunset Valley Golf Club** Sunset Rd., Highland Park. (847) 432-7140 18 holes. Par 72/72. Yards: 6,458/5,465 Mar.–Nov. High: Mar.–Aug.	Greens: Carts: Rating: Slope:	$$ $ 70.5/71.6 121/119	W L T S J

SP ☺☺	**Tamarack Golf Club** Royal Worlington Dr., Naperville. (630) 904-4004 18 holes. Par 70/70. Yards: 6,955/5,016 Mar.–Nov. High: June–Sept.	Greens: Carts: Rating: Slope:	$$–$$$ Incl. 74.2/68.8 131/114	W L T S

P ☺☺☺ DEAL	**Timber Trails Country Club** Plainfield Rd., La Grange. (708) 246-0275 18 holes. Par 71/73. Yards: 6,197/5,581 Mar.–Dec. High: May–Oct.	Greens: Carts: Rating: Slope:	$$ $$ 68.7/71.1 113/116	L T S

P ☺☺	**Urban Hills Country Club** Crawford Ave., Richton Park. (708) 747-0306 18 holes. Par 71/71. Yards: 6,650/5,266 Year-round. High: Apr.–Oct.	Greens: Carts: Rating: Slope:	$ $ 71.1/69.1 114/110	W L T S J

P ☺☺	**Village Greens of Woodridge** W. 75th St., Woodridge. (630) 985-3610 18 holes. Par 72/73. Yards: 6,650/5,847 Mar.–Nov. High: May–Sept.	Greens: Carts: Rating: Slope:	$$ $ 71.2/72.2 121/119	W L T S J

P ☺☺☺ DEAL	**Village Links of Glen Ellyn** Winchell Way, Glen Ellyn. (630) 469-8180 18 holes. Par 71/73. Yards: 6,933/5,753 Mar.–Nov. High: May–Sept.	Greens: Carts: Rating: Slope:	$$ $ 73.5/73.3 130/127	W L S J

P ☺☺☺	**Wedgewood Golf Course** Rte. 59, Joliet. (815) 741-7270	Greens: Carts:	$–$$ $	W T S J

Illinois Golf Guide

DEAL	18 holes. Par 72/72. Yards: 6,536/6,519	Rating:	72.0/72.4
	Apr.–Oct. High: June–Aug.	Slope:	119/123

P	**White Pines Golf Club**	Greens: $$	W L T
	W. Jefferson, Bensenville. (630) 766-0304	Carts: $$	
☺☺	*East Course*	Rating: 71.1/71.4	
	18 holes. Par 71/74. Yards: 6,412/5,415	Slope: 126/122	
	Year-round. High: May–Oct.		
☺☺	*West Course*	Rating: 71.5/73.4	
	18 holes. Par 72/74. Yards: 6,601/5,998	Slope: 119/121	
P	**Winnetka Golf Course**	Greens: $$	W L T
☺☺	Oak St., Winnetka. (847) 501-2050	Carts: NA	
	18 holes. Par 71/72. Yards: 6,458/5,857	Rating: 70.9/73.3	
	Apr.–Dec. High: May–Aug.	Slope: 125/124	

Kankakee Area

P	**Bon Vivant Country Club**	Greens: $–$$	
☺☺☺	Career Center Rd., Bourbonnais. (815) 935-0403	Carts: $	
DEAL	18 holes. Par 72/75. Yards: 7,498/5,979	Rating: 76.2/74.7	
	Apr.–Nov. High: May–Sept.	Slope: 128/123	
☺☺	*North Course*	Rating: NA	
	18 holes. Par 72/72. Yards: 6,653/5,181	Slope: NA	

Peoria Area

P	**Bunker Links Municipal Golf Course**	Greens: $	T
☺☺	Lincoln Park Dr., Galesburg. (309) 344-1818	Carts: $	
	18 holes. Par 71/73. Yards: 5,934/5,354	Rating: 67.4/69.4	
	Mar.–Nov. High: Apr.–Sept.	Slope: 106/108	
P	**Illinois State University Golf Course**	Greens: $	T S J
☺☺	W. Gregory St., Normal. (309) 438-8065	Carts: $	
	18 holes. Par 71/73. Yards: 6,533/5,581	Rating: 71.1/71.8	
	Mar.–Dec. High: May–Aug.	Slope: 120/119	
P	**Kellogg Golf Course**	Greens: $	W T J
☺☺	N. Radnor Rd., Peoria. (309) 691-0293	Carts: $	
	18 holes. Par 72/72. Yards: 6,735/5,675	Rating: 70.9/71.5	
	Mar.–Nov. High: June–Aug.	Slope: 117/120	
P	**Lick Creek Golf Course**	Greens: $	W T S J
☺☺☺	N. Parkway Dr., Pekin. (309) 346-0077	Carts: $	
	18 holes. Par 72/72. Yards: 6,906/5,900	Rating: 72.8/72.9	
	Apr.–Nov. High: June–Sept.	Slope: 128/125	
P	**Newman Golf Course**	Greens: $	W T J
☺☺☺	W. Nebraska, Peoria. (309) 674-1663	Carts: Inquire	
DEAL	18 holes. Par 71/74. Yards: 6,838/5,933	Rating: 71.8/74.2	
	Mar.–Nov. High: Apr.–Aug.	Slope: 119/120	
P	**Prairie Vista Golf Course**	Greens: $$	T S J
☺☺☺☺	Sale Barn Rd., Bloomington. (309) 434-2217	Carts: $	
DEAL	18 holes. Par 72/71. Yards: 6,745/5,224	Rating: 71.8/68.9	
	Mar.–Nov. High: May–Aug.	Slope: 128/114	
P	**Railside Golf Club**	Greens: $	T S J
☺☺	W. 19th St., Gibson City. (217) 784-5000	Carts: $	
	18 holes. Par 72/72. Yards: 6,801/5,367	Rating: 71.8/70.2	
	Year-round. High: May–Sept.	Slope: 122/115	

Quincy

P	**Westview Golf Course**	Greens: $	L T
☺☺☺	S. 36th St., Quincy. (217) 223-7499	Carts: $	

DEAL	18 holes. Par 71/71. Yards: 6,400/5,331		Rating:	70.1/70.2
	Jan.–Dec. High: May–Aug.		Slope:	116/114

Springfield/Decatur/Champaign Area

P	**Bunn Golf Course**		Greens:	$	S J
☺☺	S. 11th, Springfield. (217) 522-2633		Carts:	$
	18 holes. Par 72/73. Yards: 6,104/5,355		Rating:	68.7/68.4
	Mar.–Nov. High: June–July		Slope:	118/119

R	**Eagle Creek Resort Golf Course**	Greens:	$$–$$$ W L R T J
☺☺☺	Eagle Creek State Park, Findlay. (217) 756-3456	Carts:	Incl.
	18 holes. Par 72/72. Yards: 6,908/4,978	Rating:	73.5/69.1
	Year-round. High: May–Oct.	Slope:	132/115

P	**Hickory Point Golf Club**	Greens:	$ T S J
☺☺☺	Weaver Rd., Decatur. (217) 421-7444	Carts:	Inquire
DEAL	18 holes. Par 72/72. Yards: 6,855/5,896	Rating:	70.7/73.0
	Mar.–Nov. High: June–Aug.	Slope:	121/113

P	**Lake of the Woods Golf Club**	Greens:	$ S J
☺☺	Mahomet. (217) 586-2183	Carts:	$
	18 holes. Par 72/72. Yards: 6,520/5,187	Rating:	70.8/69.1
	Mar.–Dec. High: June–Aug.	Slope:	118/112

St. Louis Area

P	**Annbriar Golf Course**	Greens:	$$$ L
☺☺☺☺	Waterloo. (618) 939-4653	Carts:	Incl.
	18 holes. Par 72/72. Yards: 6,841/4,792	Rating:	72.8/66.4
	Year-round. High: Apr.–Oct.	Slope:	136/110

P	**Belk Park Golf Club**	Greens:	$–$$ W L T J
☺☺☺	Wood River. (618) 251-3115	Carts:	$$
DEAL	18 holes. Par 72/73. Yards: 6,812/5,709	Rating:	71.5/70.8
	Year-round. High: May–Sept.	Slope:	121/118

P	**Fox Creek Golf Club**	Greens:	$$ W L T J S
☺☺☺	Fox Creek Dr., Edwardsville. (618) 692-9400	Carts:	Incl.
DEAL	18 holes. Par 72/72. Yards: 7,027/5,185	Rating:	74.1/71.3
	Year-round. High: May–Sept.	Slope:	144/134

P	**Lincoln Greens Golf Course**	Greens:	$–$$ W T S J
☺☺	E. Lake Dr., Springfield. (217) 786-4000	Carts:	$
	18 holes. Par 72/72. Yards: 6,582/5,625	Rating:	70.3/70.9
	Mar.–Dec. High: June–Aug.	Slope:	112/114

P	**The Orchards Golf Club**	Greens:	$–$$ W L T S J
☺☺☺	Belleville. (618) 233-8921	Carts:	$
DEAL	18 holes. Par 71/71. Yards: 6,405/5,001	Rating:	69.0/70.1
	Year-round. High: Apr.–Oct.	Slope:	121/120

P	**The Rail Golf Club**	Greens:	$$ T S J
☺☺☺	Springfield. (217) 525-0365	Carts:	$
DEAL	18 holes. Par 72/72. Yards: 6,583/5,406	Rating:	71.1/70.6
	Mar.–Dec. High: May–Sept.	Slope:	120/116

P	**Rend Lake Golf Course**	Greens:	$$ W S
☺☺☺	Marcum Branch Rd., Benton. (618) 629-2353	Carts:	$
DEAL	27 holes. Par 72/72/72. Yards: 6,861/6,812/6,835	Rating:	72.2/71.8/73.0
	Mar.–Nov. High: May–Oct.	Slope:	130/131/133

P	**Spencer T. Olin Community Golf Course**	Greens:	$$$ W L T
☺☺☺☺	College Ave., Alton. (618) 465-3111	Carts:	Incl.
	18 holes. Par 72/72. Yards: 6,941/5,049	Rating:	73.5/65.6
	Year-round. High: Apr.–Oct.	Slope:	135/110

Indiana

The **Brickyard Crossing**, with four of its holes within auto racing's magic brick shrine in Indianapolis, is a challenging newer course. Near Louisville, Kentucky, is **Covered Bridge**, ranked as a bit less difficult but exceptionally beautiful.

Other winners near Indianapolis include **The Legends of Indiana**, **Otter Creek**, **Eagle Creek**, and the **Golf Club of Indiana**. Near Terre Haute is **Hulman Links**; in West Lafayette is the hilly South Course of **Purdue University**. Another hilly spot in this mostly flat state is the Hill Course at the **French Lick Springs Resort**, an old Donald Ross course.

The French Lick Springs Resort, the Golf Club of Indiana, Hulman Links, The Legends of Indiana, and Purdue University also make our *Golf U.S.A.* Deals list.

Many courses in Indiana are open year-round, although the best golfing—and the highest prices—can be found from spring through the end of summer.

Golf U.S.A. Leader Board: Best Public Courses in Indiana

☺☺☺☺	Brickyard Crossing Golf Club
☺☺☺☺	Covered Bridge Golf Club
☺☺☺	Eagle Creek Golf Club
☺☺☺	French Lick Springs Resort (Hill)
☺☺☺	Golf Club of Indiana
☺☺☺	Hulman Links Golf Course
☺☺☺	The Legends of Indiana Golf Course
☺☺☺	Otter Creek Golf Club
☺☺☺	Purdue University Golf Course (South)

Golf U.S.A. Leader Board: Best Deals in Indiana

$$/☺☺☺	Autumn Ridge Golf Club
$/☺☺☺	Brookwood Golf Club
$/☺☺☺	Elbel Park Golf Course
$/☺☺☺	Erskine Park Golf Club
$$/☺☺☺	Fox Prairie Golf Club
$$/☺☺☺	French Lick Springs Resort (Hill)
$/☺☺☺	Geneva Hills Golf Club
$$/☺☺☺	Golf Club of Indiana
$$/☺☺☺	Grand Oak Golf Club
$/☺☺☺	Green Acres Golf Club
$/☺☺☺	Hidden Creek Golf Club
$$/☺☺☺	Honeywell Golf Course
$$/☺☺☺	Hulman Links Golf Course
$/☺☺☺	Indiana University Golf Club
$$/☺☺☺	Juday Creek Golf Course
$$/☺☺☺	The Legends of Indiana Golf Course
$$/☺☺☺	The Links Golf Club
$/☺☺☺	Otis Park Golf Club
$$/☺☺☺	Pheasant Valley Golf Club
$/☺☺☺	Purdue University Gold Course (South)

$$/◔◔◔◔	Rock Hollow Golf Club
$$/◔◔◔	Royal Hylands Golf Club
$$/◔◔◔	Salt Creek Golf Club
$$/◔◔◔	Sultan's Run Golf Course
$/◔◔◔	Swan Lake Golf Club (East)
$/◔◔◔	Valley View Golf Club (Floyds Knobs)
$/◔◔◔	Valley View Golf Club (Middletown)
$/◔◔◔	Wabash Valley Golf Club
$/◔◔◔	Walnut Creek Golf Course
$/◔◔◔	Winchester Golf Club
$/◔◔◔	Zollner Golf Course at Tri-State University

Indiana Golf Guide

Gary Area

P
◔◔
Black Squirrel Golf Club
Hwy. 119 S., Goshen. (219) 533-1828
18 holes. Par 72/72. Yards: 6,483/5,018
Mar.–Nov. High: June–Aug.
Greens: $ W L
Carts: $
Rating: 69.8/67.8
Slope: 115/110

P
◔◔◔◔
Blackthorn Golf Club
Nimitz Pkwy., South Bend. (219) 232-4653
18 holes. Par 72/72. Yards: 7,105/5,036
Apr.–Nov. High: May–Sept.
Greens: $$$–$$$$
Carts: Incl.
Rating: 75.2/71.0
Slope: 135/120

P
◔◔
Dykeman Park Golf Course
Eberts Rd., Logansport. (219) 753-0222
18 holes. Par 70/73. Yards: 6,185/5,347
Mar.–Dec. High: Apr.–Aug.
Greens: $ T S J
Carts: $
Rating: 69.4/69.8
Slope: 118/102

P
◔◔◔
DEAL
Elbel Park Golf Course
Auten Rd., South Bend. (219) 271-9180
18 holes. Par 72/73. Yards: 6,700/5,750
Mar.–Nov. High: June–Aug.
Greens: $ W L T S J
Carts: $
Rating: 70.7/71.4
Slope: 113/114

P
◔◔◔
DEAL
Erskine Park Golf Club
Miami St., South Bend. (219) 291-3216
18 holes. Par 70/74. Yards: 6,098/5,530
Mar.–Nov. High: Apr.–Sept.
Greens: $ W T S J
Carts: $
Rating: 69.1/70.7
Slope: 121/117

P
◔◔
Forest Park Golf Course
Sheffield Dr., Valparaiso. (219) 462-5144
18 holes. Par 70/72. Yards: 5,731/5,339
Apr.–Dec. High: June–Sept.
Greens: $ T J
Carts: $
Rating: 67.4/70.7
Slope: 114/111

P
◔◔◔
DEAL
Juday Creek Golf Course
Lindy Dr., Granger. (219) 277-4653
18 holes. Par 72/72. Yards: 6,940/5,000
Mar.–Oct. High: June–Sept.
Greens: $–$$ W T S J
Carts: $
Rating: 73.3/67.1
Slope: 133/116

SP
◔◔
Maxwelton Golf Club
E. Elkhart County Line Rd., Syracuse. (219) 457-3504
18 holes. Par 72/72. Yards: 6,490/5,992
Mar.–Nov. High: May–Sept.
Greens: $
Carts: $
Rating: 70.1/73.4
Slope: 124/128

P
◔◔
Michigan City Municipal Golf Course
E. Michigan Blvd., Michigan City. (219) 873-1516
18 holes. Par 72/74. Yards: 6,169/5,363
Apr.–Nov. High: June–Aug.
Greens: $ W L J
Carts: $
Rating: 67.6/68.6
Slope: 113/113

SP
◔◔
Palmira Golf and Country Club
W. 109th St., St. John. (219) 365-4331
Greens: $–$$ W L T S J
Carts: $$

Indiana Golf Guide

	18 holes. Par 71/73. Yards: 6,421/5,863	Rating:	70.9/74.2	
	Year-round. High: May–Sept.	Slope:	118/117	
SP	**Pheasant Valley Golf Club**	Greens:	$$	W L T S J
☺☺☺	W. 141st Ave., Crown Point. (219) 663-5000	Carts:	$$	
DEAL	18 holes. Par 72/73. Yards: 6,869/6,166	Rating:	72.3/72.6	
	Apr.–Dec. High: May–Oct.	Slope:	126/NA	
P	**Rock Hollow Golf Club**	Greens:	$$$	
☺☺☺☺	County Rd., 250 W., Peru. (765) 473-6100	Carts:	Incl.	
DEAL	18 holes. Par 72/72. Yards: 6,994/4,967	Rating:	74.0/64.8	
	Mar.–Oct. High: June–Sept.	Slope:	132/112	
P	**Scherwood Golf Course**	Greens:	$–$$	W L
☺☺	E. Joliet St., Schererville. (219) 865-2554	Carts:	$	
	18 holes. Par 72/72. Yards: 6,710/5,053	Rating:	72.0/67.3	
	Apr.–Dec. High: May–Sept.	Slope:	127/108	
P	**Swan Lake Golf Club**	Greens:	$	W T S
	Plymouth LaPorte Trail, Plymouth. (219) 936-9798	Carts:	$	
☺☺☺	*East Course*	Rating:	72.4/71.7	
DEAL	18 holes. Par 72/72. Yards: 6,950/5,436	Slope:	120/109	
	Mar.–Oct. High: Apr.–June			
☺☺	*West Course*	Rating:	72.0/69.4	
	18 holes. Par 72/72. Yards: 6,942/5,436	Slope:	117/106	
P	**Wicker Memorial Park Golf Course**	Greens:	$	W L T S J
☺☺	Indianapolis Blvd., Highland. (219) 838-9809	Carts:	$	
	18 holes. Par 72/73. Yards: 6,515/5,301	Rating:	70.8/69.3	
	Year-round. High: May–Sept.	Slope:	106/107	

Fort Wayne Area

SP	**Autumn Ridge Golf Club**	Greens:	$$–$$$	L T S
☺☺☺	Old Auburn Rd., Fort Wayne. (219) 637-8727	Carts:	Incl.	
DEAL	18 holes. Par 72/72. Yards: 7,103/5,273	Rating:	73.9/70.9	
	Mar.–Dec. High: May–Sept.	Slope:	134/122	
P	**Brookwood Golf Club**	Greens:	$	
☺☺☺	Bluffton Rd., Fort Wayne. (219) 747-3136	Carts:	$	
DEAL	18 holes. Par 72/73. Yards: 6,716/5,294	Rating:	70.3/69.0	
	Mar.–Dec. High: Apr.–Sept.	Slope:	126/117	
P	**Honeywell Golf Course**	Greens:	$–$$	W L
☺☺☺	W. Division Rd., Wabash. (219) 563-8663	Carts:	$	
DEAL	18 holes. Par 71/71. Yards: 6,430/5,010	Rating:	71.2/68.9	
	Mar.–Oct. High: June–Sept.	Slope:	121/118	
P	**Riverbend Golf Course**	Greens:	$–$$	W L T S J
☺☺	St. Joe Rd., Fort Wayne. (219) 485-2732	Carts:	$	
	18 holes. Par 72/72. Yards: 6,702/5,633	Rating:	72.5/72.5	
	Mar.–Oct. High: May–Sept.	Slope:	127/124	
P	**Wabash Valley Golf Club**	Greens:	$	
☺☺☺	North Dr., Geneva. (219) 368-7388	Carts:	$	
DEAL	18 holes. Par 71/71. Yards: 6,375/4,978	Rating:	70.5/69.8	
	Mar.–Nov. High: June–Aug.	Slope:	117/106	
P	**Walnut Creek Golf Course**	Greens:	$-$$	W
☺☺☺	E. 400 S., Marion. (765) 998-7651	Carts:	$	
DEAL	18 holes. Par 72/72. Yards: 6,880/5,154	Rating:	72.1/68.5	
	Apr.–Dec. High: June–Aug.	Slope:	121/109	
P	**Zollner Golf Course at Tri-State University**	Greens:	$	
☺☺☺	W. Park St., Angola. (219) 665-4269	Carts:	$	

Indiana Golf Guide

DEAL	18 holes. Par 72/73. Yards: 6,628/5,259	Rating:	71.1/69.4
	Mar.–Dec. High: May–Sept.	Slope:	124/117

Indianapolis Area

SP	**Bear Slide Golf Club**	Greens:	$$–$$$
☺☺☺☺	E. 231 St., Cicero. (317) 984-3837	Carts:	$
	18 holes. Par 71/71. Yards: 7,041/4,848	Rating:	74.6/69.5
	Mar.–Dec. High: May–Oct.	Slope:	136/117

R	**Brickyard Crossing Golf Club**	Greens:	$$$$$
☺☺☺☺	W. 16th St., Indianapolis. (317) 484-6572	Carts:	Incl.
STATE	18 holes. Par 72/72. Yards: 6,994/5,038	Rating:	74.4/68.3
	Apr.–Oct. High: May–Oct.	Slope:	137/116

SP	**Brookshire Golf Club**	Greens:	$$ W T J
☺☺	Brookshire Pkwy., Carmel. (317) 846-7431	Carts:	Incl.
	18 holes. Par 72/75. Yards: 6,651/5,635	Rating:	71.8/74.4
	Year-round. High: May–Oct.	Slope:	123/129

P	**Coffin Golf Club**	Greens:	$ T S J
☺☺	Cold Springs Rd., Indianapolis. (317) 327-7845	Carts:	$
	18 holes. Par 72/72. Yards: 6,709/5,135	Rating:	73.7/NA
	Mar.–Dec.	Slope:	129/NA

P	**Eagle Creek Golf Club**	Greens:	$$ W L T S J
☺☺☺	W. 56th St., Indianapolis. (317) 297-3366	Carts:	$
STATE	18 holes. Par 72/72. Yards: 7,159/5,800	Rating:	74.6/68.2
	Feb.–Dec. High: June–Aug.	Slope:	139/116

P	**Forest Park Golf Course**	Greens:	$ L T
☺☺	Brazil. (812) 442-5681	Carts:	$
	18 holes. Par 71/73. Yards: 6,012/5,647	Rating:	68.0/69.8
	Year-round. High: Mar.–Nov.	Slope:	110/112

P	**Fox Prairie Golf Club**	Greens:	$–$$ W T
☺☺☺	E. 196th St., Noblesville. (317) 776-6357	Carts:	$
DEAL	18 holes. Par 72/75. Yards: 6,946/5,533	Rating:	72.6/71.4
	Mar.–Nov. High: June–Aug.	Slope:	118/114

P	**Geneva Hills Golf Club**	Greens:	$ W L T S J
☺☺☺	R.R. 3, Clinton. (765) 832-8384	Carts:	$
DEAL	18 holes. Par 72/72. Yards: 6,764/4,788	Rating:	70.2/67.3
	Year-round. High: Apr.–Oct.	Slope:	118/115

P	**Golf Club of Indiana**	Greens:	$$–$$$ L T
☺☺☺	Exit 130, Interstate 65, Lebanon. (317) 769-6388	Carts:	$
BEST	18 holes. Par 72/72. Yards: 7,084/5,498	Rating:	73.2/72.7
DEAL	Feb.–Dec. High: May–Sept.	Slope:	140/122

P	**Green Acres Golf Club**	Greens:	$–$$ L S J
☺☺☺	Green Acres Dr., Kokomo. (765) 883-5771	Carts:	$
DEAL	18 holes. Par 72/72. Yards: 6,767/5,248	Rating:	72.8/70.4
	Mar.–Dec. High: May–Oct.	Slope:	129/118

SP	**Greenfield Country Club**	Greens:	$–$$ W
☺☺	S. Morristown Pike, Greenfield. (317) 462-2706	Carts:	$
	18 holes. Par 72/73. Yards: 6,773/5,501	Rating:	71.2/73.5
	Mar.–Nov. High: May–Sept.	Slope:	119/120

SP	**Hanging Tree Golf Club**	Greens:	$$–$$$ W L T
☺☺☺	W. 161st St., Westfield. (317) 896-2474	Carts:	Incl.
	18 holes. Par 71/71. Yards: 6,519/5,151	Rating:	72.6/70.6
	Year-round. High: Apr.–Nov.	Slope:	130/122

P	**Hulman Links Golf Course**	Greens:	$$ L
☺☺☺	N. Chamberlain St., Terre Haute. (812) 877-2096	Carts:	$

Indiana Golf Guide

BEST DEAL	18 holes. Par 72/72. Yards: 7,225/5,775 Mar.–Dec. High: May–Sept.	Rating: Slope:	74.9/68.7 144/127
P ☺☺☺ DEAL	**Indiana University Golf Club** State Road 46 Bypass, Bloomington. (812) 855-7543 18 holes. Par 71/72. Yards: 6,891/5,661 Mar.–Dec. High: Apr.–Oct.	Greens: $ Carts: $ Rating: Slope:	W 72.4/73.1 129/123
P ☺☺☺ DEAL STATE	**The Legends of Indiana Golf Course** Hurricane Rd., Franklin. (317) 736-8186 27 holes. Par 72/72/72. Yards: 7,029/7,044/7,177 Mar.–Dec. High: May–Oct.	Greens: $$ Carts: $ Rating: Slope:	T 74.0/72.6/70.2 132/133/134
P ☺☺☺ DEAL	**The Links Golf Club** N. Shelby 700 W., New Palestine. (317) 861-4466 18 holes. Par 72/72. Yards: 7,054/5,117 Year-round. High: May–Sept.	Greens: $$ Carts: $ Rating: Slope:	W L T 73.3/68.4 122/100
P ☺☺☺ DEAL	**Otis Park Golf Club** Tunnelton Rd., Bedford. (812) 279-9092 18 holes. Par 72/73. Yards: 6,308/5,184 Year-round. High: May–Oct.	Greens: $ Carts: $ Rating: Slope:	 70.0/69.3 128/122
P ☺☺☺ BEST	**Otter Creek Golf Club** E. 50 N., Columbus. (812) 579-5227 18 holes. Par 72/72. Yards: 7,285/5,690 Mar.–Nov. High: May–Sept.	Greens: $$$-$$$$ Carts: Incl. Rating: Slope:	W L 74.2/72.1 137/116
P ☺☺	**Pebble Brook Golf and Country Club** Westfield Rd., Noblesville. (317) 896-5596 *South Course* 18 holes. Par 72/72. Yards: 6,557/5,261 Mar.–Dec. High: May–Sept.	Greens: $$ Carts: $ Rating: Slope:	W 70.5/71.9 121/115
☺☺	*North Course* 18 holes. Par 70/70. Yards: 6,392/5,806	Rating: Slope:	70.5/74.1 118/115
R ☺☺	**The Pointe Golf and Tennis Resort** E. Pointe Rd., Bloomington. (812) 824-4040 18 holes. Par 71/71. Yards: 6,604/5,186 Year-round. High: May–Sept.	Greens: $$-$$$ Carts: Incl. Rating: Slope:	W L T 73.0/71.2 140/126
P ☺☺☺	**Purdue University Golf Course** Cherry Lane, West Lafayette. (765) 494-3139 *Kampen Course* 18 holes. Par 72/72. Yards: 7,333/5,205	Greens: $$-$$$ Carts: $ Rating: Slope:	W L T S J 76.5/65.5 145/115
☺☺☺ DEAL STATE	*Ackerman Hills* 18 holes. Par 71/72. Yards: 6,436/5,325	Greens: $ Carts: $ Rating: Slope:	W L T S J 70.3/70.3 124/115
P ☺☺☺ DEAL	**Royal Hylands Golf Club** S. Greensboro Pike, Knightstown. (765) 345-2123 18 holes. Par 71/71. Yards: 6,452/4,590 Mar.–Dec. High: May–Aug.	Greens: $$ Carts: $ Rating: Slope:	W L J 71.9/68.8 130/122
P ☺☺☺ DEAL	**Salt Creek Golf Club** Hwy. 46 E. and Salt Creek Rd., Nashville. (812) 988-7888 18 holes. Par 72/72. Yards: 6,407/5,001 Mar.–Nov. High: May–Aug.	Greens: $$ Carts: $ Rating: Slope:	 71.2/68.8 132/122
P ☺☺	**Shady Hills Golf Course** W. Chapel Pike, Marion. (317) 668-8256 18 holes. Par 71/72. Yards: 6,513/5,595 Mar.–Nov. High: June–Aug.	Greens: $ Carts: $ Rating: Slope:	S J 71.6/71.6 123/110

Indiana Golf Guide

P ⊙⊙	**Smock Golf Course** S. County Line Rd. E., Indianapolis. (317) 888-0036 18 holes. Par 72/72. Yards: 7,055/6,230 Year-round. High: May–Sept.	Greens: $ Carts: $ Rating: 73.7/75.7 Slope: 125/127	T S J
P ⊙⊙⊙ DEAL	**Sultan's Run Golf Course** N. Meridian Rd., Jasper. (812) 482-1009 18 holes. Par 72/72. Yards: 6,859/4,911 Year-round. High: Apr.–Oct.	Greens: $$–$$$ Carts: Incl. Rating: 72.9/68.0 Slope: 132/118	W L T J
P ⊙⊙	**Valle Vista Golf Club** E. Main St., Greenwood. (317) 888-5313 18 holes. Par 70/74. Yards: 6,306/5,680 Year-round. High: May–Sept.	Greens: $–$$ Carts: $ Rating: 70.0/73.1 Slope: 117/113	W L
SP ⊙⊙⊙ DEAL	**Valley View Golf Club** W. County Rd. 850 N., Middletown. (765) 354-2698 18 holes. Par 72/72. Yards: 6,421/5,281 Mar.–Nov. High: May–Sept.	Greens: $ Carts: $ Rating: 70.3/69.9 Slope: 114/109	W S
P ⊙⊙⊙ DEAL	**Winchester Golf Club** Simpson Dr., Winchester. (765) 584-5151 18 holes. Par 72/74. Yards: 6,540/5,023 Year-round. High: Apr.–Oct.	Greens: $ Carts: $ Rating: 70.4/67.6 Slope: 115/106	W

Southwest Indiana

R ⊙⊙⊙ DEAL STATE	**French Lick Springs Resort** Hwy. 56, French Lick. (812) 936-9300, (800) 457-4042 *Hill Course* 18 holes. Par 70/73. Yards: 6,625/5,422 Mar.–Nov. High: May–Oct.	Greens: $–$$$ Carts: $ Rating: 71.5/72.2 Slope: 119/111	L R
⊙⊙⊙	*Valley Course* 18 holes. Par 70/71. Yards: 6,003/5,687	Rating: 68.0/71.7 Slope: 110/110	
P ⊙⊙	**Helfrich Golf Course** Mesker Park Dr., Evansville. (812) 435-6075 18 holes. Par 71/74. Yards: 6,306/5,506 Year-round. High: Apr.–Oct.	Greens: $ Carts: $ Rating: 69.8/71.4 Slope: 124/117	
P ⊙⊙⊙ DEAL	**Valley View Golf Club** Lawrence Banet Rd., Floyds Knobs. (812) 923-7291 18 holes. Par 71/76. Yards: 6,514/5,386 Year-round. High: Apr.–Sept.	Greens: $ Carts: $ Rating: 71.0/71.0 Slope: 125/122	W T S J

Southeast Indiana

SP ⊙⊙⊙⊙ STATE	**Fuzzy Zoeller's Covered Bridge Golf Club** Covered Bridge Rd., Sellersburg. (812) 246-8880 18 holes. Par 72/72. Yards: 6,832/4,957 Year-round. High: Apr.–Oct.	Greens: $$$–$$$$ Carts: Incl. Rating: 73.0/74.7 Slope: 128/126	W L
SP ⊙⊙⊙ DEAL	**Grand Oak Golf Club** Grand Oak Dr., W. Harrison. (812) 637-3943 18 holes. Par 71/71. Yards: 6,383/4,937 Feb.–Dec. High: Apr.–Oct.	Greens: $–$$ Carts: $ Rating: 70.3/69.4 Slope: 127/121	L S J
P ⊙⊙⊙ DEAL	**Hidden Creek Golf Club** Utica Sellersburg Rd., Sellersburg. (812) 246-2556 18 holes. Par 71/71. Yards: 6,756/5,245 Year-round. High: Mar.–Oct.	Greens: $–$$ Carts: $ Rating: 73.0/70.6 Slope: 133/123	L T S J
SP ⊙⊙	**Liberty Country Club** N. U.S. 27, Liberty. (317) 458-5664 18 holes. Par 72/72. Yards: 6,203/4,544 Year-round. High: June–Aug.	Greens: $ Carts: $ Rating: 70.5/69.3 Slope: 120/115	T

Iowa

The **Amana Colonies** course north of Cedar Rapids is a forested, hilly challenge. South of Cedar Rapids is **Finkbine**, a venerable older course that calls for long, straight shooting; it's a *Golf U.S.A.* Deal, too.

Near Des Moines, the **Bos Landen** club is one of the prettiest places to play golf in Iowa, and it's also a *Golf U.S.A.* Deal. In the northwest corner of the state is **Spencer**, another long straight-shot course.

The typical season in Iowa runs from April through October or November, with the best conditions and highest prices from May through early September.

Golf U.S.A. Leader Board: Best Public Courses in Iowa

☺☺☺	Amana Colonies Golf Course
☺☺☺☺	Bos Landen Golf Club
☺☺☺	Finkbine Golf Course
☺☺☺☺	Spencer Golf and Country Club

Golf U.S.A. Leader Board: Best Deals in Iowa

$$/☺☺☺☺	Bos Landen Golf Club
$$/☺☺☺	Emerald Hills Golf Club
$$/☺☺☺	Finkbine Golf Course
$/☺☺☺	Gates Park Golf Course
$/☺☺☺	Glynns Creek Golf Course
$/☺☺☺	Jester Park Golf Course
$$/☺☺☺	Lake Panorama National Golf Course
$/☺☺☺	Muscatine Municipal Golf Course
$/☺☺☺	Pheasant Ridge Municipal Golf Course
$/☺☺☺	Pleasant Valley Golf Club
$/☺☺☺	Sheaffer Golf Course
$$/☺☺☺☺	Spencer Golf and Country Club
$/☺☺☺	Valley Oaks Golf Club
$/☺☺☺	Veenker Memorial Golf Course
$/☺☺☺	Waveland Golf Course

Iowa Golf Guide

Sioux City Area

SP ☺☺☺ DEAL	**Emerald Hills Golf Club** Hwy. 71, Arnolds Park. (712) 332-7100 18 holes. Par 72/72. Yards: 6,609/5,687 Apr.–Oct. High: May–Sept.	Greens: Carts: Rating: Slope:	$–$$ $ 70.9/72.2 121/121	W L T J
P ☺☺	**Okoboji View Golf Course** Hwy. 86, Spirit Lake. (712) 337-3372 18 holes. Par 70/73. Yards: 6,051/5,441 Apr.–Oct. High: June–Aug.	Greens: Carts: Rating: Slope:	$$ $ 68.5/70.1 113/113	L T
SP ☺☺☺☺	**Spencer Golf and Country Club** W. 18th St., Spencer. (712) 262-2028	Greens: Carts:	$$ $$	

Iowa Golf Guide

| DEAL | 18 holes. Par 72/72. Yards: 6,888/5,412 | Rating: | 73.0/70.1 |
| STATE | Mar.–Oct. High: June–Sept. | Slope: | 127/112 |

Fort Dodge Area

P	**Briggs Wood Golf Course**	Greens:	$	W L T J
☺☺	Webster City. (515) 832-9572	Carts:	$	
	18 holes. Par 72/71. Yards: 6,502/5,267	Rating:	72.0/70.0	
	Apr.–Oct. High: Apr.–Sept.	Slope:	128/118	

Des Moines Area

P	**A.H. Blank Golf Course**	Greens:	$	L T S J
☺☺	County Line Rd., Des Moines. (515) 285-0864	Carts:	$	
	18 holes. Par 72/72. Yards: 6,815/5,617	Rating:	72.0/NA	
	Mar.–Oct. High: May–Aug.	Slope:	119/115	

P	**Beaver Run Golf Course**	Greens:	$	W S J
☺☺	N.W. Towner Dr., Grimes. (515) 986-3221	Carts:	$	
	18 holes. Par 72/73. Yards: 6,550/5,383	Rating:	70.6/70.0	
	Mar.–Nov. High: May–Aug.	Slope:	118/112	

P	**Bos Landen Golf Club**	Greens:	$$$	W L R T S J
☺☺☺☺	Pella. (515) 628-4625	Carts:	Incl.	
DEAL	18 holes. Par 72/72. Yards: 6,932/5,155	Rating:	74.0/71.0	
STATE	Apr.–Nov. High: Jun.–Sept.	Slope:	137/125	

P	**Finkbine Golf Course**	Greens:	$$	T
☺☺☺	W. Melrose Ave., Iowa City. (319) 335-9556	Carts:	$$	
DEAL	18 holes. Par 72/72. Yards: 7,030/5,645	Rating:	73.9/73.1	
STATE	Apr.–Nov. High: June–Aug.	Slope:	132/123	

P	**Jester Park Golf Course**	Greens:	$	L T S J
☺☺☺	Granger. (515) 999-2903	Carts:	$	
DEAL	18 holes. Par 72/72. Yards: 6,856/4,993	Rating:	72.9/68.4	
	Mar.–Oct. High: June–Aug.	Slope:	125/109	

R	**Lake Panorama National Golf Course**	Greens:	$$	L
☺☺☺	Clover Ridge Rd., Panora. (515) 755-2024	Carts:	Incl.	
DEAL	18 holes. Par 72/72. Yards: 7,015/5,765	Rating:	73.2/73.2	
	Apr.–Nov. High: June–Aug.	Slope:	131/121	

P	**Otter Creek Golf Club**	Greens:	$	W T
☺☺	N.E. 36th, Ankeny. (515) 965-6464	Carts:	$	
	18 holes. Par 71/73. Yards: 6,473/5,889	Rating:	71.0/73.1	
	Apr.–Oct. High: Apr.–Oct.	Slope:	117/119	

P	**Ottumwa Municipal Golf Course**	Greens:	$	
☺☺	Angle Rd., Ottumwa. (514) 683-0646	Carts:	$	
	18 holes. Par 70/70. Yards: 6,335/4,954	Rating:	70.4/66.7	
	Mar.–Nov. High: June–Aug.	Slope:	118/102	

P	**Pleasant Valley Golf Club**	Greens:	$-$$	W T S J
☺☺☺	S.E. Sand Rd., Iowa City. (319) 337-7209	Carts:	$	
DEAL	18 holes. Par 72/72. Yards: 6,472/4,754	Rating:	70.1/64.6	
	Apr.–Oct. High: June–July	Slope:	117/108	

P	**Veenker Memorial Golf Course**	Greens:	$	W J
☺☺☺	Stange Rd., Ames. (515) 294-6727	Carts:	$	
DEAL	18 holes. Par 72/73. Yards: 6,543/5,357	Rating:	71.3/65.6	
	Mar.–Nov. High: June–Aug.	Slope:	124/120	

P	**Waveland Golf Course**	Greens:	$	L T S J
☺☺☺	University Ave., Des Moines. (515) 271-8725	Carts:	$	
DEAL	18 holes. Par 72/72. Yards: 6,437/5,343	Rating:	71.4/69.4	
	Mar.–Nov. High: May–Aug.	Slope:	126/109	

Iowa Golf Guide

P
☺☺
Willow Creek Golf Club
Army Post Rd., Des Moines. (515) 285-4558
18 holes. Par 71/74. Yards: 6,465/5,758
Apr.–Oct. High: June–Sept.

Greens: $
Carts: $
Rating: 70.2/71.4
Slope: 116/112

Waterloo Area

P
☺☺☺
DEAL
Gates Park Golf Course
E. Donald St., Waterloo. (319) 291-4485
18 holes. Par 72/72. Yards: 6,833/5,635
Apr.–Dec. High: June–Aug.

Greens: $
Carts: $
Rating: 71.5/69.1
Slope: 118/113

S J

P
☺☺☺
DEAL
Pheasant Ridge Municipal Golf Course
W. 12th St., Cedar Falls. (319) 266-8266
18 holes. Par 72/72. Yards: 6,730/5,413
Apr.–Nov. High: Apr.–Sept.

Greens: $
Carts: $$
Rating: 71.5/69.7
Slope: 122/112

L S J

P
☺☺
South Hills Golf Course
Campbell, Waterloo. (319) 291-4268
18 holes. Par 72/72. Yards: 6,698/5,818
Apr.–Dec. High: June–Aug.

Greens: $
Carts: $
Rating: 71.4/NA
Slope: 108/NA

S J

Cedar Rapids Area

P
☺☺☺
STATE
Amana Colonies Golf Course
27th Ave., Amana. (319) 622-6222
18 holes. Par 72/72. Yards: 6,824/5,228
Mar.–Nov. High: June–Sept.

Greens: $$$
Carts: Incl.
Rating: 73.3/69.7
Slope: 136/115

W L T

P
☺☺
Ellis Park Municipal Golf Course
Zika Ave. N.W., Cedar Rapids. (319) 398-5180
18 holes. Par 72/72. Yards: 6,648/5,210
Apr.–Nov. High: June–Aug.

Greens: $
Carts: $
Rating: 72.0/70.8
Slope: 124/111

W T S J

Davenport Area

P
☺☺
Duck Creek Golf Club
Locust and Marlow, Davenport. (319) 326-7824
18 holes. Par 70/74. Yards: 5,900/5,500
Apr.–Nov. High: Apr.–Sept.

Greens: $
Carts: $
Rating: 67.9/72.0
Slope: 115/120

S J

P
☺☺
Emeis Golf Club
W. Central Park, Davenport. (319) 326-7825
18 holes. Par 72/74. Yards: 6,500/5,549
Apr.–Oct. High: May–Aug.

Greens: $
Carts: $
Rating: 71.9/74.0
Slope: 120/115

S J

P
☺☺☺
DEAL
Glynns Creek Golf Course
290th St., Long Grove. (319) 285-6444
18 holes. Par 72/72. Yards: 7,036/5,435
Apr.–Oct. High: June–Aug.

Greens: $
Carts: $
Rating: 73.5/70.4
Slope: 131/124

W L T S J

P
☺☺☺
DEAL
Muscatine Municipal Golf Course
Hwy. 38 N, Muscatine. (319) 263-4735
18 holes. Par 72/72. Yards: 6,471/5,471
Mar.–Nov. High: May–June

Greens: $
Carts: $
Rating: 69.7/72.5
Slope: 117/108

S J

P
☺☺
Palmer Hills Municipal Golf Course
Middle Rd., Bettendorf. (319) 332-8296
18 holes. Par 71/71. Yards: 6,535/5,923
Apr.–Dec. High: Apr.–Sept.

Greens: $
Carts: $
Rating: 71.5/74.0
Slope: 124/130

W T S J

SP
☺☺☺
DEAL
Valley Oaks Golf Club
Harts Mill Rd., Clinton. (319) 242-7221
18 holes. Par 72/73. Yards: 6,803/5,337
Mid-Mar.–Oct. High: Apr.–Oct.

Greens: $
Carts: $
Rating: 73.0/70.3
Slope: 127/121

W J

Southeast Iowa

P
☺☺☺
Sheaffer Golf Course
308th Ave., Fort Madison. (319) 528-6214

Greens: $
Carts: $

W T S J

DEAL	18 holes. Par 72/73. Yards: 6,303/5,441	Rating:	69.9/69.9
	Mar.–Nov. High: June–Aug.	Slope:	118/113

Kansas

Alvamar, southwest of Kansas City, is a public course that seems more like a country club in atmosphere. Not far away is **Deer Creek**, an interesting challenge in which the creek plays a role on almost every hole.

Terradyne Resort, east of Wichita, is set within a sea of tall prairie grass for a prairie links-style challenge.

Way out west is **Buffalo Dunes** in Garden City, which, as its name suggests, is built in and around dunes; the course underwent renovations in 1999.

Alvamar and Buffalo Dunes also earn a place on the *Golf U.S.A.* Deals list.

Most courses in Kansas operate year-round, although you'll find the best conditions and the peak prices from March through October.

Golf U.S.A. Leader Board: Best Public Courses in Kansas

◎◎◎◎ Alvamar Golf Club
◎◎◎◎ Buffalo Dunes Golf Club
◎◎◎◎ Deer Creek Golf Club
◎◎◎◎ Terradyne Resort Hotel and Country Club

Golf U.S.A. Leader Board: Best Deals in Kansas

$$/◎◎◎◎   Alvamar Golf Club
$/◎◎◎◎   Buffalo Dunes Golf Club
$$/◎◎◎   Dub's Dread Golf Club
$$/◎◎◎   Heritage Park Golf Course
$/◎◎◎   Hesston Municipal Golf Park
$/◎◎◎   Lake Shawnee Golf Course
$/◎◎◎   Mariah Hills Golf Course
$/◎◎◎   Quail Ridge Golf Course
$/◎◎◎   Rolling Meadows Golf Course
$/◎◎◎   Sunflower Hills Golf Club
$/◎◎◎   Turkey Creek Golf Course

Dodge City

P	**Mariah Hills Golf Course**	Greens:	$	T J
◎◎◎	Dodge City. (316) 225-8182	Carts:	$	
DEAL	18 holes. Par 71/73. Yards: 6,868/5,556	Rating:	72.4/71.1	
	Year-round. High: Apr.–Oct.	Slope:	118/1126	

Garden City

P	**Buffalo Dunes Golf Club**	Greens:	$	T
◎◎◎◎	Garden City. (316) 276-1210	Carts:	$$	
DEAL	18 holes. Par 72/72. Yards: 6,767/5,631	Rating:	72.5/72.0	
STATE	Year-round. High: Apr.–Oct.	Slope:	124/114	

Wichita Area

SP	**Braeburn Golf Club at Wichita State University**	Greens:	$	W L T S J
◎	E. 21st, Wichita. (316)978-4653	Carts:	$	

Kansas Golf Guide

	18 holes. Par 70/71. Yards: 6,411/5,242	Rating:	71.7/70.5
	Year-round. High: Mar.–Oct.	Slope:	128/117

P ☺☺☺ DEAL	**Hesston Municipal Golf Park** Hesston. (316) 327-2331 18 holes. Par 71/71. Yards: 6,526/5,475 Year-round. High: May–Sept.	Greens: Carts: Rating: Slope:	$ Inquire 71.4/70.9 125/113	S
P ☺☺	**Hidden Lakes Golf Course** S. Greenwich Rd., Derby. (316) 788-2855 18 holes. Par 72/71. Yards: 6,523/5,212 Year-round. High: Mar.–Oct.	Greens: Carts: Rating: Slope:	$ $ 70.8/72.2 122/120	W T S J
P ☺☺	**L.W. Clapp Golf Course** E. Harry, Wichita. (316) 688-9341 18 holes. Par 70/70. Yards: 6,087/4,965 Year-round. High: May–Aug.	Greens: Carts: Rating: Slope:	$ $ 70.0/69.7 120/110	W T S J
P ☺☺☺ DEAL	**Quail Ridge Golf Course** Winfield. (316) 221-5645 18 holes. Par 72/72. Yards: 6,824/5,442 Year-round. High: Apr.–Oct.	Greens: Carts: Rating: Slope:	$ $ 73.0/71.4 125/130	W R S J
P ☺☺	**Sim Park Golf Course** W. Murdock, Wichita. (316) 337-9100 18 holes. Par 72/72. Yards: 6,330/5,048 Year-round. High: Apr.–Sept.	Greens: Carts: Rating: Slope:	$ $ 70.5/67.9 119/103	T
R ☺☺☺☺ STATE	**Terradyne Resort Hotel and Country Club** Terradyne, Andover. (316) 733-5851 18 holes. Par 71/71. Yards: 6,843/5,048 Year-round. Resort guests only. High: Apr.–Oct.	Greens: Carts: Rating: Slope:	$$$ $ 73.8/70.2 139/121	R
P ☺☺☺ DEAL	**Turkey Creek Golf Course** Fox Run, McPherson. (316) 241-8530 18 holes. Par 70/69. Yards: 6,241/4,723 Year-round. High: Apr.–Sept.	Greens: Carts: Rating: Slope:	$ $ 71.3/66.7 125/112	W T J
P ☺☺	**Wellington Golf Club** W. Harvey, Wellington. (316) 326-7904 18 holes. Par 70/70. Yards: 6,201/5,384 Year-round. High: Apr.–Sept.	Greens: Carts: Rating: Slope:	$ $ 70.5/70.9 135/113	W T

Topeka Area

P ☺☺☺ DEAL	**Lake Shawnee Golf Course** S.E. Edge Rd., Topeka. (913) 267-2295 18 holes. Par 69/70. Yards: 6,013/5,459 Year-round. High: May–Sept.	Greens: Carts: Rating: Slope:	$ $ 68.3/70.8 107/107	W T S J
P ☺☺☺ DEAL	**Rolling Meadows Golf Course** Old Milford Rd., Milford. (913) 238-4303 18 holes. Par 72/72. Yards: 6,879/5,515 Year-round. High: Apr.–Oct.	Greens: Carts: Rating: Slope:	$ $ 74.0/70.7 134/116	W T J
SP ☺☺	**Western Hills Golf Club** S.W. 21st St., Topeka. (913) 478-4000 18 holes. Par 70/70. Yards: 6,089/4,728 Year-round. High: Apr.–Sept.	Greens: Carts: Rating: Slope:	$ $ 69.2/66.1 121/110	J

Kansas City Area

SP ☺☺☺☺ BEST DEAL	**Alvamar Golf Club** Crossgates Dr., Lawrence. (785) 842-1907 18 holes. Par 72/72. Yards: 7,092/4,892 Year-round. High: May–Sept.	Greens: Carts: Rating: Slope:	$$–$$$ $ 75.5/68.1 141/112	W L J
SP ☺☺☺☺	**Deer Creek Golf Club** W. 133rd St., Overland Park. (913) 681-3100	Greens: Carts:	$$$$ Incl.	W L T

STATE	18 holes. Par 72/72. Yards: 6,870/5,120	Rating:	74.5/68.5
	Year-round. High: Apr.–Oct.	Slope:	137/113
P	**Dub's Dread Golf Club**	Greens:	$$ W L T S J
☺☺☺	Hollingsworth Rd., Kansas City. (913) 721-1333	Carts:	$
DEAL	18 holes. Par 72/72. Yards: 6,993/5,474	Rating:	73.8/70.4
	Year-round. High: Apr.–Oct.	Slope:	133/113
P	**Heritage Park Golf Course**	Greens:	$–$$ W T S J
☺☺☺	Lackman Rd., Olathe. (913) 829-4653	Carts:	$$
DEAL	18 holes. Par 71/71. Yards: 6,876/5,797	Rating:	72.6/72.3
	Year-round. High: Mar.–Oct.	Slope:	131/121
P	**Overland Park Golf Club**	Greens:	$ T S J
	Quivira Rd., Overland Park. (913) 897-3809	Carts:	$
☺☺	*South/North/West*	Rating:	69.9/69.7/69.9
	27 holes. Par 70/70/70. Yards: 6,446/6,455/6,367	Slope:	113/119/115
	Year-round. High: Apr.–Sept.		
P	**St. Andrew's Golf Course**	Greens:	$ T S J
☺☺	W. 135 St., Overland Park. (913) 897-3804	Carts:	$
	18 holes. Par 70/70. Yards: 6,205/4,713	Rating:	69.5/67.7
	Year-round. High: June–July	Slope:	109/108
P	**Stagg Hill Golf Club**	Greens:	$
☺☺	Ft. Riley Blvd., Manhattan. (913) 539-1041	Carts:	$
	18 holes. Par 72/72. Yards: 6,697/5,642	Rating:	70.3/72.1
	Year-round. High: Apr.–Oct.	Slope:	112/117
P	**Sunflower Hills Golf Club**	Greens:	$ T S J
☺☺☺	Riverview, Bonner Springs. (913) 721-2727	Carts:	$
DEAL	18 holes. Par 72/72. Yards: 7,001/5,849	Rating:	73.3/72.6
	Year-round. High: Apr.–Sept.	Slope:	124/124

Kentucky

Lassing Pointe, a newer course located south of Cincinnati, was an immediate hit when it opened a few years back. A bit farther south is **Kearney Hill** in Lexington, with a lot of open and windy fairways and plenty of sand and grass bunkers.

To make things even better, both courses are also listed among the *Golf U.S.A.* Deals.

Most golf courses in Kentucky are open year-round, although a few close up in the bleak month of January. You'll find the best conditions and peak rates from April through September.

Golf U.S.A. Leader Board: Best Public Courses in Kentucky

☺☺☺☺ Kearney Hill Golf Links
☺☺☺☺ Lassing Pointe Golf Club

Golf U.S.A. Leader Board: Best Deals in Kentucky

$/☺☺☺   Barren River State Park Golf Course
$$/☺☺☺   Crooked Creek Golf Club
$$/☺☺☺   Doe Valley Golf Club
$/☺☺☺   Frances E. Miller Golf Course
$/☺☺☺   Gibson Bay Golf Course
$$/☺☺☺   The Golf Courses at Kenton County (Fox Run, Willows)
$$/☺☺☺☺   Kearney Hill Golf Links

$/☺☺☺	Kentucky Dam Village State Resort Park
$/☺☺☺☺	Lassing Pointe Golf Club
$$/☺☺☺	Nevel Meade Golf Course
$/☺☺☺	Quail Chase Golf Club
$/☺☺☺	Western Hills Golf Course

Kentucky Golf Guide

Paducah Area

P ☺☺☺ DEAL	**Frances E. Miller Golf Course** Pottertown Rd., Murray. (502) 762-2238 18 holes. Par 71/71. Yards: 6,592/5,058 Year-round. High: May–Aug.	Greens: Carts: Rating: Slope:	$ $ 71.6/68.9 125/117	W T S J
R ☺☺☺ DEAL	**Kentucky Dam Village State Resort Park** Hwy. 641, Gilbertsville. (502) 362-8658 18 holes. Par 72/72. Yards: 6,704/5,094 Year-round. High: Mar.–Oct.	Greens: Carts: Rating: Slope:	$$ Incl. 73.0/70.0 135/124	W

Bowling Green Area

P ☺☺☺ DEAL	**Barren River State Park Golf Course** State Park Rd., Lucas. (502) 646-4653 18 holes. Par 72/72. Yards: 6,440/4,919 Year-round. High: Apr.–Sept.	Greens: Carts: Rating: Slope:	$ $ 69.1/66.6 118/106	T
P ☺☺	**Hartland Municipal Golf Course** Wilkinson Trace, Bowling Green. (502) 843-5559 18 holes. Par 71/72. Yards: 6,512/5,044 Year-round. High: July–Aug.	Greens: Carts: Rating: Slope:	$ $ 69.9/68.3 119/113	W L T S J
P ☺☺☺ DEAL	**Western Hills Golf Course** Russellville Rd., Hopkinsville. (502) 885-6023 18 holes. Par 72/72. Yards: 6,907/3,921 Year-round. High: May–Sept.	Greens: Carts: Rating: Slope:	$ $ 73.8/64.0 134/109	W S J

Louisville Area

P ☺☺	**Charlie Vettiner Golf Course** Mary Dell Lane, Jeffersontown. (502) 267-9958 18 holes. Par 72/73. Yards: 6,914/5,388 Year-round. High: Apr.–Sept.	Greens: Carts: Rating: Slope:	$ $ 72.3/70.0 123/116	T S
SP ☺☺☺ DEAL	**Doe Valley Golf Club** Doe Valley Pkwy., Brandenburg. (502) 422-3397 18 holes. Par 71/72. Yards: 6,471/5,519 Year-round. High: Apr.–Sept.	Greens: Carts: Rating: Slope:	$–$$ $ 69.8/70.3 119/118	T S
P ☺☺	**Iroquois Golf Course** Rundill Rd., Louisville. (502) 363-9520 18 holes. Par 71/73. Yards: 6,138/5,004 Year-round. High: Apr.–Nov.	Greens: Carts: Rating: Slope:	$ $ 67.3/70.2 106/112	T S J
P ☺☺	**Lincoln Homestead State Park Golf Course** Lincoln Park Rd., Springfield. (606) 336-7461 18 holes. Par 71/73. Yards: 6,359/5,472 Year-round. High: Apr.–Oct.	Greens: Carts: Rating: Slope:	$ $ 70.0/71.0 119/118	W L T
P ☺☺	**My Old Kentucky Home State Park Golf Club** Hwy. 49, Bardstown. (502) 349-6542 18 holes. Par 70/71. Yards: 6,065/5,239 Year-round.	Greens: Carts: Rating: Slope:	$ $ 69.5/70.2 119/118	W
P ☺☺☺ DEAL	**Nevel Meade Golf Course** Nevel Meade Dr., Prospect. (502) 228-9522 18 holes. Par 72/72. Yards: 6,956/5,616 Year-round. High: Mar.–Nov.	Greens: Carts: Rating: Slope:	$–$$ $ 72.2/70.4 122/117	L T J

Kentucky Golf Guide

R	**Pine Valley Country Club & Resort**	Greens:	$	
☺☺	Pine Valley Dr., Elizabethtown. (502) 737-8300	Carts:	$	
	18 holes. Par 70/74. Yards: 6,613/5,357	Rating:	71.3/69.6	
	Year-round. High: Apr.–June	Slope:	119/114	

SP	**Quail Chase Golf Club**	Greens:	$$	W L T S J
	Cooper Chapel Rd., Louisville. (502) 239-2110	Carts:	$	
☺☺☺	*South/West/East*			
DEAL	27 holes. Par 72/72/72. Yards: 6,618/6,552/7,020	Rating:	70.5/72.0/71.7	
	Year-round. High: June–Aug.	Slope:	124/133/127	

P	**Seneca Golf Course**	Greens:	$	W T S J
☺☺	Seneca Park Rd., Louisville. (502) 458-9298	Carts:	$	
	18 holes. Par 72/73. Yards: 7,034/5,469	Rating:	73.7/71.5	
	Year-round. High: Apr.–Sept.	Slope:	130/122	

P	**Shawnee Golf Course**	Greens:	$	T
☺☺	Northwestern Pkwy., Louisville. (502) 776-9389	Carts:	Inquire	
	18 holes. Par 70/70. Yards: 6,072/5,476	Rating:	65.1/68.5	
	Year-round. High: May–Oct.	Slope:	100/105	

P	**Tanglewood Golf Course**	Greens:	$	W L R T S J
☺☺	Tanglewood Dr., Taylorsville. (502) 477-2468	Carts:	$	
	18 holes. Par 72/72. Yards: 6,626/5,275	Rating:	70.2/68.8	
	Year-round. High: May–Sept.	Slope:	121/115	

P	**Weissinger Hills Golf Course**	Greens:	$	W L T J
☺☺	Mt. Eden Rd., Shelbyville. (502) 633-7332	Carts:	$	
	18 holes. Par 72/73. Yards: 6,534/5,165	Rating:	70.8/69.0	
	Year-round. High: Apr.–Sept.	Slope:	118/112	

Lexington Area

P	**Crooked Creek Golf Club**	Greens:	$$	W L T J
☺☺☺	Crooked Creek Dr., London. (606) 877-1993	Carts:	Incl.	
DEAL	18 holes. Par 72/72. Yards: 7,007/5,087	Rating:	73.8/68.4	
	Year-round. High: Mar.–Oct.	Slope:	134/121	

SP	**Eagle's Nest Country Club**	Greens:	$$	
☺☺	Hwy. 39 N., Somerset. (606) 679-7754	Carts:	$	
	18 holes. Par 71/72. Yards: 6,404/5,010	Rating:	69.8/67.9	
	Feb.–Dec. High: May–Oct.	Slope:	117/109	

P	**Gibson Bay Golf Course**	Greens:	$	W T S J
☺☺☺	Gibson Bay Dr., Richmond. (606) 623-0225	Carts:	$	
DEAL	18 holes. Par 72/72. Yards: 7,113/4,869	Rating:	74.1/69.1	
	Year-round.	Slope:	128/115	

P	**Juniper Hills Golf Course**	Greens:	$	T
☺☺	Louisville Rd., Frankfort. (502) 875-8559	Carts:	$	
	18 holes. Par 70/74. Yards: 6,200/5,904	Rating:	68.7/67.7	
	Year-round. High: Apr.–Oct.	Slope:	111/106	

P	**Kearney Hill Golf Links**	Greens:	$$	T S J
☺☺☺☺	Kearney Rd., Lexington. (606) 253-1981	Carts:	$	
DEAL	18 holes. Par 72/72. Yards: 7,018/5,367	Rating:	73.5/70.1	
STATE	Year-round. High: Apr.–Oct.	Slope:	128/118	

R	**Marriott's Griffin Gate Resort Golf Club**	Greens:	$$–$$$$	W L T
☺☺☺	Newtown Pike, Lexington. (606) 231-5100	Carts:	Incl.	
	18 holes. Par 72/72. Yards: 6,830/4,994	Rating:	73.3/69.3	
	Year-round. High: Apr.–Oct.	Slope:	132/119	

R	**Woodson Bend Resort**	Greens:	$–$$	L J
☺☺	Woodson Bend, Bronston. (606) 561-5316	Carts:	Incl.	
	18 holes. Par 72/75. Yards: 6,189/5,155	Rating:	69.2/72.0	
	Feb.–Dec. High: May–Sept.	Slope:	117/113	

Covington/Florence Area

P ☺☺	**Boone Links** Florence. (606) 371-7550 27 holes. Par 70/72/70. Yards: 5,950/6,634/6,110 Feb.–Dec. High: May–Aug.	Greens: Carts: Rating: Slope:	$ $ 68.4/72.1/69.2 118/128/122	S J
P ☺☺☺ DEAL	**The Golf Courses at Kenton County** Richardson Rd., Independence. (606) 371-3200 *Fox Run Course* 18 holes. Par 72/72. Yards: 7,055/4,707 Apr.–Oct. High: May–Aug.	Greens: Carts: Rating: Slope:	$$ Incl. 74.8/68.1 143/123	
☺☺	*The Pioneer Course* 18 holes. Par 70/71. Yards: 6,059/5,336	Greens: Carts: Rating: Slope:	$ $ 67.9/69.5 114/115	W S J
☺☺☺ DEAL	*The Willows Course* 18 holes. Par 72/72. Yards: 6,791/5,669	Greens: Carts: Rating: Slope:	$ $ 72.5/74.0 130/129	S J
P ☺☺☺☺ DEAL STATE	**Lassing Pointe Golf Club** Double Eagle Dr., Union. (606) 384-2266 18 holes. Par 71/71. Yards: 6,724/5,153 Apr.–Nov. High: May–Sept.	Greens: Carts: Rating: Slope:	$$ $$ 72.2/69.5 132/122	S J

Michigan

The stars of northern Michigan include the scenic but difficult **Dunmaglas** in Charlevoix, the little bit of Scotland on the Gailes Course at **Lakewood Shores** in Oscoda, the woodsy charm of **Elk Ridge** in Atlanta, and the Black Forest Course at **Wilderness Valley** in Gaylord. A new driving range and learning facility was added at Wilderness Valley in 2000.

The Ross and Heather courses at **Boyne Highlands Resort** in Harbor Springs are among the best anywhere; the Ross Course re-creates many of Donald Ross's most famous holes. A new 18-hole Arthur Hills course may open at Boyne Highlands in 2000 or soon thereafter.

The better resorts near Traverse City include the spectacular Legend Course at the **Shanty Creek Resort** in Bellaire; the new Cedar River Golf Club opened there in mid-1999. It's situated among the trees around Lake Bellaire, with narrow fairways and diabolically placed water. Also worth visiting is the Bear Course (named after Jack Nicklaus, responsible for the design), and the new Wolverine (a Gary Player design) at the **Grand Traverse Resort**. And there is the Traverse City golfing supermall: the impressive **Treetops Sylvan Resort** with its top-rated Jones, Smith, and Fazio courses.

Near Grand Rapids you'll find the heavily forested **Grand Haven**. And don't miss the challenging **Thoroughbred** in Rothbury north of Muskegon; the Thoroughbred began construction in 1999 on a special course for youngsters.

The **Timber Ridge** club is the pride of the Lansing area.

The Detroit region has three local champions: **The Orchards**, **Rattle Run**, and the **University of Michigan Golf Course**.

Three courses share positions on both the *Golf U.S.A.* Best and Deals lists: Grand Haven Golf Club, High Pointe Golf Club, and Wilderness Valley Golf Club.

Most golf courses in Michigan are open from March through November, with high-season rates in effect from spring through early September. The northern latitude of the upper courses allows play late into the evening.

The Boyne Mountain and Boyne Highlands resorts offer low-season rates of as much as 40 percent off for the first half of May and the entire month of October. At Boyne Highlands, midseason rates are in effect from mid-May through early June and from the last week of August through late September. High-season rates are in effect from mid-June through late August.

Golf U.S.A. Leader Board: Best Public Courses in Michigan

⊙⊙⊙⊙ Boyne Highlands Resort (Donald Ross, Heather)
⊙⊙⊙⊙ Dunmaglas Golf Club
⊙⊙⊙⊙ Elk Ridge Golf Course
⊙⊙⊙ Grand Haven Golf Club
⊙⊙⊙⊙ Grand Traverse Resort (Bear)
⊙⊙⊙ High Pointe Golf Club
⊙⊙⊙⊙ Lakewood Shores Resort (Gailes)
⊙⊙⊙⊙ The Orchards Golf Club
⊙⊙⊙ Rattle Run Golf Course
⊙⊙⊙⊙ Shanty Creek Resort (Schuss Mountain)
⊙⊙⊙⊙ Thoroughbred Golf Club
⊙⊙⊙ Timber Ridge Golf Course
⊙⊙⊙⊙ Treetops Sylvan Resort (Jones, Smith, Fazio)
⊙⊙⊙ University of Michigan Golf Course
⊙⊙⊙⊙ Wilderness Valley Golf Club (Black Forest)

Golf U.S.A. Leader Board: Best Deals in Michigan

$$/⊙⊙⊙	Bedford Valley Golf Course
$/⊙⊙⊙	Binder Park Golf Course
$$/⊙⊙⊙	Candlestone Golf Club
$/⊙⊙⊙	Cascades Golf Course
$$/⊙⊙⊙	Clearbrook Golf Club
$$/⊙⊙⊙	Eagle Glen Golf Course
$$/⊙⊙⊙	Faulkwood Shores Golf Club
$$/⊙⊙⊙	Fox Run Country Club
$$/⊙⊙⊙	Grand Haven Golf Club
$/⊙⊙⊙	Grand View Golf Course
$$/⊙⊙⊙	Gull Lake View Golf Club (East, West)
$$/⊙⊙⊙	Heather Highlands Golf Club
$$/⊙⊙⊙	High Pointe Golf Club
$$/⊙⊙⊙	Huron Breeze Golf and Country Club
$$/⊙⊙⊙	Huron Golf Club
$$/⊙⊙⊙	Indian River Golf Club
$$/⊙⊙⊙	Katke Golf Course
$$/⊙⊙⊙	Lake Doster Golf Club
$$/⊙⊙⊙	The Links of Novi (East, South, West)

$/◎◎◎	Maple Leaf Golf Course
$$/◎◎◎	The Meadows Golf Club
$/◎◎◎	Milham Park Municipal Golf Course
$$/◎◎◎	Mistwood Golf Course
$$/◎◎◎	Pine River Golf Club
$/◎◎◎	Pleasant Hills Golf Club
$/◎◎◎	Saskatoon Golf Club (Blue, White)
$$/◎◎◎	Salem Hills Golf Club
$$/◎◎◎	Scott Lake Country Club
$/◎◎◎	Springfield Oaks Golf Course
$$/◎◎◎	Sycamore Hills Golf Club (North, South, West)
$$/◎◎◎	Tanglewood Golf Club (North, South, West)
$$/◎◎◎	Taylor Meadows Golf Club
$$/◎◎◎	Thornapple Creek Golf Club
$$/◎◎◎	Wallinwood Springs Golf Course
$$/◎◎◎◎	Wilderness Valley Golf Club

Michigan Golf Guide

Northern Michigan

P
◎◎◎
Antrim Dells Golf Club
U.S. 31, Atwood. (616) 599-2679
18 holes. Par 72/74. Yards: 6,606/5,493
Apr.–Oct. High: July–Sept.
Greens: $$–$$$ W L T J
Carts: Incl.
Rating: 72.1/71.9
Slope: 125/121

R
◎◎◎◎
Boyne Highlands Resort
600 Highland Dr., Harbor Springs. (616) 526-3029
Donald Ross Memorial Course
18 holes. Par 72/72. Yards: 6,814/4,929
May–Oct. High: June–Aug.
Greens: $$$$$ L R
Carts: Incl.
Rating: 73.4/68.5
Slope: 132/119

◎◎◎◎
Heather Course
18 holes. Par 72/72. Yards: 6,890/4,794
May–Oct. High: June–Aug.
Rating: 74.0/67.8
Slope: 131/111

◎◎◎
Moor Course
18 holes. Par 72/72. Yards: 6,809/5,061
May–Dec. High: June–Aug.
Greens: $$$$$
Carts: Incl.
Rating: 74.0/70.0
Slope: 131/118

SP
◎◎◎◎
Dunmaglas Golf Club
Boyne City Rd., Charlevoix. (616) 547-1022
18 holes. Par 72/73. Yards: 6,897/5,259
May–Oct. High: July–Aug.
Greens: $$$$$$ L T
Carts: Incl.
Rating: 73.5/69.8
Slope: 139/123

P
◎◎◎◎
Elk Ridge Golf Course
9400 Rouse Rd., Atlanta. (517) 785-2275
18 holes. Par 72/72. Yards: 7,072/5,261
May–Oct. High: June–Aug.
Greens: $$$$ W L S J
Carts: Incl.
Rating: 74.7/72.3
Slope: 143/130

P
◎◎◎
DEAL
Fox Run Country Club
5825 W. Four Mile Rd., Grayling. (517) 348-4343
18 holes. Par 72/72. Yards: 6,293/4,829
Apr.–Oct. High: June–Sept.
Greens: $$ T
Carts: $
Rating: 71.0/69.7
Slope: 128/119

R
◎◎◎
Grand Traverse Resort
U.S. 31 N., Acme. (616) 938-1620
Spruce Run Course
18 holes. Par 70/70. Yards: 6,304/4,726
Apr.–Oct. High: June–Aug.
Greens: $$$$$ L R T
Carts: Incl.
Rating: 70.8/68.2
Slope: 130/125

Michigan Golf Guide

☺☺☺☺ BEST	*The Bear* 18 holes. Par 72/72. Yards: 7,083/5,424	Greens: $$$$$$ L R T Carts: Incl. Rating: 76.8/73.1 Slope: 146/137

☺☺☺   *The Wolverine*
18 holes. Par 72/72. Yards: 7,038/5,029

Greens: $$$$$$ L R T
Carts: Incl.
Rating: 73.9/68.1
Slope: 144/121

R
☺☺☺   **Hidden Valley Resort and Club**
Gaylord. (517) 732-4653
18 holes. Par 71/71. Yards: 6,386/5,511
Mar.–Dec. High: June–Aug.

Greens: $$–$$$$ W L R T
Carts: Incl.
Rating: NA
Slope: 121/113

P
☺☺☺
DEAL   **High Pointe Golf Club**
5555 Arnold Rd., Williamsburg. (616) 267-9900
18 holes. Par 71/72. Yards: 6,849/5,101
Apr.–Oct. High: June–Aug.

Greens: $$$$$ W L R T S J
Carts: $
Rating: 72.9/69.6
Slope: 135/121

SP
☺☺☺
DEAL   **Indian River Golf Club**
3301 Chippewa Beach Rd., Indian River. (616) 238-7011
18 holes. Par 72/72. Yards: 6,735/5,277
May.–Oct. High: June–Aug.

Greens: $$ L T J
Carts: $
Rating: 72.4/71.3
Slope: 124/119

R

☺☺☺☺   **Lakewood Shores Resort**
7751 Cedar Lake Rd., Oscoda. (517) 739-2073
Gailes Course
18 holes. Par 72/73. Yards: 6,954/5,246
Apr.–Oct. High: June–Sept.

Greens: $$$ W L R T
Carts: $
Rating: 75/72.2
Slope: 138/122

☺☺☺   *Serradella Course*
18 holes. Par 72/74. Yards: 6,806/5,295
Apr.–Oct. High: June–Sept.

Greens: $$
Carts: $
Rating: 72.3/70.1
Slope: 124/116

P

☺☺☺
DEAL   **Maple Leaf Golf Course**
158 N. Mackinaw Rd., Linwood. (517) 697-3531
East/North/West
27 holes. Par 71/71/70. Yards: 5,762/5,997/5,697
Apr.–Nov. High: June–Aug.

Greens: $ W L S J
Carts: $
Rating: 67.5/68.3/66.4
Slope: 116/114/109

R

☺☺☺☺   **Shanty Creek Resort**
Bellaire. (616) 533-8621
Schuss Mountain Course
18 holes. Par 72/72. Yards: 6,922/5,383
Apr.–Oct. High: July–Aug.

Greens: $$$–$$$$ W R T L S
Carts: $
Rating: 73.4/71.2
Slope: 127/126

☺☺☺   *Summit Golf Club*
18 holes. Par 71/71. Yards: 6,260/4,679
Apr.–Oct. High: July–Aug.

Greens: $$$
Carts: $
Rating: 71.7/70.7
Slope: 120/113

☺☺☺   *Legend Course*
18 holes. Par 72/72. Yards: 6,764/4,953

Greens: $$$$$–$$$$$$$
Carts: $
Rating: 73.6/69.6
Slope: 137/124

☺☺☺   *Cedar River Golf Club*
18 holes. Par 72/72. Yards: 6,989/5,315
Apr.–Oct. High: July–Aug.

Greens: $$$$$–$$$$$$$
Carts: $
Rating: 73.6/70.5
Slope: 144/128

R

☺☺☺☺   **Treetops Sylvan Resort**
3962 Wilkinson Rd., Gaylord. (517) 732-6711
Robert Trent Jones Masterpiece Course

Greens: $$$$–$$$$$ L R T
Carts: Incl.
Rating: 75.5/70.0

	18 holes. Par 71/71. Yards: 7,060/4,972		Slope:	144/123
	Apr.–Oct. High: June–Sept.			
☺☺☺☺	*Rick Smith Signature Course*		Rating:	72.8/67.0
	18 holes. Par 70/70. Yards: 6,653/4,604		Slope:	140/123
	Apr.–Oct. High: June–Sept.			
☺☺☺☺	*Tom Fazio Premier Course*		Rating:	73.6/70.1
	18 holes. Par 72/72. Yards: 6,832/5,039		Slope:	136/125
	Apr.–Oct. High: June–Sept.			
☺☺☺☺	*Rick Smith Tradition Course*		Rating:	70.3/67.3
	18 holes. Par 71/70. Yards: 6,467/4,907		Slope:	122/109
	Apr.-Oct. High: June–Sept.			

R	**Wilderness Valley Golf Club**	Greens:	$$–$$$$ W L R T S J
	7519 Mancelona Rd., Gaylord. (616) 585-7090	Carts:	Incl.
☺☺☺☺	*Black Forest Course*	Rating:	75.3/71.8
DEAL	18 holes. Par 73/74. Yards: 7,044/5,282	Slope:	145/131
	Apr.–Oct. High: July–Aug.		
☺☺☺	*Valley Course*	Greens:	$$–$$$
	18 holes. Par 71/71. Yards: 6,519/4,889	Rating:	70.6/67.8
	Apr.–Oct. High: July–Aug.	Slope:	126/115

Grand Rapids Area

R	**Candlestone Golf Club**	Greens:	$$ W L R T
☺☺☺	8100 N. Storey, Belding. (616) 794-1580	Carts:	$
DEAL	18 holes. Par 72/74. Yards: 6,692/5,546	Rating:	72.9/73.1
	Mar.–Oct. High: May–Sept.	Slope:	130/126
SP	**Clearbrook Golf Club**	Greens:	$–$$ L
☺☺☺	6494 Clearbrook Dr., Saugatuck. (616) 857-2000	Carts:	$
DEAL	18 holes. Par 72/74. Yards: 6,516/5,153	Rating:	72.8/70.0
	Apr.–Oct. High: June–Aug.	Slope:	132/127
☺☺	*The Ravine*	Rating:	NA
	18 holes. Par 72/72. Yards: 7,105/NA	Slope:	NA
SP	**Grand Haven Golf Club**	Greens:	$$ W L R T S J
☺☺☺	17000 Lincoln St., Grand Haven. (616) 842-4040	Carts:	$
DEAL	18 holes. Par 72/72. Yards: 6,789/5,284	Rating:	73.3/70.6
	Mar.–Nov. High: June–Aug.	Slope:	134/122
P	**Grand View Golf Course**	Greens:	$ W S
☺☺☺	S. 68th Ave., New Era. (616) 861-6616	Carts:	$
DEAL	18 holes. Par 71/71. Yards: 6,258/4,737	Rating:	69.5/66.7
	Apr.–Oct. High: June–Aug.	Slope:	120/130
P	**Gull Lake View Golf Club**	Greens:	$$ W
	7417 N. 38th St., Augusta. (616) 731-4148	Carts:	$
☺☺☺	*East Course*	Rating:	69.4/68.5
DEAL	18 holes. Par 70/70. Yards: 6,002/4,918	Slope:	124/118
	Apr.–Nov. High: May–Aug.		
☺☺☺	*West Course*	Rating:	70.6/69.0
	18 holes. Par 71/72. Yards: 6,300/5,218	Slope:	123/114
	Apr.–Nov. High: May–Aug.		
P	**Katke Golf Course**	Greens:	$–$$ W L R S J
☺☺☺	1003 Perry St., Big Rapids. (616) 592-2213	Carts:	$
DEAL	18 holes. Par 72/72. Yards: 6,729/5,344	Rating:	72.5/70.8
	Apr.–Nov. High: May–Sept.	Slope:	124/119
SP	**Lake Doster Golf Club**	Greens:	$$
☺☺☺	Plainwell. (616) 685-5308	Carts:	$

Michigan Golf Guide

DEAL	18 holes. Par 72/73. Yards: 6,570/5,530	Rating:	72.7/72.8
	Apr.–Oct. High: June–Aug.	Slope:	134/128

P	**The Meadows Golf Club**	Greens: $$ W L T J	
☺☺☺	4645 W. Campus Dr., Allendale. (616) 895-1000	Carts: $	
DEAL	18 holes. Par 71/72. Yards: 6,540/4,828	Rating:	72.7/68.5
	Apr.–Oct. High: June–Sept.	Slope:	133/117

P	**Milham Park Municipal Golf Course**	Greens: $ S J	
☺☺☺	4200 Lovers Lane, Kalamazoo. (616) 344-7639	Carts: NA	
DEAL	18 holes. Par 72/72. Yards: 6,578/5,582	Rating:	71.6/71.6
	Mar.–Dec. High: June–Aug.	Slope:	130/119

P	**Saskatoon Golf Club**	Greens: $ S	
	9038 92nd St., Alto. (616) 891-9229	Carts: $	
☺☺☺	*Blue/White*	Rating:	70.7/71.7
DEAL	18 holes. Par 73/73. Yards: 6,750/6,125	Slope:	123/122
	Mar.–Dec. High: May–July		

☺☺☺	*Red/Gold*	Rating:	69.1/68.0
	18 holes. Par 71/71. Yards: 5,944/4,987	Slope:	123/113

SP	**Scott Lake Country Club**	Greens: $$ W L S J	
☺☺☺	911 Hayes Rd., Comstock Park. (616) 784-1355	Carts: $	
DEAL	18 holes. Par 72/72. Yards: 6,333/4,794	Rating:	70.8/67.6
	Apr.–Nov. High: May–Sept.	Slope:	122/110

P	**Thornapple Creek Golf Club**	Greens: $$ W L S	
☺☺☺	6415 W. F Ave., Kalamazoo. (616) 344-0040	Carts: $$	
DEAL	18 holes. Par 72/72. Yards: 6,960/4,948	Rating:	73.7/68.9
	Apr.–Nov. High: June–Aug.	Slope:	137/121

R	**Thoroughbred Golf Club**	Greens: $$$–$$$$ W L R T	
☺☺☺☺	6900 S. Water Rd., Rothbury. (616) 893-4653	Carts: Incl.	
STATE	18 holes. Par 72/72. Yards: 6,900/4,851	Rating:	74.4/69.5
	Apr.–Nov. High: June–Sept.	Slope:	147/126

SP	**Wallinwood Springs Golf Course**	Greens: $$–$$$ W L S	
☺☺☺	8152 Weatherwax, Jenison. (616) 457-9920	Carts: $	
DEAL	18 holes. Par 72/72. Yards: 6,751/5,067	Rating:	72.4/69.1
	Apr.–Nov. High: June–Aug.	Slope:	128/115

East-Central Michigan

P	**Bedford Valley Golf Course**	Greens: $–$$ W L R T	
☺☺☺	23161 Waubascon Rd., Battle Creek. (616) 965-3384	Carts: $	
DEAL	18 holes. Par 71/72. Yards: 6,876/5,104	Rating:	73.8/70.0
	Apr.–Nov. High: May–Aug.	Slope:	135/119

P	**Binder Park Golf Course**	Greens: $ S J	
☺☺☺	6723 B Drive S., Battle Creek. (616) 966-3459	Carts: $	
DEAL	18 holes. Par 72/76. Yards: 6,328/4,965	Rating:	69.8/69.8
	Apr.–Oct. High: June–Aug.	Slope:	112/108

P	**Cascades Golf Course**	Greens: $ W L T S J	
☺☺☺	1922 Warren Ave., Jackson. (517) 788-4323	Carts: NA	
DEAL	18 holes. Par 72/73. Yards: 6,614/4,320	Rating:	71.8/70.5
	Mar.–Oct. High: July–Sept.	Slope:	124/119

P	**Eagle Glen Golf Course**	Greens: $$ W L R S J	
☺☺☺	Farwell. (517) 588-9357	Carts: $	
DEAL	18 holes. Par 72/72. Yards: 6,602/5,119	Rating:	71.1/69.2
	Apr.–Oct. High: June–Oct.	Slope:	123/116

P	**Firefly Golf Links**	Greens: $–$$ W L S	
☺☺	S. Clare Ave., Clare. (517) 386-3510	Carts: $	
	18 holes. Par 72/72. Yards: 5,658/4,470	Rating:	NA
	Apr.–Oct. High: June–Aug.	Slope:	NA

Michigan Golf Guide

P ☺☺☺ DEAL	**Huron Breeze Golf and Country Club** 5200 Huron Breeze Dr., Au Gres. (517) 876-6868 18 holes. Par 72/72. Yards: 6,806/5,075 Apr.–Oct. High: May–Sept.	Greens: $$ Carts: $ Rating: 73.1/69.4 Slope: 133/123	W L T S J
P ☺☺☺ BEST	**Timber Ridge Golf Course** 16339 Park Lake Rd., East Lansing. (517) 339-8000 18 holes. Par 72/72. Yards: 6,497/5,048 Mar.–Nov. High: May–Sept.	Greens: $$–$$$ Carts: $ Rating: 72.4/70.9 Slope: 140/129	W L T S

Detroit/Ann Arbor Area

P ☺☺☺ DEAL	**Faulkwood Shores Golf Club** 300 S. Hughes Rd., Howell. (517) 546-4180 18 holes. Par 72/72. Yards: 6,828/5,431 Apr.–Nov. High: June–Sept.	Greens: $–$$ Carts: Incl. Rating: 74.3/71.8 Slope: 140/128	W L T S J
P ☺☺☺ DEAL	**Heather Highlands Golf Club** 11450 E. Holly Rd., Holly. (810) 634-6800 18 holes. Par 72/72. Yards: 6,879/5,752 Apr.–Nov. High: May–Sept.	Greens: $$$–$$$$ Carts: $ Rating: 72.6/73.4 Slope: 124/122	W L T S J
R ☺☺☺ DEAL	**Eagle Crest Golf Club** 1275 Huron St., Ypsilanti. (313) 487-2441 18 holes. Par 72/72. Yards: 6,755/5,185 Mar.–Nov. High: June–Aug.	Greens: $–$$$ Carts: Incl. Rating: 73.6/69.7 Slope: 138/124	W L T S J
P ☺☺☺ DEAL	**The Links of Novi** 50395 Ten Mile Rd., Novi. (810) 380-9595 *East/South/West* 27 holes. Par 69/70/71. Yards: 6,014/6,093/6,497 Mar.–Nov. High: June–Aug.	Greens: $$–$$$ Carts: $ Rating: 67.9/68.3/71.2 Slope: 118/119/127	T S J
P ☺☺☺ DEAL	**Mistwood Golf Course** 7568 Sweet Lake Rd., Lake Ann. (616) 275-5500 18 holes. Par 71/71. Yards: 6,715/5,070 Apr.–Nov. High: June–Aug.	Greens: $$ Carts: $ Rating: 72.4/69.6 Slope: 130/120	W L T S J
P ☺☺☺☺ STATE	**The Orchards Golf Club** 62900 Campgrounds Rd., Washington. (810) 786-7200 18 holes. Par 72/72. Yards: 7,036/5,158 Apr.–Oct. High: May–Sept.	Greens: $$–$$$$ Carts: Incl. Rating: 74.5/70.3 Slope: 136/123	W L T
P ☺☺☺ DEAL	**Pine River Golf Club** 2244 Pine River Rd., Standish. (517) 846-6819 18 holes. Par 71/74. Yards: 6,205/5,156 Apr.–Oct. High: June–Aug.	Greens: $–$$ Carts: $ Rating: 70.8/70.7 Slope: 126/126	W S J
P ☺☺☺ DEAL	**Pleasant Hills Golf Club** 4452 E. Millbrook Rd., Mt. Pleasant. (517) 772-0487 18 holes. Par 72/72. Yards: 6,012/4,607 Mar.–Dec. High: June–Aug.	Greens: $ Carts: $ Rating: 68.2/65.9 Slope: 110/107	W L T S J
P ☺☺	**Raisin River Country Club** N. Dixie Hwy., Monroe. (313) 289-3700 *East Course* 18 holes. Par 71/71. Yards: 6,930/5,580 Mar.–Nov. High: May–Sept.	Greens: $ Carts: $ Rating: 73.1/68.4 Slope: NA	L R
☺☺	*West Course* 18 holes. Par 72/72. Yards: 6,255/5,880	Rating: 68.5/NA Slope: NA	R S J
P ☺☺☺ BEST	**Rattle Run Golf Course** St. Clair Hwy., China Twnshp. (810) 329-2070 18 holes. Par 72/75. Yards: 6,891/5,085 Apr.–Nov. High: May–Sept.	Greens: $$–$$$ Carts: Incl. Rating: 73.6/70.4 Slope: 140/124	L T S J

Michigan Golf Guide

P
☺☺
Reddeman Farms Golf Course
S. Dancer Rd., Chelsea. (313) 475-3020
18 holes. Par 72/72. Yards: 6,513/5,813
Apr.–Nov. High: June–Sept.

Greens: $$ W L T S J
Carts: $
Rating: 71.4/73.4
Slope: 122/126

P
☺☺☺
DEAL
Salem Hills Golf Club
W. Six Mile Rd., Northville. (810) 437-2152
18 holes. Par 72/76. Yards: 6,966/5,874
Apr.–Nov. High: May–Sept.

Greens: $$ T S J
Carts: $
Rating: 72.9/73.4
Slope: 121/119

P
☺☺☺
DEAL
Springfield Oaks Golf Course
Andersonville Rd., Davisburg. (810) 625-2540
18 holes. Par 71/71. Yards: 6,235/5,372
Mar.–Nov. High: June–Aug.

Greens: $–$$ W L T S J
Carts: $
Rating: 69.4/70.3
Slope: 115/114

P
☺☺☺
Stonebridge Golf Club
Stonebridge Dr. S., Ann Arbor. (313) 429-8383
18 holes. Par 72/72. Yards: 6,932/5,075
Mar.–Dec. High: June–Aug.

Greens: $$–$$$ L T S J
Carts: $
Rating: 74.2/71.0
Slope: 139/128

P

☺☺☺
DEAL
Sycamore Hills Golf Club
Mt. Clemens. (810) 598-9500
North/South/West
27 holes. Par 72/72/72. Yards: 6,255/6,305/6,205
Mar.–Dec. High: May–Sept.

Greens: $$ W L T S J
Carts: $
Rating: 70.3/70.7/70.2
Slope: 123/130/132

P

☺☺☺
DEAL
Tanglewood Golf Club
W. Ten Mile Rd., S. Lyon. (810) 486-3355
North/South/West
27 holes. Par 72/72/72. Yards: 7,077/6,922/7,117
Mar.–Nov. High: May–Aug.

Greens: $$–$$$ L T S J
Carts: Incl.
Rating: 70.3/70.7/72.5
Slope: 125/127/135

P
☺☺☺
DEAL
Taylor Meadows Golf Club
Ecorse Rd., Taylor. (313) 295-0506
18 holes. Par 71/71. Yards: 6,049/4,995
Mar.–Dec. High: May–Oct.

Greens: $–$$ W L T S J
Carts: $$
Rating: 67.7/66.9
Slope: 115/110

SP
☺☺☺
STATE
University of Michigan Golf Course
E. Stadium Blvd., Ann Arbor. (313) 663-5005
18 holes. Par 71/75. Yards: 6,687/5,331
Apr.–Oct. High: May–Sept.
Open to alumni, students, faculty, and their guests.

Greens: $$$
Carts: $$
Rating: 72.5/71.0
Slope: 135/125

P

☺☺
Warren Valley Golf Course
W. Warren, Dearborn Heights. (313) 561-1040
East Course
18 holes. Par 72/72. Yards: 6,189/5,328
Mar.–Nov. High: May–Oct.

Greens: $ W L T S J
Carts: $$
Rating: 69.1/70.0
Slope: 114/113

☺☺
West Course
18 holes. Par 71/71. Yards: 6,066/5,150

Rating: 68.5/69.2
Slope: 115/114

Minnesota

The Land of 10,000 Lakes has quite a few golf courses that use the plentiful water to great advantage.

The spectacular **Edinburgh USA** club in Brooklyn Park, north of Minneapolis, is among the best public courses anywhere, with some especially challenging sand and water hazards. Even better, it's also on the *Golf U.S.A.* Deals list.

Also just outside of Minneapolis is the Platinum Course at **Majestic Oaks** in Ham Lake, another *Golf U.S.A.* Deal.

In north central Minnesota is the acclaimed **Grand View Lodge** in Nisswa, well worth the trip away from civilization.

The **Bunker Hills Golf Course** has been home to the PGA Senior Tour since 1992.

Minnesota has some tremendous extremes in weather, with an average temperature in Minneapolis of 12°F in January and a balmy 74°F in July. Most, but not all, courses in the state operate from April through November, with high-season conditions and rates in effect from June through early September.

Golf U.S.A. Leader Board: Best Public Courses in Minnesota

◔◔◔◔ Edinburgh USA Golf Club
◔◔◔◔ Grand View Lodge
◔◔◔ Majestic Oaks Golf Club (Platinum)

Golf U.S.A. Leader Board: Best Deals in Minnesota

$$/◔◔◔	Baker National Golf Course
$$/◔◔◔	Braemar Golf Course (Red, White, Blue)
$/◔◔◔	Brooktree Municipal Golf Course
$$/◔◔◔◔	Bunker Hills Golf Course
$$/◔◔◔	Cannon Golf Club
$/◔◔◔	Cedar River Country Club
$$/◔◔◔	Detroit Country Club
$$/◔◔◔◔	Edinburgh USA Golf Club
$$/◔◔◔	Fox Hollow Golf Club
$$/◔◔◔	Headwaters Country Club
$$/◔◔◔	Inverwood Golf Course
$/◔◔◔	Keller Golf Course
$$/◔◔◔	The Links at Northfork
$$/◔◔◔	Little Crow Country Club
$$/◔◔◔	Majestic Oaks Golf Club (Platinum)
$/◔◔◔	Maple Valley Golf and Country Club
$$/◔◔◔	Marshall Golf Club
$$/◔◔◔	Mississippi National Golf Links
$$/◔◔◔	Monticello Country Club
$$/◔◔◔	New Prague Golf Club
$$/◔◔◔	North Links Golf Course
$/◔◔◔	Northern Hills Golf Course
$$/◔◔◔	Northfield Golf Club
$$/◔◔◔	Oak Glen Golf Club
$/◔◔◔	Oaks Country Club
$$/◔◔◔◔	Pebble Creek Country Club
$$/◔◔◔	Pebble Lake Golf Club
$$/◔◔◔	Perham Lakeside Country Club
$$/◔◔◔	Pine Meadows Golf Course
$$/◔◔◔	Pokegama Golf Club
$$/◔◔◔	Purple Hawk Golf Club
$$/◔◔◔	Southern Hills Golf Club

$$/☺☺☺	Stonebrooke Golf Club	
$$/☺☺☺	Tianna Country Club	
$$/☺☺☺	Wedgewood Golf Club	
$$/☺☺☺	Wildflower at Fair Hills	
$$/☺☺☺☺	Willinger's Golf Club	
$/☺☺☺	Willow Creek Golf Club	

Minnesota Golf Guide

Northern Minnesota

R	**Grand View Lodge**	Greens: $$$–$$$$ W L R T
	Nisswa. (218) 963-3146	Carts: $
☺☺☺☺	*The Pines-Lakes/Woods/Marsh*	Rating: 74.2/73.9/74.3
STATE	27 holes. Par 72/72/72. Yards: 6,874/6,883/6,837	Slope: 137/139/141
	Apr.–Oct. High: June–Sept.	

SP	**Headwaters Country Club**	Greens: $–$$ L T J
☺☺☺	Cty. Rd. 99, Park Rapids. (218) 732-4832	Carts: $$
DEAL	18 holes. Par 72/72. Yards: 6,455/5,362	Rating: 70.9/71.0
	Mar.–Nov. High: June–Aug.	Slope: 120/118

R	**Madden's on Gull Lake**	Greens: $–$$ W R T
	Pine Beach Peninsula, Brainerd. (218) 829-7118	Carts: $$
☺☺	*Pine Beach East Course*	Rating: 67.9/70.9
	18 holes. Par 72/72. Yards: 5,956/5,353	Slope: 111/116
	Apr.–Oct. High: July–Aug.	

☺☺	*Pine Beach West Course*	Rating: 64.0/66.7
	18 holes. Par 67/67. Yards: 5,070/4,478	Slope: 103/107

☺☺	*Classic Course*	Greens: $$$$–$$$$$
	18 holes. Par 72/72. Yards: 7,109/4,883	Rating: 74.9/68.6
		Slope: 139/119

P	**Pine Meadows Golf Course**	Greens: $$ W L R T S J
☺☺☺	Brainerd. (218) 829-5733	Carts: $
DEAL	18 holes. Par 72/72. Yards: 6,372/4,479	Rating: 71.5/68.3
	Apr.–Oct. High: June–Aug.	Slope: 130/124

R	**Ruttger's Bay Lake Lodge**	Greens: $$–$$$ L R T
	Rte. 2, Deerwood. (218) 678-2885	Carts: $
☺☺☺	*The Lakes Course*	Rating: 72.2/69.7
	18 holes. Par 72/72. Yards: 6,626/5,052	Slope: 131/124
	Apr.–Oct. High: May–Sept.	

SP	**Tianna Country Club**	Greens: $–$$ T
☺☺☺	Walker. (218) 547-1712	Carts: $$
DEAL	18 holes. Par 72/72. Yards: 6,550/5,425	Rating: 70.7/73.5
	May–Oct. High: June–Aug.	Slope: 127/124

Duluth Area

P	**Enger Park Golf Club**	Greens: $ L T S J
☺☺	W. Skyline Blvd., Duluth. (218) 723-3451	Carts: $
	27 holes. Par 72/72/72. Yards: 6,434/6,325/6,499	Rating: 70.9/70.3/71.0
	Apr.–Nov. High: June–Aug.	Slope: 124/121/121

P	**Lester Park Golf Club**	Greens: $ L T S J
	Lester River Rd., Duluth. (218) 525-1400	Carts: $
☺	*Front/Back/Lake*	Rating: 70.8/71.7/71.7
	27 holes. Par 72/72/72. Yards: 6,371/6,606/6,599	Slope: 118/126/125
	Apr.–Nov. High: June–July	

P	**Pokegama Golf Club**	Greens: $–$$ W R T J
☺☺☺	Grand Rapids. (218) 326-3444	Carts: $

Minnesota Golf Guide

DEAL	18 holes. Par 71/72. Yards: 6,481/5,046	Rating:	70.3/67.7
	Apr.–Oct. High: June–Aug.	Slope:	121/116

Central Minnesota

P	**Detroit Country Club**	Greens:	$$	
☺☺☺	Rte. 5, Detroit Lakes. (218) 847-5790	Carts:	$$	
DEAL	18 holes. Par 71/71. Yards: 5,941/5,508	Rating:	69.2/72.3	
	May–Oct. High: June–Aug.	Slope:	122/129	

P	**Pebble Creek Country Club**	Greens:	$$	S J
	Becker. (612) 261-4653	Carts:	$	
☺☺☺☺	*Red-White/Blue-Red/White-Blue*	Rating:	73.2/72.4/72.2	
DEAL	27 holes. Par 72/72/72. Yards: 6,820/6,757/6,657	Slope:	129/129/126	
	Apr.–Oct. High: June–Sept.			

P	**Pebble Lake Golf Club**	Greens:	$–$$	L T S J
☺☺☺	Cty. Rd. 82 S., Fergus Falls. (218) 736-7404	Carts:	$	
DEAL	18 holes. Par 72/74. Yards: 6,699/5,549	Rating:	72.3/72.1	
	Apr.–Oct. High: June–Aug.	Slope:	128/126	

P	**Perham Lakeside Country Club**	Greens:	$–$$	W L R T
☺☺☺	Perham. (218) 346-6070	Carts:	$	
DEAL	18 holes. Par 72/73. Yards: 6,575/5,388	Rating:	72.5/71.1	
	Apr.–Oct. High: June–Aug.	Slope:	128/122	

P	**Wildflower at Fair Hills**	Greens:	$–$$	W L R T S J
☺☺☺	Detroit Lakes. (218) 439-3357	Carts:	$$	
DEAL	18 holes. Par 72/72. Yards: 7,000/5,299	Rating:	74.2/71.6	
	May–First snow. High: June–Aug.	Slope:	139/121	

Minneapolis/St. Paul Area

P	**Baker National Golf Course**	Greens:	$–$$	S J
☺☺☺	Parkview Dr., Medina. (612) 473-0800	Carts:	$$	
DEAL	18 holes. Par 72/74. Yards: 6,762/5,395	Rating:	74.2/72.7	
	Apr.–Oct. High: June–Aug.	Slope:	133/129	

P	**Bellwood Oaks Golf Course**	Greens:	$	S
☺☺	210th St., Hastings. (612) 437-4141	Carts:	$	
	18 holes. Par 73/74. Yards: 6,775/5,707	Rating:	71.3/71.2	
	Apr.–Nov. High: May–Sept.	Slope:	115/115	

R	**Bemidji Town and Country Club**	Greens:	$–$$	L R T
☺☺	Birchmont Dr. N.E., Bemidji. (218) 751-9215	Carts:	$	
	18 holes. Par 72/72. Yards: 6,535/5,058	Rating:	71.8/69.1	
	Year-round. High: June–Aug.	Slope:	127/120	

P	**Braemar Golf Course**	Greens:	$$	L J
	John Harris Dr., Edina. (612) 941-2072	Carts:	$$	
☺☺☺	*Red/White/Blue*	Rating:	71.8/71.6/73.0	
DEAL	27 holes. Par 71/71/72. Yards: 6,739/6,377/6,692	Slope:	124/129/134	
	Apr.–Oct. High: May–Sept.			

P	**Brooktree Municipal Golf Course**	Greens:	$
☺☺☺	Cherry St., Owatonna. (507) 444-2467	Carts:	$
DEAL	18 holes. Par 71/72. Yards: 6,684/5,534	Rating:	72.1/71.6
	Apr.–Oct. High: June–Aug.	Slope:	121/121

P	**Brookview Golf Course**	Greens:	$$
☺☺	Golden Valley. (507) 444-2467	Carts:	$$
	18 holes. Par 72/72. Yards: 6,684/5,534	Rating:	72.1/71.6
	Apr.–Oct. High: June–Sept.	Slope:	122/122

P	**Bunker Hills Golf Course**	Greens:	$$–$$$	S J
	Foley Blvd., Coon Rapids. (612) 755-4141	Carts:	$$	

Minnesota Golf Guide

☺☺☺☺ DEAL	*North-East/North-West/East-West* 27 holes. Par 72/72/72. Yards: 6,799/6,938/6,901 Apr.–Nov. High: June–Aug.	Rating: Slope:	72.5/73.4/73.5 132/133/132

SP ☺☺☺ DEAL	**Cannon Golf Club** 295th St. E., Cannon Falls. (507) 263-3126 18 holes. Par 71/71. Yards: 6,047/5,031 Apr.–Oct.	Greens: Carts: Rating: Slope:	$–$$ $$ 69.5/70.1 121/125	W S

P ☺☺	**Columbia Golf Course** Central Ave., Minneapolis. (612) 789-2627 18 holes. Par 71/71. Yards: 6,385/5,489 Apr.–Nov. High: May–Aug.	Greens: Carts: Rating: Slope:	$ $$ 70.0/71.9 121/123	T S J

P ☺☺	**Dahlgreen Golf Club** Dahlgreen Rd., Chaska. (612) 448-7463 18 holes. Par 72/72. Yards: 6,887/5,850 Mar.–Nov. High: June–Aug.	Greens: Carts: Rating: Slope:	$$ $$ 72.5/72.1 124/120	W L S J

P ☺☺	**Deer Run Golf Club** Vistoria. (612) 443-2351 18 holes. Par 71/71. Yards: 6,265/5,541 Mar.–Nov. High: June–Aug.	Greens: Carts: Rating: Slope:	$$ $$ 70.5/72.1 122/121	T S J

P ☺☺☺☺ BEST DEAL	**Edinburgh USA Golf Club** Edinbrook Crossing, Brooklyn Park. (612) 424-7060 18 holes. Par 72/72. Yards: 6,701/5,255 Apr.–Oct. High: June–Aug.	Greens: Carts: Rating: Slope:	$$ $$ 73.0/71.4 133/128	T S J

SP ☺☺☺ DEAL	**Fox Hollow Golf Club** Palmgren Lane N.E., Rogers. (612) 428-4468 18 holes. Par 72/72. Yards: 6,726/5,161 Apr.–Nov. High: June–Aug.	Greens: Carts: Rating: Slope:	$$ $$ 72.7/70.8 129/122	W L S J

P ☺☺	**Francis A. Gross Golf Course** St. Anthony Blvd., Minneapolis. (612) 789-2542 18 holes. Par 71/71. Yards: 6,575/5,824 Apr.–Nov. High: June–Aug.	Greens: Carts: Rating: Slope:	$ $$ 70.1/73.2 120/121	W T S J

P ☺☺	**Hidden Greens Golf Club** 200th St. E., Hastings. (612) 437-3085 18 holes. Par 72/72. Yards: 5,954/5,599 Apr.–Nov. High: July–Aug.	Greens: Carts: Rating: Slope:	$ $ 68.8/72.2 114/127	W S

P ☺☺☺ DEAL	**Inverwood Golf Course** Inver Grove Heights. (612) 457-3667 18 holes. Par 72/72. Yards: 6,724/5,175 Apr.–Oct. High: May–Aug.	Greens: Carts: Rating: Slope:	$$ $$ 72.5/70.3 135/124	J

R ☺☺☺	**Izaty's Golf and Yacht Club** Rte. 1, Onamia. (320) 532-3191 18 holes. Par 72/72. Yards: 6,480/4,939 Apr.–Oct. High: June–Sept.	Greens: Carts: Rating: Slope:	$$–$$$ $$ 72.1/69.7 132/127	W R T

P ☺☺☺ DEAL	**Keller Golf Course** Maplewood Dr., St. Paul. (612) 484-3011 18 holes. Par 72/73. Yards: 6,566/5,373 Mar.–Nov. High: May–Sept.	Greens: Carts: Rating: Slope:	$–$$ $$ 71.7/71.4 127/124	L T S J

P ☺☺☺ DEAL	**The Links at Northfork** 153rd Ave., Ramsey. (612) 241-0506 18 holes. Par 72/72. Yards: 6,989/5,242 Apr.–Oct. High: June–Aug.	Greens: Carts: Rating: Slope:	$–$$ $$ 73.7/66.0 127/111	W L T S J

Minnesota Golf Guide

P	**Majestic Oaks Golf Club**	Greens:	$$	W L T S J
	Bunker Lake Blvd., Ham Lake. (612) 755-2142	Carts:	$$	
☺☺	*Gold Course*	Rating:	71.2/68.4	
	18 holes. Par 72/72. Yards: 6,396/4,848	Slope:	123/120	
	Apr.–Oct. High: June–Aug.			

☺☺☺	*Platinum Course*	Rating:	73.9/71.6	
BEST, DEAL	18 holes. Par 72/72. Yards: 7,013/5,268	Slope:	129/126	

P	**Manitou Ridge Golf Course**	Greens:	$	S J
☺☺	N. McKnight Rd., White Bear Lake. (612) 777-2987	Carts:	$	
	18 holes. Par 71/71. Yards: 6,422/5,556	Rating:	70.5/71.5	
	Apr.–Oct. High: Apr.–Oct.	Slope:	120/119	

P	**Meadowbrook Golf Course**	Greens:	$	L T S J
☺☺	Meadowbrook Rd., Hopkins. (612) 929-2077	Carts:	$$	
	18 holes. Par 72/72. Yards: 6,593/5,610	Rating:	69.6/71.1	
	Apr.–Nov. High: May–Aug.	Slope:	113/122	

P	**Monticello Country Club**	Greens:	$–$$	W L S
☺☺☺	Monticello. (612) 295-4653	Carts:	$$	
DEAL	18 holes. Par 71/72. Yards: 6,390/5,243	Rating:	70.4/70.8	
	Apr.–Oct. High: Apr.–Oct.	Slope:	118/119	

P	**New Prague Golf Club**	Greens:	$$	W L R S J
☺☺☺	Lexington Ave. S., New Prague. (612) 758-3126	Carts:	$$	
DEAL	18 holes. Par 72/72. Yards: 6,335/5,032	Rating:	69.5/68.3	
	Apr.–Oct. High: May–Aug.	Slope:	121/116	

SP	**Northfield Golf Club**	Greens:	$$	
☺☺☺	Prairie St., Northfield. (507) 645-4026	Carts:	$$	
DEAL	18 holes. Par 69/71. Yards: 5,856/5,103	Rating:	68.7/70.4	
	Apr.–Oct. High: Apr.–Sept.	Slope:	128/126	

P	**Oak Glen Golf Club**	Greens:	$$	T
☺☺☺	McKusick Rd., Stillwater. (612) 439-6963	Carts:	$	
DEAL	18 holes. Par 72/72. Yards: 6,550/5,626	Rating:	72.4/73.4	
	Apr.–Nov. High: June–Aug.	Slope:	131/130	

P	**Phalen Park Golf Course**	Greens:	$	T S J
☺☺	Phalen Dr., St. Paul. (612) 778-0413	Carts:	$$	
	18 holes. Par 70/71. Yards: 6,101/5,439	Rating:	68.7/70.7	
	Mar.–Nov. High: June–Aug.	Slope:	121/121	

P	**Pheasant Run Golf Club**	Greens:	$–$$	W L T S J
☺☺	Cty. Rd., 116, Rogers. (612) 428-8244	Carts:	$$	
	18 holes. Par 71/72. Yards: 6,400/5,200	Rating:	69.9/68.7	
	Apr.–Nov. High: June–Sept.	Slope:	117/115	

SP	**Purple Hawk Golf Club**	Greens:	$–$$	T S J
☺☺☺	Cambridge. (612) 689-3800	Carts:	$$	
DEAL	18 holes. Par 72/74. Yards: 6,679/5,748	Rating:	72.3/73.5	
	Apr.–Oct. High: June–Aug.	Slope:	132/131	

SP	**Rich Spring Golf Course**	Greens:	$	S
☺☺	Cold Spring. (612) 685-8810	Carts:	$	
	18 holes. Par 72/72. Yards: 6,542/5,347	Rating:	69.7/70.0	
	Apr.–Oct. High: June–Aug.	Slope:	119/110	

P	**Rum River Hills Golf Club**	Greens:	$–$$	T S J
☺☺	St. Francis Blvd., Anoka. (612) 753-3339	Carts:	$$	
	18 holes. Par 71/71. Yards: 6,338/5,095	Rating:	71.3/70.1	
	Mar.–Nov. High: June–Aug.	Slope:	122/119	

SP	**Sawmill Golf Club**	Greens:	$–$$	L T S J
☺☺	McKusick Rd., Stillwater. (612) 439-7862	Carts:	$	

	18 holes. Par 70/71. Yards: 6,300/5,300 Apr.–Nov. High: May–Sept.	Rating: 70.2/69.5 Slope: 125/122	

P ☺☺☺ DEAL	**Southern Hills Golf Club** Chippendale Ave., Farmington. (612) 463-4653 18 holes. Par 71/71. Yards: 6,314/4,970 Apr.–Oct. High: June–Aug.	Greens: $–$$ Carts: $ Rating: 70.4/68.3 Slope: 123/116	W L T S J
SP ☺☺☺ DEAL	**Stonebrooke Golf Club** Cty. Rd., 79, Shakopee. (612) 496-3171 18 holes. Par 71/71. Yards: 6,700/5,100 Apr.–Oct. High: June–July	Greens: $$ Carts: $$ Rating: 72.4/69.7 Slope: 133/118	
P ☺☺	**Theodore Wirth Golf Course** Minneapolis. (612) 522-4584 18 holes. Par 72/72. Yards: 6,408/5,639 Apr.–Nov. High: June–Aug.	Greens: $ Carts: $ Rating: 71.7/72.8 Slope: 129/123	W L T S J
SP ☺☺☺ DEAL	**Prestwick at Wedgewood** Wedgewood Dr., Woodbury. (612) 731-4779 18 holes. Par 72/72. Yards: 6,723/5,267 Mar.–Nov. High: Apr.–Sept.	Greens: $$ Carts: $ Rating: 72.3/70.1 Slope: 127/121	W T J

Rochester Area

P ☺☺	**Eastwood Golf Club** Eastwood Rd., S.E., Rochester. (507) 281-6173 18 holes. Par 72/72. Yards: 6,178/5,289 Apr.–Nov. High: May–Aug.	Greens: $ Carts: $ Rating: 69.9/71.0 Slope: 120/121	
SP ☺☺☺ DEAL	**Maple Valley Golf and Country Club** Maple Valley Rd., S.E., Rochester. (507) 285-9100 18 holes. Par 71/71. Yards: 6,270/5,330 Mar.–Nov. High: July–Aug.	Greens: $ Carts: Inquire Rating: 70.5/71.1 Slope: 121/120	
P ☺☺☺ DEAL	**North Links Golf Course** Cty. Rd. 6, N. Mankato. (507) 947-3355 18 holes. Par 72/72. Yards: 6,073/4,659 Apr.–Nov. High: June–Aug.	Greens: $–$$ Carts: $ Rating: 69.5/66.9 Slope: 117/114	W T S J
P ☺☺☺ DEAL	**Northern Hills Golf Course** N.W. 41st Ave., Rochester. (507) 281-6170 18 holes. Par 72/72. Yards: 6,310/5,522 Apr.–Oct. High: May–Sept.	Greens: $ Carts: $ Rating: 72.0/72.0 Slope: 126/128	
SP ☺☺☺ DEAL	**Oaks Country Club** Hayfield. (507) 477-3233 18 holes. Par 72/72. Yards: 6,355/5,663 Apr.–Oct. High: June–Aug.	Greens: $ Carts: $ Rating: 69.9/72.0 Slope: 118/119	W L R
P ☺☺☺☺ DEAL	**Willinger's Golf Club** Canby Trail, Northfield. (612) 440-7000 18 holes. Par 72/72. Yards: 6,711/5,166 Apr.–Oct. High: June–Aug.	Greens: $$–$$$ Carts: $$ Rating: 73.4/71.7 Slope: 148/133	W T S J
SP ☺☺☺ DEAL	**Willow Creek Golf Club** 1700 S.W. 48th St., Rochester. (507) 285-0305 18 holes. Par 70/70. Yards: 6,053/5,293 Mar.–Nov. High: June–Aug.	Greens: $ Carts: $ Rating: 69.1/70.5 Slope: 117/121	

Southern Minnesota

P ☺☺☺ DEAL	**Cedar River Country Club** Hwy. 56 W., Adams. (507) 582-3595 18 holes. Par 72/74. Yards: 6,268/5,553 Mar.–Nov. High: June–Aug.	Greens: $ Carts: $ Rating: 70.3/72.0 Slope: 124/124	
SP ☺☺☺	**Little Crow Country Club** Hwy. 23, Spicer. (320) 354-2296	Greens: $–$$ Carts: $	W L

| DEAL | 18 holes. Par 72/72. Yards: 6,740/5,662 | Rating: | 72.3/73.1 |
| | Apr.–Nov. High: June–Aug. | Slope: | 123/125 |

SP	**Marshall Golf Club**	Greens:	$$
☺☺☺	Marshall. (507) 537-1622	Carts:	$$
DEAL	18 holes. Par 72/72. Yards: 6,600/5,136	Rating:	71.6/69.5
	Apr.–Oct. High: May–Sept.	Slope:	123/120

P	**Mississippi National Golf Links**	Greens:	$$	W
	Red Wing. (612) 388-1874	Carts:	$
☺☺☺	*Lowlands/Midlands/Highlands*	Rating:	70.0/71.5/71.1
DEAL	27 holes. Par 72/72. Yards: 6,035/6,488/6,215	Slope:	125/128/130
	Apr.–Oct. High: June–Aug.		

P	**Mount Frontenac Golf Course**	Greens:	$	W T S
☺☺	Hwy. 61, Frontenac. (612) 388-5826	Carts:	$
	18 holes. Par 70/70. Yards: 6,050/4,832	Rating:	69.2/67.7
	Apr.–Oct. High: June–Aug.	Slope:	119/117

P	**Ramsey Golf Club**	Greens:	$	L
☺☺	Autin. (507) 433-9098	Carts:	$
	18 holes. Par 71/72. Yards: 5,987/5,426	Rating:	68.2/70.7
	Apr.–Nov. High: May–Sept.	Slope:	120/117

Missouri

Foremost among Missouri's gems are the venerable **Shirkey Golf Club** near Kansas City, and the newer **Tapawingo National Golf Club**, outside of St. Louis. Shirkey, with a new clubhouse due to open in 2000, also has a spot on the *Golf U.S.A.* Deals list. Half a notch below are the lush fairways of **Eagle Lake**, in Farmington south of St. Louis, and the hilly **Osage National Golf Course**.

Golf courses in Missouri are generally open year-round. Look for peak rates from April through late September at most courses.

Golf U.S.A. Leader Board: Best Public Courses in Missouri

☺☺☺   Eagle Lake Golf Club
☺☺☺   North Port National Golf Club (Osage)
☺☺☺☺   Shirkey Golf Club
☺☺☺☺   Tapawingo National Golf Club

Golf U.S.A. Leader Board: Best Deals in Missouri

$$/☺☺☺   Bent Creek Golf Course
$$/☺☺☺   Crystal Highlands Golf Club
$$/☺☺☺   Eagle Lake Golf Club
$/☺☺☺   Honey Creek Golf Club
$/☺☺☺   Longview Lake Golf Course
$$/☺☺☺   Paradise Pointe Golf Club (Outlaw)
$$/☺☺☺☺   Shirkey Golf Club
$/☺☺☺   Swope Memorial Golf Course

Northern Missouri

| SP | **Kirksville Country Club** | Greens: | $ |
| ☺☺ | State Hwy. 63, Kirksville. (816) 665-5335 | Carts: | $ |

18 holes. Par 71/71. Yards: 6,418/5,802
Mar.–Dec. High: June–Aug.

Rating: 70.9/71.6
Slope: 118/114

Kansas City Area

SP
☺☺

Bent Oak Golf Club
S.E. 30th, Oak Grove. (816) 690-3028
18 holes. Par 72/73. Yards: 6,855/5,500
Year-round. High: May–Sept.

Greens: $ W S J
Carts: $$
Rating: 73.1/71.0
Slope: 134/119

P
☺☺

Excelsior Springs Golf Club
Excelsior Springs. (816) 630-3731
18 holes. Par 72/72. Yards: 6,650/5,450
Year-round. High: May–Sept.

Greens: $ W T
Carts: $
Rating: 69.5/67.9
Slope: 116/110

P
☺☺

Hodge Park Golf Course
N.E. Barry Rd., Kansas City. (816) 781-4152
18 holes. Par 71/71. Yards: 6,181/5,707
Year-round. High: Apr.–Oct.

Greens: $ T
Carts: Incl.
Rating: NA
Slope: 117/110

P
☺☺☺
DEAL

Longview Lake Golf Course
View High Dr., Kansas City. (816) 761-9445
18 holes. Par 72/72. Yards: 6,671/5,507
Year-round. High: May–Aug.

Greens: $ W S J
Carts: $$
Rating: 71.9/70.8
Slope: 121/113

R

☺☺☺

Marriott's Tan-Tar
Osage Beach. (573) 348-8521
The Oaks Course
18 holes. Par 71/70. Yards: 6,432/3,931
Year-round. High: May–Oct.

Greens: $$$–$$$$ W L T
Carts: Incl.
Rating: 72.1/62.5
Slope: 143/103

P

☺☺☺
DEAL

Paradise Pointe Golf Club
Smithville. (816) 532-4100
Outlaw Course
18 holes. Par 72/72. Yards: 6,988/5,322
Year-round. High: May–Oct.

Greens: $–$$ W L S
Carts: $
Rating: 73.8/67.0
Slope: 138/118

☺☺

Posse Course
18 holes. Par 72/73. Yards: 6,663/5,600

Rating: 71.8/70.0
Slope: 125/115

SP
☺☺☺☺
DEAL
STATE

Shirkey Golf Club
Wollard Blvd., Richmond. (816) 470-2582
18 holes. Par 71/74. Yards: 6,967/5,516
Year-round. High: May–Oct.

Greens: $$ W
Carts: $$
Rating: 71.3/73.1
Slope: 136/129

P
☺☺☺
DEAL

Swope Memorial Golf Course
Kansas City. (816) 523-9081
18 holes. Par 72/72. Yards: 6,274/4,517
Year-round. High: Apr.–Oct.

Greens: $ W T S J
Carts: $
Rating: 70.9/65.4
Slope: 128/107

St. Louis Area

P
☺☺☺

Cherry Hills Golf Club
Manchester Rd., Grover. (314) 458-4113
18 holes. Par 71/71. Yards: 6,389/5,359
Year-round. High: May–Aug.

Greens: $$–$$$ L T S
Carts: Incl.
Rating: 71.1/72.6
Slope: 132/120

P
☺☺☺
DEAL

Crystal Highlands Golf Club
U.S. Hwy. 61, Festus/Crystal City. (314) 931-3880
18 holes. Par 72/72. Yards: 6,480/4,946
Year-round. High: Apr.–Oct.

Greens: $$ W L T S J
Carts: $
Rating: 71.6/68.0
Slope: 135/109

P
☺☺

Eagle Springs Golf Course
Redman Rd., St. Louis. (314) 355-7277
18 holes. Par 72/72. Yards: 6,679/5,533
Year-round. High: May–Sept.

Greens: $–$$ W L S J
Carts: $
Rating: 71.4/72.3
Slope: 122/121

P
☺☺☺

Quail Creek Golf Club
Wells Rd., St. Louis. (314) 487-1988

Greens: $$$ W L T S J
Carts: Incl.

	18 holes. Par 72/72. Yards: 6,980/5,244	Rating:	73.8/69.2
	Year-round. High: Apr.–Oct.	Slope:	141/109

P	**Tapawingo National Golf Club**	Greens:	$$$$	W L T S J
	W. Watson Rd., St. Louis. (314) 349-3100	Carts:	Incl.	
◎◎◎◎	*Woodlands-Prairie/Prairie-Meramec/Woodlands-Merramec*			
STATE	27 holes. Par 72/72/72. Yards: 7,151/7,029/7,019	Rating:	75/74.3/73.7	
	Year-round. High: Apr.–Oct.	Slope:	141/141/139	

Springfield Area

P	**Bill and Payne Stewart Golf Course**	Greens:	$	W S J
◎◎	E. Norton, Springfield. (417) 833-9962	Carts:	$	
	18 holes. Par 70/72. Yards: 6,043/5,693	Rating:	68.4/71.3	
	Year-round. High: Mar.–Oct.	Slope:	113/117	

P	**Carthage Municipal Golf Course**	Greens:	$	W J
◎◎	Oak St., Carthage. (417) 358-8724	Carts:	$	
	18 holes. Par 71/73. Yards: 6,402/5,469	Rating:	69.4/70.5	
	Year-round. High: Apr.–Aug.	Slope:	124/115	

SP	**Cassville Golf Club**	Greens:	$	
◎◎	Hwy. 112 S., Cassville. (417) 847-2399	Carts:	Inquire	
	18 holes. Par 72/72. Yards: 6,620/5,802	Rating:	71.3/79.8	
	Year-round. High: Apr.–Oct.	Slope:	118/117	

SP	**Hidden Valley Golf Links**	Greens:	$	S
◎◎	Rte. 1, Clever. (417) 743-2860	Carts:	$	
	18 holes. Par 73/75. Yards: 6,611/5,288	Rating:	71.9/NA	
	Year-round. High: May–Sept.	Slope:	118/NA	

P	**Honey Creek Golf Club**	Greens:	$	
◎◎◎	Aurora. (417) 678-3353	Carts:	$	
DEAL	18 holes. Par 71/79. Yards: 6,732/5,972	Rating:	71.9/NA	
	Year-round. High: Apr.–Oct.	Slope:	118/NA	

P	**Lake Valley Golf Club**	Greens:	$$–$$$	L R T J
◎◎◎	Camdenton. (573) 346-7218	Carts:	Inquire	
	18 holes. Par 72/74. Yards: 6,405/5,268	Rating:	71.1/70.5	
	Year-round. High: Apr.–Oct.	Slope:	121/118	

P	**Schifferdecker Golf Course**	Greens:	$	T S J
◎◎	Schifferdecker, Joplin. (417) 624-3533	Carts:	$	
	18 holes. Par 71/72. Yards: 6,123/5,251	Rating:	68.7/69.7	
	Year-round. High: Apr.–Sept.	Slope:	108/117	

Southern Missouri

SP	**Bent Creek Golf Course**	Greens:	$$	W L T S J
◎◎◎	Jackson. (573) 243-6060	Carts:	Incl.	
DEAL	18 holes. Par 72/72. Yards: 6,958/5,148	Rating:	72.5/69.8	
	Year-round. High: May–Sept.	Slope:	136/112	

SP	**Eagle Lake Golf Club**	Greens:	$$	W L R T S J
◎◎◎	Hunt Rd., Farmington. (573) 756-6660	Carts:	$	
DEAL	18 holes. Par 72/72. Yards: 7,093/5,648	Rating:	73.9/71.0	
STATE	Year-round. High: Apr.–Oct.	Slope:	130/113	

R	**North Port National Golf Club (Osage)**	Greens:	$$$	W L R T S J
◎◎◎	Osage Hills Rd., Lake Ozark. (573) 365-1100	Carts:	Incl.	
STATE	18 holes. Par 72/72. Yards: 7,150/5,252	Rating:	75.6/70.5	
	Year-round. High: Apr.–Oct.	Slope:	145/122	

R	**The Lodge of Four Seasons**	Greens:	$$$–$$$$	W L T
	State Rd. HH, Lake Ozark. (573) 365-8544	Carts:	Incl.	
◎◎◎	*Robert Trent Jones Course*	Rating:	71.4/70.8	
	18 holes. Par 71/71. Yards: 6,557/5,238	Slope:	136/124	
	Apr.–Nov. High: May–Oct.			

Nebraska

Heritage Hills in McCook (southwestern Nebraska) is a hidden gem, a linkslike rolling prairie that is worth the hike from civilization. **Woodland Hills** in Eagle, outside of Lincoln, is an interesting challenge in the piney woods. Both Heritage Hills and Woodland Hills are also *Golf U.S.A.* Deals.

Some courses in Nebraska manage to stay open year-round, but most operate from March through October. Peak rates are in effect from about May through early September.

Golf U.S.A. Leader Board: Best Public Courses in Nebraska

ⓞⓞⓞⓞ   Heritage Hills Golf Course
ⓞⓞⓞⓞ   Woodland Hills Golf Course

Golf U.S.A. Leader Board: Best Deals in Nebraska

$/ⓞⓞⓞ	Grand Island Municipal Golf Course
$$/ⓞⓞⓞⓞ	Heritage Hills Golf Course
$/ⓞⓞⓞ	Highlands Golf Course
$/ⓞⓞⓞ	Himark Golf Course
$/ⓞⓞⓞ	Holmes Park Golf Course
$$/ⓞⓞⓞ	Indian Creek Golf Course
$/ⓞⓞⓞ	Meadowlark Hills Golf Course
$$/ⓞⓞⓞ	The Pines Country Club
$/ⓞⓞⓞ	Pioneers Golf Course
$/ⓞⓞⓞ	Quail Run Golf Course
$$/ⓞⓞⓞ	Tiburon Golf Club
$$/ⓞⓞⓞⓞ	Woodland Hills Golf Course

Nebraska Golf Guide

McCook and Kearney

SP ⓞⓞⓞⓞ DEAL STATE	**Heritage Hills Golf Course** McCook. (308) 345-5032 18 holes. Par 72/72. Yards: 6,715/5,445 Year-round. High: May–Sept.	Greens: $$ Carts: $ Rating: 71.5/72.3 Slope: 130/119	J
P ⓞⓞⓞ DEAL	**Meadowlark Hills Golf Course** 30th Ave., Kearney. (308) 233-3265 18 holes. Par 71/72. Yards: 6,485/4,967 Year-round.	Greens: $ Carts: $ Rating: 70.4/68.2 Slope: 119/112	L T S J

Grand Island Area

P ⓞⓞⓞ DEAL	**Grand Island Municipal Golf Course** Shady Bend Rd., Grand Island. (308) 385-5340 18 holes. Par 72/72. Yards: 6,752/5,487 Year-round. High: Apr.–Sept.	Greens: $ Carts: $ Rating: 71.3/70.5 Slope: 118/104	S J
P ⓞⓞ	**Indianhead Golf Course** Husker Hwy., Grand Island. (308) 381-4653 18 holes. Par 72/72. Yards: 6,597/5,664 Year-round. High: May–Sept.	Greens: $ Carts: $ Rating: 70.9/71.9 Slope: 122/117	W T S J

Lincoln Area

P ⓞⓞⓞ	**Highlands Golf Course** N.W. 12th St., Lincoln. (402) 441-6081	Greens: $ Carts: $	W T S J

DEAL	18 holes. Par 72/72. Yards: 7,021/5,280 Year-round. High: Apr.–Oct.	Rating: 72.5/69.4 Slope: 119/111
P ☺☺☺ DEAL	**Himark Golf Course** Pioneers Blvd., Lincoln. (402) 488-7888 18 holes. Par 71/70. Yards: 6,746/4,959 Mar.–Nov. High: June–Aug.	Greens: $ W L T S J Carts: $ Rating: 72.6/68.8 Slope: 122/111
P ☺☺☺ DEAL	**Holmes Park Golf Course** S. 70th St., Lincoln. (402) 441-8960 18 holes. Par 72/74. Yards: 6,805/6,054 Jan.–Dec. High: May–June.	Greens: $ W S J Carts: $$ Rating: 72.2/73.8 Slope: 120/126
P ☺☺	**Mahoney Golf Course** Adams St., Lincoln. (402) 441-8969 18 holes. Par 72/72. Yards: 6,300/5,607 Apr.–Nov. High: June–Aug.	Greens: $ S J Carts: $ Rating: 72.3/70.3 Slope: 125/118
P ☺☺☺ DEAL	**Pioneers Golf Course** W. Van Dorn, Lincoln. (402) 441-8966 18 holes. Par 71/74. Yards: 6,478/5,771 Year-round. High: June–Aug.	Greens: $ W T S J Carts: $$ Rating: 67.3/73.5 Slope: 108/122
P ☺☺☺☺ DEAL STATE	**Woodland Hills Golf Course** Eagle. (402) 475-4653 18 holes. Par 71/71. Yards: 6,592/4,945 Year-round. High: July–Aug.	Greens: $$ W L R S J Carts: $ Rating: 72.6/70.3 Slope: 132/122

Omaha Area

P ☺☺	**Applewood Golf Course** S. 99th St., Omaha. (402) 444-4656 18 holes. Par 72/72. Yards: 6,916/6,014 Year-round. High: May–Sept.	Greens: $ W S J Carts: $ Rating: 72.4/74.6 Slope: 121/126
SP ☺☺	**Ashland Country Club** Ashland. (402) 944-3388 18 holes. Par 70/74. Yards: 6,337/5,606 Mar.–Oct. High: June–Sept.	Greens: $–$$ Carts: $ Rating: 70.0/69.8 Slope: 112/112
P ☺☺	**Benson Park Golf Course** N. 72nd St., Omaha. (402) 444-4626 18 holes. Par 72/78. Yards: 6,814/6,085 Mar.–Dec. High: May–Sept.	Greens: $ S J Carts: $ Rating: 72.1/73.4 Slope: 120/121
P ☺☺☺ DEAL	**Indian Creek Golf Course** W. Maple Rd., Elkhorn. (402) 289-0900 27 holes. Par 72/72/72. Yards: 7,154/7,041/5,040 Mar.–Nov. High: June–July	Greens: $–$$ T S Carts: $ Rating: 74.1/73.9/68.1 Slope: 128/131112
P ☺☺	**The Knolls Golf Course** Sahler St., Omaha. (402) 493-1740 18 holes. Par 71/71. Yards: 6,300/5,111 Year-round. High: Apr.–Oct.	Greens: $ T S J Carts: $ Rating: 69.8/69.8 Slope: 123/NA
P ☺☺	**Miracle Hill Golf and Tennis Center** N. 120th St., Omaha. (402) 498-0220 18 holes. Par 70/70. Yards: 6,412/5,069 Year-round. High: May–Aug.	Greens: $–$$ T S Carts: $ Rating: 71.0/69.0 Slope: 129/117
SP ☺☺☺ DEAL	**The Pines Country Club** N. 286th St., Valley. (402) 359-4311 18 holes. Par 72/72. Yards: 6,650/5,370 Mar.–Oct. High: May–Aug.	Greens: $–$$ W S J Carts: $ Rating: 69.9/70.2 Slope: 117/117
P ☺☺☺	**Quail Run Golf Course** South 5th St., Columbus. (402) 564-1313	Greens: $ W T S J Carts: $

DEAL	18 holes. Par 72/72. Yards: 7,024/5,147	Rating:	73.1/70.1	
	Apr.–Oct. High: June–Aug.	Slope:	127/114	
SP	**Tiburon Golf Club**	Greens:	$–$$	W S J
☺☺☺	S. 168th St., Omaha. (402) 895-2688	Carts:	$	
DEAL	27 holes. Par 72/72/72. Yards: 7,005/6,530/5,435	Rating:	74.0/72.0/72.0	
	Mar.–Nov. High: June–Sept.	Slope:	131/126/127	

North Dakota

The best of North Dakota includes **Edgewood** in Fargo, a course that dates back to 1915 and provides the polished experience of a successful old-timer.

In Minot, the **Minot Country Club** is another venerable beauty, much greener than the prairies that surround it. In Bismarck, the **Riverwood Golf Club**, with its river and woods, is a tight challenge.

Most golf courses in North Dakota are open from April through October or November. Peak rates are typically in effect from June through early September.

Golf U.S.A. Leader Board: Best Public Courses in North Dakota

☺☺☺	Edgewood Golf Course
☺☺☺	Minot Country Club
☺☺☺	Riverwood Golf Club

Golf U.S.A. Leader Board: Best Deals in North Dakota

$/☺☺☺	Bois de Sioux Golf Club
$/☺☺☺	Edgewood Golf Course
$/☺☺☺	Prairie West Golf Course
$/☺☺☺	Riverwood Golf Club
$/☺☺☺	Souris Valley Golf Club

Eastern North Dakota

P	**Bois de Sioux Golf Club**	Greens:	$	W
☺☺☺	North 4th St., Wahpeton. (701) 642-3673	Carts:	$	
DEAL	18 holes. Par 72/72. Yards: 6,675/5,500	Rating:	71.3/71.4	
	Apr.–Nov. High: Apr.–Sept.	Slope:	122/119	
P	**Edgewood Golf Course**	Greens:	$	W T S J
☺☺☺	2nd St. N., Fargo. (701) 232-2824	Carts:	$	
DEAL	18 holes. Par 71/71. Yards: 6,400/5,176	Rating:	69.7/69.6	
STATE	Apr.–Nov. High: July–Aug.	Slope:	125/123	
P	**Manvel Golf Course**	Greens:	$	J
	County Rd. 5, Manvel. (701) 696-8268	Carts:	$	
☺☺	*Pioneer/Settler's*	Rating:	70.6/69.1	
	18 holes. Par 72/72. Yards: 6,357/5,146	Slope:	126/118	
	Apr.–Oct. High: Apr.–June			
P	**Rose Creek Golf Course**	Greens:	$	T S J
☺☺	Rose Creek Pkwy., Fargo. (701) 235-5100	Carts:	$	
	18 holes. Par 72/72. Yards: 6,616/5,062	Rating:	71.4/68.8	
	Apr.–Nov. High: May–Aug.	Slope:	123/114	

Western North Dakota

P	**Heart River Golf Course**	Greens:	$	J
☺☺	Dickinson. (701) 225-9412	Carts:	$	

	18 holes. Par 72/71. Yards: 6,652/5,583 Mar.–Oct. High: June–Aug.	Rating: Slope:	70.8/71.0 125/116	
SP ☺☺☺ STATE	**Minot Country Club** Hwy. 15 W., Minot. (701) 839-6169 18 holes. Par 72/72. Yards: 6,586/6,269 Apr.–Nov. High: June–Aug.	Greens: Carts: Rating: Slope:	$$ $ 69.9/70.0 124/115	W
P ☺☺☺ DEAL	**Prairie West Golf Course** Long Spur Trail, Mandan. (701) 667-3222 18 holes. Par 72/72. Yards: 6,681/5,452 Apr.–Oct. High: July–Aug.	Greens: Carts: Rating: Slope:	$ $ 71.6/70.1 127/118	S J
P ☺☺☺ DEAL STATE	**Riverwood Golf Club** Bismarck Dr., Bismarck. (701) 222-6462 18 holes. Par 72/72. Yards: 6,956/5,196 Apr.–Oct. High: June–Sept.	Greens: Carts: Rating: Slope:	$ $ 73.0/68.9 130/118	S J
P ☺☺☺ DEAL	**Souris Valley Golf Club** 14th Ave. S.W., Minot. (701) 838-4112 18 holes. Par 72/72. Yards: 6,759/5,216 Apr.–Sept. High: June–Aug.	Greens: Carts: Rating: Slope:	$ $ 71.4/69.0 115/112	T S J
P ☺	**Tom O'Leary Golf Course** N. Washington St., Bismarck. (701) 222-6462 18 holes. Par 68/68. Yards: 5,800/4,026 Apr.–Oct. High: June–Sept.	Greens: Carts: Rating: Slope:	$ $ 65.0/62.3 110/97	S J

Ohio

There are 14 courses at 12 clubs on the *Golf U.S.A.* Best list for public courses in Ohio.

Five of the favorites are in and around Cleveland: **Avalon**, **Fowler's**, **Pine Hills**, **Quail Hollow**, and **Windmill Lakes**. In nearby Akron are **Hawks Nest** and **Yankee Run**. Near Toledo is **Maumee Bay State Park**. In central Ohio near Columbus, golfers in search of the best should consider **Eagle Sticks** and **Indian Springs**.

Down south near Cincinnati are **Shaker Run** and **The Vineyard**, which is built on the rolling ground of a former vineyard.

The courses that also earn a spot on the *Golf U.S.A.* Deals list are Eagle Sticks, Hawks Nest, Indian Springs, Maumee Bay State Park, Pine Hills, The Vineyard, Windmill Lakes, and Yankee Run.

Many courses in Ohio are open year-round, with peak rates and conditions from about May to October. Other courses, including many in the snowbelts near Cleveland, operate from March through November, with peak rates in effect for the summer.

Golf U.S.A. Leader Board: Best Public Courses in Ohio

☺☺☺☺ Avalon Lakes Golf Course
☺☺☺☺ Eagle Sticks Golf Course
☺☺☺☺ Fowler's Mill Golf Club (Blue, White, Red)
☺☺☺☺ Hawks Nest Golf Club
☺☺☺☺ Indian Springs Golf Club
☺☺☺☺ Maumee Bay State Park Golf Course
☺☺☺☺ Pine Hills Golf Club
☺☺☺☺ Quail Hollow Resort

○○○○ Shaker Run Golf Course
○○○○ The Vineyard Golf Course
○○○○ Windmill Lakes Golf Club
○○○○ Yankee Run Golf Course

Golf U.S.A. Leader Board: Best Deals in Ohio

$/○○○	Apple Valley Golf Club
$/○○○	Beaver Creek Meadows Golf Course
$/○○○	Blackhawk Golf Club
$/○○○	Blacklick Woods Golf Course (Gold)
$/○○○	Blue Ash Golf Course
$$/○○○	Champions Golf Course
$$/○○○	Chardon Lakes Golf Club
$/○○○	Chippewa Golf Club
$/○○○	Country Acres Golf Club
$$/○○○○	Eagle Sticks Golf Course
$$/○○○	Fox Den Golf Club
$/○○○	Foxfire Golf Club
$$/○○○	Glenview Golf Course
$$/○○○	Granville Golf Club
$$/○○○○	Hawks Nest Golf Club
$$/○○○	Heatherwoode Golf Club
$/○○○	Hemlock Springs Golf Club
$/○○○	Hilliard Lakes Golf Club
$$/○○○	Hinckley Hills Golf Course
$$/○○○	Hueston Woods State Park Golf Resort
$$/○○○○	Indian Springs Golf Club
$/○○○	Ironwood Golf Club
$/○○○	J.E. Good Park Golf Club
$/○○○	Manakiki Golf Club
$$/○○○○	Maumee Bay State Park Golf Course
$/○○○	Miami Whitewater Forest Golf Course
$/○○○	Mill Creek Park Golf Course (North, South)
$/○○○	Mohican Hills Golf Club
$$/○○○	Orchard Hills Golf and Country Club
$/○○○	Pebble Creek Golf Club
$/○○○○	Pine Hills Golf Club
$$/○○○	Pipestone Golf Club
$$/○○○	Raintree Country Club
$/○○○	Reid Park Memorial Golf Course (North)
$$/○○○	Royal American Links Golf Club
$/○○○	Salem Hills Golf and Country Club
$/○○○	Sharon Woods Golf Course
$/○○○	Shelby Oaks Golf Club
$$/○○○	Skyland Pines Golf Club
$/○○○	Sleepy Hollow Golf Course
$$/○○○	Tam O'Shanter Golf Course (Dales, Hills)

$/☺☺☺   Thunderbird Hills Golf Club
$$/☺☺☺   Turnberry Golf Course
$$/☺☺☺   Valleywood Golf Club
$$/☺☺☺☺   The Vineyard Golf Course
$/☺☺☺   Weatherwax Golf Course (Valleyview, Highlands, Woodside,
               Meadows)
$$/☺☺☺☺   Windmill Lakes Golf Club
$$/☺☺☺   Woodland Golf Club
$$/☺☺☺☺   Yankee Run Golf Course
$/☺☺☺   Zoar Village Golf Club

Ohio Golf Guide

Toledo Area

SP ☺☺☺ DEAL	**Ironwood Golf Club** W. Leggett, Wauseon. (419) 335-0587 18 holes. Par 72/74. Yards: 6,965/5,306 Mar.–Nov. High: June–Aug.	Greens: $ Carts: $ Rating: 72.2/69.2 Slope: 112/106	W

P ☺☺☺☺ DEAL STATE	**Maumee Bay State Park Golf Course** Park Rd. 2, Oregon. (419) 836-9009 18 holes. Par 72/72. Yards: 6,941/5,221 Apr.–Oct. High: May–Aug.	Greens: $$$ Carts: Incl. Rating: 73.3/70.5 Slope: 129/118	W L T S

SP ☺☺	**Sycamore Hills Golf Club** W. Hayes Ave., Fremont. (419) 332-5716 18 holes. Par 70/72. Yards: 6,221/5,076 Mar.–Dec. High: Apr.–Sept.	Greens: $ Carts: $ Rating: 67.3/66.3 Slope: 110/107	W L S J

SP ☺☺☺ DEAL	**Valleywood Golf Club** Airport Hwy., Swanton. (419) 826-3991 18 holes. Par 71/73. Yards: 6,364/5,588 Feb.–Dec.	Greens: $–$$ Carts: $ Rating: 69.6/71.6 Slope: 115/121	S

Cleveland Area

R ☺☺☺☺ STATE	**Avalon Lakes Golf Course** Warren. (330) 856-8898 18 holes. Par 71/71. Yards: 7,001/5,324 April–Oct. High: June–Aug.	Greens: $$$ Carts: Incl. Rating: 74.3/70.1 Slope: 127/116	W L T

P ☺☺	**Big Met Golf Club** Valley Pkwy., Fairview Park. (216) 331-1070 18 holes. Par 72/74. Yards: 6,125/5,870 Year-round. High: May–Aug.	Greens: $ Carts: $ Rating: 68.0/72.0 Slope: 108/113	L S J

P ☺☺	**Briarwood Golf Course** Edgerton Rd., Broadview Heights. (216) 237-5271 *Ben/Glens/Lochs* 27 holes. Par 71/72/71. Yards: 6,405/6,985/6,500 Year-round. High: May–Sept.	Greens: $–$$ Carts: $ Rating: 70.1/72.8/70.8 Slope: 117/125/117	W L T S J

P ☺☺	**Chapel Hills Golf Course** Austinburg Rd., Ashtabula. (216) 997-3791 18 holes. Par 72/72. Yards: 5,971/4,507 Year-round. High: June–Sept.	Greens: $ Carts: $ Rating: 68.6/65.7 Slope: 112/104	W S J

P ☺☺☺ DEAL	**Chardon Lakes Golf Club** South St., Chardon. (216) 285-4653 18 holes. Par 71/73. Yards: 6,789/5,685 Apr.–Nov. High: June–Sept.	Greens: $–$$ Carts: $ Rating: 73.1/66.6 Slope: 135/111	L S J

P ☺☺	**Deer Track Golf Club** Leavitt Rd., Elyria. (216) 986-5881	Greens: $ Carts: $	L S

| | 18 holes. Par 71/71. Yards: 6,410/5,191 | Rating: | 70.3/68.7 |
| | Year-round. High: Apr.–Oct. | Slope: | 104/115 |

P
☺☺
Dorlon Park Golf Course
18000 Station Rd., Columbia Station. (216) 236-8234
18 holes. Par 72/74. Yards: 7,154/5,691
Apr.–Nov. High: May–Sept.

Greens: $ S
Carts: $
Rating: 74.0/67.4
Slope: 131/118

P
☺☺
The Elms Country Club
Manchester Rd. S.W., N. Lawrence. (216) 833-2668
27 holes. Par 72/71/73. Yards: 6,545/6,054/6,633
Feb.–Dec. High: May–Sept.

Greens: $ W L T S J
Carts: $$
Rating: 69.9/67.7/70.1
Slope: 110/104/108

P
☺☺☺☺
STATE
Fowler's Mill Golf Club
Rockhaven Rd., Chesterland. (440) 729-7569
Lake-River/Lake-Maple/River-Maple
27 holes. Par 72/72/72. Yards: 7,002/6,591/6,381
Mar.–Nov. High: June–Aug.

Greens: $$$$ W L T S J
Carts: Incl.
Rating: 74.7/72.1/70.7
Slope: 136/128/125

P
☺☺☺
DEAL
Hemlock Springs Golf Club
Cold Springs Rd., Geneva. (216) 466-4044
18 holes. Par 72/72. Yards: 6,812/5,453
Apr.–Nov. High: June–Aug.

Greens: $ W L T S J
Carts: $
Rating: 72.8/73.8
Slope: 123/115

P
☺☺☺
DEAL
Hilliard Lakes Golf Club
Hilliard Rd., Westlake. (440) 871-9578
18 holes. Par 72/75. Yards: 6,665/5,611
Mar.–Nov. High: May–Sept.

Greens: $ W S J
Carts: $$
Rating: 70.7/74.0
Slope: 124/118

P
☺☺☺
DEAL
Hinckley Hills Golf Course
Hinckley. (216) 278-4861
18 holes. Par 73/72. Yards: 6,704/5,478
Apr.–Nov. High: May–Sept.

Greens: $$
Carts: $
Rating: 73.6/70.1
Slope: 125

P
☺☺☺
DEAL
Manakiki Golf Club
Eddy Rd., Willoughby. (440) 942-2500
18 holes. Par 72/72. Yards: 6,625/5,390
Mar.–Dec. High: May–Sept.

Greens: $ L S J
Carts: $
Rating: 71.4/72.8
Slope: 128/121

P
☺☺
Maple Ridge Golf Course
Rte. 45, Austinburg. (440) 969-1368
18 holes. Par 70/70. Yards: 6,001/5,400
Mar.–Nov. High: June–Aug.

Greens: $ S J
Carts: $
Rating: 68.5/69.0
Slope: 118/118

SP
☺☺☺
DEAL
Orchard Hills Golf and Country Club
Caves Rd., Chesterland. (216) 729-1963
18 holes. Par 72/72. Yards: 6,409/5,651
Apr.–Nov. High: May–Sept.

Greens: $–$$
Carts: $$
Rating: 71.1/72.6
Slope: 126/122

P
☺
Pine Brook Golf Course
N. Durkee Rd., Grafton. (440) 748-2939
18 holes. Par 70/70. Yards: 6,062/5,225
Year-round. High: June–Aug.

Greens: $ W S J
Carts: $
Rating: 66.8/68.9
Slope: 110/109

P
☺☺☺☺
DEAL
STATE
Pine Hills Golf Club
W. 130th St., Hinckley. (330) 225-4477
18 holes. Par 72/73. Yards: 6,482/5,685
Apr.–Nov. High: May–Oct.

Greens: $$
Carts: $
Rating: 71.2/74.3
Slope: 124/126

P
☺☺
Powderhorn Golf Course
Bates Rd., Madison. (216) 428-5951
18 holes. Par 70/70. Yards: 6,004/4,881
Year-round. High: Apr.–Oct.

Greens: $ W L T S J
Carts: $
Rating: 68.5/67.6
Slope: 117/113

R
Quail Hollow Resort
Concord Hambden Rd., Concord. (440) 497-1100

Greens: $$$$–$$$$$ L T
Carts: Incl.

Ohio Golf Guide

☺☺☺☺ STATE	*Devlin Course/Von Hagge* 18 holes. Par 72/72. Yards: 6,712/4,389 Apr.–Nov. High: June–Aug.	Rating: Slope:	72.6/65.7 127/107

☺☺☺☺ *Weiskopf/Morrish Course*
18 holes. Par 71/71. Yards: 6,872/5,166
Apr.–Nov. High: June–Aug.
Rating: 73.9/70.2
Slope: 130/128

P
☺☺
Ridge Top Golf Course
Tower Rd., Medina. (330) 725-5500
18 holes. Par 71/71. Yards: 6,211/4,968
Mar.–Nov. High: June–Aug.
Greens: $ W L S J
Carts: $
Rating: 70.0/67.9
Slope: 109/106

R
☺☺☺
Sawmill Creek Golf and Racquet Club
Cleveland Rd., W. Huron. (419) 433-3789
18 holes. Par 71/74. Yards: 6,813/5,416
Apr.–Oct. High: June–Sept.
Greens: $$$ L
Carts: $$
Rating: 72.3/70.6
Slope: 128/120

P
☺☺
Shawnee Hills Golf Course
Egbert Rd., Bedford. (440) 232-7184
18 holes. Par 71/73. Yards: 6,160/6,029
Mar.–Dec. High: May–Sept.
Greens: $ L S J
Carts: $
Rating: 68.7/72.5
Slope: 112/116

P
☺☺☺
DEAL
Sleepy Hollow Golf Course
Brecksville Rd., Brecksville. (440) 526-4285
18 holes. Par 71/73. Yards: 6,630/5,715
Mar.–Dec. High: May–Sept.
Greens: $ W L S J
Carts: $
Rating: 71.9/73.5
Slope: 124/128

P

☺☺
Sweetbriar Golf
Jaycox Rd., Avon Lake. (216) 933-9001
First/Second/Third
27 holes. Par 72/72/70. Yards: 6,491/6,292/6,075
Year-round. High: May–Oct.
Greens: $ L T S J
Carts: $
Rating: 68.7/67.5/66.3
Slope: 106/104/100

P

☺☺☺
DEAL
Tam O'Shanter Golf Course
Hills and Dales Rd. N.W., Canton. (330) 477-5111
Dales Course
18 holes. Par 70/75. Yards: 6,569/5,384
Mar.–Dec. High: Apr.–Oct.
Greens: $$ W L R S J
Carts: $
Rating: 70.4/69.7
Slope: 110/109

☺☺☺
DEAL
Hills Course
18 holes. Par 70/75. Yards: 6,385/5,076
Rating: 69.1/67.4
Slope: 104/102

P
☺☺
Thunder Hill Golf Club
Griswold Rd., S. Madison. (216) 298-3473
18 holes. Par 72/72. Yards: 7,223/5,524
Apr.–Dec. High: May–Sept.
Greens: $$ L S J
Carts: Incl.
Rating: 78.0/NA
Slope: 151/127

P

☺☺☺
DEAL
Thunderbird Hills Golf Club
Mudbrook Rd., Huron. (419) 433-4552
North Course
18 holes. Par 72/74. Yards: 6,464/5,993
Year-round. High: Apr.–Nov.
Greens: $ W L S
Carts: $
Rating: 70.3/74.0
Slope: 109/121

P
☺☺☺☺
DEAL
STATE
Wind Mill Lakes Golf Club
St. Rte. 14, Ravenna. (330) 297-0440
18 holes. Par 70/70. Yards: 6,936/5,368
Mar.–Nov. High: May–Sept.
Greens: $$–$$$ W L T S J
Carts: Incl.
Rating: 73.8/70.4
Slope: 128/115

Akron Area

R
☺☺
Atwood Resort Golf Course
Lodge Rd., Dellroy. (330) 735-2211
18 holes. Par 70/70. Yards: 6,152/4,188
Year-round. High: June–Sept.
Greens: $ W L R S J
Carts: $
Rating: 65.7/62.0
Slope: 102/91

P
☺☺
Brandywine Country Club
Akron Peninsula Rd., Peninsula. (330) 657-2525
Greens: $$ W T S
Carts: $$

Ohio Golf Guide

	18 holes. Par 72/75. Yards: 7,100/5,625	Rating: 70.2/70.5
	Year-round. High: May–Sept.	Slope: 113/113

P
😊😊😊
DEAL

Chippewa Golf Club
Shank Rd., Doylestown. (330) 658-6126
18 holes. Par 71/71. Yards: 6,273/4,877
Year-round. High: Apr.–Oct.

Greens: $ W L S J
Carts: $
Rating: 69.1/67.0
Slope: 109/103

P
😊😊😊
DEAL

Fox Den Golf Club
Call Rd., Stow. (330) 673-3443
18 holes. Par 72/72. Yards: 6,447/5,473
Mar.–Nov. High: May–Sept.

Greens: $–$$ W L S J
Carts: $
Rating: 70.4/69.0
Slope: 115/114

P
😊😊😊😊
DEAL
STATE

Hawks Nest Golf Club
E. Pleasant Home Rd., Creston. (330) 435-4611
18 holes. Par 72/72. Yards: 6,680/4,767
Apr.–Dec. High: May–Oct.

Greens: $$ W S J
Carts: $
Rating: 71.5/67.9
Slope: 124/110

P
😊😊😊
DEAL

J.E. Good Park Golf Club
Nome Ave., Akron. (330) 864-0020
18 holes. Par 71/71. Yards: 6,663/4,926
Mar.–Dec. High: May–Oct.

Greens: $ L S J
Carts: $
Rating: 72.0/69.1
Slope: 123/115

P
😊😊

Maplecrest Golf Course
Tallmadge Rd., Kent. (330) 673-2722
18 holes. Par 71/72. Yards: 6,412/5,285
Mar.–Oct. High: May–Aug.

Greens: $–$$ W S
Carts: $
Rating: 69.2/67.8
Slope: 108/113

P
😊😊😊
DEAL

Mohican Hills Golf Club
Cty. Rd. 1950, Jeromesville. (330) 368-3303
18 holes. Par 72/72. Yards: 6,536/4,976
Apr.–Dec. High: June–Aug.

Greens: $ W
Carts: $
Rating: 71.1/67.9
Slope: 122/112

P

😊😊

Oak Knolls Golf Club
St. Rte. 43, Kent. (330) 673-6713
High Course
18 holes. Par 71/72. Yards: 6,483/5,279
Mar.–Nov. High: May–Sept.

Greens: $–$$ W L S J
Carts: $
Rating: 70.5/69.7
Slope: 111/107

😊😊

West Course
18 holes. Par 72/72. Yards: 6,373/5,681

Rating: 69.0/71.4
Slope: 112/112

P
😊😊

Pine Valley Golf Club
Reimer Rd., Wadsworth. (330) 335-3375
18 holes. Par 72/74. Yards: 6,097/5,268
Mar.–Nov. High: May–Oct.

Greens: $ W S J
Carts: $
Rating: 68.5/67.9
Slope: 109/107

P
😊😊

Raccoon Hill Golf Course
Judson Rd., Kent. (330) 673-2111
18 holes. Par 71/71. Yards: 6,068/4,650
Mar.–Nov. High: May–Sept.

Greens: $–$$ W L T S
Carts: $
Rating: 69.2/67.0
Slope: 115/106

SP
😊😊😊
DEAL

Raintree Country Club
Mayfair Rd., Uniontown. (330) 699-3232
18 holes. Par 72/72. Yards: 6,811/5,030
Year-round. High: Apr.–Oct.

Greens: $–$$ W L T S J
Carts: $
Rating: 73.0/68.5
Slope: 127/114

SP
😊😊😊
DEAL

Skyland Pines Golf Club
Columbus Rd. N.E., Canton. (330) 454-5131
18 holes. Par 72/72. Yards: 6,467/5,279
Feb.–Dec. High: Apr.–Nov.

Greens: $–$$ L
Carts: $
Rating: 69.6/69.6
Slope: 113/113

P
😊😊

Sunnyhill Golf Club
Sunnybrook Rd., Kent. (330) 673-1785
18 holes. Par 71/72. Yards: 6,289/5,083
Mar.–Jan. High: May–Aug.

Greens: $ W L S J
Carts: Incl.
Rating: 68.4/68.4
Slope: 110/107

Ohio Golf Guide

P	**Tannenhauf Golf Club**	Greens:	$	W L S J
☺☺	McCallum Ave., Alliance. (330) 823-4402	Carts:	$	
	18 holes. Par 72/72. Yards: 6,666/5,455	Rating:	71.0/70.8	
	Apr.–Oct. High: June–Aug.	Slope:	111/109	

P	**Valley View Golf Club**	Greens:	$	W S
☺☺	Cuyahoga St., Akron. (330) 928-9034	Carts:	$	
	27 holes. Par 72/72/72. Yards: 6,293/6,183/6,168	Rating:	68.7/68.2/68.2	
	Mar.–Nov. High: May–Sept.	Slope:	111/111/109	

P	**Yankee Run Golf Course**	Greens:	$$	W L S J
☺☺☺☺	Warren Sharon Rd., Brookfield. (330) 448-8096	Carts:	$	
DEAL	18 holes. Par 70/73. Yards: 6,501/5,140	Rating:	70.7/69.0	
STATE	Mar.–Nov. High: May–Sept.	Slope:	119/109	

P	**Zoar Village Golf Club**	Greens:	$	W S
☺☺☺	Zoar. (330) 874-4653	Carts:	$	
DEAL	18 holes. Par 72/72. Yards: 6,535/5,235	Rating:	70.7/69.7	
	Mar.–Dec. High: July–Aug.	Slope:	117/115	

Youngstown Area

P	**Beaver Creek Meadows Golf Course**	Greens:	$	W L
☺☺☺	St. Rte. 7, Lisbon. (330) 385-3020	Carts:	$	
DEAL	18 holes. Par 72/72. Yards: 6,410/5,350	Rating:	68.7/68.5	
	Year-round. High: June–Aug.	Slope:	113	

P	**Countryside Golf Course**	Greens:	$	W L S J
☺	Struthers Colt Rd., Lowellville. (330) 755-0016	Carts:	$	
	18 holes. Par 71/71. Yards: 6,461/5,399	Rating:	70.5/70.1	
	Mar.–Nov. High: May–Aug.	Slope:	NA	

P	**Mill Creek Park Golf Course**	Greens:	$	L S J
	Boardman. (330) 758-7926	Carts:	$	
☺☺☺	*North Course*	Rating:	71.9/74.4	
DEAL	18 holes. Par 70/74. Yards: 6,412/5,889	Slope:	124/117	
	Apr.–Nov. High: June–Sept.			

☺☺☺	*South Course*	Rating:	71.8/74.9	
DEAL	18 holes. Par 70/75. Yards: 6,511/6,102	Slope:	129/118	

SP	**Salem Hills Golf and Country Club**	Greens:	$	W S J
☺☺☺	Salem-Warren Rd., Salem. (330) 337-8033	Carts:	$	
DEAL	18 holes. Par 72/72. Yards: 7,146/5,597	Rating:	74.3/69.7	
	Apr.–Nov. High: June–Aug.	Slope:	126/114	

P	**Tamer Win Golf and Country Club**	Greens:	$	L S J
☺	Niles Cortland Rd. N.E., Cortland. (330) 637-2881	Carts:	$	
	18 holes. Par 71/74. Yards: 6,275/5,623	Rating:	68.8/68.8	
	Apr.–Nov. High: May–Sept.	Slope:	112/112	

Northwest Ohio

SP	**Country Acres Golf Club**	Greens:	$	S J
☺☺☺	St. Rte. 694, Ottawa. (419) 532-3434	Carts:	$	
DEAL	18 holes. Par 72/72. Yards: 6,464/4,961	Rating:	69.9/67.9	
	Year-round. High: June–Sept.	Slope:	126/113	

P	**Hickory Grove Golf Club**	Greens:	$	W T
☺☺	St. Rte. 294, Harpster. (614) 496-2631	Carts:	$$	
	18 holes. Par 72/76. Yards: 6,874/5,376	Rating:	71.0/69.1	
	Mar.–Nov. High: June–Aug.	Slope:	108/105	

P	**Miami Shores Golf Course**	Greens:	$	
☺	Rutherford Dr., Troy. (937) 335-4457	Carts:	$	
	18 holes. Par 72/73. Yards: 6,200/5,417	Rating:	67.6/68.5	
	Mar.–Dec. High: June–Aug.	Slope:	97/101	

Ohio Golf Guide

P   **Shelby Oaks Golf Club**   Greens: $ T
☺☺☺   Sidney Freyburg Rd., Sidney. (937) 492-2883   Carts: $
DEAL   27 holes. Par 72/72/72. Yards: 6,651/6,650/6,561   Rating: 71.2/60.9/70.5
  Mar.–Nov. High: May–Oct.   Slope: 115/115/115

Dayton Area

P   **Heatherwoode Golf Club**   Greens: $$ S J
☺☺☺   Heatherwoode Blvd., Springboro. (937) 748-3222   Carts: $
DEAL   18 holes. Par 71/71. Yards: 6,730/5,069   Rating: 72.9/69.8
  Mar.–Dec. High: June–Aug.   Slope: 138/127

P   **Kitty Hawk Golf Club**   Greens: $ L S J
  Chuck Wagner Lane, Dayton. (937) 237-5424   Carts: $
☺   *Eagle Course*   Rating: 72.8/74.3
  18 holes. Par 72/75. Yards: 7,115/5,887   Slope: 120/123
  Year-round. High: Apr.–Oct.

P   **Larch Tree Golf Course**   Greens: $ L J
☺☺   N. Snyder Rd., Trotwood. (937) 854-1951   Carts: $
  18 holes. Par 72/74. Yards: 6,982/5,912   Rating: 71.5/72.7
  Year-round. High: May–Aug.   Slope: 107/107

P   **Pipestone Golf Club**   Greens: $$ T
☺☺☺   Benner Rd., Miamisburg. (937) 866-4653   Carts: $
DEAL   18 holes. Par 72/72. Yards: 6,939/5,207   Rating: 72.1/69.2
  Mar.–Dec. High: June–Aug.   Slope: 137/121

P   **Sugar Isle Golf Country**   Greens: $ W S
☺☺   Dayton-Lakeview Rd., New Carlisle. (937) 845-8699   Carts: $
  18 holes. Par 72/72. Yards: 6,754/5,636   Rating: 70.2/71.1
  Year-round. High: June–Sept.   Slope: 107/110

Columbus Area

P   **Apple Valley Golf Club**   Greens: $ S
☺☺☺   Howard. (617) 397-7664   Carts: $
DEAL   18 holes. Par 72/75. Yards: 6,946/6,116   Rating: 72.4/74.9
  Year-round. High: June–Aug.   Slope: 116/120

P   **Bent Tree Golf Club**   Greens: $$$ W L T S
☺☺☺   Bent Tree Rd., Sunbury. (614) 965-5140   Carts: Incl.
  18 holes. Par 72/72. Yards: 6,805/5,280   Rating: 72.1/69.2
  Year-round. High: May–Oct.   Slope: 122/113

P   **Blackhawk Golf Club**   Greens: $ L T S
☺☺☺   Dustin Rd., Galena. (614) 965-1042   Carts: $
DEAL   18 holes. Par 71/71. Yards: 6,550/4,726   Rating: 70.6/66.0
  Mar.–Dec. High: May–Oct.   Slope: 115/106

P   **Blacklick Woods Golf Course**   Greens: $ W L T
  E. Livingston Ave., Reynoldsburg. (614) 861-3193   Carts: $
☺☺☺   *Gold Course*   Rating: 71.9/68.0
DEAL   18 holes. Par 72/72. Yards: 6,819/5,018   Slope: 124/116
  Year-round. High: May–Aug.

P   **Champions Golf Course**   Greens: $$ W L T S J
☺☺☺   Westerville Rd., Columbus. (614) 645-7111   Carts: $$
DEAL   18 holes. Par 70/72. Yards: 6,555/5,427   Rating: 71.2/71.2
  Year-round. High: May–Oct.   Slope: 127/127

SP   **Cherokee Hills Golf Course**   Greens: $ W L J
☺☺   Bellefontaine. (513) 599-3221   Carts: $
  18 holes. Par 72/72. Yards: 6,448/5,327   Rating: 70.8/70.3
  Mar.–Dec. High: May–Sept.   Slope: 115/108

P   **Darby Creek Golf Course**   Greens: $–$$ W T S
☺☺   Orchard Rd., Marysville. (513) 349-7491   Carts: $

		Greens:		
	18 holes. Par 72/72. Yards: 7,054/5,245	Rating:	72.7/68.1	
	Year-round. High: May–Oct.	Slope:	124/114	

R ◎◎
Deer Creek State Park Golf Course
Waterloo Rd., Mt. Sterling. (614) 869-3088
18 holes. Par 72/72. Yards: 7,134/5,611
Year-round. High: May–Sept.

Greens: $ W L R T S J
Carts: $
Rating: 73.7/71.7
Slope: 113/113

P ◎◎◎◎
DEAL
STATE
Eagle Sticks Golf Course
Maysville Pike, Zanesville. (740) 454-4900
18 holes. Par 70/70. Yards: 6,508/4,233
Apr.–Dec. High: June–Aug.

Greens: $$$ W L T S J
Carts: Incl.
Rating: 70.1/63.7
Slope: 120/96

P ◎
Estate Club Golf Course
Tschopp Rd., Lancaster. (614) 654-4444
18 holes. Par 71/72. Yards: 6,405/5,680
Year-round. High: June–Sept.

Greens: $ W T S J
Carts: $
Rating: 69.9/NA
Slope: 115/113

P ◎◎
Flagstone Golf Club
St. Rte. 38, Marysville. (513) 642-1816
18 holes. Par 72/72. Yards: 6,323/5,111
Year-round. High: May–Sept.

Greens: $ W L T S
Carts: $
Rating: 69.6/68.9
Slope: 115/113

P
◎◎◎
DEAL
Foxfire Golf Club
St. Rte. 104, Lockbourne. (614) 224-3694
The Foxfire Course
18 holes. Par 72/72. Yards: 6,891/5,175
Year-round. High: June–Sept.

Greens: $ L
Carts: $
Rating: 72.7/69.1
Slope: 118/112

P
◎◎◎
DEAL
Granville Golf Club
Neward Rd., Granville. (614) 587-4653
18 holes. Par 71/72. Yards: 6,612/5,413
Year-round. High: Apr.–Nov.

Greens: $-$$
Carts: $
Rating: 71.3/70.6
Slope: 126/121

P ◎◎
Hiawatha Golf Course
Beech St., Mt. Vernon. (614) 393-2886
18 holes. Par 72/74. Yards: 6,721/5,100
Year-round. High: 6,721/5,100

Greens: $ W L T S J
Carts: $
Rating: 71.5/68.5
Slope: 104

P
◎◎◎◎
DEAL
STATE
Indian Springs Golf Club
St. Rte. 161, Mechanicsburg. (937) 834-2111
Reserve-Woods/Lakes-Woods/Lakes-Reserve
27 holes. Par 72/72/72. Yards: 7,182/7,064/6,834
Mar.–Oct. High: June–Aug.

Greens: $$$ W L T
Carts: Incl.
Rating: 73.8/73.6/73.6
Slope: 126/124/125

SP ◎◎
Kings Mill Golf Course
Berringer Rd., Waldo. (614) 726-2626
18 holes. Par 70/74. Yards: 6,099/5,318
Mar.–Dec. High: May–Oct.

Greens: $ L J
Carts: $
Rating: 68.1/68.8
Slope: 106/109

P ◎◎
Licking Springs Trout and Golf Club
Horns Hill Rd., Newark. (614) 366-2770
18 holes. Par 72/72. Yards: 6,400/5,035
Year-round. High: May–Sept.

Greens: $ L S
Carts: $
Rating: 70.0/68.7
Slope: 116/107

SP ◎◎
Mill Creek Golf Club
Penn Rd., Ostrander. (614) 666-7711
18 holes. Par 72/72. Yards: 6,300/5,100
Mar.–Dec. High: June–Sept.

Greens: $ W L S J
Carts: $
Rating: 69.0/70.0
Slope: 111/111

P ◎◎
Oxbow Golf and Country Club
Cty. Rd. 85, Belpre. (614) 423-6771
18 holes. Par 71/72. Yards: 6,558/4,858
Year-round. High: May–July

Greens: $ S J
Carts: $
Rating: 70.9/68.8
Slope: 117/109

P ◎◎◎
Pebble Creek Golf Club
Algire Rd., Lexington. (419) 884-3434

Greens: $ W S J
Carts: $

Ohio Golf Guide

DEAL	18 holes. Par 72/72. Yards: 6,554/5,195 Mar.–Oct.	Rating: Slope:	70.8/69.1 117/113	
P 😊😊	**Raccoon International Golf Club** Worthington Rd. S.W., Granville. (614) 587-0921 18 holes. Par 72/72. Yards: 6,586/6,094 Year-round. High: Mar.–Oct.	Greens: Carts: Rating: Slope:	$ Incl. NA 125/116	W L
P 😊😊😊 DEAL	**Reid Park Memorial Golf Course** Bird Rd., Springfield. (513) 324-7725 *North Course* 18 holes. Par 72/72. Yards: 6,760/5,035 Year-round. High: May–Oct.	Greens: Carts: Rating: Slope:	$ $ 72.5/69.2 130/118	T
😊😊	*South Course* 18 holes. Par 72/72. Yards: 6,500/4,895	Rating: Slope:	69.0/66.5 110/102	
SP 😊😊	**Rickenbacker Golf Club** Airbase Rd., Groveport. (614) 491-5000 18 holes. Par 72/72. Yards: 7,003/5,476 Year-round. High: June–Aug.	Greens: Carts: Rating: Slope:	$ $ 72.6/71.2 117/117	W L T S J
SP 😊😊😊 DEAL	**Royal American Links Golf Club** Miller Paul Rd., Galena. (614) 965-1215 18 holes. Par 72/72. Yards: 6,839/5,172 Mar.–Dec. High: June–Sept.	Greens: Carts: Rating: Slope:	$$ $ 72.8/70.1 128/111	W L T S J
P 😊😊	**St. Albans Golf Club** Northridge Rd. N.W., Alexandria. (614) 924-8885 18 holes. Par 71/71. Yards: 6,717/5,498 Mar.–Dec. High: May–Aug.	Greens: Carts: Rating: Slope:	$ $$ 71.6/71.1 112/112	L S
P 😊😊	**Table Rock Golf Club** Wilson Rd., Centerburg. (614) 625-6859 18 holes. Par 72/72. Yards: 6,694/5,565 Year-round. High: May–Sept.	Greens: Carts: Rating: Slope:	$ $ 70.7/71.3 113/NA	W L T S
P 😊😊😊 DEAL	**Turnberry Golf Course** Pickerington. (614) 645-2582 27 holes. Par 72/73. Yards: 6,757/5,440 Year-round. High: Apr.–Oct.	Greens: Carts: Rating: Slope:	$–$$ $ 71.1/68.8 114/110	W L T S J
P 😊😊	**Whetstone Golf and Swim Club** Marion Mt. Gilead Rd., Caledonia. (614) 383-4343 18 holes. Par 72/72. Yards: 6,674/5,023 Apr.–Oct. High: Apr.–Oct.	Greens: Carts: Rating: Slope:	$ $$ 71.7/73.6 120/111	W S
P 😊😊😊 DEAL	**Woodland Golf Club** Swisher Rd., Cable. (937) 653-8875 18 holes. Par 71/71. Yards: 6,407/4,965 Year-round. High: Mar.–Sept.	Greens: Carts: Rating: Slope:	$–$$ $ 70.1/67.7 116/110	W L T S J

Cincinnati Area

P 😊😊😊 DEAL	**Blue Ash Golf Course** Cooper Rd., Cincinnati. (513) 745-8577 18 holes. Par 72/72. Yards: 6,643/5,125 Year-round. High: May–Sept.	Greens: Carts: Rating: Slope:	$–$$ $$ 72.6/70.3 127/124	L S J
P 😊😊	**California Golf Course** Kellogg Ave., Cincinnati. (513) 231-4734 18 holes. Par 70/71. Yards: 6,216/5,626 Year-round. High: Apr.–Sept.	Greens: Carts: Rating: Slope:	$ $ 70.0/71.4 116/113	L
P 😊😊	**Fairfield Golf Club** John Gray Rd., Fairfield. (513) 867-5385 18 holes. Par 70/70. Yards: 6,250/4,900 Mar.–Dec. High: June–Aug.	Greens: Carts: Rating: Slope:	$ $$ 69.5/68.8 123/113	S J

Ohio Golf Guide

P ☺☺☺ DEAL	**Glenview Golf Course** Springfield Pike, Cincinnati. (513) 771-1747 18 holes. Par 72/72. Yards: 6,965/5,091 Year-round. High: May–Sept.	Greens: Carts: Rating: Slope:	$$ $$ 72.3/69.9 132/110	L S J
R ☺☺☺	**The Golf Center at Kings Island** Mason. (513) 398-7700 *North/South/West* 27 holes. Par 71/72/72. Yards: 6,130/6,146/6,242 Mar.–Dec. High: May–Sept.	Greens: Carts: Rating: Slope:	$$–$$$$ $ 70.3/69.6/69.9 130/128/126	W L T
P ☺☺	**Hickory Woods Golf Course** Hickory Woods Dr., Loveland. (513) 575-3900 18 holes. Par 70/71. Yards: 6,105/5,115 Year-round. High: Apr.–Aug.	Greens: Carts: Rating: Slope:	$–$$ $ 70.1/69.4 119/113	L S J
R ☺☺☺ DEAL	**Hueston Woods State Park Golf Resort** Brown Rd., Oxford. (513) 523-8081 18 holes. Par 72/72. Yards: 7,005/5,176 Apr.–Oct. High: June–Sept.	Greens: Carts: Rating: Slope:	$–$$ $$ 73.1/68.9 132/NA	W T S
P ☺☺☺ DEAL	**Miami Whitewater Forest Golf Course** Mt. Hope Rd., Harrison. (513) 367-4627 18 holes. Par 72/72. Yards: 6,780/5,093 Mar.–Dec. High: June–Aug.	Greens: Carts: Rating: Slope:	$ $ 71.9/68.8 120/104	S J
P ☺☺	**Neumann Golf Course** Bridgetown Rd., Cincinnati. (513) 574-1320 *White/Blue/Red* 27 holes. Par 71/70/71. Yards: 6,218/6,115/5,989 Year-round. High: Mar.–Nov.	Greens: Carts: Rating: Slope:	$ $ 69.0/68.5/68.4 109/109/111	L S J
P ☺☺	**Pleasant Hill Golf Club** Hankins Rd., Middletown. (513) 539-7220 18 holes. Par 71/71. Yards: 6,586/4,723 Year-round. High: June–July	Greens: Carts: Rating: Slope:	$ $ 70.2/65.6 111/101	W L S J
P ☺☺☺☺ STATE	**Shaker Run Golf Course** Greentree Rd., Lebanon. (513) 727-0007 *Woodlands/Lakeside/Meadow* 27 holes. Par 72/72/72. Yards: 7,064/6,862/7,120 Mar.–Dec. High: May–Oct.	Greens: Carts: Rating: Slope:	$$$$ Incl. 74.0/73.7/74.1 138/136/134	W L T S J
P ☺☺☺ DEAL	**Sharon Woods Golf Course** Cincinnati. (513) 769-4325 18 holes. Par 70/70. Yards: 6,652/5,288 Mar.–Dec. High: Apr.–Sept.	Greens: Carts: Rating: Slope:	$ $ 72.3/68.3 131/116	S J
P ☺☺☺☺ DEAL STATE	**The Vineyard Golf Course** Nordyke Rd., Cincinnati. (513) 474-3007 18 holes. Par 71/71. Yards: 6,789/4,747 Mar.–Nov. High: May–Sept.	Greens: Carts: Rating: Slope:	$$ $ 72.8/67.9 132/114	S J
P ☺☺☺ DEAL	**Weatherwax Golf Course** Mosiman Rd., Middletown. (513) 425-7886 *Valleyview/Highlands* 18 holes. Par 72/72. Yards: 6,756/5,253 Year-round. High: Apr.–Nov.	Greens: Carts: Rating: Slope:	$ $ 72.0/69.8 120/114	S J
☺☺☺ DEAL	*Woodside/Meadows* 18 holes. Par 72/72. Yards: 7,174/5,669	Rating: Slope:	73.4/71.5 116/112	
P ☺☺	**Winton Woods Golf Club** W. Sharon Rd., Cincinnati. (513) 825-3770 18 holes. Par 72/72. Yards: 6,376/4,554 Mar.–Dec. High: May–Sept.	Greens: Carts: Rating: Slope:	$ $ 70.0/66.6 120/108	S J

South Dakota

The best of South Dakota's public courses may be the **Meadowbrook Golf Course** in Rapid City. It boasts flat fairways, the meandering Rapid Creek, and views of Mount Rushmore.

In Sioux Falls is **Willow Run**, where every hole presents a different challenge. In Yankton, about 50 miles to the southwest, is the worthy **Hillcrest**.

North in Aberdeen is **Moccasin Creek**, fair but challenging with lots of trees.

The good news is that all four of South Dakota's best also reside on the *Golf U.S.A.* Deals list.

Courses in South Dakota are generally open from April to November, with peak rates in effect in the summer months. Some courses are open year-round.

Golf U.S.A. Leader Board: Best Public Courses in South Dakota

ＯＯＯＯ   Hillcrest Golf and Country Club
ＯＯＯＯ   Meadowbrook Golf Course
ＯＯＯＯ   Moccasin Creek Country Club
ＯＯＯＯ   Willow Run Golf Course

Golf U.S.A. Leader Board: Best Deals in South Dakota

$/ＯＯＯ   Fox Run Golf Course
$$/ＯＯＯＯ   Hillcrest Golf and Country Club
$/ＯＯＯ   Meadowbrook Golf Course
$$/ＯＯＯＯ   Moccasin Creek Country Club
$/ＯＯＯ   Two Rivers Golf Course
$/ＯＯＯＯ   Willow Run Golf Course

South Dakota Golf Guide

Rapid City and Western South Dakota

P ＯＯ	**Hillsview Golf Club** Hwy. 34, Pierre. (605) 224-6191 18 holes. Par 72/72. Yards: 6,828/5,470 Apr.–Oct. High: June–Aug.	Greens: Carts: Rating: Slope:	$ $ 71.4/73.9 122/119	J
P ＯＯＯ BEST DEAL	**Meadowbrook Golf Course** Jackson Blvd., Rapid City. (605) 394-4191 18 holes. Par 72/72. Yards: 7,054/5,603 Year-round. High: Apr.–Oct.	Greens: Carts: Rating: Slope:	$ $ 73.0/71.1 138/130	L T S J

Sioux City and Eastern South Dakota

P ＯＯ	**Elmwood Golf Course** W. Russell, Sioux Falls. (605) 367-7092 18 holes. Par 72/72. Yards: 6,850/5,750 Apr.–Oct. High: May–Aug.	Greens: Carts: Rating: Slope:	$ $ 72.1/72.0 129/125	
P ＯＯＯ DEAL	**Fox Run Golf Course** W. 27th St., Yankton. (605) 668-5205 18 holes. Par 72/72. Yards: 6,731/5,209 Mar.–Oct. High: May–Aug.	Greens: Carts: Rating: Slope:	$ $ 70.8/68.6 122/115	W
SP ＯＯＯＯ DEAL STATE	**Hillcrest Golf and Country Club** Mulberry, Yankton. (605) 665-4621 18 holes. Par 72/73. Yards: 6,874/5,726 Apr.–Nov. High: June–Aug.	Greens: Carts: Rating: Slope:	$$–$$$ $ 72.2/72.2 130/130	W

South Dakota Golf Guide

P	**Lakeview Golf Course**	Greens:	$	J
☺☺	N. Ohlman, Mitchell. (605) 996-1424	Carts:	$	
	18 holes. Par 72/73. Yards: 6,670/5,808	Rating:	71.3/72.6	
	Apr.–Oct. High: June–Aug.	Slope:	124/125	
SP	**Moccasin Creek Country Club**	Greens:	$$	
☺☺☺☺	40th Ave. N.E., Aberdeen. (605) 226-0989	Carts:	$	
DEAL	18 holes. Par 72/73. Yards: 7,096/5,408	Rating:	72.5/69.4	
STATE	Apr.–Nov. High: June–Aug.	Slope:	138/127	
P	**Prairie Green Golf Course**	Greens:	$–$$	W T
☺☺	E. 69th St., Sioux Falls. (605) 339-6076	Carts:	$	
	18 holes. Par 72/72. Yards: 7,179/5,250	Rating:	74.2/70.2	
	Apr.–Oct. High: May–Sept.	Slope:	134/122	
P	**Two Rivers Golf Course**	Greens:	$	L
☺☺☺	S. Oak Tree Lane, Dakota Dunes. (605) 232-3241	Carts:	$	
DEAL	18 holes. Par 70/70. Yards: 5,820/5,246	Rating:	69.0/71.0	
	Apr.–Oct. High: June–Sept.	Slope:	120/112	
P	**Watertown Municipal Golf Course**	Greens:	$	T
☺☺	S. Lake Dr., Watertown. (605) 886-3618	Carts:	$	
	18 holes. Par 72/78. Yards: 5,220/5,858	Rating:	67.4/71.3	
	Apr.–Oct. High: May–Sept.	Slope:	106/114	
P	**Willow Run Golf Course**	Greens:	$$	W T S J
☺☺☺☺	E. Hwy. 38/42, Sioux Falls. (605) 335-5900	Carts:	$	
DEAL	18 holes. Par 71/71. Yards: 6,500/4,895	Rating:	71.1/68.7	
STATE	Mar.–Nov. High: May–Oct.	Slope:	127/119	

West Virginia

The gem of West Virginia is the spectacular **Greenbrier** in White Sulphur Springs; the Greenbrier Course is the best of three there, although the venerable Old White Course, designed in 1910, is still a major favorite.

In second place in the state is the **Hawthorne Valley Golf Course**, a hilly modern course near the ski mountain at Snowshoe. The **Glade Springs Resort** in Daniels, south of Beckley, is a wide-open course, especially difficult in the wind.

The **Lakeview Resort** in Morgantown lies next to the Greenbrier and has its own woodsy, narrow challenge along Cheat Lake.

Mountain-region and snowbelt courses in West Virginia usually operate from April to November, with peak rates in the summer months. Elsewhere in the state many courses are open year-round, also with summertime peak rates.

The lovely Greenbrier in White Sulphur Springs operates year-round with room rates (including breakfast and dinner) as high as $300 weekdays and $350 weekends per person in the high season of April 1 through October 31; that same superior room drops in price to $216 from November 1 through March 31. Less-opulent accommodations are available from a high-season rate of $235 per person to a low-season rate of about $190 per night.

Golf greens fees are free to guests in December, January, and February. In March and November, greens fees are about $45, and in the high season—April through October—it'll cost you $90 to tee it up at the Greenbrier.

Golf U.S.A. Leader Board: Best Public Courses in West Virginia

☺☺☺☺ Glade Springs Resort
☺☺☺☺ The Greenbrier (Greenbrier, Old White)
☺☺☺☺ Hawthorne Valley Golf Course
☺☺☺ Lakeview Resort & Conference Center (Lakeview)

Golf U.S.A. Leader Board: Best Deals in West Virginia

$$/☺☺☺ Cacapon State Park Resort Golf Course
$$/☺☺☺ Canaan Valley State Park Resort Golf Course
$/☺☺☺ Greenhills Country Club
$$/☺☺☺ Lakeview Resort & Conference Center (Lakeview)
$$/☺☺☺ Locust Hill Golf Course
$$/☺☺☺ Oglebay Park (Speidel)
$$/☺☺☺ The Woods Resort

West Virginia Golf Guide

Wheeling

P	**Oglebay Park**	Greens: $$	W R
	Oglebay Park, Wheeling. (304) 243-4050	Carts: $	
☺	*Crispin Course*	Rating: 66.6/68.4	
	18 holes. Par 71/71. Yards: 5,760/5,100	Slope: 103/108	
	Mar.–Nov. High: May–Aug.		
☺☺☺	*Speidel Course*	Rating: 72.7/72.0	
DEAL	18 holes. Par 71/71. Yards: 7,000/5,515	Slope: 126/120	

Clarksburg Area

R	**Canaan Valley State Park Resort Golf Course**	Greens: $$	S
☺☺☺	Rte. 1, Davis. (304) 866-4121	Carts: $$	
DEAL	18 holes. Par 72/72. Yards: 6,982/5,820	Rating: 73.4/71.8	
	Apr.–Nov. High: June–Aug.	Slope: 125/115	
R	**Lakeview Resort & Conference Center**	Greens: $$-$$$	W L R J
	Rte. 6, Morgantown. (304) 594-2011	Carts: $	
☺☺☺	*Lakeview Course*	Rating: 72.8/71.8	
DEAL	18 holes. Par 72/72. Yards: 6,800/5,432	Slope: 130/118	
STATE	Year-round. High: June–Sept.		
☺☺	*Mountainview Course*	Rating: 70.7/69.4	
	18 holes. Par 72/72. Yards: 6,447/5,242	Slope: 119/122	
SP	**Locust Hill Golf Course**	Greens: $-$$	W L T
☺☺☺	St. Andrews Dr., Charles Town. (304) 728-7300	Carts: $	
DEAL	18 holes. Par 72/72. Yards: 7,005/5,112	Rating: 73.5/72.0	
	Year-round. High: May–Oct.	Slope: 128/120	
R	**The Woods Resort**	Greens: $$	W L T S J
	Mtn. Lake Road, Hedgesville. (304) 754-7222	Carts: $	
☺☺☺	*Mountain View Golf Course*	Rating: 72.2/68.5	
DEAL	18 holes. Par 72/71. Yards: 6,608/4,900	Slope: 121/107	
	Year-round. High: Apr.–Sept.		

Berkeley Springs/Northeast Region

R	**Cacapon State Park Resort Golf Course**	Greens: $-$$	L S
☺☺☺	Rte. 1, Berkeley Springs. (304) 258-1022	Carts: $	
DEAL	18 holes. Par 72/72. Yards: 6,940/5,510	Rating: 72.3/70.8	
	Year-round. High: Apr.–Oct.	Slope: 126/118	

Charleston Area

SP	**Greenhills Country Club**	Greens:	$	W L R
☺☺☺	Rte. 56, Ravenswood. (304) 273-3396	Carts:	$	
DEAL	18 holes. Par 72/74. Yards: 6,056/5,018	Rating:	68.6/69.0	
	Year-round. High: Apr.–Oct.	Slope:	119/108	

P	**Lavalette Golf Club**	Greens:	$	
☺☺	Lynn Oak Dr., Lavalette. (304) 525-7405	Carts:	$	
	18 holes. Par 71/71. Yards: 6,262/5,257	Rating:	69.5/72.6	
	Year-round. High: May–Sept.	Slope:	118/120	

SP	**Scarlet Oaks Country Club**	Greens:	$$
☺☺	Dair Rd., Poca. (304) 755-8079	Carts:	Incl.
	18 holes. Par 72/72. Yards: 6,700/5,036	Rating:	72.3/69.3
	Mar.–Dec. High: June–July	Slope:	129/109

Beckley Area

R	**Glade Springs Resort**	Greens:	$$$-$$$$	L R J
☺☺☺☺	Lake Dr., Daniels. (304) 763-2050	Carts:	Incl.	
STATE	18 holes. Par 72/72. Yards: 6,841/4,884	Rating:	73.2/69.2	
	Year-round. High: May–Oct.	Slope:	139/124	

R	**The Greenbrier**	Greens:	$$$$$-$$$$$$	L R
	White Sulphur Springs. (304) 536-1110	Carts:	Incl.	
☺☺☺☺	*Greenbrier Course*	Rating:	73.1/70.3	
BEST	18 holes. Par 72/72. Yards: 6,675/5,095	Slope:	135/120	
	Mar.–Nov. High: Apr.–Oct.			

☺☺☺	*The Meadows Course*	Rating:	73.3/68.0
	18 holes. Par 71/71. Yards: 6,807/5,001	Slope:	130/111

☺☺☺☺	*Old White Course*	Rating:	72.1/69.7
STATE	18 holes. Par 70/70. Yards: 6,652/5,179	Slope:	130/119

R	**Hawthorne Valley Golf Course**	Greens:	$$$-$$$$	W L R
☺☺☺☺	Snowshoe Dr., Snowshoe. (304) 572-1000	Carts:	Incl.	
STATE	18 holes. Par 72/72. Yards: 7,045/4,363	Rating:	75.5/65.3	
	May–Nov. High: July–Sept.	Slope:	142/120	

P	**Twin Falls State Park Golf Course**	Greens:	$-$$	W L S
☺☺	Mullens. (304) 294-4044	Carts:	Inquire	
	18 holes. Par 71/71. Yards: 6,382/5,202	Rating:	70.1/69.5	
	Year-round. High: June–Oct.	Slope:	122/112	

Wisconsin

Although few are national names, Wisconsin has more than its share of fine golf courses. Among the best are the River Course at the **Blackwolf Run Golf Club** in Kohler, about 50 miles north of Milwaukee, and **Brown Deer** in Milwaukee proper. Blackwolf Run Golf Club added Whistling Straits in 1999, joining the respected River Course, and Meadow Valleys Course. Blackwolf plans to open yet another 18-hole course in late 2000.

Also worth a trip are the Palmer and Trevino courses at **Geneva National Golf Club** in Lake Geneva, about 50 miles southwest of Milwaukee, and the Briar Patch Course and the Brute Course at the **Grand Geneva Resort and Spa** in Lake Geneva.

The tight woods challenge of **Old Hickory** is in Beaver Dam, about 30 miles north of Madison. The **Brown County Golf Course** is in Oneida, about seven miles west of Green Bay.

Courses in and around Oshkosh include the acclaimed Links Course and the almost-as-wonderful Woodlands at **The Golf Courses of Lawsonia** in Green Lake, some 35 miles southwest of Oshkosh. There's also the **Lake Arrowhead Golf Course** in Nekoosa, south of Wisconsin Rapids.

In the northern portion of the state there are the superb sand traps and the famed "Flower Hole" No. 16 (with nearly 100,000 flowers planted in beds around the green) at **Sentryworld** in Stevens Point. Also worth a visit are the East and West pair at **Nemadji** in Superior, the **New Richmond Golf Club** in New Richmond, and the **Northwood Golf Course** in Rhinelander. Some 90 miles south of Duluth is the challenging **Turtleback Golf and Country Club** in Rice Lake.

Near Madison is the difficult **University Ridge Golf Course** in Verona, with rolling hills, lots of water, and plenty of woods.

Joint residents of the *Golf U.S.A.* Best and *Golf U.S.A.* Deals lists are Lake Arrowhead, New Richmond, Northwood, and Turtleback. New Richmond added a new 9-hole links course in 1999.

Courses in Wisconsin generally are open from April to October, with peak rates from June to early September.

Golf U.S.A. Leader Board: Best Public Courses in Wisconsin

◎◎◎◎ Blackwolf Run Golf Club (Meadow Valleys, River)
◎◎◎◎ Brown County Golf Course
◎◎◎◎ Brown Deer Golf Course
◎◎◎◎ Geneva National Golf Club (Palmer, Trevino)
◎◎◎◎ The Golf Courses of Lawsonia (Links, Woodlands)
◎◎◎◎ Grand Geneva Resort and Spa (Brute, Briar Patch)
◎◎◎◎ Lake Arrowhead Golf Course
◎◎◎◎ Nemadji Golf Course (East, West)
◎◎◎◎ New Richmond Golf Club
◎◎◎◎ Northwood Golf Course
◎◎◎◎ Old Hickory Golf Club
◎◎◎◎ Sentryworld Golf Course
◎◎◎◎ Turtleback Golf and Country Club
◎◎◎◎ University Ridge Golf Course

Golf U.S.A. Leader Board: Best Deals in Wisconsin

$$/◎◎◎◎ Brighton Dale Golf Club (Blue Spruce, White Birch)
$/◎◎◎ Dretzka Park Golf Course
$$/◎◎◎ Eagle River Golf Course
$$/◎◎◎ Evergreen Golf Club
$/◎◎◎ Ives Grove Golf Links
$/◎◎◎ Johnson Park Golf Course
$$/◎◎◎ Kettle Hills Golf Course (Ponds, Woods)
$$/◎◎◎◎ Lake Arrowhead Golf Course
$/◎◎◎ Maplecrest Country Club
$$/◎◎◎ Mascoutin Golf Club
$/◎◎◎ Mill Run Golf Course
$/◎◎◎ Naga-Waukee Golf Course
$/◎◎◎◎ Nemadji Golf Course (East, West)

$$/☺☺☺☺	New Richmond Golf Club	
$$/☺☺☺☺	Northwood Golf Course	
$/☺☺☺	Oakwood Park Golf Course	
$$/☺☺☺	Petrifying Springs Golf Course	
$$/☺☺☺	Quit-Qui-Oc Golf Club	
$$/☺☺☺	Rainbow Springs Golf Club	
$$/☺☺☺	Reedsburg Country Club	
$$/☺☺☺	Riverside Golf Course	
$$/☺☺☺	Spooner Golf Club	
$/☺☺☺	Spring Valley Country Club	
$/☺☺☺☺	Turtleback Golf and Country Club	

Wisconsin Golf Guide

Duluth Area and Northern Wisconsin

P ☺☺☺ DEAL	**Eagle River Golf Course** McKinley Blvd., Eagle River. (715) 479-8111 18 holes. Par 71/72. Yards: 6,103/5,105 May–Oct. High: July–Aug.	Greens: Carts: Rating: Slope:	$$ $ 69.4/69.0 121/119	L R T J
P ☺☺☺ DEAL	**Mill Run Golf Course** Kane Rd., Eau Claire. (715) 834-1766 18 holes. Par 70/71. Yards: 6,065/4,744 Apr.–Oct.	Greens: Carts: Rating: Slope:	$ $ 68.7/66.6 116/109	S J
P ☺☺☺☺ DEAL STATE	**Nemadji Golf Course** N. 58th St. E., Superior. (715) 394-0266 *East/West* 18 holes. Par 72/72. Yards: 6,701/5,252 Apr.–Oct. High: June–Aug.	Greens: Carts: Rating: Slope:	$$ $$ 72.7/70.7 133/124	L T J
☺☺	*North/South* 18 holes. Par 71/71. Yards: 6,362/4,983	Rating: Slope:	69.7/67.8 120/114	
SP ☺☺☺☺ DEAL STATE	**New Richmond Golf Club** 180th Ave., New Richmond. (715) 246-6724 18 holes. Par 72/73. Yards: 6,713/5,488 Apr.–Oct. High: June–Aug.	Greens: Carts: Rating: Slope:	$$ $ 72.5/71.1 136/129	W S
P ☺☺☺☺ DEAL STATE	**Northwood Golf Course** Hwy. 8 W., Rhinelander. (715) 282-6565 18 holes. Par 72/72. Yards: 6,724/5,338 Apr.–Oct. High: June–Sept.	Greens: Carts: Rating: Slope:	$$ $$ 73.1/71.3 140/129	J
P ☺☺☺☺ BEST	**Sentryworld Golf Course** N. Michigan Ave., Stevens Point. (715) 345-1600 18 holes. Par 72/72. Yards: 6,951/5,108 Apr.–Oct. High: June–Aug.	Greens: Carts: Rating: Slope:	$$$$ Incl. 74.4/71.0 142/126	L T J
SP ☺☺☺ DEAL	**Spooner Golf Club** Spooner. (715) 635-3580 18 holes. Par 71/72. Yards: 6,407/5,084 Apr.–Oct. High: June–Aug.	Greens: Carts: Rating: Slope:	$–$$ $ 70.9/68.8 128/117	W T
P ☺☺☺☺ DEAL STATE	**Turtleback Golf and Country Club** W. Allen Rd., Rice Lake. (715) 234-7641 18 holes. Par 71/71. Yards: 6,604/5,163 Apr.–Oct. High: June–Aug.	Greens: Carts: Rating: Slope:	$$ $ 72.0/70.6 129/120	W

Green Bay Area

P ☺☺☺☺ BEST	**Brown County Golf Course** Riverdale Dr., Oneida. (920) 497-1731 18 holes. Par 72/73. Yards: 6,749/5,801 Apr.–Oct. High: May–Aug.	Greens: Carts: Rating: Slope:	$$ $$ 72.1/72.7 133/127	S J

Wisconsin Golf Guide

P ☺☺	**Cherry Hills Golf Course** Dunn Rd., Sturgeon Bay. (920) 743-3240 18 holes. Par 72/72. Yards: 6,163/5,432 Apr.–Oct. High: June–Aug.	Greens: Carts: Rating: Slope:	$–$$ $ 69.2/71.0 121/122	W L T S J
P ☺☺	**Idlewild Golf Course** Sturgeon Bay. (920) 743-3334 18 holes. Par 72/76. Yards: 6,889/5,886 Apr.–Oct. High: June–Sept.	Greens: Carts: Rating: Slope:	$$ $ 72.7/73.4 130/128	T S J
P ☺☺	**Shawano Lake Golf Club** Lake Dr., Shawano. (715) 524-4890 18 holes. Par 71/71. Yards: 6,231/6,181 Apr.–Nov. High: June–Sept.	Greens: Carts: Rating: Slope:	$–$$ $–$$ 72.9/70.4 128/128	W R

Oshkosh Area

P ☺☺	**Chaska Golf Course** Hwys. 10 and 45, Appleton. (920) 757-5757 18 holes. Par 72/72. Yards: 6,854/5,847 Apr.–Nov. High: May–Aug.	Greens: Carts: Rating: Slope:	$ $$ 72.5/73.1 128/126	T S J
R ☺☺☺☺ BEST	**The Golf Courses of Lawsonia** S. Valley View Dr., Green Lake. (920) 294-3320 *Links Course* 18 holes. Par 72/71. Yards: 6,764/5,078 Apr.–Nov. High: June–Aug.	Greens: Carts: Rating: Slope:	$$$–$$$$ Incl. 72.8/65.2 130/115	L R T
☺☺☺☺ STATE	*The Woodlands* 18 holes. Par 72/72. Yards: 6,618/5,106	Rating: Slope:	71.5/69.1 129/120	
P ☺☺☺☺ DEAL STATE	**Lake Arrowhead Golf Course** Apache Lane, Nekoosa. (715) 325-2929 *The Pines* 18 holes. Par 72/72. Yards: 6,624/5,213 Apr.–Oct. High: May–Sept.	Greens: Carts: Rating: Slope:	$$$–$$$$ Incl. 72.1/70.1 132/122	L T
☺☺☺☺	*The Lakes* 18 holes. Par 72/72. Yards: 7,105/5,272	Rating: Slope:	74.8/71.0 140/124	
P ☺☺	**Lake Shore Golf Course** Punhoqua St., Oshkosh. (920) 235-6200 18 holes. Par 70/71. Yards: 6,030/5,162 Apr.–Nov. High: June–Aug.	Greens: Carts: Rating: Slope:	$ Inquire 68.2/69.4 120/119	S J

Key to Symbols

Rating: 1 to 4 Golf Balls

☺	Worth a Visit
☺☺	Above Average
☺☺☺	Exceptional
☺☺☺☺	Very Best

Course Type

P	Public
R	Resort
SP	Semiprivate

BEST	*Golf U.S.A.* Best American Courses
DEAL	*Golf U.S.A.* Best Golfing Deals
STATE	*Golf U.S.A.* Best in State

Price Ranges

$	<$20	Bargain
$$	$20–$39	Budget
$$$	$40–$59	Moderate
$$$$	$60–$79	Expensive
$$$$$	$80–$100	Very Expensive
$$$$$$	$100+	Exclusive

Discounts

W	Weekdays
L	Low Season
R	Resort Guests
T	Twilight
S	Seniors
J	Juniors

Wisconsin Golf Guide

| πP
☺☺☺
DEAL | **Mascoutin Golf Club**
Berlin. (920) 361-2360
18 holes. Par 72/73. Yards: 6,821/5,133
Apr.–Oct. High: May–Sept. | Greens:
Carts:
Rating:
Slope: | $$
$
72.8/69.9
130/122 | W L T S J |

Madison Area

| SP
☺☺ | **Baraboo Country Club**
Lake St., Baraboo. (608) 356-8195
18 holes. Par 72/72. Yards: 6,570/5,681
Apr.–Oct. High: June–Aug. | Greens:
Carts:
Rating:
Slope: | $$
$$
71.3/72.5
124/124 | W L T |

| R
☺☺ | **Devil's Head Resort and Convention Center**
Bluff Rd., Merrimac. (608) 493-2251
18 holes. Par 73/73. Yards: 6,725/5,141
Apr.–Oct. High: June–Aug. | Greens:
Carts:
Rating:
Slope: | $$
Incl.
71.6/64.4
127/113 | L T |

| P
☺☺ | **Evansville Country Club**
Cemetery Rd., Evansville. (608) 882-6524
18 holes. Par 72/72. Yards: 6,559/5,366
Apr.–Oct. High: June–Aug. | Greens:
Carts:
Rating:
Slope: | $
$$
71.0/70.3
127/122 | L J |

| SP
☺☺☺
DEAL | **Reedsburg Country Club**
Hwy. 33, Reedsburg. (608) 524-6000
18 holes. Par 72/73. Yards: 6,300/5,324
Mar.–Nov. High: June–Aug. | Greens:
Carts:
Rating:
Slope: | $$
$
70.5/70.3
129/124 | T |

| P
☺☺☺
DEAL | **Riverside Golf Course**
Janesville. (608) 757-3080
18 holes. Par 72/72. Yards: 6,508/5,147
Apr.–Nov. High: June–Aug. | Greens:
Carts:
Rating:
Slope: | $–$$
$
70.7/68.9
123/116 | W S J |

| P
☺☺☺ | **Trappers Turn Golf Club**
Wisconsin Dells. (608) 253-7000
18 holes. Par 72/72. Yards: 6,550/5,013
Apr.–Oct. High: July–Aug. | Greens:
Carts:
Rating:
Slope: | $$–$$$
Incl.
72.0/69.5
131/122 | W L R T |

| P
☺☺☺☺
STATE | **University Ridge Golf Course**
County Trunk Pd., Verona. (608) 845-7700
18 holes. Par 72/72. Yards: 6,888/5,005
Apr.–Oct. High: May–Sept. | Greens:
Carts:
Rating:
Slope: | $$$–$$$$
$
73.2/68.9
142/121 | L T J |

| P

☺☺ | **Yahara Hills Golf Course**
East Broadway, Madison. (608) 838-3126
East Course
18 holes. Par 72/72. Yards: 7,200/6,115
Apr.–Nov. High: Apr.–Aug. | Greens:
Carts:
Rating:
Slope: | $
$$
71.9/73.4
116/118 | L S J |

| ☺☺ | *West Course*
18 holes. Par 72/72. Yards: 7,000/5,705 | Rating:
Slope: | 71.6/71.4
118/116 | |

Milwaukee Area

| R
☺☺☺ | **Abbey Springs Golf Course**
Fontana on Geneva Lake. (414) 275-6111
18 holes. Par 72/72. Yards: 6,466/5,439
Apr.–Nov. High: June–Sept. | Greens:
Carts:
Rating:
Slope: | $$$$
Incl.
71.4/72.4
133/129 | L J |

| R

☺☺☺☺
STATE | **Blackwolf Run Golf Club**
Riverside Dr., Kohler. (920)457-4446
Meadow Valleys Course
18 holes. Par 72/72. Yards: 7,142/5,065
Apr.–Oct. High: June–Sept. | Greens:
Carts:
Rating:
Slope: | $$$$–$$$$$$
$
74.7/69.5
143/125 | L T |

| ☺☺☺☺
BEST | *River Course*
18 holes. Par 72/72. Yards: 6,991/5,115 | Greens:
Carts:
Rating:
Slope: | $$$$$$
$
74.9/70.7
151/128 | |

Wisconsin Golf Guide

☺☺☺☺	*Whistling Straits* 18 holes. Par 72/72. Yards: 7,288/5,381	Greens: Carts: Rating: Slope:	$$$$$$ Not allowed 76.8/72.2 152/132
P ☺☺☺ DEAL	**Brighton Dale Golf Club** 248th Ave., Kansasville. (414) 878-1440 *White Birch Course* 18 holes. Par 72/72. Yards: 6,977/5,859 Apr.–Nov. High: May–Sept.	Greens: Carts: Rating: Slope:	$–$$ W L $$ 73.3/73.2 130/126
☺☺☺☺ DEAL	*Blue Spruce* 18 holes. Par 72/72. Yards: 6,687/5,628	Rating: Slope:	72.0/72.1 129/125
P ☺☺☺☺ STATE	**Brown Deer Golf Course** N. Green Bay Rd., Milwaukee. (414) 352-8080 18 holes. Par 71/73. Yards: 6,716/5,927 Year-round. High: June–Sept.	Greens: Carts: Rating: Slope:	$$–$$$$ W $$ 72.6/73.9 132/132
P ☺☺	**Browns Lake Golf Course** Burlington. (414) 763-6065 18 holes. Par 72/75. Yards: 6,449/6,206 Mar.–Oct. High: June–Sept.	Greens: Carts: Rating: Slope:	$ S J $ 70.2/75.8 122/132
P ☺☺☺	**Country Club of Wisconsin** Grafton. (414) 375-2444 18 holes. Par 72/72. Yards: 7,108/5,499 Apr.–Nov. High: May–Sept.	Greens: Carts: Rating: Slope:	$$–$$$ W T S J $ 74.7/72.4 137/126
P ☺☺☺ DEAL	**Dretzka Park Golf Course** W. Bradley Rd., Milwaukee. (414) 354-7300 18 holes. Par 72/72. Yards: 6,832/5,680 Mar.–Nov. High: May–Sept.	Greens: Carts: Rating: Slope:	$ T S J $ 70.8/74.6 124/123
P ☺☺☺ DEAL	**Evergreen Golf Club** Hwys. 12 and 67 N., Elkhorn. (414) 723-5722 *North/East/South* 27 holes. Par 72/72/72. Yards: 6,431/6,501/6,280 Mar.–Dec. High: May–Sept.	Greens: Carts: Rating: Slope:	$$ W L T J $ 71.7/71.7/70.8 128/127/125
R ☺☺☺☺ STATE	**Geneva National Golf Club** Lake Geneva. (414) 245-7000 *Palmer Course* 18 holes. Par 72/72. Yards: 7,177/4,892 Mar.–Oct. High: May–Sept.	Greens: Carts: Rating: Slope:	$$$$$–$$$$$$ W L R Incl. 74.7/68.5 140/122
☺☺☺☺ STATE	*Trevino Course* 18 holes. Par 72/72. Yards: 7,116/5,261	Rating: Slope:	74.2/70.2 135/124
☺☺☺☺	*Gary Player Course* (opening June 2000) 18 holes. Par 72/72. Yards: 7,039 (est.)/NA	Rating: Slope:	NA/NA NA/NA
R ☺☺☺ STATE	**Grand Geneva Resort and Spa** Hwys. 50 and 12, Lake Geneva. (414) 248-2556 *The Highlands* 18 holes. Par 71/71. Yards: 6,170/5,038 Apr.–Nov. High: May–Sept.	Greens: Carts: Rating: Slope:	$$$$$–$$$$$$ L T Incl. 71.7/65.0 133/117
☺☺☺☺ STATE	*The Brute Course* 18 holes. Par 72/74. Yards: 6,997/5,244	Rating: Slope:	73.8/71.9 136/131
P ☺☺	**Grant Park Golf Course** Hawthorne Ave., S. Milwaukee. (414) 762-4646 18 holes. Par 67/71. Yards: 5,174/5,147 Year-round. High: June–Aug.	Greens: Carts: Rating: Slope:	$ W L T S J $$ 64.1/68.4 110/103

Wisconsin Golf Guide

SP ☺☺	**Hartford Golf Club** Lee Rd., Hartford. (414) 673-2710 18 holes. Par 72/74. Yards: 6,406/5,850 Apr.–Dec. High: May–Sept.	Greens: Carts: Rating: Slope:	$$ $ 69.7/72.9 114/119	T

P ☺☺	**Hawthorne Hills Golf Club** Hwy. 1, Saukville. (414) 692-2151 18 holes. Par 72/72. Yards: 6,595/5,307 Apr.–Oct.	Greens: Carts: Rating: Slope:	$ $$ 70.5/69.1 118/114	S J

SP ☺☺	**Hillmoor Golf Club** Hwy. 50, Lake Geneva. (414) 248-4570 18 holes. Par 72/72. Yards: 6,350/5,360 Mar.–Dec. High: May–Oct.	Greens: Carts: Rating: Slope:	$$ $ 71.0/65.3 123/113	W L T J

P ☺☺☺ DEAL	**Ives Grove Golf Links** Washington Ave., Sturtevant. (414) 878-3714 *Red/White/Blue* 27 holes. Par 72/72/72. Yards: 6,965/6,985/7,000 Mar.–Nov. High: May–Sept.	Greens: Carts: Rating: Slope:	$ $$ 72.9/73.0/73.0 130/131/131	S J

P ☺☺☺ DEAL	**Johnson Park Golf Course** Northwestern Ave., Racine. (414) 637-2840 18 holes. Par 72/74/. Yards: 6,683/5,732 Apr.–Nov. High: June–Aug.	Greens: Carts: Rating: Slope:	$ $ 70.8/73.0 117/120	W L S J

P ☺☺☺ DEAL	**Kettle Hills Golf Course** Hwy. 167 W., Richfield. (414) 255-2200 *Ponds/Woods* 18 holes. Par 72/72. Yards: 6,787/5,171 Apr.–Nov. High: May–Sept.	Greens: Carts: Rating: Slope:	$$ $ 72.5/69.6 128/123	L T S J

R ☺☺	**Lake Lawn Golf Course** Hwy. 50 E., Delavan. (414) 728-7950 18 holes. Par 70/70. Yards: 6,418/5,215 Apr.–Oct. High: June–Aug.	Greens: Carts: Rating: Slope:	$$$ Incl. 69.2/64.1 120/107	W L R T S J

P ☺☺	**Lake Park Golf Course** Mequon Rd., Germantown. (414) 255-4200 *Red/White/Blue* 27 holes. Par 72/72/72. Yards: 6,979/6,781/6,642 Apr.–Oct. High: May–Sept.	Greens: Carts: Rating: Slope:	$–$$ $ 73.4/72.7/71.9 131/126/126	W L T S

SP ☺☺☺ DEAL	**Maplecrest Country Club** 18th St., Kenosha. (414) 859-2887 18 holes. Par 70/70. Yards: 6,396/5,056 Mar.–Nov. High: May–Sept.	Greens: Carts: Rating: Slope:	$ Inquire 70.9/71.0 121/124	L T S

P ☺☺☺ DEAL	**Naga-Waukee Golf Course** Maple Ave., Pewaukee. (414) 367-2153 18 holes. Par 72/72. Yards: 6,772/5,796 Apr.–Dec. High: May–Sept.	Greens: Carts: Rating: Slope:	$–$$ $ 71.8/72.9 125/125	W L T S J

P ☺☺☺ DEAL	**Oakwood Park Golf Course** W. Oak Ridge Rd., Franklin. (414) 281-6700 18 holes. Par 72/72. Yards: 6,972/6,179 Apr.–Oct. High: June–Aug.	Greens: Carts: Rating: Slope:	$ $$ 71.4/74.4 118/123	W S J

SP ☺☺☺☺ STATE	**Old Hickory Golf Club** Hwy. 33 E., Beaver Dam. (920) 887-7577 18 holes. Par 72/72. Yards: 6,721/5,372 Apr.–Oct. High: June–Aug.	Greens: Carts: Rating: Slope:	$$$ $ 72.6/71.2 129/124	L

R ☺☺	**Olympia Resort Golf Club** Royale Mile Rd., Oconomowoc. (414) 567-2577	Greens: Carts:	$$ $	L T S J

Wisconsin Golf Guide

	18 holes. Par 72/71. Yards: 6,458/5,735	Rating:	70.5/72.4
	Apr.–Nov. High: June–Sept.	Slope:	118/119

P	**Petrifying Springs Golf Course**	Greens:	$–$$	
☺☺☺	7th St., Kenosha. (414) 552-9052	Carts:	$	
DEAL	18 holes. Par 71/72. Yards: 5,979/5,588	Rating:	67.8/70.9	
	Apr.–Oct. High: July	Slope:	119/122	

P	**Quit-Qui-Oc Golf Club**	Greens:	$–$$	W L T S J
☺☺☺	Elkhart Lake. (414) 876-2833	Carts:	$	
DEAL	18 holes. Par 70/71. Yards: 6,178/5,134	Rating:	69.6/64.9	
	Apr.–Nov. High: May–Sept.	Slope:	119/109	

SP	**Rainbow Springs Golf Club**	Greens:	$$	W L T S J
☺☺☺	Hwy. 99, Mukwonago. (414) 363-4550	Carts:	Incl.	
DEAL	18 holes. Par 72/72. Yards: 6,914/5,382	Rating:	73.4/71.5	
	Apr.–Nov. High: June–Sept.	Slope:	132/123	

SP	**Rivermoor Country Club**	Greens:	$$	L T S
☺☺	Waterford Dr., Waterford. (414) 534-2500	Carts:	$	
	18 holes. Par 70/72. Yards: 6,508/5,147	Rating:	68.7/72.7	
	Apr.–Nov. High: June–Aug.	Slope:	121/125	

P	**Spring Valley Country Club**	Greens:	$	W L T S
☺☺☺	23913 Wilmot Rd., Salem. (414) 862-2626	Carts:	$	
DEAL	18 holes. Par 70/70. Yards: 6,354/5,135	Rating:	69.8/68.9	
	Year-round. High: Apr.–Nov.	Slope:	119/113	

SP	**Tuscumbia Golf Club**	Greens:	$$	L T S J
☺☺	Illinois Ave., Green Lake. (414) 294-3240	Carts:	$$	
	18 holes. Par 71/71. Yards: 6,301/5,619	Rating:	70.1/73.2	
	Apr.–Oct. High: June–Sept.	Slope:	122/123	

P	**Whitnall Park Golf Course**	Greens:	$$	L T S J
☺☺	S. 92nd St., Hales Corners. (414) 425-7931	Carts:	$	
	18 holes. Par 71/74. Yards: 6,216/5,778	Rating:	69.9/72.1	
	Apr.–Nov. High: June–Sept.	Slope:	117/119	

The South

Alabama	North Carolina
Arkansas	Oklahoma
Florida	South Carolina
Georgia	Tennessee
Louisiana	Texas
Mississippi	

Alabama

Among the crown jewels of Alabama, and among America's premier golf tours open to the public, is the Robert Trent Jones Golf Trail, a collection of 18 superb courses in seven Alabama cities. The largest golf course construction project ever attempted, the trail was initiated in the late 1980s with funding from the state pension fund.

The courses include Cambrian Ridge in Greenville, Grand National in Opelika, Hampton Cove in Huntsville, Highland Oaks in Dothan, Magnolia Grove in Mobile, Oxmoor Valley in Birmingham, and Silver Lakes near Anniston.

The **Cambrian Ridge Golf Club** offers 27 holes of championship-level golf at public-course rates in Greenville, 40 miles south of Montgomery. The Canyon and Sherling courses there are the best of the lot and also are *Golf U.S.A.* Deals.

The Grand National Golf Club in Opelika, east of Montgomery, is Alabama's golfing mall, with 54 holes of superior golf at the Lake, Links, and Short courses. And even better, they are on our list of *Golf U.S.A.* Deals. The Lake Course is considered one for the scrapbooks of traveling golfers. The Links Course is the toughest of the three at Grand National.

We also give high marks to the **Highland Oaks Golf Club** in Dothan, considered by some to be the most difficult challenge on the Jones Trail.

The Crossings and Falls courses at **Magnolia Grove Golf Club** in Semmes, west of Mobile, are handsome, challenging courses and *Golf U.S.A.* Deals.

Most golf courses and resorts in Alabama operate year-round, with high-season prices in effect from spring to fall. Some courses, though, may drop to a mid-season rate for the hottest months of summer.

The Robert Trent Jones Golf Trail offers three-, five-, and seven-day passes and other special deals. Contact any of the courses for information.

Golf U.S.A. Leader Board: Best Public Courses in Alabama

ⓖⓖⓖⓖ Cambrian Ridge Golf Club (Canyon, Sherling)
ⓖⓖⓖⓖ Grand National Golf Club (Lake, Links)
ⓖⓖⓖⓖ Highland Oaks Golf Club (Highland, Magnolia, Marshwood)
ⓖⓖⓖ   Lagoon Park Golf Course
ⓖⓖⓖⓖ Magnolia Grove Golf Club (Crossings, Falls)
ⓖⓖⓖ   Rock Creek Golf Club
ⓖⓖⓖⓖ Timbercreek Golf Club (Dogwood, Magnolia, Pines)

Golf U.S.A. Leader Board: Best Deals in Alabama

$$/ⓖⓖⓖ   Auburn Links
$$/ⓖⓖⓖⓖ   Cambrian Ridge Golf Club
$$/ⓖⓖⓖ   Eagle Point Golf Club
$$/ⓖⓖⓖⓖ   Grand National Golf Club
$$/ⓖⓖⓖ   Hampton Cove Golf Club
$/ⓖⓖⓖ   Lagoon Park Golf Course
$$/ⓖⓖⓖⓖ   Magnolia Grove Golf Club (Crossings, Falls)
$$/ⓖⓖⓖ   Silver Lakes Golf Course
$$/ⓖⓖⓖⓖ   Timbercreek Golf Club (Dogwood, Magnolia, Pines)

Alabama Golf Guide

Birmingham Area

R ⓖ	**Alpine Bay Golf and Country Club** Renfore Rd., Alpine (205) 268-9410 18 holes. Par 72/72. Yards: 6,518/5,518 Year-round. High: May–Sept.	Greens: Carts: Rating: Slope:	$–$$ W R T $ 70.9/69.8 129/120
P ⓖⓖⓖ	**Bent Brook Golf Course** Dickey Springs Rd., Bessemer. (205) 424-2368 27 holes. Par 71/71/70. Yards: 6,934/7,053/6,847 Year-round.	Greens: Carts: Rating: Slope:	$$ $ 71.8/71.7/71.1 119/121/121

Alabama Golf Guide

P ☺☺☺	**Eagle Point Golf Club** Eagle Point Dr., Birmingham. (205) 991-9070 18 holes. Par 71/70. Yards: 6,470/4,691 Year-round. High: Apr.–Sept.	Greens: Carts: Rating: Slope:	$$ S $ 70.2/61.9 127/108
P ☺	**Oak Mountain State Park Golf Course** Findley Dr., Pelham. (205) 620-2522 18 holes. Par 72/72. Yards: 6,748/5,540 Year-round. High: May–Sept.	Greens: Carts: Rating: Slope:	$ S $ 71.5/NA 127/124
P ☺☺	**Oxmoor Valley Golf Club** Sunbelt Pkwy., Birmingham. (205) 942-1177 *Ridge Course* 18 holes. Par 72/72. Yards: 7,053/4,869 Year-round. High: Apr.–Nov.	Greens: Carts: Rating: Slope:	$$ W L T S J $ 73.5/68.6 140/130
☺☺	*Valley Course* 18 holes. Par 72/72. Yards: 7,240/4,866	Rating: Slope:	73.9/65.4 135/118
P ☺☺☺ DEAL	**Silver Lakes Golf Course** Sunbelt Pkwy., Glencoe. (205) 892-3268 *Mindbreaker/Heartbreaker/Backbreaker* 27 holes. Par 72/72/72. Yards: 7,407/7,674/7,425 Year-round. High: Mar.-May/Sept.-Nov.	Greens: Carts: Rating: Slope:	$$ W L T S J $ 75.5/76.7/75.2 132/131/127

Huntsville Area

R ☺☺	**Goose Pond Colony Golf Course** Ed Hembree Dr., Scottsboro. (205) 574-5353 18 holes. Par 72/72. Yards: 6,860/5,370 Year-round. High: Apr.–Aug.	Greens: Carts: Rating: Slope:	$–$$ W R S J $ 71.7/70.0 125/115
P ☺☺☺ DEAL	**Hampton Cove Golf Club** Old Hwy. 431 S., Owens Cross Roads. (205) 551-1818 *Highlands* 18 holes. Par 72/72. Yards: 7,262/4,766 Year-round High: July–Sept.	Greens: Carts: Rating: Slope:	$$ W T J $ 74.1/66.0 134/118
☺☺☺	*River Course* 18 holes. Par 72/72. Yards: 7,507/5,283	Rating: Slope:	75.6/67.0 135/118
R ☺	**Joe Wheeler State Park Golf Club** Rte. 4, Rogersville. (205) 247-9308 18 holes. Par 72/72. Yards: 7,251/6,055 Year-round.	Greens: Carts: Rating: Slope:	$ R S $ 73.1/67.7 120/109
P ☺☺	**Lake Guntersville Golf Club** St. Hwy. 227. Guntersville. (205) 582-0379 18 holes. Par 72/72. Yards: 6,785/5,776 Year-round. High: July–Aug.	Greens: Carts: Rating: Slope:	$ S $ 71.2/70.3 128/124
P ☺☺	**Point Mallard Golf Course** Point Mallard Dr., Decatur. (205) 351-7776 18 holes. Par 72/73. Yards: 7,113/5,437 Year-round. High: Apr.–Sept.	Greens: Carts: Rating: Slope:	$ W L S J $ 73.7/NA 125/NA

Mobile Area

P ☺☺	**Azalea City Golf Club** Gaillard Dr., Mobile. (334) 342-4221 18 holes. Par 72/72. Yards: 6,765/6,491 Year-round. High: Mar.–Oct.	Greens: Carts: Rating: Slope:	$ T $ 70.9/69.8 124/121
SP ☺☺☺	**Cotton Creek Club** Cotton Creek Blvd., Gulf Shores. (334) 968-7766 *North/West/East* 27 holes. Par 72/72/72. Yards: 7,028/6,971/6,975 Year-round. High: Mar.–Oct.	Greens: Carts: Rating: Slope:	$$$ W L $ 73.9/73.0/73.2 132/127/131

Alabama Golf Guide

SP	**Glenlakes Country Club**	Greens: $$	L R T J
	Foley. (334) 943-8000	Carts: Incl.	
☺	*Dunes Course*	Rating: 69.1/70.5	
	18 holes. Par 72/72. Yards: 6,680/5,019	Slope: 126/120	
	Year-round. High: Jan.–Mar.		

P	**Gulf State Park Golf Course**	Greens: $	R S
☺☺	20115 St. Hwy. 135, Gulf Shores. (334) 948-4653	Carts: $	
	18 holes. Par 72/72. Yards: 6,563/5,310	Rating: 72.5/70.4	
	Year-round. High: Feb.–Apr., June–Aug.	Slope: NA	

P	**Isle Dauphine Golf Club**	Greens: $	W
☺	Orleand Dr., Dauphin Island. (334) 861-2433	Carts: $	
	18 holes. Par 72/72. Yards: 6,620/5,619	Rating: NA	
	Year-round. High: Feb.–May	Slope: 123/122	

P	**The Linksman Golf Club**	Greens: $	W R T S J
☺	St. Andres Dr., Mobile. (334) 661-0018	Carts: $	
	18 holes. Par 72/72. Yards: 6,275/5,416	Rating: 70.1/71.0	
	Year-round. High: Mar.–June	Slope: 123/121	

P	**Magnolia Grove Golf Club**	Greens: $$$	L J
	Lamplighter Dr., Semmes. (334) 645-0075	Carts: $	
☺☺☺☺	*Crossings Course*	Rating: 74.6/70.4	
DEAL	18 holes. Par 72/72. Yards: 7,150/5,184	Slope: 134/131	
STATE	Year-round. High: Feb.–Apr.		

☺☺☺☺	*Falls Course*	Rating: 75.1/71.0	
DEAL	18 holes. Par 72/72. Yards: 7,240/5,253	Slope: 137/126	
STATE			

R	**Marriott's Lakewood Golf Club**	Greens: $$$$	J
	Hwy. 98, Point Clear. (334) 990-6312	Carts: Incl.	
☺☺	*Azalea Course*	Rating: 72.5/71.3	
	18 holes. Par 72. Yards: 6,770/5,307	Slope: 128/118	
	Year-round.		

☺☺☺	*Dogwood Course*	Rating: 72.1/72.6	
	18 holes. Par 71/72. Yards: 6,676/5,532	Slope: 124/122	

P	**Quail Creek Golf Course**	Greens: $	T
☺	Quail Creek Dr., Fairhope. (334) 990-0240	Carts: $	
	18 holes. Par 72/72. Yards: 6,426/5,305	Rating: 70.1/69.6	
	Year-round. High: Jan.–Apr.	Slope: 112/114	

SP	**Rock Creek Golf Club**	Greens: $$–$$$	T
☺☺☺	Fairhope. (334) 928-4223	Carts: $	
STATE	18 holes. Par 72/72. Yards: 6,400/5,800	Rating: 72.2/68.4	
	Year-round. High: Spring and Fall	Slope: 129/117	

P	**Timbercreek Golf Club**	Greens: $$$	W R T J
	Timbercreek Blvd., Daphne. (334) 621-9900	Carts: Incl.	
☺☺☺☺	*Dogwood/Magnolia/Pines*	Rating: 73.8/72.9/74.3	
DEAL	27 holes. Par 72/72/72. Yards: 7,062/6,928/7,090	Slope: 144/137/143	
STATE	Year-round. High: March and Apr.		

Montgomery Area

P	**Auburn Links**	Greens: $$	L R S J
☺☺☺	Shell-Toomer Pkwy., Auburn. (334) 887-5151	Carts: $	
DEAL	18 holes. Par 72/72. Yards: 7,145/5,320	Rating: 72.5/68.5	
	Year-round. High: June–Oct.	Slope: 129/121	

P	**Cambrian Ridge Golf Club**	Greens: $$$	W T J
	Sunbelt Pkwy., Greenville. (334) 382-9787	Carts: Incl.	
☺☺☺☺	*Canyon/Sherling/Loblolly*	Rating: 75.4/74.6/73.9	
DEAL	27 holes. Par 72/71/71. Yards: 7,424/7,297/7,232	Slope: 142/140/133	
STATE	Year-round. High: Mar.-May/Sept.-Nov.		

Alabama Golf Guide

P	**Grand National Golf Club**	Greens:	$$-$$$	L J
	Sunbelt Pkwy., Opelika. (334) 749-9042	Carts:	$	
☺☺☺☺	*Lake Course*	Rating:	74.9/68.7	
DEAL	18 holes. Par 72/72. Yards: 7,149/4,910	Slope:	138/117	
STATE	Year-round. High: Mar.–Oct.			

☺☺☺☺	*Links Course*	Rating:	74.9/69.6	L J
DEAL	18 holes. Par 72/72. Yards: 7,311/4,843	Slope:	141/113	
STATE				

P	**Lagoon Park Golf Course**	Greens:	$-$$	W L
☺☺☺	Lagoon Park Dr., Montgomery. (334) 271-7000	Carts:	$	
BEST	18 holes. Par 72/72. Yards: 6,773/5,342	Rating:	71.1/69.6	
DEAL	Year-round. High: Apr.–Oct.	Slope:	124/113	

R	**Still Waters Resort**	Greens:	$$	W L J
☺☺	Still Waters Dr., Dadeville. (205) 825-7021	Carts:	$	
	18 holes. Par 72/72. Yards: 6,407/5,287	Rating:	69.9/71.5	
	Year-round. High: Mar.–Oct.	Slope:	124/125	

Southern Alabama

P	**Highland Oaks Golf Club**	Greens:	$$–$$$	W L T J
	Royal Parkway, Dothan. (334) 712-2820	Carts:	$	
☺☺☺☺	*Highland/Magnolia/Marshwood*	Rating:	76.9/76.0/75.7	
STATE	27 holes. Par 72/72/72. Yards: 7,704/7,591/7,511	Slope:	138/135/133	
	Year-round. High: Mar.–Oct.			

R	**Lakepoint Resort Golf Course**	Greens:	$	S
☺☺	Hwy. 431, Eufala. (334) 687-6677	Carts:	$	
	18 holes. Par 72/72. Yards: 6,752/5,363	Rating:	73.6/69.2	
	Year-round. High: Mar.–June	Slope:	123	

SP	**Olympia Spa Golf Resort**	Greens:	$	T
☺	Hwy. 231 S., Dothan. (334) 677-3326	Carts:	$	
	18 holes. Par 72/72. Yards: 7,242/5,470	Rating:	74.5/71.1	
	Year-round. High: Mar.–June	Slope:	123/113	

Arkansas

Not known as a golf state, Arkansas nevertheless has a decent collection of courses of varying quality. The best of the lot available to the public is probably **Mountain Ranch Golf Club**, a resort in Fairfield Bay, way north of Little Rock. It's hidden away in the hills, and features more than its share of water and sand hazards. Also worthy are the mountain and meadow South Course at **Cherokee Village** and the **Prairie Creek Country Club** in Rogers, a tough hilltop challenge.

Most courses in Arkansas operate year-round. Expect to find peak prices during the summer, with the best deals in the fall through spring.

Golf U.S.A. Leader Board: Best Public Courses in Arkansas

☺☺☺ Cherokee Village (South)
☺☺☺☺ Mountain Ranch Golf Club
☺☺☺ Prairie Creek Country Club

Golf U.S.A. Leader Board: Best Deals in Arkansas

$$/☺☺☺ Cherokee Village (South)
$$/☺☺☺ Quapaw Golf Links
$$/☺☺☺ Prairie Creek Country Club
$$/☺☺☺☺ Mountain Ranch Golf Club

Arkansas Golf Guide

Fayetteville Area

R ☺☺	**Dawn Hill Golf Club** Dawn Hill Rd., Siloam Springs. (501) 524-4838 18 holes. Par 72/73. Yards: 6,852/5,330 Year-round. High: May–Oct.	Greens: Carts: Rating: Slope:	$–$$ Inquire 71.3/69.1 114/110	T
SP ☺☺☺ DEAL STATE	**Prairie Creek Country Club** Hwy. 12 E., Rogers. (501) 925-2414 18 holes. Par 72/72. Yards: 6,707/5,599 Year-round. High: Apr.–Sept.	Greens: Carts: Rating: Slope:	$ $ 73.1/67.8 135/109	W R T

Fort Smith

P ☺☺	**Ben Green Regional Park Golf Course** S. Zero, Fort Smith. (501) 646-5301 18 holes. Par 72/73. Yards: 6,782/5,023 Year-round. High: Apr.–Oct.	Greens: Carts: Rating: Slope:	$ $$ 71.7/67.7 120/109	W T S J

Little Rock Area

P ☺☺	**DeGray State Park Golf Course** Bismarck. (501) 865-2807 18 holes. Par 72/72. Yards: 6,930/5,731 Year-round. High: Apr.–Sept.	Greens: Carts: Rating: Slope:	$ $ 60.7/67.0 134/123	S
P ☺☺	**Hindman Park Golf Course** Brookview Dr., Little Rock. (501) 565-6450 18 holes. Par 72/72. Yards: 6,393/4,349 Year-round. High: May–Aug.	Greens: Carts: Rating: Slope:	$ $ 68.9/NA 109/NA	L T S J
R ☺☺☺	**Hot Springs Country Club** Malvern Ave., Hot Springs. (501) 624-2661 *Arlington Course* 18 holes. Par 72/74. Yards: 6,690/6,017 Year-round. High: Mar.–Oct.	Greens: Carts: Rating: Slope:	$$$$ Incl. 74.2/75.6 127/137	W R
☺☺	*Majestic Course* 18 holes. Par 72/72. Yards: 6,761/6,429	Greens: Carts: Rating: Slope:	$$$ Incl. 71.5/71.1 120/121	W R
SP ☺☺	**Longhills Golf Club** Hwy. 5 N., Benton. (501) 794-9907 18 holes. Par 72/73. Yards: 6,539/5,350 Year-round. High: Apr.–Sept.	Greens: Carts: Rating: Slope:	$ $ 69.9/69.5 110/110	J
P ☺☺☺ DEAL	**Quapaw Golf Links** St. Hwy. 391 N., North Little Rock. (501) 945-0945 18 holes. Par 72/72. Yards: 6,972/5,118 Year-round. High: Mar.–Oct.	Greens: Carts: Rating: Slope:	$–$$ $ 72.4/70.3 119/120	W L T S J
R ☺☺	**The Red Apple Inn and Country Club** Heber Springs. (501) 362-3131 18 holes. Par 72/72. Yards: 6,402/5,137 Year-round. High: Apr.–Nov.	Greens: Carts: Rating: Slope:	$$ $ 70.0/69.0 121/110	

Northern Arkansas

R ☺☺☺ DEAL STATE	**Cherokee Village** Laguna Dr., Cherokee Village. (870) 257-2555 *South* 18 holes. Par 72/72. Yards: 7,058/5,270 Year-round. High: May–Sept.	Greens: Carts: Rating: Slope:	$–$$ $ 73.5/70.4 128/116	
R ☺☺☺☺ DEAL STATE	**Mountain Ranch Golf Club** Lost Creek Pkwy., Fairfield Bay. (501) 884-3400 18 holes. Par 72/72. Yards: 6,780/5,235 Year-round. High: May–Oct.	Greens: Carts: Rating: Slope:	$$–$$$ Incl. 71.8/69.8 129/121	W L R T

Florida

The Sunshine State is probably best known for beaches, Mickey Mouse's home away from home, and golf. And if you really want to, you can combine all three on a single visit. In fact, the **Walt Disney World** megaresort near Orlando has turned into a golf factory, with five major first-class resorts located on the grounds of the sprawling theme park. There are at least that many superb courses at hotels and resorts outside of the park.

Of more than 1,000 courses in the state; about half are open to the public.

Orlando and Walt Disney World

Some of the best courses in Florida—or anywhere else—are in and around Orlando, but that's not the best reason to go there. No, the best reasons to play golf in the area are all of the other things to do: Walt Disney World's rides, water sports, entertainment, and more; Universal Studios Florida; Sea World Orlando; and so much more. If these things don't appeal to you, they may still offer you the chance to take the spouse and kids with you on a golf vacation and not worry about whether they'll be able to entertain themselves.

Walt Disney World's Magic Linkdom includes no fewer than five fabulous 18-hole courses—any one of which would be among the best in any other state. The best of the best is generally acknowledged to be the Osprey Ridge Golf Course, a long, difficult challenge with elevated tees. The circulating layout features holes that play in all possible directions.

Close behind in challenge level is the Palm Golf Course, one of the most difficult resort courses in the country, with lots of sand and water, and an 18th hole rated among the most challenging on the PGA Tour.

Other winners at Disney World include Eagle Pines Golf Course, a Pete Dye design with deep-dish fairways that keep the ball at tree level.

The Magnolia Golf Course is named for the more than 1,500 magnolia trees on the land; it is used as the setting for the final round of the Walt Disney World Golf Classic held each mid-October. It features elevated tees and greens, and a real Mickey Mouse of a hazard on the 6th hole.

Disney's Lake Buena Vista Golf Course is perhaps the easiest here, but it is also one of the few courses anywhere that has played host to a PGA Tour event, an LPGA event, *and* a USGA event.

There's even the Oak Trail 9-hole "executive" course nearby to the Magnolia, featuring some of the most challenging holes at the resort and a miniature-golf course. Oh, and I'm told there are a couple of big theme parks nearby.

Non-Disney resorts worth noting include **Arnold Palmer's Bay Hill Club**, one of the top resorts in Florida and the nation.

There are 45 superb holes (18 at the New Course and 9 holes each at the North and South courses are the best of the lot) at the **Grand Cypress Resort** in Orlando. The New Course is a near-replica of the Old Course at St. Andrews (including 145 bunkers). Grand Cypress is a palatial resort, sort of an art museum–cum–golf course and hotel . . . or is it the other way around? In any case, this is a five-star hotel with a four-star golf course (and a private trolley system that runs between the two).

The **Grenelefe Golf and Tennis Resort**, about 25 miles south of Walt Disney World in Haines City, has 54 holes of golf, including the top-rated and very long West Course near and along Lake Marion. Some 75 miles north of Orlando is the **Golden Ocala Golf Course**, which includes eight replicas of famous holes, including samples of St. Andrews, Muirfield, Baltusrol, and Augusta National.

Miami

The **Doral Golf Resort and Spa** offers no fewer than 72 superb holes created out of the swamps near Miami, including the top-rated Blue Course, better known as the Blue Monster, the home of the Doral Ryder Open on the PGA Tour. It is a long, difficult course with lots of sand and water. The killer hole is the 18th, a dogleg left with water at the tee and on the approach. More than 30 years ago, Doral was built in the middle of nowhere on land that was considered wasted; what exists today is a showplace with some of the most beautifully manicured lawns anywhere, including more than 1,000 bunkers, 100 acres of water, and some sumptuous resort and spa amenities.

The **Links at Key Biscayne** is a challenging course along the waterfront, a bit more difficult when the wind blows through the coconut palms.

The **Golf Club of Miami**, a close contender for a *Golf U.S.A.* Best rating, deserves mention for something else: the club was one of the first to equip many of its golf carts with specialized Global Positioning System receivers that tell golfers the distance, within four feet, from the cart to the pin. How did we ever get along without this?

West Palm Beach

The **PGA National Resort and Spa** has 90 holes of superb golf, topped by the Champion Course in Palm Beach Gardens. This is the home of the PGA of America itself (along with the U.S. Croquet Association, in case you were wondering where *that* was). The Champion was originally designed by George and Tom Fazio, and was redesigned by Jack Nicklaus in 1990; it stretches more than 7,000 yards.

Among West Palm Beach's best is the **Emerald Dunes Golf Club**, a plush though pricey course that includes all sorts of grass, dunes, and water hazards.

The **Palm Beach Polo and Country Club** has water on 14 holes of its Dunes Course. Alas, it went private in 1998; perhaps you can find a long-lost relative with a membership and a polo mallet. The resort is the center of the universe for the sport of polo; over the last decade the resort has expanded to offer golf challenges that entertain the horsey crowd. The acclaimed Cypress Course is a Pete Dye design, a 7,116-yard monster; the Dunes, laid out by Rong Garl and Jerry Pate, is a slightly shorter, slightly easier world-class links challenge.

Tampa

There are two top-rated courses at the **Innisbrook Hilton Resort** in Palm Harbor, northwest of Tampa: the challenging Copperhead Course and the gorgeous Island Course. Copperhead is practically mountainous (by Florida standards);

well, it does go up and down a lot more than other challenges in the state. The Island Course, as befits its name, has more than 50 sand bunkers and a dozen water hazards.

About 60 miles north of Tampa are a pair of outstanding courses that are greener and more manicured than most other Florida courses: the Pine Barrens Course and the Rolling Oaks Course at **World Woods Golf Club** in Brooksville.

The **Eastwood Golf Course** is an exceptionally attractive municipal course in Fort Myers that includes an abundance of wildlife and some long-distance over-water calls.

Also in Fort Myers is the **Gateway Golf and Country Club**, a links-type course in the marshes and trees.

Jacksonville

By most rankings the Stadium Course at the famed **Tournament Players Club at Sawgrass** in Ponte Vedra Beach is among the top 10 resorts nationwide; the difficult course includes treacherous greens, huge bunkers, and its famed 17th-hole island—shades of a similar challenge at the TPC Stadium Course at PGA West Resort in California. Water comes into play on all 18 holes.

The famed **Amelia Island Plantation** near Jacksonville offers a quartet of memorable challenges, including the Oceanside, which runs along and amidst the dunes; the Oakmarsh, which plunges deep into the oak and palmetto woods; the marshy Oysterbay; and the Long Point, which combines forests and dunes. The courses are known for tight fairways, small greens, and spectacular beach-side links.

The Panhandle

Water, water everywhere—that's the unofficial motto at **Marriott's Bay Point Resort** near Panama City beach, and The Lagoon Legend is considered among the most difficult in the nation. In fact, it has the highest slope rating—152—of any public course listed in this book. If the water or the sand doesn't get you, the marsh and the Tai Tai Swamp will. The front nine is somewhat easier, but we're only speaking in relative terms here.

Sunshine State Deals

Florida offers year-round golfing; its high season is in the winter when temperatures are moderate and the snowbirds (northerners) are in town. Expect to pay peak rates from about December through April, including spring break. You can find deep discounts during the heat of the summer; be aware, though, that in and around Orlando, hotel rooms may be at peak or near-peak levels in the summer, too, because of young people on school vacation.

Winter rates at the Doral Golf Resort and Spa—including a room, 18 holes of golf with a cart, breakfast, a clinic, and other amenities—start at about $265 per person for a double room.

Rates for the basic package begin slightly higher spring and fall. The resort offers summer packages from late May through the end of September, including a $129 per-person (double-occupancy). In past seasons, Doral has offered a summer package including room, breakfast, golf clinic, carts, and unlimited rounds of golf; check with the resort for details.

At the Walt Disney World golf complex you'll have lots of company from Christmas through late spring; be sure to book as early as possible. Guests at hotels at the Walt Disney World resort have priority. But the links are much less crowded from May through December. If you are a Florida Resident or Magic Kingdom Club member, you can pay about $50 for a Disney VIP Golf Membership which offers discounts year-round after 10 A.M., plus 20 percent off on golf instruction, and admission to the Walt Disney World Golf Classic in October, a $35 value in itself.

Golf U.S.A. Leader Board: Best Public Courses in Florida

⊙⊙⊙	Amelia Island Plantation (Oakmarsh, Oysterbay, Oceanside, Long Point)
⊙⊙⊙⊙	Baytree National Golf Links
⊙⊙⊙	Cimarrone Golf and Country Club
⊙⊙⊙	The Country Club at Jacaranda West
⊙⊙⊙	Doral Golf Resort and Spa (Blue)
⊙⊙⊙	Doral Park Golf and Country Club (Silver)
⊙⊙⊙	Eastwood Golf Course
⊙⊙⊙⊙	Emerald Dunes Golf Club
⊙⊙⊙	Gateway Golf and Country Club
⊙⊙⊙	Golden Ocala Golf Course
⊙⊙⊙	The Golf Club at Cypress Creek
⊙⊙⊙	The Golf Club at Marco
⊙⊙⊙	Golf Club of Jacksonville
⊙⊙⊙⊙	Grand Cypress Resort (New, North, South, East)
⊙⊙⊙⊙	Grenelefe Golf and Tennis Resort (West)
⊙⊙⊙	Hunter's Creek Golf Course
⊙⊙⊙⊙	Innisbrook Hilton Resort (Copperhead, Island)
⊙⊙⊙⊙	Links at Key Biscayne
⊙⊙⊙⊙	Marriott's Bay Point Resort (The Lagoon Legend)
⊙⊙⊙⊙	PGA National Resort and Spa (Champion)
⊙⊙⊙⊙	Tournament Players Club at Sawgrass (Stadium)
⊙⊙⊙⊙	Walt Disney World Resort (Osprey Ridge)
⊙⊙⊙	West Palm Beach Municipal Country Club
⊙⊙⊙⊙	World Woods Golf Club (Pine Barrens, Rolling Oaks)

Golf U.S.A. Leader Board: Best Deals in Florida

$$/⊙⊙⊙	Bluewater Bay Resort (Magnolia, Marsh, Bay, Lake)
$$/⊙⊙⊙	Cimarrone Golf and Country Club
$$/⊙⊙⊙	Cocoa Beach Golf Course (River, Dolphin, Lakes)
$$/⊙⊙⊙	The Country Club at Jacaranda West
$$/⊙⊙⊙	The Country Club at Silver Springs Shores

$$/○○○	DeBary Golf and Country Club
$$/○○○	Delray Beach Golf Club
$$/○○○	Fairwinds Golf Course
$$/○○○	The Golf Club at Cypress Creek
$$/○○○	The Golf Club at Marco
$$/○○○	Golf Club of Jacksonville
$$/○○○	Golf Club of Miami (East, West)
$/○○○	Habitat Golf Course
$/○○○	Halifax Plantation Golf Club
$$/○○○	Killearn Country Club and Inn (South, East, North)
$/○○○	Mangrove Bay Golf Course
$$/○○○○	Marcus Pointe Golf Club
$$/○○○	Marriott at Sawgrass Resort (Oak Bridge Golf Club)
$$/○○○	The Moors Golf Club
$$/○○○	Oak Hills Golf Club
$$/○○○	Pelican Bay Country Club (South)
$/○○○	St. Johns Country Golf Club
$$/○○○	Sandridge Golf Club (Dunes, Lakes)
$$/○○○	Seven Hills Golfers Club
$$/○○○	Seville Golf and Country Club
$$/○○○	Sherman Hills Golf Club
$$/○○○	Summerfield Golf Club
$$/○○○	Tatum Ridge Golf Links
$$/○○○	Viera East Golf Club
$$/○○○	West Palm Beach Municipal Country Club

Florida Golf Guide

Pensacola Area

R	**Bluewater Bay Resort**	Greens:	$$	L R J
	Bluewater Blvd., Niceville. (904) 897-3241	Carts:	$	
○○○	*Magnolia/Marsh*	Rating:	71.6/68.4	
DEAL	18 holes. Par 72/72. Yards: 6,669/5,048	Slope:	127/114	
	Year-round. High: Feb.–May			

○○○	*Bay/Lake*	Rating:	73.0/70.6
DEAL	18 holes. Par 72/72. Yards: 6,803/5,378	Slope:	140/124

SP	**The Club at Hidden Creek**	Greens:	$$–$$$	W L T J
○○○○	PGA Blvd., Navarre. (850) 939-1939	Carts:	Incl.	
	18 holes. Par 72/72. Yards: 6,862/5,213	Rating:	73.2/70.1	
	Year-round. High: Jan.–Apr.	Slope:	139/124	

SP	**Emerald Bay Golf Course**	Greens:	$$$–$$$$	W L R J
○○○○	Emerald Coast Pkwy., Destin. (850) 837-7420	Carts:	Incl.	
	18 holes. Par 72/72. Yards: 6,802/5,184	Rating:	73.1/70.1	
	Year-round. High: Mar.–Nov.	Slope:	135/122	

P	**Fort Walton Beach Municipal Golf Course**	Greens:	$	T
	Fort Walton Beach. (904) 862-3922	Carts:	$	
○○	*Oaks Course.* 1909 Lewis Turner Blvd.	Rating:	70.2/67.8	
	18 holes. Par 72/72. Yards: 6,409/5,366	Slope:	119/107	
	Year-round. High: Feb.–Aug.			

○○	*Pines Course.* 699 Country Club Dr.	Rating:	69.9/69.1
	18 holes. Par 72/72. Yards: 6,802/5,320	Slope:	110/107

Florida Golf Guide

P ☺☺	**Hilaman Park Municipal Golf Course** Blairstone Rd., Tallahassee. (904) 891-3935 18 holes. Par 72/72. Yards: 6,364/5,365 Year-round. High: Mar.–June	Greens: Carts: Rating: Slope:	$ $ 70.1/70.8 121/116	W T S J
SP ☺☺☺	**Hombre Golf Club** Coyote Pass, Panama City Beach. (904) 234-3673 18 holes. Par 72/74. Yards: 6,820/4,800 Year-round. High: Mar.–Apr., June–July	Greens: Carts: Rating: Slope:	$$$$ Incl. 73.4/67.2 136/118	L R T J
SP ☺☺☺	**Indian Bayou Golf and Country Club** Destin. (850) 837-6191 *Seminole/Choctaw/Creek* 27 holes. Par 72/72/72. Yards: 6,958/6,893/7,016 Year-round. High: Feb.–Aug.	Greens: Carts: Rating: Slope:	$$–$$$ Inquire 73.3/73.1/73.7 126/129/128	
R ☺☺☺ DEAL	**Killearn Country Club and Inn** Tyron Circle, Tallahassee. (850) 893-2144, (800) 476-4101 *South/East/North* 27 holes. Par 72/72. Yards: 7,025/6,760/6,899 Year-round. High: Mar.–Aug.	Greens: Carts: Rating: Slope:	$$ Inquire 73.9/73.1/73.3 133/131/132	W T
P ☺☺☺☺ DEAL	**Marcus Pointe Golf Club** Oak Pointe Dr., Pensacola. (850) 484-9770 18 holes. Par 72/72. Yards: 6,737/5,185 Year-round. High: Feb.–May	Greens: Carts: Rating: Slope:	$$$ Incl. 72.3/69.6 129/119	W L T J
SP ☺☺☺	**Marriott's Bay Point Resort** Dellwood Beach Rd., Panama City Beach. (850) 235-6937 *Club Meadows Course* 18 holes. Par 72/72. Yards: 6,913/4,999 Year-round. High: Feb.–June	Greens: Carts: Rating: Slope:	$$$$ Incl. 73.0/68.0 126/118	L R J
P ☺☺☺ BEST	*The Lagoon Legend* Marriott Dr., Panama City Beach. (850) 235-6937 18 holes. Par 72/72. Yards: 6,885/4,942 Year-round. High: June–Oct.	Greens: Carts: Rating: Slope:	$$$$ Incl. 75.3/69.8 152/127	L R T J
P ☺☺☺ DEAL	**The Moors Golf Club** Avalon Blvd., Milton. (850) 995-4653 18 holes. Par 70/70. Yards: 6,828/5,259 Year-round. High: Apr.–May, Sept.–Oct.	Greens: Carts: Rating: Slope:	$$ $ 72.9/70.3 126/117	W R J
R ☺☺☺	**Perdido Bay Golf Club** Doug Ford Dr., Pensacola. (904) 492-1223 18 holes. Par 72/72. Yards: 7,154/5,478 Year-round. High: Jan.–Apr.	Greens: Carts: Rating: Slope:	$$–$$$ Incl. 73.6/71.4 125/121	R T J
R ☺☺☺	**Sandestin Beach Hilton Golf and Tennis Resort** Hwy. 98 W., Destin *Baytowne: Troon/Dunes/Harbor.* (850) 267-8155 27 holes. Par 72/72/72. Yards: 7,185/6,890/6,891 Year-round. High: Mar.–Apr., Sept.–Oct.	Greens: Carts: Rating: Slope:	$$$–$$$$$ $ 74.6/73.4/73.9 128/127/127	L R T J
☺☺☺	*Burnt Pines Golf Course.* (850) 267-6500 18 holes. Par 72/72. Yards: 7,046/5,950	Rating: Slope:	74.1/69.4 135/124	R J
☺☺☺	*The Links Course.* (850) 267-6500 18 holes. Par 72/72. Yards: 6,710/4,969	Rating: Slope:	72.8/69.2 124/115	L R T J
P ☺☺	**Scenic Hills Country Club** Burning Tree Rd., Pensacola. (904) 476-0611 18 holes. Par 71/71. Yards: 6,689/5,187 Year-round. High: Feb.–Apr.	Greens: Carts: Rating: Slope:	$$ Incl. NA 135/116	W L R T

Florida Golf Guide

R ☺☺☺	**Seascape Resort** Seascape Dr., Destin. (904) 654-7888 18 holes. Par 71/71. Yards: 6,480/5,014 Year-round. High: Mar.–Oct.	Greens: $$–$$$ L R J Carts: Incl. Rating: 71.5/70.3 Slope: 120/113
P ☺☺	**Seminole Golf Club** Pottsdamer St., Tallahassee. (850) 644-2582 18 holes. Par 72/72. Yards: 7,033/5,930 Year-round.	Greens: $ W R T J Carts: $ Rating: 73.4/73.0 Slope: 121/111
SP ☺☺	**Shalimar Pointe Golf and Country Club** Shalimar. (904) 651-1416 18 holes. Par 72/72. Yards: 6,765/5,427 Year-round. High: Jan.–Apr.	Greens: $$–$$$ W L R T Carts: Incl. Rating: 72.9/70.7 Slope: 125/115
P ☺☺	**Tanglewood Golf and Country Club** Tanglewood Dr., Milton. (904) 623-6176 18 holes. Par 72/72. Yards: 6,455/5,295 Year-round. High: Apr.–Nov.	Greens: $–$$ L S Carts: $ Rating: 70.0/69.9 Slope: 115/118
SP ☺☺☺	**Tiger Point Golf and Country Club** Gulf Breeze. (904) 932-1333 *East Course* 18 holes. Par 72/72. Yards: 7,033/5,217 Year-round. High: Feb.–Apr., Oct.–Nov.	Greens: $$–$$$ W L T Carts: Incl. Rating: 73.8/70.2 Slope: 132/125
☺☺	*West Course* 18 holes. Par 72/72. Yards: 6,715/5,314	Greens: $$ Carts: Incl. Rating: 72.2/70.2 Slope: 119/121

Jacksonville Area

R ☺☺☺ STATE	**Amelia Island Plantation** 1st Coast Hwy., Amelia Island. (904) 277-5907 *Oakmarsh/Oysterbay/Oceanside* 27 holes. Par 72/71/71. Yards: 6,502/6,026/6,140 Year-round. High: Mar.–May	Greens: $$$$–$$$$$ L R T J Carts: Incl. Rating: 70.7/68.6/69.3 Slope: 127/117/120
☺☺☺ BEST	*Long Point Golf Club* 18 holes. Par 72/72. Yards: 6,775/4,927	Greens: $$$$$–$$$$$$ Carts: Incl. Rating: 72.9/69.1 Slope: 129/121
SP ☺☺	**Baymeadows Golf Club** Baymeadows Circle W., Jacksonville. (904) 731-5701 18 holes. Par 72/72. Yards: 7,002/5,309 Year-round. High: Year-round	Greens: $$ T Carts: Incl. Rating: 73.7/72.2 Slope: 130/130
SP ☺☺	**Champions Club at Julington Creek** Durbin Creek Blvd., Jacksonville. (904) 287-4653 18 holes. Par 72/72. Yards: 6,872/4,994 Year-round. High: Mar.–May, Oct.–Dec.	Greens: $$–$$$ W T R S J Carts: Incl. Rating: 72.8/68.6 Slope: 126/114
SP ☺☺☺ DEAL STATE	**Cimarrone Golf and Country Club** Cimarrone Blvd., Jacksonville. (904) 287-2000 18 holes. Par 72/72. Yards: 6,891/4,707 Year-round. High: Apr.–May, Sept.–Oct.	Greens: $$–$$$ W L T Carts: Incl. Rating: 72.7/67.8 Slope: 132/115
P ☺☺	**Deerfield Lakes Golf Course** Lem Turner Rd., Callahan. (904) 879-1210 18 holes. Par 72/74. Yards: 6,700/5,266 Year-round. High: Oct.–Mar.	Greens: $$ W Carts: Incl. Rating: 70.2/69.0 Slope: 114/102
SP ☺☺☺☺	**Eagle Harbor Golf Club** Eagle Harbor Pkwy., Orange Park. (904) 269-9300	Greens: $$–$$$ W T J Carts: Incl.

| | 18 holes. Par 72/72. Yards: 6,840/4,980 | Rating: | 73.3/70.3 |
| | Year-round. High: Apr.–June | Slope: | 138/122 |

P
☺☺
Fernandina Beach Municipal Golf Course
Bill Melton Rd., Fernandina Beach. (904) 227-7370
North/West/South
27 holes. Par 72/71/73. Yards: 6,806/6,412/7,027
Year-round.

Greens: $ W J
Carts: $
Rating: 71.5/69.7/72.6
Slope: 118/121/123

R
☺☺☺
The Golf Club of Amelia Island
Amelia Island Pkwy., Amelia Island. (904) 277-8015
18 holes. Par 72/72. Yards: 6,681/5,039
Year-round. High: May–Sept.

Greens: $$$$$ L R T S J
Carts: Incl.
Rating: 71.7/70.6
Slope: 127/122

P
☺☺☺
DEAL
STATE
Golf Club of Jacksonville
Jacksonville. (904) 779-0800
18 holes. Par 71/71. Yards: 6,620/5,021
Year-round. High: Mar.–June

Greens: $$ W T S J
Carts: Incl.
Rating: 70.7/68.0
Slope: 120/115

P
☺☺
Jacksonville Beach Golf Course
S. Penman Rd., Jacksonville. (904) 249-8600
18 holes. Par 72/72. Yards: 6,510/5,245
Year-round. High: Spring and Fall

Greens: $ W L T J
Carts: Inquire
Rating: 70.5/69.2
Slope: 119/114

R
☺☺☺
DEAL
Oak Bridge Golf Club
Alta Mar Dr., Ponte Vedra Beach. (904) 285-0204
18 holes. Par 70/70. Yards: 6,383/4,869
Year-round. High: Feb.–May

Greens: $$
Carts: $
Rating: 70.3/67.8
Slope: 126/116

SP
☺☺
Meadowbrook Golf Club
N.W. 37th Place, Gainesville. (352) 332-0577
18 holes. Par 72/72. Yards: 6,289/4,720
Year-round. High: Jan.–Apr.

Greens: $-$$ W L T
Carts: Inquire
Rating: 69.9/66.7
Slope: 119/117

P
☺☺
Mill Cove Golf Club
Monument Rd., Jacksonville. (904) 646-4653
18 holes. Par 71/71. Yards: 6,671/4,719
Year-round.

Greens: $-$$ W L T S J
Carts: $
Rating: 71.7/66.3
Slope: 129/112

R
☺☺
Ponce de Leon Golf and Conference Resort
U.S. Hwy. 1 N., St. Augustine. (904) 829-5314
18 holes. Par 72/72. Yards: 6,823/5,308
Year-round. High: Feb.–May, Oct.–Nov.

Greens: $$-$$$ L R T
Carts: $
Rating: 72.9/70.7
Slope: 131/125

R

☺☺☺
Ponte Vedra Inn and Club
Ponte Vedra Blvd., Ponte Vedra Beach. (904) 285-1111
Lagoon Course
18 holes. Par 70/70. Yards: 5,574/4,641

Greens: $$$$-$$$$$
Carts: Incl.
Rating: 66.2/66.9
Slope: 110/113

☺☺☺
Ocean Course
18 holes. Par 72/72. Yards: 6,573/5,237

Rating: 71.3/69.6
Slope: 120/119

SP
☺☺☺
Ravines Golf and Country Club
Ravines Rd., Middleburg. (904) 282-7888
18 holes. Par 72/70. Yards: 6,733/4,817
Year-round. High: Mar.–May

Greens: $$-$$$
Carts: Incl.
Rating: 72.4/67.4
Slope: 133/120

P
☺☺☺
DEAL
St. Johns Country Golf Club
Cypress Links Blvd., Ecton. (904) 825-4900
18 holes. Par 72/72. Yards: 6,926/5,173
Year-round. High: Jan.–Apr.

Greens: $ T
Carts: $
Rating: 72.9/68.8
Slope: 130/117

R

☺☺☺☺
Tournament Players Club at Sawgrass
TPC Blvd., Ponte Vedra Beach. (904) 273-3235
Stadium Course

Greens: $$$$$-$$$$$$ L J
Carts: Incl.
Rating: 73.3/64.9

Florida Golf Guide

BEST	18 holes. Par 72/72. Yards: 6,937/5,000 Year-round. High: Mar.–June	Slope:	138/120
☺☺☺☺	*Valley Course* 18 holes. Par 72/72. Yards: 6,864/5,126 Year-round. High: Mar.–June	Greens: Carts: Rating: Slope:	$$$$–$$$$$ Incl. 72.8/68.7 130/120
P ☺☺☺	**Windsor Parke Golf Club** Hodges Blvd., Jacksonville. (904) 223-4653 18 holes. Par 72/72. Yards: 6,740/5,206 Year-round. High: Mar.–May	Greens: Carts: Rating: Slope:	$$$ W T J Incl. 71.9/69.4 133/123

Daytona Area

SP ☺☺	**Cypress Knoll Golf Club** E. Hampton Blvd., Palm Coast. (904) 437-5807 18 holes. Par 72/72. Yards: 6,591/5,386 Year-round. High: Nov.–Apr.	Greens: Carts: Rating: Slope:	$$–$$$ W L Incl. 71.6/69.3 130/117
P ☺	**Daytona Beach Golf Course** Wilder Blvd., Daytona Beach. (904) 258-3119 *North Course* 18 holes. Par 72/72. Yards: 6,567/5,247 Year-round. High: Nov.–May	Greens: Carts: Rating: Slope:	$ W L T $ 71.0/69.1 111/111
☺	*South Course* 18 holes. Par 71/71. Yards: 6,229/5,346	Rating: Slope:	69.7/69.6 106/106
P ☺☺☺ DEAL	**The Golf Club at Cypress Head** Palm Vista St., Port Orange. (904) 756-5449 18 holes. Par 72/72. Yards: 6,814/4,909 Year-round. High: Jan.–Apr.	Greens: Carts: Rating: Slope:	$$ W L R T J Incl. 72.4/68.3 133/116
SP ☺☺☺ DEAL	**Halifax Plantation Golf Club** Old Dixie Hwy., Ormond Beach. (904) 676-9600 18 holes. Par 72/72. Yards: 7,128/4,971 Year-round. High: Nov.–Apr.	Greens: Carts: Rating: Slope:	$ W L R T $ 73.9/67.6 129/113
SP ☺☺☺	**Indigo Lakes Golf Club** Indigo Dr., Daytona Beach. (904) 254-3607 18 holes. Par 72/72. Yards: 7,168/5,159 Year-round. High: Jan.–May	Greens: Carts: Rating: Slope:	$$–$$$ W L T Incl. 73.5/69.1 128/123
P ☺☺	**LPGA International** Daytona Beach. (904) 274-3880 18 holes. Par 72/72. Yards: 7,088/5,131 Year-round. High: Nov.–Dec.	Greens: Carts: Rating: Slope:	$$–$$$$ L T Incl. 74.0/68.9 134/122
SP ☺☺☺	**Matanzas Woods Golf Club** Lakeview Dr., Palm Coast. (904) 446-6360 18 holes. Par 72/72. Yards: 6,985/5,336 Year-round. High: Jan.–Apr.	Greens: Carts: Rating: Slope:	$$–$$$ L R T J Incl. 73.3/71.2 132/126
SP ☺☺	**Palm Harbor Golf Club** Palm Harbor Pkwy., Palm Coast. (904) 445-0845 18 holes. Par 72/72. Yards: 6,572/5,346 Year-round. High: Jan.–May	Greens: Carts: Rating: Slope:	$$–$$$ L R T J Incl. 71.8/71.2 127/128
P ☺☺☺ DEAL	**Pelican Bay Country Club** Sea Duck Dr., Daytona Beach. (904) 788-6496 *South Course* 18 holes. Par 72/72. Yards: 6,561/5,260 Year-round. High: Dec.–Apr.	Greens: Carts: Rating: Slope:	$-$$ W L T Incl. 71.9/70.8 123/127
SP ☺☺	**Pine Lakes Country Club** Pine Lakes Pkwy., Palm Coast. (904) 445-0852	Greens: Carts:	$$–$$$ L R T J Incl.

	18 holes. Par 72/72. Yards: 7,074/5,166	Rating: 73.5/71.4
	Year-round. High: Jan.–Apr.	Slope: 126/124

SP
☺☺☺
River Bend Golf Club
Airport Rd., Ormond Beach. (904) 673-6000
18 holes. Par 72/72. Yards: 6,821/5,112
Year-round. High: Jan.–Apr.

Greens: $$–$$$ W L T J
Carts: Incl.
Rating: 72.3/69.6
Slope: 126/120

SP
☺☺
Spruce Creek Country Club
Daytona Beach. (904) 756-6114
18 holes. Par 72/72. Yards: 6,751/5,157
Year-round. High: Jan.–Apr.

Greens: $$ L R T J
Carts: Incl.
Rating: 72.2/70.3
Slope: 125/121

SP

☺☺☺
Sugar Mill Country Club
New Smyrna Beach. (904) 426-5210
Red/White/Blue
27 holes. Par 72/72/72. Yards: 6,766/6,695/6,749
Year-round. High: Jan.–Apr. Open to public May–Dec. only.

Greens: $$–$$$$ L
Carts: Incl.
Rating: 72.1/72.4/72.6
Slope: 125/128/129

Orlando Area

SP
☺☺☺☺
STATE
Baytree National Golf Links
National Dr., Melbourne. (407) 259-9060
18 holes. Par 72/72. Yards: 7,043/4,803
Year-round. High: Jan.–Mar.

Greens: $$$$–$$$$$ L R T
Carts: Incl.
Rating: 74.4/68.6
Slope: 138/118

SP
☺☺
Bella Vista Golf and Yacht Club
Hwy. 48, Howey In The Hills. (352) 324-3233
(800) 955-7001
18 holes. Par 71/71. Yards: 6,321/5,386
Year-round. High: Sept.–Apr.

Greens: $–$$ W L R T S J
Carts: Incl.
Rating: 68.4/71.9
Slope: 119/123

P
☺☺☺
DEAL
Cocoa Beach Golf Course
Tom Warriner Blvd., Cocoa Beach. (407) 868-3351
River/Dolphin/Lakes
27 holes. Par 71/71/72. Yards: 6,363/6,393/6,714
Year-round. High: Dec.–Apr.

Greens: $–$$ W L T J
Carts: $
Rating: 69.9/70.1/71.7
Slope: 116/115/119

SP
☺☺☺
DEAL
The Country Club at Silver Springs Shores
Silver Rd., Ocala. (904) 687-2828
18 holes. Par 72/72. Yards: 6,857/5,188
Year-round. High: Dec.–Apr.

Greens: $–$$ L T
Carts: Incl.
Rating: 73.7/70.2
Slope: 131/120

SP
☺☺☺
Country Club of Mount Dora
Mount Dora. (352) 735-2263
18 holes. Par 72/72. Yards: 6,571/5002
Year-round. High: Jan.–Mar.

Greens: $$–$$$ W L R T
Carts: Incl.
Rating: 72.1/71.0
Slope: 125/120

SP
☺☺☺
DEAL
DeBary Golf and Country Club
Plantation Dr., DeBary. (407) 668-2061
18 holes. Par 72/72. Yards: 6,776/5,060
Year-round. High: Feb.–Apr.

Greens: $$ L J
Carts: Incl.
Rating: 72.3/68.8
Slope: 128/122

SP
☺☺☺
Deltona Hills Golf and Country Club
Elkcam Blvd., Deltona. (904) 789-4911
18 holes. Par 72/73. Yards: 6,892/5,623
Year-round. High: Jan.–Apr.

Greens: $$–$$$ W L R T J
Carts: Incl.
Rating: 72.9/72.8
Slope: 125/127

P
☺☺☺
BEST
Eastwood Golf Club
Golfway Blvd., Orlando. (407) 281-4653
18 holes. Par 72/72. Yards: 7,176/5,393
Year-round. High: Jan.–Apr.

Greens: $$–$$$$ W L R T J
Carts: Incl.
Rating: 73.9/70.5
Slope: 124/117

SP
☺☺☺
Ekana Golf Club
Ekana Dr., Oviedo. (407) 366-1211
18 holes. Par 72/72. Yards: 6,683/5,544
Year-round. High: Jan.–Apr.

Greens: $$–$$$$ W L T
Carts: Incl.
Rating: 71.3/72.7
Slope: 127/127

Florida Golf Guide

P ☺☺☺	**Falcon's Fire Golf Club** Seralago Blvd., Kissimmee. (407) 239-5445 18 holes. Par 72/72. Yards: 6,901/5,417 Year-round. High: Jan.–Apr.	Greens: Carts: Rating: Slope:	$$$–$$$$ L J Incl. 72.5/70.4 125/118
P ☺☺☺ STATE	**Golden Ocala Golf Course** U.S. Hwy. 27 N.W., Ocala. (904) 622-0198 18 holes. Par 72/72. Yards: 6,735/5,595 Year-round. High: Nov.–Apr.	Greens: Carts: Rating: Slope:	$$$ L T Incl. 72.2/72.2 132/124
SP ☺☺	**Golf Hammock Country Club** Golf Hammock Dr., Sebring. (941) 382-2151 18 holes. Par 72/72. Yards: 6,431/5,352 Year-round. High: Oct.–Apr.	Greens: Carts: Rating: Slope:	$$ L R T J Incl. 71.0/70.2 127/118
R ☺☺☺☺ BEST	**Grand Cypress Resort** N. Jacaranda, Orlando. (407) 239-1904 *New Course* 18 holes. Par 72/72. Yards: 6,773/5,314	Greens: Carts: Rating: Slope:	$$$$$–$$$$$$ L T J R Incl. 72.2/69.8 122/115
☺☺☺☺ BEST	*North/South/East* 27 holes. Par 72/72/72. Yards: 6,993/6,906/6,955 Year-round. High: Sept.–Apr.	Rating: Slope:	75.1/74.7/75.0 137/138/139
SP ☺☺☺	**Grenelefe Golf and Tennis Resort** State Rd., 546, Haines City. (941) 422-7511 *South Course* 18 holes. Par 71/71. Yards: 6,869/5,174 Year-round. High: Jan.–Mar.	Greens: Carts: Rating: Slope:	$$$$$–$$$$$$ W L R T Incl. 72.6/69.5 124/115
☺☺☺☺	*East Course* 18 holes. Par 72/72. Yards: 6,802/5,095	Rating: Slope:	72.7/69.5 131/118
☺☺☺☺ STATE	*West Course* 18 holes. Par 72/72. Yards: 7,325/5,398	Rating: Slope:	75.6/71.3 133/124
P ☺☺☺ DEAL	**Habitat Golf Course** Fairgreen St., Valkaria. (407) 952-6312 18 holes. Par 72/72. Yards: 6,836/4,969 Year-round. High: Dec.–Mar.	Greens: Carts: Rating: Slope:	$-$$ W L R J $ 72.9/68.2 129/115
P ☺☺	**Harder Hall Country Club** Golfview Dr., Sebring. (941) 382-0500 18 holes. Par 72/72. Yards: 6,300/5,003 Year-round. High: Jan.–Apr.	Greens: Carts: Rating: Slope:	$–$$ L R T Incl. 70.0/68.5 116/114
P ☺☺☺ STATE	**Hunter's Creek Golf Course** Sports Club Way, Orlando. (407) 240-4653 18 holes. Par 72/72. Yards: 7,432/5,755 Year-round. High: Jan.–Mar.	Greens: Carts: Rating: Slope:	$$–$$$ W L T Incl. 75.2/72.5 127/120
SP ☺☺	**Kissimmee Bay Country Club** Kissimmee Bay Blvd., Kissimmee. (407) 348-4653 18 holes. Par 71/71. Yards: 6,846/5,171 Year-round. High: Jan.–Apr.	Greens: Carts: Rating: Slope:	$$–$$$$ W L T Incl. 70.1/71.0 119/109
SP ☺☺	**Kissimmee Golf Club** Florida Coach Dr., Kissimmee. (407) 847-2816 18 holes. Par 72/72. Yards: 6,537/5,083 Year-round. High: Dec.–Apr.	Greens: Carts: Rating: Slope:	$$–$$$ L R T Incl. 71.4/68.6 119/109
R ☺☺	**Marriott's Orlando World Center** World Center Dr., Orlando. (407) 238-8660 18 holes. Par 71/71. Yards: 6,307/4,988 Year-round. High: Jan.–Apr.	Greens: Carts: Rating: Slope:	$$$$–$$$$$$ R T J Incl. 69.8/68.5 121/115

Florida Golf Guide

SP ☺☺☺	**Metrowest Country Club** S. Hiawasee Rd., Orlando. (407) 299-1099 18 holes. Par 72/72. Yards: 7,051/5,325 Year-round. High: Jan.–May	Greens: Carts: Rating: Slope:	$$$–$$$$ L T J Incl. 73.1/69.6 126/117
SP ☺☺☺	**Mission Inn Golf and Tennis Resort** County Road 48, Howie-in-the-Hills. (352) 324-3885 *El Campeon Course* 18 holes. Par 72/73. Yards: 6,852/4,709 Year-round. High: Feb.–Apr.	Greens: Carts: Rating: Slope:	$$–$$$$ W L T S J Incl. 73.6/67.3 133/118
☺☺☺	*Las Colinas Course* 18 holes. Par 72/71. Yards: 6,879/4,651	Rating: Slope:	73.2/64.3 128/103
R ☺☺	**Orange Lake Country Club** W. Irlo Bronson Mem. Blvd., Kissimmee. (407) 239-1050 27 holes. Par 72/72/72. Yards: 6,531/6,670/6,571 Year-round. High: Jan.–Apr.	Greens: Carts: Rating: Slope:	$$–$$$$ W L R T J Incl. 72.6/72.6/72.3 132/131/131
SP ☺☺☺	**Palisades Golf Club** Palisades Blvd., Clermont. (904) 394-0085 18 holes. Par 72/72. Yards: 7,004/5,524 Year-round. High: Jan.–Apr.	Greens: Carts: Rating: Slope:	$$–$$$ W L R T S J Incl. 73.8/72.1 127/122
R ☺☺	**Plantation Inn and Golf Resort** West Fort Island Trail, Crystal River. (352) 795-7211 *Championship Course* 18 holes. Par 72/72. Yards: 6,502/5,395 Year-round. High: Feb.–Apr.	Greens: Carts: Rating: Slope:	$–$$ W L R T J Incl. 71.6/71.1 126/117
R ☺☺	**Poinciana Golf and Racquet Resort** E. Cypress Pkwy., Kissimmee. (407) 933-5300 18 holes. Par 72/72. Yards: 6,700/4,938 Year-round. High: Jan.–Apr.	Greens: Carts: Rating: Slope:	$$–$$$$ L R T J Incl. 72.2/68.4 125/118
SP ☺☺☺	**Ridgewood Lakes Golf Club** Eagle Ridge Dr., Davenport. (941) 424-8688 18 holes. Par 72/72. Yards: 7,016/5,217 Year-round. High: Nov.–Apr.	Greens: Carts: Rating: Slope:	$–$$$ Incl. 73.7/69.9 129/116
SP ☺☺	**Royal Oak Golf Course** Titusville. (407) 268-1550 18 holes. Par 71/72. Yards: 6,709/5,471 Year-round. High: Jan.–Mar.	Greens: Carts: Rating: Slope:	$–$$$ W L R T S J Incl. 72.3/71.5 126/128
SP ☺☺	**Sabal Point Country Club** Sabal Club Way, Longwood. (407) 869-4622 18 holes. Par 72/72. Yards: 6,603/5,278 Year-round. High: Jan.–Apr.	Greens: Carts: Rating: Slope:	$$–$$$ W L T J Incl. 71.6/70.0 129/119
P ☺☺	**Sebastian Municipal Golf Course** E. Airport Dr., Sebastian. (407) 589-6801 18 holes. Par 72/72. Yards: 6,717/4,579 Year-round. High: Dec.–Apr.	Greens: Carts: Rating: Slope:	$–$$ L T J Incl. 71.0/64.6 112/101
P ☺☺☺☺	**Southern Dunes Golf and Country Club** Southern Dunes Blvd., Haines City. (941) 421-4653 18 holes. Par 72/72. Yards: 7,227/4,987 Year-round. High: Oct.–Apr.	Greens: Carts: Rating: Slope:	$$$$$–$$$$$$ W L T Incl. 74.7/68.8 135/118
R ☺☺	**Spring Lake Golf and Tennis Resort** Sebring. (941) 655-1276 *Osprey/Hawk/Eagle* 27 holes. Par 71/71/72. Yards: 6,531/6,398/6,673 Year-round. High: Jan.–Mar.	Greens: Carts: Rating: Slope:	$–$$ R T Incl. 71.3/70.1/71.8 127/116/125
SP ☺☺☺	**Timacuan Golf and Country Club** Timacuan Blvd., Lake Mary. (407) 321-0010	Greens: Carts:	$$–$$$$$ W L R T J Incl.

	18 holes. Par 72/72. Yards: 6,915/5,243 Year-round. High: Jan.–Apr.	Rating: 73.2/74.8 Slope: 133/109

P
☺☺ **Turtle Creek Golf Club**
Admiralty Blvd., Rockledge. (407) 632-2520
18 holes. Par 72/72. Yards: 6,709/4,880
Year-round. High: Jan.–Apr.

Greens: $$–$$$ W L T J
Carts: Incl.
Rating: 70.1/68.8
Slope: 129/113

P
☺☺☺
DEAL **Viera East Golf Club**
Viera. (407) 639-6500
18 holes. Par 72/72. Yards: 6,720/5,428
Year-round. High: Dec.–Apr.

Greens: $$ L R T J
Carts: Incl.
Rating: 72.1/71.0
Slope: 129/122

R
☺☺☺☺ **Walt Disney World Resort**
Lake Buena Vistaq
Eagle Pines Golf Course. (407) 824-2675
18 holes. Par 72/72. Yards: 6,772/4,838
Year-round. High: Jan.–Apr.

Greens: $$$$$–$$$$$$ L R T
Carts: Incl.
Rating: 72.3/67.6
Slope: 131/116

☺☺☺ *Lake Buena Vista Golf Course.* (407) 828-3741
18 holes. Par 72/72. Yards: 6,819/5,194
Year-round. High: Jan.–Apr.

Greens: $$$$$–$$$$$$ L R T
Carts: Incl.
Rating: 72.7/69.4
Slope: 128/120

☺☺☺☺ *Magnolia Golf Course.* (407) 824-2288
18 holes. Par 72/72. Yards: 7,190/5,232
Year-round. High: Jan.–Apr.

Greens: $$$$$–$$$$$$ L R T
Carts: Incl.
Rating: 74.9/69.4
Slope: 136/125

☺☺☺☺
STATE *Osprey Ridge Golf Course.* (407) 824-2675
18 holes. Par 72/72. Yards: 7,101/5,402
Year-round. High: Jan.–Apr.

Greens: $$$$$–$$$$$$ L R T
Carts: Incl.
Rating: 73.9/70.4
Slope: 135/124

☺☺☺☺ *Palm Golf Course.* (407) 824-2288
18 holes. Par 72/72. Yards: 6,957/5,311
Year-round. High: Jan.–Apr.

Greens: $$$$$–$$$$$$ L R T
Carts: Incl.
Rating: 73.9/69.5
Slope: 138/126

SP
☺☺ **Zellwood Station Country Club**
Spillman Dr., Zellwood. (407) 886-3303
18 holes. Par 72/74. Yards: 6,400/5,377
Year-round. High: Nov.–Apr.

Greens: $$ L T
Carts: Incl.
Rating: 70.5/71.1
Slope: 122/122

Tampa Area

P
☺☺ **Apollo Beach Golf and Sea Club**
Golf & Sea Blvd., Apollo Beach. (813) 645-6212
18 holes. Par 72/72. Yards: 7,040/4,831
Year-round. High: Nov.–Mar.

Greens: $$ L T S J
Carts: Incl.
Rating: 73.9/69.1
Slope: 130/115

P
☺☺ **Bardmoor North Golf Club**
Bardmoor Blvd., Largo. (813) 397-0483
18 holes. Par 72/72. Yards: 6,960/5,269
Year-round. High: Dec.–Apr.

Greens: $$–$$$$ W L T J
Carts: Incl.
Rating: 72.4/71.8
Slope: 126/118

R
☺☺ **Belleview Mido Country Club**
Indian Rocks Rd., Belleair. (813) 581-5498
18 holes. Par 72/74. Yards: 6,655/5,703
Year-round. High: Jan.–Apr.

Greens: $$–$$$$ L R
Carts: $
Rating: 70.7/72.1
Slope: 118/119

SP
☺☺☺ **Bloomingdale Golfer's Club**
Nature's Way Blvd., Valrico. (813) 685-4105
18 holes. Par 72/73. Yards: 7,165/5,506
Year-round. High: Dec.–Apr.

Greens: $$–$$$
Carts: $
Rating: 74.4/72.1
Slope: 131/132

P

☺ **Bobby Jones Golf Complex**
Azinger Way, Sarasota. (941) 365-4653
American Course

Greens: $ L T J
Carts: $
Rating: 68.4/65.1

18 holes. Par 71/71. Yards: 6,009/4,453 Year-round. High: Dec.–Apr.	Slope: 117/107

☺ *British Course*
18 holes. Par 72/72. Yards: 6,468/5,695

Rating: 70.0/71.8
Slope: 111/115

SP **Citrus Hills Golf and Country Club**
E. Hartford St., Hernando. (352) 746-4425
☺☺ *Meadows Course*
18 holes. Par 70/70. Yards: 5,885/4,585

Greens: $$ L T
Carts: NA
Rating: 68.5/66.9
Slope: 114/112

☺☺☺ *Oaks Course*
18 holes. Par 70/70. Yards: 6,323/4,647
Year-round. High: Dec.–Apr.

Rating: 68.7/67.7
Slope: 117/114

P **The Club at Oak Ford**
Palm View Rd., Sarasota. (941) 371-3680
☺☺☺ *Myrtle/Palms/Live Oaks*
27 holes. Par 72/72. Yards: 6,743/5,051
Year-round. High: Jan.–Apr.

Greens: $$ L
Carts: Incl.
Rating: 72.7/69.0
Slope: 131/118

SP **The Country Club at Jacaranda West**
☺☺☺ Jacaranda Blvd., Venice. (941) 493-2664
DEAL 18 holes. Par 72/72. Yards: 6,589/5,314
STATE Year-round. High: Jan.–Apr.

Greens: $$-$$$ L T J
Carts: Incl.
Rating: 71.9/70.7
Slope: 130/117

SP **Dunedin Country Club**
☺☺ Palm Blvd., Dunedin. (813) 733-7836
18 holes. Par 72/73. Yards: 6,565/5,726
Year-round. High: Dec.–Apr.

Greens: $$-$$$ L T
Carts: Incl.
Rating: 70.3/73.1
Slope: 115/121

SP **The Eagles Golf Club**
Nine Eagles Dr., Odessa. (813) 920-6681
☺☺☺ *Forest/Lakes/Oaks*
27 holes. Par 72/72/72. Yards: 7,134/7,194/7,068
Year-round. High: Jan.–Apr.

Greens: $$-$$$ W L T
Carts: Incl.
Rating: 70.3/70.3/70.3
Slope: 130/130/130

P **Fox Hollow Golf Club**
☺☺☺ Robert Trent Jones Pkwy., New Port Richey
(813) 376-6333
18 holes. Par 71/71. Yards: 7,138/4,454
Year-round. High: Jan.–Mar.

Greens: $$-$$$$ W L J
Carts: Incl.
Rating: 74.3/65.7
Slope: 137/112

SP **The Golf Club at Cypress Creek**
☺☺☺ Cypress Village Blvd., Ruskin. (813) 634-8888
DEAL 18 holes. Par 72/72. Yards: 6,839/4,640
STATE Year-round. High: Feb.–Apr.

Greens: $$ W L R T
Carts: Incl.
Rating: 74.0/66.0
Slope: 133/114

R **The Golf Club at Marco**
☺☺☺ Marriott Club Dr., Naples. (941) 793-6060
DEAL 18 holes. Par 72/72. Yards: 6,898/5,416
STATE Year-round. High: Jan.–Apr.

Greens: $$-$$$$$
Carts: Incl.
Rating: 73.4/70.9
Slope: 137/122

SP **Huntington Hills Golf and Country Club**
☺☺☺ Duff Rd., Lakeland. (941) 859-3689
18 holes. Par 72/72. Yards: 6,631/5,011
Year-round. High: Dec.-Mar.

Greens: $$ W L T
Carts: Incl.
Rating: 72.5/68.7
Slope: 122/115

SP **Imperial Lakes Golf Club**
☺☺ Buffalo Rd., Palmetto. (941) 747-4653
18 holes. Par 72/72. Yards: 6,658/5,270
Year-round. High: Nov.–Apr.

Greens: $-$$ W L T J
Carts: Incl.
Rating: 71.5/69.7
Slope: 123/117

R **Innisbrook Hilton Resort**
Hwy. 19 N., Palm Harbor. (727) 942-2000
☺☺☺☺ *Copperhead Course*

Greens: $$$$-$$$$$ L R J
Carts: Incl.
Rating: 74.4/71.8

Florida Golf Guide

BEST	18 holes. Par 71/71. Yards: 7,087/5,537 Year-round. High: Nov.–Apr.	Slope:	140/130
☺☺☺☺ BEST	*Island Course* 18 holes. Par 72/72. Yards: 6,999/5,578	Rating: Slope:	74.1/73.0 132/129
☺☺☺☺	*Eagle's Watch* 18 holes. Par 71/71. Yards: 6,635/4,975	Rating: Slope:	72.0/68.9 127/121
☺☺☺☺	*Hawk's Run* 18 holes. Par 71/71. Yards: 6,445/4,970	Rating: Slope:	70.5/68.4 125/118

SP
☺☺
Lansbrook Golf Club
Village Center Dr., Palm Harbor. (813) 784-7333
18 holes. Par 72/72. Yards: 6,719/5,264
Year-round. High: Dec.–Apr.
Greens: $$–$$$ W L T
Carts: Incl.
Rating: 71.6/69.3
Slope: 126/119

SP
☺☺
The Links of Lake Bernadette
Links Lane, Zephyr Hills. (813) 788-4653
18 holes. Par 71/71. Yards: 6,392/5,031
Year-round. High: Jan.–Apr.
Greens: $$ W L T
Carts: Incl.
Rating: 70.0/68.0
Slope: 117/118

R

☺☺☺
Longboat Key Club
Gulf of Mexico Dr., Longboat Key. (941) 383-0781
Islandside Course
18 holes. Par 72/72. Yards: 6,792/5,198
Year-round. High: Dec.–May. Note: Resort guests only.
Greens: $$$$$ L T
Carts: Incl.
Rating: NA
Slope: 138/121

P
☺☺☺
DEAL
Mangrove Bay Golf Course
62nd Ave. N.E., St. Petersburg. (813) 893-7800
18 holes. Par 72/72. Yards: 6,779/5,204
Year-round. High: Nov.–Feb., Apr.–May
Greens: $$ L T
Carts: Incl.
Rating: 71.5/68.5
Slope: 120/112

SP
☺☺
Northdale Golf Club
Northdale Blvd., Tampa. (813) 962-0428
18 holes. Par 72/72. Yards: 6,791/5,397
Year-round. High: Dec.–Apr.
Greens: $$ T
Carts: Incl.
Rating: 72.1/71.0
Slope: 119/113

P
☺☺☺
DEAL
Oak Hills Golf Club
Northcliff Blvd., Spring Hill. (352) 683-6830
18 holes. Par 72/72. Yards: 6,791/5,397
Year-round. High: Dec.–Mar.
Greens: $–$$ T
Carts: Incl.
Rating: 72.1/71.0
Slope: 119/113

SP

☺☺☺
Plantation Golf and Country Club
Rockley Blvd., Venice. (941) 493-2000
Bobcat Course
18 holes. Par 72/72. Yards: 6,840/5,073
Year-round. High: Oct.–Apr.
Greens: $$–$$$ L R
Carts: $
Rating: 73.0/70.6
Slope: 130/121

☺☺☺
Panther Course
18 holes. Par 72/72. Yards: 6,311/4,751
Rating: 70.7/68.0
Slope: 124/117

P
☺☺☺
The River Club
River Club Blvd., Bradenton. (941) 751-4211
18 holes. Par 72/72. Yards: 7,026/5,157
Year-round. High: Jan.–Apr.
Greens: $$ L T
Carts: Incl.
Rating: 74.1/70.4
Slope: 135/121

SP
☺☺☺
River Hills Country Club
New River Hills Pkwy., Valrico. (941) 653-3323
18 holes. Par 72/72. Yards: 7,007/5,236
Year-round. High: Jan.–Apr.
Greens: $$–$$$
Carts: $
Rating: 74.0/70.4
Slope: 132/124

SP
☺☺☺☺
Riverwood Golf Club
Riverwood Dr., Port Charlotte. (941) 764-6661
18 holes. Par 72/72. Yards: 6,938/4,695
Year-round. High: Dec.–Apr.
Greens: $$$–$$$$$ L R T
Carts: Incl.
Rating: 73.8/66.8
Slope: 133/114

Florida Golf Guide

P ☺☺	**Rogers Park Golf Course** N. 30th St., Tampa. (813) 234-1911 18 holes. Par 72/72. Yards: 6,500/5,900 Year-round. High: Jan.–Apr.	Greens: Carts: Rating: Slope:	$$ $ 71.0/67.0 120/114	W L T S J
SP ☺☺☺	**Rosedale Golf and Country Club** 87th St. E., Bradenton. (941) 756-0004 18 holes. Par 72/72. Yards: 6,779/5,169 Year-round. High: Oct.–May	Greens: Carts: Rating: Slope:	$$–$$$ Incl. 72.9/70.4 134/114	L R T
R ☺☺☺	**Saddlebrook Resort** Saddlebrook Way, Wesley Chapel. (813) 973-1111 *Palmer Course* 18 holes. Par 71/71. Yards: 6,469/5,212 Year-round. High: Nov.–Apr.	Greens: Carts: Rating: Slope:	$$–$$$$$ Incl. 71.0/70.2 126/121	L R
☺☺☺	*Saddlebrook Course* 18 holes. Par 70/70. Yards: 6,603/5,183	Rating: Slope:	72.0/70.8 124/124	
SP ☺☺	**Sandpiper Golf and Country Club** Sandpipers Dr., Lakeland. (941) 859-5461 18 holes. Par 70/70. Yards: 6,442/5,024 Year-round. High: Jan.–Mar.	Greens: Carts: Rating: Slope:	$$ Incl. 70.4/67.7 120/109	W L T
SP ☺☺	**Sarasota Golf Club** N. Leewynn Dr., Sarasota. (941) 371-3431 18 holes. Par 72/72. Yards: 7,066/5,004 Year-round. High: Jan.–Apr.	Greens: Carts: Rating: Slope:	$$ Incl. 73.0/67.4 120/106	L R T S J
SP ☺☺	**Schalamar Creek Golf and Country Club** U.S. Hwy. 92 E., Lakeland. (941) 666-1623 18 holes. Par 72/72. Yards: 6,399/4,363 Year-round. High: Jan.–Apr.	Greens: Carts: Rating: Slope:	$–$$ $ 70.9/64.8 124/106	W L T
SP ☺☺☺ DEAL	**Seven Hills Golfers Club** Fairchild Rd., Spring Hill. (352) 688-8888 18 holes. Par 72/72. Yards: 6,715/4,902 Year-round. High: Dec.–Apr.	Greens: Carts: Rating: Slope:	$$ Incl. 70.5/66.5 126/109	W L T
SP ☺☺☺	**Seven Springs Golf and Country Club** Trophy Blvd., New Port Richey. (813) 376-0035 *Championship Course* 18 holes. Par 72/72. Yards: 6,566/5,250 Year-round. High: Jan.–Apr.	Greens: Carts: Rating: Slope:	$$ Incl. NA 123/112	L T
P ☺☺☺ DEAL	**Seville Golf and Country Club** Weeki Wachee. (352) 596-7888 18 holes. Par 72/72. Yards: 7,140/5,236 Year-round. High: Jan.–Apr.	Greens: Carts: Rating: Slope:	$–$$ Incl. 74.9/70.8 138/126	W L T
P ☺☺☺ DEAL	**Sherman Hills Golf Club** Eagle Falls Dr., Brooksville. (352) 544-0990 18 holes. Par 72/72. Yards: 6,778/4,959 Year-round. High: Oct.–Apr.	Greens: Carts: Rating: Slope:	$–$$ Incl. 72.1/68.2 118/110	W L T
SP ☺☺	**Silver Oaks Golf and Country Club** Zephyr Hills. (813) 788-1225 18 holes. Par 72/72. Yards: 6,632/5,147 Year-round. High: Dec.–May	Greens: Carts: Rating: Slope:	$–$$ Incl. 71.1/68.8 120/109	W L R T S J
R ☺☺	**Stouffer Vinoy Golf Club** Snell Isle Blvd. N.E., St. Petersburg. (813) 896-8000 18 holes. Par 70/71. Yards: 6,267/4,818 Year-round. High: Jan.–Apr.	Greens: Carts: Rating: Slope:	$$$$ Inquire 70.0/67.3 118/111	T
SP ☺☺☺	**Summerfield Golf Club** Summerfield Blvd., Riverview. (813) 671-3311	Greens: Carts:	$–$$ Incl.	

DEAL	18 holes. Par 71/71. Yards: 6,903/5,139 Year-round. High: Jan.–Apr.	Rating: Slope:	73.0/69.6 125/114

SP ☺☺	**Tarpon Woods Golf and Country Club** Tarpon Woods Blvd., Palm Harbor. (813) 784-2273 18 holes. Par 72/72. Yards: 6,466/5,205 Year-round. High: Jan.–May	Greens: Carts: Rating: Slope:	$$–$$$ W L T Incl. 71.2/69.5 128/115

SP ☺☺☺ DEAL	**Tatum Ridge Golf Links** North Tatum Rd., Sarasota. (941) 378-4211 18 holes. Par 72/72. Yards: 6,757/5,149 Year-round. High: Nov.–May	Greens: Carts: Rating: Slope:	$–$$ L S Incl. 71.9/68.9 124/114

SP ☺☺	**Tournament Players Club of Tampa Bay** Terrain de Golf Dr., Lutz. (813) 949-0091 18 holes. Par 71/71. Yards: 6,898/5,036 Year-round. High: Jan.–Apr.	Greens: Carts: Rating: Slope:	$$$–$$$$ W L T J Incl. 73.4/69.1 130/119

P ☺☺	**University of South Florida Golf Course** 46th St., Tampa. (813) 974-2071 18 holes. Par 72/72. Yards: 6,942/5,393 Year-round. High: Nov.–Apr.	Greens: Carts: Rating: Slope:	$ W L T S J Inquire 73.1/69.8 131/115

SP ☺☺☺☺	**University Park Country Club** Park Blvd., University Park. (941) 359-9999 27 holes. Par 72/72/72. Yards: 7,001/7,152/7,247 Year-round. High: Nov.–Apr.	Greens: Carts: Rating: Slope:	$$$$–$$$$$ L T Incl. 73.6/74.0/74.4 138/134/132

P ☺☺☺	**Waterford Golf Club** Gleneagles Dr., Venice. (941) 484-6621 *Gleneagles/Turnberry/Sawgrass* 27 holes. Par 72/72. Yards: 6,454/6,670/6,498 Year-round. High: Jan.–Apr.	Greens: Carts: Rating: Slope:	$$$ L Incl. 71.5/72.3/71.4 126/128/124

SP ☺☺	**Wedgewood Golf and Country Club** Carpenter's Way, Lakeland. (941) 858-4451 18 holes. Par 72/72. Yards: 6,401/4,885 Year-round. High: Nov.–May	Greens: Carts: Rating: Slope:	$–$$ L T Incl. 69.1/68.1 115/113

P ☺☺☺	**Westchase Golf Club** Radcliffe Dr., Tampa. (813) 854-2331 18 holes. Par 72/72. Yards: 6,710/5,205 Year-round. High: Jan.–Apr.	Greens: Carts: Rating: Slope:	$$–$$$ W L T J Incl. 71.8/69.1 130/121

R ☺☺☺☺ STATE	**World Woods Golf Club** Ponce De Leon Blvd., Brooksville. (352) 796-5500 *Pine Barrens Course* 18 holes. Par 71/71. Yards: 6,902/5,301 Year-round. High: Jan.–Apr.	Greens: Carts: Rating: Slope:	$$$$–$$$$$ W L Incl. 73.7/70.9 140/132

☺☺☺☺ STATE	*Rolling Oaks Course* 18 holes. Par 72/72. Yards: 6,985/5,245	Rating: Slope:	73.5/70.7 136/128

Fort Myers Area

P ☺☺	**Cape Coral Golf and Tennis Resort** Palm Tree Blvd., Cape Coral. (941) 542-7879 18 holes. Par 72/72. Yards: 6,649/5,464 Year-round. High: Jan.–Mar.	Greens: Carts: Rating: Slope:	$–$$$$ L R T J Incl. 71.6/71.2 122/119

P ☺☺	**Coral Oaks Golf Course** N.W. 28th Ave., Cape Coral. (941) 283-4100 18 holes. Par 72/72. Yards: 6,623/4,803 Year-round. High: Dec.–Apr.	Greens: Carts: Rating: Slope:	$$ Incl. 71.7/68.9 123/117

P ☺☺☺	**Eastwood Golf Course** Bruce Herd Lane, Fort Myers. (941) 275-4848	Greens: Carts:	$$–$$$ W L T Incl.

	18 holes. Par 72/72. Yards: 6,772/5,116	Rating: 73.3/68.9
	Year-round. High: Dec.–Mar.	Slope: 130/120

P ☺☺	**Fort Myers Country Club** McGregor Blvd., Fort Myers. (941) 936-2457 18 holes. Par 71/71. Yards: 6,414/5,135 Year-round. High: Dec.–Apr.	Greens: $$ Carts: $ Rating: NA Slope: 118/117	W L T

SP ☺☺☺ STATE	**Gateway Golf and Country Club** Fort Myers. (941) 561-1010 18 holes. Par 72/72. Yards: 6,974/5,323 Year-round. High: Jan.–Mar.	Greens: $$$$–$$$$$ Carts: Incl. Rating: 73.7/70.6 Slope: 130/120	L T

P ☺☺☺☺	**Lely Flamingo Island Club** Lely Resort Blvd., Naples. (941) 793-2223 *Flamingo* 18 holes. Par 72/72. Yards: 7,171/5,377 Year-round. High: Nov.–Apr.	Greens: $$$$$–$$$$$$ Carts: Incl. Rating: 75.0/71.4 Slope: 136/123	L T

☺☺☺☺	*Mustang* 18 holes. Par 72/72. Yards: 7,217/5,197 Year-round. High: Nov.–Apr.	Rating: 75.2/70.5 Slope: 141/120

SP ☺☺	**Lochmoor Country Club** Orange Grove Blvd., North Fort Myers. (941) 995-0501 18 holes. Par 72/72. Yards: 7,908/5,152 Year-round. High: Jan.–Apr.	Greens: $$–$$$ Carts: Incl. Rating: 73.1/69.1 Slope: 128/116	L T

P ☺☺	**Marco Shores Country Club** Mainsail Dr., Naples. (941) 394-2581 18 holes. Par 72/72. Yards: 6,879/5,634 Year-round. High: Jan.–Apr.	Greens: $$–$$$$ Carts: Incl. Rating: 73.0/72.3 Slope: 125/121	L T J

SP ☺☺	**Naples Beach Hotel and Golf Club** Gulf Shore Blvd. N., Naples. (941) 261-2222 18 holes. Par 72/72. Yards: 6,500/5,300 Year-round. High: Jan.–Apr.	Greens: $$–$$$$$ Carts: Incl. Rating: 71.2/70.1 Slope: 122/115	R

Palm Beach Area

R ☺☺☺	**Atlantis Country Club** Atlantis Blvd., Atlantis. (561) 968-1300 18 holes. Par 72/72. Yards: 6,537/5,258 Year-round. High: Oct.–Mar.	Greens: $$–$$$ Carts: $ Rating: 71.5/70.9 Slope: 128/123	W L R

SP ☺☺☺	**Binks Forest Golf Course** Binks Forest Dr., Wellington. (561) 795-0595 18 holes. Par 72/72. Yards: 7,065/5,599 Year-round. High: Nov.–Apr.	Greens: $$–$$$$ Carts: Incl. Rating: 75.0/71.9 Slope: 138/127	W L R T

R ☺	**Boca Raton Resort and Club** E. Camino Real, Boca Raton. (561) 395-3000, ext. 3076 *Country Club Course* 18 holes. Par 72/72. Yards: 6,564/5,565 Year-round. High: Oct.–May	Greens: $$$$ Carts: Incl. Rating: NA Slope: 126/124	L T

☺☺	*Resort Course* 18 holes. Par 71/71. Yards: 6,682/5,518	Rating: NA Slope: 122/124

P ☺☺	**Boynton Beach Municipal Golf Course** Jog Rd., Boynton Beach. (561) 969-2201 *Red/White/Blue* 27 holes. Par 71/66/65. Yards: 6,316/5,290/5,062	Greens: $ Carts: $ Rating: 70.1/65.0/63.9 Slope: 129/NA/NA	L J

R ☺☺	**The Breakers Club** South County Rd., Palm Beach. (561) 659-8407 18 holes. Par 70/72. Yards: 6,017/5,582 Year-round. High: Dec.–Mar.	Greens: $$$$$ Carts: Incl. Rating: 69.3/72.6 Slope: 121/122	R T J

Florida Golf Guide

SP ☺☺☺	**Breakers West Country Club** Flagler Pkwy., W. Palm Beach. (561) 653-6320 18 holes. Par 71/71. Yards: 6,905/5,197 Year-round. High: Nov.–Apr.	Greens: Carts: Rating: Slope:	$$$$–$$$$$ Incl. 73.9/71.1 135/123
P ☺☺☺	**The Champions Club at Summerfield** S.E. Summerfield Way, Stuart. (561) 283-1500 18 holes. Par 72/72. Yards: 6,809/4,914 Year-round. High: Nov.–Apr.	Greens: Carts: Rating: Slope:	$$–$$$ L T J Incl. 72.8/71.0 131/120
P ☺☺☺	**Cypress Creek** North Military Trail, Boynton Beach. (888) 650-4653 18 holes. Par 72/72. Yards: 6,808/5,425 Year-round. High: Dec.–Apr.	Greens: Carts: Rating: Slope:	$$$$ W L T S J Incl. 72.0/72.3 129/127
P ☺☺☺ DEAL	**Delray Beach Golf Club** Highland Ave., Delray Beach. (561) 243-7380 18 holes. Par 72/72. Yards: 6,907/5,189 Year-round. High: Dec.–Mar.	Greens: Carts: Rating: Slope:	$–$$ L J Incl. 73.0/69.8 126/117
SP ☺☺	**Dodger Pines Country Club** 26th St., Vero Beach. (561) 569-4400 18 holes. Par 73/74. Yards: 6,692/5,776 Year-round. High: Jan.–Apr.	Greens: Carts: Rating: Slope:	$–$$$ $ 71.2/72.3 122/124
SP ☺☺☺☺ STATE	**Emerald Dunes Golf Club** Emerald Dunes Dr., W. Palm Beach. (888) 650-4653 18 holes. Par 72/72. Yards: 7,006/4,676 Year-round. High: Dec.–Apr.	Greens: Carts: Rating: Slope:	$$$$$–$$$$$$ L T J Incl. 73.8/67.1 133/115
P ☺☺☺ DEAL	**Fairwinds Golf Course** Fairwinds Dr., Fort Pierce. (407) 466-4653 18 holes. Par 72/72. Yards: 6,783/5,392 Year-round. High: Jan.–Apr.	Greens: Carts: Rating: Slope:	$$ L J Incl. 71.1/68.5 119/112
P ☺☺	**Lake Worth Golf Club** 7th Ave. N., Lake Worth. (561) 582-9713 18 holes. Par 70/70. Yards: 6,113/5,413 Year-round. High: Jan.–Mar.	Greens: Carts: Rating: Slope:	$–$$ W T J Inquire 68.6/69.6 116/113
P ☺☺	**Martin County Golf and Country Club** S.E. Saint Lucie Blvd., Stuart. (561) 287-3747 *Blue/Gold* 18 holes. Par 72/72. Yards: 5,900/5,236 Year-round. High: Dec.–Apr.	Greens: Carts: Rating: Slope:	$–$$ L J Inquire 67.5/69.1 120/120
☺☺	*Red/White* 18 holes. Par 72/73. Yards: 6,200/5,400	Rating: Slope:	69.1/70.4 116/120
P ☺☺	**North Palm Beach Country Club** U.S. Hwy. 1, N. Palm Beach. (561) 626-4344 18 holes. Par 72/72. Yards: 6,275/5,055 Year-round. High: Nov.–May	Greens: Carts: Rating: Slope:	$$–$$$ L J Incl. 70.0/69.0 117/115
P ☺☺	**Palm Beach Gardens Municipal Golf Course** Northlake Blvd., Palm Beach Gardens. (561) 775-2556 18 holes. Par 72/72. Yards: 6,375/4,663 Year-round. High: Dec.–Apr.	Greens: Carts: Rating: Slope:	$$ W L T S J Incl. 71.1/66.5 125/110
P ☺☺☺	**Polo Trace** 13481 Polo Trace Dr., Delray Beach. (888) 650-4653 18 holes. Par 72/72. Yards: 7,105/5,314 Year-round. High: Dec.–Apr.	Greens: Carts: Rating: Slope:	$$$$$$ W L T S J Incl. 74.8/71.6 138/125
R ☺☺☺☺	**PGA National Resort and Spa** Ave. of Champions, Palm Beach Gardens. (561) 627-1800 *Champion Course*	Greens: Carts: Rating:	$$$$$$ L $$ 73.7/71.1

Florida Golf Guide

BEST	18 holes. Par 72/72. Yards: 6,777/5,266 Year-round. High: Jan.–Apr.	Slope:	140/131
☺☺☺	*Estate Course* (561) 627-1614 18 holes. Par 72/72. Yards: 6,694/4,943	Greens: Carts: Rating: Slope:	$$$$–$$$$$ $$ 72.5/69.1 138/118
☺☺☺	*General Course* 18 holes. Par 72/72. Yards: 6,768/5,327	Greens: Carts: Rating: Slope:	$$$$–$$$$$$ $$ 72.6/71.2 132/121
☺☺☺	*Haig Course* 18 holes. Par 72/72. Yards: 6,806/5,645	Greens: Carts: Rating: Slope:	$$$$–$$$$$$ $$ 73.5/72.9 135/129
☺☺☺	*Squire Course* 18 holes. Par 72/72. Yards: 6,465/4,975	Greens: Carts: Rating: Slope:	$$$$–$$$$$$ $$ 72.1/69.8 132/123
P ☺☺☺ DEAL	**Sandridge Golf Club** 73rd St., Vero Beach. (561) 770-5000 *Dunes Course* 18 holes. Par 72/72. Yards: 6,817/4,944 Year-round. High: Jan.–Mar.	Greens: Carts: Rating: Slope:	$–$$　　　W L T J Incl. 72.2/69.1 123/114
☺☺☺ DEAL	*Lakes Course* 18 holes. Par 72/72. Yards: 6,152/4,625	Rating: Slope:	69.3/66.6 120/109
P ☺☺☺ DEAL STATE	**West Palm Beach Municipal Country Club** Parker Ave., West Palm Beach. (561) 582-2019 18 holes. Par 72/72. Yards: 6,789/5,884 Year-round. High: Dec.–Apr.	Greens: Carts: Rating: Slope:	$–$$　　　L T J $ 72.8/73.3 124/126
SP ☺☺☺	**Westchester Golf and Country Club** Westchester Club Dr., Boynton Beach. (561) 734-6300 18 holes. Par 72/72. Yards: 6,760/4,886 Year-round. High: Nov.–Apr.	Greens: Carts: Rating: Slope:	$$–$$$　　W L R Incl. 72.0/67.5 128/111
P ☺☺☺	**Winston Trails Golf Club** Winston Trails Blvd., Lake Worth. (561) 439-3700 18 holes. Par 72/72. Yards: 6,835/5,405 Year-round. High: Mar.–Nov.	Greens: Carts: Rating: Slope:	$$–$$$$　W L T Incl. 73.0/71.1 130/119

Fort Lauderdale Area

P ☺☺☺	**Bonaventure** Fort Lauderdale. (888) 650-4653 *East Course* 18 holes. Par 72/72. Yards: 7,011/5,304 Year-round. High: Dec.–Apr.	Greens: Carts: Rating: Slope:	$$$$　　　W L T S J Incl. 74.2/71.6 132/122
☺☺☺	*West Course* 18 holes. Par 70/70. Yards: 6,189/4,993 Year-round. High: Dec.–Apr.	Rating: Slope:	71.0/69.0 118/114
P ☺☺	**Crystal Lake Country Club** Crystal Lake Dr., Pompano Beach. (954) 942-1900 *Tam O'Shanter North Course* 18 holes. Par 70/72. Yards: 6,390/5,205 Year-round. High: Nov.–Apr.	Greens: Carts: Rating: Slope:	$$–$$$　　L T Incl. 71.0/70.0 121/118
☺☺	*South Course* 18 holes. Par 72/72. Yards: 6,610/5,458	Rating: Slope:	71.7/71.5 112/109

Florida Golf Guide

SP	**Deer Creek Golf Club**	Greens:	$$–$$$$$$ W L R J
☺☺☺	Deerfield Beach. (954) 421-5550	Carts:	Incl.
	18 holes. Par 72/72. Yards: 7,038/5,319	Rating:	74.8/71.6
	Year-round. High: Dec.–Apr.	Slope:	133/120

R	**Grand Palms Golf and Country Club Resort**	Greens:	$$–$$$ W L R T
	Grand Palms Dr., Pembroke Pines. (954) 437-3334	Carts:	Incl.
☺☺	*Grand/Royal/Sabal*	Rating:	71.6/71.9/71.5
	27 holes. Par 72/73/71. Yards: 6,757/6,736/6,653	Slope:	127/128/124
	Year-round. High: Dec.–Apr.		

P	**Jacaranda Golf Club**	Greens:	$$$–$$$$ W L T
	W. Broward Blvd., Plantation. (954) 472-5836	Carts:	Incl.
☺☺☺	*East Course*	Rating:	NA
	18 holes. Par 72/72. Yards: 7,170/5,668	Slope:	130/121
	Year-round. High: Nov.–May		

☺☺☺	*West Course*	Rating:	NA
	18 holes. Par 72/72. Yards: 6,729/5,314	Slope:	135/129

R	**Palm Aire Spa Resort and Country Club**	Greens:	$$–$$$
	Palm Aire Dr. N., Pompano Beach. (954) 974-7699	Carts:	$
☺☺	*Palms Course*	Rating:	73.7/70.9
	18 holes. Par 72/72. Yards: 6,932/5,434	Slope:	128/120
	Year-round. High: May–Sept.		

R	**Palm Aire Spa Resort and Country Club**	Greens:	$$–$$$
	Pompano Beach. (954) 978-1737	Carts:	$
☺☺	*The Oaks*	Rating:	72.2/70.4
	18 holes. Par 72/72. Yards: 6,747/5,402	Slope:	122/114
	Year-round. High: May–Sept.		

☺☺	*The Cypress*	Rating:	73.3/70.8
	18 holes. Par 72/72. Yards: 6,868/5,447	Slope:	128/118

P	**Pompano Beach Golf Course**	Greens:	$$
	N. Federal Hwy., Pompano Beach. (954) 781-0426	Carts:	NA
☺☺	*Palms Course*	Rating:	69.4/70.2
	18 holes. Par 72/72. Yards: 6,356/5,426	Slope:	113/114
	Year-round. High: Jan.–Apr.		

☺☺	*Pines Course*	Rating:	69.4/70.2
	18 holes. Par 72/74. Yards: 6,886/5,980	Slope:	113/114

R	**Raintree Golf Course**	Greens:	$$–$$$ W L R T S J
☺☺☺	S. Hiatus Rd., Pembroke Pines. (954) 432-4400	Carts:	Incl.
	18 holes. Par 72/72. Yards: 6,456/5,274	Rating:	70.8/70.2
	Year-round. High: Nov.–Apr.	Slope:	126/122

R	**Rolling Hills Hotel and Golf Resort**	Greens:	$$–$$$ W L R T
☺☺	W. Rolling Hills Circle, Fort Lauderdale. (954) 475-3010	Carts:	Incl.
	18 holes. Par 72/72. Yards: 6,905/5,630	Rating:	72.7/71.7
	Year-round. High: Jan.–Apr.	Slope:	124/121

R	**Turnberry Isle Resort and Club**	Greens:	$$$–$$$$$ L
	W. Country Club Dr., Aventura. (305) 933-6929	Carts:	$
☺☺	*North Course*	Rating:	70.3/67.9
	18 holes. Par 70/70. Yards: 6,403/4,991	Slope:	127/107
	Year-round. High: Nov.–Apr.		

☺☺☺	*South Course*	Rating:	73.7/71.3
	18 holes. Par 72/72. Yards: 7,003/5,581	Slope:	136/116

Miami Area

P	**The Biltmore Golf Course**	Greens:	$$$
☺☺	Anastasia Ave., Coral Gables. (305) 460-5364	Carts:	Incl.

Florida Golf Guide

	18 holes. Par 71/74. Yards: 6,642/5,237	Rating: 71.5/70.1
	Year-round. High: Nov.–Apr.	Slope: 119/115

P

Colony West Country Club
N.W. 88th Ave., Tamarac. (305) 726-8430
☺☺☺ *Championship Course*
18 holes. Par 71/71. Yards: 7,271/5,422
Year-round. High: Dec.–Apr.

Greens: $$–$$$$ W L T
Carts: Incl.
Rating: 75.8/71.6
Slope: 138/127

P
☺☺

Don Shula's Golf Club
Miami Lakes Dr., Miami Lake. (305) 821-1150
18 holes. Par 72/72. Yards: 7,055/5,639
Year-round. High: Jan.–Apr.

Greens: $$–$$$ W L R T
Carts: $
Rating: 73.0/70.5
Slope: 124/120

R

☺☺☺
BEST

Doral Golf Resort and Spa
N.W. 87th Ave., Miami. (305) 592-2000
Blue Course
18 holes. Par: 72/72. Yards: 6,935/5,786
Year-round. High: Nov.–Apr.

Greens: $$$–$$$$$$ W L S R T
Carts: Incl.
Rating: 73.2/73.0
Slope: 127/124

☺☺☺

Gold Course
18 holes. Par: 70/70. Yards: 6,361/5,422

Rating: 70.6/71.4
Slope: 127/123

☺☺☺

Red Course
18 holes. Par: 71/71. Yards: 6,210/5,254

Rating: 69.9/70.6
Slope: 118/118

☺☺☺

White Course
18 holes. Par: 72/72. Yards: 6,208/5,286

Rating: 69.7/70.1
Slope: 117/116

SP

☺☺☺
STATE

Doral Park Golf and Country Club
N.W. 104th Ave., Miami. (305) 594-0954
Silver Course
18 holes. Par 71/71. Yards: 6,614/4,661
Year-round. High: Jan.–Apr.

Greens: $$$–$$$$ W L R
Carts: Incl.
Rating: 72.0/66.6
Slope: 129/113

P

☺

Fontainebleau Golf Course
Fontainebleau Blvd., Miami. (305) 221-5181
East Course
18 holes. Par 72/72. Yards: 7,035/5,586
Year-round. High: Nov.–Apr.

Greens: $$ W L
Carts: Incl.
Rating: 73.3/71.5
Slope: 122/119

☺

West Course
18 holes. Par 72/72. Yards: 6,944/5,565

Rating: 72.5/71.0
Slope: 120/118

P

☺☺☺
DEAL

Golf Club of Miami
Miami Gardens Dr., Miami. (305) 829-4700
East Course
18 holes. Par 70/70. Yards: 6,553/5,025
Year-round. High: Feb.–Nov.

Greens: $$ L T
Carts: Incl.
Rating: 70.3/68.8
Slope: 124/117

☺☺☺
DEAL

West Course
18 holes. Par 72/72. Yards: 7,017/5,298

Rating: 73.5/70.1
Slope: 130/123

P
☺☺☺☺
BEST

Links at Key Biscayne
Crandon Blvd., Key Biscayne. (305) 361-9129
18 holes. Par 72/72. Yards: 7,180/5,423
Year-round. High: Dec.–May

Greens: $$$$–$$$$$ W L T
Carts: Incl.
Rating: 75.4/71.8
Slope: 129/125

SP
☺☺☺

The Links at Polo Trace
Hagen Ranch Rd., Delray Beach. (407) 459-5300
18 holes. Par 72/72. Yards: 7,096/5,314
Year-round. High: Dec.–Apr.

Greens: $$–$$$$$ W L T S J
Carts: Incl.
Rating: 73.4/71.0
Slope: 134/124

SP
☺☺

Miami Shores Country Club
Biscayne Blvd., Miami Shores. (305) 795-2366

Greens: $$–$$$ W L T
Carts: Incl.

	18 holes. Par 71/72. Yards: 6,400/5,400	Rating:	70.6/71.3	
	Year-round. High: Dec.–Apr.	Slope:	121/126	
P	**Normandy Shores Golf Course**	Greens:	$$–$$$	W L T
☺☺	Biarritz Dr., Miami Beach. (305) 868-6502	Carts:	Incl.	
	18 holes. Par 71/73. Yards: 6,402/5,527	Rating:	70.5/71.0	
	Year-round. High: Nov.–Apr.	Slope:	120/119	
P	**Palmetto Golf Course**	Greens:	$–$$	W L T J
☺☺	S.W. 152nd St., Miami. (305) 238-2922	Carts:	$	
	18 holes. Par 70/73. Yards: 6,713/5,725	Rating:	72.7/73.4	
	Year-round. High: Jan.–Mar.	Slope:	128/125	

Georgia

The most famous of the more than 300 courses in Georgia is the Augusta National Golf Club, site of the Masters; alas, it is not open to the public. You can, though, practice your skills to prepare for the PGA Tour yourself at several hundred other interesting courses.

Atlanta Area

The Boulders Course at Lake Acworth is a tough lakeside course with an especially challenging back nine.

There are two topflight choices at **Reynold's Plantation** in Eatonton, in the rural countryside between Macon and Atlanta: the superb Nicklaus-designed Great Waters Course, which runs along a lake, and the lush Plantation Course. Reynolds will add 9 more holes in the spring of 2001.

The Stonemont and Woodmont courses at **Stone Mountain Park Golf Course** in Stone Mountain east of Atlanta are both ranked among the best public courses in the nation, with some demanding and very scenic holes.

The **Renaissance PineIsle Resort** juts out into Lake Lanier and includes eight holes along the water and at least one that tempts the golfer into trying to cut the corner with two water carries to an island green. Another handsome challenge is at the **Port Armor Club** in Greensboro, with rolling terrain, tall pines, and marshes along Lake Oconee.

Augusta Area

The **Jones Creek Golf Club** in Evans is a fine public course that also earns a spot on the *Golf U.S.A.* Deals list.

Columbus Area

The Mountain View Course at the **Callaway Gardens Resort** in Pine Mountain is home to a PGA event. It's a long-distance call from tee to green on many holes.

The West Course at **Bull Creek Golf Course** near Columbus is considered one of the nation's best public courses, with heavy woods, a wandering creek, and some unusual challenges.

Southern Georgia

The **Osprey Cove Golf Club** in St. Marys, on the state's southern border near

Jacksonville, Florida, is a gem of an oceanside links-style course through the woods, across marshlands, and along several small lakes.

Alas, the Seaside/Plantation pair at the **Sea Island Golf Club** on St. Simons Island has gone private; see if you can wangle an invite from a member. Seaside, designed by Bobby Jones, has one of golf's memorable holes at No. 4, a shot across an open marsh.

Georgia on Your Mind

Most courses in Georgia operate year-round. Expect off-peak prices in the winter, with highest prices from late spring through midfall.

Golf U.S.A. Leader Board: Best Public Courses in Georgia

⊙⊙⊙⊙	Cobblestone Golf Course at Lake Acworth
⊙⊙⊙	Bull Creek Golf Course (West)
⊙⊙⊙⊙	Callaway Gardens Resort (Mountain View)
⊙⊙⊙	Jones Creek Golf Club
⊙⊙⊙⊙	Osprey Cove Golf Club
⊙⊙⊙	Port Armor Golf and Country Club
⊙⊙⊙⊙	Reynold's Plantation (Great Waters, Plantation)
⊙⊙⊙	Stone Mountain Park Golf Course (Lakemont, Woodmont, Stonemont)
⊙⊙⊙	Stouffer Renaissance PineIsle Resort

Golf U.S.A. Leader Board: Best Deals in Georgia

$$/⊙⊙⊙	Barrington Hall Golf Club
$$/⊙⊙⊙	Bull Creek Golf Course (East, West)
$$/⊙⊙⊙	Chattahoochee Golf Club
$$/⊙⊙⊙	Chicopee Woods Golf Course
$$/⊙⊙⊙	Fields Ferry Golf Club
$$/⊙⊙⊙	Forest Hills Golf Club
$$/⊙⊙⊙	Foxfire Golf Club
$$/⊙⊙⊙	Georgia Veterans State Park Golf Course
$$/⊙⊙⊙	Jekyll Island Golf Resort (Indian Mound, Oleander, Pine Lakes)
$$/⊙⊙⊙	Jones Creek Golf Club
$$/⊙⊙⊙	Landings Golf Club (Trestle, Bluff, Creek)
$$/⊙⊙⊙	Lane Creek Golf Club
$/⊙⊙⊙	Maple Ridge Golf Club
$/⊙⊙⊙	Nob North Golf Course
$$/⊙⊙⊙	The Oaks Golf Course
$$/⊙⊙⊙	Orchard Hills Golf Club
$$/⊙⊙⊙⊙	Osprey Cove Golf Club
$$/⊙⊙⊙	Port Armor Golf and Country Club
$$/⊙⊙⊙	Southbridge Golf Club
$$/⊙⊙⊙	Stone Mountain Park Golf Course (Lakemont, Woodmont, Stonemont)
$$/⊙⊙⊙	University of Georgia Golf Club
$$/⊙⊙⊙	Wallace Adams Golf Course

Georgia Golf Guide

Atlanta Area

SP ☺☺☺ DEAL	**Barrington Hall Golf Club** Zebulon Rd., Macon. (912) 757-8358 18 holes. Par 72/72. Yards: 7,062/5,012 Year-round. High: Apr.–May	Greens: $–$$ Carts: $ Rating: 73.8/69.3 Slope: 138/118	W
P ☺☺☺☺ STATE	**Cobblestone Golf Course at Lake Acworth** Nance Rd., Acworth. (770) 917-5151 18 holes. Par 71/71. Yards: 6,759/5,400 Year-round. High: Mar.–Oct.	Greens: $$–$$$ Carts: Incl. Rating: 73.1/71.5 Slope: 140/129	W L T S
P ☺☺	**Browns Mill Golf Course** Cleveland Ave., Atlanta. (404) 366-3573 18 holes. Par 72/72. Yards: 6,539/5,545 Year-round. High: Mar.–Oct.	Greens: $–$$ Carts: $ Rating: 71.0/71.4 Slope: 123/118	W T S J
P ☺☺	**Centennial Golf Club** Woodstock Rd., Acworth. (770) 975-1000 18 holes. Par 72/72. Yards: 6,850/5,095 Year-round. High: June–Oct.	Greens: $$–$$$ Carts: Incl. Rating: 73.1/69.5 Slope: 134/122	T S J
SP ☺☺☺	**The Champions Club of Atlanta** Hopewell Rd., Alpharetta. (770) 343-9700 18 holes. Par 72/72. Yards: 6,725/4,470 Year-round. High: Mar.–Dec.	Greens: $$$ Carts: Incl. Rating: 72.9/65.2 Slope: 131/108	T
R ☺☺☺	**Chateau Elan Golf Club** Braselton. (770) 271-6050 18 holes. Par 71/71. Yards: 7,030/5,092 Year-round. High: Apr.–Oct.	Greens: $$$–$$$$ Carts: Incl. Rating: 73.5/70.8 Slope: 136/124	
P ☺☺☺ DEAL	**Chattahoochee Golf Club** Tommy Aaron Dr., Gainesville. (770) 532-0066 18 holes. Par 71/71. Yards: 6,700/5,000 Year-round. High: Apr.–Oct.	Greens: $–$$ Carts: $ Rating: 72.1/64.5 Slope: 125/110	T S J
P ☺☺☺ DEAL	**Chicopee Woods Golf Course** Atlanta Hwy., Gainesville. (770) 534-7322 18 holes. Par 72/72. Yards: 7,040/5,001 Year-round. High: Apr.–Sept.	Greens: $$ Carts: $ Rating: 74.0/69.0 Slope: 135/117	T
SP ☺☺☺	**Eagle Watch Golf Club** Eagle Watch Dr., Woodstock. (770) 591-1000 18 holes. Par 72/72. Yards: 6,900/5,243 Year-round. High: June–Aug.	Greens: $$$–$$$$ Carts: Incl. Rating: 72.6/68.9 Slope: 136/126	W L R T S J
P ☺☺	**Georgia National Golf Club** Lake Dow Rd., McDonough. (770) 914-9994 18 holes. Par 71/71. Yards: 6,874/5,741 Year-round. High: Apr.–Sept.	Greens: $$–$$$ Carts: Incl. Rating: 73.3/73.0 Slope: 132/130	S J
SP ☺☺	**Harbor Club** Greensboro. (706) 453-4414 18 holes. Par 72/72. Yards: 6,988/5,207 Year-round. High: Mar.–Oct.	Greens: $$–$$$$ Carts: Inquire Rating: 73.7/70.2 Slope: 135/123	T S J
P ☺☺	**Hard Labor Creek State Park Golf Course** Knox Chapel Rd., Rutledge. (706) 557-3006 18 holes. Par 72/75. Yards: 6,437/4,854 Year-round. High: Mar.–Oct.	Greens: $ Carts: $ Rating: 71.5/68.8 Slope: 129/123	T S J
P ☺☺	**Innsbruck Resort and Golf Club** Bahn Innsbruck, Helen. (706) 878-2100, (800) 642-2709 18 holes. Par 72/72. Yards: 6,748/5,174 Year-round. High: Apr.–Oct.	Greens: $$–$$$ Carts: Incl. Rating: 72.4/NA Slope: 136/118	L R T S J

Georgia Golf Guide

R ⛳⛳⛳	**Lake Lanier Islands Hilton Resort** Holiday Rd., Lake Lanier. (404) 945-8787 18 holes. Par 72/72. Yards: 6,341/4,935 Year-round. High: Apr.–Sept.	Greens: Carts: Rating: Slope:	$$$ Incl. 70.1/68.3 124/117	W L T
P ⛳⛳	**Lakeside Country Club** Old Fairburn Rd., Atlanta. (404) 344-3629 18 holes. Par 71/71. Yards: 6,522/5,279 Year-round. High: Mar.–May	Greens: Carts: Rating: Slope:	$$ Incl. 71.4/70.7 127/121	W L T S
P, ⛳⛳⛳ DEAL	**Lane Creek Golf Club** Cole Springs Rd., Bishop. (706) 769-6699 18 holes. Par 72/72. Yards: 6,752/5,293 Year-round. High: Year-round	Greens: Carts: Rating: Slope:	$$ Incl. 72.6/68.4 134/115	W T S J
SP ⛳⛳⛳	**Metropolitan Golf Club** Fairington Pkwy., Lithonia. (404) 981-7976 18 holes. Par 72/72. Yards: 6,030/5,966 Year-round. High: Apr.–Sept.	Greens: Carts: Rating: Slope:	$$–$$$ Incl. 74.2/74.8 138/131	W T
P ⛳⛳	**Mystery Valley Golf Course** Shadowrock Dr., Lithonia. (770) 469-6913 18 holes. Par 72/75. Yards: 6,705/5,928 Year-round. High: Mar.–Sept.	Greens: Carts: Rating: Slope:	$ $ 71.5/67.9 124/115	W S J
P ⛳⛳⛳ DEAL	**Nob North Golf Course** Nob North Dr., Cohutta. (706) 694-8505 18 holes. Par 72/72. Yards: 6,573/5,448 Year-round. High: Mar.–Nov.	Greens: Carts: Rating: Slope:	$ Inquire 71.7/71.7 128/126	S J
P ⛳⛳	**North Fulton Golf Course** W. Wieuca Rd., Atlanta. (404) 255-0723 18 holes. Par 71/71. Yards: 6,570/5,120 Year-round. High: July	Greens: Carts: Rating: Slope:	$ Inquire 71.8/69.5 126/118	W L T S J
P ⛳⛳⛳ DEAL	**The Oaks Golf Course** Brown Bridge Rd., Covington. (770) 786-3801 18 holes. Par 70/70. Yards: 6,437/4,663 Year-round. High: Apr.–Sept.	Greens: Carts: Rating: Slope:	$$ Incl. 69.5/64.5 118/107	W L R T S J
SP ⛳⛳⛳	**Olde Atlanta Golf Club** Olde Atlanta Pkwy., Suwanee. (770) 497-0097 18 holes. Par 71/71. Yards: 6,800/5,147 Year-round. High: Apr.–Sept.	Greens: Carts: Rating: Slope:	$$–$$$ Incl. 73.1/69.3 132/120	T S
P ⛳⛳⛳ DEAL	**Orchard Hills Golf Club** E. Hwy. 16, Newnan. (770) 251-5683 18 holes. Par 72/72. Yards: 7,100/5,304 Year-round. High: Apr.–May	Greens: Carts: Rating: Slope:	$$ $$ 73.7/69.5 132/116	W L T S J
R ⛳⛳⛳ DEAL STATE	**Port Armor Golf and Country Club** Port Armor Pkwy., Greensboro. (706) 453-4564 18 holes. Par 72/72. Yards: 6,926/5,177 Year-round. High: Apr.–Oct.	Greens: Carts: Rating: Slope:	$$$–$$$$ Incl. 74.0/72.8 140/131	L R
R ⛳⛳⛳ STATE	**Renaissance Pinelsle Resort** Holiday Rd., Lake Lanier Islands. (404) 945-8922 18 holes. Par 72/72. Yards: 6,527/5,297 Year-round. High: Apr.–Oct.	Greens: Carts: Rating: Slope:	$$$ Incl. 71.6/70.6 132/127	
SP ⛳⛳⛳	**River's Edge Golf Course** Fayetteville. (770) 460-1098 18 holes. Par 71/71. Yards: 6,810/5,641 Year-round. High: Mar.–Oct.	Greens: Carts: Rating: Slope:	$$–$$$ Incl. 72.9/69.9 135/121	W T S J

Georgia Golf Guide

P ☺☺☺	**Riverpines Golf Club** Old Alabama Rd., Alpharetta. (770) 442-5960 18 holes. Par 70/70. Yards: 6,511/4,279 Year-round. High: Apr.–Sept.	Greens: $$$ J Carts: Incl. Rating: 71.3/64.7 Slope: 126/107
SP ☺☺☺	**Royal Lakes Golf and Country Club** Royal Lakes Dr., Flowery Branch. (770) 535-8800 18 holes. Par 72/72. Yards: 6,871/5,325 Year-round. High: Mar.–Sept.	Greens: $$–$$$ W T J Carts: Incl. Rating: 72.0/70.4 Slope: 131/125
SP ☺☺	**Royal Oaks Golf Club** Summit Ridge Dr., Cartersville. (770) 382-3999 18 holes. Par 71/75. Yards: 6,309/4,890 Year-round. High: Apr.–Oct.	Greens: $$ W L T S J Carts: $ Rating: 70.0/71.0 Slope: 124/121
P ☺☺	**St. Marlo Golf Club** St. Marlo Country Club Pkwy., Duluth. (770) 813-8259 18 holes. Par 71/75. Yards: 6,900/5,300 Year-round. High: Apr.–Oct.	Greens: $$$–$$$$ W J Carts: $ Rating: 73.6/70.3 Slope: 137/121
R ☺☺☺	**Sconti Golf Club** Big Canoe. (706) 268-3323 *Choctaw/Cherokee/Creek* 27 holes. Par 72/72/72. Yards: 6,371/6,276/6,247 Year-round. High: Apr.–Oct.	Greens: $$–$$$ W L Carts: Incl. Rating: 71.0/70.2/70.4 Slope: 136/132/134
SP ☺☺☺	**Southerness Golf Club** Flat Bridge Rd., Stockbridge. (770) 808-6000 18 holes. Par 72/72. Yards: 6,766/4,956 Year-round. High: Apr.–Sept.	Greens: $$–$$$ T Carts: Incl. Rating: 72.2/69.0 Slope: 127/119
R ☺☺☺ BEST DEAL	**Stone Mountain Park Golf Course** Stone Mountain. (770) 498-5715 *Lakemont/Woodmont* 18 holes. Par 72/72. Yards: 6,595/5,231 Year-round. High: Apr.–Oct.	Greens: $$ Carts: Incl. Rating: 71.6/69.4 Slope: 130/120
☺☺☺ BEST, DEAL	*Stonemont* 18 holes. Par 72/72. Yards: 6,683/5,020	Rating: 72.6/69.1 Slope: 133/121
P ☺	**Sugar Hill Golf Club** Suwanee Dam Rd., Sugar Hill. (770) 271-0519 18 holes. Par 72/72. Yards: 6,423/4,207 Year-round. High: Apr.–Oct.	Greens: $$–$$$ L T S J Carts: Incl. Rating: 70.7/65.3 Slope: 127/112
P ☺☺	**Towne Lake Hills Golf Club** Towne Lake Hills E., Woodstock. (770) 592-9969 18 holes. Par 72/72. Yards: 6,757/4,984 Year-round. High: May–Oct.	Greens: $$–$$$ L T Carts: Incl. Rating: 72.3/69.0 Slope: 133/116
P ☺☺☺ DEAL	**University of Georgia Golf Club** Riverbend Rd., Athens. (706) 369-5739 18 holes. Par 72/73. Yards: 6,890/5,713 Year-round. High: Mar.–June	Greens: $–$$ W T Carts: $ Rating: 74.2/74.0 Slope: 135/128
P ☺☺	**White Columns Golf Club** White Columns Dr., Alpharetta. (770) 343-9025 18 holes. Par 72/72. Yards: 6,739/4,909 Year-round. High: Mar.–Oct.	Greens: $$$$–$$$$$ Carts: Incl. Rating: 72.3/68.2 Slope: 133/123

Augusta Area

P ☺☺	**Belle Meade Country Club** Twin Pine Rd. N.W., Thomson. (706) 595-4511 18 holes. Par 72/73. Yards: 6,212/5,362 Year-round. High: May–Aug.	Greens: $–$$ W S Carts: Inquire Rating: 69.9/68.6 Slope: 120/113

Georgia Golf Guide

SP ◎◎	**The Fields Golf Club** S. Smith Rd., LaGrange. (706) 845-7425 18 holes. Par 72/72. Yards: 6,650/5,000 Year-round. High: Mar.–Oct.	Greens: Carts: Rating: Slope:	$ W L T S $ 71.4/67.4 128/113
P ◎◎◎ DEAL	**Forest Hills Golf Club** Comfort Rd., Augusta. (706) 733-0001 18 holes. Par 72/72. Yards: 6,780/4,875 Year-round. High: Mar.–Oct.	Greens: Carts: Rating: Slope:	$–$$ J $ 72.8/69.8 124/117
SP ◎◎	**Goshen Plantation Country Club** Augusta. (706) 793-1168 18 holes. Par 72/72. Yards: 6,902/5,688 Year-round. High: Mar.–Oct.	Greens: Carts: Rating: Slope:	$$ W L T S J Incl. 72.6/70.9 130/125
P ◎◎◎ BEST DEAL	**Jones Creek Golf Club** Hammond's Ferry Rd., Evans. (706) 860-4228 18 holes. Par 72/72. Yards: 7,008/5,430 Year-round. High: Apr.–Aug.	Greens: Carts: Rating: Slope:	$$ S J $ 73.8/72.4 137/130

Macon/Warner Robins Area

P ◎◎◎ DEAL	**Georgia Veterans State Park Golf Course** Hwy. 280 W., Cordel. (912) 276-2377 18 holes. Par 72/72. Yards: 7,088/5,171 Year-round. High: Apr.–Sept.	Greens: Carts: Rating: Slope:	$–$$ W T S J $ 72.1/73.5 130/124
SP ◎◎◎ DEAL	**Landings Golf Club** Statham's Way, Warner Robins. (912) 923-5222 *Trestle/Bluff/Creek* 27 holes. Par 72/72/72. Yards: 6,998/6,671/6,819 Year-round. High: Mar.–Dec.	Greens: Carts: Rating: Slope:	$–$$ W $ 73.1/71.9/72.6 133/130/131
R ◎◎◎◎ STATE	**Reynold's Plantation** Wood Crest Dr. N.E., Eatonton. (706) 485-0235 *Great Waters Course* 18 holes. Par 72/72. Yards: 7,048/5,082 Year-round. Resort guests only. High: Apr.–Oct.	Greens: Carts: Rating: Slope:	$$$$$–$$$$$$ W $$ 73.8/69.2 135/114
◎◎◎◎ STATE	*Plantation Course* 18 holes. Par 72/72. Yards: 6,698/5,121 Year-round. Resort guests only. High: Apr.–Aug.	Greens: Carts: Rating: Slope:	$$$$$–$$$$$$ W $ 71.7/68.9 128/115
◎◎◎◎ STATE	*National Course* 18 holes. Par 72/72. Yards: 7,015/5,292 Year-round. Resort guests only. High: Apr.–June	Greens: Carts: Rating: Slope:	$$$$$–$$$$$$ W $ 73.5/71.7 131/127
P ◎◎◎ DEAL	**Wallace Adams Golf Course** Hwy. 441 N., McRae. (912) 868-6651 18 holes. Par 72/72. Yards: 6,625/5,001 Year-round. High: Spring/Fall	Greens: Carts: Rating: Slope:	$–$$ R S Inquire 70.8/69.1 128/120

Columbus Area

P ◎◎◎ DEAL	**Bull Creek Golf Course** Lynch Rd., Columbus. (706) 561-1614 *East Course* 18 holes. Par 72/74. Yards: 6,705/5,430 Year-round. High: Apr.–Aug.	Greens: Carts: Rating: Slope:	$ W S J $ 71.2/69.8 124/114
◎◎◎ BEST, DEAL	*West Course* 18 holes. Par 72/74. Yards: 6,921/5,385	Rating: Slope:	72.5/69.9 130/121
R ◎◎◎	**Callaway Gardens Resort** U.S. Hwy. 27, Pine Mountain. (706) 663-2281, (800) 282-8181 *Garden View Course*	Greens: Carts: Rating:	$$$–$$$$ L T Incl. 70.9/73.4

	18 holes. Par 72/72. Yards: 6,391/5,848 Year-round. High: Mar.–May.	Slope:	119/125

☺☺☺ *Lake View Course*
18 holes. Par 70/71. Yards: 6,006/5,452

Greens: $$$–$$$$
Carts: Incl.
Rating: 69.4/70.3
Slope: 115/122

☺☺☺☺ *Mountain View Course*
BEST 18 holes. Par 72/74. Yards: 7,057/5,848

Greens: $$$$$–$$$$$$
Carts: Incl.
Rating: 73.9/74.3
Slope: 136/131

P **Fields Ferry Golf Club**
☺☺☺ Fields Ferry Dr., Calhoun. (706) 625-5666
sDEAL 18 holes. Par 72/72. Yards: 6,824/5,355
Year-round. High: Apr.–Oct.

Greens: $–$$ W T S J
Carts: $
Rating: 71.8/70.5
Slope: 123/120

P **Maple Ridge Golf Club**
☺☺☺ Maple Ridge Trail, Columbus. (706) 569-0966
DEAL 18 holes. Par 71/71. Yards: 6,652/5,030
Year-round. High: Apr.–July

Greens: $ W L T S J
Carts: Inquire
Rating: 72.2/68.9
Slope: 123/127

R **Sky Valley Golf Club**
☺☺☺ Sky Valley. (706) 746-5303
18 holes. Par 72/72. Yards: 6,452/5,017
Year-round. High: Apr.–Oct.

Greens: $$–$$$ L R T
Carts: Incl.
Rating: 71.7/69.0
Slope: 128/118

Savannah Area

SP **Foxfire Golf Club**
☺☺☺ Foxfire Dr., Vidalia. (912) 538-8670
DEAL 18 holes. Par 72/71. Yards: 6,118/4,757
Year-round. High: Mar.–Sept.

Greens: $$ W S J
Carts: Incl.
Rating: 69.3/67.5
Slope: 125/116

R **Sheraton Savannah Resort & Country Club**
☺☺☺ Wilmington Island Rd., Savannah. (912) 897-1615
18 holes. Par 72/72. Yards: 6,876/5,328
Year-round. High: Apr.–Oct.

Greens: $$–$$$ W L R T S J
Carts: Incl.
Rating: 73.5/70.6
Slope: 137/128

SP **Southbridge Golf Club**
☺☺☺ Southbridge Blvd., Savannah. (912) 651-5455
DEAL 18 holes. Par 72/72. Yards: 6,990/5,181
Year-round. High: Apr.–May

Greens: $$ W L S
Carts: Incl.
Rating: 73.4/69.2
Slope: 136/118

Southern Georgia

P **Francis Lake Golf Course**
☺☺ Lake Park. (912) 559-7961
18 holes. Par 72/72. Yards: 6,458/5,709
Year-round. High: Mar.–Aug.

Greens: $–$$ W R T J
Carts: Incl.
Rating: 71.4/70.1
Slope: 124/117

SP **Hampton Club**
☺☺☺ Tabbystone, St. Simons Island. (912) 634-0255
18 holes. Par 72/72. Yards: 6,400/5,233
Year-round. High: Mar.–Apr.

Greens: $$$$ R J
Carts: $
Rating: 71.4/71.0
Slope: 130/123

R **Jekyll Island Golf Resort**
Captain Wylly Rd., Jekyll Island. (912) 635-2368
☺☺☺ *Indian Mound Course*
DEAL 18 holes. Par 72/72. Yards: 6,596/5,345
Year-round. High: Feb.–Apr.

Greens: $$ T
Carts: $
Rating: 71.3/70.0
Slope: 127/122

☺☺☺ *Oleander Course*
DEAL 18 holes. Par 72/72. Yards: 6,679/5,654

Rating: 72.0/72.6
Slope: 128/124

☺☺☺ *Pine Lakes Course*
DEAL 18 holes. Par 72/72. Yards: 6,802/5,742

Rating: 71.9/71.9
Slope: 130/124

SP	**Osprey Cove Golf Club**	Greens:	$$$–$$$$ J W L
☺☺☺☺	Osprey Dr., St. Marys. (912) 882-5575	Carts:	Incl.
DEAL	18 holes. Par 72/72. Yards: 6,791/5,145	Rating:	72.9/69.7
STATE	Year-round. High: Feb.–July	Slope:	132/120

P	**St. Simons Island Club**	Greens:	$$$ L R T J
☺☺☺	Kings Way, St. Simons Island. (912) 638-5130	Carts:	$
	18 holes. Par 72/72. Yards: 6,490/5,361	Rating:	71.8/70.0
	Year-round. High: Mar.–Apr.	Slope:	133/124

R	**Sea Palms Resort**	Greens:	$$–$$$ W L R T J
	Frederica Rd., St. Simons Island. (912) 638-9041	Carts:	$
☺☺	*Tall Pines/Great Oaks/Sea Palms*	Rating:	71.3/71.1/69.7
	27 holes. Par 72/72/72. Yards: 6,658/6,350/6,198	Slope:	128/126/124
	Year-round. High: Feb.–May		

Louisiana

The distinguishing feature of many of the courses in Louisiana is water: open water, swamp, and bayou. The best public resort course in Louisiana is the surprisingly up-and-down challenge of the **Bluffs on Thompson Creek** in St. Francisville, located to the north of Baton Rouge.

Louisiana's *Golf U.S.A.* Deals include the swampy bayou course at **Belle Terre Country Club**, west of New Orleans, and the long and hard **Mallard Cove** in Lake Charles. Mallard plans to rebuild its greens in 2001.

Down south in Louisiana the courses generally are open all year long. Peak rates usually are in effect from April through September. Off-season covers the fall through spring, and some courses also reduce prices slightly in the hottest months of summer.

Golf U.S.A. Leader Board: Best Public Course in Louisiana

☺☺☺☺   Bluffs on Thompson Creek Golf Club

Golf U.S.A. Leader Board: Best Deals in Louisiana

$/☺☺☺	Bayou Oaks Golf Courses (Championship)
$$/☺☺☺	Belle Terre Country Club
$/☺☺☺	Mallard Cove Golf Course
$$/☺☺☺	Santa Maria Golf Course

Louisiana Golf Guide

Shreveport Area

P	**Huntington Park Golf Course**	Greens:	$ W T S J
☺☺	Pines Rd., Shreveport. (318) 673-7765	Carts:	$
	18 holes. Par 72/74. Yards: 7,294/6,171	Rating:	73.3/74.7
	Year-round. High: May–Sept.	Slope:	NA

R	**Toro Hills Lodge**	Greens:	$$ W
☺☺	Florien. (318) 586-4661	Carts:	$
	18 holes. Par 72/72. Yards: 6,550/6,300	Rating:	NA
	Year-round. High: Apr.–Sept.	Slope:	120/118

Lake Charles

P	**Mallard Cove Golf Course**	Greens:	$ W T S J
☺☺☺	Chennault Air Base, Lake Charles. (318) 491-1204	Carts:	$$

Louisiana Golf Guide

DEAL	18 holes. Par 72/72. Yards: 6,903/5,294 Year-round. High: Apr.–Oct.	Rating: Slope:	72.4/70.1 125/117

Baton Rouge Area

R ☺☺☺☺ STATE	**Bluffs on Thompson Creek Golf Club** Hwy. 965, St. Francisville. (225) 634-5551 18 holes. Par 72/72. Yards: 7,154/4,781 Year-round. High: Spring/Fall	Greens: Carts: Rating: Slope:	$$$$–$$$$$ W L R Incl. 74.6/69.0 143/123
P ☺☺☺ DEAL	**Santa Maria Golf Course** Old Perkins Rd., Baton Rouge. (225) 752-9667 18 holes. Par 72/72. Yards: 7,051/5,267 Year-round. High: Apr.–Oct.	Greens: Carts: Rating: Slope:	$$ T S J W Incl. 72.9/69.6 124/120

New Orleans Area

P ☺	**Bayou Oaks Golf Courses** Filmore, New Orleans. (504) 483-9396 *Lakeside Course* 18 holes. Par 70/70. Yards: 6,054/5,872 Year-round. High: Apr.–June, Sept.–Oct.	Greens: Carts: Rating: Slope:	$ T S J $ 68.5/70.5 110/103
☺☺☺ DEAL	*Championship Course* 18 holes. Par 72/72. Yards: 7,061/6,013	Rating: Slope:	71.5/73.3 116/118
☺☺	*Wisner Course* 18 holes. Par 72/72. Yards: 6,465/5,707	Rating: Slope:	70.5/71.8 111/116
SP ☺☺☺ DEAL	**Belle Terre Country Club** La Place. (504) 652-5000 18 holes. Par 72/72. Yards: 6,840/5,510 Year-round. High: Apr.–Oct.	Greens: Carts: Rating: Slope:	$$$ W Incl. 72.2/71.6 130/122
P ☺☺☺	**Oak Harbor Golf Club** Oak Harbor Blvd., Slidell. (504) 646-0110 18 holes. Par 72/72. Yards: 6,885/5,208 Year-round. High: Apr.–July	Greens: Carts: Rating: Slope:	$$–$$$ T J Incl. 72.2/68.8 132/115

Mississippi

The best semi-private course in Mississippi may be the 27 holes of **Timberton** in Hattiesburg; the fact that it is a *Golf U.S.A.* Deal makes it even better.

Other recommended courses include **Kirkwood National** in Holly Springs in the northern reach of the state, and **Windance Country Club** in Gulfport on the Gulf of Mexico.

Courses in Mississippi generally are open year-round. Expect peak rates and conditions from about February through April at most courses; some, though, extend their peak through the hot summer as well.

Golf U.S.A. Leader Board: Best Public Courses in Mississippi

☺☺☺☺   Kirkwood National Golf Club
☺☺☺☺   Timberton Golf Club
☺☺☺☺   Windance Country Club

Golf U.S.A. Leader Board: Best Deals in Mississippi

$$/☺☺☺   Diamondhead Country Club (Cardinal, Pine)
$$/☺☺☺   Mississippi National Golf Club

$/☺☺☺   Mississippi State University Golf Course
$/☺☺☺   Ole Miss Golf Club
$$/☺☺☺   Plantation Golf Course
$$/☺☺☺☺   Timberton Golf Club
$$/☺☺☺   Wedgewood Golf Course

Mississippi Golf Guide

Northern Mississippi

SP ☺☺☺☺ STATE	**Kirkwood National Golf Club** Holly Springs. (601) 252-4888 18 holes. Par 72/72. Yards: 7,129/4,898 Year-round. High: May–Sept.	Greens: Carts: Rating: Slope:	$$–$$$ Incl. 73.6/68.2 135/116	W L T S J
P ☺☺☺ DEAL	**Ole Miss Golf Club** College Hill Rd., Oxford. (601) 234-4816 18 holes. Par 72/72. Yards: 6,682/5,276 Year-round. High: May–Aug.	Greens: Carts: Rating: Slope:	$ $ 72.8/70.9 129/120	
SP ☺☺☺ DEAL	**Plantation Golf Course** Plantation Rd., Olive Branch. (601) 895-3530 18 holes. Par 72/72. Yards: 6,773/5,055 Year-round. High: Apr.-Oct.	Greens: Carts: Rating: Slope:	$$–$$$ Incl. 72.0/64.4 122/109	W L T S J
SP ☺☺☺ DEAL	**Wedgewood Golf Course** Olive Branch. (601) 521-8275 18 holes. Par 72/72. Yards: 6,863/5,627 Year-round. High: May–Sept.	Greens: Carts: Rating: Slope:	$$ $ 72.8/69.1 127/118	W L R T S J

Tupelo Area

SP ☺☺	**Natchez Trace Golf Club** Beech Springs Rd., Saltillo. (601) 869-2166 18 holes. Par 72/72. Yards: 6,841/4,791 Year-round. High: June–Aug.	Greens: Carts: Rating: Slope:	$–$$ $ 72.3/69.3 116/108	W

Columbus Area

P ☺☺☺ DEAL	**Mississippi State University Golf Course** Old Hwy. 82 E., Starkville. (601) 325-3028 18 holes. Par 72/72. Yards: 6,926/5,443 Year-round. High: Mar.–Sept.	Greens: Carts: Rating: Slope:	$ $ 73.5/71.8 130/121	W J

Jackson Area

P ☺☺	**Eagle Ridge Golf Course** Hwy. 18 S., Raymond. (601) 857-5993 18 holes. Par 70.5/NA. Yards: 6,500/5,135 Year-round. High: Mar.–Aug.	Greens: Carts: Rating: Slope:	$ $ 70.5/NA 113/NA	W S

Hattiesburg Area

SP ☺☺☺☺ DEAL STATE	**Timberton Golf Club** Hattiesburg. (601) 584-4653 *Creekside-Lakeview/Valley-Lakeview/Creekside-Valley* 27 holes. Par 72/72/72. Yards: 6,740/6,753/7,003 Year-round. High: Mar.–Apr.	Greens: Carts: Rating: Slope:	$$$ Incl. 73.1/72.7/73.4 133/131/135	T

Gulfport/Biloxi Area

R ☺☺	**Broadwater Resort** Beach Dr., Gulfport. (601) 385-4085 *Sea Course* 18 holes. Par 72/72. Yards: 6,214/5,403 Year-round. High: Feb.–May	Greens: Carts: Rating: Slope:	$$$ Incl. 70.0/72.0 118/113	L
☺☺	*Sun Course* Beauvoir, Biloxi. (601) 385-4081 18 holes. Par 72/72. Yards: 7,168/5,485	Rating: Slope:	72.0/72.0 126/120	

Mississippi Golf Guide

R	**Diamondhead Country Club**	Greens: $$-$$$	L R J
	Diamondhead. (601) 255-3910	Carts: Incl.	
☺☺☺	*Cardinal Course*	Rating: 72.7/68.9	
DEAL	18 holes. Par 72/72. Yards: 6,831/5,065	Slope: 132/117	
	Year-round. High: Feb.–May		

☺☺☺	*Pine Course*	Rating: 73.6/71.1
DEAL	18 holes. Par 72/72. Yards: 6,817/5,313	Slope: 133/118

P	**Mississippi National Golf Club**	Greens: $$-$$$	W L R
☺☺☺	Hickory Hill Dr., Gautier. (601) 497-2372	Carts: $	
DEAL	18 holes. Par 72/72. Yards: 7,003/5,229	Rating: 73.1/69.6	
	Year-round. High: Feb.–Apr.	Slope: 128/113	

SP	**Pass Christian Isles Golf Club**	Greens: $$
☺☺	Pass Christian. (601) 452-3830	Carts: $
	18 holes. Par 72/72. Yards: 6,438/5,428	Rating: 69.7/71.6
	Year-round. High: Feb.–Apr.	Slope: 124/120

SP	**Pine Island Golf Club**	Greens: $–$$	W L R T
☺	Beachview Dr., Ocean Springs. (601) 875-1674	Carts: $	
	18 holes. Par 71/71. Yards: 6,369/4,915	Rating: 70.9/67.8	
	Year-round. High: Feb.–Apr.	Slope: 129/109	

SP	**St. Andrews Country Club**	Greens: $–$$
☺☺	Ocean Springs. (601) 875-7730	Carts: $
	18 holes. Par 72/72. Yards: 6,460/4,960	Rating: 69.7/67.8
	Year-round. High: Feb.–Mar.	Slope: 119/111

SP	**Southwind Country Club**	Greens: $$
☺☺	Dismuke Dr., Biloxi. (601) 392-0400	Carts: $
	18 holes. Par 72/72. Yards: 6,202/5,577	Rating: 65.0/66.0
	Year-round. High: Feb.–Apr.	Slope: 113/113

R	**Sunkist Country Club**	Greens: $$	W L T
☺☺	Sunkist Country Club Rd., Biloxi. (601) 388-3961	Carts: Incl.	
	18 holes. Par 72/72. Yards: 6,000/5,300	Rating: 69.0/71.0	
	Year-round. High: Feb.–Apr.	Slope: 117/121	

P	**Tramark Golf Course**	Greens: $	J
☺☺	Gulfport. (601) 863-7808	Carts: $	
	18 holes. Par 72/72. Yards: 6,350/5,800	Rating: 68.5/69.5	
	Year-round. High: Feb.–Apr.	Slope: 116/109	

SP	**Windance Country Club**	Greens: $$$$	R L
☺☺☺☺	Champion Circle, Gulfport. (228) 832-4871	Carts: Incl.	
STATE	18 holes. Par 72/72. Yards: 6,660/5,208	Rating: 73.1/70.1	
	Year-round. High: Feb.–Apr.	Slope: 129/120	

North Carolina

North Carolina sometimes seems like one big, beautiful golf course, interrupted by a few towns, roads, and mountains. And that is the way many golfers think of the Tarheel State. There is something for just about everyone in this state, which features spectacular courses chiseled out of the Great Smoky Mountains and the Blue Ridge Mountains, sprawling across the improbably green heartland, or hugging the coast and barrier islands. Among the nearly 500 courses in North Carolina is one of the game's meccas, Pinehurst.

North Carolina is, of course, one of the temples of golf in this country, and this is proved by the fact there are 19 *Golf U.S.A.* Best–rated courses around the state. And in a state where some of the courses are among the priciest anywhere, there are nevertheless four Best–rated courses on the *Golf U.S.A.* Deals list.

The most famous of the North Carolina courses are at **Pinehurst Plantation** and **Pinehurst Resort**, located in the center of the state, east of Charlotte. Pinehurst was created around the turn of the century when a Boston soda-fountain inventor used some of his riches to purchase 5,000 acres of sandy barrens left behind by timber harvesters. The original intent was to create a winter haven for frozen northerners; the impressive Pinehurst Hotel was erected in 1901.

The Pinehurst Resort boasts no fewer than 144 championship holes, including the all-but-incomparable No. 2, first designed by Donald Ross in 1907 and adjusted by him for decades afterward. It rolls through tall pines with mounds and bunkers that offer a touch of Scotland. Ross also created numbers 1, 3, and 4, although the last one has been updated by someone else. In 1996, the spectacular No. 8 joined the ranks and was an immediate goal for visitors. Pinehurst No. 2 was home to the 1999 U.S. Open, one of the last wins by Payne Stewart.

Also worth checking out in the area is **Pine Needles**, another Donald Ross design in the tall pines, this one dating from 1927; if Pinehurst weren't such a close neighbor, this one might be famous. Nearby is **The Pit Golf Links**, an unusual challenge that sends golfers down into the pit of a former sand mine for the front nine, only to make them work back alongside and across a lake.

Near Winston-Salem is **Tanglewood Park**. Around Greensboro is **Bryan Park**, a superb public course carved out of the forest and running along Lake Townsend; it is in regular use for tournaments. The Champions Course there was renovated in 1999 and a new clubhouse added. Also in Greensboro is **Oak Hollow**. In the Raleigh-Durham area are fine courses at **Duke University**, **Keith Hills**, and **Porters Neck**. All the way west near Asheville is the mountain course at **Linville**.

Along the southern coast of Cape Fear near Wilmington is the well-regarded **North Shore Country Club**. Also of note is **Bald Head Island**, the southernmost point of North Carolina, served by a private passenger ferry. Bald Head has some 14 miles of nearly untouched beach, a seaside forest, and a superb, difficult course that uses the ocean as a backdrop and more than a dozen marshes and creeks as punishment for letting your mind wander.

Oyster Bay features an island green built from oyster shells. The **Marsh Harbour Golf Links**, on the border between the Carolinas, almost floats above marshes and wetlands. At **Sandpiper Bay**, the course features marshes, numerous lakes, alligators, sandpipers, and the occasional eagle of the bird variety.

Joint members of the *Golf U.S.A.* Best and *Golf U.S.A.* Deals lists are Bryan Park, Keith Hills, Linville, and Oak Hollow.

A great collection of courses also lies along and nearby the spectacular Blue Ridge Parkway that cuts through the Appalachian Mountains in the western portion of the state. The road itself dates back to a rough passage cut by Daniel Boone; in 1934 nearly 500 miles of paved road was developed as a link between two national parks, the Great Smoky Mountains in North Carolina and Shenandoah in Virginia. Courses along the "golfway" are located in and near Asheville, Waynesville, Morganton, and up to Roanoke in Virginia.

The off-peak season for courses in North Carolina is generally mid-November through mid-March and June through August; peak season runs from mid-March through May, and mid-September through mid-November.

At the Pinehurst Resort and Country Club, peak prices are in effect from early March through early June and again from early September to mid-November. Off-season rates are in effect from late November through early March.

Golf U.S.A. Leader Board: Best Public Courses in North Carolina

☺☺☺☺	Bald Head Island Club
☺☺☺☺	Bryan Park and Golf Club (Champions)
☺☺☺	Duke University Golf Club
☺☺☺☺	Keith Hills Country Club
☺☺☺☺	Linville Golf Course
☺☺☺	Marsh Harbour Golf Links
☺☺☺☺	North Shore Country Club
☺☺☺	Oak Hollow Golf Course
☺☺☺	Oyster Bay Golf Links
☺☺☺☺	Pine Needles Golf Club
☺☺☺☺	Pinehurst Plantation Golf Club
☺☺☺☺	Pinehurst Resort and Country Club (No. 2, No. 7, No. 8)
☺☺☺	The Pit Golf Links
☺☺☺	Porters Neck Country Club
☺☺☺	Sandpiper Bay Golf and Country Club
☺☺☺☺	Talamore Resort
☺☺☺☺	Tanglewood Park Golf Courses (Championship)

Golf U.S.A. Leader Board: Best Deals in North Carolina

$$/☺☺☺	Boone Golf Club
$$/☺☺☺☺	Bryan Park and Golf Club (Champions, Players)
$/☺☺☺	Carolina Lakes Golf Club
$$/☺☺☺	Cleghorn Plantation Golf and Country Club
$$/☺☺☺	Devil's Ridge Golf Club
$$/☺☺☺	Etowah Valley Country Club (South, West, North)
$/☺☺☺	Jamestown Park Golf Club
$$/☺☺☺	Jefferson Landing Club
$$/☺☺☺☺	Keith Hills Country Club
$$/☺☺☺	Lane Tree Golf Course
$$/☺☺☺☺	Linville Golf Course
$$/☺☺☺	Maggie Valley Resort Golf Club
$$/☺☺☺	Mount Mitchell Golf Club
$$/☺☺☺	The Neuse Golf Club
$/☺☺☺	Oak Hollow Golf Course
$/☺☺☺	River Bend Golf Club
$$/☺☺☺	Stoney Creek Golf Club
$$/☺☺☺	Woodbridge Golf Links

North Carolina Golf Guide

Asheville Area

R	**Etowah Valley Country Club**	Greens:	$$	L
	Brickyard Rd., Etowah. (704) 891-7141	Carts:	$	
☺☺☺	*South/West/North*	Rating:	73.3/73.1/72.4	
DEAL	27 holes. Par 72/73/73. Yards: 6,880/6,700/6,604	Slope:	123/122/121	
	Year-round. High: Apr.–Oct.			

R	**Fairfield Mountains**	Greens:	$$$	L
	Blvd. of the Mountains, Lake Lure. (704) 625-2888	Carts:	Incl.	
☺☺☺	*Apple Valley Golf Club*	Rating:	72.6/66.3	
	18 holes. Par 72/72. Yards: 6,726/4,661	Slope:	125/112	
	Year-round. High: Apr.–Oct.			

☺☺	*Bald Mountain Golf Club*	Greens:	$$	L
	18 holes. Par 72/72. Yards: 6,575/4,808	Carts:	Incl.	
		Rating:	70.9/66.9	
		Slope:	127/118	

R	**Foxfire Resort and Country Club**	Greens:	$$–$$$$	L R J
	Jackson Springs. (910) 295-5555	Carts:	Incl.	
☺☺	*East Course*	Rating:	70.5/72.8	
	18 holes. Par 72/72. Yards: 6,851/5,256	Slope:	130/119	
	Year-round. High: Mar.–June, Sept.			

☺☺☺	*West Course*	Rating:	70.1/72.8
	18 holes. Par 72/72. Yards: 6,742/5,273	Slope:	125/114

SP	**Glen Cannon Country Club**	Greens:	$$–$$$	L T
☺☺☺	Wilson Rd., Brevard. (704) 884-9160	Carts:	Incl.	
	18 holes. Par 72/72. Yards: 6,548/5,172	Rating:	71.7/69.1	
	Year-round. High: Apr.–Oct.	Slope:	124/117	

R	**The Grove Park Inn Resort**	Greens:	$$–$$$	L T
☺☺	Macon Ave., Asheville. (704) 252-2711	Carts:	Inquire	
	18 holes. Par 72/72. Yards: 6,520/4,687	Rating:	71.7/68.6	
	Year-round. High: Apr.–Nov.	Slope:	125/111	

R	**High Hampton Inn and Country Club**	Greens:	$–$$	L R T
☺☺	Hwy. 107 S., Cashiers. (704) 743-2450	Carts:	$	
	18 holes. Par 72/72. Yards: 6,012	Rating:	68.5	
	Year-round. High: June–Aug.	Slope:	120	

R	**Holly Forest Country Club**	Greens:	$$$	L
☺☺☺	Hwy. 64 W., Sapphire. (704) 743-1174	Carts:	Incl.	
	18 holes. Par 70/70. Yards: 6,185/5,690	Rating:	69.3/65.9	
	Year-round. High: May–Sept.	Slope:	127/114	

SP	**Hound Ears Club**	Greens:	$$–$$$$
☺☺☺	Blowing Rock. (704) 963-5831	Carts:	$
	18 holes. Par 72/73. Yards: 6,165/4,959	Rating:	69.4/66.8
	Apr.–Nov. High: June–Sept.	Slope:	122/110

R	**Linville Golf Course**	Greens:	$$$$
☺☺☺☺	Linville Ave., Linville. (828) 733-4363	Carts:	Incl.
DEAL	18 holes. Par 72/72. Yards: 6,780/5,086	Rating:	72.5/69.3
STATE	May–Oct.	Slope:	134/121

R	**Maggie Valley Resort Golf Club**	Greens:	$–$$	W L T J
☺☺☺	Maggie Valley. (704) 926-6013	Carts:	$	
DEAL	18 holes. Par 72/73. Yards: 6,336/5,195	Rating:	69.8/69.4	
	Year-round. High: Mar.–Nov.	Slope:	121/117	

P	**Mount Mitchell Golf Club**	Greens:	$$–$$	W L R
☺☺☺	Hwy. 80 S., Burnsville. (704) 675-5454	Carts:	Incl.	
DEAL	18 holes. Par 72/72. Yards: 6,475/5,455	Rating:	70.0/69.5	
	Apr.–Nov. High: May–Oct.	Slope:	121/117	

North Carolina Golf Guide

SP ☺☺☺	**Reems Creek Golf Club** Pink Fox Cove Rd., Weaverville. (704) 645-4393 18 holes. Par 72/72. Yards: 6,477/4,605 Year-round. High: Mar.–Oct.	Greens: $$–$$$ W L R Carts: Incl. Rating: 70.5/66.9 Slope: 130/114
SP ☺☺☺	**Springdale Country Club** Rte. 2, Canton. (704) 235-8451 18 holes. Par 72/72. Yards: 6,812/5,421 Year-round. High: Apr.–May	Greens: $$ T Carts: Incl. Rating: 72.4/72.2 Slope: 126/121
R ☺☺	**Waynesville Country Club Inn** Ninevah Rd., Waynesville. (704) 452-4617 27 holes. Par 70/70/70. Yards: 5,798/5,803/5,943 Year-round. High: Mar.–Oct.	Greens: $–$$ L R Carts: $ Rating: 66.4/66.4/66.8 Slope: 103/105/104

Charlotte Area

P ☺☺	**Charlotte Golf Links** Providence Rd., Charlotte. (704) 846-7990 18 holes. Par 71/72. Yards: 6,700/5,279 Year-round. High: Apr.–Nov.	Greens: $–$$ L T S J Carts: $ Rating: 71.5/70.3 Slope: 121/117
P ☺☺☺	**Highland Creek Golf Club** Highland Creek Pkwy., Charlotte. (704) 875-9000 18 holes. Par 72/72. Yards: 7,008/5,080 Year-round. High: Apr.–Sept.	Greens: $$$ W Carts: Incl. Rating: 73.3/70.1 Slope: 133/128
P ☺☺	**Monroe Country Club** Hwy. 601 S., Monroe. (704) 282-4661 18 holes. Par 72/72. Yards: 6,759/4,964 Year-round. High: May–Aug.	Greens: $ W Carts: $ Rating: 71.8/68.6 Slope: 118/117
P ☺☺☺ DEAL	**River Bend Golf Club** Longwood Dr., Shelby. (704) 482-4286 18 holes. Par 72/72. Yards: 6,750/4,920 Year-round. High: May–Oct.	Greens: $ S J Carts: $ Rating: 72.0/66.0 Slope: 131/102
P ☺☺☺ DEAL	**Woodbridge Golf Links** Kings Mountain. (704) 482-0353 18 holes. Par 72/72. Yards: 6,743/5.151 Year-round. High: Apr.–Oct.	Greens: $$ Carts: Incl. Rating: 71.9/69.3 Slope: 131/116

Winston-Salem Area

P ☺☺☺ DEAL	**Boone Golf Club** Boone. (704) 264-8760 18 holes. Par 71/75. Yards: 6,401/5,172 Apr.–Nov. High: June–Aug.	Greens: $$ W L T Carts: $ Rating: 70.1/69.1 Slope: 120/113
P ☺☺☺ DEAL	**Jefferson Landing Club** Jefferson. (910) 246-5555 18 holes. Par 72/72. Yards: 7,111/4,960 Mar.–Nov. High: June–Sept.	Greens: $$ W L R T Carts: Incl. Rating: 72.3/66.0 Slope: 121/103
P ☺☺	**Mountain Aire Golf Club** W. Jefferson. (910) 877-4716 18 holes. Par 71/71. Yards: 6,107/4,143 Year-round. High: June–Aug.	Greens: $ W L T J Carts: $ Rating: 71.0/66.0 Slope: 113/113
P ☺☺☺☺ BEST	**Tanglewood Park Golf Courses** 4201 Hwy. 158 W., Clemmons. (336) 778-6321 *Championship Course* 18 holes. Par 70/74. Yards: 7,018/5,119 Year-round. High: Spring/Fall	Greens: $$$ W R T S J Carts: $ Rating: 74.5/70.9 Slope: 140/130
☺☺☺	*Reynolds Course* 18 holes. Par 72/72. Yards: 6,537/5,308	Rating: 71.8/71.5 Slope: 135/122

North Carolina Golf Guide

Greensboro Area

P	**Bryan Park and Golf Club**	Greens:	$–$$ W L T S J
	Bryan Park Rd., Browns Summit. (336) 375-2200	Carts:	$
☺☺☺☺	*Champions Course*	Rating:	74.0/72.0
DEAL	18 holes. Par 72/72. Yards: 7,135/5,395	Slope:	130/123
STATE	Year-round. High: Apr.–Sept.		
☺☺☺	*Players Course*	Rating:	73.7/69.5
DEAL	18 holes. Par 72/72. Yards: 7,076/5,260	Slope:	131/122
P	**Cleghorn Plantation Golf and Country Club**	Greens:	$$ W
☺☺☺	Rutherfordton. (704) 286-9117	Carts:	Incl.
DEAL	18 holes. Par 72/73. Yards: 6,903/4,751	Rating:	74.6/68.1
	Year-round. High: Apr.–Sept.	Slope:	134/111
P	**Jamestown Park Golf Club**	Greens:	$ W S J
☺☺☺	E. Fork Rd., Jamestown. (910) 584-7871	Carts:	$
DEAL	18 holes. Par 72/72. Yards: 6,665/5,298	Rating:	72.6/70.7
	Year-round. High: May–Sept.	Slope:	126/118
P	**Oak Hollow Golf Course**	Greens:	$ S J
☺☺☺	Oakview Rd., High Point. (910) 883-3260	Carts:	$
BEST	18 holes. Par 72/72. Yards: 6,564/4,825	Rating:	72.1/68.5
DEAL	Year-round. High: Apr.–Aug.	Slope:	131/120
P	**Stoney Creek Golf Club**	Greens:	$$ W L T S J
☺☺☺	E. Stoney Creek. (910) 449-5688	Carts:	$
DEAL	18 holes. Par 72/72. Yards: 7,063/4,737	Rating:	74.1/69.8
	Year-round. High: Spring/Fall	Slope:	144/123

Raleigh-Durham Area

SP	**Devil's Ridge Golf Club**	Greens:	$$ W L T S J
☺☺☺	Linksland Dr., Holly Springs. (919) 557-6100	Carts:	$
DEAL	18 holes. Par 72/72. Yards: 7,002/5,244	Rating:	73.7/69.8
	Year-round. High: June–Aug.	Slope:	138/121
R	**Duke University Golf Club**	Greens:	$$–$$$ W L T S J
☺☺☺	Rte. 741, Durham. (919) 681-2288	Carts:	$
STATE	18 holes. Par 72/73. Yards: 7,045/5,505	Rating:	73.9/71.2
	Year-round. High: Mar.–Sept.	Slope:	137/124
SP	**Keith Hills Country Club**	Greens:	$–$$$ J W L
☺☺☺☺	Blues Creek. (910) 893-5051	Carts:	Incl.
DEAL	18 holes. Par 72/72. Yards: 6,703/5,225	Rating:	71.6/69.6
STATE	Year-round. High: Mar.–June	Slope:	129/120
SP	**Lane Tree Golf Course**	Greens:	$–$$ W L R
☺☺☺	Salem Church Rd., Goldsboro. (919) 734-1245	Carts:	$
DEAL	18 holes. Par 72/72. Yards: 6,962/5,168	Rating:	72.4/68.9
	Year-round. High: Apr.–Sept.	Slope:	131/120
SP	**The Neuse Golf Club**	Greens:	$–$$ W L T S J
☺☺☺	Birkdale Dr., Clayton. (919) 550-0550	Carts:	$
DEAL	18 holes. Par 72/72. Yards: 7,010/5,478	Rating:	73.5/72.2
	Year-round. High: Apr.–Oct.	Slope:	136/126
SP	**Porters Neck Country Club**	Greens:	$$–$$$$ W L R T
☺☺☺	Porters Neck Rd., Wilmington. (910) 686-1177	Carts:	Incl.
STATE	18 holes. Par 72/72. Yards: 7,209/5,268	Rating:	75.6/71.2
	Year-round. High: Feb.–May	Slope:	140/124
SP	**Quail Ridge Golf Course**	Greens:	$$ W L T S J
☺☺	Quail Ridge Dr., Sanford. (919) 776-6623	Carts:	Incl.
	18 holes. Par 72/72. Yards: 6,875/5,280	Rating:	73.2/70.8
	Year-round. High: Spring/Fall	Slope:	125/117

North Carolina Golf Guide

P ☺☺	**Reedy Creek Golf Club** Reedy Creek Rd., Four Oaks. (919) 934-7502 18 holes. Par 72/72. Yards: 6,401/5,115 Year-round. High: Apr.–Sept.	Greens: Carts: Rating: Slope:	$–$$ $ 70.5/68.5 117/115	W R T S J
R ☺☺☺	**Woodlake Country Club** Vass. (910) 245-4686 *Lake Shore/Cypress Creek* 18 holes. Par 72/72. Yards: 7,012/5,255 Year-round. High: Mar.–May	Greens: Carts: Rating: Slope:	$$–$$$$ Incl. 73.4/71.4 134/128	W L R T
☺☺☺	*Arnold Palmer Course* 18 holes. Par 72/72. Yards: 6,962/5,223	Greens: Carts: Rating: Slope:	$$–$$$$ Incl. 73.4/69.6 133/118	W L R T
☺☺☺	*Ellis Maples Course* 18 holes. Par 72/72. Yards: 7,043/5,303	Greens: Carts: Rating: Slope:	$$–$$$$ Incl. 74.4/71.6 136/118	W L R T

Fayetteville/Pinehurst Area

P ☺☺☺ DEAL	**Carolina Lakes Golf Club** Rte. 6, Sanford. (919) 499-5421 18 holes. Par 70/70. Yards: 6,397/5,010 Year-round. High: Mar.–May	Greens: Carts: Rating: Slope:	$ $ 70.7/67.0 117/110	W L R T S J
SP ☺☺☺	**The Club at Longleaf** Midland Rd., Southern Pines. (910) 692-6100 18 holes. Par 71/71. Yards: 6,600/4,719 Year-round. High: Mar.–May, Oct.	Greens: Carts: Rating: Slope:	$$–$$$ Incl. 69.7/65.7 117/108	L R T J
SP ☺☺☺	**Country Club of Whispering Pines** Whispering Pines. (910) 949-2311 *East Course* 18 holes. Par 72/72. Yards: 7,138/5,542 Year-round. High: Mar.–Oct.	Greens: Carts: Rating: Slope:	$$$ $ 73.9/72.0 125/123	L R J
☺☺☺	*West Course* 18 holes. Par 71/71. Yards: 6,363/5,135	Rating: Slope:	70.3/69.8 128/121	
P ☺☺	**Cypress Lakes Golf Course** Rte. 1, Hope Mills. (910) 483-0359 18 holes. Par 72/74. Yards: 7,240/5,685 Year-round. High: Spring/Fall	Greens: Carts: Rating: Slope:	$ Inquire 74.2/72.1 126/116	W
SP ☺☺☺	**Deercroft Golf and Country Club** Deercroft Dr., Wagram. (910) 369-3107 18 holes. Par 72/72. Yards: 6,745/5,443 Year-round. High: Spring/Fall	Greens: Carts: Rating: Slope:	$$$–$$$$ Incl. 72.2/67.0 125/113	W L T S J
SP ☺☺☺	**Gates Four Country Club** Irongate Dr., Fayetteville. (910) 425-2176 18 holes. Par 72/72. Yards: 6,865/5,368 Year-round. High: Spring/Fall	Greens: Carts: Rating: Slope:	$–$$ $ 73.4/70.5 122/115	W L R
P ☺☺	**Hyland Hills Golf Club** U.S. 1 N., Southern Pines. (910) 692-3752 18 holes. Par 72/72. Yards: 6,726/4,677 Year-round. High: Mar.–May, Oct.	Greens: Carts: Rating: Slope:	$–$$ $ 70.4/66.8 124/109	
P ☺☺☺	**Legacy Golf Links** U.S. 15, Aberdeen. (910) 944-8825 18 holes. Par 72/72. Yards: 7,018/4,948 Year-round. High: Spring/Fall	Greens: Carts: Rating: Slope:	$$–$$$$ Incl. 73.2/68.3 132/120	L R J

North Carolina Golf Guide

R ☺☺☺	**Mid Pines Golf Club** Midland Rd., Southern Pines. (910) 692-9362 18 holes. Par 72/75. Yards: 6,515/5,592 Year-round.	Greens: Carts: Rating: Slope:	$$$$$–$$$$$$ L R T $ 71.4/72.3 127/128
R ☺☺☺☺ STATE	**Pine Needles Golf Club** Midland Rd., Southern Pines. (910) 692-8611 18 holes. Par 71/71. Yards: 6,708/5,039 Year-round. High: Spring/Fall	Greens: Carts: Rating: Slope:	$$$$$–$$$$$$ L R J Incl. 72.2/68.6 131/124
SP ☺☺☺☺ STATE	**Pinehurst Plantation Golf Club** Midland Rd., Pinehurst. (910) 695-3193 18 holes. Par 72/72. Yards: 7,123/4,845 Year-round. High: Mar.–May.	Greens: Carts: Rating: Slope:	$$$$$–$$$$$$ Incl. 70.0/68.9 140/123
R ☺☺☺	**Pinehurst Resort and Country Club** Carolina Vista St., Pinehurst. (910) 295-8141 *Pinehurst No. 1* 18 holes. Par 70/73. Yards: 6,128/5,297 Year-round. High: Spring/Fall	Greens: Carts: Rating: Slope:	$$$$$–$$$$$$ L T Incl. 69.4/70.5 116/117
☺☺☺☺ BEST	*Pinehurst No. 2* 18 holes. Par 72/74. Yards: 7,254/5,825	Greens: Carts: Rating: Slope:	$$$$$$+ L T Incl. 75.9/74.6 138/130
☺☺☺	*Pinehurst No. 3* 18 holes. Par 70/71. Yards: 5,682/5,232	Greens: Carts: Rating: Slope:	$$$$–$$$$$$ L T Incl. 67.2/69.9 115/117
☺☺☺	*Pinehurst No. 4* (reopens January 2000) 18 holes. Par NA/NA. Yards: NA/NA	Greens: Carts: Rating: Slope:	$$$$$$ L T Incl. NA/NA NA/NA
☺☺☺	*Pinehurst No. 5* 18 holes. Par 72/73. Yards: 6,848/5,248	Greens: Carts: Rating: Slope:	$$$$$–$$$$$$ L T Incl. 73.4/70.1 137/119
☺☺☺	*Pinehurst No. 6* 18 holes. Par 72/72. Yards: 7,157/5,430	Greens: Carts: Rating: Slope:	$$$$–$$$$$$ L T Incl. 75.6/71.2 139/125
☺☺☺☺ BEST	*Pinehurst No. 7* 18 holes. Par 72/72. Yards: 7,125/4,996	Greens: Carts: Rating: Slope:	$$$$$$ L T Incl. 74.4/69.7 140/122
☺☺☺☺ BEST	*Pinehurst No. 8: Centennial Course* 18 holes. Par 72/72. Yards: 7,092/5,177	Greens: Carts: Rating: Slope:	$$$$$$ L T Incl. 74.2/69.8 135/122
P BEST ☺☺☺	**The Pit Golf Links** Hwy. 5, Pinehurst. (910) 944-1600 18 holes. Par 72/72. Yards: 6,600/4,759 Year-round. High: Mar., May–Oct.	Greens: Carts: Rating: Slope:	$$–$$$$ L T J $ 72.3/68.4 139/121
SP ☺☺☺	**Rock Barn Club of Golf** Conover. (704) 459-9279 18 holes. Par 72/72. Yards: 6,778/4,812 Year-round. High: Apr.–Oct.	Greens: Carts: Rating: Slope:	$$ W S $ 72.2/67.7 132/117

North Carolina Golf Guide

SP ☺☺☺	**Seven Lakes Country Club** West End. (910) 673-1092 18 holes. Par 72/73. Yards: 6,927/5,192 Year-round. High: Spring/Fall	Greens: Carts: Rating: Slope:	$$–$$$ L J $ 74.4/70.6 136/124
SP ☺☺☺	**Southern Pines Golf Course** Southern Pines. (910) 692-6551 18 holes. Par 71/74. Yards: 6,500/5,400 Year-round. High: Mar.–Oct.	Greens: Carts: Rating: Slope:	$$–$$$ W L R T $ 70.3/71.1 124/118
SP ☺☺	**Star Hill Golf and Country Club** Cape Carteret. (919) 393-8111 *Sands/Pines/Lakes* 27 holes. Par 72/71/71. Yards: 6,301/6,448/6,361 Year-round. High: June–Aug.	Greens: Carts: Rating: Slope:	$–$$ L R T $ 70.5/70.2/70.9 115/113/118
P ☺☺☺☺ STATE	**Talamore Resort** Midland Rd., Southern Pines. (910) 692-5884 18 holes. Par 71/71. Yards: 6,900/4,993 Year-round. High: Spring/Fall	Greens: Carts: Rating: Slope:	$$$–$$$$$L R T Incl. 72.9/69.0 142/125
SP ☺☺	**Whispering Woods Golf Club** Sandpiper Dr., Whispering Pines. (910) 949-4653 18 holes. Par 72/72. Yards: 6,334/4,924 Year-round. High: Spring/Fall	Greens: Carts: Rating: Slope:	$$–$$$ L T S J $ 70.5/68.7 122/122

North Carolina Shore

R ☺☺☺☺ STATE	**Bald Head Island Club** Bald Head Island. (910) 457-7310 18 holes. Par 72/72. Yards: 6,855/4,810 Year-round. High: May–Sept.	Greens: Carts: Rating: Slope:	$$$–$$$$$$$ L R J $ 74.3/70.1 139/117
SP ☺☺	**Brandywine Bay Golf & Country Club** Hwy. 70 W., Morehead City. (919) 247-2541 18 holes. Par 71/71. Yards: 6,609/5,191 Year-round. High: Mar.–Oct.	Greens: Carts: Rating: Slope:	$–$$ L T $ 72.2/68.5 119/119
R ☺☺	**Brick Landing Plantation** Goose Creek Rd., Ocean Isle Beach. (910) 754-5545 18 holes. Par 72/71. Yards: 6,752/4,707 Year-round. High: Mar.–Apr., Oct.	Greens: Carts: Rating: Slope:	$$–$$$$ T J Incl. 72.1/67.0 141/116
R ☺☺☺	**Brunswick Plantation Golf Links** Hwy. 17 N., Calabash. (910) 287-7888 18 holes. Par 72/72. Yards: 6,779/5,210 Year-round. High: Mar.–Apr., Oct.	Greens: Carts: Rating: Slope:	$$–$$$$ W L R T Incl. 72.7/70.4 131/115
SP ☺☺	**Duck Woods Country Club** Dogwood Trail, Kitty Hawk. (919) 261-2609 18 holes. Par 72/72. Yards: 6,650/5,407 Year-round. High: May–Sept.	Greens: Carts: Rating: Slope:	$$–$$$ $ 71.3/70.7 132/127
R ☺☺☺	**Lion's Paw Golf Links** Ocean Ridge Pkwy., Sunset Beach. (910) 287-1717 18 holes. Par 72/72. Yards: 7,003/5,363 Year-round. High: Spring/Fall	Greens: Carts: Rating: Slope:	$$–$$$$ W L R T J $ 74.6/69.1 138/118
P ☺☺☺ BEST	**Marsh Harbour Golf Links** Hwy. 179, Calabash. (910) 579-3161 18 holes. Par 71/71. Yards: 6,690/4,795 Year-round. High: Mar.–Apr., Oct.	Greens: Carts: Rating: Slope:	$$$–$$$$$ L R Incl. 72.4/67.7 134/115
R ☺☺☺	**Nags Head Golf Links** S. Seachase Dr., Nags Head. (919) 441-8073 18 holes. Par 71/71. Yards: 6,126/5800 Year-round. High: June–Aug.	Greens: Carts: Rating: Slope:	$$–$$$$ W L R T S J Incl. 68.8/66.9 130/126

North Carolina Golf Guide

P ☺☺	**Ocean Isle Beach Golf Course** Ocean Isle Beach. (910) 579-2610 18 holes. Par 72/72. Yards: 6,626/5,075 Year-round. High: Mar.–May, Sept–Nov.	Greens: Carts: Rating: Slope:	$$ Incl. NA 126/116	T
P ☺☺☺ BEST	**Oyster Bay Golf Links** Hwy. 179, Sunset Beach. (910) 579-3528 18 holes. Par 70/70. Yards: 6,685/4,825 Year-round. High: Mar.–Apr., Oct.	Greens: Carts: Rating: Slope:	$$–$$$$ $ 74.1/68.0 136/117	L R
P ☺☺☺	**The Pearl Golf Links** Pearl Blvd., S.W., Sunset Beach. (910) 579-8132 *East Course* 18 holes. Par 72/72. Yards: 7,008/5,188 Year-round. High: Spring/Fall	Greens: Carts: Rating: Slope:	$$–$$$$ Incl. 73.1/73.9 135/129	T J
☺☺☺	*West Course* 18 holes. Par 72/72. Yards: 7,000/5,188	Rating: Slope:	73.2/73.4 132/127	
P ☺☺☺ STATE	**Sandpiper Bay Golf and Country Club** Sandpiper Bay Dr., Sunset Beach. (910) 579-9120 18 holes. Par 71/71. Yards: 6,503/4,869 Year-round. High: Spring/Fall	Greens: Carts: Rating: Slope:	$$$–$$$$ Incl. 71.6/68.3 119/113	W L
R ☺☺	**Sea Scape Golf Course** Eckner St., Kitty Hawk. (919) 261-2158 18 holes. Par 72/72. Yards: 6,409/5,536 Year-round. High: May–Oct.	Greens: Carts: Rating: Slope:	$$–$$$$ Incl. 70.4/70.9 120/115	L R T J
R ☺☺☺	**Sea Trail Plantation and Golf Links** Sunset Beach. (910) 287-1122 *Willard Byrd Course* 18 holes. Par 72/72. Yards: 6,750/4,697 Year-round. High: Mar.–Apr., Oct.	Greens: Carts: Rating: Slope:	$–$$$ $ 72.1/67.9 128/111	R J
☺☺☺	*Dan Maples Course* 18 holes. Par 72/72. Yards: 6,751/5,090	Rating: Slope:	72.4/69.0 129/115	
☺☺☺	*Rees Jones Course* 18 holes. Par 72/72. Yards: 6,761/4,912	Rating: Slope:	72.4/68.5 132/115	

Wilmington Area

SP ☺☺	**Beau Rivage Plantation Country Club** Carolina Beach Rd., Wilmington. (910) 392-9022 18 holes. Par 72/72. Yards: 6,709/4,612 Year-round. High: Mar.–Sept.	Greens: Carts: Rating: Slope:	$$–$$$ Incl. 72.5/69.0 136/114	W L R T S J
P ☺☺	**Belvedere Plantation Golf and Country Club** Hampstead. (910) 270-2703 18 holes. Par 71/72. Yards: 6,401/4,992 Year-round. High: Mar.–May	Greens: Carts: Rating: Slope:	$$–$$$ Incl. 128/113 71.2/68.5	L R T J
SP ☺☺	**Brierwood Golf Club** Hwy. 179, Shallotte. (910) 754-4660 18 holes. Par 72/72. Yards: 6,607/4,810 Year-round. High: Apr.–Oct.	Greens: Carts: Rating: Slope:	$–$$ Incl. 71.8/67.0 127/112	W L T S
SP ☺☺	**Cape Golf and Racquet Club** The Cape Blvd., Wilmington. (910) 799-3110 18 holes. Par 72/72. Yards: 6,790/4,948 Year-round. High: Apr.	Greens: Carts: Rating: Slope:	$–$$$ Incl. 73.1/69.3 133/118	W L T S
SP ☺☺	**Echo Farms Golf and Country Club** Echo Farms Blvd., Wilmington. (910) 791-9318 18 holes. Par 72/72. Yards: 7,014/5,142 Year-round. High: Apr.–Oct.	Greens: Carts: Rating: Slope:	$$ Incl. 74.2/70.7 132/121	L R

North Carolina Golf Guide

SP ☺☺☺	**The Emerald Golf Club** New Bern. (919) 633-4440 18 holes. Par 72/72. Yards: 6,924/5,287 Year-round. High: Mar.–May, Oct.	Greens: Carts: Rating: Slope:	$$–$$$ L T J Incl. 74.0/71.3 125/119
SP ☺☺	**Fairfield Harbour Country Club** Pelican Dr., New Bern. (919) 514-0050 *Harbour Pointe Course* 18 holes. Par 72/72. Yards: 6,650/5,100 Year-round. High: Spring/Fall	Greens: Carts: Rating: Slope:	$$ L T $ 71.8/68.6 125/111
☺☺	*Shoreline Course* 18 holes. Par 72/72. Yards: 6,802/5,200 Year-round. High: Spring/Fall	Rating: Slope:	72.1/70.0 128/118
SP ☺☺☺	**The Gauntlet at St. James Plantation** Hwy. 211, Southport. (910) 253-3008 18 holes. Par 72/72. Yards: 7,050/5,003 Year-round. High: Mar.–May	Greens: Carts: Rating: Slope:	$$$–$$$$ L T S Incl. 75.0/69.7 142/119
SP ☺☺☺	**Lockwood Golf Links** Supply. (910) 842-5666 18 holes. Par 72/72. Yards: 6,836/5,524 Year-round. High: Spring/Fall	Greens: Carts: Rating: Slope:	$$–$$$$ L R J Incl. 73.5/70.0 135/121
SP ☺	**Magnolia Country Club** Magnolia Lane, Magnolia. (910) 289-2126 18 holes. Par 71/71. Yards: 6,400/4,600 Year-round. High: June–Aug.	Greens: Carts: Rating: Slope:	$ W R T S J $ 69.8/68.3 116/109
SP ☺☺☺☺ STATE	**North Shore Country Club** N. Shore Dr., Sneads Ferry. (910) 327-2410 18 holes. Par 72/72. Yards: 6,866/5,039 Year-round. High: Mar.–Nov.	Greens: Carts: Rating: Slope:	$$–$$$ W L T J Incl. 72.8/68.7 134/122
P ☺☺	**Oak Island Golf and Country Club** Caswell Beach Rd., Caswell Beach. (910) 278-5275 18 holes. Par 72/72. Yards: 6,608/5,437 Year-round. High: June–Oct.	Greens: Carts: Rating: Slope:	$$ W L Incl. NA 128
SP ☺☺☺	**Olde Point Country Club** Hwy. 17 N., Hampstead. (910) 270-2403 18 holes. Par 72/72. Yards: 6,913/5,133 Year-round. High: Mar.–May	Greens: Carts: Rating: Slope:	$$–$$$ W L Incl. 73.1/69.8 130/118

Oklahoma

The cream of the public golf course crop in Oklahoma is the **Karsten Creek Golf Course** in Stillwater, about 50 miles northeast of Oklahoma City; Karsten opens a new clubhouse in late 2000.

Also a worthy course is **Forest Ridge** in Broken Arrow, southeast of Tulsa.

Beyond these, there is an unusually large number of *Golf U.S.A.* Deals in Oklahoma, good deals for quality golf.

Golf courses in Oklahoma generally are open year-round. Expect peak rates from late spring through early fall.

Golf U.S.A. Leader Board: Best Public Courses in Oklahoma

☺☺☺☺ Forest Ridge Golf Club
☺☺☺☺ Karsten Creek Golf Course

Golf U.S.A. Leader Board: Best Deals in Oklahoma

$$/☺☺☺	Bailey Golf Ranch
$/☺☺☺	Boiling Springs Golf Club
$/☺☺☺	Cedar Valley Golf Club (Augusta)
$/☺☺☺	Cimarron National Golf Club (Cimarron)
$$/☺☺☺	Coffee Creek Golf Course
$/☺☺☺	Earlywine Park Golf Course
$$/☺☺☺	Falconhead Ranch and Country Club
$/☺☺☺	Heritage Hills Golf Course
$/☺☺☺	John Conrad Regional Golf Course
$/☺☺☺	Kickingbird Golf Course
$/☺☺☺	Lake Hefner Golf Club (North)
$/☺☺☺	Lakeview Golf Course
$/☺☺☺	Lew Wentz Memorial Golf Course
$/☺☺☺	Page Belcher Golf Course (Old Page, Stone Creek)
$$/☺☺☺	Silverhorn Golf Club
$/☺☺☺	Sunset Hills Golf Course

Oklahoma Golf Guide

Western Oklahoma

P ☺☺☺ DEAL	**Boiling Springs Golf Club** Woodward. (405) 256-1206 18 holes. Par 71/75. Yards: 6,454/4,944 Year-round. High: Apr.–Oct.	Greens: $ Carts: $ Rating: 69.6/68.6 Slope: 117/117	W L T S J
R ☺☺	**Quartz Mountain Golf Course** Lone Wolf. (405) 563-2520 18 holes. Par 71/71. Yards: 6,595/5,706 Year-round. High: May–Aug.	Greens: $ Carts: $ Rating: 70.8 Slope: 119	R T S J

Oklahoma City Area

P ☺☺☺ DEAL	**Cedar Valley Golf Club** Guthrie. (405) 282-4800 *Augusta Course* 18 holes. Par 70/72. Yards: 6,602/5,170 Year-round. High: May–Aug.	Greens: $ Carts: $ Rating: 70.3/69.1 Slope: 108/117	W
☺☺	*International Course* 18 holes. Par 70/72. Yards: 6,520/4,955	Rating: 71.1/68.4 Slope: 112/115	
P ☺☺	**Cimarron National Golf Club** Duffy's Way, Guthrie. (405) 282-7888 *Aqua Canyon Course* 18 holes. Par 70/71. Yards: 6,358/5,720 Year-round. High: May–Sept.	Greens: $ Carts: $ Rating: 69.6/66.4 Slope: 114/110	W L S
☺☺☺ DEAL	*Cimarron Course* 18 holes. Par 70/70. Yards: 6,653/5,559	Rating: 68.1/66.1 Slope: 120/113	
P ☺☺☺ DEAL	**Coffee Creek Golf Course** N. Kelly, Edmond. (405) 340-4653 18 holes. Par 70/70. Yards: 6,700/5,559 Year-round. High: May–Sept.	Greens: $–$$ Carts: $ Rating: 71.5/70.5 Slope: 129/122	W T S J
P ☺☺☺	**Earlywine Park Golf Course** S. Portland, Oklahoma City. (405) 691-1727 *South Course*	Greens: $ Carts: $ Rating: 69.5/71.6	W L T S J

Oklahoma Golf Guide

DEAL	18 holes. Par 71/71. Yards: 6,728/5,388 Year-round. High: Mar.–Nov.	Slope:	107/117
☺☺☺	*North Course* 18 holes. Par 72/72. Yards: 6,721/4,843	Rating: Slope:	71.9/70.4 126/122
P ☺☺	**Fire Lake Golf Course** S. Gordon Cooper, Shawnee. (405) 275-4471 18 holes. Par 70/71. Yards: 6,335/4,992 Year-round. High: May–July	Greens: $ Carts: $ Rating: 69.6/NA Slope: 121/NA	W T S J
P ☺☺☺ DEAL	**John Conrad Regional Golf Course** S. Douglas Blvd., Midwest City. (405) 732-2209 18 holes. Par 72/74. Yards: 6,854/5,511 Year-round. High: Apr.–Oct.	Greens: $ Carts: $ Rating: 72.0/70.8 Slope: 122/119	T S J
SP ☺☺☺☺ BEST	**Karsten Creek Golf Course** Stillwater. (405) 743-1658 18 holes. Par 72/72. Yards: 7,095/4,906 Year-round. High: Apr.–Sept.	Greens: $$$$$$+ Carts: Incl. Rating: 74.8/70.1 Slope: 142/127	
P ☺☺☺ DEAL	**Kickingbird Golf Course** E. Danforth Rd., Edmond. (405) 341-5350 18 holes. Par 71/72. Yards: 6,816/4,801 Year-round. High: May–Sept.	Greens: $ Carts: $ Rating: 71.4/68.5 Slope: 127/117	T S J
P ☺☺☺ DEAL	**Lake Hefner Golf Club** S. Lake Hefner Dr., Oklahoma City. (405) 843-1565 *North Course* 18 holes. Par 72/72. Yards: 6,970/5,169 Year-round. High: Mar.–Sept.	Greens: $ Carts: $ Rating: 74.2/69.6 Slope: 128/117	T S J
☺☺	*South Course* 18 holes. Par 70/73. Yards: 6,305/5,393	Rating: 68.9/71.2 Slope: 111/115	
R ☺☺	**Lake Texoma Golf Resort** Kingston. (405) 564-3333 18 holes. Par 71/74. Yards: 6,145/5,145 Year-round. High: Apr.–Oct.	Greens: $ Carts: $ Rating: 67.8/68.7 Slope: 112/108	W L R T S J
P ☺☺	**Lincoln Park Golf Course** N.E. Grand Blvd., Oklahoma City. (405) 424-1421 *East Course* 18 holes. Par 70/71. Yards: 6,508/5,467 Year-round. High: Apr.–Sept.	Greens: $ Carts: Inquire Rating: 70.0/66.2 Slope: 120/112	W T S J
☺☺	*West Course* 18 holes. Par 70/71. Yards: 6,508/5,587	Rating: 70.7/68.4 Slope: 121/115	
SP ☺☺☺ DEAL	**Silverhorn Golf Club** N. Kelley Ave., Oklahoma City. (405) 752-1181 18 holes. Par 71/71. Yards: 6,800/4,943 Year-round. High: Apr.–Sept.	Greens: $$ Carts: $ Rating: 73.4/71.0 Slope: 128/113	W L T S J
P ☺☺	**University of Oklahoma Golf Course** Norman. (405) 325-6716 18 holes. Par 72/72. Yards: 7,197/5,310 Year-round. High: Apr.–Oct.	Greens: $-$$ Carts: $$ Rating: 74.9/71.6 Slope: 134/119	W L T S J
P ☺☺	**Westwood Park Golf Course** Westport Dr., Norman. (405) 321-0433 18 holes. Par 72/72. Yards: 6,015/5,525 Year-round. High: Apr.–Sept.	Greens: $ Carts: $ Rating: 67.7/71.0 Slope: 108/120	W T S

Tulsa Area

P ☺☺	**Adams Municipal Golf Course** E. Tuxedo Blvd., Bartlesville. (918) 337-5313	Greens: $ Carts: $	W T S J

18 holes. Par 72/74. Yards: 6,819/5,655 Year-round. High: Mar.–Oct.	Rating: 72.0/71.8 Slope: 119/117

P
☺☺☺
DEAL

Bailey Golf Ranch
Larkin Bailey Blvd., Owasso. (918) 272-9339
18 holes. Par 72/72. Yards: 6,752/4,898
Year-round. High: Apr.–Oct.

Greens: $–$$ W L T S J
Carts: $
Rating: 73.1/68.4
Slope: 132/115

P
☺☺☺☺
STATE

Forest Ridge Golf Club
E. Kenosha, Broken Arrow. (918) 357-2282
18 holes. Par 71/72. Yards: 7,069/5,341
Year-round. High: Mar.–Oct.

Greens: $$$–$$$$ W L T
Carts: Incl.
Rating: 74.8/73.3
Slope: 137/132

P
☺☺

Fountainhead State Park Golf Course
Checotah. (918) 689-3209
18 holes. Par 72/72. Yards: 6,919/4,864
Year-round. High: Mar.–Oct.

Greens: $ T S J
Carts: $
Rating: 71.3/67.3
Slope: 116/98

P
☺☺☺
DEAL

Heritage Hills Golf Course
Claremore. (918) 341-0055
18 holes. Par 71/72. Yards: 6,760/4,909
Year-round. High: Apr.–Sept.

Greens: $ W T S J
Carts: $
Rating: 72.6/70.0
Slope: 120/117

P
☺☺

Lafortune Park Golf Club
S. Yale Ave., Tulsa. (918) 596-8627
18 holes. Par 72/73. Yards: 6,970/5,780
Year-round. High: Mar.–Aug.

Greens: $ T S J
Carts: $
Rating: 71.4/68.5
Slope: 127/117

P
☺☺☺
DEAL

Lew Wentz Memorial Golf Course
Cann Dr., Ponca City. (405) 767-0433
18 holes. Par 71/70. Yards: 6,400/5,450
Year-round. High: Apr.–Oct.

Greens: $ W S J
Carts: $
Rating: 70.0/71.8
Slope: 125/123

P

☺☺

Mohawk Park Golf Club
E. 41st St. N., Tulsa. (918) 425-6871
Woodbine Course
18 holes. Par 72/76. Yards: 6,898/6,202
Year-round. High: June–July

Greens: $ T S J
Carts: $
Rating: 71.0/73.9
Slope: 115/127

☺

Pecan Valley Course
18 holes. Par 70/70. Yards: 6,499/5,130

Rating: 71.6/69.6
Slope: 124/119

P

☺☺☺
DEAL

Page Belcher Golf Course
S. Union Ave., Tulsa. (918) 446-1529
Old Page Course
18 holes. Par 71/71. Yards: 6,826/5,532
Year-round. High: Apr.–Oct.

Greens: $ W T S J
Carts: $
Rating: 72.0/71.5
Slope: 121/118

☺☺☺
DEAL

Stone Creek Course
18 holes. Par 71/71. Yards: 6,539/5,144

Rating: 72.3/69.9
Slope: 126/127

P
☺☺

Sand Springs Municipal Golf Course
N. McKinley, Sand Springs. (918) 245-7551
18 holes. Par 71/70. Yards: 6,113/4,692
Year-round. High: Apr.–Oct.

Greens: $ W L T S J
Carts: $
Rating: 68.9/68.4
Slope: 115/118

R

☺☺☺

Shangri-La Golf Resort
Afton. (918) 257-4204
Blue Course
18 holes. Par 72/73. Yards: 7,012/5,892
Year-round. High: Apr.–Oct.

Greens: $$$–$$$$ W L R
Carts: Incl.
Rating: 74.0/74.8
Slope: 132/126

☺☺☺

Gold Course
18 holes. Par 70/71. Yards: 6,800/4,943

Rating: 66.8/66.8
Slope: 123/112

Oklahoma Golf Guide

P	South Lakes Golf Course	Greens:	$	T S J
☺☺	S. Elwood, Jenks. (918) 746-3760	Carts:	$	
	18 holes. Par 71/71. Yards: 6,340/5,242	Rating:	68.6/70.4	
	Year-round. High: Apr.–Sept.	Slope:	113/116	

SP	Spunky Creek Country Club	Greens:	$	W L T S J
☺☺	Catoosa. (918) 266-2207	Carts:	$	
	18 holes. Par 71/74. Yards: 6,732/5,748	Rating:	71.5/72.9	
	Year-round. High: Mar.–Oct.	Slope:	124/127	

SP	White Hawk Golf Club	Greens:	$$	W L T S J
☺☺	S. York Ave., Bixby. (918) 366-4653	Carts:	$	
	18 holes. Par 72/72. Yards: 6,982/5,148	Rating:	74.1/NA	
	Year-round. High: May–Oct.	Slope:	134/NA	

Southern Oklahoma

R	Cedar Creek Golf Course	Greens:	$	W L R T S J
☺☺	Broken Bow. (405) 494-6456	Carts:	$	
	18 holes. Par 72/72. Yards: 6,724/5,762	Rating:	72.1/NA	
	Year-round. High: Apr.–Oct.	Slope:	132/NA	

SP	Falconhead Ranch and Country Club	Greens:	$–$$	S
☺☺☺	Burneyville. (405) 276-9284	Carts:	$	
DEAL	18 holes. Par 72/71. Yards: 6,400/5,280	Rating:	69.9/70.3	
	Year-round. High: Apr.–Oct.	Slope:	118/120	

P	Lakeview Golf Course	Greens:	$	W T S J
☺☺☺	N. Commerce, Ardmore. (405) 223-4260	Carts:	$	
DEAL	18 holes. Par 71/72. Yards: 6,881/5,032	Rating:	71.2/67.5	
	Year-round. High: Apr.–Sept.	Slope:	114/113	

P	Sunset Hills Golf Course	Greens:	$	T
☺☺☺	Guymon. (405) 338-7404	Carts:	$	
DEAL	18 holes. Par 71/74. Yards: 6,236/5,204	Rating:	70.3/69.0	
	Year-round. High: June–Aug.	Slope:	120/117	

South Carolina

The Palmetto State has a collection of some of the best oceanside courses anywhere. On and nearby Hilton Head Island, a large barrier island at the southern end of the state's coastline, are three of the best of the best. The breathtaking **Harbour Town** is on the island. So too is the Arthur Hills Course at **Palmetto Hall Plantation**, a superb melding of woods and water, located near its corporate cousin, the renowned Palmetto Dunes Resort.

Hilton Head National Golf Club is a traditional course with a varying cast of traps and challenges that will reward the accurate shooter. Hilton Head, about 42 square miles, has become a year-round destination and home; parts of the island look a bit like the worst of tourist America, with fast-food outlets and miniature golf, while other sections feature near-pristine beaches, marshes, and forests. The island has 12 miles of beaches, more than 20 golf courses, and dozens of superb resorts. The commercial center is Harbour Town.

The lovely Harbour Town Golf Links was scheduled to be closed for much of 2000 for a complete remake. In nearby Beaufort is the **Callawassie Island Club**, a bit less well known but no less beautiful or challenging.

The **Kiawah Island Resort** near Charleston has three great courses in one location, plus a new clubhouse opening in 2000. The Ocean Course there is one of the most spectacular and difficult in the country, stretching nearly three miles along the beach, with views of the ocean at every hole, and 10 holes directly on the water. Some say it is the best course anywhere. The Osprey Point Course is beautiful but not quite as hard; it is blessed, though, with a huge new clubhouse. The Turtle Point Course is right along the sea, featuring beaches, bikinis, and the occasional alligator. For those times when you aren't holding a club, the posh resort facilities on the island offer tennis, boating, fishing, and much more.

Nearby in Isle of Palms is the **Wild Dunes Resort**, which has one of the nation's best links courses, with the last two holes oceanside and spectacular. The resort there and its courses were all but erased by Hurricane Hugo in 1989, but the restoration has polished this gem even brighter.

At Myrtle Beach is the intriguingly named **The Witch**, a lovely, isolated beach-and-wetlands course that uses bridges and walkways to cross marshlands; your ball will have to take the aerial route to the greens.

Another Myrtle Beach favorite is the Heathland Course at **Legends**, which re-creates a links feeling on its treeless rolling land and has its own version of the famed clubhouse at St. Andrews.

The Tidewater Golf Club in North Myrtle Beach underwent a total facelift in 1999.

Finally, **Cedar Creek** at Aiken, 25 miles west of Augusta, presents a deceptively difficult inland challenge. Cedar Creek is also South Carolina's only joint member of the *Golf U.S.A.* Best and *Golf U.S.A.* Deals lists.

Most courses in South Carolina are open year-round; look for peak rates from spring through fall. Some courses offer discounts during the hottest months of the summer

The Kiawah Island Resort offers value-season rates from about November 15 through about March 30. Peak season includes Easter and spring-break periods and mid-June through mid-August. In recent years, a basic room with a scenic (not ocean) view sold for $180 at peak rates and $115 in value season; a luxury oceanfront two-bedroom villa sold for a high of $475 per night and a low of $240 per night.

Golf U.S.A. Leader Board: Best Public Courses in South Carolina

◎◎◎◎ Caledonia Golf and Fish Club
◎◎◎◎ Callawassie Island Club (Palmetto, Dogwood, Magnolia)
◎◎◎◎ Cedar Creek Golf Club
◎◎◎◎ Harbour Town Golf Links
◎◎◎◎ Heather Glen Golf Links
◎◎◎◎ Heritage Club
◎◎◎   Hilton Head National Golf Club
◎◎◎◎ Kiawah Island Resort (Osprey Point, Ocean, Turtle Point)
◎◎◎◎ Legends (Heathland)
◎◎◎◎ The Long Bay Club
◎◎◎◎ Palmetto Hall Plantation (Arthur Hills)
◎◎◎◎ Tidewater Golf Club

⊙⊙⊙⊙ Wild Dunes Resort (Links)
⊙⊙⊙⊙ Wild Wing Plantation (Avocet, Wood Stork)
⊙⊙⊙⊙ The Witch

Golf U.S.A. Leader Board: Best Deals in South Carolina

$$/⊙⊙⊙⊙	Cedar Creek Golf Club
$$/⊙⊙⊙	Cobb's Glen Country Club
$$/⊙⊙⊙	Crowfield Golf and Country Club
$/⊙⊙⊙	Fox Creek Golf Club
$/⊙⊙⊙	Hickory Knob Golf Club
$$/⊙⊙⊙	Northwoods Golf Club
$/⊙⊙⊙	Persimmon Hill Golf Club
$$/⊙⊙⊙	River Falls Plantation
$/⊙⊙⊙	Stoney Point Golf Club
$$/⊙⊙⊙	Timberlake Plantation Golf Club
$$/⊙⊙⊙	The Wellman Club

South Carolina Golf Guide

Greenville/Anderson Area

SP **Carolina Springs Country Club**
⊙⊙ Scuffletown Rd., Fountain Inn. (864) 862-3551
Willows/Pines/Cedar
27 holes. Par 72/72/72. Yards: 6,676/6,815/6,643
Year-round. High: Apr.–Sept.
Greens: $–$$ W L T S J
Carts: $
Rating: 71.7/72.1/71.2
Slope: 125/121/121

SP **Cobb's Glen Country Club**
⊙⊙⊙ Cobb's Way, Anderson. (864) 226-7688
DEAL 18 holes. Par 72/72. Yards: 7,005/5,312
Year-round. High: Apr.–Oct.
Greens: $$ W S J
Carts: $
Rating: 72.3/72.0
Slope: 129/121

SP **Falcon's Lair Golf Course**
⊙ Falcon Dr., Walhalla. (864) 638-0000
18 holes. Par 72/72. Yards: 6,955/5,238
Year-round. High: Mar.–Oct.
Greens: $$ W L T S J
Carts: $
Rating: 72.1/70.6
Slope: 124/123

P **Cherokee Valley Golf Club**
⊙⊙ Chinquapin Rd., Tigerville. (864) 895-6758
18 holes. Par 72/72. Yards: 6,713/4,545
Year-round. High: Mar.–Oct.
Greens: $$ W L T S J
Carts: Incl.
Rating: 72.1/69.7
Slope: 133/117

P **River Falls Plantation**
⊙⊙⊙ Duncan. (864) 433-9192
DEAL 18 holes. Par 72/72. Yards: 6,697/4,802
Year-round. High: Apr.–Aug.
Greens: $$–$$$ L R S J
Carts: Incl.
Rating: 72.8/68.2
Slope: 132/125

SP **Saluda Valley Country Club**
⊙⊙ Beaver Dam Rd., Williamston. (864) 847-7102
18 holes. Par 72/72. Yards: 6,430/5,126
Year-round. High: Apr.–Sept.
Greens: $ W
Carts: $
Rating: 70.8/69.4
Slope: 119/114

SP **Stoney Point Golf Club**
⊙⊙⊙ Swing About Rd., Greenwood. (864) 942-0900
DEAL 18 holes. Par 72/72. Yards: 6,686/5,457
Year-round. High: Spring/Fall
Greens: $$ T S
Carts: Incl.
Rating: 72.1/69.4
Slope: 122/125

R **Verdae Greens Golf Club**
⊙⊙⊙ Verdae Blvd., Greenville. (864) 676-1500
18 holes. Par 72/72. Yards: 7,041/5,012
Year-round. High: Mar.–Nov.
Greens: $$–$$$ L R S J
Carts: Incl.
Rating: 74.2/68.1
Slope: 140/116

South Carolina Golf Guide

Columbia Area

SP ☺☺	**Calhoun Country Club** Rte. 3, St. Matthews. (803) 823-2465 18 holes. Par 71/71. Yards: 6,339/4,812 Year-round. High: Mar.–Apr.	Greens: Carts: Rating: Slope:	$–$$ Incl. 70.0/66.4 119/110	W T S J
SP ☺☺	**Coldstream Country Club** Hwy. 60, Irmo. (803) 781-0114 18 holes. Par 71/71. Yards: 6,155/5,097 Year-round. High: Apr.–Oct.	Greens: Carts: Rating: Slope:	$$ Incl. 70.1/68.7 122/NA	W L R T S J
P ☺☺	**Hillcrest Golf Club** Orangeburg. (803) 533-6030 18 holes. Par 72/72. Yards: 6,722/5,208 Year-round. High: Mar.–May	Greens: Carts: Rating: Slope:	$ $ 70.5/67.8 119/107	L
P ☺☺☺	**Lake Marion Golf Club** Santee. (803) 854-2554 18 holes. Par 72/72. Yards: 6,670/5,254 Year-round. High: Mar.–May	Greens: Carts: Rating: Slope:	$$–$$$ Incl. 72.1/69.8 121/112	
SP ☺☺	**Linrick Golf Course** Campground Rd., Columbia. (803) 754-6331 18 holes. Par 73/73. Yards: 6,919/5,243 Year-round. High: Mar.–Sept.	Greens: Carts: Rating: Slope:	$ $ 72.2/69.4 125/NA	S J
P ☺☺☺ DEAL	**Northwoods Golf Club** Powell Rd., Columbia. (803) 786-9242 18 holes. Par 72/72. Yards: 6,800/5,000 Year-round. High: May–Oct.	Greens: Carts: Rating: Slope:	$–$$ $ 71.6/67.6 135/113	W L T
P ☺☺	**Oak Hills Golf Club** Fairfield Rd., Columbia. (803) 735-9830 18 holes. Par 72/72. Yards: 6,894/4,574 Year-round. High: Apr.-May, Sept.-Oct.	Greens: Carts: Rating: Slope:	$$ Incl. 72.3/65.6 131/111	W L T S J
SP ☺☺☺ DEAL	**Timberlake Plantation Golf Club** Amicks Ferry Rd., Chapin. (803) 345-9909 18 holes. Par 72/72. Yards: 6,703/5,111 Year-round. High: Apr.–May, Aug.–Nov.	Greens: Carts: Rating: Slope:	$–$$ $ 73.2/69.8 132/118	W L J S

Florence Area

P ☺☺☺	**Cheraw State Park Golf Course** Cheraw. (803) 537-2215 18 holes. Par 72/72. Yards: 6,900/5,408 Year-round. High: Mar.–June	Greens: Carts: Rating: Slope:	$ $ NA 130/120	W T
SP ☺☺☺ DEAL	**Fox Creek Golf Club** Hwy. 15 S., Lydia. (803) 332-0613 18 holes. Par 72/72. Yards: 6,903/5,271 Year-round. High: Feb.–May, Sept.–Nov.	Greens: Carts: Rating: Slope:	$ $ 72.7/67.9 128/106	W R S J

Myrtle Beach Region

P ☺☺☺	**Arcadian Shores Golf Club** Hilton Rd., Myrtle Beach. (843) 449-5217 18 holes. Par 72/72. Yards: 6,857/5,113 Year-round. High: Mar.–May, Oct.	Greens: Carts: Rating: Slope:	$$$–$$$$$ Incl. 73.1/69.9 137/117	L R
P ☺☺☺	**Arrowhead Golf Club** Burcal Rd., Myrtle Beach. (843) 236-3243 *Lakes/Waterway/Cypress* 27 holes. Par 72/72. Yards: 6,600/6,754/6,898 Year-round. High: Spring/Fall	Greens: Carts: Rating: Slope:	$$–$$$$$ Incl. 71.4/71.4/71.4 132/134/136	
P ☺☺	**Azalea Sands Golf Club** Hwy. 17 S., N. Myrtle Beach. (843) 272-6191	Greens: Carts:	$$–$$$ Incl.	L R T

	18 holes. Par 72/72. Yards: 6,902/5,172		Rating:	72.5/70.2
	Year-round. High: Spring/Fall		Slope:	123/119

P	**Bay Tree Golf Plantation**		Greens:	$–$$$ L
	N. Myrtle Beach. (843) 249-1487		Carts:	$
☺☺	*Gold Course*		Rating:	72.0/69.7
	18 holes. Par 72/72. Yards: 6,942/5,264		Slope:	135/117
	Year-round. High: Mar.–Apr.			

☺☺	*Green Course*		Rating:	72.5/69.0
	18 holes. Par 72/72. Yards: 7,044/5,362		Slope:	135/118

☺☺	*Silver Course*		Rating:	70.5/69.0
	18 holes. Par 72/72. Yards: 6,871/5,417		Slope:	131/116

R	**Blackmoor Golf Club**		Greens:	$$–$$$$ L R J
☺☺☺	Longwood Rd., Murrells Inlet. (843) 650-5555		Carts:	$
	18 holes. Par 72/72. Yards: 6,614/4,807		Rating:	71.1/67.9
	Year-round. High: Apr.–Oct.		Slope:	126/115

P	**Buck Creek Golf Plantation**		Greens:	$$–$$$$ L T J
	Bucks Trail, Hwy. 9, Longs. (843) 399-2806		Carts:	$
☺☺	*Meadow/Cypress/Tupelo*		Rating:	71.1/72.4/71.6
	27 holes. Par 72/72/72. Yards: 6,751/6,865/6,726		Slope:	126/132/128
	Year-round. High: Spring/Fall			

R	**Burning Ridge Golf Club**		Greens:	$$$ W L T
	Hwy. 501 W., Conway. (843) 347-0538		Carts:	Incl.
☺☺	*East Course*		Rating:	72.8/65.4
	18 holes. Par 72/72. Yards: 6,780/4,524		Slope:	128/111
	Year-round. High: Feb.–Oct.			

☺☺	*West Course*		Rating:	71.8/67.2
	18 holes. Par 72/72. Yards: 6,714/4,831		Slope:	122/118

P	**Caledonia Golf and Fish Club**		Greens:	$$$$$–$$$$$$$ L
☺☺☺☺	Caledonia Dr., Pawleys Island. (843) 237-3675		Carts:	Incl.
STATE	18 holes. Par 70/70. Yards: 6,526/4,957		Rating:	70.9/68.2
	Year-round. High: Spring/Fall		Slope:	132/113

P	**Colonial Charters Golf Club**		Greens:	$$$$
☺☺☺	Charter Dr., Longs. (843) 249-8809		Carts:	Incl.
	18 holes. Par 72/72. Yards: 6,901/6,372		Rating:	71.8/68.6
	Year-round. High: Spring/Fall		Slope:	124/115

R	**Deer Track Golf Resort**		Greens:	$$–$$$ W L R T J
	Platt Blvd., Surfside Beach. (843) 650-2146		Carts:	Incl.
☺☺	*North Course*		Rating:	73.5/69.6
	18 holes. Par 72/72. Yards: 7,203/5,353		Slope:	121/119
	Year-round. High: Spring/Fall			

☺☺	*South Course*		Rating:	73.5/69.6
	18 holes. Par 71/71. Yards: 6,916/5,226		Slope:	119/120

R	**Eagle Nest Golf Club**		Greens:	$–$$$ R T
☺☺☺	Hwy. 17 N., N. Myrtle Beach. (843) 399-3375		Carts:	$
	18 holes. Par 72/72. Yards: 6,901/5,105		Rating:	73.0/69.8
	Year-round. High: Mar.–Apr., Oct.		Slope:	120/116

P	**Eastport Golf Club**		Greens:	$–$$ W
☺☺	Hwy. 17, N. Myrtle Beach. (843) 249-3997		Carts:	Incl.
	18 holes. Par 70/70. Yards: 6,202/4,698		Rating:	69.1/65.7
	Year-round. High: Mar.–May		Slope:	121/114

P	**Gator Hole Golf Course**		Greens:	$$–$$$ T J
☺☺☺	Hwy. 17, N. Myrtle Beach. (843) 249-3543		Carts:	Incl.

South Carolina Golf Guide

	18 holes. Par 70/70. Yards: 6,000/4,685	Rating:	69.8/65.9
	Year-round. High: Mar.–May	Slope:	116/112

R	**Heather Glen Golf Links**	Greens:	$$$–$$$$ L
	Hwy. 17 N., Little River. (843) 249-9000	Carts:	Incl.
☺☺☺☺	*Red/White/Blue*	Rating:	72.4/72.4/72.4
BEST	27 holes. Par 72/72/72. Yards: 6,783/6,882/6,831	Slope:	130/130/127
	Year-round. High: Mar.–May, Oct.		

P	**Heritage Club**	Greens:	$$$–$$$$$$ W L R T
☺☺☺☺	Hwy. 17 S., Pawleys Island. (843) 237-3424	Carts:	Incl.
BEST	18 holes. Par 71/71. Yards: 6,985/5,315	Rating:	74.1/71.0
	Year-round. High: Mar.–Apr., Oct.	Slope:	142/125

P	**Heron Point Golf Club**	Greens:	$$–$$$ W L R T J
☺☺	Blue Heron Blvd., Myrtle Beach. (843) 650-6664	Carts:	Incl.
	18 holes. Par 72/72. Yards: 6,477/4,734	Rating:	70.9/69.2
	Year-round. High: Spring/Fall	Slope:	129/121

P	**Indian Wells Golf Club**	Greens:	$–$$$ L R T J
☺☺	Woodlake Dr., Garden City. (843) 651-1505	Carts:	$
	18 holes. Par 72/72. Yards: 6,624/4,872	Rating:	71.9/68.2
	Year-round. High: Spring/Fall	Slope:	125/118

P	**Indigo Creek Golf Club**	Greens:	$$–$$$$ L T
☺☺	Surfside Beach. (843) 650-0381	Carts:	Incl.
	18 holes. Par 72/72. Yards: 6,750/4,921	Rating:	72.4/69.2
	Year-round. High: Spring/Fall	Slope:	134/120

R	**Legends Resorts**	Greens:	$$$–$$$$$ L R
	Hwy. 501, Myrtle Beach. (843) 236-9318	Carts:	Incl.
☺☺☺☺	*Heathland at the Legends*	Rating:	72.3/71.0
STATE	18 holes. Par 71/71. Yards: 6,785/5,115	Slope:	127/121
	Year-round. High: Mar.–May, Oct.		

☺☺☺	*Moorland at the Legends*	Rating:	72.8/72.8
	18 holes. Par 72/72. Yards: 6,799/4,905	Slope:	135/118

☺☺☺	*Parkland at the Legends*	Rating:	74.9/71.0
	18 holes. Par 72/72. Yards: 7,170/5,543	Slope:	137/125

P	**The Links at Cypress Bay**	Greens:	$$–$$$ L R T J
☺☺	Little River. (843) 249-1025	Carts:	$
	18 holes. Par 72/72. Yards: 6,502/5,004	Rating:	70.0/69.0
	Year-round. High: Mar.–June, Sept.	Slope:	118/113

R	**Litchfield Country Club**	Greens:	$$$–$$$$$ L J
☺☺☺	Hwy. 17, Pawleys Island. (843) 448-3331	Carts:	Incl.
	18 holes. Par 72/72. Yards: 6,752/5,304	Rating:	72.6/70.8
	Year-round. High: Spring/Fall	Slope:	130/119

SP	**The Long Bay Club**	Greens:	$$$$–$$$$$$ L R J
☺☺☺☺	Hwy. 9, Longs. (843) 399-2222	Carts:	$
STATE	18 holes. Par 72/72. Yards: 7,025/5,640	Rating:	74.3/72.1
	Year-round. High: Mar.–Apr., Oct.	Slope:	140/127

R	**Myrtle Beach National Golf Club**	Greens:	$–$$$$$ L R J
	National Dr., Myrtle Beach. (843) 448-2308	Carts:	$
☺☺☺	*North Course*	Rating:	72.6/67.0
	18 holes. Par 72/72. Yards: 7,017/4,816	Slope:	136/122
	Year-round. High: Mar.–Apr., Oct.		

☺☺☺	*Southcreek Course*	Rating:	70.5/66.5
	18 holes. Par 72/72. Yards: 6,416/4,723	Slope:	123/109

☺☺☺	*West Course*	Rating:	73.0/69.0
	18 holes. Par 72/72. Yards: 6,866/5,307	Slope:	119/109

South Carolina Golf Guide

P ☺☺	**Myrtle West Golf Club** Hwy. 9 W., N. Myrtle Beach. (843) 756-0550 18 holes. Par 72/72. Yards: 6,787/4,859 Year-round. High: Spring/Fall	Greens: Carts: Rating: Slope:	$$–$$$ L Incl. 72.7/67.9 132/113
SP ☺☺☺	**Myrtlewood Golf Club** Hwy. 17, Myrtle Beach. (843) 449-5134 *Palmetto Course* 18 holes. Par 72/72. Yards: 6,953/5,176 Year-round. High: Spring/Fall	Greens: Carts: Rating: Slope:	$$$–$$$$ L R J Incl. 72.7/70.1 121/117
☺☺☺	*Pinehills Course* 18 holes. Par 72/72. Yards: 6,640/4,906	Rating: Slope:	72.0/67.4 125/113
SP ☺☺☺	**Pine Lakes International Country Club** Woodside Ave., Myrtle Beach. (843) 449-3321 18 holes. Par 71/71. Yards: 6,609/5,376 Year-round. High: Mar.–Apr.	Greens: Carts: Rating: Slope:	$$$–$$$$$ R $$ T 71.5/71.6 125/122
R ☺☺	**Possum Trot Golf Club** N. Myrtle Beach. (843) 272-5341 18 holes. Par 72/72. Yards: 6,966/5,153 Year-round. High: Mar.–Apr., Oct.	Greens: Carts: Rating: Slope:	$$–$$$ W T J L Incl. 73.1/68.6 127/111
R ☺☺☺	**The River Club** Hwy. 17 S., Pawley's Island. (843) 873-7110 18 holes. Par 72/72. Yards: 6,704/4,963 Year-round. High: Mar.–Apr., Oct.	Greens: Carts: Rating: Slope:	$$–$$$ L R $ 71.8/67.7 125/118
P ☺☺☺	**River Hills Golf and Country Club** Cedar Creek Run, Little River. (843) 399-2100 18 holes. Par 72/72. Yards: 6,918/5,030 Year-round. High: Apr.–Oct.	Greens: Carts: Rating: Slope:	$–$$$ T $ 73.3/67.7 136/120
R ☺☺	**River Oaks Golf Plantation** River Oaks Dr., Myrtle Beach. (843) 236-2222 *Otter/Bear/Fox* 27 holes. Par 72/72/72. Yards: 6,877/6,778/6,791 Year-round. High: Mar.–Apr.	Greens: Carts: Rating: Slope:	$$–$$$ L R T J Incl. 72.5/72.0/71.7 125/126/125
P ☺☺	**Robbers Roost Golf Course** Hwy. 17 N., Myrtle Beach. (843) 249-1471 18 holes. Par 72/72. Yards: 7,148/5,387 Year-round. High: Mar.–Apr.	Greens: Carts: Rating: Slope:	$$–$$$ L T Incl. 74.4/70.2 137/116
P ☺☺	**Rolling Hills Golf Course** Hwy. 501, Galavants Ferry. (843) 358-4653 18 holes. Par 72/72. Yards: 6,749/5,141 Year-round. High: Spring/Fall	Greens: Carts: Rating: Slope:	$–$$ W L R T S J $ 71.4/86.3 120/109
P ☺☺	**Sea Gull Golf Club** Pawleys Island. (843) 237-4285 18 holes. Par 72/72. Yards: 6,910/5,250 Year-round. High: Spring/Fall	Greens: Carts: Rating: Slope:	$$$–$$$$ L Incl. 74.0/74.4 134/120
SP ☺☺☺☺	**Surf Golf and Beach Club** Springland Lane, N. Myrtle Beach. (843) 249-1524 18 holes. Par 72/72. Yards: 6,842/5,960 Year-round. High: Spring/Fall	Greens: Carts: Rating: Slope:	$$$–$$$$$L Incl. 72.6/68.4 126/114
P ☺☺☺☺ STATE	**Tidewater Golf Club** Little River Neck Rd., N. Myrtle Beach. (843) 249-3829 18 holes. Par 72/72. Yards: 7,078/4,615 Year-round. High: Mar. - May	Greens: Carts: Rating: Slope:	$$$$$–$$$$$$ W L J Incl. 74.8/67.1 144/115
R	**Waterway Hills Golf Club** Hwy. 17 N., Myrtle Beach. (843) 449-6488	Greens: Carts:	$–$$$ L R $

South Carolina Golf Guide

☺☺	*Oaks/Lakes/Ravines* 27 holes. Par 72/72/72. Yards: 6,461/6,339/6,470 Year-round. High: Mar.–Apr., Oct.	Rating: Slope:	71.0/70.6/70.8 120/122/121

SP
☺☺ **Wedgefield Plantation Country Club**
129 Clubhouse Ln., Georgetown. (843) 546-8587
18 holes. Par 72/73. Yards: 6,705/5,249
Year-round. High: Spring/Fall

Greens: $$–$$$　L T
Carts: Incl.
Rating: 72.7/69.9
Slope: 132/119

SP
☺☺☺
DEAL **The Wellman Club**
Johnsonville. (843) 386-2521
18 holes. Par 72/72. Yards: 7,018/5,281
Year-round. High: Feb.–May

Greens: $–$$　W L R J
Carts: $
Rating: 73.9/69.5
Slope: 129/105

R
☺☺☺☺
STATE **Wild Wing Plantation**
Wild Wing Blvd., Conway. (843) 347-5900
Avocet Course
18 holes. Par 72/72. Yards: 7,127/5,298
Year-round. High: Sept.–Nov.; Feb.–June

Greens: $$$–$$$$$$　W L R T
Carts: Incl.
Rating: 74.1/70.4
Slope: 129/118

☺☺☺ *Falcon Course*
18 holes. Par 72/72. Yards: 7,082/5,190

Greens: $$$–$$$$$$　W L R T
Carts: Incl.
Rating: 74.4/70.4
Slope: 134/118

☺☺☺ *Hummingbird Course*
18 holes. Par 72/72. Yards: 6,853/5,168

Greens: $$$–$$$$$$　W L R T
Carts: Incl.
Rating: 73.6/69.5
Slope: 135/123

☺☺☺☺
STATE *Wood Stork Course*
18 holes. Par 72/72. Yards: 7,044/5,409

Greens: $$$–$$$$$$　W L R T
Carts: Incl.
Rating: 74.1/70.7
Slope: 130/124

R
☺☺☺ **Willbrook Plantation Golf Course**
Hwy. 17, Pawleys Island. (843) 237-4900
18 holes. Par 72/72. Yards: 6,704/4,963
Year-round. High: Mar.–Apr.

Greens: $$–$$$$　R
Carts: Incl.
Rating: 71.8/67.9
Slope: 125/118

R
☺☺☺☺
STATE **The Witch**
Hwy. 544, Conway. (843) 347-2706
18 holes. Par 71/71. Yards: 6,702/4,812
Year-round. High: Feb.–May, Sept.–Nov.

Greens: $$$–$$$$$T L J
Carts: Incl.
Rating: 71.2/69.0
Slope: 133/109

Augusta Area

SP
☺☺☺☺
DEAL
STATE **Cedar Creek Golf Club**
Aiken. (803) 648-4206
18 holes. Par 72/72. Yards: 7,206/5,182
Year-round. High: Apr.–Sept.

Greens: $$–$$$　W S J T
Carts: Incl.
Rating: 74.1/68.6
Slope: 142/113

R
☺☺☺
DEAL **Hickory Knob Golf Club**
Hwy. 378, McCormick. (864) 391-2450
18 holes. Par 72/72. Yards: 6,560/4,905
Year-round. High: Apr.–Oct.

Greens: $　T S R
Carts: $
Rating: 70.5/67.3
Slope: 119/120

P
☺☺☺
DEAL **Persimmon Hill Golf Club**
Rte. 3, Saluda. (803) 275-3522
18 holes. Par 72/72. Yards: 6,925/5,449
Year-round. High: Mar.–May

Greens: $　W L T
Carts: $
Rating: 72.3/71.1
Slope: 122/121

Charlotte Area

P
☺☺ **Charleston Municipal Golf Course**
Maybank Hwy., Charleston. (843) 795-6517
18 holes. Par 72/72. Yards: 6,411/5,202
Year-round. High: Spring/Fall

Greens: $　T S J
Carts: $
Rating: 70.2/69.2
Slope: 112/114

South Carolina Golf Guide

SP ☺☺☺	**Charleston National Country Club** National Dr., Mt. Pleasant. (843) 884-7799 18 holes. Par 72/72. Yards: 6,928/5,054 Year-round. High: Spring/Fall	Greens: Carts: Rating: Slope:	$$–$$$ W L T Incl. 73.5/70.8 137/126
R ☺☺☺	**The Club at Seabrook Island** Landfall Way, Seabrook Island. (843) 768-1000 *Crooked Oaks Course* 18 holes. Par 72/72. Yards: 6,832/5,250 Year-round. High: Feb.–Aug.	Greens: Carts: Rating: Slope:	$$$–$$$$ Incl. 73.2/70.1 126/119
☺☺☺	*Ocean Winds Course* 18 holes. Par 72/72. Yards: 6,805/5,524	Rating: Slope:	73.2/70.1 126/119
SP ☺☺☺ DEAL	**Crowfield Golf and Country Club** Hamlet Circle, Goose Creek. (843) 764-4618 18 holes. Par 72/72. Yards: 7,003/5,682 Year-round. High: Spring	Greens: Carts: Rating: Slope:	$$ W L T $ 73.7/67.3 134/NA
SP ☺☺☺	**The Dunes West Golf Club** Wando Plantation Way, Mt. Pleasant. (843) 856-9000 18 holes. Par 72/72. Yards: 6,871/5,278 Year-round. High: Mar.–May, Oct.	Greens: Carts: Rating: Slope:	$$–$$$$ W L J Incl. 73.4/69.2 131/118
R ☺☺	**Edisto Beach Golf Club** Edisto Island. (843) 869-1111 18 holes. Par 71/72. Yards: 6,212/5,306 Year-round. High: Apr.–Oct.	Greens: Carts: Rating: Slope:	$$$ W L R J Incl. 69.9/70.3 120/120
SP ☺☺	**Fort Mill Golf Club** Fort Mill. (803) 547-2044 18 holes. Par 72/72. Yards: 6,865/5,448 Year-round. High: Apr.–Sept.	Greens: Carts: Rating: Slope:	$ $$ 72.5/70.0 123/123
R ☺☺	**Kiawah Island Resort** Kiawah Island. (843) 768-2121 *Cougar Point Course* 18 holes. Par 68/72. Yards: 6,887/4,776 Year-round. High: Spring/Fall	Greens: Carts: Rating: Slope:	$$$$$–$$$$$$ L R T J Incl. 73/67.6 134/118
☺☺☺☺ BEST	*Osprey Point Course* 18 holes. Par 72/72. Yards: 6,871/5,023	Greens: Carts: Rating: Slope:	$$$$$–$$$$$$ L R T J Incl. 72.9/69.6 137/120
☺☺☺☺ BEST	*The Ocean Course* 18 holes. Par 72/72. Yards: 7,296/5,327	Greens: Carts: Rating: Slope:	$$$$$–$$$$$$ L R T J Incl. 78/72.9 152/133
☺☺☺☺ BEST	*Turtle Point Course* 18 holes. Par 72/72. Yards: 6,925/5,205	Greens: Carts: Rating: Slope:	$$$$$–$$$$$$ L R T J $ 74/71.1 142/126
P ☺☺	**The Links at Stono Ferry** Forest Oaks Dr., Hollywood. (843) 763-1817 18 holes. Par 72/72. Yards: 6,606/4,928 Year-round. High: Mar.–May, Oct.	Greens: Carts: Rating: Slope:	$–$$ W L T S Incl. 68.3/69.2 115/119
P ☺☺☺	**Oak Point Golf Course** Bohicket Rd., Johns Island. (843) 768-7431 18 holes. Par 72/72. Yards: 6,759/4,484 Year-round. High: Apr.–Oct.	Greens: Carts: Rating: Slope:	$$–$$$$ L T J Incl. 71.0/69.8 132/121
P ☺☺	**Patriots Point Links** Mt. Pleasant. (843) 881-0042	Greens: Carts:	$–$$ W L T $

South Carolina Golf Guide

18 holes. Par 72/72. Yards: 6,838/5,562
Year-round. High: Spring/Fall

Rating: 72.1/71.0
Slope: 118/115

SP
☺☺☺
Pine Forest Country Club
Congressional Blvd., Summerville. (843) 851-1193
18 holes. Par 72/72. Yards: 6,905/4,990
Year-round. High: Spring/Fall

Greens: $$–$$$ W L T
Carts: Incl.
Rating: 73.6/67.7
Slope: 140/120

SP
☺☺
Pinetuck Golf Club
Tuckaway Rd., Rock Hill. (803) 327-1141
18 holes. Par 72/72. Yards: 6,567/4,870
Year-round. High: Mar.–Oct.

Greens: $–$$ W T S
Carts: $
Rating: 71.7/68.2
Slope: 127/111

R
☺☺
Santee National Golf Club
Hwy. 6 W., Santee. (843) 854-3531
18 holes. Par 72/72. Yards: 6,858/4,748
Year-round. High: Mar.–Apr., Oct.

Greens: $$ R S J
Carts: Incl.
Rating: 72.1/68.2
Slope: 120/116

SP
☺☺
Shadowmoss Plantation Golf Club
Dunvegan Dr., Charleston. (843) 556-8251
18 holes. Par 72/72. Yards: 6,700/5,200
Year-round. High: Mar.–May

Greens: $–$$ W L R T S J
Carts: $
Rating: 72.4/70.2
Slope: 123/120

SP
☺☺
Spring Lake Country Club
Spring Lake Rd., York. (803) 684-4898
18 holes. Par 72/72. Yards: 6,748/4,975
Year-round. High: May–Oct.

Greens: $$ W J
Carts: Incl.
Rating: 72.8/67.3
Slope: 127/116

R

☺☺☺
Wild Dunes Resort
Palmetto Dr., Isle of Palms. (843) 886-2301
Harbor Course
18 holes. Par 70/70. Yards: 6,446/4,774
Year-round. High: Spring/Fall

Greens: $$$–$$$$$$ W L R T
Carts: Incl.
Rating: 70.9/68.1
Slope: 124/117

☺☺☺☺
BEST
Links Course. (843) 886-2180
18 holes. Par 72/72. Yards: 6,722/4,849

Greens: $$$$$–$$$$$$ W L R T
Carts: Incl.
Rating: 73.1/69.1
Slope: 132/121

Hilton Head

SP
☺☺
Country Club of Beaufort
Barnwell Dr., Beaufort. (843) 522-1605
18 holes. Par 72/72. Yards: 6,506/4,880
Year-round. High: Spring/Fall

Greens: $$–$$$ T J
Carts: Incl.
Rating: 71.2/67.8
Slope: 123/120

SP
☺☺☺
Country Club of Hilton Head
Skull Creek Dr., Hilton Head Isle. (843) 681-2582
18 holes. Par 72/72. Yards: 6,919/5,373
Year-round. High: Spring/Fall

Greens: $$$–$$$$ L T
Carts: Incl.
Rating: 73.6/71.3
Slope: 132/123

R
☺☺☺☺
BEST
Harbour Town Golf Links
Lighthouse Lane, Hilton Head Isle. (843) 363-4485
18 holes. Par 71/71. Yards: 6,916/5,019
Year-round. High: Spring/Fall
Closed for much of 2000 for renovation. Call to check reopening date.

Greens: $$$$$$+   L R T J
Carts: Incl.
Rating: 74.0/69.0
Slope: 136/117

P
☺☺☺
STATE
Hilton Head National Golf Club
Hilton Head Isle. (843) 842-5900
18 holes. Par 72/72. Yards: 6,779/5,589
Year-round. High: Spring/Fall
9 new holes opening winter '99.

Greens: $$$–$$$$$
Carts: $
Rating: 69.9/66.2
Slope: 124/109

SP
☺☺
Golden Bear Golf Club
Colonial Dr., Hilton Head Isle. (843) 689-2200
18 holes. Par 72/72. Yards: 7,012/4,974
Year-round. High: Mar.–May, Oct.

Greens: $$–$$$ L R T J
Carts: $
Rating: 73.7/69.3
Slope: 132/120

South Carolina Golf Guide

R ☺☺	**Island West Golf Club** U.S. Hwy. 278, Bluffton. (843) 689-6660 18 holes. Par 72/72. Yards: 6,803/4,938 Year-round. High: Mar.–Apr., Oct.	Greens: Carts: Rating: Slope:	$$–$$$ L R T J $ 72.1/66.5 129/116
P ☺☺☺	**Old South Golf Links** Buckingham Plantation Dr., Bluffton. (843) 785-5353 18 holes. Par 72/72. Yards: 6,772/4,776 Year-round. High: Mar.–Apr.	Greens: Carts: Rating: Slope:	$$–$$$$ L R T J Incl. 72.4/69.6 129/123
SP ☺☺☺	**Oyster Reef Golf Club** High Bluff Rd., Hilton Head Isle. (843) 681-2184 18 holes. Par 72/72. Yards: 7,027/5,288 Year-round. High: Spring/Fall	Greens: Carts: Rating: Slope:	$$$–$$$$$ L R J Incl. 73.7/70.1 131/118
R ☺☺☺	**Palmetto Dunes Resort** Hilton Head Isle. (843) 785-1199 *Arthur Hills Course* 18 holes. Par 72/72. Yards: 6,651/4,999 Year-round. High: Mar.–Oct.	Greens: Carts: Rating: Slope:	$$$–$$$$$ R Incl. 71.4/68.5 127/118
☺☺☺	*George Fazio Course* 18 holes. Par 72/72. Yards: 6,875/5,273	Greens: Carts: Rating: Slope:	$$$–$$$$ R Incl. 74.2/69.2 132/117
☺☺☺	*Robert Trent Jones Course* 18 holes. Par 72/72. Yards: 6,710/5,525	Greens: Carts: Rating: Slope:	$$$–$$$$ R Incl. 72.2/70.7 123/117
R ☺☺☺☺ STATE	**Palmetto Hall Plantation** Fort Howell Dr., Hilton Head Isle. (843) 689-4100 *Arthur Hills Course* 18 holes. Par 72/72. Yards: 6,918/4,956 Year-round. High: Spring/Fall	Greens: Carts: Rating: Slope:	$$$$–$$$$$ R J Incl. 74.0/68.6 140/119
☺☺	*Robert Cupp Course* 18 holes. Par 72/72. Yards: 7,079/5,220	Rating: Slope:	75.2/71.1 144/126
R ☺☺	**Port Royal Golf Club** Glasslawn Ave., Hilton Head Isle. (843) 686-8801 *Barony Course* 18 holes. Par 72/72. Yards: 6,530/5,253 Year-round. High: Apr.–Sept., Mar.–May	Greens: Carts: Rating: Slope:	$$$–$$$$$ L R T J Incl. 71.6/70.1 129/115
☺☺	*Planter's Row Course* 18 holes. Par 72/72. Yards: 6,520/5,126	Rating: Slope:	71.7/69.9 133/116
☺☺☺	*Robber's Row Course* 18 holes. Par 72/72. Yards: 6,642/5,000	Rating: Slope:	72.6/70.4 134/115
R ☺☺☺	**Sea Pines Sports and Conference Center** Hilton Head Isle. (843) 842-8484 *Ocean Course* 18 holes. Par 72/72. Yards: 6,906/5,325 Year-round. High: Spring/Fall	Greens: Carts: Rating: Slope:	$$$$–$$$$$ L R T J Incl. 72.8/71.1 133/124
☺☺	*Sea Marsh Course* 18 holes. Par 72/72. Yards: 6,515/5,054	Rating: Slope:	70.0/69.8 120/123
☺☺	*Harbortown Course* 18 holes. Par 71/71. Yards: 6900/5019	Rating: Slope:	74.0/69.0 136/117
SP ☺☺	**South Carolina National Golf Club** Waveland Ave., Beaufort. (843) 524-0300	Greens: Carts:	$$–$$$ R T J Incl.

18 holes. Par 71/71. Yards: 6,625/4,970	Rating: 72.0/67.4
Year-round. High: Spring/Fall	Slope: 126/116

Tennessee

The hills and dales of Tennessee have more than their share of golfing challenges.

In Fairfield Glade, 60 miles west of Knoxville, **Stonehenge Golf Club** is a mountain-and-forest challenge ranked as one of the best resort courses in the nation. The **Graysburg Hills Golf Course** is a hidden jewel. It's situated in a valley with three lakes in Chuckey, which is east of Knoxville and north of Greeneville—be sure to call for directions. The challenging and handsome course at **River Islands** is in Kodak, east of Knoxville.

Fall Creek Falls is a green hideaway in a state park with spectacular waterfalls in Pikeville, 70 miles north of Chattanooga.

In Franklin, south of Nashville, The North and South courses at the **Legends Club of Tennessee** are a pair of gems. The North Course is long and open; the South is more like a links challenge with mounding.

The tight and tricky **Springhouse Golf Club** in Nashville is a regular on the Senior PGA Tour. **Fall Creek** and **Graysburg** are also on the *Golf U.S.A.* Deals list.

Most courses in Tennessee are open year-round, with peak rates in effect from about April to September.

Golf U.S.A. Leader Board: Best Public Courses in Tennessee

☺☺☺	Fall Creek Falls State Park Golf Course
☺☺☺☺	Graysburg Hills Golf Course
☺☺☺☺	Legends Club of Tennessee
☺☺☺☺	River Islands Golf Club
☺☺☺	Springhouse Golf Club
☺☺☺☺	Stonehenge Golf Club

Golf U.S.A. Leader Board: Best Deals in Tennessee

$$/☺☺☺	Big Creek Golf Club
$$/☺☺☺	Briarwood Golf Course
$/☺☺☺	Eastland Green Golf Course
$/☺☺☺	Fall Creek Falls State Park Golf Course
$$/☺☺☺☺	Graysburg Hills Golf Course
$/☺☺☺	Henry Horton State Park Golf Course
$$/☺☺☺	Hermitage Golf Course
$/☺☺☺	Montgomery Bell State Park Golf Course
$$/☺☺☺	Nashboro Village Golf Course
$/☺☺☺	Orgill Park Golf Course
$$/☺☺☺	Quail Ridge Golf Course
$$/☺☺☺	Roan Valley Golf Estates
$$/☺☺☺	Stonebridge Golf Course
$/☺☺☺	Three Ridges Golf Course
$$/☺☺☺	Willow Creek Golf Club

Tennessee Golf Guide

Memphis Area

SP ☺☺☺ DEAL	**Big Creek Golf Club** Woodstock-Cuba Rd., Millington. (901) 353-1654 18 holes. Par 72/72. Yards: 7,052/5,086 Year-round. High: Apr.–Sept.	Greens: Carts: Rating: Slope:	$–$$ $ 72.8/69.6 121/111	W L T S J

SP ☺☺☺	**Marriott's Golf Club at Shiloh Falls** Pickwick Dam. (901) 689-5050 18 holes. Par 72/72. Yards: 6,713/5,156 Year-round. High: Apr.–Oct.	Greens: Carts: Rating: Slope:	$$–$$$ Incl. 73.6/71.2 131/122	W L R J

P ☺☺☺ DEAL	**Orgill Park Golf Course** Bethuel Rd., Millington. (901) 872-3610 18 holes. Par 72/72. Yards: 6,284/4,574 Year-round. High: Apr.–Sept.	Greens: Carts: Rating: Slope:	$ Inquire 66.8/68.3 109/108	W S J

P ☺☺☺ DEAL	**Quail Ridge Golf Course** Altruria Rd., Bartlett. (901) 386-6951 18 holes. Par 71/70. Yards: 6,600/5,206 Year-round. High: Apr.–Oct.	Greens: Carts: Rating: Slope:	$$ $ 71.8/70.8 128/117	W T S J

P ☺☺☺ DEAL	**Stonebridge Golf Course** Davies Plantation Rd., Memphis. (901) 382-1886 18 holes. Par 71/71. Yards: 6,788/5,012 Year-round. High: Apr.–Sept.	Greens: Carts: Rating: Slope:	$$ $ 73.3/66.8 133/113	W L

P ☺☺	**T.O. Fuller Golf Course** Pavilion Dr., Memphis. (901) 543-7771 18 holes. Par 72/73. Yards: 6,000/5,656 Year-round. High: May–Dec.	Greens: Carts: Rating: Slope:	$ $ 71.0/72.0 117/110	W L S

Nashville Area

P ☺☺	**Country Hills Golf Course** Saundersville Rd., Hendersonville. (615) 824-1100 18 holes. Par 72/72. Yards: 6,100/4,800 Year-round. High: Mar.–Oct.	Greens: Carts: Rating: Slope:	$–$$ $ 71.2/67.8 119/114	W L T S J

P ☺☺☺ DEAL	**Eastland Green Golf Course** Clarksville. (615) 358-9051 18 holes. Par 72/72. Yards: 6,437/4,790 Year-round. High: July–Aug.	Greens: Carts: Rating: Slope:	$ $ 71.5/68.4 123/116	W T S J

P ☺☺	**Forrest Crossing Golf Course** Riverview Dr., Franklin. (615) 794-9400 18 holes. Par 72/72. Yards: 6,968/5,011 Year-round. High: Apr.–Sept.	Greens: Carts: Rating: Slope:	$–$$ $ 73.6/69.1 125/114	W L T

P ☺☺	**Harpeth Hills Golf Course** Old Hickory Blvd., Nashville. (615) 862-8493 18 holes. Par 72/72. Yards: 6,900/5,200 Year-round. High: May–Sept.	Greens: Carts: Rating: Slope:	$ $ 73.1/71.2 126/124	

P ☺☺☺ DEAL	**Henry Horton State Park Golf Course** Nashville Hwy., Chapel Hill. (615) 364-2319 18 holes. Par 72/72. Yards: 7,060/5,625 Year-round. High: May–June	Greens: Carts: Rating: Slope:	$ $ 74.3/72.1 128/117	S J

P ☺☺☺ DEAL	**Hermitage Golf Course** Old Hickory Blvd., Old Hickory. (615) 847-4001 18 holes. Par 72/72. Yards: 6,775/5,475 Year-round. High: Apr.–Oct.	Greens: Carts: Rating: Slope:	$$ $ 71.9/70.8 122/120	T

P ☺☺	**Indian Hills Golf Club** Calumet Trace, Murfreesboro. (615) 898-0152 18 holes. Par 71/71. Yards: 6,495/5,686 Year-round. High: Apr.–Oct.	Greens: Carts: Rating: Slope:	$–$$ $ 72.8/70.3 125/118	W L T S J

Tennessee Golf Guide

SP	**Legends Club of Tennessee**	Greens:	$$–$$$$$ W T
	Franklin. (615) 790-1300	Carts:	Incl.
☺☺☺☺	*Ropers Knob*	Rating:	75.0/71.4
STATE	18 holes. Par 71/71. Yards: 7,100/5,286	Slope:	132/121
	Year-round. High: Spring and Fall.		

P	**Montgomery Bell State Park Golf Course**	Greens:	$ S J
☺☺☺	Hotel Ave., Burns. (615) 797-2578	Carts:	$
DEAL	18 holes. Par 71/72. Yards: 6,146/4,961	Rating:	69.3/68.8
	Year-round. High: Apr.–Nov.	Slope:	121/116

P	**Nashboro Village Golf Course**	Greens:	$–$$ W L R T J
☺☺☺	Murfreesboro Rd., Nashville. (615) 367-2311	Carts:	$
DEAL	18 holes. Par 72/75. Yards: 6,887/5,485	Rating:	73.5/72.3
	Year-round. High: Apr.–Sept.	Slope:	134/121

R	**Springhouse Golf Club**	Greens:	$$$$–$$$$$L S
☺☺☺	Springhouse Lane, Nashville. (615) 871-7759	Carts:	Incl.
STATE	18 holes. Par 72/72. Yards: 7,007/5,126	Rating:	74.0/70.2
	Year-round. High: Apr.–Oct.	Slope:	133/118

P	**Ted Rhodes Golf Course**	Greens:	$ S J
☺☺	Ed Temple Blvd., Nashville. (615) 862-8463	Carts:	$
	18 holes. Par 72/72. Yards: 6,660/5,732	Rating:	71.8/68.3
	Year-round. High: May–Sept.	Slope:	120/115

P	**Two Rivers Golf Course**	Greens:	$
☺☺	McGavock Pike, Nashville. (615) 889-2675	Carts:	Inquire
	18 holes. Par 72/72. Yards: 6,595/5,336	Rating:	71.5/70.4
	Year-round. High: Apr.–Sept.	Slope:	120/116

P	**Windtree Golf Course**	Greens:	$$ T
☺☺	Nonaville Rd., Mt. Juliet. (615) 754-4653	Carts:	Inquire
	18 holes. Par 72/72. Yards: 6,557/5,126	Rating:	71.1/69.6
	Year-round. High: Apr.–Sept.	Slope:	124/117

Chattanooga Area

P	**Brainerd Golf Course**	Greens:	$ W L
☺☺	Old Mission Rd., Chattanooga. (615) 855-2692	Carts:	$
	18 holes. Par 72/72. Yards: 6,468/5,408	Rating:	69.8/69.9
	Year-round. High: Apr.–Sept.	Slope:	119/118

P	**Fall Creek Falls State Park Golf Course**	Greens:	$ S J
☺☺☺	Rte. 3, Pikeville. (423) 881-5706	Carts:	$
BEST	18 holes. Par 72/72. Yards: 6,669/6,051	Rating:	71.6/74.8
DEAL	Year-round. High: May–Oct.	Slope:	127/126

P	**Moccasin Bend Golf Club**	Greens:	$ S J
☺☺	Moccasin Bend Rd., Chattanooga. (423) 267-3585	Carts:	$
	18 holes. Par 72/72. Yards: 6,469/5,290	Rating:	69.6/69.0
	Year-round. High: Apr.–Oct.	Slope:	111/109

Knoxville Area

R	**Bent Creek Golf Resort**	Greens:	$–$$ L R T
☺☺	E. Parkway, Gatlinburg. (423) 436-3947	Carts:	$
	18 holes. Par 72/72. Yards: 6,182/5,111	Rating:	70.3/69.2
	Year-round. High: Mar.–Nov.	Slope:	127/117

P	**Briarwood Golf Course**	Greens:	$$ W L
☺☺☺	Crab Orchard. (423) 484-5285	Carts:	Incl.
DEAL	18 holes. Par 72/72. Yards: 6,689/5,021	Rating:	74.2/70.9
	Year-round. High: Apr.–Oct.	Slope:	132/123

P	**Egwani Farms Golf Course**	Greens:	$$$ J
☺☺☺	Singleton Station Rd., Rockford. (423) 970-7132	Carts:	Incl.
	18 holes. Par 72/72. Yards: 6,708/4,680	Rating:	71.9/66.1
	Year-round. High: Apr.–Oct.	Slope:	126/113

Tennessee Golf Guide

P ◎◎	**Gatlinburg Golf Course** Dollywood Lane, Pigeon Forge. (423) 453-3912 18 holes. Par 71/72. Yards: 6,281/4,718 Year-round. High: May–Oct.	Greens: Carts: Rating: Slope:	$$ T J $ 72.3/68.9 125/117
P ◎◎◎◎ DEAL STATE	**Graysburg Hills Golf Course** Graysburg Hills Rd., Chuckey. (423) 234-8061 *Knobs/Fodderstack/Chimneytop* 27 holes. Par 72/72/72. Yards: 6,834/6,875/6,743 Year-round. High: Mar.–Oct.	Greens: Carts: Rating: Slope:	$$ W L T Incl. 72.8/73.0/72.2 128/134/133
SP ◎◎	**Lambert Acres Golf Club** Tuckaleechee Park, Maryville. (423) 982-9838 27 holes. Par 72/72/72. Yards: 6,480/6,282/6,292 Year-round. High: May–Oct.	Greens: Carts: Rating: Slope:	$ $ 70.8/70.1/69.6 118/121/119
P ◎◎◎◎ STATE	**River Islands Golf Club** Kodak Rd., Kodak. (423) 933-0100 18 holes. Par 72/72. Yards: 7,001/4,973 Year-round. High: Apr.–Oct.	Greens: Carts: Rating: Slope:	$$–$$$ W L T Incl. 75.4/69.4 133/118
R ◎◎◎◎ BEST	**Stonehenge Golf Club** Fairfield Blvd., Fairfield Glade. (931) 484-3731 18 holes. Par 72/72. Yards: 6,549/5,043 Mar.–Nov. High: Sept.–Oct.	Greens: Carts: Rating: Slope:	$$–$$$$ R T J Incl. 71.5/70.2 131/124
P ◎◎◎ DEAL	**Three Ridges Golf Course** Wise Springs Rd., Knoxville. (423) 687-4797 18 holes. Par 72/72. Yards: 6,825/5,225 Year-round. High: Apr.–Oct.	Greens: Carts: Rating: Slope:	$ W T S J $ 73.2/70.7 128/121
R ◎◎	**Thunder Hollow Golf Club** Tennessee Ave., Crossville. (423) 456-4060 18 holes. Par 72/72. Yards: 6,411/4,844 Year-round. High: Apr.–Sept.	Greens: Carts: Rating: Slope:	$$ Incl. 71.9/70.0 124/121
P ◎◎	**Warrior's Path State Park Golf Course** Kingsport. (423) 323-4990 18 holes. Par 72/72. Yards: 6,581/5,328 Year-round. High: July–Aug.	Greens: Carts: Rating: Slope:	$ W L S J $ 71.2/72.4 115/117
P ◎◎◎ DEAL	**Willow Creek Golf Club** Kingston Pike, Knoxville. (423) 675-0100 18 holes. Par 72/74. Yards: 7,266/5,557 Year-round. High: Apr.–Oct.	Greens: Carts: Rating: Slope:	$$ L J $ 73.5/71.9 130/119

Johnson City Area

P ◎◎	**Elizabethton Municipal Golf Club** Elizabethton. (423) 542-8051 18 holes. Par 72/72. Yards: 6,339/6,051 Year-round. High: Apr.–Sept.	Greens: Carts: Rating: Slope:	$–$$ Incl. 71.2/67.7 129/118
SP ◎◎◎ DEAL	**Roan Valley Golf Estates** Hwy. 421 S., Mountain City. (423) 727-7931 18 holes. Par 72/72. Yards: 6,736/4,370 Apr.–Nov. High: May–Oct.	Greens: Carts: Rating: Slope:	$$ W L J Incl. 71.8/68.9 120/107

Texas

The **Barton Creek Resort** in Austin sports three superb courses, including two that are among the best in the state: the Fazio Course and the Palmer-Lakeside Course. The Lakeside Course is on high ground above Lake Travis.

Another triumvirate of golfing challenges can be found at **Horseshoe Bay Resort**. Ram Rock there is a difficult beauty; Applerock is a stunning challenge with lots of beach and water, and Slick Rock is a bit easier but still picturesque, including a broad waterfall across the fairway of No. 14.

In Houston, the Masters Course at **Bear Creek Golf World** is tree-lined, full of sand and water . . . and long. In New Ulm, 60 miles west of Houston, **The Falls Country Club** is a tight challenge with all sorts of hazards.

One of the most unusual offerings in Texas or anywhere else is **Tour 18** in Humble, about 15 miles northeast of Houston. The club re-creates 18 holes from famous courses around the world.

Waterwood National Resort and Country Club in Huntsville, about 75 miles north of Houston, delivers water with Lake Livingston and wood from the neighboring Sam Houston National Forest, a difficult but rewarding challenge.

There are two commendable courses at **The Woodlands Resort and Country Club**, located in The Woodlands, 25 miles north of Houston. The better of the two is TPC at the Woodlands, with unrelenting challenges on every hole. The North Course has enough sand to start its own beach. **Buffalo Creek** is a rolling challenge in Rockwall, located about 15 miles east of Dallas.

A very difficult, spectacular course is at **The Cliffs** in Graford, about 75 miles northwest of Fort Worth. The **Squaw Valley Golf Course** in Glen Rose, 60 miles southwest of Fort Worth, is full of tricks, with links out front and a tighter back nine.

The **Hill Country Golf Club** in San Antonio delivers hills and lots of trees and a good challenge. **The Quarry Golf Club** is set in an old quarry, which gives it some unusual fairways and tees. Another worthy course nearby is **Pecan Valley**; it's an older long course.

The **Painted Dunes Desert Golf Course** in El Paso is dry as, err, a desert, but it's an enjoyable challenge; it was expanded to 27 holes in 1999.

Painted Dunes and Squaw Valley also have positions on the *Golf U.S.A.* Deals list.

Most courses in Texas are open year-round, with peak rates in effect from about April to October. Some courses may offer lower rates during the hottest summer months.

Golf U.S.A. Leader Board: Best Public Courses in Texas

ⓞⓞⓞⓞ   Barton Creek Resort and Country Club (Fazio, Palmer-Lakeside)
ⓞⓞⓞ   Bear Creek Golf World (Masters)
ⓞⓞⓞⓞ   Buffalo Creek Golf Club
ⓞⓞⓞⓞ   The Cliffs Golf Club
ⓞⓞⓞⓞ   The Falls Country Club
ⓞⓞⓞⓞ   Hill Country Golf Club
ⓞⓞⓞⓞ   Horseshoe Bay Resort (Ram Rock, Slick Rock)
ⓞⓞⓞⓞ   Painted Dunes Desert Golf Course
ⓞⓞⓞ   Pecan Valley Golf Club
ⓞⓞⓞⓞ   The Quarry Golf Club
ⓞⓞⓞⓞ   Squaw Valley Golf Course
ⓞⓞⓞ   Tour 18
ⓞⓞⓞ   Waterwood National Resort and Country Club
ⓞⓞⓞⓞ   The Woodlands Resort and Country Club (TPC at the Woodlands)

Golf U.S.A. Leader Board: Best Deals in Texas

$/◎◎◎	Andrews County Golf Course
$/◎◎◎	Bay Forest Golf Course
$/◎◎◎	Cielo Vista Golf Course
$$/◎◎◎	Delaware Springs Golf Course
$$/◎◎◎	Firewheel Golf Park (Lakes, Old)
$$/◎◎◎	Flying L Ranch Golf Course
$$/◎◎◎	Galveston Island Municipal Golf Course
$/◎◎◎	Garden Valley Golf Resort (Hummingbird)
$/◎◎◎	Hidden Hills Public Golf Course
$$/◎◎◎	Indian Creek Golf Club (Creeks, Lakes)
$$/◎◎◎	Iron Horse Golf Club
$/◎◎◎	J.F. Sammons Park Golf Course
$/◎◎◎	Lady Bird Johnson Municipal Golf Course
$/◎◎◎	Mission del Lago Golf Course
$/◎◎◎◎	Painted Dunes Desert Golf Course
$$/◎◎◎	Peach Tree Golf Club (Oakhurst)
$$/◎◎◎	Rayburn Country Club and Resort
$$/◎◎◎	Rio Colorado Golf Course
$/◎◎◎	San Saba Municipal Golf Course
$$/◎◎◎◎	Squaw Valley Golf Course
$$/◎◎◎	Sugartree Golf Club
$$/◎◎◎	Tanglewood Resort

Texas Golf Guide

Amarillo Area

P ◎◎	**Comanche Trail Golf Club** S. Grand, Amarillo. (806) 378-4281 18 holes. Par 72/72. Yards: 7,180/5,524 Year-round. High: Mar.–Sept.	Greens: $ Carts: $ Rating: 72.9/70.0 Slope: 117/108	S J
P ◎◎◎ DEAL	**Hidden Hills Public Golf Course** N. Hwy. 70, Pampa. (806) 669-5866 18 holes. Par 71/71. Yards: 6,463/5,196 Year-round. High: May–Sept.	Greens: $ Carts: $ Rating: 69.4/68.0 Slope: 122/116	W T S J

El Paso

P ◎◎◎ DEAL	**Cielo Vista Golf Course** Hawkins, El Paso. (915) 591-4927 18 holes. Par 71/71. Yards: 6,411/5,421 Year-round. High: Apr.–Oct.	Greens: $ Carts: $ Rating: 69.4/69.4 Slope: 122/113	W T
P ◎◎◎◎ DEAL STATE	**Painted Dunes Desert Golf Course** McCombs, El Paso. (915) 821-2122 *Hueco-Franklin/Franklin-Organ/Organ-Hueco* 27 holes. Par 72/72/72. Yards: 6,925/6,941/6,904 Year-round. High: Apr.–May, Sept.	Greens: $$ Carts: Incl. Rating: 72.7/72.6/72.3 Slope: 134/131/128	W T S J

Odessa Area

| P
◎◎◎
DEAL | **Andrews County Golf Course**
Andrews. (915) 524-1462
18 holes. Par 70/72. Yards: 6,300/5,348
Year-round. High: May–July | Greens: $
Carts: $
Rating: 68.9/69.7
Slope: 116/110 | |

Texas Golf Guide

San Antonio Area

P ☺☺☺	**Cedar Creek Golf Course** Vista Colina, San Antonio. (210) 695-5050 18 holes. Par 72/72. Yards: 7,103/5,535 Year-round.	Greens: $–$$$ Carts: $ Rating: 73.4/70.8 Slope: 132/113	W L T S J
R ☺☺☺ DEAL	**Flying L Ranch Golf Course** Bandera. (210) 460-3001 18 holes. Par 72/72. Yards: 6,646/5,442 Year-round. High: Apr.–Sept.	Greens: $$ Carts: $ Rating: 71.0/69.9 Slope: 123/109	W L R T S J
R ☺☺☺☺ STATE	**Hill Country Golf Club** Hyatt Resort Dr., San Antonio. (210) 520-4040 18 holes. Par 72/72. Yards: 6,913/4,781 Year-round. High: Spring/Fall	Greens: $$$$$$ Carts: Incl. Rating: 73.9/67.8 Slope: 136/114	W L T J
P ☺☺☺ DEAL	**Lady Bird Johnson Municipal Golf Course** Hwy. 16 S., Fredericksburg. (210) 997-4010 18 holes. Par 72/72. Yards: 6,432/5,092 Year-round. High: Mar.–Nov.	Greens: $ Carts: $ Rating: 70.3/68.0 Slope: 125/112	W
P ☺☺☺ DEAL	**Mission del Lago Golf Course** Mission Grande, San Antonio. (210) 627-2522 18 holes. Par 72/72. Yards: 7,004/5,301 Year-round. High: Mar.–July, Oct.–Dec.	Greens: $ Carts: $ Rating: 72.6/69.2 Slope: 127/113	W L R T S J
P ☺☺☺ BEST	**Pecan Valley Golf Club** San Antonio. (210) 333-9018 18 holes. Par 71/72. Yards: 7,071/5,621 Year-round. High: Spring/Fall	Greens: $$–$$$ Carts: Incl. Rating: 74.5/73.0 Slope: 136/126	W L T S J
P ☺☺☺☺ STATE	**The Quarry Golf Club** E. Basse Rd., San Antonio. (210) 824-4500 18 holes. Par 71/71. Yards: 6,740/4,897 Year-round. High: Mar.–Nov.	Greens: $$$$–$$$$$ Carts: Incl. Rating: 72.4/67.4 Slope: 128/115	W T
P ☺☺	**Riverside Municipal Golf Course** McDonald, San Antonio. (210) 533-8371 18 holes. Par 72/72. Yards: 6,729/5,730 Year-round. High: Apr.–Sept.	Greens: $ Carts: $ Rating: 72.0/72.0 Slope: 128/121	W L R T S J
R ☺☺☺	**Tapatio Springs Resort and Conference Center** West Johns Rd., Boerne. (210) 537-4197 18 holes. Par 72/72. Yards: 6,504/5,185 Year-round. High: Spring/Fall	Greens: $$$$ Carts: Incl. Rating: 70.9/69.5 Slope: 122/118	R J

Austin Area

R ☺☺☺	**Barton Creek Resort and Country Club** Austin. (512) 329-4608 *Crenshaw and Coore Course* 18 holes. Par 71/71. Yards: 6,678/4,843 Year-round. High: Spring/Fall	Greens: $$$$$ Carts: $ Rating: 71.0/67.2 Slope: 124/110	W
☺☺☺☺ BEST	*Fazio Course* 18 holes. Par 72/72. Yards: 6,956/5,207	Greens: $$$$$$+ Carts: $ Rating: 74.0/69.4 Slope: 135/120	W
☺☺☺☺ STATE	*Palmer-Lakeside Course* 18 holes. Par 71/71. Yards: 6,657/5,067	Greens: $$$$$ Carts: $ Rating: 71.0/74.0 Slope: 124/135	W
P ☺☺	**Bluebonnet Hill Golf Club** Decker Lane, Austin. (512) 272-4228 18 holes. Par 72/72. Yards: 6,503/5,241 Year-round. High: Mar.–Aug.	Greens: $ Carts: $ Rating: 70.0/68.2 Slope: 113/107	W T S J

Texas Golf Guide

P ☺☺☺	**Circle C Golf Club** Austin. (512) 288-4297 18 holes. Par 72/72. Yards: 6,859/5,236 Year-round. High: Spring/Fall	Greens: Carts: Rating: Slope:	$$–$$$ Incl. 72.7/69.9 122/120	W L T J
P ☺☺☺ DEAL	**Delaware Springs Golf Course** Hwy. 281 S., Burnet. (512) 756-8951 18 holes. Par 72/71. Yards: 6,819/5,770 Year-round. High: Mar.–Sept.	Greens: Carts: Rating: Slope:	$$ $ 72.0/66.9 121/108	T S J
P ☺☺☺	**Forest Creek Golf Club** Twin Ridge Pkwy., Round Rock. (512) 388-2874 18 holes. Par 72/72. Yards: 7,084/5,601 Year-round. High: Mar.-Oct.	Greens: Carts: Rating: Slope:	$$–$$$ Incl. 72.8/71.9 130/124	W L T S J
R ☺☺☺☺	**Horseshoe Bay Resort** Bay West Blvd., Horseshoe Bay. (210) 598-6561 *Applerock Course* 18 holes. Par 72/72. Yards: 6,999/5,509 Year-round. High: Mar.–Nov.	Greens: Carts: Rating: Slope:	$$$$–$$$$$ $ 73.9/71.6 134/117	W L R J
☺☺☺☺ BEST	*Ram Rock Course* 18 holes. Par 71/71. Yards: 6,946/5,306	Rating: Slope:	73.9/71.4 137/121	
☺☺☺☺ STATE	*Slick Rock Course* 18 holes. Par 72/72. Yards: 6,834/5,832	Rating: Slope:	72.6/70.2 125/115	
P ☺☺☺ DEAL	**J.F. Sammons Park Golf Course** Temple. (817) 778-8282 18 holes. Par 70/70. Yards: 6,007/4,979 Year-round. High: Mar.–Aug.	Greens: Carts: Rating: Slope:	$ $ 69.6/65.8 129/110	W L T S J
P ☺☺	**Jimmy Clay Golf Course** Austin. (512) 444-0999 18 holes. Par 72/72. Yards: 6,857/5,036 Year-round. High: Aug.	Greens: Carts: Rating: Slope:	$ $ 72.4/68.5 124/110	W T S J
P ☺☺	**Lions Municipal Golf Course** Enfield Rd., Austin. (512) 477-6963 18 holes. Par 72/72. Yards: 6,001/4,931 Year-round. High: June–Aug.	Greens: Carts: Rating: Slope:	$ $ NA 118/NA	T
R ☺☺☺	**Mill Creek Golf and Country Club** Old Mill Rd., Salado. (817) 947-5698 18 holes. Par 71/73. Yards: 6,486/5,250 Year-round. High: Mar.–Oct.	Greens: Carts: Rating: Slope:	$$–$$$ $ 72.1/69.6 128/114	W R
SP ☺☺☺	**River Place Golf Club** Austin. (512) 346-6784 18 holes. Par 71/71. Yards: 6,611/4,878 Year-round. High: Mar.–Oct.	Greens: Carts: Rating: Slope:	$$$ Incl. 72.0/65.5 128/113	T S J
P ☺☺	**Riverside Golf Course** Grove Blvd., Austin. (512) 389-1070 18 holes. Par 71/71. Yards: 6,562/5,334 Year-round. High: May–Aug.	Greens: Carts: Rating: Slope:	$ $ 70.3/69.6 122/112	W T S J
P ☺☺☺ DEAL	**San Saba Municipal Golf Course** San Saba. (915) 372-3212 18 holes. Par 72/72. Yards: 6,904/5,246 Year-round. High: Mar.–Oct.	Greens: Carts: Rating: Slope:	$ $ 72.5/69.0 119/113	

Dallas/Fort Worth Area

SP ☺☺	**Briarwood Golf Club** Briarwood Dr., Tyler. (903) 593-7741	Greens: Carts:	$–$$ $	L

	18 holes. Par 71/71. Yards: 6,512/4,735 Year-round. High: May–June	Rating: Slope:	70.6/66.1 118/111

P
☺☺☺☺
STATE

Buffalo Creek Golf Club
Rockwall. (972) 771-1779
18 holes. Par 71/71. Yards: 7,018/5,209
Year-round. High: Apr.-Oct.

Greens: $$–$$$$ W L T S J
Carts: Incl.
Rating: 73.8/67.0
Slope: 133/113

P
☺☺

Cedar Crest Golf Course
Southerland, Dallas. (214) 670-7615
18 holes. Par 71/75. Yards: 6,550/5,594
Year-round. High: Apr.–Sept.

Greens: $ T S J
Carts: $
Rating: 71.0/76.0
Slope: 121/116

P
☺☺

Chester W. Ditto Golf Club
Brown Blvd., Arlington. (817) 275-5941
18 holes. Par 72/72. Yards: 6,727/5,555
Year-round. High: Apr.–Sept.

Greens: $ W T S J
Carts: $
Rating: 70.8/71.2
Slope: 117/116

R
☺☺☺☺
STATE

The Cliffs Golf Club
Graford. (940) 779-3926
18 holes. Par 71/71. Yards: 6,808/4,876
Year-round. High: Apr.–Sept.

Greens: $$$-$$$$ W L T S J
Carts: $
Rating: 73.9/68.4
Slope: 143/124

P
☺☺

Connally Golf Course
Concord Rd., Waco. (254) 799-6561
18 holes. Par 72/73. Yards: 6,975/5,950
Year-round. High: Apr.–Sept.

Greens: $ T S J
Carts: $
Rating: 72.5/73.8
Slope: 116/120

P
☺☺

Cottonwood Creek Golf Course
Bagby Dr., Waco. (254) 752-2474
18 holes. Par 72/72. Yards: 7,123/5,724
Year-round. High: Mar.–Oct.

Greens: $ W L S J
Carts: $
Rating: 73.3/71.9
Slope: 129/120

P
☺☺

Country View Golf Club
W. Beltline Rd., Lancaster. (972) 227-0995
18 holes. Par 71/71. Yards: 6,609/5,048
Year-round. High: Apr.–Oct.

Greens: $ L T S J
Carts: $$
Rating: 71.0/68.2
Slope: 120/114

P

☺☺☺
DEAL

Firewheel Golf Park
W. Blackburn Rd., Garland. (972) 205-2795
Lakes Course
18 holes. Par 71/71. Yards: 6,625/5,215
Year-round. High: June–Aug.

Greens: $–$$ T S
Carts: $
Rating: 72.0/69.1
Slope: 126/110

☺☺☺
DEAL

Old Course
18 holes. Par 72/72. Yards: 7,054/5,692

Rating: 74.1/71.7
Slope: 129/117

R

☺☺☺

Four Seasons Resort and Club
N. MacArthur Blvd., Irving. (214) 717-2530
TPC Course
18 holes. Par 70/70. Yards: 6,899/5,340
Year-round. High: Feb.–Oct.

Greens: $$$$–$$$$$$+ L R T
Carts: Incl.
Rating: 73.5/70.6
Slope: 135/116

R

☺☺☺

Garden Valley Golf Resort
Lindale. (903) 882-6107
Dogwood Course
18 holes. Par 72/72. Yards: 6,754/5,532
Year-round. High: Apr.–Oct.

Greens: $$$ W L T S
Carts: $
Rating: 72.4/72.5
Slope: 132/130

☺☺☺
DEAL

Hummingbird Course
18 holes. Par 71/71. Yards: 6,446/5,131

Greens: $
Carts: $
Rating: 71.0/69.0
Slope: NA

P

☺☺

Grand Prairie Municipal Golf Course
S.E. 14th St., Grand Prairie. (972) 263-0661
Blue/Red/White

Greens: $ T S J
Carts: $
Rating: 71.0/69.5/69.5

Texas Golf Guide

---

27 holes. Par 72/71/71. Yards: 6,500/6,309/6,219
Year-round. High: May–Sept.

Slope: 118/112/94

P
☺☺
Grapevine Golf Course
Grapevine. (817) 481-0421
18 holes. Par 72/72. Yards: 6,953/5,786
Year-round. High: Apr.–Sept.

Greens: $ T S J
Carts: $
Rating: 72.0/72.5
Slope: 113/113

P
☺☺
Grover C. Keaton Golf Course
Jim Miller Rd., Dallas. (214) 670-8784
18 holes. Par 72/72. Yards: 6,511/5,054
Year-round. High: Mar.–Aug.

Greens: $ W L T S J
Carts: $
Rating: 70.6/68.1
Slope: 113/113

P

☺☺☺
Hyatt Bear Creek Golf and Racquet Club
Bear Creek Court, DFW Airport. (214) 615-6800
East Course
18 holes. Par 72/72. Yards: 6,670/5,620
Year-round. High: Apr.–Nov.

Greens: $$$–$$$$ W L T S J
Carts: $
Rating: 72.5/72.4
Slope: 127/124

☺☺☺
West Course
18 holes. Par 72/72. Yards: 6,675/5,570

Rating: 72.7/72.5
Slope: 130/122

P
☺☺☺
DEAL
Indian Creek Golf Club
W. Frankford, Carrollton. (972) 492-3620
Creeks Course
18 holes. Par 72/72. Yards: 7,218/4,967
Year-round. High: Mar.–Oct.

Greens: $$ W T S J
Carts: $
Rating: 74.7/68.2
Slope: 136/114

☺☺☺
DEAL
Lakes Course
18 holes. Par 72/72. Yards: 7,060/5,367

Rating: 72.9/69.9
Slope: 135/114

P
☺☺☺
DEAL
Iron Horse Golf Club
Skylark Circle, N. Richland Hills. (817) 485-6666
18 holes. Par 70/70. Yards: 6,580/5,083
Year-round. High: Apr.–Aug.

Greens: $$ W T S J
Carts: $
Rating: 71.8/69.6
Slope: 130/119

P
☺☺☺
Marriott's Golf Club at Fossil Creek
Fort Worth. (817) 847-1900
18 holes. Par 72/72. Yards: 6,865/5,066
Year-round. High: Mar.–June, Sept.

Greens: $$$–$$$$ W T
Carts: Incl.
Rating: 73.6/68.5
Slope: 131/111

SP
☺☺☺
DEAL
Peach Tree Golf Club
Bullard. (903) 894-7079
Oakhurst Course
18 holes. Par 72/72. Yards: 6,813/5,086
Year-round. High: Apr.–Sept.

Greens: $–$$ W T S
Carts: $
Rating: 72.1/68.4
Slope: 126/113

P
☺☺
Plantation Resort Golf Club
Frisco. (972) 335-4653
18 holes. Par 72/72. Yards: 6,382/5,945
Year-round.

Greens: $$–$$$ W T
Carts: Incl.
Rating: NA
Slope: 122/117

SP
☺☺☺
The Ranch Country Club
Glen Oaks Dr., McKinney. (972) 529-5990
18 holes. Par 72/72. Yards: 7,087/5,053
Year-round. High: May–Sept.

Greens: $$–$$$ W L R T
Carts: $
Rating: 73.8/69.4
Slope: 130/117

P
☺☺
Riverchase Golf Club
Coppell. (972) 462-8281
18 holes. Par 71/71. Yards: 6,593/6,041
Year-round. High: Apr.–Oct.

Greens: $$–$$$ W L T
Carts: Incl.
Rating: NA
Slope: 124/114

P
☺☺☺
Riverside Golf Club
Riverside Pkwy., Grand Prairie. (817) 640-7800
18 holes. Par 72/72. Yards: 7,025/5,175
Year-round. High: Mar.–Oct.

Greens: $$$ W T S J
Carts: Incl.
Rating: 74.4/69.5
Slope: 132/113

Texts Golf Guide

P	**Sherill Park Golf Course**	Greens: $	W L T S J
	E. Lookout Dr., Richardson. (214) 234-1416	Carts: $	
☺☺	*Course No. 1*	Rating: 72.6/72.0	
	18 holes. Par 72/72. Yards: 6,800/5,455	Slope: 126/118	
	Year-round. High: May–Nov.		

P	**Squaw Valley Golf Course**	Greens: $$	W T S
☺☺☺☺	Hwy. 67, Glen Rose. (254) 897-7956	Carts: $$	
DEAL	18 holes. Par 72/72. Yards: 7,062/5,014	Rating: 73.6/70.0	
STATE	Year-round. High: Apr.–Oct.	Slope: 130/117	

P	**Stevens Park Golf Course**	Greens: $	W L T S J
☺☺	N. Montclair, Dallas. (214) 670-7506	Carts: $	
	18 holes. Par 71/71. Yards: 6,005/5,000	Rating: 65.0/68.0	
	Year-round. High: Spring/Fall	Slope: 98/118	

SP	**Sugartree Golf Club**	Greens: $–$$	W L T S J
☺☺☺	Hwy. 1189, Dennis. (817) 441-8643	Carts: $	
DEAL	18 holes. Par 71/71. Yards: 6,775/5,254	Rating: 72.8/71.0	
	Year-round. High: Mar.–Oct.	Slope: 138/125	

R	**Tanglewood Resort**	Greens: $$	T
☺☺☺	Hwy. 120 N., Pottsboro. (903) 786-4140	Carts: $	
DEAL	18 holes. Par 72/72. Yards: 6,993/4,925	Rating: 73.7/67.5	
	Year-round. High: Spring/Fall	Slope: 128/104	

P	**Tenison Park Golf Course**	Greens: $	W L T S J
	Samuell, Dallas. (214) 670-1402	Carts: $	
☺☺	*East Course*	Rating: 72.0/70.2	
	18 holes. Par 72/75. Yards: 6,802/5,444	Slope: 123/113	
	Year-round. High: Apr.–Oct.		

☺☺	*West Course*	Rating: 72.0/72.2
	18 holes. Par 72/72. Yards: 6,902/5,747	Slope: 121/118

P	**Timarron Golf and Country Club**	Greens: $$$–$$$$	W
☺☺☺	Byron Nelson Pkwy., South Lake. (817) 481-7529	Carts: Incl.	
	18 holes. Par 72/72. Yards: 7,012/5,330	Rating: 74.2/71.3	
	Year-round. High: Mar.–Apr.	Slope: 137/120	

SP	**Western Oaks Country Club**	Greens: $	W L R T J
☺☺	Waco. (817) 772-8100	Carts: $	
	18 holes. Par 70/70. Yards: 6,400/5,040	Rating: 70.7/68.7	
	Year-round. High: Apr.–Nov.	Slope: 122/120	

SP	**White Bluff Golf Club**	Greens: $$$–$$$$$	T
☺☺☺	Whitney. (254) 694-3656	Carts: Incl.	
	18 holes. Par 72/72. Yards: 6.845/5,292	Rating: 73.3/72.4	
	Year-round. High: Apr.–Oct.	Slope: 132/128	

☺☺☺	*New Course*	Rating: NA
	18 holes. Par 72/72. Yards: 6,964/5,589	Slope: NA

Houston Area

P	**Bay Forest Golf Course**	Greens: $	T S
☺☺☺	LaPorte. (281) 471-4653	Carts: $	
DEAL	18 holes. Par 72/72. Yards: 6,756/5,094	Rating: 72.4/69.0	
	Year-round. High: Apr.–Oct.	Slope: 126/113	

P	**Bayou Din Golf Club**	Greens: $	T S
	Rte. 2, Beaumont. (409) 796-1327	Carts: $	
☺☺	*Front/Back/New*	Rating: 68.5/70.6/72.1	
	27 holes. Par 71/71/72. Yards: 6,285/6,495/7,020	Slope: 108/118/116	
	Year-round. High: Mar.–Aug.		

P	**Bayou Golf Club**	Greens: $	T S
☺☺	Ted Dudley Dr., Texas City. (409) 643-5850	Carts: $	

Texas Golf Guide

	18 holes. Par 72/73. Yards: 6,665/5,448 Year-round.	Rating: 71.0/73.0 Slope: 114/118	

P
⊙⊙

Bear Creek Golf World
Clay Rd., Houston. (281) 855-4720
Challenger Course
18 holes. Par 66/66. Yards: 5,295/4,432
Year-round. High: Apr.–Oct.

Greens: $–$$$ W L T S J
Carts: $
Rating: 64.2/64.7
Slope: 103/103

⊙⊙⊙
BEST

Masters Course
18 holes. Par 72/72. Yards: 7,131/5,544

Rating: 74.1/72.1
Slope: 133/125

⊙⊙

President's Course
18 holes. Par 72/72. Yards: 6,562/5,728

Rating: 69.1/70.6
Slope: 110/111

R
⊙⊙⊙

Columbia Lakes Golf Club
Freeman Blvd., W. Columbia. (409) 345-5455
18 holes. Par 72/72. Yards: 6,967/5,280
Year-round. High: Apr.–June

Greens: $$$ W L R
Carts: Incl.
Rating: 75.7/71.7
Slope: 131/122

P
⊙⊙⊙

Cypresswood Golf Club
Cypresswood Dr., Spring. (713) 821-6300
Creek Course
18 holes. Par 72/72. Yards: 6,937/5,549
Year-round. High: Mar.–Oct.

Greens: $$–$$$ W T S J
Carts: $
Rating: 72.0/69.1
Slope: 124/113

⊙⊙⊙

Cypress Course
18 holes. Par 72/72. Yards: 6,906/5,599

Rating: 71.8/67.6
Slope: 123/111

R
⊙⊙⊙

Del Lago Resort
Montgomery. (409) 582-6100
18 holes. Par 72/72. Yards: 7,007/5,854
Year-round. High: May–Oct.

Greens: $$–$$$ W R T
Carts: $
Rating: 73.0/69.1
Slope: 131/122

SP
⊙⊙⊙⊙
STATE

The Falls Country Club
N. Falls Dr., New Ulm. (409) 992-3128
18 holes. Par 72/73. Yards: 6,757/5,326
Year-round. High: Mar.–July

Greens: $$$–$$$$ W R
Carts: Incl.
Rating: 72.3/70.0
Slope: 133/123

P
⊙⊙⊙
DEAL

Galveston Island Municipal Golf Course
Sydnor Lane, Galveston. (409) 744-2366
18 holes. Par 72/73. Yards: 6,969/5,407
Year-round. High: Apr.–Oct.

Greens: $–$$ W R T S J
Carts: $
Rating: 73.0/71.4
Slope: 131/121

P
⊙⊙

Glenbrook Golf Course
N. Bayou Dr., Houston. (713) 649-8089
18 holes. Par 71/71. Yards: 6,427/5,258
Year-round. High: Apr.–Oct.

Greens: $ W L T S J
Carts: $
Rating: 70.7/70.7
Slope: 120/117

P
⊙⊙⊙

The Golf Club at Cinco Ranch
Katy. (713) 395-4653
18 holes. Par 72/72. Yards: 7,044/5,263
Year-round. High: Apr.–June

Greens: $$–$$$ T S J
Carts: Incl.
Rating: 73.7/70.3
Slope: 132/118

P
⊙⊙⊙

Greatwood Golf Club
Greatwood Pkwy., Sugar Land. (281) 343-9999
18 holes. Par 72/72. Yards: 6,836/5,220
Year-round. High: Mar.–Oct.

Greens: $$$ T
Carts: Incl.
Rating: 72.6/70.0
Slope: 130/125

P
⊙⊙

Jersey Meadow Golf Course
Rio Grande, Houston. (281) 896-0900
Red/White/Blue
27 holes. Par 72/72/72. Yards: 6,583/6,383/6,400
Year-round. High: Apr.–Oct.

Greens: $$ W L T S J
Carts: Incl.
Rating: 70.5/70.4/68.9
Slope: 120/118/118

P
⊙⊙

Kingwood Cove Golf Club
Hamblen Rd., Kingswood. (281) 358-1155

Greens: $$ W L T S J
Carts: $

18 holes. Par 71/71. Yards: 6,722/5,601
Year-round. High: Spring/Fall

| Rating: | 71.9/73.2 |
| Slope: | 118/114 |

P
◎◎
Lake Houston Golf Club
Afton Way, Huffman. (281) 324-1841
18 holes. Par 72/74. Yards: 6,850/5,759
Year-round. High: Spring/Fall

Greens:	$$	W T S J
Carts:	Incl.	
Rating:	72.6/73.3	
Slope:	128/131	

P
◎◎
The Links at Tennwood
Magnolia Rd., Hockley. (713) 757-5465
18 holes. Par 72/73. Yards: 6,880/5,238
Year-round. High: Spring/Fall

Greens:	$–$$	W T S J
Carts:	$	
Rating:	70.8/68.3	
Slope:	120/109	

P
◎◎
Memorial Park Golf Course
Memorial Loop Park E., Houston. (713) 862-4033
18 holes. Par 72/72. Yards: 7,380/6,140
Year-round. High: Apr.–Aug.

Greens:	$	W T
Carts:	$	
Rating:	NA	
Slope:	111	

P

◎◎◎
Old Orchard Golf Club
Richmond. (281) 277-3300
Stables/Barn/Range
27 holes. Par 72/72/72. Yards: 6,888/6,927/6,687
Year-round. High: Spring/Fall

Greens:	$$–$$$	T S J
Carts:	Incl.	
Rating:	73.5/73.6/71.7	
Slope:	130/127/124	

R
◎◎◎
DEAL
Rayburn Country Club and Resort
Wingate Blvd., Sam Rayburn. (409) 698-2958
27 holes. Par 72/72/72. Yards: 6,731/6,719/6,728
Year-round. High: Spring/Fall

Greens:	$$	W L T J
Carts:	$$	
Rating:	71.3/72.5/72.2	
Slope:	116/129/124	

P
◎◎◎
DEAL
Rio Colorado Golf Course
Riverside Park, Bay City. (409) 244-2955
18 holes. Par 72/72. Yards: 6,824/5,020
Year-round. High: Apr.–Oct.

Greens:	$–$$	L T S J
Carts:	$	
Rating:	73.1/69.1	
Slope:	127/116	

P
◎◎◎
Southwyck Golf Club
Pearland. (713) 436-9999
18 holes. Par 72/72. Yards: 6,914/5,145
Year-round. High: Spring/Fall

Greens:	$$–$$$	W L T S J
Carts:	Incl.	
Rating:	73.2/70.5	
Slope:	127/120	

◎◎◎
BEST
Tour 18
Humble. (281) 540-1818
18 holes. Par 72/72. Yards: 6,807/5,583
Year-round. High: Apr.–May/Sept.–Nov.

Greens:	$$$$	T J
Carts:	Incl.	
Rating:	72.2/66.6	
Slope:	126/113	

R
◎◎◎
STATE
Waterwood National Resort and Country Club
Huntsville. (409) 891-5050
18 holes. Par 71/73. Yards: 6,872/5,029
Year-round. High: Apr.–June

Greens:	$$–$$$	L T S J
Carts:	$	
Rating:	73.7/68.0	
Slope:	142/117	

P
◎◎
Wedgewood Golf Club
Hwy. 105 W., Conroe. (409) 441-4653
18 holes. Par 72/72. Yards: 6,817/5,071
Year-round. High: Spring/Fall

Greens:	$–$$	W T S J
Carts:	$	
Rating:	73.7/69.6	
Slope:	134/128	

R

◎◎◎◎
The Woodlands Resort and Country Club
N. Millbend Dr., The Woodlands. (281) 367-1100
North Course
18 holes. Par 72/72. Yards: 6,881/5,245
Year-round. High: Spring/Fall

Greens:	$$$–$$$$$	W L T
Carts:	$	
Rating:	72.2/72.1	
Slope:	126/120	

◎◎◎◎
STATE
TPC at the Woodlands
18 holes. Par 72/72. Yards: 7,045/5,302

| Rating: | 73.6/70.3 |
| Slope: | 135/120 |

The West, Alaska, and Hawaii

Alaska	Nevada
Arizona	New Mexico
California	Oregon
Colorado	Utah
Hawaii	Washington
Idaho	Wyoming
Montana	

Alaska

Let's be charitable here: Alaska is not the most hospitable location for golfing. The population is small and very spread out, and the tourists who come to the 49th state do not often arrive in search of the perfect 350-yard wooded dogleg. The courses may not be as fabulous as some you'll find in the lower 48 states, but some of the views—from mountains to moose—are incomparable.

The best course in Alaska may be the **Anchorage Golf Course**, set at the base of the Chugach Mountains with a view of Anchorage and, on clear days, distant vistas of Mount McKinley.

The state has about a dozen courses of various descriptions, including the **Eagleglen Golf Course** at Elmendorf Air Force Base in Anchorage. Yet another Robert Trent Jones course, it is a very scenic watery challenge.

We expect you already know that it gets cold and snowy in much of Alaska in the winter. Most courses are open from about May to October, with high-season rates in effect for the heart of the summer. Expect the best deals in the spring and fall. The summer days are longer than anywhere else in the nation, while winter days may not last much longer than 18 holes and lunch.

Golf U.S.A. Leader Board: Best Public Course in Alaska

☺☺ Anchorage Golf Course
☺ Any course that is within a few hours of where you are and open

Golf U.S.A. Leader Board: Best Deal in Alaska

$$/☺☺ Anchorage Golf Course

Alaska Golf Guide

Anchorage Area

P	**Anchorage Golf Course**	Greens:	$$-$$$	R S J
☺☺	O'Malley Rd., Anchorage. (907) 522-3363	Carts:	$	
DEAL	18 holes. Par 70/70. Yards: 5,966/4,429	Rating:	69.1/65.9	
STATE	May–Oct. High: June–Aug.	Slope:	123/114	
P	**Eagleglen Golf Course**	Greens:	$-$$	L T S
☺☺	Elmendorf A.F.B., Anchorage. (907) 552-3821	Carts:	Inquire	
	18 holes. Par 72/72. Yards: 6,689/5,457	Rating:	71.6/70.4	
	May–Oct. High: June–Aug.	Slope:	126/123	

P	**Palmer Golf Course**	Greens:	$$	S J
☺	Lepak Ave., Palmer. (907) 745-4653	Carts:	$	
	18 holes. Par 72/73. Yards: 7,125/5,895	Rating:	74.5/68.8	
	Apr.-Oct. High: May–July	Slope:	132/121	

Fairbanks

SP	**North Star Golf Course**	Greens:	$$	W R J
☺	Fairbanks. (907) 457-4653	Carts:	$	
	9 holes. Par 72/72. Yards: 6,521/5,226	Rating:	69.9/69.7	
	May–Oct. High: June–Sept.	Slope:	114/118	

Arizona

There are *a lot* of golf courses in the mostly arid and mountainous land of Arizona, proof positive of the state's lure to retirees and tourists. In fact, the state counts more than 225 courses. Some of the resort courses are kept quite green, but the lack of water in much of the state means you can expect to find a lot of sand and some unusual conditions including cactus, creosote bushes, and wildlife not common in cooler and wetter climes.

The state's best includes **The Boulders Club** in Carefree, north of Phoenix. The North Course is a desert classic, and the South Course is equally challenging.

Another desert delight is the **Los Caballeros Golf Club** in Wickenburg, a bit farther north out of Phoenix.

In Sedona you'll find the **Sedona Golf Resort**, a breathtaking mountain course amidst the red rocks of Oak Creek Canyon.

And then there is **Troon North Golf Club** in Scottsdale, a national treasure with unreal greens in a desert setting.

The Stadium Course of the **Tournament Players Club** near Scottsdale is the site of the annual Phoenix Open, where some 400,000 fans squeeze onto the viewing mounds during tournament week.

Ventana Canyon Golf and Racquet Club offers a pair of memorable courses in Tucson. The Canyon Course is set at the base of the Catalina Mountains and

---

Key to Symbols

Rating: 1 to 4 Golf Balls		**Course Type**	
☺	Worth a Visit	P	Public
☺☺	Above Average	R	Resort
☺☺☺	Exceptional	SP	Semiprivate
☺☺☺☺	Very Best		

BEST	*Golf U.S.A.* Best American Courses
DEAL	*Golf U.S.A.* Best Golfing Deals
STATE	*Golf U.S.A.* Best in State

Price Ranges			**Discounts**	
$	<$20	Bargain	W	Weekdays
$$	$20–$39	Budget	L	Low Season
$$$	$40–$59	Moderate	R	Resort Guests
$$$$	$60–$79	Expensive	T	Twilight
$$$$$	$80–$100	Very Expensive	S	Seniors
$$$$$$	$100+	Exclusive	J	Juniors

plays into the Esperanto Canyon. The Mountain Course presents a high-desert challenge. Also in Tucson is the superlative **Westin La Paloma**, with three nine-hole desert courses. They are so desertlike that not a splash of water is likely to interfere with your game; instead count on a lot of bunkers, mounds, and other dry natural obstructions.

At **Ocotillo** in Chandler, water is nearby on 23 of the 27 holes.

In the northern portion of the state, where there is a bit of green, the best golfing runs from late spring through the summer. In the desert around Phoenix and the rest of southern Arizona, golfing is best in the cooler fall and winter.

The posh **Wigwam Resort** in Litchfield Park, west of Phoenix, was built in 1918 as lodging for visiting executives of the Goodyear Tire and Rubber Company. Although it has undergone extensive renovation over the years, it still retains its old-time appeal, a five-star resort with 331 *casitas* for guests.

There are three courses at the resort, including a pair designed by Robert Trent Jones, Sr. The Gold Course is a huge course, sprawling across nearly twice the acreage of most modern courses.

High season is in the winter from early January through mid-May. In 1999 rooms rented for about $330–$475 per night. Fall rates (September through the end of the year) range from about $245 to $380 per night. Prices in the summer, from mid-June through early September, drop to $145–$225. Golf packages, some including meals and other amenities, are also available. One example is a midweek high-season price of $680 per person for three nights and three rounds of golf; the same package drops to $432 per person in the spring, $483 in the fall and $279 in the low summer season.

Golf U.S.A. Leader Board: Best Public Courses in Arizona

◗◗◗◗ The Boulders Club (North, South)
◗◗◗◗ Los Caballeros Golf Club
◗◗◗◗ Ocotillo Golf Club (Blue, White, Gold)
◗◗◗◗ Sedona Golf Resort
◗◗◗◗ Starr Pass Golf Club
◗◗◗ Tonto Verde Golf Club
◗◗◗◗ Tournament Players Club of Scottsdale (Stadium)
◗◗◗◗ Troon North Golf Club
◗◗◗◗ Ventana Canyon Golf and Racquet Club (Mountain, Canyon)
◗◗◗ Westin La Paloma Country Club (Ridge, Canyon, Hill)
◗◗◗ Wigwam Golf and Country Club (Gold)

Golf U.S.A. Leader Board: Best Deals in Arizona

$$/◗◗◗ Antelope Hills Golf Course
$/◗◗◗ Desert Hills Golf Course
$$/◗◗◗ Emerald Canyon Golf Course
$$/◗◗◗ Great Eagle Golf Club at Happy Trails
$$/◗◗◗ Papago Golf Course
$$/◗◗◗ Pueblo El Mirage Country Club
$$/◗◗◗ Silver Creek Golf Club

Arizona Golf Guide

Flagstaff Area

P	**Elden Hills Golf Club**	Greens: $$ W L T J
☺☺	N. Oakmont Dr., Flagstaff. (520) 527-7999	Carts: $
	18 holes. Par 72/73. Yards: 6,029/5,280	Rating: 66.6/70.5
	Mar.–Nov. High: May–Sept.	Slope: 115/120

SP	**Oakcreek Country Club**	Greens: $$$ T J
☺☺☺	Bell Rock Blvd., Sedona. (520) 284-1660	Carts: Incl.
	18 holes. Par 72/72. Yards: 6,854/5,555	Rating: 71.0/71.0
	Year-round. High: June–Oct.	Slope: 129/128

P	**Sedona Golf Resort**	Greens: $$$–$$$$ W T
☺☺☺☺	Hwy. 179, Sedona. (520) 284-9355	Carts: Incl.
STATE	18 holes. Par 71/71. Yards: 6,646/5,059	Rating: 70.3/67.0
	Year-round. High: Mar.–Nov.	Slope: 129/114

Lake Havasu City

P	**London Bridge Golf Club**	Greens: $$–$$$ L T J
	Lake Havasu City. (520) 855-2719	Carts: Incl.
☺☺	*London Bridge Course*	Rating: 70.4/73.5
	18 holes. Par 71/72. Yards: 6,618/5,756	Slope: 122/133
	Year-round. High: Jan.–Apr.	

☺☺	*Stonebridge Course*	Rating: 68.8/68.6
	18 holes. Par 72/68. Yards: 6,140/5,045	Slope: 114/118

Phoenix Area

P	**The 500 Club**	Greens: $$–$$$ W J
☺☺☺	W. Pinnacle Peak Rd., Glendale. (602) 492-9500	Carts: $
	18 holes. Par 72/73. Yards: 6,599/5,557	Rating: 71.0/69.8
	Year-round. High: Nov.–Apr.	Slope: 121/112

SP	**Ahwatukee Country Club**	Greens: $$–$$$$ W L T
☺☺	S. 48th St., Phoenix. (602) 893-1161	Carts: Incl.
	18 holes. Par 72/72. Yards: 6,713/5,506	Rating: 71.5/70.3
	Year-round. High: Jan.–Mar.	Slope: 124/118

P	**Antelope Hills Golf Course**	Greens: $$–$$$ L T J
	Perkins Dr., Prescott. (520) 776-7888	Carts: Inquire
☺☺☺	*North Course*	Rating: 72.1/72.7
DEAL	18 holes. Par 72/72. Yards: 6,829/6,029	Slope: 128/127
	Year-round. High: Apr.–Oct.	

☺☺	*South Course*	Rating: 71.3/69.9
	18 holes. Par 72/72. Yards: 7,014/5,570	Slope: 124/118

R	**Arizona Golf Resort**	Greens: $$$$ W L R T
☺☺	S. Power Rd., Mesa. (602) 832-1661	Carts: Incl.
	18 holes. Par 71/72. Yards: 6,574/6,195	Rating: 71.2/68.4
	Year-round. High: Jan.–Mar.	Slope: 124/109

SP	**Arizona Biltmore Country Club**	Greens: $$–$$$$$ L
	24th St. and Missouri, Phoenix. (602) 955-9655	Carts: Incl.
☺☺☺	*Adobe Course*	Rating: 70.1/72.2
	18 holes. Par 72/73. Yards: 6,449/5,796	Slope: 119/118
	Year-round. High: Jan.–May	

☺☺☺	*Links Course*	Rating: 69.7/66.5
	18 holes. Par 71/71. Yards: 6,300/4,747	Slope: 126/106

R	**The Boulders Club**	Greens: $$$$$$ L
	N. Tom Darlington Dr., Carefree. (602) 488-9028	Carts: Incl.
☺☺☺☺	*North Course*	Rating: NA
BEST	18 holes. Par 72/72. Yards: 6,731/4,893	Slope: 135/113
	Year-round. High: Feb.–May	

Arizona Golf Guide

☺☺☺☺ STATE	*South Course* 18 holes. Par 71/71. Yards: 6,589/4,715	Rating: Slope:	NA 137/107

P ☺☺☺	**Club West Golf Club** S. 14th Ave., Phoenix. (602) 460-4400 18 holes. Par 72/72. Yards: 7,057/4,985 Year-round. High: Jan.–Apr.	Greens: Carts: Rating: Slope:	$$–$$$$$ L T Incl. 73.1/63.5 129/104

P ☺☺☺	**Coyote Lakes Golf Club** N. Coyote Lakes Pkwy., Surprise. (602) 566-2323 18 holes. Par 71/71. Yards: 6,200/4,708 Year-round. High: Jan.–Apr.	Greens: Carts: Rating: Slope:	$$–$$$ W L T J Incl. 68.9/68.0 114/106

P ☺☺☺ DEAL	**Desert Hills Golf Course** Desert Hills Dr., Yuma. (520) 344-4653 18 holes. Par 72/73. Yards: 6,800/5,726 Year-round. High: Dec.–Apr.	Greens: Carts: Rating: Slope:	$ L J $ 71.7/72.4 117/122

SP ☺☺	**Eagle's Nest Country Club at Pebble Creek** Goodyear. (602) 935-6750 18 holes. Par 72/72. Yards: 6,790/5,115 Year-round. High: Dec.-Apr.	Greens: Carts: Rating: Slope:	$$–$$$ L Incl. 72.6/61.1 130/107

P ☺☺☺ DEAL	**Emerald Canyon Golf Course** Emerald Canyon Dr., Parker. (520) 667-3366 18 holes. Par 72/71. Yards: 6,657/4,754 Year-round. High: Nov.–Mar.	Greens: Carts: Rating: Slope:	$–$$ W L T J Incl. 71.5/66.2 131/119

P ☺☺	**Encanto Park Golf Course** N. 15th Ave., Phoenix. (602) 253-3963 18 holes. Par 72/72. Yards: 6,386/5,731 Year-round. High: Feb.–Apr.	Greens: Carts: Rating: Slope:	$–$$ L T S J $ 69.0/70.5 111/111

P ☺☺	**Estrella Mountain Golf Course** Goodyear. (609) 932-3714 18 holes. Par 71/73. Yards: 6,767/5,383 Year-round. High: Dec.–Apr.	Greens: Carts: Rating: Slope:	$–$$ L T S J Inquire 71.2/71.2 121/116

P ☺☺☺	**The Foothills Golf Club** Phoenix. (602) 460-4653 18 holes. Par 72/72. Yards: 6,958/5,438 Year-round. High: Jan.–Mar.	Greens: Carts: Rating: Slope:	$$–$$$$$ W L T J Incl. 73.2/70.5 132/117

SP ☺☺☺	**Fountain Hills Golf Club** Indian Wells Dr., Fountain Hills. (602) 837-1173 18 holes. Par 71/71. Yards: 6,087/5,035 Year-round. High: Jan.–Apr.	Greens: Carts: Rating: Slope:	$$–$$$$ L T J Incl. 68.9/68.4 119/114

R ☺☺	**Francisco Grande Resort and Golf Club** Gila Bend Hwy., Casa Grande. (520) 426-9205 18 holes. Par 72/72. Yards: 7,594/5,554 Year-round. High: Nov.–Apr.	Greens: Carts: Rating: Slope:	$$–$$$$ L J Incl. 74.9/69.9 126/112

R ☺☺☺	**Gainey Ranch Golf Club** Scottsdale. (602) 483-2582 *Dunes/Lakes/Arroyo* 27 holes. Par 72/72/72. Yards: 6,800/6,614/6,662 Year-round. High: Jan.–Apr.	Greens: Carts: Rating: Slope:	$$$$–$$$$$$ L Incl. 71.9/70.7 128/126/124

R ☺☺☺	**Gold Canyon Golf Club** S. Kings Rd., Apache Junction. (602) 982-9449 *Dinosaur Mountain Golf Course* 18 holes. Par 71/67. Yards: 6,584/4,768 Year-round. High: Jan.–Mar.	Greens: Carts: Rating: Slope:	$$$–$$$$$ W L R T Incl. 70.9/67.4 138/111

☺☺	*Sidewinder Golf Course* 18 holes. Par 71/71. Yards: 6,481/4,534	Rating: Slope:	71.8/NA 133/NA
P ☺☺	**Grayhawk Golf Club** N. Pima Rd., Scottsdale. (602) 502-1800 *Talon Course* 18 holes. Par 72/72. Yards: 7,001/5,143 Year-round. High: Jan.-Apr.	Greens: Carts: Rating: Slope:	$$$$–$$$$$$+ L Incl. 74.3/70.0 141/121
☺☺	*Raptor Course* 18 holes. Par 72/72. Yards: 7,108/5,300	Greens: Carts: Rating: Slope:	$$$$$–$$$$$$+ L Incl. 74.0/71.3 136/127
SP ☺☺☺ DEAL	**Great Eagle Golf Club at Happy Trails** W. Bell Rd., Surprise. (602) 584-6000 18 holes. Par 72/72. Yards: 6,646/5,939 Year-round. High: Nov.–Apr.	Greens: Carts: Rating: Slope:	$–$$ W L R T J Incl. 71.3/67.9 124/118
P ☺☺☺	**Hillcrest Golf Club** Star Ridge Rd., Sun City West. (602) 584-1500 18 holes. Par 72/72. Yards: 6,960/5,880 Year-round. High: Nov.–May	Greens: Carts: Rating: Slope:	$$$ W L R T Incl. 71.8/72.5 126/119
P ☺☺☺	**Karsten Golf Course at ASU** E. Rio Salado Pkwy., Tempe. (602) 921-8070 18 holes. Par 72/72. Yards: 7,057/4,765 Year-round. High: Jan.-Apr.	Greens: Carts: Rating: Slope:	$$–$$$$$ W L J Incl. 74.3/67.5 133/116
P ☺☺	**Ken McDonald Golf Club** Tempe. (602) 350-5256 18 holes. Par 72/73. Yards: 6,743/5,872 Year-round. High: Nov.–Apr.	Greens: Carts: Rating: Slope:	$ T $ 70.8/70.8 115/112
P ☺☺☺	**Kokopelli Golf Resort** W. Guadalupe, Gilbert. (602) 926-3589 18 holes. Par 72/72. Yards: 6,716/4,992 Year-round. High: Jan.-Apr.	Greens: Carts: Rating: Slope:	$$–$$$$ W L R T Incl. 72.2/68.8 132/120
P ☺☺☺	**The Legend Golf Resort at Arrowhead** N. 67th Ave., Glendale. (602) 561-1902 18 holes. Par 72/72. Yards: 7,005/5,233 Year-round. High: Jan.-Apr.	Greens: Carts: Rating: Slope:	$$–$$$$$ W L T Incl. 73.0/71.2 129/119
R ☺☺☺☺ STATE	**Los Caballeros Golf Club** S. Vulture Mine Rd., Wickenburg. (520) 684-2704 18 holes. Par 72/72. Yards: 6,962/5,690 Year-round. High: Feb.–Apr.	Greens: Carts: Rating: Slope:	$$$–$$$$$ L R Incl. 73.5/71.2 138/124
R ☺☺	**Marriott's Camelback Golf Club** N. Mockingbird Lane, Scottsdale. (602) 948-6770 *Indian Bend Course* 18 holes. Par 72/72. Yards: 7,014/5,917 Year-round. High: Jan.-Apr.	Greens: Carts: Rating: Slope:	$$–$$$$$ W L R T Incl. 71.9/72.0 117/118
☺☺	*Padre Course* 18 holes. Par 71/73. Yards: 6,559/5,626	Rating: Slope:	70.3/71.1 115/113
P ☺☺	**Maryvale Golf Course** W. Indian School Rd., Phoenix. (602) 846-4022 18 holes. Par 72/72. Yards: 6,539/5,656 Year-round. High: Nov.–Apr.	Greens: Carts: Rating: Slope:	$–$$ W L T S J Inquire 69.8/70.2 115/113
R	**McCormick Ranch Golf Club** E. McCormick Pkwy., Scottsdale. (602) 948-0260	Greens: Carts:	$$–$$$$$ W L T Incl.

Arizona Golf Guide

| ☺☺☺ | *Palm Course*
 18 holes. Par 72/72. Yards: 7,187/5,057
 Year-round. High: Jan.–June | Rating: 74.4/68.7
 Slope: 135/114 |

| ☺☺☺ | *Pine Course*
 18 holes. Par 72/72. Yards: 7,187/5,333 | Rating: 74.4/69.9
 Slope: 135/117 |

| P
 ☺☺☺☺
 STATE | **Ocotillo Golf Club**
 Chandler. (602) 917-6660
 Blue/White/Gold
 27 holes. Par 72/72. Yards: 6,729/5,128
 Year-round. High: Jan.–Apr. | Greens: $$–$$$$$ L
 Carts: Incl.
 Rating: 71.3/71.3
 Slope: 131/128 |

| R
 ☺☺ | **Orange Tree Golf Club**
 N. 56th St., Scottsdale. (602) 948-3730
 18 holes. Par 72/72. Yards: 6,762/5,632
 Year-round. High: Jan.–Mar. | Greens: $$–$$$$$
 Carts: Incl.
 Rating: 71.3/71.8
 Slope: 122/116 |

| SP
 ☺☺☺ | **Palm Valley Golf Club**
 N. Litchfield Rd., Goodyear. (602) 935-2500
 18 holes. Par 72/72. Yards: 7,015/5,300
 Year-round. High: Jan.–Mar. | Greens: $–$$$ W L T J
 Carts: $
 Rating: 72.8/68.7
 Slope: 130/109 |

| P
 ☺☺☺
 DEAL | **Papago Golf Course**
 E. Moreland St., Phoenix. (602) 275-8428
 18 holes. Par 72/72. Yards: 7,068/5,781
 Year-round. High: Jan.–May | Greens: $–$$ L T S J
 Carts: $
 Rating: 73.3/72.4
 Slope: 132/119 |

| R
 ☺☺ | **Phantom Horse Golf Club**
 S. Pointe Pkwy., Phoenix. (602) 431-6480
 18 holes. Par 70/70. Yards: 6,003/4,550
 Year-round. High: Jan.–Apr. | Greens: $$–$$$$$ L T
 Carts: Incl.
 Rating: 68.1/66.2
 Slope: 117/107 |

| R
 ☺☺☺ | **The Phoenician Golf Club**
 E. Camelback Rd., Scottsdale. (602) 423-2449
 Oasis/Desert
 27 holes. Par 71/71. Yards: 5,842/5,024
 Year-round. High: Oct.–May | Greens: $$$$–$$$$$$+ L R
 Carts: Incl.
 Rating: 69.0/74.5
 Slope: 122/114 |

| ☺☺☺ | *Canyon/Oasis*
 Yards: 5,839/4,871 | Rating: 68.1/73.3
 Slope: 127/119 |

| ☺☺☺ | *Desert/Canyon*
 Yards: 5,691/4,771 | Rating: 67.8/73.0
 Slope: 124/116 |

| P
 ☺ | **Pohlcat Mountain View Golf Club**
 W. Baseline Rd., Laveen. (602) 237-4567
 East Course
 18 holes. Par 72/74. Yards: 6,875/5,945
 Year-round. High: Dec.–Mar. | Greens: $–$$ W L T S J
 Carts: $
 Rating: 71.7/72.3
 Slope: 119/114 |

| ☺ | *West Course*
 18 holes. Par 71/71. Yards: 6,646/5,770 | Greens: $$ W L T S J
 Carts: $
 Rating: 70.9/71.6
 Slope: 121/116 |

| R
 ☺☺☺ | **The Pointe Golf Club on Lookout Mountain**
 N. 7th St., Phoenix. (602) 866-6356
 18 holes. Par 72/72. Yards: 6,617/4,552
 Year-round. High: Nov.–May | Greens: $$$–$$$$$$+ W L R T
 Carts: Incl.
 Rating: 71.7/65.3
 Slope: 131/113 |

| SP
 ☺☺☺
 DEAL | **Pueblo El Mirage Country Club**
 N. El Mirage Rd., El Mirage. (602) 583-0425
 18 holes. Par 72/72. Yards: 6,521/5,563
 Year-round. High: Nov.–Mar. | Greens: $–$$ W L T J
 Carts: Incl.
 Rating: 71.1/67.6
 Slope: 125/117 |

Arizona Golf Guide

SP ☺☺	**Rancho Mañana Golf Course** E. Rancho Mañana Blvd., Cave Creek. (602) 488-0398 18 holes. Par 70/70. Yards: 6,999/4,436 Year-round. High: Jan.–Apr.	Greens: $$–$$$$ W L T Carts: Incl. Rating: 67.8/70.0/65.2 Slope: 125/131/114
SP ☺☺☺	**Red Mountain Ranch Country Club** E. Teton, Mesa. (602) 985-0285 18 holes. Par 72/72. Yards: 6,797/4,982 Year-round. High: Jan.–Apr.	Greens: $$–$$$$$$+ W L T Carts: Incl. Rating: 73.3/69.4 Slope: 144/120
SP ☺☺☺	**San Marcos Golf & Country Club** N. Dakota St., Chandler. (602) 963-3358 18 holes. Par 72/72. Yards: 6,501/5,386 Year-round. High: Jan.–Apr.	Greens: $$–$$$$ W L T Carts: Incl. Rating: 70.0/69.4 Slope: 117/112
SP ☺☺	**Scottsdale Country Club** E. Shea Blvd., Scottsdale. (602) 948-6000 27 holes. Par 70/71/71. Yards: 6,085/6,335/6,292 Year-round. High: Jan.–Apr.	Greens: $$–$$$$$ W L T Carts: Incl. Rating: 69.3/69.6/70.1 Slope: 120/118/121
P ☺☺☺ DEAL	**Silver Creek Golf Club** Silver Lake Blvd., White Mountain Lake. (520) 537-2744 18 holes. Par 71/71. Yards: 6,813/5,193 Year-round. High: June–Sept.	Greens: $–$$ W L T S J Carts: $ Rating: 71.5/68.0 Slope: 131/126
SP ☺☺☺	**Stonecreek, The Golf Club** Paradise Valley. (602) 953-9111 18 holes. Par 71/71. Yards: 6,871/5,018 Year-round. High: Jan.–Apr.	Greens: $$–$$$$$ W L Carts: Incl. Rating: 72.6/68.4 Slope: 134/119
R ☺☺☺	**Superstition Springs Golf Club** E. Baseline Rd., Mesa. (602) 985-5622 18 holes. Par 72/72. Yards: 7,005/5,328 Year-round. High: Oct.–Apr.	Greens: $$–$$$$$ W L T Carts: Incl. Rating: 74.1/70.9 Slope: 135/120
P ☺☺☺	**Tatum Ranch Golf Club** N. Tatum Ranch Dr., Cave Creek. (602) 585-2399 18 holes. Par 72/72. Yards: 6,870/5,609 Year-round. High: Nov.–Apr.	Greens: $$–$$$$$ W L T J Carts: Incl. Rating: 73.4/71.5 Slope: 128/116
SP ☺☺☺ STATE	**Tonto Verde Golf Club** El Circulo Dr., Rio Verde. (602) 471-2710 18 holes. Par 72/72. Yards: 6,744/5,376 Year-round. High: Dec.–Apr.	Greens: $$–$$$$$ L Carts: Incl. Rating: 67.5/70.6 Slope: 122/127
R ☺☺	**Tournament Players Club of Scottsdale** N. Hayden Rd., Scottsdale. (602) 585-3939 *Desert Course* 18 holes. Par 71/71. Yards: 6,552/4,715 Year-round. High: Oct.–Apr.	Greens: $ L T S Carts: Inquire Rating: 71.4/65.9 Slope: 112/105
☺☺☺☺ STATE	*Stadium Course* 18 holes. Par 71/71. Yards: 6,992/5,567	Greens: $$–$$$$ L T Carts: Inquire Rating: 73.9/71.6 Slope: 131/122
SP ☺☺☺☺ BEST	**Troon North Golf Club** E. Dynamite Blvd., Scottsdale. (602) 585-5300 *Monument Course* 18 holes. Par 72/72. Yards: 7,028/5,901 Year-round. High: Nov.–May	Greens: $$$$–$$$$$$+ L Carts: Incl. Rating: 73.3/74.4 Slope: 147/128
☺☺☺	*Pinnacle Course* 18 holes. Par 72/72. Yards: 7,044/5,765	Rating: 73.4/74.4 Slope: 147/128
R	**The Wigwam Golf and Country Club** N. Litchfield Rd., Litchfield Park. (602) 272-4653	Greens: $$–$$$$$ L R Carts: Incl.

☺☺☺	*Blue Course*	Rating:	67.9/69.8
	18 holes. Par 72/72. Yards: 6,130/5,235	Slope:	115/112
	Year-round. High: Jan.–May		

| ☺☺☺ | *Gold Course* | Rating: | 73.6/72.2 |
| STATE | 18 holes. Par 72/72. Yards: 7,021/5,737 | Slope: | 129/120 |

| ☺☺☺ | *Red Course* | Rating: | 71.8/71.9 |
| | 18 holes. Par 72/72. Yards: 6,867/5,821 | Slope: | 118/115 |

Tucson Area

P	**San Ignacio Golf Club**	Greens:	$$–$$$	L
☺☺☺	S. Camino Del Sol, Green Valley. (520) 648-3468	Carts:	$	
	27 holes. Par 71/72. Yards: 6,704/5,200	Rating:	71.8/68.7	
	Year-round. High: Jan.–Apr.	Slope:	136/116	

R	**Sheraton El Conquistador Country Club**	Greens:	$$$–$$$$$$	L R
	N. La Canada, Tucson. (520) 544-1800	Carts:	Incl.	
☺☺☺	*Sunrise Course*	Rating:	72.5/71.1	
	18 holes. Par 72/72. Yards: 6,819/5,255	Slope:	139/126	
	Year-round. High: Feb.–Apr.			

| ☺☺☺ | *Sunset Course* | Rating: | 72.2/71.2 |
| | 18 holes. Par 72/72. Yards: 6,763/5,323 | Slope: | 130/123 |

SP	**Starr Pass Golf Club**	Greens:	$$$–$$$$$ L R T
☺☺☺☺	W. Starr Pass Blvd., Tucson. (520) 670-0400	Carts:	Incl.
STATE	18 holes. Par 71/71. Yards: 6,910/5,071	Rating:	139/121
	Year-round. High: Jan.–Apr.	Slope:	74.6/70.7

R	**Tucson National Resort and Conference Center**	Greens:	$$$–$$$$$$+ R
	Tucson. (520) 575-7540	Carts:	Incl.
☺☺☺	*Orange/Gold/Green*	Rating:	74.8/74.7/74.6
	27 holes. Par 73/73/72. Yards: 7,108/6,860/6,692	Slope:	136/135/134
	Year-round. High: Oct.–May		

R	**Ventana Canyon Golf and Racquet Club**	Greens:	$$$$–$$$$$$+ L R
	Tucson. (520) 577-4061	Carts:	Incl.
☺☺☺	*Canyon Course*	Rating:	72.7/68.3
STATE	18 holes. Par 72/72. Yards: 6,819/4,919	Slope:	141/114
	Year-round. High: Oct.–May		

| ☺☺☺☺ | *Mountain Course* | Rating: | 74.2/68.3 |
| BEST | 18 holes. Par 72/72. Yards: 6,926/4,789 | Slope: | 146/117 |

R	**Westin La Paloma Country Club**	Greens:	$$$$–$$$$$$
	Tucson. (520) 299-1500	Carts:	Incl.
☺☺☺☺	*Ridge/Canyon/Hill*	Rating:	75.4/75.4/74.6
BEST	27 holes. Par 72/72/72. Yards: 7,088/7,017/6,997	Slope:	155/155/155
	Year-round. High: Jan.–May		

California

Let's do lunch . . . at the club. There are some spectacular private and resort club-houses in the Golden State . . . and more than a few fantastic golf courses too.

The state is so large that there are at least three regions that claim some sort of golf immortality: Pebble Beach in Monterey, the Palm Springs area, and the greater San Diego region. They may all be right; the only challenge may come from the fact that spotted around California are a number of other gems that would earn best-of-state ratings almost anywhere else.

In portions of the state—desert courses in and around Palm Springs among them—the summer climate can be brutal, with temperatures climbing well into triple digits. If you must play in the hot season, try to take advantage of early morning or late afternoon tee times; you can also expect to be rewarded with discounts of as much as 50 percent on hotels and greens fees for golfing between mid-May and mid-October.

The celebrity-filled history of California had a lot to do with the development of golf as we know it. Star golfer Bing Crosby is credited with launching much of the glitzy industry in 1946 when he hosted a tournament at Rancho Santa Fe, which is located north of San Diego; a year later, Crosby moved his party to the Monterey Peninsula, spreading the seeds of high-profile golf there. Another important figure in California golf was comedian Bob Hope, who helped establish the Coachella Valley and the Palm Springs area as two of the sport's meccas and the heart of the local social scene.

Pebble Beach/Monterey Area

The Monterey Peninsula on the central coast brings together the beauty of the sand, the green hills, the sea, the fog, and the golf.

Perhaps the most famous course in California and by some ratings the best in America is **Pebble Beach Golf Links** on the spectacular 17-Mile Drive. The course opened in 1919 and has been at or near the pinnacle of American golfing dreams ever since, serving as the site of three U.S. Opens. The course dates back to 1910, when the land was purchased from the Del Monte fruit company by businessman and artist Samuel F. B. Morse. Among the most difficult challenges is the 8th hole, which includes a nearly 200-yard carry over a deep chasm to a green surrounded by bunkers and backed up by a cliff; the finishing 18th hole brings you along the shores of Carmel Bay. Tee times can be difficult to obtain and, at around $200, difficult to rationalize, but few golfers complain about the experience. The U.S. Open is scheduled to be held there in June of 2000.

Almost as wonderful is the **Spyglass Hill Golf Course**, a very difficult course with gorgeous ocean and forest views. Also in the Pebble Beach area, there is **The Links at Spanish Bay**, a beach course not as famous as Pebble Beach itself, but considered by many to be almost as good and slightly less exorbitantly priced—expect to pay at least $125 for a round. Spanish Bay is considered one of the best classic links-style courses in America. It's a Robert Trent Jones, Jr., design that includes huge sand dunes, thick underbrush, and strong ocean winds.

Pebble Beach, Spyglass Hill, and Spanish Bay are all owned by the same company and are open to the public—although, as mentioned earlier, tee times can be very difficult to obtain.

The **Pasatiempo Golf Club** in Santa Cruz on the other side of Monterey Bay is a classic older course that is often compared to the Pebble Beach offerings. It includes the 395-yard 16th hole, a blind drive where you must trust in your skills—and the course map from the tee.

Other exceptional recreational opportunities include fishing and visiting the spectacular Monterey Bay Aquarium and the Carmel Mission, which dates back to 1771. Shopping opportunities abound near Cannery Row, a place immortalized by author John Steinbeck. An extraordinary visual entertainment is a car or bicycle tour along the gorgeous 17-Mile Drive, which goes down to the ocean, passing Pebble Beach, Cypress Point, and Spanish Bay.

Palm Springs/Coachella Valley Area

The self-proclaimed golf capital of the world in the Coachella Valley boasts some 90 courses in a 150-square-mile area. It features tracks by name designers including Jack Nicklaus, Arnold Palmer, Gary Player, Pete Dye, and Robert Trent Jones, Jr. Marquee tournaments at the courses are also likely to draw Hollywood stars.

To the north of Palm Springs, **Desert Dunes Golf Club** is a desert course considered an absolute pleasure except when the wind is blowing, which happens often. The Mountain Course at **La Quinta Resort and Club** about 15 miles east of Palm Springs is a spectacular desert track. The La Quinta Hotel, which dates back to 1926—making it a California antiquity—was an important extension of Hollywood in the 1930s and 1940s. The three golf courses, all designed by Pete Dye, were added in the 1970s and 1980s.

Another beauty in the area is the **Westin Mission Hills North Golf Course** in Rancho Mirage, a meticulously manicured challenge. The original course is a relatively forgiving Pete Dye design; the North Course, planned by Gary Player, wends its way among sand dunes, waterfalls, and rock formations set against the San Jacinto Mountains.

At the **PGA West Resort** in La Quinta there are two national stars: the Jack Nicklaus Resort Course and the TPC Stadium Course, which includes a famed island green on the 17th hole and the almost unbearably challenging Eternity 11th hole. The Stadium Course was designed to be as difficult as possible, and by most accounts that goal was met. A new Greg Norman–designed course was due to open by early in 2000.

The **Ojai Valley Inn** is another link to old Hollywood, the setting for Frank Capra's famous 1937 film *Lost Horizon*. The old course there was reworked in the 1980s and is a regular stop on the tournament circuit.

By the way, if you want to mix with the horsey set, the polo season in Palm Springs runs from November through April.

Los Angeles Area

South of Los Angeles in Newport Coast, the **Pelican Hill Golf Club's** highly rated Links and Ocean courses have both been compared to the Pebble Beach standard. Up the coast, above Santa Barbara, is the **Sandpiper Golf Course** on the sea cliffs in Goleta, one of the best and most spectacular public courses.

The **Redhawk Golf Club** is in Temecula, midway between Los Angeles and San Diego, and is considered a beautifully manicured destination from either direction. The Temecula Valley, a rich grape-growing region, benefits from cool ocean breezes most afternoons.

San Diego Area

San Diego claims the title of Sports Town USA, thanks to its more than 80 courses and its other outdoor appeals, including some 70 miles of Pacific Ocean beaches to the west and the Laguna and Palomar mountain ranges to the east.

La Costa Resort in Carlsbad
Courtesy of San Diego Convention & Visitors Bureau

San Diego won its golfing fame through the South Course at the **Torrey Pines Golf Course** in La Jolla, just north of San Diego, with its majestic coastal cliffs. The North Course is only slightly less wonderful. Torrey Pines is on the most-favored list of many golfers and the site of a PGA Tour tourney.

Aviara Golf Club, the only Arnold Palmer–designed course in the area, in Carlsbad, north of San Diego, sprawls across hills and valleys and on some holes overlooks Batiquitos Lagoon. The lush hotel facilities are managed by Four Seasons Hotels.

The **La Costa Resort and Spa** will host the World Golf Championships in February of 2000 and again in 2002. La Costa is open to guests and club members, with some of the most sumptuous facilities of any golf resort in the world.

California is a huge state, with widely varying climates and conditions. The northern California and mountain areas offer cool summers and cool-to-temperate winters. Central areas deliver hot summers and moderate winters. And desert and southern areas can be absolutely brutal in the summer, with midday temperatures reaching as high as 120°F with frightening regularity.

Because of this variation, the off-peak seasons around the state differ. Most courses are open year-round. Check the listings in this book for high seasons.

Golf U.S.A. Leader Board: Best Public Courses in California

- ◔◔ Ancil Hoffman Golf Course
- ◔◔◔◔ Aviara Golf Club
- ◔◔◔◔ Desert Dunes Golf Club
- ◔◔◔◔ La Quinta Resort and Club (Mountain)
- ◔◔◔◔ The Links at Spanish Bay
- ◔◔◔◔ Oak Valley Golf Club
- ◔◔◔◔ Ojai Valley Inn
- ◔◔◔◔ Pasatiempo Golf Club
- ◔◔◔◔ Pebble Beach Golf Links
- ◔◔◔◔ Pelican Hill Golf Club (Links, Ocean)
- ◔◔◔◔ PGA West Resort (Nicklaus, Stadium)
- ◔◔◔◔ Sandpiper Golf Course

◎◎◎◎   Spyglass Hill Golf Course
◎◎◎◎   Torrey Pines Golf Course (South, North)

Golf U.S.A. Leader Board: Best Deals in California

$$/◎◎◎	Avila Beach Resort Golf Course
$$/◎◎◎	Beau Pre Golf Club
$$/◎◎◎	Castle Oaks Golf Club
$$/◎◎◎	Coronado Golf Course
$$/◎◎◎	Delaveaga Golf Club
$$/◎◎◎	Dry Creek Ranch Golf Course
$$/◎◎◎	Elkins Ranch Golf Club
$$/◎◎◎	El Rivino Country Club
$$/◎◎◎◎	Fall River Valley Golf and Country Club
$$/◎◎◎	Graeagle Meadows Golf Course
$$/◎◎◎	Horse Thief Country Club
$$/◎◎◎	Hunter Ranch Golf Course
$$/◎◎◎	La Contenta Golf Club
$$/◎◎◎◎	La Purisma Golf Course
$$/◎◎◎	Lake Tahoe Golf Course
$$/◎◎◎	Los Serranos Lakes Golf and Country Club (North, South)
$$/◎◎◎	Morro Bay Golf Course
$$/◎◎◎	Mountain Meadows Golf Club
$$/◎◎◎	Oakmont Golf Club (West)
$$/◎◎◎	Pacific Grove Municipal Golf Links
$$/◎◎◎	Paradise Valley Golf Course
$$/◎◎◎	Rancho Solano Golf Course
$$/◎◎◎	Santa Teresa Golf Club
$$/◎◎◎	Shandin Hills Golf Club
$$/◎◎◎	Singing Hills Country Club (Oak Glen, Willow Glen)
$$/◎◎◎	Soule Park Golf Course
$$/◎◎◎	Tijeras Creek Golf Club

California Golf Guide

North and North Central California

SP ◎◎◎ DEAL	**Beau Pre Golf Club** Norton Rd., McKinleyville. (707) 839-2342 18 holes. Par 72/72. Yards: 5,824/4,869 Year-round. High: May–Sept.	Greens: $–$$ Carts: $ Rating: 69.0/66.8 Slope: 118/111	W T J
P ◎◎	**Bidwell Park Golf Course** Wildwood Ave., Chico. (530) 891-8417 18 holes. Par 72/72. Yards: 6,363 Year-round. High: June–July	Greens: $ Carts: $ Rating: 68.5/70.2 Slope: 117/123	T S J
P ◎◎◎◎ DEAL	**Fall River Valley Golf and Country Club** Fall River Mills. (530) 336-5555 18 holes. Par 72/72. Yards: 7,365/6,832 Apr.–Nov. High: May–Sept.	Greens: $$ Carts: $$ Rating: 74.9/73.9 Slope: 131/127	W T S J
R ◎◎◎	**Graeagle Meadows Golf Course** Hwy. 89, Graeagle. (530) 836-2323	Greens: $$ Carts: $$	T

California Golf Guide

DEAL	18 holes. Par 72/72. Yards: 6,680/5,640 Apr.–Nov. High: July–Aug.	Rating: Slope:	70.7/71.3 119/127
R ☺☺☺	**Lake Shastina Golf Resort** Weed. (530) 938-3205 *Championship Course* 18 holes. Par 72/72. Yards: 6,969/5,530 Year-round. High: May–Sept.	Greens: Carts: Rating: Slope:	**$$–$$$**　　L R T J **$** 72.6/70.2 126/114
P ☺☺☺ DEAL	**Morro Bay Golf Course** State Park Rd., Morro Bay. (805) 772-4341 18 holes. Par 71. Yards: 6,360/5,055 Year-round. High: Apr.–Aug.	Greens: Carts: Rating: Slope:	**$$**　　　　T S J **$** 70.4/69.5 118/117

Sacramento Area

SP ☺☺☺	**Alta Sierra Golf and Country Club** Tammy Way, Grass Valley. (530) 273-2010 18 holes. Par 72/72. Yards: 6,537/5,984 Year-round. High: Apr.–June	Greens: Carts: Rating: Slope:	**$$$**　　　W J **$** 71.2/74.6 128/128
P ☺☺ STATE	**Ancil Hoffman Golf Course** Tarshes Dr., Carmichael. (916) 482-5660 18 holes. Par 72/73. Yards: 6,794/5,954 Year-round.	Greens: Carts: Rating: Slope:	**$–$$**　　　T S Inquire 72.5/73.4 128/123
P ☺☺☺ DEAL	**Castle Oaks Golf Club** Castle Oaks Dr., Ione. (209) 274-0167 18 holes. Par 71/71. Yards: 6,739/4,953 Year-round. High: Spring/Fall	Greens: Carts: Rating: Slope:	**$$–$$$**　　W T S J Incl. 72.7/67.3 131/114
P ☺☺	**Cherry Island Golf Course** Elverta Rd., Elverta. (916) 575-GOLF 18 holes. Par 72/72. Yards: 6,562/5,163 Year-round. High: Apr.–Nov.	Greens: Carts: Rating: Slope:	**$–$$**　　　L T S J **$** 71.1/70.0 122/117
P ☺☺	**Diamond Oaks Golf Club** Diamond Oaks Rd., Roseville. (916) 783-4947 18 holes. Par 72/72. Yards: 6,283/5,608 Year-round. High: Apr.–Oct.	Greens: Carts: Rating: Slope:	**$**　　　　W T S J **$** 69.5/71.5 115/112
P ☺☺☺ DEAL	**Dry Creek Ranch Golf Course** Crystal Way, Galt. (209) 745-4653 18 holes. Par 72/74. Yards: 6,773/5,952 Year-round. High: Apr.–July	Greens: Carts: Rating: Slope:	**$–$$**　　　W L T **$** 72.7/73.9 129/128
P ☺☺	**Green Tree Golf Club** Leisure Town Rd., Vacaville. (707) 448-1420 18 holes. Par 72/72. Yards: 6,301/6,008 Year-round. High: Mar.–Nov.	Greens: Carts: Rating: Slope:	**$**　　　　W T S J **$** 70.2/68.5 119/114
P ☺	**Haggin Oaks Golf Course** Fulton Ave., Sacramento. (916) 481-4507 *North Course* 18 holes. Par 72/72. Yards: 6,631/5,853 Year-round. High: Apr.–Sept.	Greens: Carts: Rating: Slope:	**$**　　　　W T **$$** 71.4/71.7 115/111
☺☺	*South Course* 18 holes. Par 72/72. Yards: 6,602/5,732	Rating: Slope:	70.6/71.4 113/113
SP ☺☺☺	**Rancho Murieta Country Club** Alameda Dr., Rancho Murieta. (916) 354-3440 *North Course* 18 holes. Par 72/72. Yards: 6,839/5,608 Year-round. High: Apr.–Oct.	Greens: Carts: Rating: Slope:	**$$$–$$$$**　R J Incl. 72.6/66.8 136/124

California Golf Guide

☺☺☺	*South Course* 18 holes. Par 72/72. Yards: 6,894/5,583	Rating: Slope:	72.9/66.6 129/121

P
☺☺☺
DEAL
Rancho Solano Golf Course
Rancho Solano Pkwy., Fairfield. (707) 429-4653
18 holes. Par 72/72. Yards: 6,705/5,206
Year-round. High: June–Sept.

Greens: $$ W T S J
Carts: Inquire
Rating: 72.1/69.6
Slope: 128/117

San Francisco Area

P
☺☺
Adobe Creek Golf Club
Frates Rd., Petaluma. (707) 765-3000
18 holes. Par 72/72. Yards: 6,825/5,027
Year-round. High: May–Oct.

Greens: $–$$$$ W T S J
Carts: $
Rating: 73.8/69.4
Slope: 131/120

P
☺☺☺
Aptos Seascape Golf Course
Aptos. (408) 688-3213
18 holes. Par 72/72. Yards: 6,116/5,576
Year-round. High: June–Oct.

Greens: $–$$$ W L R T S J
Carts: $$
Rating: 69.8/72.6
Slope: 126/127

P
☺☺
Bennett Valley Golf Course
Yulupa Ave., Santa Rosa. (707) 528-3673
18 holes. Par 72/72. Yards: 6,600/5,958
Year-round. High: May–Sept.

Greens: $ W T S J
Carts: $
Rating: 70.6/72.5
Slope: 112/123

R
☺☺☺
Bodega Harbour Golf Links
Heron Dr., Bodega Bay. (707) 875-3538
18 holes. Par 70/71. Yards: 6,260/4,749
Year-round. High: Apr.–Oct.

Greens: $$–$$$$ W L R T
Carts: $
Rating: 71.9/67.7
Slope: 130/120

P
☺☺☺
Canyon Lakes Country Club
Bollinger Canyon Way, San Ramon. (510) 735-6511
18 holes. Par 70/71. Yards: 6,731/5,234
Year-round. High: Feb.–Oct.

Greens: $$$–$$$$
Carts: Incl.
Rating: 70.9/69.9
Slope: 124/121

SP

☺☺
The Chardonnay Golf Club
Jameson Canyon Rd., Napa. (707) 257-8950
The Club Shakespeare
18 holes. Par 72/72. Yards: 6,811/5,463
Year-round. High: Apr.–Oct.

Greens: $$$$–$$$$$$ W L T S J
Carts: Incl.
Rating: 74.5/72.3
Slope: 137/128

☺☺☺
The Vineyards Course
18 holes. Par 71/71. Yards: 6,816/5,223

Greens: $$$–$$$$
Carts: Incl.
Rating: 73.7/70.1
Slope: 133/126

P

☺☺
Chuck Corica Golf Complex
Alameda. (510) 522-4321
Earl Fry Course
18 holes. Par 71/72. Yards: 6,141/5,560
Year-round. High: May–Oct.

Greens: $–$$ W T S J
Carts: $
Rating: 69.2/71.0
Slope: 119/114

☺☺
Jack Clark South Course
18 holes. Par 71/71. Yards: 6,559/5,473

Rating: 70.8/70.0
Slope: 119/110

P
☺☺☺
DEAL
Delaveaga Golf Club
Upper Park Rd., Santa Cruz. (408) 423-7214
18 holes. Par 72/72. Yards: 6,010/5,331
Year-round.

Greens: $$ W T
Carts: Inquire
Rating: 70.4/70.6
Slope: 133/125

P
☺☺
Diablo Creek Golf Course
Port Chicago Hwy., Concord. (510) 686-6262
18 holes. Par 71/72. Yards: 6,866/5,872
Year-round.

Greens: $ W T S J
Carts: $
Rating: 72.2/72.5
Slope: 122/119

SP
☺☺☺
Fountaingrove Resort and Country Club
Fountaingrove Pkwy., Santa Rosa. (707) 579-4653

Greens: $$$–$$$$ W T
Carts: Incl.

California Golf Guide

	18 holes. Par 72/72. Yards: 6,940/5,424	Rating:	73.3/71.0
	Year-round. High: May–Oct.	Slope:	135/125

P
☺☺
Franklin Canyon Golf Course	Greens:	$$	W L T S J
Hwy. 4, Rodeo. (510) 799-6191	Carts:	$
18 holes. Par 72/72. Yards: 6,776/5,516	Rating:	70.9/71.2
Year-round.	Slope:	118/123

R
☺☺☺
Half Moon Bay Golf Links	Greens:	$$$$$	W R T
Half Moon Bay. (415) 726-4438	Carts:	Incl.
18 holes. Par 72/72. Yards: 7,131/5,769	Rating:	75.0/73.3
Year-round.	Slope:	135/128

P
☺☺
Harding Park Golf Club	Greens:	$$	W T S J
Skyline Blvd., San Francisco. (415) 664-4690	Carts:	$$
18 holes. Par 72/73. Yards: 6,743/6,205	Rating:	72.1/74.1
Year-round. High: Apr.–Nov.	Slope:	124/120

SP
☺☺☺
DEAL
La Contenta Golf Club	Greens:	$$	W R T S J
Hwy. 26, Valley Springs. (209) 772-1081	Carts:	$
18 holes. Par 71/72. Yards: 6,425/5,120	Rating:	70.2/70.8
Year-round. High: Mar.–Oct.	Slope:	125/120

P
☺☺
Lincoln Park Golf Course	Greens:	$$	W T J
34th Ave., San Francisco. (415) 221-9911	Carts:	$$
18 holes. Par 68/70. Yards: 5,194/4,984	Rating:	64.4/67.4
Year-round. High: Apr.–Nov.	Slope:	106/108

P
☺☺
Micke Grove Golf Links	Greens:	$–$$	W T S J
Lodi. (209) 369-4410	Carts:	$
18 holes. Par 72/72. Yards: 6,565/5,286	Rating:	71.1/69.7
Year-round. High: Mar.–Nov.	Slope:	118/111

P

☺☺
Mountain Shadows Golf Course	Greens:	$$	W T S J
Rohnert Park. (707) 584-7766	Carts:	$
North Course	Rating:	72.1/70.5
18 holes. Par 72/72. Yards: 7,035/5,503	Slope:	NA
Year-round. High: Apr.–Oct.		

☺
| *South Course* | Rating: | 70.1/71.4 |
| 18 holes. Par 72/72. Yards: 6,720/5,805 | Slope: | 115/122 |

P
☺☺
Mountain Springs Golf Club	Greens:	$–$$	T S J
Sonora. (209) 532-1000	Carts:	$
18 holes. Par 72/71. Yards: 6,665/5,195	Rating:	70.8/71.7
Year-round. High: Apr.–Sept.	Slope:	124/120

P
☺☺
Napa Municipal Golf Club	Greens:	$–$$	W L T S J
Streblow Dr., Napa. (707) 255-4333	Carts:	$$
18 holes. Par 72/73. Yards: 6,730/5,956	Rating:	71.7/76.8
Year-round. High: Apr.–Nov.	Slope:	127/137

SP

☺☺☺
DEAL
Oakmont Golf Club	Greens:	$$	T
Oakmont Dr., Santa Rosa. (707) 539-0415	Carts:	$
West Course	Rating:	70.5/71.9
18 holes. Par 72/72. Yards: 6,379/5,573	Slope:	121/128
Year-round.		

P
☺☺☺
Paradise Valley Golf Course	Greens:	$$	W L R T
Paradise Valley Dr., Fairfield. (707) 426-1600	Carts:	$
18 holes. Par 72/72. Yards: 6,993/5,413	Rating:	74.1/71.1
Year-round.	Slope:	135/119

R
| **Ridgemark Golf and Country Club** | Greens: | $$$ | T |
| Airline Hwy., Hollister. (408) 637-1010 | Carts: | Incl. |

California Golf Guide

☺☺☺	*Diablo Course* 18 holes. Par 72/72. Yards: 6,603/5,475 Year-round.	Rating: Slope:	71.9/72.0 123/123
☺☺	*Gabilan Course* 18 holes. Par 72/72. Yards: 6,781/5,683	Rating: Slope:	72.0/72.7 124/124

P
☺☺
Riverside Golf Club
Monterey Rd., Coyote. (408) 463-0622
18 holes. Par 72/73. Yards: 6,881/5,942
Year-round.

Greens: $$ W L T S J
Carts: Inquire
Rating: 72.2/72.5
Slope: 127/118

SP
☺☺☺
San Geronimo Golf Club
Sir Francis Drake Blvd., San Geronimo. (415) 488-4030
18 holes. Par 72/72. Yards: 6,801/5,140
Year-round. High: Mar.–Oct.

Greens: $$–$$$ W T S J
Carts: Inquire
Rating: 73.8/69.9
Slope: 135/125

P
☺☺
San Jose Municipal Golf Course
Oakland Rd., San Jose. (408) 441-4653
18 holes. Par 72/72. Yards: 6,602/5,594
Year-round.

Greens: $$ W T S J
Carts: Inquire
Rating: 70.1/69.7
Slope: 108/112

SP
☺
San Ramon Royal Vista Golf Club
Fircrest Lane, San Ramon. (510) 828-6100
18 holes. Par 72/73. Yards: 6,560/5,770
Year-round. High: May–Sept.

Greens: $$ T S J
Carts: Inquire
Rating: 70.9/72.7
Slope: 115/119

P
☺☺☺
DEAL
Santa Teresa Golf Club
Bernal Rd., San Jose. (408) 225-2650
18 holes. Par 71/73. Yards: 6,742/6,032
Year-round. High: Apr.–Sept.

Greens: $$ W T S J
Carts: Inquire
Rating: 71.1/73.5
Slope: 121/125

R

☺☺☺
Silverado Country Club and Resort
Atlas Peak Rd., Napa. (707) 257-5460
South Course
18 holes. Par 72/72. Yards: 6,685/5,672
Year-round. High: Mar.–Nov.

Greens: $$$–$$$$$$ L R T
Carts: Incl.
Rating: 72.4/71.8
Slope: 129/123

☺☺☺
North Course
18 holes. Par 72/72. Yards: 6,900/5,857

Rating: 73.4/73.1
Slope: 131/128

P
☺☺
Skywest Golf Club
Hayward. (520) 278-6188
18 holes. Par 72/73. Yards: 6,930/6,171
Year-round.

Greens: $–$$ S J
Carts: Inquire
Rating: 72.8/74.3
Slope: 121/123

P
☺☺☺☺
Sonoma Golf Club
Arnold Dr., Sonoma. (707) 996-0300
18 holes. Par 72/72. Yards: 7,087/5,511
Year-round. High: Apr.–Oct.

Greens: $$$$–$$$$$$ W L T
Carts: Incl.
Rating: 74.1/71.8
Slope: 132/125

P

☺☺
Sunol Valley Golf Course
Mission Rd., Sunol.
Palm Course. (510) 862-0414
18 holes. Par 72/74. Yards: 6,843/5,997
Year-round. High: Apr.–Sept.

Greens: $$$ T
Carts: Incl.
Rating: 72.2/74.4
Slope: 118/124

☺☺
Cypress Course. (510) 862-2404
18 holes. Par 72/72. Yards: 6,195/5,458

Rating: 69.1/70.1
Slope: 115/115

P
☺☺
Tilden Park Golf Course
Shasta Rd., Berkeley. (510) 848-7373
18 holes. Par 72/72. Yards: 6,300/5,400
Year-round. High: Apr.–Oct.

Greens: $–$$ W T S J
Carts: $$
Rating: 69.9/69.2
Slope: 120/116

California Golf Guide

P 😊😊	**Van Buskirk Park Golf Course** Houston Ave., Stockton. (209) 937-7357 18 holes. Par 72/74. Yards: 6,928/5,927 Year-round.	Greens: Carts: Rating: Slope:	$ $$ 72.2/72.2 118/113	T S J
P 😊😊	**Willow Park Golf Club** Redwood Rd., Castro Valley. (510) 537-8989 18 holes. Par 71/71. Yards: 6,227/5,193 Year-round.	Greens: Carts: Rating: Slope:	$–$$ Inquire 67.4/69.2 110/117	
P 😊😊😊	**Windsor Golf Club** Skylane Blvd., Windsor. (707) 838-7888 18 holes. Par 72/72. Yards: 6,650/5,116 Year-round.	Greens: Carts: Rating: Slope:	$$ Inquire 72.3/69.3 126/125	W T S J

Modesto

P 😊😊	**Dryden Park Golf Course** Sunset Ave., Modesto. (209) 577-5359 18 holes. Par 72/74. Yards: 6,574/6,048 Year-round. High: May–Sept.	Greens: Carts: Rating: Slope:	$ $ 69.8/72.5 119/115	W T S J

Monterey Area

P 😊😊😊	**Fort Ord Golf Course** McClure Way, Fort Ord. (408) 899-2351 *Bayonet Course* 18 holes. Par 72/72. Yards: 6,982/5,680 Year-round. High: Mar.–Nov.	Greens: Carts: Rating: Slope:	$–$$$ $ 74.0/73.7 132/134	T
😊😊😊	*Blackhorse Course* 18 holes. Par 72/72. Yards: 6,396/5,613	Rating: Slope:	71.3/72.5 128/129	
P 😊😊😊	**Laguna Seca Golf Club** York Rd., Monterey. (408) 373-3701 18 holes. Par 72/72. Yards: 6,125/5,186 Year-round. High: June–Aug.	Greens: Carts: Rating: Slope:	$$$ $$ 70.4/70.2 123/119	T
R 😊😊😊😊 BEST	**The Links at Spanish Bay** 17 Mile Dr., Pebble Beach. (831) 647-7495 18 holes. Par 72/72. Yards: 6,820/5,309 Year-round. High: Sept.–Nov.	Greens: Carts: Rating: Slope:	$$$$$$+ $$ 74.8/70.6 146/129	R T
P 😊😊😊	**Old Del Monte Golf Course** Sylvan Rd., Monterey. (408) 373-2700 18 holes. Par 72/74. Yards: 6,339/5,526 Year-round. High: Apr.–Oct.	Greens: Carts: Rating: Slope:	$$$ $ 71.6/71.0 125/120	R T S J
P 😊😊😊 DEAL	**Pacific Grove Municipal Golf Links** Asilomar Blvd., Pacific Grove. (408) 648-3175 18 holes. Par 70/72. Yards: 5,732/5,305 Year-round.	Greens: Carts: Rating: Slope:	$$ $ 67.5/70.5 117/114	T J
P 😊😊😊	**Pajaro Valley Golf Club** Salinas Rd., Watsonville. (408) 724-3851 18 holes. Par 72/72. Yards: 6,234/5,694 Year-round. High: Apr.–Nov.	Greens: Carts: Rating: Slope:	$$–$$$ $$ 70.0/72.3 122/123	W T
SP 😊😊😊😊 BEST	**Pasatiempo Golf Club** Santa Cruz. (831) 459-9155 18 holes. Par 70/72. Yards: 6,445/5,629 Year-round. High: June–Sept.	Greens: Carts: Rating: Slope:	$$$$$$ $$ 72.3/73.6 140/135	W T
R 😊😊😊😊 BEST	**Pebble Beach Golf Links** 17 Mile Dr., Pebble Beach. (831) 624-3811 18 holes. Par 72/72. Yards: 6,719/5,198 Year-round. High: Sept.–Oct.	Greens: Carts: Rating: Slope:	$$$$$$+++ Incl. 73.8/71.9 142/130	T

California Golf Guide

P ☺☺☺☺	**Poppy Hills Golf Course** Lopez Rd., Pebble Beach. (831) 625-2154 18 holes. Par 72/72. Yards: 6,835/5,408 Year-round. High: May–Aug.	Greens: Carts: Rating: Slope:	$$$–$$$$$$ J Incl. 74.6/72.1 144/131
P ☺☺☺	**Rancho Canada Golf Club** Carmel Valley Rd., Carmel. (408) 624-0111 *East Course* 18 holes. Par 71/72. Yards: 6,109/5,267 Year-round. High: Apr.–Oct.	Greens: Carts: Rating: Slope:	$$$ T $ 68.7/69.4 120/114
☺☺☺	*West Course* 18 holes. Par 72/73. Yards: 6,349/5,568	Greens: Carts: Rating: Slope:	$$$$ T $ 70.4/71.9 125/118
R ☺☺☺☺ BEST	**Spyglass Hill Golf Course** Spyglass Hill Rd., Pebble Beach. (831) 625-8563 18 holes. Par 72/74. Yards: 6,855/5,618 Year-round. High: May–Nov.	Greens: Carts: Rating: Slope:	$$$$$$+++ R T $$ 75.1/73.7 147/133

Bakersfield Area

P ☺☺	**Kern River Golf Course** Rudal Rd., Bakersfield. (805) 872-5128 18 holes. Par 70/73. Yards: 6,458/5,971 Year-round.	Greens: Carts: Rating: Slope:	$ W T S $ 70.5/72.3 117/116
P ☺☺☺☺ BEST	**Sandpiper Golf Course** Hollister Ave., Goleta. (805) 968-1541 18 holes. Par 72/73. Yards: 7,068/5,701 Year-round. High: May–Oct.	Greens: Carts: Rating: Slope:	$$$$–$$$$$$ W $$ 74.5/73.3 134/125
P ☺☺	**Wasco Valley Rose Golf Course** N. Leonard Ave., Wasco. (805) 758-8301 18 holes. Par 72/72. Yards: 6,862/5,356 Year-round. High: Apr.–June, Oct.	Greens: Carts: Rating: Slope:	$ W L T S J $$ 72.5/70.5 121/119

Fresno Area

SP ☺☺	**Fig Garden Golf Club** N. Van Ness Blvd., Fresno. (209) 439-2928 18 holes. Par 72/72. Yards: 6,621/5,605 Year-round.	Greens: Carts: Rating: Slope:	$$ W T J $$ 70.6/71.9 113/120
P ☺☺	**Fresno West Golf and Country Club** W. Whitesbridge Rd., Kerman. (209) 846-8655 18 holes. Par 72/72. Yards: 6,959/6,000 Year-round.	Greens: Carts: Rating: Slope:	$ W L T S J $$ 67.7/69.2 103/111
P ☺☺	**Riverside of Fresno Golf Club** N. Josephine, Fresno. (209) 275-5900 18 holes. Par 72/72. Yards: 6,621/6,008 Year-round. High: Apr.–Oct.	Greens: Carts: Rating: Slope:	$ T S J $ 71.2/73.9 122/125
P ☺☺	**Sherwood Forest Golf Club** N. Frankwood Ave., Sanger. (209) 787-2611 18 holes. Par 71/72. Yards: 6,205/5,605 Year-round. High: Apr.–June	Greens: Carts: Rating: Slope:	$ J Inquire 67.5/70.8 110/115

Lake Tahoe Area

P ☺☺☺ DEAL	**Lake Tahoe Golf Course** Emerald Bay Rd., S. Lake Tahoe. (530) 577-0788 18 holes. Par 71/72. Yards: 6,741/5,703 May–Oct. High: June–Sept.	Greens: Carts: Rating: Slope:	$$$ L T $$ 70.8/66.7 126/109
R ☺☺☺	**Northstar-at-Tahoe Resort Golf Course** Hwy. 267, Truckee. (530) 562-2490	Greens: Carts:	$$$$ L R T S J Incl.

		Rating:	72.0/70.8
18 holes. Par 72/72. Yards: 6,897/5,470		Slope:	137/136
May–Oct. High: July–Aug.			

R	**Resort at Squaw Creek**	Greens:	$$$$$$	W L T
☺☺☺	Squaw Creek Rd., Olympic Valley. (530) 583-6300	Carts:	Incl.	
	18 holes. Par 71/71. Yards: 6,931/5,097	Rating:	72.9/68.9	
	May–Oct. High: July–Aug.	Slope:	140/127	

Santa Barbara Area

R	**The Alisal Ranch Golf Course**	Greens:	$$$$
☺☺☺	Alisal Rd., Solvang. (805) 688-4215	Carts:	$$
	18 holes. Par 72/72. Yards: 6,472/5,767	Rating:	71.0/74.4
	Year-round. High: May–Oct.	Slope:	124/130

P	**Avila Beach Resort Golf Course**	Greens:	$$	T J
☺☺☺	Avila Beach. (805) 595-2307	Carts:	$	
	18 holes. Par 72/72. Yards: 6,443/5,116	Rating:	70.9/69.9	
	Year-round. High: Apr.–Nov.	Slope:	122/126	

R	**Black Lake Golf Club**	Greens:	$$$	W L R T S J
	Nipoma. (805) 343-1214	Carts:	$$	
☺☺☺	*Oaks/Canyon/Lakes*	Rating:	69.3/69.7/70.9	
	27 holes. Par 72/72. Yards: 6,034/6,501/6,285	Slope:	121/121/123	
	Year-round. High: May–Sept.			

P	**Elkins Ranch Golf Club**	Greens:	$$	W T S J
☺☺☺	Chambersburg Rd., Fillmore. (805) 524-1440	Carts:	$	
DEAL	18 holes. Par 71/73. Yards: 6,302/5,650	Rating:	69.9/72.6	
	Year-round. High: Apr.–Oct.	Slope:	117/122	

R	**Horse Thief Country Club**	Greens:	$$	W T S J
☺☺☺	Stallion Spring, Tehachapi. (805) 822-5581	Carts:	Inquire	
	18 holes. Par 72/72. Yards: 6,678/5,677	Rating:	72.1/72.1	
	Year-round. High: May–Sept.	Slope:	124/124	

P	**Hunter Ranch Golf Course**	Greens:	$$	J
☺☺☺	Hwy. 46 E., Paso Robles. (805) 237-7444	Carts:	$$	
DEAL	18 holes. Par 72/72. Yards: 6,741/5,629	Rating:	72.2/72.8	
	Year-round. High: May–Oct.	Slope:	128/132	

P	**La Purisma Golf Course**	Greens:	$$$–$$$$	J
☺☺☺☺	St. Hwy. 246, Lompoc. (805) 735-8395	Carts:	$$	
DEAL	18 holes. Par 72/72. Yards: 7,105/5,763	Rating:	74.9/74.3	
	Year-round. High: May–Oct.	Slope:	143/131	

P	**Rancho Maria Golf Club**	Greens:	$–$$	W T S J
☺☺	Casmalia Rd., Santa Maria. (805) 937-2019	Carts:	$	
	18 holes. Par 72/73. Yards: 6,390/5,504	Rating:	70.2/71.3	
	Year-round.	Slope:	119/123	

P	**River Course at the Alisal**	Greens:	$$–$$$	W R S J
☺☺☺	Alisal Rd., Solvang. (805) 688-6042	Carts:	$	
	18 holes. Par 72/72. Yards: 6,820/5,815	Rating:	73.1/73.4	
	Year-round. High: Jan.–Mar.	Slope:	126/127	

P	**Santa Barbara Golf Club**	Greens:	$–$$	W T S J
☺☺	McCaw Ave., Santa Barbara. (805) 687-7087	Carts:	$	
	18 holes. Par 70/72. Yards: 6,014/5,541	Rating:	67.6/71.9	
	Year-round. High: May–Sept.	Slope:	113/121	

P	**Soule Park Golf Course**	Greens:	$–$$	W T S J
☺☺☺	E. Ojai Ave., Ojai. (805) 646-5633	Carts:	Inquire	
DEAL	18 holes. Par 72/72. Yards: 6,435/5,894	Rating:	70.1/73.0	
	Year-round.	Slope:	120/124	

Los Angeles Area

P	**Anaheim Hills Golf Course**	Greens:	$$	T S
☺☺	Nohl Ranch Rd., Anaheim. (714) 748-8900	Carts:	Incl.	

California Golf Guide

		Rating:	70.0/70.0
18 holes. Par 71/72. Yards: 6,218/5,356		Slope:	119/115
Year-round.			

P	**Brookside Golf Club**	Greens:	$–$$	W T S J
	N. Rosemont Ave., Pasadena. (818) 796-8151	Carts:	$
☺☺	*C.W. Koiner Course*	Rating:	74.5/74.7
	18 holes. Par 72/75. Yards: 7,037/6,104	Slope:	134/128
	Year-round. High: Apr.–Oct.		

| ☺☺ | *E.O. Nay Course* | Rating: | 68.4/70.5 |
| | 18 holes. Par 70/71. Yards: 6,046/5,377 | Slope: | 115/117 |

P	**Camarillo Springs Golf Course**	Greens:	$$–$$$$	W R T S J
☺☺	Camarillo Springs Rd., Camarillo. (805) 484-1075	Carts:	Incl.
	18 holes. Par 72/72. Yards: 6,375/5,297	Rating:	70.2/70.2
	Year-round. High: May–Aug.	Slope:	115/116

P	**Cypress Golf Club**	Greens:	$$$–$$$$$	W T S
☺☺☺	Katella Ave., Los Alamitos. (714) 527-1800	Carts:	Incl.
	18 holes. Par 71/71. Yards: 6,510/5,188	Rating:	71.4/70.8
	Year-round. High: Apr.–Oct.	Slope:	129/129

P	**Debell Golf Club**	Greens:	$	W L T S J
☺☺	Walnut Ave., Burbank. (818) 845-0022	Carts:	$
	18 holes. Par 71/73. Yards: 5,610/5,412	Rating:	67.4/70.8
	Year-round.	Slope:	108/118

P	**El Prado Golf Courses**	Greens:	$–$$	W L T S J
	Pine Ave., Chino. (909) 597-1751	Carts:	$
☺☺	*Butterfield Stage Course*	Rating:	69.7/70.2
	18 holes. Par 72/73. Yards: 6,508/5,503	Slope:	108/118
	Year-round.		

| ☺☺ | *Chino Creek Course* | Rating: | 71.0/70.8 |
| | 18 holes. Par 72/73. Yards: 6,671/5,596 | Slope: | 114/115 |

P	**El Rivino Country Club**	Greens:	$–$$	W T
☺☺☺	El Rivino Rd., Riverside. (909) 684-8905	Carts:	$
DEAL	18 holes. Par 73/73. Yards: 6,466/5,863	Rating:	71.8/70.8
	Year-round.	Slope:	111/113

P	**Green River Golf Course**	Greens:	$$	J
	Green River Rd., Corona. (909) 737-7393	Carts:	$
☺☺	*Orange Course*	Rating:	70.4/75.7
	18 holes. Par 71/72. Yards: 6,416/5,744	Slope:	119/125
	Year-round.		

| ☺☺ | *Riverside Course* | Rating: | 69.2/73.9 | T J |
| | 18 holes. Par 71/71. Yards: 6,275/5,467 | Slope: | 117/121 |

P	**Griffith Park**	Greens:	$–$$	W T S J
	Crystal Springs Dr., Los Angeles. (213) 664-2255	Carts:	$
☺☺	*Harding Course*	Rating:	70.4/72.5
	18 holes. Par 72/73. Yards: 6,536/6,028	Slope:	112/118
	Year-round. High: Mar.–Sept.		

| ☺☺ | *Wilson Course* | Rating: | 72.7/74.6 |
| | 18 holes. Par 72/73. Yards: 6,942/6,330 | Slope: | 115/119 |

SP	**Hesperia Golf and Country Club**	Greens:	$–$$	J
☺☺☺	Bangor Ave., Hesperia. (619) 244-9301	Carts:	$$
	18 holes. Par 72/72. Yards: 6,996/6,136	Rating:	73.5/73.9
	Year-round. High: Spring/Fall	Slope:	131/124

P	**Indian Hills Golf Course**	Greens:	$–$$	W L T S J
☺☺	Riverside. (909) 360-2090	Carts:	Inquire
	18 holes. Par 70/72. Yards: 6,104/5,562	Rating:	70.0/70.7
	Year-round. High: Nov.–June	Slope:	126/118

California Golf Guide

R ☺☺☺	**Industry Hills Sheraton Resort** City of Industry. (818) 810-4653 *Eisenhower Course* 18 holes. Par 72/73. Yards: 6,735/5,589 Year-round. High: Apr.–July	Greens: Carts: Rating: Slope:	$$$ W L T S J Incl. 72.9/73.1 136/135
☺☺☺	*Babe Didrikson Zaharias Course* 18 holes. Par 71/71. Yards: 6,600/5,363	Rating: Slope:	72.5/72.4 134/133
P ☺☺	**Jurupa Hills Country Club** Morage Ave., Riverside. (909) 685-7214 18 holes. Par 70/71. Yards: 6,022/5,773 Year-round.	Greens: Carts: Rating: Slope:	$–$$ W L T S J Incl. 68.2/73.4 112/121
P ☺☺	**La Mirada Golf Course** E. Alicante Rd., La Mirada. (310) 943-7123 18 holes. Par 72/72. Yards: 6,044/5,632 Year-round.	Greens: Carts: Rating: Slope:	$–$$ W T S J $ 67.2/71.7 109/115
SP ☺	**Los Angeles Royal Vista Golf Course** E. Colima Rd., Walnut. (909) 595-7441 *North/South/East* 27 holes. Par 71/71/72. Yards: 6,381/6,071/6,182 Year-round. High: Apr.–Sept.	Greens: Carts: Rating: Slope:	$–$$ W L R T S J Incl. 69.0/67.6/68.5 115/110/112
P ☺☺	**Los Robles Golf Club** S. Moorpark Rd., Thousand Oaks. (805) 495-6171 18 holes. Par 70/70. Yards: 6,274/5,333 Year-round.	Greens: Carts: Rating: Slope:	$–$$ W T S J $ 69.4/70.1 118/117
P ☺☺☺ DEAL	**Los Serranos Lakes Golf and Country Club** Yorba Ave., Chino Hills. (909) 597-1711 *North Course* 18 holes. Par 72/74. Yards: 6,430/5,949 Year-round. High: Mar.–June	Greens: Carts: Rating: Slope:	$$ W T S $ 71.3/73.9 129/125
☺☺☺ DEAL	*South Course* 18 holes. Par 74/74. Yards: 7,080/5,957	Rating: Slope:	74.0/73.9 134/128
P ☺☺	**Los Verdes Golf Course** Rancho Palos Verdes. (310) 377-0338 18 holes. Par 71/72. Yards: 6,651/5,738 Year-round. High: June–Sept.	Greens: Carts: Rating: Slope:	$–$$ W T S J $ 72.4/71.8 122/118
P ☺☺☺	**Malibu Country Club** Encinal Canyon Rd., Malibu. (818) 889-6680 18 holes. Par 72/72. Yards: 6,740/5,627 Year-round.	Greens: Carts: Rating: Slope:	$$$–$$$$ S Incl. 72.3/71.4 130/120
SP ☺☺☺	**Menifee Lakes Country Club** Menifee. (909) 672-3090 27 holes. Par 72/72. Yards: 6,503/6,435/6,392 Year-round.	Greens: Carts: Rating: Slope:	$$–$$$ W T J Incl. 71.1/70.7/70.5 122/121/120
P ☺☺	**Mile Square Golf Club** Warner Ave., Fountain Valley. (714) 968-4556 18 holes. Par 72/72. Yards: 6,629/5,545 Year-round. High: Mar.–Sept.	Greens: Carts: Rating: Slope:	$$ T $$ 71.4/70.5 121/109
P ☺☺	**Montebello Golf Club** Via San Clemente, Montebello. (213) 723-2971 18 holes. Par 72/72. Yards: 6,671/5,979 Year-round. High: Apr.–Oct.	Greens: Carts: Rating: Slope:	$–$$ $$ 70.4/72.4 114/117
P ☺☺☺	**Moreno Valley Ranch Golf Club** JFK Dr., Moreno Valley. (909) 924-4444 *Mountain/Lake/Valley*	Greens: Carts: Rating:	$$–$$$ W L T S J Incl. 73.1/74.1/74.2

California Golf Guide

	27 holes. Par 72/72/72. Yards: 6,684/6,898/6,880 Year-round. High: Nov.–May	Slope: 139/138/140

P ◔◔◔ DEAL	**Mountain Meadows Golf Club** N. Fairplex Dr., Pomona. (909) 623-3704 18 holes. Par 72/72. Yards: 6,440/5,519 Year-round. High: May–Aug.	Greens: $–$$ W L T S J Carts: $ Rating: 70.4/71.4 Slope: 120/122
P ◔◔◔◔ STATE	**Oak Valley Golf Club** 14th St., Beaumont. (909) 769-7200 18 holes. Par 72/72. Yards: 7,003/5,349 Year-round.	Greens: $$$–$$$$ W T Carts: Incl. Rating: 74.0/71.1 Slope: 136/122
R ◔◔◔◔ STATE	**Ojai Valley Inn** Ojai. (805) 646-2420 18 holes. Par 70/71. Yards: 6,235/5,225 Year-round. High: Mar.–Oct.	Greens: $$$$$$ R T Carts: Incl. Rating: 70.2/70.2 Slope: 122/123
P ◔◔	**Olivas Park Golf Course** Ventura. (805) 642-4303 18 holes. Par 72/72. Yards: 6,760/5,501 Year-round. High: May–Sept.	Greens: $–$$ T J Carts: $$ Rating: 71.3/71.3 Slope: 119/117
SP ◔◔◔	**Palos Verdes Golf Club** Via Campesina, Palos Verdes Estates. (310) 375-2759 18 holes. Par 72/72. Yards: 6,116/5,506 Year-round. High: June–Aug.	Greens: $$$$$ J Carts: Incl. Rating: 70.4/73.3 Slope: 131/128
R ◔◔◔◔ STATE	**Pelican Hill Golf Club** Pelican Hill Rd., Newport Coast. (949) 640-0238 *The Links Course* 18 holes. Par 71/71. Yards: 6,856/5,800 Year-round.	Greens: $$$$$$++ R T Carts: Incl. Rating: 73.6/73.0 Slope: 136/125
◔◔◔◔ STATE	*The Ocean Course* 18 holes. Par 70/70. Yards: 6,634/5,409	Rating: 72.8/72.5 Slope: 138/124
P ◔◔◔	**Recreation Park Golf Course** Deukmejian Dr., Long Beach. (562) 494-5000 18 holes. Par 72/74. Yards: 6,317/5,793 Year-round.	Greens: $–$$ W T S J Carts: $ Rating: 69.0/72.6 Slope: 112/120
SP ◔◔◔◔	**Redhawk Golf Club** Redhawk Pkwy., Temecula. (909) 302-3850 18 holes. Par 72/72. Yards: 7,180/5,515 Year-round.	Greens: $$$–$$$$ T J Carts: Incl. Rating: 75.7/72.0 Slope: 149/124
P ◔◔◔	**Rio Hondo Golf Club** Old River School Rd., Downey. (310) 927-2329 18 holes. Par 72/72. Yards: 6,344/5,080 Year-round.	Greens: $$ T S J Carts: Inquire Rating: 70.2/69.4 Slope: 119/117
P ◔◔	**San Bernardino Golf Club** S. Waterman, San Bernardino. (909) 885-2414 18 holes. Par 72/72. Yards: 5,782/5,226 Year-round. High: Apr.–May, Sept.–Oct.	Greens: $–$$ W T S J Carts: $ Rating: 67.4/70.0 Slope: 112/112
P ◔◔	**San Dimas Canyon Golf Club** Terrebonne Ave., San Dimas. (909) 599-2313 18 holes. Par 72/72. Yards: 6,314/5,571 Year-round. High: Apr.–Sept.	Greens: $–$$ W T S J Carts: Inquire Rating: 70.2/73.9 Slope: 118/123
P ◔◔	**Santa Anita Golf Course** S. Santa Anita Ave., Arcadia. (818) 447-7156 18 holes. Par 71/74. Yards: 6,368/5,908 Year-round.	Greens: $–$$ T S J Carts: $$ Rating: 70.4/73.1 Slope: 122/121

California Golf Guide

P	**Shandin Hills Golf Club**	Greens:	$–$$ W T S J
☺☺☺	Little Mountain Dr., San Bernardino. (909) 886-0669	Carts:	$
DEAL	18 holes. Par 72/72. Yards: 6,517/5,592	Rating:	70.3/71.6
	Year-round. High: Oct.	Slope:	120/122

P	**Tijeras Creek Golf Club**	Greens:	$–$$ W T S J
☺☺☺	Rancho Santa Margarita. (714) 589-9793	Carts:	$$
DEAL	18 holes. Par 72/72. Yards: 6,601/5,400	Rating:	69.9/69.2
	Year-round. High: Apr.–Oct.	Slope:	120/116

P	**Tustin Ranch Golf Club**	Greens:	$$$$–$$$$$ W S J
☺☺☺	Tustin Ranch Rd., Tustin. (714) 730-1611	Carts:	Incl.
	18 holes. Par 72/72. Yards: 6,736/5,204	Rating:	72.4/65.0
	Year-round. High: June–Oct.	Slope:	129/110

SP	**Upland Hills Country Club**	Greens:	$–$$
☺☺	E. 16th St., Upland. (909) 946-4711	Carts:	$
	18 holes. Par 70/70. Yards: 5,827/4,813	Rating:	67.1/66.5
	Year-round.	Slope:	111/106

SP	**Victorville Municipal Golf Course**	Greens:	$–$$ W L R T S J
☺☺	Green Tree Blvd., Victorville. (619) 245-4860	Carts:	$
	18 holes. Par 72/72. Yards: 6,640/5,878	Rating:	71.2/72.7
	Year-round. High: May–Sept.	Slope:	121/118

Palm Springs Area

P	**Desert Dunes Golf Club**	Greens:	$$$–$$$$$ W L R T J
☺☺☺☺	Palm Dr., Desert Hot Springs. (760) 251-5366	Carts:	Incl.
BEST	18 holes. Par 72/72. Yards: 6,876/5,359	Rating:	73.8/70.7
	Year-round. High: Jan.–May	Slope:	142/116

SP	**Desert Falls Country Club**	Greens:	$$–$$$$$$$+ L T
☺☺☺	Desert Falls Pkwy., Palm Desert. (760) 340-5646	Carts:	Incl.
	18 holes. Par 72/72. Yards: 7,017/5,313	Rating:	75.0/71.7
	Year-round. High: Nov.–Apr.	Slope:	145/124

R	**Desert Princess Country Club and Resort**	Greens:	$$$–$$$$$ W L R T
	Landau Blvd., Cathedral City. (760) 322-2280	Carts:	Incl.
☺☺☺	*La Vista/El Cielo/Los Lagos*	Rating:	72.5/71.2/71.8
	27 holes. Par 72/72/72. Yards: 6,764/6,587/6,667	Slope:	126/121/123
	Year-round. High: Nov.–May		

R	**Golf Resort at Indian Wells**	Greens:	$$$–$$$$$$ W L R T
	Indian Wells Lane, Indian Wells. (760) 346-4653	Carts:	Incl.
☺☺☺	*East Course*	Rating:	71.7/71.5
	18 holes. Par 72/72. Yards: 6,631/5,516	Slope:	122/118
	Year-round. High: Jan.–May		

☺☺☺	*West Course*	Rating:	70.7/71.0
	18 holes. Par 72/72. Yards: 6,500/5,408	Slope:	120/127

SP	**La Quinta Resort and Club**	Greens:	$$$$$$ W L R T
	Vista Bonita, La Quinta. (760) 564-4111	Carts:	Incl.
☺☺☺☺	*Mountain Course*	Rating:	74.1/69.1
STATE	18 holes. Par 72/72. Yards: 6,756/5,005	Slope:	140/123
	Year-round. High: Nov.–Apr.		

☺☺☺	*Dunes Course*	Rating:	73.1/70.7
	18 holes. Par 72/72. Yards: 6,747/4,997	Slope:	137/125

SP	**Lawrence Welk's Desert Oasis Country Club**	Greens:	$$–$$$$$ W L T
	Cathedral Canyon Dr., Cathedral City. (760) 328-6571	Carts:	Incl.
☺☺	*Lakeview/Mountain/Resort*	Rating:	71.6/70.9/70.3
	27 holes. Par 72/72/72. Yards: 6,505/6,477/6,366	Slope:	128/119/118
	Year-round. High: Jan.–Apr.		

California Golf Guide

R	**Marriott's Desert Springs Resort and Spa**	Greens:	$$$$–$$$$$$ W L R T
	Palm Desert. (760) 341-2211	Carts:	Incl.
☺☺☺	*Palm Course*	Rating:	72.0/70.8
	18 holes. Par 72/72. Yards: 6,761/5,492	Slope:	124/116
	Year-round. High: Oct.–May		
☺☺☺	*Valley Course*	Rating:	72.1/69.6
	18 holes. Par 72/72. Yards: 6,679/5,330	Slope:	124/110
R	**Marriott's Rancho Las Palmas Resort**	Greens:	$$$–$$$$$ W L R T
	Bob Hope Dr., Rancho Mirage. (760) 568-0955	Carts:	Inquire
☺☺	*North/South/West*	Rating:	67.2/65.5/65.3
	27 holes. Par 71/69/70. Yards: 6,019/5,569/5,550	Slope:	115/106/105
	Year-round. High: Jan.–Apr.		
P	**Mesquite Golf and Country Club**	Greens:	$$$$ W L T
☺☺☺	E. Mesquite Ave., Palm Springs. (760) 323-1502	Carts:	Incl.
	18 holes. Par 72/72. Yards: 6,328/5,244	Rating:	67.9/69.2
	Year-round. High: Nov.–May	Slope:	117/118
P	**Mission Hills North Golf Course**	Greens:	$$$$$$+ W L R T
☺☺☺☺	Ramon Rd., Rancho Mirage. (760) 770-9496	Carts:	Incl.
	18 holes. Par 72/72. Yards: 7,062/4,907	Rating:	73.9/68.0
	Year-round. High: Oct.–Apr.	Slope:	134/118
SP	**Mission Lakes Country Club**	Greens:	$$–$$$$ W L R T J
☺☺☺	Desert Hot Springs. (760) 329-8061	Carts:	Incl.
	18 holes. Par 72/72. Yards: 6,737/5,390	Rating:	72.8/70.6
	Year-round. High: Jan.–May	Slope:	131/115
R	**Palm Desert Resort Country Club**	Greens:	$$$$–$$$$$ W L T
☺☺☺	Palm Desert. (760) 345-2791	Carts:	Incl.
	18 holes. Par 72/72. Yards: 6,585/5,549	Rating:	70.8/71.8
	Nov.–Sept. High: Nov.–Apr.	Slope:	117/121
R	**PGA West Resort**	Greens:	$$$$$$+++ WLRT
	La Quinta. (760) 564-7170	Carts:	Incl.
☺☺☺☺	*Jack Nicklaus Resort Course*	Rating:	74.7/69.0
BEST	18 holes. Par 72/72. Yards: 7,204/5,023	Slope:	139/116
	Year-round. High: Jan.–Apr.		
☺☺☺☺	*TPC Stadium Course*	Greens:	$$$$$$ W L R T
BEST	18 holes. Par 72/72. Yards: 7,261/5,087	Carts:	Incl.
		Rating:	75.9/69.0
		Slope:	150/124
SP	**Soboda Springs Country Club**	Greens:	$$–$$$ T J
☺☺☺	Soboda Rd., San Jacinto. (909) 654-9354	Carts:	Incl.
	18 holes. Par 72/72. Yards: 6,888/5,762	Rating:	72.8/72.7
	Year-round. High: Oct.–May	Slope:	133/130
R	**Sun City Palm Springs Golf Club**	Greens:	$$–$$$$ W L T
☺☺☺	Del Webb Blvd., Bermuda Dunes. (760) 772-2200	Carts:	Incl.
	18 holes. Par 72/72. Yards: 6,720/5,305	Rating:	73.0/70.3
	Year-round.	Slope:	131/118
SP	**Sun Lakes Country Club**	Greens:	$$$ T J
☺☺☺	Banning. (909) 845-2135	Carts:	Incl.
	18 holes. Par 72/72. Yards: 7,006/5,550	Rating:	68.471.9
	Year-round. High: Apr.–Oct.	Slope:	115/120
R	**Tahquitz Creek Palm Springs Golf Course**	Greens:	$–$$ L T
	Palm Springs. (760) 328-1956	Carts:	$$
☺☺	*Old Course*	Rating:	69.5/72.6
	18 holes. Par 71/73. Yards: 6,040/5,800	Slope:	107/115
	Year-round. High: Jan.–May		

California Golf Guide

☺☺	*Resort Course* 18 holes. Par 72/72. Yards: 6,705/5,206	Rating: Slope:	71.4/70.0 120/119

R ☺☺☺	**The Westin Mission Hills Resort** Dinah Shore Dr., Rancho Mirage. (760) 328-3198 18 holes. Par 70/70. Yards: 6,706/4,841 Year-round. High: Oct.–Apr.	Greens: Carts: Rating: Slope:	$$$–$$$$$$+ R Incl. 73.5/67.4 137/107

San Diego Area

R ☺☺☺☺ STATE	**Aviara Golf Club** Batiquitos Dr., Carlsbad. (760) 603-6900 18 holes. Par 72/72. Yards: 7,007/5,007 Year-round. High: Apr.–Aug.	Greens: Carts: Rating: Slope:	$$$$$$ W T Incl. 74.2/69.1 137/119

R ☺☺☺	**Carlton Oaks Country Club** Inwood Dr., Santee. (619) 448-8500 18 holes. Par 72/72. Yards: 7,088/4,548 Year-round.	Greens: Carts: Rating: Slope:	$$$–$$$$ R T Incl. 74.6/67.1 137/114

R ☺☺	**Carmel Highland Doubletree Resort** Penasquitos Dr., San Diego. (619) 672-9100 18 holes. Par 72/72. Yards: 6,428/5,361 Year-round. High: Jan.–Apr.	Greens: Carts: Rating: Slope:	$$$ W L R T S J Incl. 70.7/71.9 123/125

P ☺☺☺	**Carmel Mountain Ranch Country Club** Carmel Ridge Rd., San Diego. (619) 487-9224 18 holes. Par 72/72. Yards: 6,529/5,228 Year-round.	Greens: Carts: Rating: Slope:	$$$–$$$$ T S J Incl. 71.9/71.0 131/122

SP ☺☺	**Castle Creek Country Club** Circle R Dr., Escondido. (619) 749-2422 18 holes. Par 72/72. Yards: 6,396/4,800 Year-round. High: Jan.–Apr.	Greens: Carts: Rating: Slope:	$$ W T $ 70.8/67.4 124/108

P ☺☺	**Chula Vista Municipal Golf Course** Bonita Rd., Bonita. (619) 479-4141 18 holes. Par 73/74. Yards: 6,759/5,776 Year-round. High: July–Sept.	Greens: Carts: Rating: Slope:	$–$$ W T S J $ 72.3/72.7 128/124

P ☺☺☺ DEAL	**Coronado Golf Course** Visalia Row, Coronado. (619) 435-3121 18 holes. Par 72/72. Yards: 6,633/5,784 Year-round.	Greens: Carts: Rating: Slope:	$$ T J $ 71.8/73.7 124/126

P ☺☺☺	**Eagle Crest Golf Club** Cloverdale Rd., Escondido. (619) 737-9762 18 holes. Par 72/72. Yards: 6,417/4,941 Year-round. High: Jan.–Apr.	Greens: Carts: Rating: Slope:	$$–$$$ T S J Incl. 71.6/69.6 136/123

P ☺☺☺	**Eastlake Country Club** Chula Vista. (619) 482-5757 18 holes. Par 72/72. Yards: 6,225/5,118 Year-round. High: Jan.–June	Greens: Carts: Rating: Slope:	$$$–$$$$ W S J Incl. 70.1/70.2 116/120

R ☺☺☺	**La Costa Resort and Spa** Costa Del Mar Rd., Carlsbad. (619) 438-9111 *North Course* 18 holes. Par 72/73. Yards: 6,987/5,939 Year-round.	Greens: Carts: Rating: Slope:	$$$$$$++ W R T Incl. 74.8/74.0 137/127

California Golf Guide

☺☺☺ | *South Course* | Rating: | 74.4/72.1
| 18 holes. Par 72/74. Yards: 6,894/5,612 | Slope: | 138/123

SP | **Meadow Lake Country Club** | Greens: | $$ | W R T J
☺☺ | Meadow Glen Way, Escondido. (619) 749-1620 | Carts: | $
| 18 holes. Par 72/74. Yards: 6,521/5,758 | Rating: | 72.5/72.8
| Year-round. | Slope: | 131/123

R | **Monarch Beach Golf Links** | Greens: | $$$$–$$$$$$
☺☺☺ | Stonehill Dr., Dana Point. (714) 240-8247 | Carts: | Incl.
| 18 holes. Par 70/70. Yards: 6,344/5,046 | Rating: | 69.2/68.5
| Year-round. | Slope: | 128/119

SP | **Mt. Woodson Country Club** | Greens: | $$–$$$ | W T J
☺☺☺ | N. Woodson Dr., Ramona. (619) 788-3555 | Carts: | Incl.
| 18 holes. Par 70/70. Yards: 6,180/4,441 | Rating: | 68.8/64.7
| Year-round. | Slope: | 130/108

R | **Pala Mesa Resort** | Greens: | $$–$$$$ | W L R T J
☺☺☺ | S. Hwy. 395, Fallbrook. (619) 728-5881 | Carts: | Incl.
| 18 holes. Par 72/72. Yards: 6,528/5,848 | Rating: | 72.0/74.5
| Year-round. High: Jan.–May | Slope: | 131/128

R | **Rancho Bernardo Inn and Country Club** | Greens: | $$$–$$$$ | W R T J
☺☺☺ | Bernardo Oaks Dr., San Diego. (619) 675-8470 | Carts: | Incl.
| 18 holes. Par 72/72. Yards: 6,458/5,448 | Rating: | 70.6/71.2
| Year-round. High: Dec.–May | Slope: | 122/119

P | **The SCGA Members' Club at Rancho California** | Greens: | $$$ | W T J
☺☺☺ | Murrieta Hot Springs Rd., Murrieta. (909) 677-7446 | Carts: | Incl.
| 18 holes. Par 72/72. Yards: 7,059/5,355 | Rating: | 73.9/70.5
| Year-round. High: Jan.–May | Slope: | 132/116

P | **San Clemente Municipal Golf Club** | Greens: | $–$$ | W T S J
☺☺ | E. Magdalena, San Clemente. (714) 492-1997 | Carts: | $
| 18 holes. Par 72/73. Yards: 7,008/5,355 | Rating: | 73.7/70.5
| Year-round. High: June–Aug. | Slope: | 131/116

R | **San Luis Rey Downs Country Club** | Greens: | $$–$$$ | T J
☺☺ | Bonsall. (619) 758-9699 | Carts: | Incl.
| 18 holes. Par 72/72. Yards: 6,750/5,493 | Rating: | 72.6/71.4
| Year-round. High: Jan.–May | Slope: | 128/124

SP | **San Vicente Golf Club** | Greens: | $$–$$$ | T
☺☺☺ | San Vicente Rd., Ramona. (619) 789-3477 | Carts: | Incl.
| 18 holes. Par 72/72. Yards: 6,610/5,543 | Rating: | 71.5/72.8
| Year-round. | Slope: | 123/128

R | **Singing Hills Country Club** | Greens: | $$ | W T J
| Dehesa Rd., El Cajon. (619) 442-3425 | Carts: | Inquire
☺☺☺ | *Oak Glen Course* | Rating: | 71.3/71.4
DEAL | 18 holes. Par 72/72. Yards: 6,597/5,549 | Slope: | 122/124
| Year-round.

☺☺☺ | *Willow Glen Course* | Rating: | 72.0/72.8
DEAL | 18 holes. Par 72/72. Yards: 6,605/5,585 | Slope: | 124/122

P | **Steele Canyon Golf Club** | Greens: | $$$–$$$$ | T S J
| Stonefield Dr., Jamul. (619) 441-6900 | Carts: | Incl.
☺☺☺ | *Canyon/Ranch/Meadow* | Rating: | 72.7/74.0/72.2
| 27 holes. Par 71/72/71. Yards: 6,741/7,001/6,672 | Slope: | 135/137/134
| Year-round. High: Dec.–May

R | **Temecula Creek Inn** | Greens: | $$–$$$ | W L R T J
| Rainbow Canyon Rd., Temecula. (909) 676-2405 | Carts: | Inquire

☺☺☺	*Creek/Oaks/Stonehouse* 27 holes. Par 72/72/72. Yards: 6,784/6,693/6,605 Year-round.	Rating: Slope:	72.6/72.6/71.8 125/130/123
P ☺☺☺ BEST	**Torrey Pines Golf Course** N. Torrey Pines Rd., La Jolla. (619) 452-3226 *North Course* 18 holes. Par 72/74. Yards: 6,647/6,118 Year-round.	Greens: Carts: Rating: Slope:	$$$–$$$$ $$ 72.1/75.4 129/134
☺☺☺☺ BEST	*South Course* 18 holes. Par 72/76. Yards: 7,055/6,457	Rating: Slope:	74.6/77.3 136/139
P ☺☺☺	**The Vineyard at Escondido** San Pasqual Rd., Escondido. (760) 735-9545 18 holes. Par 70/70. Yards: 6,531/5,073 Year-round.	Greens: Carts: Rating: Slope:	$$$–$$$$ W L T S J Incl. 70.3/70.3 125/117
SP ☺	**Whispering Palms Lodge and Country Club** Rancho Santa Fe. (619) 756-2471 *East/South/North* 27 holes. Par 71/72/71. Yards: 6,141/6,443/6,346 Year-round.	Greens: Carts: Rating: Slope:	$$–$$$ T $ 68.8/70.2/69.7 110/112/112

Colorado

Colorado contains luxurious and interesting Rocky Mountain resorts *and* plains with surprisingly green greens. Whichever you choose, remember to check the operating season—mountain resorts may be open only from May to October, while some flatland courses operate year-round. With a bit of luck it may be possible to combine a golf and ski vacation in the same trip.

Rocky Mountain Highs

When skiers leave, golfers arrive to populate the condos and hotels at the base of the mountains and play on the lush courses that have come out from beneath their winter white. Among the best of the mountain tracks is the **Breckenridge Golf Club** at the ski resort of the same name. The **Keystone Ranch Golf Course** at Keystone is a handsome mountain challenge set in a former cattle ranch 9,300 feet above sea level. **Pole Creek Golf Club** is a gem at the base of the ski area at Winter Park.

The well-maintained **Sonnenalp Golf Club** is in Edwards, just west of Vail. The lovely **Tamarron Resort** in Durango is set among cliffs and canyons and high mountain meadows.

East of the Mountains

Among the best in the eastern foothills are the 54 holes at the **Broadmoor Golf Club,** on the grounds of the famed hotel of the same name in Colorado Springs. The East Course was designed in 1918 by Donald Ross; the West Course came half a century later, courtesy of Robert Trent Jones, Sr. And in 1976, Arnold Palmer and Ed Seay added the South Course, the toughest of the trio.

Also highly regarded is the **Arrowhead Golf Club** in Littleton south of Denver, which has some of the most spectacular geologic formations you'll ever find on the grounds of a golf course. Just west of Denver are the 27 holes of the **Fox Hollow at Lakewood Golf Course**, which are among the state jewels.

About 10 miles north of Denver is the challenging Dunes Course at the **Riverdale Golf Club**. Some 15 miles south of Denver is the **Plum Creek Golf and Country Club**, a links-type course designed as a stadium course with room for visitors, wide-open fairways, and views of the Rockies above.

All the way south, 45 miles below Pueblo, is the **Grandote Golf and Country Club** in La Veta, a hidden treasure and a great deal.

Most high-mountain courses and resorts in Colorado are closed for the winter; high season is the summer, with midlevel rates in the spring and fall. Plateau courses, mostly to the east of the Rockies, may be open year-round, with high-season rates in the summer and deepest discounts in the winter.

The renowned Broadmoor Hotel is a grand Colorado Springs resort built in 1918. This is a world of Italian Renaissance formality, with grand lobbies and staircases and works of art. There are 700 rooms and suites in the five-star hotel.

The Broadmoor overlooks a trio of 18-hole championship courses, including one designed by Donald Ross and a second by Robert Trent Jones, Sr.

Golf packages, including a room and greens fees, can range from a high-season (May 1 to the end of September) price of about $275 per person for double occupancy to about $170 per person in the late fall. The lowest rates are in November near the closing of the season.

Golf U.S.A. Leader Board: Best Public Courses in Colorado

Rating	Course
⊙⊙⊙	Arrowhead Golf Club
⊙⊙⊙⊙	Breckenridge Golf Club
⊙⊙⊙⊙	Broadmoor Golf Club (East, West, South)
⊙⊙⊙	The Courses at Hyland Hills
⊙⊙⊙⊙	Fox Hollow at Lakewood Golf Course (Canyon, Meadow, Links)
⊙⊙⊙	Keystone Ranch Golf Course
⊙⊙⊙⊙	Legacy Ridge Golf Course
⊙⊙⊙	Plum Creek Golf and Country Club
⊙⊙⊙⊙	Pole Creek Golf Club
⊙⊙⊙⊙	Riverdale Golf Club (Dunes)
⊙⊙⊙⊙	Sonnenalp Golf Club
⊙⊙⊙⊙	Tamarron Resort

Golf U.S.A. Leader Board: Best Deals in Colorado

Rating	Course
$$/⊙⊙⊙	Battlement Mesa Golf Club
$/⊙⊙⊙	Boomerang Links
$$/⊙⊙⊙	Coal Creek Golf Course
$/⊙⊙⊙	The Courses at Hyland Hills (Hyland Hills Gold)
$$/⊙⊙⊙⊙	Dalton Ranch Golf Club
$$/⊙⊙⊙	Fairfield Pagosa Golf Club
$$/⊙⊙⊙	Highland Hills Golf Course
$$/⊙⊙⊙	Indian Peaks Golf Club

$$/☺☺☺☺	Legacy Ridge Golf Course	
$$/☺☺☺	Loveland Golf Club	
$$/☺☺☺☺	Mariana Butte Golf Course	
$$/☺☺☺	The Meadows Golf Club	
$$/☺☺☺	Pine Creek Golf Club	
$/☺☺☺	Pueblo West Golf Course	
$$/☺☺☺☺	Riverdale Golf Club (Dunes)	
$/☺☺☺☺	Walking Stick Golf Course	

Colorado Golf Guide

Grand Junction Area

P
☺☺
Adobe Creek National Golf Course
Fruita. (970) 858-0521
18 holes. Par 72/72. Yards: 6,997/4,980
May–Dec. High: May–Sept.

Greens: $–$$ W L T S J
Carts: $
Rating: 71.2/55.1
Slope: 119/97

Rocky Mountain Region

P
☺☺
Aspen Golf Course
E. Cooper, Aspen. (970) 925-2145
18 holes. Par 71/72. Yards: 7,165/5,591
Apr.–Oct. High: July–Sept.

Greens: $$–$$$ L S J
Carts: $
Rating: 72.2/69.9
Slope: 125/116

P
☺☺☺
DEAL
Battlement Mesa Golf Club
N. Battlement Pkwy., Parachute. (970) 285-7274
18 holes. Par 72/72. Yards: 7,309/5,386
Mar.–Nov. High: June–Aug.

Greens: $–$$ W L S J
Carts: $
Rating: 73.9/69.2
Slope: 132/116

R
☺☺☺
Beaver Creek Golf Club
Avon. (970) 845-5775
18 holes. Par 70/70. Yards: 6,752/5,200
May–Oct. High: May–June

Greens: $$$$$$ L R
Carts: Inquire
Rating: 69.2/70.2
Slope: 133/121

P
☺☺☺☺
STATE
Breckenridge Golf Club
Breckenridge. (970) 453-9104
18 holes. Par 72/72. Yards: 7,279/5,066
May–Oct. High: July–Sept.

Greens: $$$–$$$$ L T
Carts: $
Rating: 73.1/67.7
Slope: 146/118

SP
☺☺☺
The Club at Cordillera
Edwards. (970) 926-5100
18 holes. Par 72/72. Yards: 6,186/5,226
May–Oct.

Greens: $$$$$$++
Carts: Incl.
Rating: 68.0/68.6
Slope: 130/128

R
☺☺
Copper Mountain Resort
Copper Creek Golf Club
Wheeler Circle, Copper Mountain. (970) 968-2882
18 holes. Par 70/70. Yards: 6,094/4,374
June–Oct. High: July–Aug.

Greens: $$$–$$$$ L R T
Carts: Incl.
Rating: 67.7/63.8
Slope: 124/100

P
☺☺☺
Eagle Vail Golf Club
Eagle Dr., Avon. (970) 949-5267
18 holes. Par 72/72. Yards: 6,819/4,856
May–Oct. High: June–Sept.

Greens: $$$–$$$$ L T
Carts: Incl.
Rating: 70.9/67.3
Slope: 131/114

P
☺☺
Eagles Nest Golf Club
Golden Eagle Rd., Silverthorne. (970) 468-0681
18 holes. Par 72/72. Yards: 7,024/5,556
May–Oct. High: July–Sept.

Greens: $$–$$$$ W L T J
Carts: Incl.
Rating: 72.6/71.9
Slope: 141/126

P
☺☺
Estes Park Golf Course
S. Saint Vrain Ave., Estes Park. (970) 586-8146
18 holes. Par 71/72. Yards: 6,326/5,250
Apr.–Oct. High: June–Sept.

Greens: $$ L T
Carts: $
Rating: 68.3/68.3
Slope: 118/115

Colorado Golf Guide

P ☺☺☺	**Grand Lake Golf Course** County Rd. 48, Grand Lake. (970) 627-8008 18 holes. Par 72/74. Yards: 6,542/5,685 May–Oct. High: July–Aug.	Greens: Carts: Rating: Slope:	$$$ Inquire 70.5/70.9 131/123
R ☺☺☺ BEST	**Keystone Ranch Golf Course** Keystone. (970) 468-4250 18 holes. Par 72/72. Yards: 7,090/5,596 May–Oct. High: June–Sept.	Greens: Carts: Rating: Slope:	$$$$$-$$$$$$ L R T J Incl. 71.4/70.7 130/129
P ☺☺☺☺ BEST	**Pole Creek Golf Club** Winter Park. (970) 726-8847 18 holes. Par 72/72. Yards: 7,107/5,006 May–Oct. High: June–Sept.	Greens: Carts: Rating: Slope:	$$-$$$$ W L T J $ 72.9/69.9 139/119
SP ☺☺	**Rifle Creek Golf Course** St. Hwy. 325, Rifle. (970) 625-1093 18 holes. Par 72/72. Yards: 6,241/5,131 Mar.–Nov. High: June–Sept.	Greens: Carts: Rating: Slope:	$-$$ W S J $ 69.3/68.5 123/109
R ☺☺☺	**Sheraton Steamboat Resort** Steamboat Springs. (970) 879-1391 18 holes. Par 72/72. Yards: 6,902/5,536 May–Oct. High: June–Aug.	Greens: Carts: Rating: Slope:	$$$-$$$$$ L R T S $ 71.2/71.5 133/127
SP ☺☺☺☺	**Skyland Mountain Golf Course** Crested Butte. (970) 349-6131 18 holes. Par 72/72. Yards: 7,208/5,702 May–Oct. High: July–Aug.	Greens: Carts: Rating: Slope:	$$-$$$$ L R T Incl. 71.7/68.0 133/120
R ☺☺☺☺ BEST	**Sonnenalp Golf Club** Berry Creek Rd., Edwards. (970) 926-3533 18 holes. Par 71/71. Yards: 7,059/5,293 Apr.–Oct. High: June–Sept.	Greens: Carts: Rating: Slope:	$$$$-$$$$$$ WLRTJ Incl. 72.3/70.0 138/115
R ☺☺☺	**The Snowmass Club Golf Course** Snowmass Village. (970) 923-3148 18 holes. Par 71/71. Yards: 6,662/5,056 May–Oct. High: June–Sept.	Greens: Carts: Rating: Slope:	$$$-$$$$$ L R T J Incl. 71.5/67.5 134/127
P ☺☺☺	**Vail Golf Club** Vail Valley Dr., Vail. (970) 479-2260 18 holes. Par 77/72. Yards: 7,100/5,291 May–Oct. High: June–Sept.	Greens: Carts: Rating: Slope:	$$$-$$$$$ L Incl. 70.8/69.5 121/114

Denver Area

P ☺☺	**Applewood Golf Course** W. 32nd Ave., Golden. (303) 279-3003 18 holes. Par 72/72. Yards: 6,229/5,374 Year-round. High: Apr.–Oct.	Greens: Carts: Rating: Slope:	$-$$ W T S J $ 68.2/69.0 122/118
P ☺☺☺ BEST	**Arrowhead Golf Club** W. Sundown Trail, Littleton. (303) 973-9614 18 holes. Par 70/72. Yards: 6,682/5,465 Mar.–Nov. High: June–Sept.	Greens: Carts: Rating: Slope:	$$$-$$$$$ W L T S Incl. 70.9/70.0 134/123
P ☺☺☺ DEAL	**Coal Creek Golf Course** S. Lark Ave., Louisville. (303) 666-7888 18 holes. Par 72/72. Yards: 6,957/5,168 Year-round. High: Apr.–Sept.	Greens: Carts: Rating: Slope:	$-$$ W L T S J $ 71.1/68.4 130/114
P ☺☺	**Flatirons Golf Course** Arapahoe Rd., Boulder. (303) 442-7851 18 holes. Par 70/71. Yards: 6,765/5,615 Year-round. High: Mar.–Sept.	Greens: Carts: Rating: Slope:	$ $ 69.9/71.1 125/115

Colorado Golf Guide

P ☺☺	**Foothills Golf Course** S. Carr St., Denver. (303) 989-3901 18 holes. Par 72/74. Yards: 6,908/6,028 Year-round. High: Apr.–Oct.	Greens: $ Carts: $ Rating: 71.1/73.4 Slope: 122/118
P ☺☺☺☺ STATE	**Fox Hollow at Lakewood Golf Course** W. Morrison Rd., Lakewood. (303) 986-7888 *Canyon/Meadow/Links* 27 holes. Par 71/72/71. Yards: 6,806/6,888/7,030 Year-round. High: Apr.–Oct.	Greens: $$ S J Carts: $ Rating: 71.2/71.1/72.3 Slope: 138/132/134
P ☺☺☺ DEAL	**Indian Peaks Golf Club** Indian Peaks Trail, Lafayette. (303) 666-4706 18 holes. Par 72/72. Yards: 7,083/5,468 Year-round. High: May–Sept.	Greens: $$ Carts: $$ Rating: 72.5/69.9 Slope: 134/116
R ☺☺☺☺	**Inverness Golf Course** Englewood. (303) 799-9660 18 holes. Par 70/70. Yards: 6,948/6,407 Year-round. High: June–Aug.	Greens: $$$$ T Carts: Incl. Rating: 70.6 Slope: 136/129
P ☺☺	**John F. Kennedy Golf Club** E. Hampden Ave., Aurora. (303) 755-0105 27 holes. Par 71/71/72. Yards: 6,868/6,753/7,009 Year-round. High: Apr.–Sept.	Greens: $ S J Carts: $$ Rating: 71.6/70.9/71.7 Slope: 131/125/118
SP ☺☺	**Lake Valley Golf Club** Lake Valley Dr., Longmont. (303) 444-2114 18 holes. Par 70/720. Yards: 6,725/5,713 Year-round. High: Apr.–Aug.	Greens: $$ W T S J Carts: $ Rating: 69.6/71.8 Slope: 121/119
P ☺☺☺☺ DEAL STATE	**Legacy Ridge Golf Course** Westminster. (303) 438-8997 18 holes. Par 72/72. Yards: 7,251/5,383 Year-round. High: Apr.–Oct.	Greens: $$ W S J Carts: $ Rating: 74.0/70.6 Slope: 134/122
P ☺☺	**Lone Tree Golf Club** Sunningdale Blvd., Littleton. (303) 799-9940 18 holes. Par 72/72. Yards: 7,012/5,340 Year-round. High: Apr.–Oct.	Greens: $$–$$$ S Carts: $ Rating: 72.1/70.6 Slope: 127/120
P ☺☺☺	**Meadow Hills Golf Course** S. Dawson St., Aurora. (303) 690-2500 18 holes. Par 70/72. Yards: 6,717/5,481 Year-round. High: May–Sept.	Greens: $–$$ W T S J Carts: $ Rating: 70.9/70.5 Slope: 133/117
P ☺	**Park Hill Golf Club** E. 35th Ave., Denver. (303) 333-5411 18 holes. Par 71/72. Yards: 6,585/5,811 Year-round. High: May–Aug.	Greens: $–$$ Carts: $$ Rating: 69.4/73.4 Slope: 120/124
SP ☺☺☺ STATE	**Plum Creek Golf and Country Club** Castle Rock. (303) 688-2611 18 holes. Par 72/72. Yards: 6,700/4,875 Year-round. High: June–Sept.	Greens: $$$$–$$$$$ W L T Carts: Incl. Rating: 70.1/68.3 Slope: 131/118
P ☺☺☺☺ BEST DEAL	**Riverdale Golf Club** Riverdale Rd., Brighton. (303) 659-6700 *Dunes Course* 18 holes. Par 72/72. Yards: 7,030/4,903 Year-round. High: May–Sept.	Greens: $-$$ Carts: $$ Rating: 72.1/67.5 Slope: 129/109
☺☺	*Knolls Course* 18 holes. Par 71/73. Yards: 6,756/5,931	Rating: 70.2/72.2 Slope: 118/117

Colorado Golf Guide

P	**The Courses at Hyland Hills**	Greens: $-$$
	Westminster. (303) 428-6526	Carts: $$
☺☺☺	*Hyland Hills Gold Course*	Rating: 71.9/71.9
BEST	18 holes. Par 72/73. Yards: 7,021/5,654	Slope: 132/120
DEAL	Year-round. High: June–Aug.	

P	**The Meadows Golf Club**	Greens: $-$$ L S J
☺☺☺	S. Simms, Littleton. (303) 972-8831	Carts: $$
DEAL	18 holes. Par 72/72. Yards: 6,995/5,416	Rating: 71.6/71.1
	Year-round. High: May–Sept.	Slope: 130/123

P	**Thorncreek Golf Club**	Greens: $$ T S J
☺☺	N. Washington St., Thornton. (303) 450-7055	Carts: $
	18 holes. Par 72/72. Yards: 7,268/5,547	Rating: 73.7/70.5
	Year-round. High: May–Sept.	Slope: 136/120

P	**Wellshire Golf Course**	Greens: $-$$ W S J
☺☺	S. Colorado Blvd., Denver. (303) 757-1352	Carts: $$
	18 holes. Par 71/73. Yards: 6,608/5,890	Rating: 70.1/69.3
	Year-round. High: Apr.–Sept.	Slope: 124/121

P	**West Woods Golf Club**	Greens: $$ J
☺☺	Quaker St., Arvada. (303) 424-3334	Carts: $
	18 holes. Par 72/72. Yards: 7,035/5,197	Rating: 72.1/69.5
	Year-round. High: Apr.–Aug.	Slope: 135/112

Fort Collins Area

P	**Boomerang Links**	Greens: $ W L T S J
☺☺☺	W. 4th St., Greeley. (303) 351-8934	Carts: $
DEAL	18 holes. Par 72/72. Yards: 7,214/5,285	Rating: 72.6/68.5
	Year-round. High: June–Sept.	Slope: 131/113

P	**Collindale Golf Club**	Greens: $ W L T S J
☺☺	E. Horsetooth Rd., Fort Collins. (970) 221-6651	Carts: $
	18 holes. Par 71/73. Yards: 7,011/5,472	Rating: 71.5/69.9
	Year-round. High: May–Sept.	Slope: 126/113

P	**Fort Morgan Golf Course**	Greens: $ W
☺☺	Colorado Rd., Fort Morgan. (970) 867-5990	Carts: Inquire
	18 holes. Par 73/74. Yards: 6,470/5,615	Rating: 69.7/70.1
	Year-round. High: Apr.–Oct.	Slope: 117/113

P	**Highland Hills Golf Course**	Greens: $-$$ W L T S J
☺☺☺	Greeley. (970) 330-7327	Carts: Inquire
DEAL	18 holes. Par 71/75. Yards: 6,723/6,459	Rating: 71.4/70.2
	Year-round. High: May–Oct.	Slope: 128/126

P	**Loveland Golf Club**	Greens: $ W T J
☺☺☺	W. 29th St., Loveland. (970) 667-5256	Carts: Inquire
DEAL	18 holes. Par 72/71. Yards: 6,827/5,498	Rating: 70.9/70.6
	Year-round. High: May–Sept.	Slope: 125/124

P	**Mariana Butte Golf Course**	Greens: $-$$ W L T
☺☺☺☺	Loveland. (970) 667-8308	Carts: $
DEAL	18 holes. Par 72/72. Yards: 6,572/5,420	Rating: 70.6/70.2
	Year-round. High: May–Sept.	Slope: 130/121

SP	**Ptarmigan Country Club**	Greens: $$-$$$ W L T S J
☺☺☺	Vardon Way, Fort Collins. (970) 226-6600	Carts: $$
	18 holes. Par 72/72. Yards: 7,201/5,327	Rating: 73.0/69.0
	Year-round. High: May–Sept.	Slope: 135/116

P	**Southridge Golf Club**	Greens: $ W L T S J
☺☺	S. Lemay Ave., Fort Collins, (970) 226-2828	Carts: $

Colorado Golf Guide

	18 holes. Par 71/71. Yards: 6,363/5,508	Rating:	69.1/69.3
	Year-round. High: Apr.–Sept.	Slope:	122/118

Colorado Springs Area

P
☺☺
Appletree Golf Course
Rolling Ridge Rd., Colorado Springs. (719) 382-3649
18 holes. Par 72/72. Yards: 6,407/5,003
Year-round. High: May–Sept.

Greens: $–$$ W L S J
Carts: $$
Rating: 68.6/66.9
Slope: 122/113

R

☺☺☺☺
BEST
Broadmoor Golf Club
Pourtales Dr., Colorado Springs. (719) 577-5790
East Course
18 holes. Par 72/73. Yards: 7,091/5,873
Year-round. High: Apr.–Oct.

Greens: $$$$$
Carts: $
Rating: 73.0/74.1
Slope: 129/126

☺☺☺
STATE
South Course
18 holes. Par 72/72. Yards: 6,781/4,834

Rating: 72.1/68.4
Slope: 135/117

☺☺☺☺
BEST
West Course
18 holes. Par 72/72. Yards: 6,937/5,505

Rating: 73.0/71.6
Slope: 133/122

P
☺☺☺
DEAL
Pine Creek Golf Club
Colorado Springs. (719) 594-9999
18 holes. Par 72/72. Yards: 7,194/5,314
Year-round. High: Apr.–Oct.

Greens: $$ W L T S J
Carts: $$
Rating: 72.6/70.2
Slope: 139/122

P
☺☺☺
DEAL
Pueblo West Golf Course
S. McCulloch Blvd., Pueblo West. (719) 547-2280
18 holes. Par 72/72. Yards: 7,368/5,688
Year-round. High: Apr.–Sept.

Greens: $ W S J
Carts: $
Rating: 73.3/71.4
Slope: 125/117

P
☺☺☺☺
DEAL
Walking Stick Golf Course
Pueblo. (719) 584-3400
18 holes. Par 72/72. Yards: 7,147/5,181
Year-round. High: May–Sept.

Greens: $ W T
Carts: $
Rating: 72.6/69.0
Slope: 130/114

Southern Colorado

SP
☺☺☺☺
DEAL
Dalton Ranch Golf Club
Rte. 252, Durango. (970) 247-8774
18 holes. Par 72/72. Yards: 6,934/5,539
Apr.–Nov. High: June–Sept.

Greens: $$ L R T
Carts: $
Rating: 72.4/71.7
Slope: 135/127

R

☺☺☺
DEAL
Pagosa Springs Golf Club
Pines Club Place, Pagosa Springs. (970) 731-4755
Pinon/Ponderosa/Meadows
27 holes. Par 71/72/71. Yards: 6,677/7,228/6,913
Apr.–Oct. High: July–Aug.

Greens: $–$$ L T J
Carts: $
Rating: 69.4/72.9/70.9
Slope: 119/125/123

R
☺☺☺☺
Grandote Golf and Country Club
Hwy. 12, La Veta. (719) 742-3390
18 holes. Par 72/72. Yards: 7,085/5,608
Apr.–Oct. High: July–Sept.

Greens: $$–$$$ W L
Carts: $$
Rating: 72.8/70.7
Slope: 133/117

R
☺☺☺
Great Sand Dunes Country Club
Hwy. 150, Mosca. (719) 378-2357
18 holes. Par 72/72. Yards: 7,006/5,327
May–Oct. High: July–Sept.

Greens: $$$$
Carts: Inquire
Rating: 71.2/67.8
Slope: 126/118

SP
☺☺
Hillcrest Golf Club
Rim Dr., Durango. (970) 247-1499
18 holes. Par 71/71. Yards: 6,838/5,252
Mar.–Nov. High: June–Aug.

Greens: $ T
Carts: $
Rating: 71.3/68.1
Slope: 127/111

R

☺☺☺☺
STATE
Tamarron Resort
Durango. (970) 259-2000
The Cliffs
18 holes. Par 72/72. Yards: 6,885/5,330
May–Nov. High: June–Sept.

Greens: $$$$–$$$$$ L R T S J
Carts: Incl.
Rating: 73.0/71.9
Slope: 142/126

Hawaii

The Hawaiian Islands boast some of the lushest and priciest golf resorts anywhere; they also have more than their share of hidden bargains. Hawaii has two glorious seasons: summer and almost-summer.

Hawaii

The Big Island of Hawaii is larger than all of the other islands in the chain combined, and six times larger than the most populous island of Oahu, but the core of this island is mostly empty. Part of the reason lies in the landscape, which features the active Kilauea Crater, the Mauna Loa volcano, and Mauna Kea peak. The mountains in the center split the island into two miniclimates. The wet and windy side is east, including the major city of Hilo; on the west side the weather is generally better, and it is there that most of the golf resorts are clustered.

The famed **Mauna Kea Beach Golf Course** in Kamuela is sure not to disappoint, with spectacular ocean views and a memorable No. 3 that belongs in any collection of golfing memories—a 200-yard carry over an ocean bay. There are also more than 100 sand traps. The Robert Trent Jones design that sprawls across the lava flows is at the Mauna Kea Beach Hotel, one of the Rockefeller Resorts.

The **Mauna Lani Resort** in Kohala Coast has two first-class challenges that mix black lava flows, ultragreen fairways, and deep blue water. The transcendent South Course is nearly matched by the nearby North holes.

The Kings' Golf Course at the **Waikoloa Beach Resort** in Kamuela is considered by some to be the best on the island. The course is literally carved out of lava flows from the Mauna Kea volcano; it offers links-style challenges where the ocean breezes come into play on most holes.

If your golf game alone is not thrill enough, consider playing a round at the **Volcano Golf and Country Club**, set at the base of still-active Mauna Loa.

Things to do—besides golf, that is—include visiting Hawaii Volcanoes National Park on the east side of Mauna Loa.

Kauai

Kauai is the most unspoiled of the major Hawaiian Islands, although the pace of development has picked up in recent years. There are a double handful or so of first-class golf resorts on Kauai, all about as good as they come. And the pace of life on Kauai is more relaxed than on the bigger and more tourist-bound islands.

The Kiele Course at **Kauai Lagoons Resort** is considered a picturesque, difficult challenge. Another well-thought-of course on the island is the **Poipu Bay Resort Golf Club** in Koloa, where the windy back nine lies along the ocean.

Among the most famous resorts on Kauai is the Princeville Resort, home of the top-rated **Princeville Makai** golf club's three courses. The Ocean and Lakes courses are considered the best here.

Nearby is **The Prince Golf Club**, one of the best resort courses in Hawaii and the nation. Its emphasis is on the varied natural attractions and obstacles of the area, including waterfalls, ravines, and unusual trees and plants. The Prince Course has five tee boxes for most holes, with the back pair restricted to players with handicaps in the single digits. Whichever box you shoot from, unless you are a touring pro or a scratch amateur you can probably expect to enjoy the course more for the challenge and the scenery than for the score on your souvenir card. One of the signature holes at The Prince is No. 12, the par-4 Eagle's Nest. The tee perches 100 feet above a narrow fairway lined by a dense jungle. The Anini Stream comes into play on all sides of the fern-green backdrop on the second shot.

Sights include the spectacular Waimea Canyon in the western portion, and Kawaikini peak on Mount Waialeale in the center of the island. One of the rainiest places on earth, it receives an average of more than 450 inches of rain each year. By contrast, the southern coast is very dry year-round, and the northern coast, including the Princeville Resort, has a more moderate climate. The lovely Lumahai Beach and Hanalei Bay in the north look little different from when they were used in the filming of *South Pacific* in 1957, or for thousands of years before that, for that matter.

Lanai

Lanai is one of the smallest of the Hawaiian Islands, a privately owned pineapple plantation with just a few thousand residents. Although the island lies just off the northern end of Maui, it is nevertheless a relatively untouched paradise.

A jewel of the isles is **The Challenge at Manele** in Lanai City, with fairways set between lava fields and the ocean.

For an even more impressive setting, there is **The Experience at Koele**, also in Lanai City. The experience begins 500 feet above the elegant lodge, and the front nine is mostly downhill from there into tropical canyons; the back nine is more open, including an island green on the 17th hole.

Maui

The second-largest island was created by two volcanoes, Haleakala on the larger eastern portion and Puu Kukui and the West Maui range at the other end.

A minimall of great golf can be found at the **Kapalua Golf Club**, a resort with no fewer than three top-rated courses. The best of the best is the Plantation Course, a long and wide challenge along the ocean with fairways in the middle of pineapple fields. How long and wide? The famed No. 18 stretches 663 yards, but it runs downhill and usually downwind, making the return home a reasonable par 5 for most players. Next in line is the Village Course with mountain views and uphill shots into the wind; the third jewel is the Bay Course. The beach at Kapalua, by the way, is regularly listed on charts of the world's best strands.

Two more gems can be found at the **Makena Resort Golf Course** in Kihei, where the North and South courses each are on the best-of-state list. The North features views of Haleakala Crater, with most of the natural obstacles of the area (including rock walls, gullies, and lava) left intact. The South Course includes views way out to sea from the 15th and 16th holes.

The Gold Course at **Wailea Golf Club** in Wailea has two kinds of traps: an abundance of sand and some spectacular views including the Mount Haleakala Crater.

Molokai

The rugged island of Molokai features the lovely and relatively uncrowded **Kalu-**

akoi Golf Course on the western coast. Kaluakoi is a rolling course that takes golfers through the woods and along Kepuhi Beach.

Oahu

Oahu is the center of the Hawaiian tourist scene, including Honolulu and Waikiki Beach; it is the most populous of the islands, with more than 80 percent of the state's population. It also has nearly half of the 70 or so golf courses in the state. Many of those courses are private or limited to military personnel and families.

Near the top of any list of courses in Hawaii is the **Koolau Golf Course** in Kaneohea, a very long, very tough public course—in fact it has some of the most difficult ratings in the nation.

A newer rising star, already considered one of the best resorts in the nation, is **Ko Olina** on Oahu's west coast. There is a lot of water on the course, from placid ponds to tumbling waterfalls; the fairways are alive with native plants, and it is all set against the foreboding silhouette of the local volcano range. The resort itself, developed by a Japanese company, has plans for major expansion in coming years for half a dozen luxury hotels, a marina, and more.

Some of the many other appeals of Oahu include the famed Waikiki Beach, Manoa Falls, and the museums and memorials of Pearl Harbor.

As befits a collection of island paradises, golf courses and resorts on Hawaii operate year-round, with little variation in climate except for rainy periods. Variations in rates are more related to the times of year when visitors from distant places crowd the courses and beaches. Expect peak prices in the winter months; some courses also have peak prices in the heart of the summer.

In general, the hottest months of the year are August and September, with temperature readings commonly reaching the 90s; the relatively coolest time is December through February, with lows all the way down to the low 60s. Of more importance for some visitors are the rainy periods, which coincide with the cool period on most of the islands; some places, including Kauai and its famed Princeville Resort, are very rainy all year-round, while the Kohala Coast on the Big Island receives little annual rain.

Golf U.S.A. Leader Board: Best Public Courses in Hawaii

Hawaii, the Big Island
ⓞⓞⓞⓞ Makalei Hawaii Country Club
ⓞⓞⓞⓞ Mauna Kea Beach Golf Course
ⓞⓞⓞⓞ Mauna Lani Resort (South)
ⓞⓞⓞ Waikoloa Beach Resort (Kings)

Kauai
ⓞⓞⓞⓞ Kauai Lagoons Resort (Kiele)
ⓞⓞⓞ Poipu Bay Resort Golf Club
ⓞⓞⓞⓞ The Prince Golf Club
ⓞⓞⓞⓞ Princeville Makai (Ocean, Lakes, Woods)
ⓞⓞⓞ Wailua Golf Course

Lanai
ⓞⓞⓞⓞ The Challenge at Manele
ⓞⓞⓞ The Experience at Koele

Maui
◎◎◎◎   Kapalua Golf Club (Bay, Plantation, Village)
◎◎◎◎   Makena Resort Golf Course (North, South)
◎◎◎   Wailea Golf Club (Blue, Gold)
Molokai
◎◎◎   Kaluakoi Golf Course
Oahu
◎◎◎   Ko Olina Golf Club
◎◎◎   Koolau Golf Course

Golf U.S.A. Leader Board: Best Deals in Hawaii

$$/◎◎	Olomana Golf Links (Oahu)
$$/◎◎◎	Pali Municipal Golf Course (Oahu)
$$/◎◎	Seamountain Golf Course (Hawaii)
$$/◎◎◎	Wailua Golf Course (Kauai)
$/◎◎◎	West Loch Golf Course (Oahu)

Hawaii Golf Guide

Hawaii, the Big Island

R ◎◎◎	**Hapuna Golf Course** Kauna'oa Dr., Kamuela. (808) 880-3000 18 holes. Par 72/72. Yards: 6,875/5,067 Year-round. High: Nov.–Apr.	Greens: $$$$$ R J Carts: Inquire Rating: 72.5/68.9 Slope: 134/117
P ◎◎◎	**Kona Surf Resort and Country Club** Alii Dr., Kailua-Kona. (808) 322-2595 *Mountain Course* 18 holes. Par 72/72. Yards: 6,471/4,906 Year-round. High: Jan.–Mar.	Greens: $$$$–$$$$$$ T Carts: Incl. Rating: 71.5/69.2 Slope: 133/125
◎◎◎	*Ocean Course* 18 holes. Par 72/73. Yards: 6,579/5,499	Rating: 71.6/71.9 Slope: 129/127
SP ◎◎◎◎ STATE	**Makalei Hawaii Country Club** Hawaii Belt Rd., Kailua-Kona. (808) 325-6625 18 holes. Par 72/72. Yards: 7,091/5,242 Year-round. High: Dec.–Mar.	Greens: $$$$$$ R T Carts: Incl. Rating: 73.5/64.9 Slope: 143/125
R ◎◎◎◎ BEST	**Mauna Kea Beach Golf Course** Mauna Kea Beach Dr., Kamuela. (808) 880-3480 18 holes. Par 72/72. Yards: 7,114/5,277 Year-round. High: Nov.–Apr.	Greens: $$$$$–$$$$$$ R Carts: Incl. Rating: 73.6/69.4 Slope: 133/129
R ◎◎◎◎	**Mauna Lani Resort** Kohala Coast. (808) 885-6655 *North Course* 18 holes. Par 72/72. Yards: 6,913/5,383 Year-round. High: Nov.–Apr.	Greens: $$$$$–$$$$$$ L T Carts: Incl. Rating: 73.2/70.6 Slope: 136/120
◎◎◎◎ STATE	*South Course* 18 holes. Par 72/72. Yards: 6,938/5,128	Rating: 72.8/69.6 Slope: 133/117
R ◎◎ DEAL	**Seamountain Golf Course** Punaluu. (808) 928-6222 18 holes. Par 72/72. Yards: 6,416/5,590 Year-round. High: Jan.–Feb.	Greens: $$–$$$ R J Carts: Incl. Rating: 71.1/70.9 Slope: 129/116
P ◎◎	**Volcano Golf and Country Club** Volcano National Park. (808) 967-7331	Greens: $$$ Carts: Incl.

Hawaii Golf Guide

	18 holes. Par 72/72. Yards: 6,547/5,567	Rating:	70.8/70.7
	Year-round. High: July–Sept.	Slope:	128/117

R	**Waikoloa Beach Resort**	Greens:	$$$$$	R T
☺☺☺	Kamuela. (808) 885-6060	Carts:	Incl.	
	Beach Golf Course	Rating:	71.5/69.4	
	18 holes. Par 70/70. Yards: 6,566/5,094	Slope:	133/119	
	Year-round. High: Dec.–Mar.			

☺☺☺	*Kings Golf Course.* (808) 885-4647	Rating:	73.9/71.0
BEST	18 holes. Par 72/72. Yards: 7,074/5,459	Slope:	133/121

R	**Waikoloa Village Golf Club**	Greens:	$$$–$$$$ T J
☺☺☺	68-1792 Melia St., Waikoloa. (808) 883-9621	Carts:	Incl.
	18 holes. Par 72/72. Yards: 6,791/5,479	Rating:	71.8/72.1
	Year-round. High: Dec.–Feb.	Slope:	132/119

Kauai

R	**Kauai Lagoons Resort**	Greens:	$$$$$$++ R
	Hoolaulea Way, Lihue. (808) 241-6000	Carts:	Incl.
☺☺☺☺	*Kiele Course*	Rating:	73.7/66.5
BEST	18 holes. Par 72/72. Yards: 7,070/5,417	Slope:	137/123
	Year-round. High: Jan.–Mar., Aug.		

	Lagoons Course	Greens:	$$$$$$ R
☺☺☺	18 holes. Par 72/72. Yards: 6,960/5,607	Carts:	Incl.
		Rating:	73.1/71.8
		Slope:	127/116

R	**Kiahuna Golf Club**	Greens:	$$$$ R T
☺☺	Kiahuna Plantation Dr., Poipu. (808) 742-9595	Carts:	Incl.
	18 holes. Par 70/70. Yards: 6,353/5,631	Rating:	69.7/71.4
	Year-round. High: Nov.–Mar.	Slope:	128/119

R	**Poipu Bay Resort Golf Club**	Greens:	$$$$$–$$$$$$+ RTJ
☺☺☺	Ainako St., Koloa. (808) 742-8711	Carts:	Incl.
STATE	18 holes. Par 72/72. Yards: 6,959/5,241	Rating:	73.4/70.9
	Year-round. High: Jan.–May	Slope:	132/121

R	**The Prince Golf Club**	Greens:	$$$$$$++ R J
☺☺☺☺	Kuhio Hwy., Princeville. (808) 826-5000	Carts:	Incl.
BEST	18 holes. Par 72/72. Yards: 7,309/5,338	Rating:	75.3/72.0
	Year-round.	Slope:	145/127

R	**Princeville Makai**	Greens:	$$$$–$$$$$$ L R T J
	Lei O Papa Rd., Princeville. (808) 826-3580	Carts:	Incl.
☺☺☺☺	*Ocean/Lakes/Woods*	Rating:	73.0/72.6/72.4
BEST	27 holes. Par 72/72/72. Yards: 6,875/6,886/6,901	Slope:	134/132/133
	Year-round. High: Nov.–Mar.		

P	**Wailua Golf Course**	Greens:	$–$$ T S
☺☺☺	Kuhio Hwy., Lihue. (808) 241-6666	Carts:	$
BEST	18 holes. Par 72/72. Yards: 6,585/5,974	Rating:	71.9/73.1
DEAL	Year-round. High: Jan.–Apr.	Slope:	125/122

Lanai

R	**The Challenge at Manele**	Greens:	$$$$$$ R
☺☺☺☺	Lanai City. (808) 565-2222	Carts:	Incl.
STATE	18 holes. Par 72/72. Yards: 7,039/5,024	Rating:	73.3/68.8
	Year-round. High: Nov.–Feb.	Slope:	132/119

R	**The Experience at Koele**	Greens:	$$$$$$+++ J R
☺☺☺	Lanai Ave., Lanai City. (808) 565-4653	Carts:	Incl.
STATE	18 holes. Par 72/72. Yards: 7,014/5,425	Rating:	73.3/66.0
	Year-round. High: Dec.–May	Slope:	141/123

Hawaii Golf Guide

Maui

R ☺☺☺	**Kaanapali Golf Course** Kaanapali Resort, Lahaina. (808) 661-3691 *South Course* 18 holes. Par 71/71. Yards: 6,555/5,485 Year-round. High: Dec.–Apr.	Greens: $$$$$$ L R T Carts: Incl. Rating: 70.7/69.8 Slope: 127/120
☺☺☺	*North Course* 18 holes. Par 71/72. Yards: 6,994/5,417	Rating: 72.8/71.1 Slope: 134/123
R ☺☺☺☺ BEST	**Kapalua Golf Club** Kapalua Dr., Kapalua. *The Bay Course.* (808) 669-8820 18 holes. Par 72/72. Yards: 6,600/5,124 Year-round. High: Dec.–Mar.	Greens: $$$$$$ R T J Carts: Incl. Rating: 71.7/69.6 Slope: 138/121
☺☺☺☺ BEST	*The Plantation Course.* (808) 669-8877 18 holes. Par 73/75. Yards: 7,263/5,627	Rating: 75.2/73.2 Slope: 142/129
☺☺☺ BEST	*The Village Course.* (808) 669-8835 18 holes. Par 71/71. Yards: 6,632/5,134	Rating: 73.3/70.9 Slope: 139/12
R ☺☺☺☺ STATE	**Makena Resort Golf Course** Makena Alanui, Kihei. (808) 879-3344 *North Course* 18 holes. Par 72/72. Yards: 6,914/5,303 Year-round. High: Dec.–Apr., Aug., Oct.	Greens: $$$$$$ R T J Carts: Incl. Rating: 72.1/70.9 Slope: 139/128
☺☺☺☺ STATE	*South Course* 18 holes. Par 72/72. Yards: 7,017/5,529	Rating: 72.6/71.1 Slope: 138/130
P ☺☺	**Pukalani Country Club** Pukalani St., Pukalani. (808) 572-1314 18 holes. Par 72/74. Yards: 6,494/5,612 Year-round. High: Jan.–Mar.	Greens: $$$–$$$$ L T Carts: Incl. Rating: 70.6/71.6 Slope: 121/119
P ☺☺☺	**Sandalwood Golf Course** Honoapiilani Hwy., Wailuku. (808) 242-4653 18 holes. Par 72/72. Yards: 6,469/5,162 Year-round. High: Jan.–Apr.	Greens: $$$ R Carts: Incl. Rating: 71.2/67.8 Slope: 129/119
P ☺☺	**Silversword Golf Club** Piilani Hwy., Kiehi. (808) 874-0777 18 holes. Par 71/71. Yards: 6,801/5,265 Year-round. High: Jan.–Mar.	Greens: $$$–$$$$ L T Carts: Incl. Rating: 72.0/70.0 Slope: 124/118
P ☺☺	**Waiehu Golf Course** Wailuku. (808) 244-5934 18 holes. Par 72/73. Yards: 6,330/5,511 Year-round. High: Nov.–Mar.	Greens: $$ Carts: $ Rating: 69.8/70.6 Slope: 111/115
R ☺☺☺ BEST	**Wailea Golf Club** Kaukahi St., Wailea. (808) 875-5111 *Blue Course* 18 holes. Par 72/72. Yards: 6,758/5,291 Year-round. High: Dec.–Apr.	Greens: $$$$$$ R Carts: Incl. Rating: 71.6/72.0 Slope: 130/117
☺☺	*Emerald Course* 18 holes. Par 72/72. Yards: 6,825/5,454	Rating: NA Slope: 134
☺☺☺ STATE	*Gold Course* 18 holes. Par 72/72. Yards: 7,070/5,317	Rating: 73.0/70.3 Slope: 139/121

Molokai

R ☺☺☺	**Kaluakoi Golf Course** Maunaloa. (808) 552-2739	Greens: $$$$ L R Carts: Incl.

Hawaii Golf Guide

| STATE | 18 holes. Par 72/72. Yards: 6,564/5,461
Year-round. High: Dec.–Mar. | Rating:
Slope: | 72.3/73.0
129/126 |

Oahu

R ☺☺☺ BEST	**Ko Olina Golf Club** Aliinui Dr., Kapolei. (808) 676-5300 18 holes. Par 72/72. Yards: 6,867/5,361 Year-round. High: Dec.–Feb.	Greens: Carts: Rating: Slope:	$$$$$–$$$$$$ R T Incl. 72.8/71.3 137/125
P ☺☺☺ BEST	**Koolau Golf Course** Kionaole, Kaneohe. (808) 236-4653 18 holes. Par 72/72. Yards: 7,310/5,119 Year-round.	Greens: Carts: Rating: Slope:	$$$$$–$$$$$$ L T Incl. 76.5/72.9 155/134
P ☺☺☺	**Makaha Valley Country Club** Makaha Valley Rd., Waianae. (808) 695-7111 18 holes. Par 71/71. Yards: 6,369/5,720 Year-round. High: Dec.–Mar.	Greens: Carts: Rating: Slope:	$$$–$$$$$ W L Incl. 69.2/72.7 133/120
SP ☺☺ DEAL	**Olomana Golf Links** Kalanianaole Hwy., Waimanalo. (808) 259-7926 18 holes. Par 72/73. Yards: 6,326/5,456 Year-round. High: July–Aug.	Greens: Carts: Rating: Slope:	$$-$$$ W T S Incl. 70.3/72.4 129/128
P ☺☺☺ DEAL	**Pali Municipal Golf Course** Kamehameha Hwy., Kaneohe. (808) 266-7612 18 holes. Par 72/74. Yards: 6,493/6,080 Year-round. High: June–Aug.	Greens: Carts: Rating: Slope:	$$ S J $ 78.8/70.4 126/127
P ☺☺☺	**Pearl Country Club** Kaonohi St., Aiea. (808) 487-3802 18 holes. Par 72/72. Yards: 6,787/5,536 Year-round.	Greens: Carts: Rating: Slope:	$$$$$ T Incl. 72.0/72.1 135/130
P ☺☺☺	**Sheraton Makaha Resort and Country Club** Makaha Valley Rd., Waianae. (808) 695-9544 18 holes. Par 72/72. Yards: 7,077/5,856 Year-round. High: Jan.–Mar.	Greens: Carts: Rating: Slope:	$$$$$–$$$$$$ WT Incl. 73.2/73.9 139/129
R ☺☺☺	**Turtle Bay Hilton Golf and Tennis Resort** Kamehameha Hwy., Kahuku. (808) 293-8574 *The Links at Kuilima* 18 holes. Par 72/72. Yards: 7,199/4,851 Year-round. High: Dec.–Mar.	Greens: Carts: Rating: Slope:	$$$$–$$$$$$+ R Incl. 75.0/64.3 141/121
SP ☺☺☺	**Waikele Golf Club** Paioa Place, Waipahu. (808) 676-9000 18 holes. Par 72/72. Yards: 6,663/5,226 Year-round. High: Jan.–Feb.	Greens: Carts: Rating: Slope:	$$$$$–$$$$$$ W T Incl. 71.7/65.6 126/113
P ☺☺☺ DEAL	**West Loch Golf Course** Okupe St., Ewa Beach. (808) 671-2292 18 holes. Par 72/72. Yards: 6,479/5,296 Year-round.	Greens: Carts: Rating: Slope:	$$$ S J Incl. 70.3/68.6 123/117

Idaho

The **Coeur d'Alene Resort Golf Course** reminds you of one of its most distinct features with its address, 900 Floating Green Drive. The famed 14th hole ends on a green built on a floating pontoon about 75 yards into Lake Coeur d'Alene and reachable only by boat; you've got two tries to land on the green before you must drop a ball on board. You'll find the best deals on lodging in the spring or fall.

Equally famous around the nation is the **Sun Valley Resort Golf Course** on the grounds of the well-known ski resort.

Most courses in Idaho operate from about March through October or November; expect peak rates to be in effect from spring through the end of summer.

Golf U.S.A. Leader Board: Best Public Courses in Idaho

ⓞⓞⓞⓞ   Coeur d'Alene Resort Golf Course
ⓞⓞⓞⓞ   Sun Valley Resort Golf Course

Golf U.S.A. Leader Board: Best Deals in Idaho

$$/ⓞⓞⓞ	Avondale Golf Club
$/ⓞⓞⓞ	Blackfoot Municipal Golf Course
$$/ⓞⓞⓞ	The Highlands Golf and Country Club
$/ⓞⓞⓞ	Pinecrest Municipal Golf Course
$/ⓞⓞⓞ	Quail Hollow Golf Club

Idaho Golf Guide

Coeur d'Alene Area

SP ⓞⓞⓞ DEAL	**Avondale Golf Club** Avondale Loop Rd., Hayden Lake. (208) 772-5963 18 holes. Par 72/74. Yards: 6,573/5,357 Mar.–Oct. High: June–Aug.	Greens: Carts: Rating: Slope:	$$ L T J $$ 71.8/70.9 124/123
R ⓞⓞⓞⓞ BEST	**Coeur d'Alene Resort Golf Course** Floating Green Dr., Coeur d'Alene. (208) 667-4653 18 holes. Par 71/71. Yards: 6,309/5,428 Apr.–Oct. High: June–Sept.	Greens: Carts: Rating: Slope:	$$$$$$+ L R Incl. 69.6/70.3 121/118
P ⓞⓞⓞ DEAL	**The Highlands Golf and Country Club** Inverness Dr., Post Falls. (208) 773-3673 18 holes. Par 72/73. Yards: 6,369/5,115 Mar.–Oct. High: June–Aug.	Greens: Carts: Rating: Slope:	$$ W L S J $$ 70.7/69.5 125/121
R ⓞⓞ	**Stoneridge Golf Club** Blanchard Rd., Blanchard. (208) 437-4682 18 holes. Par 72/72. Yards: 6,522/5,678 Apr.–Oct. High: May–Sept.	Greens: Carts: Rating: Slope:	$$ T S J $$ 71.4/72.8 127/126
SP ⓞⓞ	**Twin Lakes Village Golf Course** Rathdrum. (208) 687-1311 18 holes. Par 71/72. Yards: 6,277/5,363 Apr.–Oct. High: June–Aug.	Greens: Carts: Rating: Slope:	$–$$ L T S J $$ 70.0/70.5 121/118
P ⓞⓞ	**University of Idaho Golf Course** Nez Perce, Moscow. (208) 885-6171 18 holes. Par 72/72. Yards: 6,639/5,770 Mar.–Oct. High: May–Aug.	Greens: Carts: Rating: Slope:	$ W T S J $$ 72.0/73.0 130/130

Boise Area

P ⓞⓞ	**Eagle Hills Golf Course** N. Edgewood Lane, Eagle. (208) 939-0402 18 holes. Par 72/72. Yards: 6,485/5,305 Year-round. High: Mar.–Oct.	Greens: Carts: Rating: Slope:	$ W L T S J $ 70.5/70.2 118/114
R ⓞⓞⓞ	**Elkhorn Country Club** Elkhorn Rd., Sun Valley. (208) 622-3300 18 holes. Par 72/72. Yards: 7,101/5,424 May–Oct. High: June–Aug.	Greens: Carts: Rating: Slope:	$$$$ R Incl. 72.4/69.2 133/120

P ☺☺	**Purple Sage Golf Course** Caldwell. (208) 459-2223 18 holes. Par 71/71. Yards: 6,747/5,343 Mar.–Dec. High: May–Aug.	Greens: Carts: Rating: Slope:	$ W $ 70.7/68.9 117/111
SP ☺☺☺ DEAL	**Quail Hollow Golf Club** N. 36th St., Boise. (208) 344-7807 18 holes. Par 70/70. Yards: 6,444/4,530 Year-round. High: Mar.–Oct.	Greens: Carts: Rating: Slope:	$ W L S J $ 70.7/68.0 128/129
P ☺	**Warm Springs Golf Course** Warm Springs Ave., Boise. (208) 343-5661 18 holes. Par 72/72. Yards: 6,719/5,660 Year-round. High: May–Sept.	Greens: Carts: Rating: Slope:	$ W T $ NA 113/113

Sun Valley

R ☺☺☺☺ BEST	**Sun Valley Resort Golf Course** Sun Valley. (208) 622-2251 18 holes. Par 72/73. Yards: 6,565/5,241 Apr.–Oct. High: June–Sept.	Greens: Carts: Rating: Slope:	$$$–$$$$$ L R Incl. 71.1/70.4 128/125

Pocatello Area

P ☺☺☺ DEAL	**Blackfoot Municipal Golf Course** Teeples Dr., Blackfoot. (208) 785-9960 18 holes. Par 72/75. Yards: 6,899/6,385 Mar.–Nov. High: May–Oct.	Greens: Carts: Rating: Slope:	$ W L $ 71.5/75.0 123/124
P ☺☺	**Highland Golf Course** Von Elm Rd., Pocatello. (208) 237-9922 18 holes. Par 72/76. Yards: 6,512/6,100 Mar.–Oct. High: May–Sept.	Greens: Carts: Rating: Slope:	$ S J $ 67.5/73.0 114/117
P ☺☺☺ DEAL	**Pinecrest Municipal Golf Course** E. Elva St., Idaho Falls. (208) 529-1485 18 holes. Par 70/77. Yards: 6,394/6,123 Mar.–Nov. High: May–Sept.	Greens: Carts: Rating: Slope:	$ $ 69.5/74.0 116/125
P ☺☺	**Riverside Golf Course** S. Bannock Hwy., Pocatello. (208) 232-9515 18 holes. Par 72/72. Yards: 6,397/5,710 Mar.–Oct. High: May–Aug.	Greens: Carts: Rating: Slope:	$ $ 69.7/72.2 114/119
P ☺☺	**Sand Creek Golf Club** S. 25th E., Idaho Falls. (208) 529-1115 18 holes. Par 72/73. Yards: 6,805/5,770 Mar.–Nov. High: June–Aug.	Greens: Carts: Rating: Slope:	$ S J $ 70.5/72.2 115/116

Montana

The golfing high points of Montana are the Ridge and Lakes courses of **Eagle Bend** in Bigfork near Kalispell, a long and breathtaking challenge with gorgeous views and abundant wildlife all around.

Not far away in Whitefish are the North and South courses of the **Whitefish Lake Golf Club,** with more mountain scenery and good golfing challenges. Whitefish Lake is also a *Golf U.S.A.* Deal.

The mountain and high-plateau courses of Montana are generally open from about March through November, although snowstorms can eat away at either end of the schedule. Peak rates are usually in effect from April or May through September.

Golf U.S.A. Leader Board: Best Public Courses in Montana

☺☺☺   Eagle Bend Golf Club
☺☺☺   Whitefish Lake Golf Club (North)

Golf U.S.A. Leader Board: Best Deals in Montana

$$/☺☺☺   Buffalo Hill Golf Course
$/☺☺☺   Larchmont Golf Course
$$/☺☺☺   Meadow Lake Golf Resort
$$/☺☺☺   Mission Mountain Country Club
$$/☺☺☺   Polson Country Club
$$/☺☺☺   Whitefish Lake Golf Club (North, South)

Montana Golf Guide

Kalispell Area

P	**Buffalo Hill Golf Course**	Greens:	$$	L T
	North Main St., Kalispell. (406) 756-4547	Carts:	$	
☺☺☺	*Championship Course*	Rating:	71.4/70.3	
DEAL	18 holes. Par 72/72. Yards: 6,525/5,258	Slope:	131/125	
	Apr.–Oct. High: May–Sept.			
P	**Eagle Bend Golf Club**	Greens:	$$–$$$	L T J
	Bigfork. (406) 837-7302	Carts:	$	
☺☺☺	*Ridge/Lakes Course*	Rating:	71.4/70.0	
STATE	18 holes. Par 72/72. Yards: 6,639/5,382	Slope:	124/122	
	Apr.–Oct. High: June–Aug.			
R	**Meadow Lake Golf Resort**	Greens:	$$	L R T
☺☺☺	St. Andrews Dr., Columbia Falls. (406) 892-2111	Carts:	$	
DEAL	18 holes. Par 72/73. Yards: 6,714/5,344	Rating:	70.9/69.8	
	Apr.–Nov. High: June–Sept.	Slope:	124/121	
P	**Polson Country Club**	Greens:	$$	
☺☺☺	Bayview Dr., Polson. (406) 883-8230	Carts:	$	
DEAL	18 holes. Par 72/72. Yards: 6,756/5,215	Rating:	70.9/68.4	
	Mar.–Nov. High: June–Aug.	Slope:	119/114	
P	**Whitefish Lake Golf Club**	Greens:	$$	R T
	Hwy. 93 N., Whitefish. (406) 862-5960	Carts:	$	
☺☺☺	*North Course*	Rating:	69.8/70.1	
DEAL	18 holes. Par 72/72. Yards: 6,556/5,556	Slope:	118/115	
STATE	Apr.–Oct. High: June–Sept.			
☺☺☺	*South Course*	Rating:	70.5/70.3	
DEAL	18 holes. Par 71/72. Yards: 6,563/5,358	Slope:	122/120	

Missoula Area

P	**Larchmont Golf Course**	Greens:	$	W S J
☺☺☺	Old Fort Rd., Missoula. (406) 721-4416	Carts:	$$	
DEAL	18 holes. Par 72/72. Yards: 7,114/5,580	Rating:	71.9/69.4	
	Mar.–Oct. High: May–Aug.	Slope:	117/110	
SP	**Mission Mountain Country Club**	Greens:	$$	
☺☺☺	Stagecoach Trail, Ronan. (406) 676-4653	Carts:	$$	
DEAL	18 holes. Par 72/73. Yards: 6,479/5,125	Rating:	70.1/69.1	
	Mar.–Oct. High: June–Aug.	Slope:	115/115	

Butte Area

R	**Fairmont Hot Springs Resort**	Greens:	$$	R
☺☺	Fairmont Rd., Anaconda. (406) 797-3241	Carts:	$$	
	18 holes. Par 72/72. Yards: 6,741/5,921	Rating:	68.5/70.7	
	Mar.–Oct. High: June–Aug.	Slope:	107/109	

Helena

P
😊😊

Bill Roberts Municipal Golf Course
Cole Ave., Helena. (406) 442-2191
18 holes. Par 72/72. Yards: 6,782/4,700
Mar.–Nov. High: Apr.–Sept.

Greens: $ S J
Carts: $$
Rating: 70.5/65.1
Slope: 117/101

Bozeman Area

P
😊😊

Big Sky Ski and Summer Resort
Meadow Village, Big Sky. (406) 995-4706
18 holes. Par 72/72. Yards: 6,748/5,374
May–Oct. High: June–Aug.

Greens: $$ T J
Carts: $$
Rating: 69.0/67.4
Slope: 111/104

Billings Area

SP
😊

Lake Hills Golf Course
Billings. (406) 252-9244
18 holes. Par 72/74. Yards: 6,802/6,105
Year-round. High: May–Sept.

Greens: $ L S J
Carts: $
Rating: 70.1/72.3
Slope: 112/109

P
😊😊

Peter Yegen Jr. Golf Club
Grand Ave., Billings. (406) 656-8099
18 holes. Par 71/71. Yards: 6,617/4,994
Year-round. High: Apr.–Oct.

Greens: $ W
Carts: $
Rating: 69.7/67.0
Slope: 112/109

R
😊😊

Red Lodge Mountain Golf Course
Upper Continental Dr., Red Lodge. (406) 446-3344
18 holes. Par 72/72. Yards: 6,865/5,678
May–Oct. High: July–Aug.

Greens: $$ W L T J
Carts: $
Rating: 69.3/70.4
Slope: 115/115

Nevada

There are patches of green spread about the great deserts of Nevada—most are in the shadows of the fabulous gambling resorts of the state in and around Las Vegas and Lake Tahoe. (If you're looking to mix a bit of resort travel, you might want to check out another book, *Econoguide '00—Las Vegas, Reno, Laughlin, Lake Tahoe* by Corey Sandler.)

Among the best public and resort courses in Nevada is the **Edgewood Tahoe Golf Course** in Stateline at the south end of Lake Tahoe, a mountain course with fabulous views and incomparable facilities; the 17th hole uses a beach on Lake Tahoe as a sand hazard. At the north end of the lake is the Championship Course at the **Incline Village Golf Resort**, a very highly regarded open desert course located 6,400 feet above sea level.

On the other side of the Sierra Nevadas, within easy reach of Reno and Lake Tahoe, is **The Golf Club at Genoa Lakes** in Genoa, a challenging course with lots of water . . . and wind. It also is open year-round, even when there is 20 feet of snow on the other side of the range. In nearby Dayton is the **Dayton Valley Country Club**, a superb challenge that is also open year-round.

In Las Vegas, the **Sheraton Desert Inn Golf Club** is worth breaking away from the tables for; although it is right off the Strip, it is so rich with trees, water, and attention to detail you just might be able to forget you are within a wood shot or so of an Egyptian pyramid, a 100-foot-tall lion, and Elvis on Ice. Also worth visiting is the **Las Vegas Hilton Country Club**, the former Sahara Country Club. The **Sun City Las Vegas Golf Club**, a semiprivate facility not affiliated with a casino, has two worthy courses, Highland Falls and Palm Valley.

In Henderson, 10 miles south of Las Vegas, there is **The Legacy Golf Club**, a challenging desert course with a touch of Scotland mixed in.

Courses to the east of the Sierra Nevadas, including those in Las Vegas and Laughlin and some on the plateaus near Reno, are open year-round, with peak-season prices in effect from spring through fall. Some courses reduce their rates in the desert heat of midsummer.

In the high mountain resorts in and around Lake Tahoe, the golfing season runs from May through October, with high-season rates in effect from June through September.

Golf U.S.A. Leader Board: Best Public Courses in Nevada

☺☺☺	Dayton Valley Country Club
☺☺☺☺	Edgewood Tahoe Golf Course
☺☺☺☺	The Golf Club at Genoa Lakes
☺☺☺☺	Incline Village Golf Resort
☺☺☺	Las Vegas Hilton Country Club
☺☺☺	The Legacy Golf Club
☺☺☺	Sheraton Desert Inn Golf Club
☺☺☺	Sun City Las Vegas Golf Club (Highland Falls, Palm Valley)

Golf U.S.A. Leader Board: Best Deals in Nevada

$$/☺☺☺	Eagle Valley Golf Club (East, West)
$$/☺☺☺	Northgate Golf Course
$$/☺☺☺	Rosewood Lakes Golf Course
$/☺☺☺	Ruby View Golf Course

Desert oasis—Las Vegas style
Courtesy of the Sheraton Desert Inn Golf Club, Las Vegas, Nevada

Nevada Golf Guide

Reno/Carson City Area

SP ☺☺☺ STATE	**Dayton Valley Country Club** Palmer Dr., Dayton. (702) 246-7888 18 holes. Par 72/72. Yards: 7,218/5,161 Year-round. High: May–Oct.	Greens: $$–$$$$ W L T J Carts: Incl. Rating: 72.1/68.4 Slope: 143/121
P ☺☺☺ DEAL	**Eagle Valley Golf Club** Centennial Park Dr., Carson City. (702) 887-2380 *East Course* 18 holes. Par 72/72. Yards: 6,658/5,980 Year-round. High: May–Sept.	Greens: $ T Carts: $ Rating: 68.7/72.5 Slope: 117/127
☺☺☺ DEAL	*West Course* 18 holes. Par 72/72. Yards: 6,851/5,293	Greens: $$ T Carts: Incl. Rating: 73.5/71.8 Slope: 131/127
P ☺☺☺	**Lakeridge Golf Course** Razorback Rd., Reno. (702) 825-2200 18 holes. Par 71/71. Yards: 6,703/5,159 Mar.–Dec. High: Apr.–Oct.	Greens: $$–$$$ L T Carts: Incl. Rating: 70.8/68.5 Slope: 127/121
R ☺☺☺ DEAL	**Northgate Golf Course** Reno. (702) 747-7577 18 holes. Par 72/72. Yards: 6,966/5,521 Year-round. High: June–Sept.	Greens: $$ W L R T Carts: Incl. Rating: 72.3/70.2 Slope: 131/127
P ☺☺☺ DEAL	**Rosewood Lakes Golf Course** Pembroke Dr., Reno. (702) 857-2892 18 holes. Par 72/72. Yards: 6,693/5,073 Year-round. High: Apr.–Nov.	Greens: $–$$ L T S J Carts: $ Rating: 71.1/67.8 Slope: 127/117
P ☺	**Washoe County Golf Club** S. Arlington, Reno. (702) 828-6640 18 holes. Par 72/72. Yards: 6,695/5,863 Year-round. High: Apr.–Oct.	Greens: $–$$ L T S J Carts: Inquire Rating: 70.0/72.9 Slope: 119/122

Lake Tahoe Area

R ☺☺☺☺ BEST	**Edgewood Tahoe Golf Course** U.S. Hwy. 50, Stateline. (702) 588-3566 18 holes. Par 72/72. Yards: 7,491/5,749 May–Oct. High: July–Sept.	Greens: $$$$$$+ Carts: Incl. Rating: 75.1/71.5 Slope: 136/130
P ☺☺☺☺ STATE	**The Golf Club at Genoa Lakes** Genoa. (702) 782-4653 18 holes. Par 72/72. Yards: 7,263/5,008 Year-round. High: June–Sept.	Greens: $$$–$$$$$ W L T Carts: Incl. Rating: 73.5/67.6 Slope: 134/117
R ☺☺☺☺ BEST	**Incline Village Golf Resort** Incline Village. (702) 832-1143/(888) 236-8725 *Championship Course* 18 holes. Par 72/72. Yards: 6,931/5,245 May–Oct. High: June–Sept.	Greens: $$$$$$ L T Carts: Incl. Rating: 72.2/70.0 Slope: 133/131

Central Nevada

SP ☺☺☺	**Calvada Valley Golf and Country Club** Mt. Charleston Rd., Pahrump. (702) 727-4653 18 holes. Par 71/73. Yards: 7,025/5,948 Year-round. High: Feb.–May, Sept.–Nov.	Greens: $$$ S J Carts: Incl. Rating: 73.2/74.3 Slope: 124/123
R ☺☺☺	**Oasis Resort Hotel Casino** Hillside Dr., Mesquite. (702) 346-5232 *Palms Golf Course* 18 holes. Par 72/72. Yards: 7,008/6,284 Year-round. High: Jan.–May, Oct.–Nov.	Greens: $$$$–$$$$$ W L R T Carts: Incl. Rating: 74.9/70.4 Slope: 137/122

| P
☺☺☺
DEAL | **Ruby View Golf Course**
Elko. (702) 738-6212
18 holes. Par 72/72. Yards: 6,928/5,958
Mar.–Nov. High: June–Aug. | Greens: $ T
Carts: $
Rating: 70.5/72.5
Slope: 118/123 |

Las Vegas Area

P ☺☺	**Angel Park Golf Club** S. Rampart Blvd., Las Vegas. (702) 254-4653 *Mountain Course* 18 holes. Par 71/72. Yards: 6,722/5,164 Year-round. High: Feb.–June, Sept.–Nov.	Greens: $$$–$$$$$ L T J Carts: Incl. Rating: 72.4/69.9 Slope: 128/119
☺☺	*Palm Course* 18 holes. Par 70/70. Yards: 6,530/4,570	Rating: 72.6/67.6 Slope: 130/110
P ☺☺	**Boulder City Golf Club** Boulder City. (702) 293-9236 18 holes. Par 72/72. Yards: 6,561/5,566 Year-round. High: Spring/Fall	Greens: $$ L T Carts: Inquire Rating: 70.2/70.7 Slope: 110/113
P ☺☺	**Las Vegas Golf Club** W. Washington, Las Vegas. (702) 646-3003 18 holes. Par 72/72. Yards: 6,631/5,715 Year-round.	Greens: $$ T S J Carts: Inquire Rating: 71.8/71.2 Slope: 117/118
R ☺☺☺ STATE	**Las Vegas Hilton Country Club** E. Desert Inn Rd., Las Vegas. (702) 796-0013 18 holes. Par 71/71. Yards: 6,815/5,741 Year-round. High: Feb.–May	Greens: $$$$$$+ W L T R J Carts: Inquire Rating: 72.1/72.9 Slope: 130/127
P ☺☺☺ STATE	**The Legacy Golf Club** Henderson. (702) 897-2187 18 holes. Par 72/72. Yards: 7,233/5,340 Year-round. High: Sept.–June	Greens: $$$$$$ T Carts: Incl. Rating: 74.9/71.0 Slope: 136/120
P ☺☺☺	**Painted Desert Golf Club** Painted Mirage Way, Las Vegas. (702) 645-2568 18 holes. Par 72/72. Yards: 6,840/5,711 Year-round. High: Sept.–June	Greens: $$$$$ W L T J Carts: Incl. Rating: 73.7/72.7 Slope: 136/120
R ☺☺☺ BEST	**Desert Inn Golf Club** Las Vegas Blvd. S., Las Vegas. (702) 733-4290 18 holes. Par 72/72. Yards: 7,066/5,791 Year-round. High: Feb.–May	Greens: $$$$$–$$$$$$ L R Carts: Incl. Rating: 73.9/72.7 Slope: 124/121
SP ☺☺☺ STATE	**Sun City Las Vegas Golf Club** Las Vegas. (702) 254-7010 *Highland Falls Course.* Sun City Blvd. 18 holes. Par 72/72. Yards: 6,512/5,099 Year-round. High: Oct.–May	Greens: $$–$$$$$ W L J Carts: Incl. Rating: 71.2/68.8 Slope: 126/110
☺☺☺ STATE	*Palm Valley Course.* Del Webb Blvd. 18 holes. Par 72/72. Yards: 6,849/5,502	Rating: 72.3/71.5 Slope: 127/124
R ☺☺	**Wild Horse Golf Club** Showboat Club Dr., Henderson. (702) 434-9009 18 holes. Par 72/72. Yards: 7,053/5,372 Year-round. High: Oct.–May	Greens: $$$$–$$$$$ L T J Carts: Incl. Rating: 75.2/71.3 Slope: 135/125

Laughlin

| P
☺☺ | **Emerald River Golf Course**
W. Casino Dr., Laughlin. (702) 298-0061
18 holes. Par 72/72. Yards: 6,809/5,205
Year-round. High: Jan.–May, Oct.–Nov. | Greens: $$–$$$ W L R T S J
Carts: Incl.
Rating: NA
Slope: 144/129 |

New Mexico

The best of the public courses in New Mexico is probably the **Piñon Hills Golf Course** in Farmington in the remote northwest corner of the state; it is described as a fair but challenging course in a spectacular setting with views of the La Plata Mountains across the border near Durango, Colorado.

Another winner is the Tamaya and Rio Grande nines at the **Santa Ana Golf Course** in Bernalillo, just north of Albuquerque along the Rio Grande River. In Albuquerque itself is the long, hilly, and otherwise demanding Championship Course at the **University of New Mexico**.

The **Taos Country Club** is a spectacular desert challenge located just north of Santa Fe. **Cochiti Lake** lies about 35 miles southwest of Santa Fe; it's an excellent challenge with spectacular views.

The **Links at Sierra Blanca** is in Ruidoso, north of Alamogordo; it's a remote high-altitude course. Nearby is the **Inn of the Mountain Gods** in Mescalero. A beautiful place with devilish greens, it is owned by the Mescalero Apache tribe.

Our *Golf U.S.A.* Deals list includes Cochiti Lake, Piñon Hills, Santa Ana, and the Taos Country Club.

In the mountains of New Mexico, courses generally are open from March through November, with peak rates during the summer months of June through September. Year-round courses elsewhere in the state have peak rates in effect in the summer; some courses offer discounts in the hottest part of the summer.

Golf U.S.A. Leader Board: Best Public Courses in New Mexico

☺☺☺ Cochiti Lake Golf Course
☺☺☺☺ Inn of the Mountain Gods Golf Club
☺☺☺ The Links at Sierra Blanca
☺☺☺☺ Piñon Hills Golf Course
☺☺☺ Santa Ana Golf Course (Tamaya, Rio Grande)
☺☺☺☺ Taos Country Club
☺☺☺☺ University of New Mexico Golf Course (Championship)

Golf U.S.A. Leader Board: Best Deals in New Mexico

$$/☺☺☺ Cochiti Lake Golf Course
$/☺☺☺ New Mexico State University Golf Course
$/☺☺☺ New Mexico Tech Golf Course
$/☺☺☺☺ Piñon Hills Golf Course
$$/☺☺☺ Santa Ana Golf Course
$$/☺☺☺☺ Taos Country Club

New Mexico Golf Guide

Albuquerque Area

P ☺☺	**Arroyo del Oso Municipal Golf Course** Osuna Rd. N.E., Albuquerque. (505) 884-7505 18 holes. Par 72/73. Yards: 6,892/5,998 Year-round. High: Apr.–Nov.	Greens: $ Carts: $ Rating: 72.3/72.3 Slope: 125/120	T S J

New Mexico Golf Guide

P ☺☺	**Ladera Golf Course** Ladera Dr. N.W., Albuquerque. (505) 836-4449 18 holes. Par 72/72. Yards: 7,107/5,966 Year-round. High: Apr.–Sept.	Greens: $ W L T S J Carts: Inquire Rating: 73.0/72.8 Slope: 123/116
P ☺☺	**Los Altos Golf Course** Copper St. N.E., Albuquerque. (505) 298-1897 18 holes. Par 72/72. Yards: 6,459/5,895 Year-round. High: May–Aug.	Greens: $ L T S J Carts: Inquire Rating: 69.9/71.9 Slope: 110/113
P ☺☺☺ DEAL	**New Mexico Tech Golf Course** Canyon Rd., Socorro. (505) 835-5335 18 holes. Par 72/73. Yards: 6,688/5,887 Year-round. High: Apr.–Oct.	Greens: $ W T J Carts: Inquire Rating: 71.2/72.8 Slope: 126/122
P ☺☺	**Paradise Hills Golf Club** Albuquerque. (505) 898-7001 18 holes. Par 72/74. Yards: 6,801/6,090 Year-round. High: Apr.–Sept.	Greens: $–$$ L T S Carts: $ Rating: 71.7/73.5 Slope: 125/118
P ☺☺☺☺ DEAL STATE	**Piñon Hills Golf Course** Sunrise Pkwy., Farmington. (505) 326-6066 18 holes. Par 72/72. Yards: 7,249/5,522 Year-round. High: May–Oct.	Greens: $ W Carts: $ Rating: 74.3/71.1 Slope: 140/126
P ☺☺☺ DEAL STATE	**Santa Ana Golf Course** Prairie Star Rd., Bernalillo. (505) 867-9464 *Tamaya/Cheena/Star* 27 holes. Par 72/71/72. Yards: 6,500/6,500/6,500 Year-round. High: Mar.–Oct. 18 new holes due in 1999.	Greens: $$ W L T S J Carts: $ Rating: 71.1/70.3/70.9 Slope: 127/126/128
SP ☺☺	**Tierra del Sol Golf Course** Belen. (505) 865-5056 18 holes. Par 72/72. Yards: 6,659/5,462 Year-round. High: Apr.–Oct.	Greens: $–$$ W T J Carts: Inquire Rating: 70.8/69.7 Slope: 120/118
P ☺☺☺☺ BEST	**University of New Mexico Golf Course** University Blvd. S.E., Albuquerque. (505) 277-4546 *Championship Course* 18 holes. Par 72/73. Yards: 7,248/6,031 Year-round. High: May–Sept.	Greens: $–$$$ W T S J Carts: $$ Rating: 74.7/75.1 Slope: 138/131

Santa Fe Area

R ☺☺	**Angel Fire Country Club** Angel Fire. (505) 377-3055 18 holes. Par 72/72. 6,624/5,328 May–Oct. High: June–Sept.	Greens: $$$ L R Carts: $ Rating: NA Slope: 128/118
P ☺☺☺ BEST DEAL	**Cochiti Lake Golf Course** Cochiti Hwy., Cochiti Lake. (505) 465-2239 18 holes. Par 72/72. Yards: 6,451/5,292 Year-round. High: Mar.–Oct.	Greens: $–$$ W Carts: $ Rating: 71.2/70.6 Slope: 131/121
P ☺☺☺ STATE	**The Links at Sierra Blanca** Sierra Blanca Dr., Ruidoso. (505) 258-5330 18 holes. Par 72/72. Yards: 6,793/5,071 Year-round. High: June–Sept.	Greens: $$–$$$$ W L T S J Carts: Incl. Rating: 71.0/63.0 Slope: 121/105
P ☺☺	**Los Alamos Golf Club** Diamond Dr., Los Alamos. (505) 662-8139 18 holes. Par 71/74. Yards: 6,440/5,499 Year-round. High: June–Sept.	Greens: $ W Carts: $ Rating: 69.7/69.8 Slope: 118/113
SP ☺☺☺☺	**Taos Country Club** Hwy. 570 W., Rancho de Taos. (505) 758-7300	Greens: $$–$$$ W T Carts: $$

New Mexico Golf Guide

DEAL STATE	18 holes. Par 72/72. Yards: 7,302/5,343 Mar.–Nov. High: June–Sept.		Rating: Slope:	73.6/69.0 129/125

Southern New Mexico

R ☺☺☺☺ STATE	**Inn of the Mountain Gods Golf Club** Rte. 4, Mescalero. (505) 257-5141 18 holes. Par 72/72. Yards: 6,834/5,478 Mar.–Dec.	Greens: Carts: Rating: Slope:	$$$ $$ 72.1/65.5 132/128	
P ☺☺☺ DEAL	**New Mexico State University Golf Course** Las Cruces. (505) 646-3219 18 holes. Par 72/72. Yards: 7,040/5,858 Year-round. High: Spring/Fall	Greens: Carts: Rating: Slope:	$ $ 74.1/70.7 133/120	W T
P ☺☺	**Ocotillo Park Golf Course** N. Lovington Hwy., Hobbs. (505) 397-9297 18 holes. Par 72/72. Yards: 6,716/5,245 Year-round. High: Apr.–Aug.	Greens: Carts: Rating: Slope:	$ $ 70.5/69.0 121/108	W T S J

Oregon

Portland is Oregon's golfing capital, with four of the state's best in and around the city. The best is probably the Ghost Creek Course at the **Pumpkin Ridge Golf Club** in Cornelius, about 20 miles west of Portland but still inland from the coast. **Eastmoreland** and **Heron Lakes** (its Great Blue Course the best of two there) are in the city itself; both are among the best public courses anywhere.

The best public oceanside course in Oregon—challenging, windy, and full of weather—may be the **Sandpines Golf Resort** in Florence, west of Eugene. Another excellent seaside course is **Salishan Golf Links** in Gleneden Beach, on the coast due west of Salem.

The other direction out of Eugene on the fringes of the Willamette National Forest is the **Tokatee Golf Club** in Blue River, a hidden gem carved out of the mountains, with thousands of pines framing views of the snow-capped Three Sisters.

On the other side of the mountain range, near Bend, is the superb **Sunriver Lodge and Resort**, where the North Woodlands Course is a difficult woodsy challenge and a lovely resort. Northeast of Bend is the **Black Butte Ranch**, with the wide-open Big Meadow and the tight mountain track of Glaze Meadow.

Eastmoreland, Heron Lakes, Salishan, and Tokatee are also on both the *Golf U.S.A.* Best and Deals lists.

Many courses in Oregon operate most of the year, generally from about March through November, with peak rates through the summer months. Some courses, including a number around Portland and Salem, are open year-round, with peak rates from about May through October.

Golf U.S.A. Leader Board: Best Public Courses in Oregon

☺☺☺	Black Butte Ranch (Big Meadow, Glaze Meadow)
☺☺☺	Eastmoreland Golf Course
☺☺☺	Heron Lakes Golf Course (Great Blue)
☺☺☺☺	Pumpkin Ridge Golf Club (Ghost Creek)
☺☺☺	Salishan Golf Links
☺☺☺☺	Sandpines Golf Resort

⊙⊙⊙⊙ Sunriver Lodge and Resort (North Woodlands)
⊙⊙⊙⊙ Tokatee Golf Club

Golf U.S.A. Leader Board: Best Deals in Oregon

$$/⊙⊙⊙	Eagle Crest Resort (Resort, Ridge)
$/⊙⊙⊙	Eastmoreland Golf Course
$$/⊙⊙⊙	Emerald Valley Golf Club
$$/⊙⊙⊙	Forest Hills Golf Course
$$/⊙⊙⊙	Heron Lakes Golf Course (Great Blue, Greenback)
$$/⊙⊙⊙	Meadow Lakes Golf Course
$/⊙⊙⊙	Quail Valley Golf Course
$$/⊙⊙⊙	River's Edge Golf Course
$$/⊙⊙⊙	Salem Golf Club
$$/⊙⊙⊙	Salishan Golf Links
$$/⊙⊙⊙⊙	Tokatee Golf Club
$$/⊙⊙⊙	Trysting Tree Golf Club

Oregon Golf Guide

Portland Area

P
⊙⊙
Broadmoor Golf Course
N.E. Columbia Blvd., Portland. (503) 281-1337
18 holes. Par 72/74. Yards: 6,498/5,384
Year-round. High: May–Sept.
Greens: $–$$ W L
Carts: $
Rating: 70.3/69.9
Slope: 118/110

P
⊙⊙
Colwood National Golf Club
N.E. Columbia Blvd., Portland. (503) 254-5515
18 holes. Par 72/77. Yards: 6,400/5,800
Year-round. High: Apr.–Oct.
Greens: $ J
Carts: $$
Rating: 70.2/71.5
Slope: 113/111

P
⊙⊙⊙
**BEST
DEAL**
Eastmoreland Golf Course
S.E. Bybee Blvd., Portland. (503) 775-2900
18 holes. Par 72/74. Yards: 6,529/5,646
Year-round. High: June–Sept.
Greens: $–$$ S J
Carts: $$
Rating: 71.7/71.4
Slope: 123/117

SP
⊙⊙⊙
DEAL
Forest Hills Golf Course
S.W. Tongue Lane, Cornelius. (503) 357-3347
18 holes. Par 72/74. Yards: 6,173/5,673
Year-round. High: May–Sept.
Greens: $$ J
Carts: $$
Rating: 69.7/71.7
Slope: 122/114

P

⊙⊙
Glendoveer Golf Course
N.E. Glisan, Portland. (503) 253-7507
East Course
18 holes. Par 73/75. Yards: 6,296/5,142
Year-round. High: May–Sept.
Greens: $ S J
Carts: $$
Rating: 69.3/73.5
Slope: 119/120

P

⊙⊙⊙
**BEST
DEAL**
Heron Lakes Golf Course
N. Victory Blvd., Portland. (503) 289-1818
Great Blue Course
18 holes. Par 72/72. Yards: 6,916/5,285
Year-round. High: Mar.–Oct.
Greens: $–$$ W L S J
Carts: $–$$
Rating: 73.6/69.8
Slope: 132/120

⊙⊙⊙
DEAL
Greenback Course
18 holes. Par 72/72. Yards: 6,595/5,224
Rating: 71.4/69.4
Slope: 124/113

P

⊙⊙⊙⊙
BEST
Pumpkin Ridge Golf Club
Old Pumpkin Ridge Rd., Cornelius. (503) 647-9977
Ghost Creek Course
18 holes. Par 71/71. Yards: 6,839/5,206
Year-round. High: Apr.–Oct.
Greens: $$$-$$$$ W L T
Carts: $$
Rating: 73.6/70.4
Slope: 135/117

Oregon Golf Guide

P ☺☺☺ DEAL	**Quail Valley Golf Course** N.W. Aerts Rd., Banks. (503) 324-4444 18 holes. Par 72/72. Yards: 6,603/5,519 Year-round. High: June–Sept.	Greens: Carts: Rating: Slope:	$$ $$ 71.6/71.5 122/117

R ☺☺	**The Resort at the Mountain** Welches. (503) 622-3151 27 holes. Par 72/70/70. Yards: 6,443/5,776/6,032 Year-round. High: May–Oct.	Greens: Carts: Rating: Slope:	$$ W L R T J $$ 70.0/68.0/68.0 119/116/116

P ☺☺☺ DEAL	**Salem Golf Club** Salem. (503) 363-6652 18 holes. Par 72/72. Yards: 6,200/5,163 Year-round. High: July–Sept.	Greens: Carts: Rating: Slope:	$$ L J $$ 68.4/68.1 114/113

R ☺☺☺ BEST DEAL	**Salishan Golf Links** Gleneden Beach. (541) 764-3632 18 holes. Par 72/72. Yards: 6,439/5,693 Year-round. High: June–Oct.	Greens: Carts: Rating: Slope:	$$ J $$ 72.1/73.6 128/127

P ☺☺	**Santiam Golf Club** Aumsville. (503) 769-3485 18 holes. Par 72/72. Yards: 6,392/5,469 Year-round. High: July–Sept.	Greens: Carts: Rating: Slope:	$$ S J $$ 70.4/72.2 115/122

P ☺☺☺ DEAL	**Trysting Tree Golf Club** Electric Rd., Corvallis. (541) 752-3332 18 holes. Par 72/72. Yards: 7,014/5,516 Year-round. High: May–Oct.	Greens: Carts: Rating: Slope:	$$ J $ 73.9/71.3 129/118

Eugene Area

SP ☺☺☺ DEAL	**Emerald Valley Golf Club** Dale Kuni Rd., Creswell. (541) 895-2174 18 holes. Par 72/73. Yards: 6,873/5,371 Year-round. High: June–Sept.	Greens: Carts: Rating: Slope:	$$ W T S J $ 71.7/71.4 123/117

P ☺☺	**The Knolls Golf Club** Sutherlin. (541) 459-4422 18 holes. Par 72/73. Yards: 6,346/5,427 Year-round. High: June–Aug.	Greens: Carts: Rating: Slope:	$ T $ 70.3/71.5 121/122

P ☺☺	**Ocean Dunes Golf Links** Munsel Lake Rd., Florence. (541) 997-3232 18 holes. Par 70/72. Yards: 5,670/4,868 Year-round. High: Apr.–Nov.	Greens: Carts: Rating: Slope:	$$ T S J $ 68.5/69.5 124/124

P ☺☺	**Riveredge Golf Course** N. Delta, Eugene. (541) 345-9160 18 holes. Par 71/71. Yards: 6,256/5,146 Year-round. High: May–Sept.	Greens: Carts: Rating: Slope:	$–$$ L T S J $$ 68.6/67.7 116/112

P ☺☺☺☺ BEST	**Sandpines Golf Resort** 35th St., Florence. (541) 997-1940 18 holes. Par 72/72. Yards: 6,954/5,346 Year-round. High: June–Oct.	Greens: Carts: Rating: Slope:	$$–$$$ T $$ 74.0/65.8 129/111

P ☺☺☺☺ BEST DEAL	**Tokatee Golf Club** McKenzie Hwy., Blue River. (541) 822-3220 18 holes. Par 72/72. Yards: 6,842/5,651 Feb.–Nov. High: June–Sept.	Greens: Carts: Rating: Slope:	$$ J $ 72.0/71.2 126/115

Bend Area

SP ☺☺☺	**Awbrey Glen Golf Club** Bend. (541) 388-8526 18 holes. Par 72/72. Yards: 7,007/5,459 Mar.–Oct. High: May–Sept.	Greens: Carts: Rating: Slope:	$$$ L J $ 73.7/69.6 135/119

Oregon Golf Guide

R	**Black Butte Ranch**	Greens:	$$–$$$ W L T
	Hwy. 20, Black Butte. (541) 595-6689	Carts:	$$
☺☺☺	*Big Meadow Course*	Rating:	72.0/70.5
STATE	18 holes. Par 72/72. Yards: 6,870/5,716	Slope:	127/115
	Mar.–Nov. High: June–Sept.		
☺☺☺	*Glaze Meadow Course*	Rating:	71.5/72.1
STATE	18 holes. Par 72/72. Yards: 6,560/5,616	Slope:	128/120
R	**Eagle Crest Resort**	Greens:	$$ L R J
	Cline Falls Rd., Redmond. (541) 923-4653	Carts:	$$
☺☺☺	*Resort Course*	Rating:	71.5/69.8
DEAL	18 holes. Par 72/72. Yards: 6,673/5,395	Slope:	123/109
	Year-round. High: Apr.–Oct.		
☺☺☺	*Ridge Course*	Rating:	70.8/NA
DEAL	18 holes. Par 72/72. Yards: 6,477/4,773	Slope:	123/NA
P	**Meadow Lakes Golf Course**	Greens:	$$ L
☺☺☺	Prineville. (541) 447-7113	Carts:	$
DEAL	18 holes. Par 72/72. Yards: 6,731/5,155	Rating:	73.1/69.0
	Year-round. High: June–Sept.	Slope:	131/121
P	**River's Edge Golf Course**	Greens:	$$ L R T J
☺☺☺	N.W. Mt. Washington Dr., Bend. (541) 389-2828	Carts:	$
DEAL	18 holes. Par 72/73. Yards: 6,647/5,380	Rating:	72.2/71.8
	Year-round. High: May–Sept.	Slope:	139/135
R	**Sunriver Lodge and Resort**	Greens:	$$–$$$
	Sunriver. (541) 593-1221	Carts:	Incl.
☺☺☺☺	*North Woodlands Course*	Rating:	70.4/72.2
BEST	18 holes. Par 72/72. Yards: 6,880/5,446	Slope:	115/122
	Apr.–Oct. High: June–Aug.		
☺☺☺	*South Meadows Course*	Greens:	$$–$$$$ L R T J
	18 holes. Par 72/72. Yards: 6,960/5,847	Carts:	Incl.
		Rating:	72.9/71.7
		Slope:	130/116

Medford Area

P	**Cedar Links Golf Course**	Greens:	$$
☺☺	Medford. (541) 773-4373	Carts:	$
	18 holes. Par 70/71. Yards: 6,142/5,145	Rating:	68.9/68.7
	Year-round. High: May–Sept.	Slope:	114/112
P	**Harbor Links Golf Course**	Greens:	$$ W L T S J
☺☺	Harbor Isles Blvd., Klamath Falls. (541) 882-0609	Carts:	$$
	18 holes. Par 72/72. Yards: 6,272/5,709	Rating:	69.3/71.2
	Year-round. High: June–Sept.	Slope:	117/119
R	**Kah-Nee-Ta Resort Golf Club**	Greens:	$–$$ L S J
☺☺	Warm Springs. (541) 553-1112	Carts:	$$
	18 holes. Par 72/73. Yards: 6,352/5,195	Rating:	73.1/70.0
	Year-round. High: Mar.–Oct.	Slope:	123/116

Utah

The **Green Spring Golf Course** in Washington, in the southwest corner of Utah at the Arizona border, is a very difficult canyon course with desert and forest holes. In nearby St. George is the **Sunbrook Golf Club**, a tough mountain course and perhaps the best course in the state.

Park Meadows Golf Club is a spectacular challenge way up in the ski town of Park City, about 30 miles east of Salt Lake City on the back side of the mountains that face the city. **Homestead Golf Club** is another attractive high-mountain course, located in Midway not far from the Alta and Brighton ski areas.

North of Salt Lake City in Layton is **Valley View Golf Course**, an up-and-down long challenge.

And if you've got a few hours to kill before flying away, **Wingpointe** is a tough challenge just outside of downtown Salt Lake City near the airport.

Hobble Creek, in Springville between Salt Lake City and Provo, is a mountain gem and a great deal.

All six of Utah's *Golf U.S.A.* Best–rated courses are also on the *Golf U.S.A.* Deals list.

High-mountain resorts in Utah are generally open from April to October, with peak rates in effect from June to September. Other courses, including some in the valleys around Salt Lake City, operate year-round, with peak rates in the summer. Does that sound like you could combine skiing in the Wasatch and golfing down below? You bet.

Golf U.S.A. Leader Board: Best Public Courses in Utah

ꙮꙮꙮ   Green Spring Golf Course
ꙮꙮꙮꙮ   Hobble Creek Golf Club
ꙮꙮꙮ   Homestead Golf Club
ꙮꙮꙮꙮ   Sunbrook Golf Club
ꙮꙮꙮꙮ   Valley View Golf Course
ꙮꙮꙮ   Wingpointe Golf Course

Golf U.S.A. Leader Board: Best Deals in Utah

$/ꙮꙮꙮ   Bonneville Golf Course
$/ꙮꙮꙮ   Bountiful City Golf Course
$/ꙮꙮꙮ   Davis Park Golf Course
$/ꙮꙮꙮ   Eagle Mountain Golf Course
$/ꙮꙮꙮ   Eaglewood Golf Course
$/ꙮꙮꙮ   Gladstan Golf Club
$$/ꙮꙮꙮ   Green Spring Golf Course
$/ꙮꙮꙮꙮ   Hobble Creek Golf Club
$$/ꙮꙮꙮ   Homestead Golf Club
$/ꙮꙮꙮ   Logan River Golf Course
$/ꙮꙮꙮ   Moab Golf Club
$/ꙮꙮꙮ   Mountain Dell Golf Club (Canyon, Lake)
$$/ꙮꙮꙮ   Park City Golf Course
$/ꙮꙮꙮ   Spanish Oaks Golf Club
$/ꙮꙮꙮꙮ   Sunbrook Golf Club
$/ꙮꙮꙮ   Tri-City Golf Course
$/ꙮꙮꙮꙮ   Valley View Golf Course
$/ꙮꙮꙮ   West Ridge Golf Course
$/ꙮꙮꙮ   Wingpointe Golf Course
$$/ꙮꙮꙮ   Wolf Creek Resort Golf Course

Utah Golf Guide

Salt Lake City Area

P	**Bonneville Golf Course**	Greens: $	S J
☺☺☺	Connor St., Salt Lake City. (801) 583-9513	Carts: $	
DEAL	18 holes. Par 72/74. Yards: 6,824/5,860	Rating: 71.0/71.6	
	Mar.–Nov. High: Apr.–Sept.	Slope: 120/119	

P	**Bountiful City Golf Course**	Greens: $	S J
☺☺☺	S. Bountiful Blvd., Bountiful. (801) 298-6040	Carts: $	
DEAL	18 holes. Par 71/72. Yards: 6,630/5,012	Rating: 70.1/68.6	
	Mar.–Nov. High: May–Aug.	Slope: 117/115	

P	**Davis Park Golf Course**	Greens: $	S J
☺☺☺	E. Nicholls Rd., Fruit Heights. (801) 546-4154	Carts: $	
DEAL	18 holes. Par 71/71. Yards: 6,481/5,295	Rating: 69.3/68.7	
	Mar.–Nov. High: May–Aug.	Slope: 117/114	

P	**Eagle Mountain Golf Course**	Greens: $	
☺☺☺	E. 700 S., Brigham City. (801) 723-3212	Carts: $	
DEAL	18 holes. Par 71/71. Yards: 6,769/4,767	Rating: 71.4/65.4	
	Mar.–Nov. High: Apr.–Sept.	Slope: 119/101	

P	**Eaglewood Golf Course**	Greens: $	W L J
☺☺☺	E. Eaglewood Dr., N. Salt Lake City. (801) 299-0088	Carts: $	
DEAL	18 holes. Par 71/71. Yards: 6,769/4,767	Rating: 71.1/68.8	
	Mar.–Nov. High: Apr.–Sept.	Slope: 121/112	

P	**Glendale Golf Course**	Greens: $	W S J
☺☺	W. 2100 S., Salt Lake City. (801) 974-2403	Carts: $	
	18 holes. Par 72/73. Yards: 7,000/5,930	Rating: 70.9/72.5	
	Mar.–Nov. High: May–Aug.	Slope: 117/120	

P	**Glenmoor Golf and Country Club**	Greens: $	W S
☺☺	S. 4800 W., S. Jordan. (801) 280-1742	Carts: $	
	18 holes. Par 72/72. Yards: 6,900/5,800	Rating: 70.9/72.0	
	Year-round. High: June–July	Slope: 117/118	

R	**Homestead Golf Club**	Greens: $–$$	W L R T S
☺☺☺	N. Homestead Dr., Midway. (435) 654-5588	Carts: $	
DEAL	18 holes. Par 72/72. Yards: 7,017/5,091	Rating: 73.0/68.8	
STATE	Apr.–Oct. High: June–Sept.	Slope: 135/118	

P	**Logan River Golf Course**	Greens: $	S J
☺☺☺	W. 1000 S., Logan. (435) 750-0123	Carts: $	
DEAL	18 holes. Par 71/71. Yards: 6,502/5,048	Rating: 70.5/78.9	
	Apr.–Oct. High: June–Sept.	Slope: 124/117	

P	**Mount Ogden Golf Course**	Greens: $	
☺☺	Constitution Way, Ogden. (801) 629-8700	Carts: $	
	18 holes. Par 71/72. Yards: 6,300/4,980	Rating: 70.5/69.5	
	Mar.–Nov. High: Apr.–Oct.	Slope: 121/111	

P	**Mountain Dell Golf Club**	Greens: $	W T S J
	Cummings Rd., Salt Lake City. (801) 582-3812	Carts: $	
☺☺☺	*Canyon Course*	Rating: 71.3/71.1	
DEAL	18 holes. Par 72/73. Yards: 6,787/5,447	Slope: 126/112	
	Apr.–Nov. High: June–Aug.		

☺☺☺	*Lake Course*	Rating: 72.2/67.6
DEAL	18 holes. Par 71/71. Yards: 6,709/5,066	Slope: 129/109

P	**Murray Parkway Golf Club**	Greens: $	J
☺☺	Murray. (801) 262-4653	Carts: $	
	18 holes. Par 72/72. Yards: 6,800/5,800	Rating: 71.3/71.0	
	Mar.–Nov. High: June–Aug.	Slope: 120/118	

P	**Park City Golf Course**	Greens: $$	L
☺☺☺	Lower Park Ave., Park City. (801) 649-8701	Carts: $	

Utah Golf Guide

DEAL	18 holes. Par 72/72. Yards: 6,754/5,600 Apr.–Oct. High: May–Sept.	Rating: Slope:	71.7/71.4 127/123

P 😊😊	**Rose Park Golf Club** N. Redwood Rd., Salt Lake City. (801) 596-5030 18 holes. Par 72/75. Yards: 6,696/5,816 Feb.–Dec. High: May–Sept.	Greens: $ Carts: $ Rating: 69.6/70.8 Slope: 109/112	S J
P 😊😊	**Schneiter's Riverside Golf Course** S. Weber Dr., Ogden. (801) 399-4636 18 holes. Par 71/71. Yards: 6,177/5,217 Mar.–Nov. High: May–Aug.	Greens: $ Carts: $ Rating: 68.4/68.5 Slope: 114/113	S J
P 😊😊	**Stansbury Park Golf Club** Tooele. (801) 328-1483 18 holes. Par 72/72. Yards: 6,831/5,722 Feb.–Nov. High: June–Aug.	Greens: $ Carts: $ Rating: 71.6/71.5 Slope: 125/121	W L
P 😊😊😊 DEAL	**Tri-City Golf Course** N. 200 E., American Fork. (801) 756-3594 18 holes. Par 72/75. Yards: 7,077/6,304 Mar.–Oct. High: May–Aug.	Greens: $ Carts: $ Rating: 73.0/75.0 Slope: 125/127	S J
P 😊😊😊😊 DEAL STATE	**Valley View Golf Course** E. Gentile, Layton. (801) 546-1630 18 holes. Par 72/74. Yards: 6,652/5,755 Mar.–Nov. High: May–Sept.	Greens: $ Carts: $ Rating: 71.0/73.2 Slope: 123/125	S J
P 😊😊	**West Bountiful City Golf Course** N. 1100 W., W. Bountiful. (801) 295-1019 18 holes. Par 71/72. Yards: 6,030/4,895 Mar.–Oct. High: June–Aug.	Greens: $ Carts: $ Rating: 67.2/66.5 Slope: 113/115	S J
P 😊😊😊 DEAL	**West Ridge Golf Course** W. Valley City. (801) 966-4653 18 holes. Par 71/71. Yards: 6,734/5,027 Mar.–Nov. High: Apr.–Aug.	Greens: $ Carts: $ Rating: 72.2/68.1 Slope: 125/118	W S J
P 😊😊😊 DEAL STATE	**Wingpointe Golf Course** W. 100 N., Salt Lake City. (801) 575-2345 18 holes. Par 72/72. Yards: 7,101/5,228 Year-round. High: May–Oct.	Greens: $ Carts: $ Rating: 73.3/72.0 Slope: 131/125	W L S J
R 😊😊😊 DEAL	**Wolf Creek Resort Golf Course** N. Wolf Creek Dr., Eden. (801) 745-3365 18 holes. Par 72/72. Yards: 6,845/5,332 Mar.–Nov. High: May–Sept.	Greens: $$ Carts: $ Rating: NA Slope: 134/127	W L R T

Provo Area

P 😊😊	**East Bay Golf Course** S. East Bay Blvd., Provo. (801) 379-6612 18 holes. Par 71/72. Yards: 6,932/5,125 Mar.–Nov. High: May–Sept.	Greens: $ Carts: $ Rating: 67.6/66.6 Slope: 116/106	
P 😊😊😊 DEAL	**Gladstan Golf Club** Payson. (801) 465-2549 18 holes. Par 71/71. Yards: 6,509/4,782 Mar.–Nov. High: May–Aug.	Greens: $ Carts: $ Rating: 70.7/67.4 Slope: 121/111	S J
P 😊😊😊😊 DEAL STATE	**Hobble Creek Golf Club** E. Hobble Creek Canyon, Springville. (801) 489-6297 18 holes. Par 71/73. Yards: 6,315/5,435 Mar.–Nov. High: July–Sept.	Greens: $ Carts: $ Rating: 69.4/69.5 Slope: 120/117	S J
P 😊😊😊	**Spanish Oaks Golf Club** Powerhouse Rd., Spanish Fork. (801) 798-9816	Greens: $ Carts: $	T S J

DEAL	18 holes. Par 72/73. Yards: 6,358/5,319	Rating:	68.7/68.9
	Mar.–Oct. High: May–Sept.	Slope:	116/113

Southern Utah/St. George

P	**Green Spring Golf Course**	Greens:	$$ W L T J
☺☺☺	N. Green Spring Dr., Washington. (801) 673-7888	Carts:	$
DEAL	18 holes. Par 71/71. Yards: 6,717/5,042	Rating:	72.6/69.8
STATE	Year-round. High: Oct.–May	Slope:	131/119

P	**Moab Golf Club**	Greens:	$ J
☺☺☺	S.E. Bench Rd., Moab. (801) 259-6488	Carts:	$
DEAL	18 holes. Par 72/72. Yards: 6,819/4,725	Rating:	72.2/69.6
	Year-round. High: Spring/Fall	Slope:	125/110

P	**St. George Golf Club**	Greens:	$$
☺☺	S. 1400 E., St. George. (801) 634-5854	Carts:	Incl.
	18 holes. Par 73/73. Yards: 7,211/5,216	Rating:	73.1/68.9
	Year-round. High: Oct.–May	Slope:	126/114

P	**Southgate Golf Club**	Greens:	$$ L T J
☺☺	S. Tonaquint Dr., St. George. (801) 628-0000	Carts:	$
	18 holes. Par 70/70. Yards: 6,400/4,463	Rating:	70.2/66.8
	Year-round. High: Oct.–Apr.	Slope:	120/112

P	**Sunbrook Golf Club**	Greens:	$$ L
☺☺☺☺	St. George. (801) 634-5866	Carts:	$
DEAL	27 holes. Par 72/72. Yards: 6,828/6,758/5,286	Rating:	74.0/73.8/71.1
STATE	Year-round. High: Oct.-May	Slope:	134/133/121

Washington

Way up in the northwest corner of the state on the Canadian border is the **Semiahmoo Golf and Country Club** in Blaine, a spectacular desert course. In Bellingham, the **Shuksan Golf Club** is an exciting newer public course.

The **Classic Country Club** in Spanaway, about 60 miles south of Seattle, is a long, tight challenge with distant views of Mount Rainier. **Kayak Point** in Stanwood, 45 miles south of Seattle, is another narrow, hilly challenge. The **McCormick Woods Golf Course** winds its way through the woods in Port Orchard, about 20 miles northwest of Tacoma. The Tide and Timber nines at the **Port Ludlow Golf Course** in Port Ludlow, about 20 miles northwest of Seattle, are among the most picturesque and difficult in the state. The Timber Course includes hundreds of stumps of old cedar trees, which were cut down by loggers and left in place as seminatural obstacles.

Indian Canyon is the best of the public courses near Spokane and one of the best in the country, an older course with a challenging heavily wooded track in the hills with views down to the city from the first and tenth holes. The **Meadowwood Golf Course** in Liberty Lake east of Spokane is a hidden gem with some difficult challenges on the back nine.

The **Desert Canyon Golf Resort** in Orondo in the center of the state offers spectacular views of the Columbia River and some excellent desert golf.

Apple Tree in Yakima is set in an apple orchard with an apple-shaped 17th hole.

Indian Canyon, Kayak Point, and Meadowwood are also on the *Golf U.S.A.* Best and *Golf U.S.A.* Deals lists.

Some of Washington's coastal courses are open year-round, with peak rates in effect from May to September. Other courses typically operate from March to October, with peak rates in the summer.

Golf U.S.A. Leader Board: Best Public Courses in Washington

☺☺☺☺ Apple Tree Golf Course
☺☺☺ Classic Country Club
☺☺☺☺ Desert Canyon Golf Resort
☺☺☺ Indian Canyon Golf Course
☺☺☺☺ Kayak Point Golf Course
☺☺☺☺ McCormick Woods Golf Course
☺☺☺☺ Meadowwood Golf Course
☺☺☺☺ Port Ludlow Golf Course (Tide, Timber, Trail)
☺☺☺☺ Semiahmoo Golf and Country Club
☺☺☺☺ Shuksan Golf Club

Golf U.S.A. Leader Board: Best Deals in Washington

$$/☺☺☺ Canyon Lakes Golf Course
$$/☺☺☺ Capitol City Golf Club
$$/☺☺☺ The Creek at Qualchan Golf Course
$/☺☺☺ Downriver Golf Club
$$/☺☺☺ Dungeness Golf and Country Club
$$/☺☺☺ Gold Mountain Golf Course
$/☺☺☺ Hangman Valley Golf Course
$$/☺☺☺ Indian Canyon Golf Course
$$/☺☺☺☺ Kayak Point Golf Course
$$/☺☺☺ Lake Padden Golf Course
$/☺☺☺ Lake Spanaway Golf Course
$/☺☺☺ Leavenworth Golf Club
$/☺☺☺☺ Meadowwood Golf Course
$$/☺☺☺ Riverside Country Club
$$/☺☺☺ Snohomish Golf Course
$$/☺☺☺ Sudden Valley Golf and Country Club

Washington Golf Guide

Seattle/Tacoma/Bellingham Area

R ☺☺	**Alderbrook Golf and Yacht Club** Union. (360) 898-2560 18 holes. Par 72/73. Yards: 6,326/5,500 Year-round. High: Apr.–Oct.	Greens: Carts: Rating: Slope:	$$ $ 70.9/72.2 122/125	W L R S
P ☺☺	**Brookdale Golf Course** Tacoma. (253) 537-4400 18 holes. Par 71/74. Yards: 6,425/5,847 Year-round. High: Apr.–Oct.	Greens: Carts: Rating: Slope:	$ $ 69.6/72.2 112/123	L T S J
P ☺☺☺	**Capitol City Golf Club** Yelm Hwy. S.E., Olympia. (360) 459-3459	Greens: Carts:	$–$$ $	W L T S J

DEAL	18 holes. Par 72/72. Yards: 6,536/5,510	Rating:	70.9/71.7	
	Year-round. High: June–Aug.	Slope:	123/122	
P	**Classic Country Club**	Greens:	$$–$$$	W L T S J
☺☺☺	208th St. E., Spanaway. (253) 847-4440	Carts:	$$	
STATE	18 holes. Par 72/72. Yards: 6,793/5,580	Rating:	73.6/73.3	
	Year-round. High: May–Oct.	Slope:	133/128	
SP	**Dungeness Golf and Country Club**	Greens:	$–$$	W T J
☺☺☺	Woodcock Rd., Sequim. (206) 683-6344	Carts:	$$	
DEAL	18 holes. Par 72/72. Yards: 6,372/5,344	Rating:	70.4/70.1	
	Year-round. High: Apr.–Oct.	Slope:	121/119	
SP	**Echo Falls Country Club**	Greens:	$$–$$$	W L R T S J
☺☺	121st Ave. S.E., Snohomish. (360) 668-3030	Carts:	$	
	18 holes. Par 70/71. Yards: 6,123/4,357	Rating:	68.9/64.6	
	Year-round. High: June–Aug.	Slope:	126/115	
P	**Gold Mountain Golf Course**	Greens:	$–$$	T S J
	W. Belfair Valley Rd., Bremerton. (360) 415-5432	Carts:		
☺☺☺	*Olympic Course*	Rating:	73.1/69.2	
DEAL	18 holes. Par 72/75. Yards: 7,003/5,220	Slope:	128/115	
	Year-round. High: Apr.–Oct.			
P	**Harbour Pointe Golf Club**	Greens:	$$–$$$	W L T S J
☺☺☺	Mukilteo. (425) 355-6060	Carts:	$	
	18 holes. Par 72/72. Yards: 6,862/4,842	Rating:	72.8/68.8	
	Year-round. High: May–Oct.	Slope:	135/117	
P	**High Cedars Golf Club**	Greens:	$$	W T S J
☺☺	149th St., Orting. (360) 893-3171	Carts:	$$	
	18 holes. Par 71/72. Yards: 6,303/5,651	Rating:	70.2/75.6	
	Year-round. High: Apr.–Nov.	Slope:	116/126	
P	**Kayak Point Golf Course**	Greens:	$$	W S J
☺☺☺☺	Marine Dr., Standwood. (360) 652-9676	Carts:	$$	
BEST	18 holes. Par 72/72. Yards: 6,719/5,346	Rating:	72.7/72.8	
DEAL	Year-round. High: May–Sept.	Slope:	133/129	
P	**Lake Padden Golf Course**	Greens:	$–$$	S J
☺☺☺	Samish Way, Bellingham. (360) 676-6989	Carts:	$$	
DEAL	18 holes. Par 72/72. Yards: 6,675/5,496	Rating:	71.3/71.9	
	Year-round. High: May–Sept.	Slope:	122/126	
P	**Lake Spanaway Golf Course**	Greens:	$	W S J
☺☺☺	Pacific Ave., Tacoma. (253) 531-3660	Carts:	$$	
DEAL	18 holes. Par 72/74. Yards: 6,810/5,935	Rating:	701.8/73.4	
	Year-round. High: May–Oct.	Slope:	121/123	
SP	**Leavenworth Golf Club**	Greens:	$	
☺☺☺	Icicle Rd., Leavenworth. (509) 548-7267	Carts:	$$	
DEAL	18 holes. Par 71/71. Yards: 5,711/5,343	Rating:	67.0/69.6	
	Apr.–Nov. High: Apr.–Oct.	Slope:	110/112	
P	**Lipoma Firs Golf Course**	Greens:	$–$$	W L T S J
	110th Ave. E., Puyallup. (206) 841-4396	Carts:	$	
☺☺	*Green/Gold/Blue*	Rating:	72.2/72.1/72.0	
	27 holes. Par 72/72/72. Yards: 6,722/6,805/6,687	Slope:	122/122/122	
	Year-round. High: Apr.–Oct.			
P	**Madrona Links Golf Course**	Greens:	$$	T S J
☺☺	22nd Ave. N.W., Gig Harbor. (253) 851-5193	Carts:	$	
	18 holes. Par 71/73. Yards: 5,602/4,737	Rating:	65.5/68.1	
	Year-round. High: Mar.–Oct.	Slope:	110/115	
P	**McCormick Woods Golf Course**	Greens:	$$–$$$	W L T S
☺☺☺☺	Port Orchard. (360) 895-0130	Carts:	$$	

Washington Golf Guide

BEST		18 holes. Par 72/72. Yards: 7,040/5,299 Year-round. High: June–Sept.	Rating: 74.1/71.1 Slope: 135/122
P ☺☺	**Meadow Park Golf Course** Lakewood Dr. W., Tacoma. (253) 473-3033 18 holes. Par 71/73. Yards: 6,093/5,262 Year-round. High: May–Sept.		Greens: $-$$ W S J Carts: $ Rating: 69.0/70.3 Slope: 114/118
P ☺☺	**Mount Si Golf Course** Snoqualmie. (425) 881-1541 18 holes. Par 72/72. Yards: 6,304/5,439 Year-round. High: Apr.–Sept.		Greens: $$ L S J Carts: $ Rating: NA Slope: 111
P ☺☺	**North Shore Golf and Country Club** N. Shore Blvd. N.E., Tacoma. (253) 927-1375 18 holes. Par 71/73. Yards: 6,305/5,442 Year-round. High: May–Sept.		Greens: $$ W L T J Carts: $$ Rating: 69.9/70.7 Slope: 120/119
R ☺☺	**Ocean Shores Golf Course** Canal Dr. N.E., Ocean Shores. (360) 289-3357 18 holes. Par 71/72. Yards: 6,252/5,173 Year-round. High: May–Sept.		Greens: $-$$ L S J Carts: $$ Rating: 70.2/69.6 Slope: 115/115
R ☺☺☺☺ BEST	**Port Ludlow Golf Course** Highland Dr., Port Ludlow. (360) 437-0272 *Tide/Timber/Trail* 27 holes. Par 72/72/72. Yards: 6,746/6,683/6,787 Year-round. High: May–Sept.		Greens: $$-$$$ W L R T Carts: $ Rating: 73.6/73.1/72.7 Slope: 138/138/131
P ☺☺	**Riverbend Golf Complex** W. Meeker St., Kent. (253) 854-3673 18 holes. Par 72/72. Yards: 6,603/5,538 Year-round. High: Apr.–Sept.		Greens: $-$$ W L S J Carts: $$ Rating: 71.8/70.4 Slope: 125/124
P ☺☺☺ DEAL	**Riverside Country Club** N.W. Airport Rd., Chehalis. (360) 748-8182 18 holes. Par 71/72. Yards: 6,155/5,456 Year-round. High: Apr.–Sept.		Greens: $-$$ L J Carts: $$ Rating: 69.3/71.2 Slope: 118/116
R ☺☺☺☺ BEST	**Semiahmoo Golf and Country Club** Semiahmoo Pkwy., Blaine. (360) 371-7005 18 holes. Par 72/72. Yards: 7,005/5,288 Year-round. High: July–Sept.		Greens: $$-$$$$ W L R T Carts: $ Rating: 74.5/71.6 Slope: 130/126
P ☺☺☺☺ STATE	**Shuksan Golf Club** E. Axton Rd., Bellingham. (360) 398-8888 18 holes. Par 72/72. Yards: 6,706/5,253 Year-round. High: Apr.–Oct.		Greens: $ W L T S J Carts: Incl. Rating: 70.4/72.7 Slope: 121/123
P ☺☺☺ DEAL	**Snohomish Golf Course** 147th Ave. S.E., Snohomish. (360) 568-2676 18 holes. Par 72/74. Yards: 6,858/5,980 Year-round. High: May–Sept.		Greens: $$ T S J Carts: $$ Rating: 72.7/74.1 Slope: 126/129
SP ☺☺☺ DEAL	**Sudden Valley Golf and Country Club** Lake Whatcom Blvd., Bellingham. (360) 734-6435 18 holes. Par 72/72. Yards: 6,553/5,627 Year-round. High: July–Sept.		Greens: $$ W L T J Carts: $$ Rating: 71.8/72.8 Slope: 128/124
P ☺☺	**Tumwater Valley Golf Club** Tumwater Valley Dr., Tumwater. (360) 943-9500 18 holes. Par 72/72. Yards: 7,154/5,504 Year-round. High: May–Oct.		Greens: $-$$ W L T S J Carts: $$ Rating: 73.1/70.4 Slope: 120/114
P ☺☺	**West Seattle Golf Course** 35th Ave. S.W., Seattle. (206) 935-5187		Greens: $ T S J Carts: $

	18 holes. Par 72/72. Yards: 6,600/5,700	Rating:	70.9/72.6
	Year-round. High: May–Sept.	Slope:	119/123

Southern Washington/Yakima Area

P	**Apple Tree Golf Course**	Greens:	$$–$$$ W L T S J
☺☺☺☺	Occidental Ave., Yakima. (509) 966-5877	Carts:	$
STATE	18 holes. Par 72/72. Yards: 6,892/5,428	Rating:	73.3/72.0
	Year-round. High: Mar.–Oct.	Slope:	129/124

P	**Canyon Lakes Golf Course**	Greens:	$–$$ J
☺☺☺	Kennewick. (509) 582-3736	Carts:	$$
DEAL	18 holes. Par 72/72. Yards: 6,973/5,565	Rating:	73.7/71.1
	Year-round. High: Mar.–Nov.	Slope:	135/132

P	**Cedars Golf Club**	Greens:	$ J
☺☺	N.E. 181st St., Brush Prairie. (360) 687-4233	Carts:	$$
	18 holes. Par 72/73. Yards: 6,423/5,216	Rating:	71.2/71.1
	Year-round. High: May–Oct.	Slope:	129/117

SP	**Desert Aire Golf Course**	Greens:	$
☺☺	Desert Aire. (509) 932-4439	Carts:	$
	18 holes. Par 72/73. Yards: 6,501/5,786	Rating:	73.6/73.3
	Year-round. High: June–Oct.	Slope:	133/128

R	**Desert Canyon Golf Resort**	Greens:	$$–$$$$ W L T S J
☺☺☺☺	Brays Rd., Orondo. (509) 784-1111	Carts:	Incl.
STATE	18 holes. Par 72/72. Yards: 7,293/4,899	Rating:	74.0/67.5
	Mar.–Nov. High: July–Aug.	Slope:	127/104

P	**Quail Ridge Golf Course**	Greens:	$ J
☺☺	Swallows Nest Dr., Clarkston. (509) 758-8501	Carts:	$$
	18 holes. Par 71/71. Yards: 5,861/4,720	Rating:	68.1/66.2
	Year-round. High: Apr.–Sept.	Slope:	114/107

P	**Three Rivers Golf Course**	Greens:	$ L T S J
☺☺	S. River Rd., Kelso. (360) 423-4653	Carts:	$$
	18 holes. Par 72/72. Yards: 6,846/5,455	Rating:	72.1/68.5
	Year-round. High: May–Sept.	Slope:	127/120

SP	**Tri-City Country Club**	Greens:	$$ J
☺☺	N. Underwood, Kennewick. (509) 783-6014	Carts:	$$
	18 holes. Par 65/65. Yards: 4,700/4,400	Rating:	62.5/65.2
	Year-round. High: May–Sept.	Slope:	112/115

Spokane Area

SP	**Chewelah Golf and Country Club**	Greens:	$ S J
☺☺	Sand Canyon Rd., Chewelah. (509) 935-6807	Carts:	$$
	18 holes. Par 72/74. Yards: 6,511/5,672	Rating:	70.9/72.2
	Apr.–Oct. High: May–Sept.	Slope:	125/124

P	**Downriver Golf Club**	Greens:	$
☺☺☺	Columbia Circle, Spokane. (509) 327-5269	Carts:	$$
DEAL	18 holes. Par 71/73. Yards: 6,130/5,592	Rating:	68.8/70.9
	Feb.–Nov. High: May–Sept.	Slope:	115/114

P	**Hangman Valley Golf Course**	Greens:	$ S J
☺☺☺	Spokane. (509) 448-1212	Carts:	$$
DEAL	18 holes. Par 72/71. Yards: 6,906/5,699	Rating:	71.9/71.8
	Mar.–Oct. High: May–Sept.	Slope:	126/125

P	**Indian Canyon Golf Course**	Greens:	$$ T J
☺☺☺	Spokane. (509) 747-5353	Carts:	$$
BEST	18 holes. Par 72/72. Yards: 6,255/5,943	Rating:	70.7/65.9
DEAL	Mar.–Oct. High: May–Sept.	Slope:	126/115

P ☺☺	Liberty Lake Golf Club Liberty Lake. (509) 255-6233 18 holes. Par 70/74. Yards: 6,398/5,886 Year-round. High: June–Sept.	Greens: Carts: Rating: Slope:	$ $$ 69.8/75.7 121/134	S J
P ☺☺☺☺ DEAL STATE	Meadowwood Golf Course Liberty Lake. (509) 255-9539 18 holes. Par 72/72. Yards: 6,874/5,880 Mar.–Nov. High: May–Aug.	Greens: Carts: Rating: Slope:	$ $$ 72.4/74.1 126/127	S J
P ☺☺☺ DEAL	The Creek at Qualchan Golf Course E. Meadowlane Rd., Spokane. (509) 448-9317 18 holes. Par 72/72. Yards: 6,599/5,538 Mar.–Oct. High: May–Sept.	Greens: Carts: Rating: Slope:	$–$$ $$ 71.6/72.3 127/126	J
P ☺☺	Wandermere Golf Course Division St., Spokane. (509) 466-8023 18 holes. Par 70/73. Yards: 6,095/5,760 Mar.–Nov. High: June–Sept.	Greens: Carts: Rating: Slope:	$ $$ 68.6/72.2 119/126	S J

Wyoming

The spectacular **Jackson Hole Golf and Tennis Club** is by most accounts the best course in Wyoming and among the best in the nation. Set at the base of Jackson Hole's ski mountain, it offers spectacular views of the Tetons. The Gros Ventre River winds its way through and alongside 12 holes. Nearby in Jackson is the nearly as wonderful, watery **Teton Pines Resort and Country Club**.

Near Sheridan in the north of the state is the well-regarded **Kendrick Golf Course**; in Cody is the **Olive Glenn Golf and Country Club**. Kendrick and Olive Glenn share positions on the *Golf U.S.A.* Best and *Golf U.S.A.* Deals lists.

High mountain courses are generally open from April to October, with peak rates in effect from June to early September. A handful of lower-altitude courses are in operation year-round, again with summer peak rates.

Golf U.S.A. Leader Board: Best Public Courses in Wyoming

☺☺☺☺   Jackson Hole Golf and Tennis Club
☺☺☺   Kendrick Golf Course
☺☺☺   Olive Glenn Golf and Country Club
☺☺☺☺   Teton Pines Resort and Country Club

Golf U.S.A. Leader Board: Best Deals in Wyoming

$/☺☺☺   Bell Nob Golf Club
$/☺☺☺   Buffalo Golf Club
$/☺☺☺   Kendrick Golf Course
$$/☺☺☺   Olive Glenn Golf and Country Club
$$/☺☺☺   Riverton Country Club

Northern Wyoming

| P ☺☺☺ | Bell Nob Golf Club
Overdale Dr., Gillette. (307) 686-7069 | Greens:
Carts: | $
$ |

Wyoming Golf Guide

DEAL	18 holes. Par 72/72. Yards: 7,024/5,555	Rating:	70.8/70.6
	Apr.–Oct. High: May–July	Slope:	119/116

P	**Buffalo Golf Club**	Greens:	$
☺☺☺	Buffalo. (307) 684-5266	Carts:	Inquire
DEAL	18 holes. Par 71/72. Yards: 6,684/5,512	Rating:	70.9/69.8
	Mar.–Nov. High: May–Sept.	Slope:	116/115

P	**Green Hills Municipal Golf Course**	Greens:	$ J
☺☺	Airport Rd., Worland. (307) 347-8972	Carts:	$
	18 holes. Par 72/73. Yards: 6,444/5,104	Rating:	69.3/68.0
	Apr.–Oct. High: June–Aug.	Slope:	113/113

P	**Kendrick Golf Course**	Greens:	$ J
☺☺☺	Big Goose Rd., Sheridan. (307) 674-8148	Carts:	Inquire
DEAL	18 holes. Par 72/73. Yards: 6,667/5,180	Rating:	70.7/68.0
STATE	Apr.–Oct. High: June–Aug.	Slope:	114/111

SP	**Olive Glenn Golf and Country Club**	Greens:	$$ J
☺☺☺	Meadow Lane, Cody. (307) 587-5551	Carts:	$
DEAL	18 holes. Par 72/72. Yards: 6,880/5,654	Rating:	71.6/71.2
STATE	Apr.–Oct. High: June–Aug.	Slope:	124/120

R	**Jackson Hole Golf and Tennis Club**	Greens:	$$$–$$$$ L T
☺☺☺☺	Spring Gulch Rd., Jackson. (307) 733-3111	Carts:	Incl.
BEST	18 holes. Par 72/73. Yards: 7,168/5,410	Rating:	72.5/72.5
	Apr.–Oct. High: June–Aug.	Slope:	126/127

R	**Teton Pines Resort and Country Club**	Greens:	$$$–$$$$$ W L R J
☺☺☺☺	Jackson. (307) 733-1733	Carts:	Incl.
BEST	18 holes. Par 72/72. Yards: 7,412/5,486	Rating:	74.2/70.8
	May–Oct. High: June–Sept.	Slope:	137/117

Casper Area

P	**Casper Municipal Golf Course**	Greens:	$ W
☺☺	Allendale, Casper. (307) 234-2405	Carts:	$
	18 holes. Par 70/72. Yards: 6,234/5,472	Rating:	67.9/69.2
	Mar.–Oct. High: May–Aug.	Slope:	112/112

P	**Douglas Community Club**	Greens:	$ W
☺☺	Douglas. (307) 358-5099	Carts:	$
	18 holes. Par 71/72. Yards: 6,253/5,323	Rating:	68.4/68.5
	Apr.–Oct. High: June–Aug.	Slope:	107/103

SP	**Riverton Country Club**	Greens:	$$
☺☺☺	Riverton. (307) 856-4779	Carts:	$
DEAL	18 holes. Par 72/72. Yards: 7,064/5,549	Rating:	72.2/71.0
	Mar.–Oct. High: June–Aug.	Slope:	128/119

Cheyenne Area

P	**Francis E. Warren AFB Golf Course**	Greens:	$ T
☺☺	Randall Ave., Warren AFB. (307) 775-3556	Carts:	$
	18 holes. Par 71/75. Yards: 6,585/5,186	Rating:	68.2/67.0
	Year-round. High: Apr.–Oct.	Slope:	105/102

P	**Glenn "Red" Jacoby Golf Club**	Greens:	$ J
☺☺	30th and Willett, Laramie. (307) 745-3111	Carts:	$
	18 holes. Par 70/72. Yards: 6,540/5,395	Rating:	67.3/68.1
	Mar.–Nov. High: June–Aug.	Slope:	108/109

Special Offers to *Golf U.S.A.* Readers

Look to your left, look to your right. One of you three people on vacation is paying the regular price for airfare, hotels, meals, and shopping. One is paying premium price for a less-than-first rate package. And one pays a deeply discounted special rate.

Which one would you rather be?

In this book you've learned about strategies to obtain the lowest prices on airfare, the best times to take a trip, and ideas on how to negotiate just about every element of travel.

And now, we're happy to present a special section of discount coupons for Econoguide readers.

All of the offers represent real savings. Be sure to read the coupons carefully, though, because of exclusions during holiday periods and other fine print.

The author and publisher of this book do not endorse any of the businesses whose coupons appear here, and the presence of a coupon in this section does not in any way affect the author's opinions expressed in this book.

SixFlags®
MAGIC MOUNTAIN

Minutes north of Hollywood off I-5

Save $5

On Six Flags Magic Mountain General Use Tickets
Excitement You'll Flip Over!

Present this coupon at a Six Flags Magic Mountain ticket booth & save $5.00 on each full-price general use ticket. Limit six (6) general use tickets per coupon. Does not apply to special ticketed events or special price tickets for kids (under 48"), Senior Citizens (55+), or Hurricane Harbor general admission.

Coupon cannot be sold or combined with any other discount or promotional offer. Not valid at any other Six Flags park.

Cash value not to exceed $.001.

GL01-42

Expires Dec. 31, 2001

37734

HRN REBATE COUPON

HOTEL RESERVATIONS NETWORK

(800) 964-6835
www.hoteldiscount.com

Major Cities - Rooms for Soldout Dates - Special Rates
$10 REBATE with 2-Night Booking
$20 REBATE with 4-Night Booking
$30 REBATE with 5-Night Booking
$50 REBATE with 7-Night Booking

Name: _____

Booking Number: _____

Hotel: _____

Dates of Stay: _____

See reverse side for rules.

GL01-29

SixFlags®
MAGIC MOUNTAIN

Come to Six Flags Magic Mountain and explore ten themed lands of fun, fantasy, and adventure. Discover the most exciting rides and action-packed shows on earth. Six Flags Magic Mountain is open weekends and selected holidays all year and daily April to mid-September. Park opens at 10 A.M. Call for specific operating days and hours. Schedule subject to change.

26101 Magic Mountain Pky.,Valencia, CA 91355, (661) 255-4129

HRN REBATE COUPON

Coupon Rules:

1. Must return this coupon to receive rebate.
2. Coupon expires 12/31/01.
3. Rebate mailed after check-out.
4. Coupons non-combinable.
5. Not retroactive.
6. After check-out, send this coupon with self-addressed stamped envelope to:
   HRN 8140 Walnut Hill Lane, Suite 203, Dallas, TX 75231.
7. Rebate check mailed within 2-3 weeks.
8. One rebate per customer.

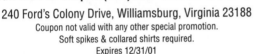

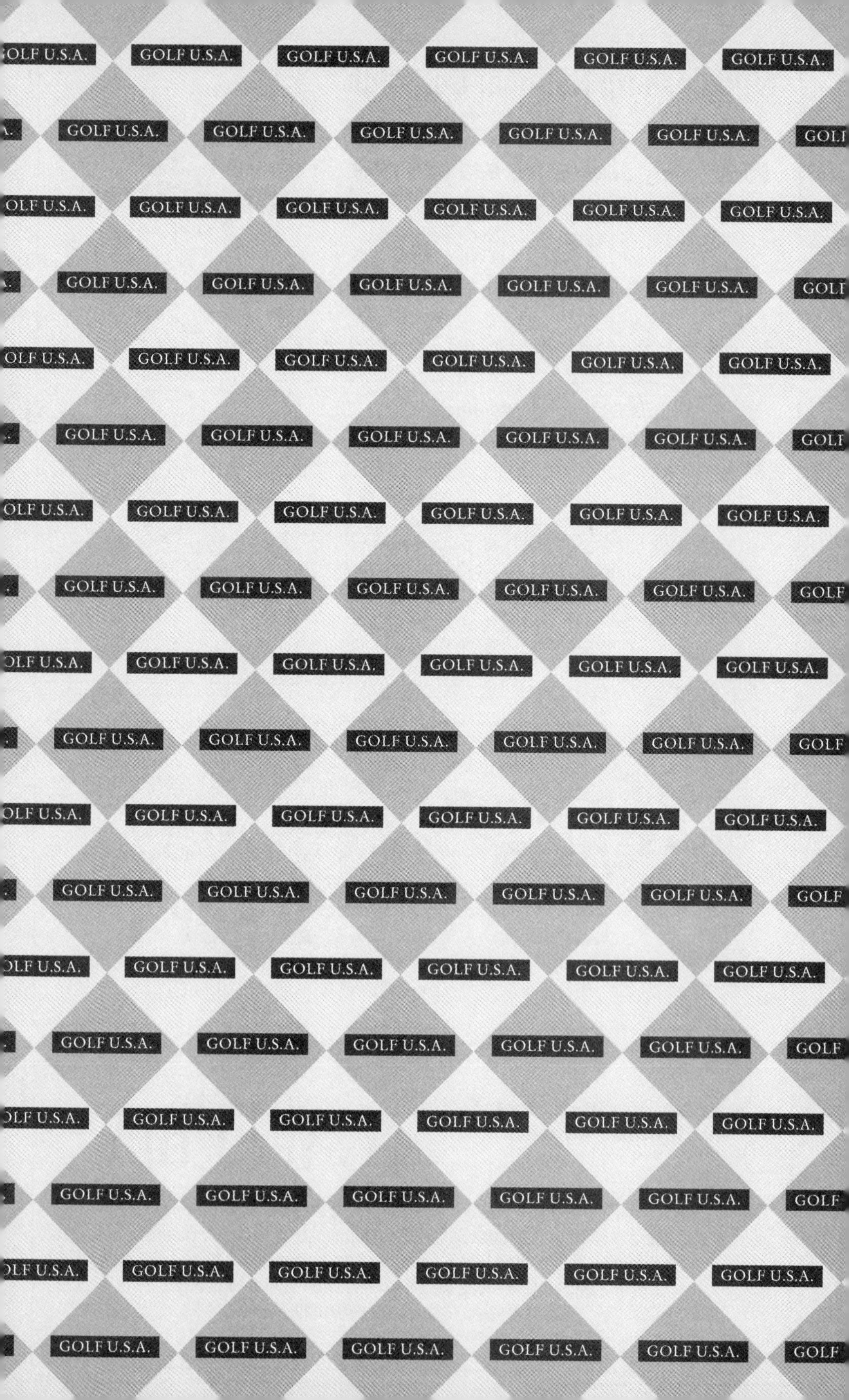

Quick-Find Index to Golf Courses

(See also the detailed Contents)